A History of Modern French Literature

A History of Modern French Literature

FROM THE SIXTEENTH CENTURY
TO THE TWENTIETH CENTURY

Edited by Christopher Prendergast

Princeton University Press
Princeton & Oxford

Copyright © 2017 by Princeton University Press

Published by Princeton University Press, 41 William Street, Princeton, New
  Jersey 08540

In the United Kingdom: Princeton University Press, 6 Oxford Street,
  Woodstock, Oxfordshire OX20 1TR

press.princeton.edu

Library of Congress Cataloging-in-Publication Data

Names: Prendergast, Christopher, editor.
Title: A history of modern French literature : from the sixteenth century to
  the twentieth century / edited by Christopher Prendergast.
Description: Princeton, New Jersey : Princeton University Press, 2016. |
  Includes index.
Identifiers: LCCN 2016009876 | ISBN 9780691157726 (hardcover : alk.
  paper)
Subjects: LCSH: French literature—History and criticism.
Classification: LCC PQ103 .H57 2016 | DDC 840.9–dc23 LC record
  available at https://lccn.loc.gov/2016009876

British Library Cataloging-in-Publication Data is available

This book has been composed in Janson Text LT Std

Printed on acid-free paper. ∞

Printed in the United States of America

10 9 8 7 6 5 4 3 2 1

CONTENTS

List of Contributors, ix

Introduction (1): Aims, Methods, Stories, 1
CHRISTOPHER PRENDERGAST

Introduction (2): The Frenchness of French Literature, 20
DAVID COWARD

Erasmus and the "First Renaissance" in France, 47
EDWIN M. DUVAL

Rabelais and the Low Road to Modernity, 71
RAYMOND GEUSS

Marguerite de Navarre: Renaissance Woman, 91
WES WILLIAMS

Ronsard: Poet Laureate, Public Intellectual, Cultural
Creator, 113
TIMOTHY J. REISS

Du Bellay and *La deffence et illustration de la
langue françoyse*, 137
HASSAN MELEHY

Montaigne: Philosophy before Philosophy, 155
TIMOTHY HAMPTON

Molière, Theater, and Modernity, 171
CHRISTOPHER BRAIDER

Racine, *Phèdre*, and the French Classical Stage, 190
NICHOLAS PAIGE

Lafayette: *La Princesse de Clèves* and the Conversational
Culture of Seventeenth-Century Fiction, 212
KATHERINE IBBETT

From Moralists to Libertines, 229
ERIC MÉCHOULAN

Travel Narratives in the Seventeenth Century: La Fontaine and Cyrano de Bergerac, 250
JUDITH SRIBNAI

The Quarrel of the Ancients and the Moderns, 269
LARRY F. NORMAN

Voltaire's *Candide*: Lessons of Enlightenment and the Search for Truth, 291
NICHOLAS CRONK

Disclosures of the Boudoir: The Novel in the Eighteenth Century, 312
PIERRE SAINT-AMAND

Women's Voices in Enlightenment France, 330
CATRIONA SETH

Comedy in the Age of Reason, 351
SUSAN MASLAN

Diderot, *Le neveu de Rameau*, and the Figure of the *Philosophe* in Eighteenth-Century Paris, 371
KATE E. TUNSTALL

Rousseau's First Person, 393
JOANNA STALNAKER

Realism, the Bildungsroman, and the Art of Self-Invention: Stendhal and Balzac, 414
ALEKSANDAR STEVIĆ

Hugo and Romantic Drama: The (K)night of the Red, 436
SARAH ROCHEVILLE AND ETIENNE BEAULIEU

Flaubert and *Madame Bovary*, 451
PETER BROOKS

Baudelaire, Verlaine, Rimbaud: Poetry, Consciousness, and Modernity, 470
CLIVE SCOTT

Mallarmé and Poetry: Stitching the Random, 495
ROGER PEARSON

Becoming Proust in Time, 514
MICHAEL LUCEY

Céline/Malraux: Politics and the Novel in the 1930s, 534
STEVEN UNGAR

Breton, Char, and Modern French Poetry, 554
MARY ANN CAWS

Césaire: Poetry and Politics, 575
MARY GALLAGHER

Sartre's *La Nausée* and the Modern Novel, 595
CHRISTOPHER PRENDERGAST

Beckett's French Contexts, 615
JEAN-MICHEL RABATÉ

Djebar and the Birth of "Francophone" Literature, 634
NICHOLAS HARRISON

Acknowledgments, 653

Index, 655

CONTRIBUTORS

Etienne Beaulieu, Cégep de Drummondville, Canada

Christopher Braider, University of Colorado–Boulder

Peter Brooks, Princeton University

Mary Ann Caws, City University of New York Graduate Center

David Coward, University of Leeds

Nicholas Cronk, University of Oxford

Edwin M. Duval, Yale University

Mary Gallagher, University College Dublin

Raymond Geuss, Cambridge University

Timothy Hampton, University of California–Berkeley

Nicholas Harrison, King's College London

Katherine Ibbett, University College, London

Michael Lucey, University of California–Berkeley

Susan Maslan, University of California–Berkeley

Eric Méchoulan, Université de Montréal

Hassan Melehy, University of North Carolina

Larry F. Norman, University of Chicago

Nicholas Paige, University of California–Berkeley

Roger Pearson, University of Oxford

Christopher Prendergast, King's College, Cambridge

Jean-Michel Rabaté, University of Pennsylvania

Timothy J. Reiss, New York University

Sarah Rocheville, University of Sherbrooke, Canada

Pierre Saint-Amand, Yale University

Clive Scott, University of East Anglia

Catriona Seth, University of Oxford

Judith Sribnai, Université du Québec à Montréal

Joanna Stalnaker, Columbia University

Aleksandar Stević, King's College, Cambridge

Kate E. Tunstall, University of Oxford

Steven Ungar, University of Iowa

Wes Williams, University of Oxford

* *

Introduction (1)

Aims, Methods, Stories

CHRISTOPHER PRENDERGAST

All the main terms of our title call for some clarification ("history," "modern," "French," "literature"), and the introductory chapter that follows this one, by David Coward, is in part devoted to providing that. But, in explaining the basic aims of the book, it is also important to highlight what might otherwise go unnoticed, the normally anodyne indefinite article; it is in fact meant to do quite a lot of indicative work. The initial "a" has a dual purpose. It is designed, first, to avoid the imperiousness of the definite article and thus to mark the fact this is but *a* history, modestly taking its place as just one among many other English-language histories, with no claim whatsoever on being "definitive"; on the contrary, it is highly selective in its choice of authors and texts, and very specific in its mode of address. This in turn connects with a second purpose: the indefinite article is also meant to highlight a history that is primarily intended for a particular readership. In the sphere of scholarly publication, the general reader (or "common reader," in the term made famous by Dr. Johnson in the eighteenth century and Virginia Woolf in the twentieth) is often invoked, but less often actually or effectively addressed. We take the term seriously, while of course remaining cognizant of the fact that conditions of readership and reading have changed hugely since Virginia Woolf's time, let alone Dr. Johnson's. While we naturally hope the book will prove useful in the more specialized worlds of study inhabited by the student and the teacher, the readers we principally envision are those with an active but nonspecialist interest in French literature, whether read in the original or in translation, and on a spectrum from the sustained to the sporadic (one version of Woolf's common reader is someone "guided" by "whatever odds or ends he can come by," a nontrivial category when one bears in mind that a collection of Samuel Beckett texts goes under the title of *Ends and Odds*).

This has various consequences for the book's character as *a* history. The first concerns what it does not attempt: what is often referred to, unappetizingly, as "coverage," the panoramic view that sweeps across centuries in the attempt to say something about everything. We too sweep across centuries (five of them), but more in the form of picking out selected "landmarks," to resurrect the term used by Virginia Woolf's contemporary, Lytton Strachey, in his *Landmarks of French Literature*, a book also written for the general reader, if from within the conditions and assumptions of another time and another world. One point of departure adopted for the direction of travel has been to work out from what is most likely to be familiar to our readership. There are dangers as well as advantages to this trajectory. The familiar will be for the most part what is historically closest, which in turn can color interests and expectations in ways that distort understanding of what is not close. One name for this is "presentism," whereby we read history "backward," approaching the past through the frame of the present or the more distant past through the frame of the recent past. In some respects, this is inevitable, a natural feature of the culture of reading, and in some cases it is even enabling as a check to imaginative inertia (what in his essay "Tradition and the Individual Talent," T. S. Eliot described as the desirable practice of interpreting a past writer from a point of view that "will not find it preposterous that the past should be altered by the present as much as the present is directed by the past"). Eliot's contemporary, Paul Valéry famously claimed that a reader in 1912 taking pleasure in a work from 1612 is very largely a matter of chance, but one obvious source of the pleasure we take in the remoter past is viewing it through our own cultural spectacles (Valéry reading 1612 via his own historical location in 1912, for instance). The risk, however, is the loss of the historical sense as that which demands that we try to understand and appreciate the past (here the literary past) on its terms rather than our own, while remaining aware that we can never fully see the past from the point of view of the past. On the other hand, if the past is another country, it is not another planet, nor are its literary and other idioms, for us, an unintelligible babble. One of the implicit invitations of this book is for the reader to use the familiar as a steering device for journeys to places unknown or underexplored, while not confusing the ship's wheel with the design of the ship itself or the nature of the places to which it takes us. Indeed the literature itself provides examples and models for just this approach, most notably the genre of travel writing, both documentary and fictional, from the Renaissance onward, a complex literary phenomenon at once freighted with the preconceptions (and prejudices) of the society in which it is produced, but also often urging its readers to try to see other cultures through other, indigenous, eyes (think Montaigne's essay, "Des Cannibales" or Diderot's *Supplément au voyage de Bougainville*).

The balance of the familiar and the unfamiliar goes some way (but only some) to account for the content of this volume. All histories (including those that aim for "coverage") are necessarily selective, but the principles governing our own inclusions, and hence, by necessary implication, the exclusions, need some further explaining. Where are Maurice Scève and Louise Labé, both important Renaissance poets, both also based in Lyons (and thus reflections of the fact that Paris was not, as became the case later, the only serious center of cultural life in the sixteenth century)? Where, for the nineteenth, is Nerval and, above all, the great wordsmith, Hugo (the poet; he is there in connection with nineteenth-century theater)? Or where indeed, for the twentieth, is Valéry? The list is indefinitely extendable; even a list of exclusions itself excludes. But the particular examples mentioned here are chosen to illustrate a specific and important issue for this history: the case of poetry. Access to the nature and history of the sound worlds of French verse, along with the character and evolution of its prosodic and rhythmic forms, is fundamental to understanding it as both poetry in general and French poetry in particular. But that is difficult, verging on impossible, without a degree of familiarity not only with French but also with French verse forms that we cannot reasonably assume on the part of most readers of this volume. This has heavily constrained the amount of space given over to poetry and determined a restriction of focus for the most part to what, historically speaking, are the two absolutely key moments or turning points.

There is the sixteenth-century remodeling of poetry, under the influence of Petrarch (often posited as the first "modern" European poet) and the form of the Petrarchan sonnet. Edwin Duval's contribution gives us some insight into the role of Clément Marot in the earlier chapter of this Renaissance story, while Hassan Melehy's chapter sheds light on the later generation of "Pléiade" poets to which du Bellay belonged. The key figure, however, is Pierre de Ronsard, founder and leader of the Pléiade group. Timothy Reiss's account of Ronsard's multidimensional significance as poet and public intellectual includes the invention of a foundational prosody based on the use of the twelve-syllable alexandrine verse form later codified, naturalized, and perpetuated in a manner that was to dominate most of the subsequent history of French poetry. In fact, Ronsard's own stance was marked by hesitation and fluctuation, given the image of the decasyllabic line as more fitting for the "heroic" register favored by the ruling elites. Furthermore, the novel uses to which the alexandrine was put by Ronsard in many ways reflects the exact opposite of the normative and hierarchical status this metrical form was to acquire; for Ronsard it was seen and used more as a binding, inclusive form, bringing together, in the very act of poetry, the natural, the human, and the divine in a spirit of "amity" beyond the contemporary experience of strife and civil war. It is, in short, a rich and complex story of shifting values and fluctuating practices.

But where more extensive formal analysis of poetic language—and especially prosody—is concerned, the main focus here is directed to a moment more familiar by virtue of being closer to us in time, the nineteenth century, specifically the later nineteenth century and the constellation Baudelaire, Verlaine, Rimbaud, and Mallarmé. This is the moment of Mallarmé's *crise de vers*, when the historical institution of French regular verse is, if not demolished (Mallarmé remained a staunch defender of the alexandrine even while recognizing that the days of its largely unquestioned hegemony were over), certainly challenged by the emergence of new forms developed to match new kinds of sensibility. Its most radical manifestations will be the prose poem and free verse, both of which will undergo further transformations in the twentieth century via Apollinaire, surrealism, and its aftermath (a glimpse of which is provided by Mary Ann Caws's contribution on

André Breton and René Char). The most extended engagements with the technical details of versification, prosody, syntax, typography, and page layout are in the chapters by Clive Scott and Roger Pearson. This is sometimes quite demanding, but the rewards are more than worth the effort of concentration required. There is also here an intentionally invoked line of continuity (Reiss highlights it) linking the modern period to early modern developments in the history of French poetry.

More generally, the conversation about what's in and what's out can go on forever, and rightly so (however explained and defended in any given case, it is simply impossible to avoid a whiff of the arbitrary, along with the difficulty of transcending mere personal preferences). The important thing in respect to *this* history of French literature is to avoid its conversation becoming another eruption of disputes over membership in the canon. This is not to suggest avoiding it, period. To the contrary, the issue remains real and pressing. In fact, it never goes away, and is indissolubly bound up with histories and relations of cultural power. On the other hand, discussion can all too readily congeal into empty sloganizing orchestrated by the dead hand of academic habit. The question for this particular volume is more what, for a specific purpose or audience, will best work by way of providing windows onto a history and historical understanding. That too is indefinitely debatable. Short of the comprehensive survey, which this is not and does not aspire to be, what will count as best serving those aims is something on which reasonable people can disagree. The list of inclusions will nevertheless to a very large extent look like a roll call of the usual canonical suspects, and, leaving to one side futile infighting over promotions and demotions, this does raise some basic questions of approach and method regarding what this history purports to be.

A limited but useful distinction is sometimes drawn between "history of literature" and "literary history." In its most developed form, this is a long story, with a number of theoretical complications that don't belong here. A compacted version would describe history of literature as essentially processional, rather like the "kings and queens" model of history, with the great works paraded in regal succession—grand, colorful, arresting, but a parade lacking in historical "depth." Literary history, on the other hand, is the child of a developing historical consciousness in Europe from the Enlightenment through Romanticism to positivism, one that is increasingly attuned to cultural relativities, deploys the methods of philological inquiry to reconstruct the past, and finally emerges as a fully constituted discipline. In France, this kind of scholarly inquiry began with the archival compilations of the Benedictines of Saint Maur in the eighteenth century, and then in the nineteenth century, via the critical journalism of Sainte-Beuve, eventually penetrated the university as a professional academic pursuit (the key figure in this connection was Gustave Lanson). The overarching category to emerge from these developments and that came to guide the literary-historical enterprise is "context," the social and cultural settings in and from which literary works are produced, the minor as well as the major. Indeed, in the emergence, and then later the explicit formulation, of the new discipline, the "minor," as barometer of a "context" comes to assume for literary-historical purposes a major role. A hierarchy of value is, if not abolished outright (that is a move that will be attempted much later, with only partial success), partly flattened toward the horizontal plane in order to get a sense of broader swathes of the historical time of "literature."

Our venture might, on the face of it, look as if it conforms to the processional template of history of literature (this is, after all, the expression used in the book's title) rather than to that of the context-reconstructing endeavors of literary history. In reality, however, it is a hybrid mix of the two, using the first (the great works) as a lever for entry into a variety of historically framed contextual worlds. The resurrection of Lytton Strachey's term "landmarks" acquires its proper force in relation to this hybrid blend: the "mark" as mark of importance or distinction, designating membership of a canon, but also "mark" as that which marks the spot, the historical spot, landmarks as signposts for a historical mapping. To this end, we also routinely, though not exclusively, deploy a particular method: focus on a single author and even a single work, reading out from text to context and then back again, in a series of mutually informing feedback loops within which the known (and often much-loved) texts are allowed to "breathe" a history. This does not, however, entail a dogmatic commitment to the position whereby "close reading" is the only road or the royal road to literary-historical understanding. It merely reflects the pragmatic view that this method works well for the intended audience. In addition, what here counts as a context is flexible. In some cases, it is strictly literary, and often generic in focus. Thus, the account of Racine's *Phèdre* takes us to some of the more general features of tragedy in the early modern period. The chapter on Voltaire's *Candide* runs the discussion of its hero's adventures and misadventures into the legacy of picaresque narrative and the history of eighteenth-century imaginative travel writing. The detailed analysis of Flaubert's *Madame Bovary* is set in the context of ideas about literary "realism" and related developments in the history of the nineteenth-century novel, with a side glance at nineteenth-century painting. Proust's *A la recherche du temps perdu* is similarly contextualized in a surrounding literary world (including Gide and Colette). "Context," however, can also be taken in nonliterary senses: for example, the Wars of Religion in connection with Rabelais and Montaigne; modern urban history in connection with Baudelaire; the economic and political crises of the 1930s in relation to Malraux and Céline.

⁂ ⁂ ⁂ ⁂

I have already used the word "glimpse" in connection with one of the contributions. The term could be generalized to encompass the whole book as a collection of glimpses, angled and partial snapshots (which, with variations of scale, is all history can ever be). On the other hand, it is not just an assortment of self-framing windows onto the French literary-historical world. Its unfolding describes, if in patchwork and fragmentary form, the arc of a story centered on the nexus of language, nation, and modernity. David Coward outlines this story in terms of "the idea of a national literary culture" built on and in turn reinforcing notions of "Frenchness." The story begins in the Renaissance, crucially with du Bellay's "defense" of a new form of linguistic self-consciousness and his affirmation of the literary prospects for French as a national language and as a modern literary language on a par with other languages both modern and ancient. The seventeenth century was to confer both political legitimacy and institutional authority on this new self-confidence, with Richelieu's creation of the Académie française and then more broadly under Louis XIV in the context of the developing process of centralized state formation initiated in the sixteenth century by François I and Henri IV. It was also the moment when—notwithstanding the continuing power of the Church, the sonorously commanding tones of Bossuet's orations, or the more radical defense of faith by the members of the Port-Royal group—the practices of literature and the expectations of the public came to embody a more distinctly "modern" look by virtue of a turn toward more secular interests: in science and philosophy; in moral psychology; in drama, both tragedy and comedy; and in the novel, with the whole notionally presided over by the rationally administering monarch and the worldly codes and manners of court and salon, even when the latter were ruthlessly dissected and exposed, whether in the comedies of Molière or the aphorisms of La Rochefoucauld.

The modernizing impulse generated a turbulent dynamic of tradition and innovation, characterized by public disputes over governing values, norms, and models. With du Bellay's polemic, we enter the age of the Quarrel, and its later offshoot, the Manifesto. To be sure, literary quarreling was not unknown in the Middle Ages, the most prominent the "querelle du *Roman de la Rose*," with Christine de Pizan in the leading role as critic of the terms for the representation of women (more precisely "ladies") in the later medieval romance. The paradigm of the modern quarrel was the seventeenth-century *Querelle des anciens et des modernes*, not least because of the institutional setting in which it was launched (the presentation on January 27, 1687, by the arch-modern, Charles Perrault of *Le siècle de Louis le Grand*, in the hallowed precincts of the Académie française). We may now see these disputes as self-advertising, transient blips on the surface of culture, the place where "public" discourse becomes mere publicity. But the quarrel in fact ran for decades, and if we have included a whole chapter on it, this is because the basic thrust of the case made by the Moderns (namely, that the modern equals the new) was to be the hallmark of all subsequent interventions of this type, the most noteworthy of which—also getting a chapter to itself—was the famous first night of Hugo's play, *Hernani*, in 1830. Beneath the stridency, the bitterness, and the misunderstandings (paradoxically none were more "modern" than the Ancients, Boileau, and Racine), the importance of the quarrel consists in its being an index of an emergent literary self-consciousness. It was no wonder that there were intense debates and acute differences over how "literature" was to be defined and who was to take ownership of the definition. What was fundamentally at stake was the significance of literature as part of a modern national patrimony, what later would be viewed and fought over as the canon of the "national classics" ("our classic authors," as Voltaire would put it).

The attempt to build and secure the treasure house of the national classic would run and run, well into the nineteenth century, largely under the banner of "classicism," an ideology in which the "classic" (as timeless great work) and "classical" as a set of literary and cultural values associated with the seventeenth century became fused in the rearguard enterprise of making historical time stand still or even go backward. There was however another, and altogether more influential, strain of literary self-consciousness underlying the polemical clash of opinion, one that pulled literature away from institutionalized centers of power, patronage, and control toward an ever greater sense of its own autonomy. This was partly a consequence of professionalization. In the seventeenth century, the idea of the professional literary "career" (as against the earlier image of the "amateur" associated in particular with Montaigne) was largely anchored in and governed by institutional settings. It would not, however, be long before being a professional was about the writer coming to operate more in the commercial networks of a modern market society, beginning in the publishers' offices and coffeehouses of the eighteenth century and accelerating with the invention of new technologies of paper manufacture and printing, new outlets of distribution, and a huge expansion of the reading public. David Coward describes several of these developments in some detail. Their great nineteenth-century chronicler and diagnostician would be Balzac, above all in his novel *Illusions perdues* (one of the works discussed in the chapter on Stendhal and Balzac). But there was also another type of separation, geared less to moneymaking than to opposition, the writer as rebel and outsider. In the eighteenth century, Voltaire, master of the marketplace, was also the exile on the run from the authorities, as close as possible to the Swiss border in Ferney. After his death, he was belatedly folded back into the embrace of state and nation with the transfer of his remains to the Panthéon in 1791, his public funeral a statement on a grand scale, a spectacle repeated almost a century later with the funeral procession of that other exile from the reach of power, Victor Hugo (also a skillful player in the literary marketplace, especially the heavily commercialized theater).

Separation also meant what subsequently came to be understood as "alienation." Rousseau is a key figure, his "solitary walker" and styles of first-personal meditation staging a new relation of nonbelonging between interiority, self, and society; Beaumarchais's Figaro speaks (out) in a manner virtually unthinkable in earlier periods; Diderot's vagabond-beggar lives at the edge in more ways than one; the ultimate outsider, the incandescent Marquis de Sade, travels a trajectory from incarceration in the Bastille to confinement in the Charenton asylum. In the nineteenth century, Stendhal would use his heroes and their narratives to probe, expose, ironize, and finally reject accommodation with the social world. Baudelaire, Verlaine, and Rimbaud would use the medium of verse and prose poetry to introduce new kinds of edge, at the very margin of society (associated with the world of the Bohème, in reality a very different thing from its sentimental representations) and a new experience of edginess, captured in the nervous rhythms of a vagabond consciousness never anywhere at home. It would all come to a head as the militancy that characterizes the age of the Manifesto comes into outright conflict with the state, most dramatically in two famous nineteenth-century literary trials, of Baudelaire's *Les fleurs du mal* and Flaubert's *Madame Bovary*, both in 1857, on charges variously relating to obscenity, blasphemy, and insult to public decency. There had been trials aplenty in the eighteenth century—though more commonly imprisonment without trial—but these reflected more contests of belief, ideology, and opinion. With the nineteenth-century trials it was the very idea of "literature" and its proper tasks that was at stake. In his correspondence, Flaubert repeatedly states his loathing of the nineteenth century (Baudelaire called it the Age of the Undertaker), opposing to it an insistence on the unconditional autonomy of literature. Whence his dream of the "book about nothing," the novel as pure aesthetic artifact held together only by the force of "style" and disaffiliated from both the demands of the marketplace and the imperatives of institutional belonging; literary art was in the process of becoming Art, self-conscious in the sense of being more and more about itself and hence internally self-supporting (the slogan "art for art's sake" captured something of the spirit of this development).

These challenges to both state and market in their exercise of cultural power had another effect, increasingly felt in the twentieth century: ever-increasing critical pressure on the idea of literature as the reflection of a self-sealing national identity and the expression of a unique and distinctive "Frenchness," culminating (for now) in the twenty-first century with yet another manifesto, resurrecting Goethe's cosmopolitan idea of *Weltliteratur* for the age of globalization—"pour une *littérature-monde* en français" [for a world literature in French], published in *Le Monde* in 2007. On the other hand, apart from the more self-absorbed periods of nation-state building buttressed by notions of France as the cultural center of Europe and of French as a *lingua franca*, there has nearly always been an international dimension to the history of French literature from the Renaissance onward (not the least irony here is the fact that this history begins with a figure—Erasmus—who was not French). If du Bellay's literary nationalism is a pitch for the singularity of French, his argument for the cultivation of a national language and the growth of a national literature paradoxically required an international soil: France was playing catch-up, borrowing and assimilating from the ancients, but also from modern Italian (above all the exemplary "modern" European poet, Petrarch). The thought was that, initially inferior, French would learn from other languages and literary cultures, but through processes of ingestion and osmosis would emerge the other side as the superior language of Europe. But this also points to something more general about the French sixteenth century. It was the most seriously multilingual of the European literary Renaissances, from Marguerite de Navarre's creative interaction with Boccaccio to Rabelais's "polyglossia" and riotous play with idiolects of French along with multiple other languages, both real and invented.

The seventeenth century is often seen, in these terms, as a hiatus, self-occupied with the projection of French monarchical aura and the creation of grand national-cultural institutions. But, while true to a very great extent, this is to accept the terms of the projection itself, often just kingly propaganda. In reality, the internationalist dimension of French literary and intellectual culture remained alive and well, for example, in the epistolary circuits of the Republic of Letters and the influence of both Italian and Spanish sources on the theatre (though not English ones). It is an intriguing exercise in counterfactual literary history (of which more later) to reflect on what might have been the case if Shakespeare had been read and absorbed in the seventeenth century. The "discovery" of Shakespeare had to await the eighteenth century, followed by his consecration as the Master by the nineteenth-century Romantics. The Enlightenment more generally was to develop a pronounced obsession with things English (Voltaire's *Lettres sur les Anglais* will imply that England is everything that France is not but should be). It also expands hugely the genre of travel writing, often positing the "Other" as both reference and device in a running campaign of opposition to authority. This in turn fed into Romantic cosmopolitanism, an imaginative and actual border-crossing phenomenon on multiple axes from Europe to the Near East, North Africa, and North America, with, in the European context, a strong focus on Germany (Mme de Staël's *De l'Allemagne* is a key text). This was a literary and cultural opening to the world with another quarrel as its background, mobilized to sustain the challenge of the Romantics to an increasingly threadbare conservative nationalism based on a claim to the eternal validity of a French seventeenth-century "classicism" at once idealized and petrified (Sainte-Beuve memorably described the work of one of its nineteenth-century spokesmen as a form of "transcendental chauvinism"). Resistance thus there was, and there would be more to come, especially when in the late nineteenth century nationalism moved further to the right. These were dangerously regressive forces, exploding into public life and discourse around the Dreyfus affair, with a literary politics that glorified a "classical" past alongside a politics of ethnicity, blood, and soil as an attempted check to the "rootless" cosmopolitanism of modernity ("cosmopolitan" had already become a code word in racist discourse).

Boundary crossing was, however, unstoppable, creating internal fragmentation and placing great strain on any assumption of a stable relation between nation, state, and literature, and in particular the idea of a coherent and transmissible national literary culture (what Sainte-Beuve called the Tradition). In the late nineteenth century into the twentieth, this was to touch the very cornerstone of the tradition, the language itself. Mallarmé's *crise de vers* is a key turning point—a "landmark" if ever there were one—and his own poetry, in both verse and prose, actively estranges language from the known and the predictable comforts of easy consumption. His was a practice of language designed to unsettle, as it notably did, many of the writers and intellectuals who would cluster around Action française and its ultranationalist offshoots, clinging desperately to fictions of seventeenth-century political and cultural order to ward off the threats of both "strangeness" and "foreignness": for Charles Maurras, Mallarmé was "un-French," while later Robert Brasillach accused him of having acted "against the French language." Proust's narrator in *A la recherche du temps perdu* remarks that "each great artist is the citizen of an unknown homeland which even he has forgotten," and Proust himself, the prose writer whose work is deeply soaked in the history of French prose from the seventeenth century, claimed that "beautiful books are written in a kind of foreign language." (Sydney Schiff, Proust's friend and the translator of the last volume of the *Recherche*, described Proust's style as "exotic and anticlassical," one that it is "difficult to believe that any pure-bred Frenchman could have evolved.") Breton and the surrealists took the modernist project of "making it strange" into an encounter of the language of poetry with the oneiric worlds of the unconscious, a place where the fabled French qualities of "clarity and "reason" no longer had purchase. From an entirely different direction, Céline (who hated Proust) launched an assault on the institution of "literary" writing by means of a radical use of demotic, creating in effect a style as anti-style. Camus, creator of the best-known "outsider" figure in twentieth-century French literature (along with the existentially dislocated hero of Sartre's *La nausée*) also captures the "stranger" in the term of his title, *L'étranger*, injecting into the tradition of first-personal writing the estranging force of a kind of stylistic blankness (the "zero degree" style made famous by the critic-theoretician, Roland Barthes, which would become associated with the cool and flat tones of the *nouveau roman*).

Camus's title also carries a third meaning, the *étranger* as foreigner, the Frenchman situated—in terms that have proved endlessly controversial—on the shores of colonial North Africa. The opening of French literature, that is, of literature in French, to forms of foreignness, a locus beyond France and the nation-bound definitions and understandings of "Frenchness," is where the story ends, in a terminus reflected through the work and example of three figures. There is the Irishman, Samuel Beckett, migrating inward to Paris from Dublin and into French from English (while also often acting as his own translator). Beckett interrogates and recasts the basic forms of both drama and novel around "where now?"—as questions about writing itself (an interrogation also at work in the experimental moves of the French novel from Maurice Blanchot to Alain Robbe-Grillet). As an Irishman writing in French, Beckett's work also raises issues to do with the "identity" of (French) literature as well as other kinds of identity, existential and cultural. These too are issues for "francophone" culture beyond the shores of France itself, here represented by two key moments and two key writers: in the first instance, the writings of Aimé Césaire and their engagement with questions of colonialism, native land, and literary heritage; in the second, the novels of Assia Djebar as a window onto so-called "postcolonial" writing from the perspective of an Algerian woman whose family had roots in both Arab and Berber cultures. "Francophone" appears here within quotation marks for all the reasons stated and explored in the chapters on both Césaire and Djebar. A shorthand for this might be the curiously awkward terms (highlighted by Harrison) of Pierre-Jean Rémy's welcoming address on Djebar's admission to that august institution where in many ways much of the story of the relation between "literature" and "nation" begins—the Académie française.

∗ ∗ ∗ ∗

The entire history illustrated in this volume by a sequence of "landmarks" is thus framed in a very precise way: it begins (in the Renaissance) with a strong focus on the formation of a "national" literary consciousness but ends with its dispersal into a much wider arena in the age when the category of "nation" starts to crack and dissolve. It is a compelling narrative that, like all linear stories of this type, should carry some provisos. It is, quite simply, too neat. A first caveat concerns the temporal framing of the narrative, what's called "periodization" and its basic unit of division and measurement—the century (a topic also touched on by David Coward). Ours is arranged as a succession of five centuries in the sense of each as the nicely rounded number of one hundred years. This notionally helpful, because tidy, division of historical time has rarely worked to anyone's satisfaction other than the purveyors of certain kinds of textbooks. Thus we have the "long" sixteenth century and the "short" twentieth century to accommodate realities and interpretations that overflow or fall short of the magical round number. Even more important is the fact that the "century" as we understand it is itself a historical invention, late in that other invention, "millennial" time (it was not until the latter part of the second millennium that "century" came to mean one hundred years). In Shakespeare's time "century" didn't mean a hundred years; it meant a hundred of *anything*. When we come across, in English translation, Nostradamus's sixteenth-century "Prophecies," gathered as a collection of "centuries," we might well be inclined to read this as reflecting prophecy on a grand scale, the epic sweep of apocalyptic vision across the expanse of "centuries" toward the End Time. In fact "centuries" here (a translation of *cents*) refers to the grouping of the prophecies in bundles of one hundred. As for the French term *siècle*, this didn't originally mean a hundred years either. A derivative of the Latin *saeculum*, it signified an "age" (the sense of the term in Perrault's encomium to Louis XIV). This, however, changed in the late seventeenth century. The older meaning of "age" remained, but the new more mathematical sense in the "age" of mathematics established itself. Perrault in fact was also instrumental in bringing about the semantic turn whereby, for a whole complex of reasons, the term eventually came to mean what it does today.

But, apart from the large quotient of both the arbitrary and the contingent in the shaping of the history as a set of numerically identical periods, there are other major shortcomings to the story. For example, just as "century" was a historical invention, so too was the image of the Renaissance as the origin of a postmedieval "modernity." This was in fact an invention of the Renaissance itself, in many ways a self-promoting historical fiction and one that proved robustly durable. Even Sainte-Beuve, the greatest of the nineteenth-century French critics, claimed that French literature only properly "began" in the sixteenth century. There are of course problems with assigning the place of medieval literature in the scheme of things "French," most notably the glorious flowering of Occitan troubadour poetry; it is not so much that Occitan became "French" as that Occitania became part of France through military conquest and political annexation by the French monarchy. But the picture of a "backward" *medium aevum* to be left behind in the name of a modernizing project was tendentious to a degree. It helped to secure a version of the Renaissance as providing both momentum for a form of "take-off" and a bedrock for a purposefully driven history. Secular modernity was intellectually designed to challenge the providentialist views of history sanctioned by theology, but that did not prevent it from installing its own teleology, the conception of history as governed by laws of ineluctability and sustained by a whole fable of "progress" whereby historical change is also felt to be improvement on the past. In the literary sphere this was most marked in the great quarrels and the argument advanced by the Moderns that what they stood for was not just different from, but superior to, the Ancients. It was a natural feature of the polemic running from the seventeenth century through nineteenth-century Romanticism to the self-advertisements of the twentieth-century avant-garde. But it was, and remains, also symptomatic of a wider cultural paradigm, an entire way of thinking conducted under the hoisted banner of the Modern.

There are, however, other ways of thinking, which capture what the mono-track linear history preferred by the myth of modernity leaves out. Raymond Williams sketched a model for cultural history incorporating literary history that is based on the tripartite schema he defined as the dominant, the emergent, and the residual. All cultural formations combine these three features, if in varying degrees. The myth of modernity always favors the dominant (winners' history as "progress" story), while modernism would fall in love with the "emergent." The "residual," however, is what is left behind, discarded by the forward march of the modern, its sole function that of pasture for nostalgic reaction. A curious echo of some, but crucially only some, of this is to be found in a passage from Alfred de Musset's *Confession d'un enfant du siècle*, with which Sarah Rocheville and Etienne Beaulieu conclude their account of the Romantic movement:

> The life offered to the youths of that time was made up of three elements: behind them was a past that was never destroyed and which still stirred about its ruins, with all the fossils of the centuries of absolutism; in front of them was the dawn of a vast horizon, the first light of the future; and in between these two worlds . . . something similar to the Ocean which divides the old continent from the young America, something vague and floating, a stormy sea full of shipwrecks, crossed from time to time by some white sail or by some ship blowing heavy steam. In other words, the present century, which separates the past from the future, which is neither one nor the other and which resembles both at once, where one does not know, at every step, whether he is walking on a seed or on remains.

This is an instance of the notorious *mal du siècle* held to characterize a key dimension of Romantic sensibility and outlook. The moment between the forms of the residual and the horizon of the emergent is "dominant," but as a moment of uncertainty and confusion, adrift on an ocean without a compass, a non-place (Musset here is an uninhibited mixer of metaphors) between seeds and remains. But there are other values that can attach to the residual (if not precisely to the cultural and literary remnants Musset has in mind), enabling us to approach the past in terms of what pseudo-providentialist accounts exclude. One form of the "residual" is as the trace of the might-have-beens of history and involves the thought that much of the story could have unfolded otherwise. This returns us to the intriguing possibilities offered by the counterfactual in history mentioned earlier in connection with the French seventeenth century and the absence of Shakespeare from its world of literary reference and influence. I would like to conclude this "introduction" with two further counterfactuals, if only to highlight the deep questions that remain when trying to "introduce" something as vast and complex as a "history" of French literature.

The first takes us back to the staple of "periodization," the division of time into centuries. Apart from the latter being a relatively late historical invention, endowed moreover with adaptive flexibility (expandable to "long" and contractable to "short" as need arises), the entire temporal arrangement could have been different. The historian Daniel Milo has shown how the dating of chronology in the Christian era could have gone in a different direction, when disputes over how to date the Easter cycle led some Church figures to suggest dating the year 1 CE from the Passion rather than the Nativity, thus pushing everything "back" thirty-three years. This thirty-three-year delay would of course have had many consequences for where we delimit centuries, place literary movements, and locate authors. Proust, for example, situated "between two centuries," would be wholly a nineteenth-century writer. The dwindling band still clinging to the view that French literature "begins" with the Renaissance in the sixteenth century would have a problem with dating the Renaissance itself. Then enrich the counterfactual by mapping what would have been the case if the Republican calendar introduced in 1793 (and backdated to 1792) to celebrate the foundational character of the French Revolution had stuck. Between them, the sixth-century monks and the eighteenth-century revolutionaries would have ensured an outcome whereby year 1 would have been in 1759, *Du côté de chez Swann* would have appeared in 154, and this volume in 258.

The second example concerns the relationship between counterfactuals and the idea of history as turning points, forks in the road, those taken and those not but which might or could have been. It is represented here in the chapter on Rabelais by Raymond Geuss. I have spoken of literary history as the seeing of literary works in context, by which is meant primarily the (manifold) contexts to which they belong at the moment of their own production (genres, publics, mentalities, etc.). But there is another sense of "context" that matters to historical understanding, that of a writer's or a work's "posterity," the futures of reading and rereading into which the work is sent out without any foreknowledge of the postbox to which it will be delivered. As David Coward notes, literary history is also a history of readings, the transformation of the successive environments in which works are read. Returning to Valéry's example of the work written in

1612 interesting a reader in 1912, there is nothing here that guarantees that outcome. The work is not sent out into the future with a certificate of survival attached (nor, by the same token, of extinction). This imparts to literary history an element of haphazard convergences and disjunctions of taste and interest over time. In the standard literary histories (the ones that prefer tidiness to disorder), the posterity of the work, its historical afterlife, often comes out as a tale of "influence," sometimes, moreover, converted into a strong causal account of literary-historical change. It is also a way of exercising imaginary control of the field, the principle of "influence" grasped as a kind of fathering process, granting a quasi-paternal authority over what comes after. The alternative to this lies in the sphere of imagining alternatives. This is intellectually risky and can easily degenerate into preference fantasies (the "if only" and "what if" that so often confuse the might-have-been with what we would like to have been). But in its more disciplined guises, counterfactual history may hold lessons for literary history. For Geuss, part of the point of reading Rabelais is not just to recover a literary past but also a set of possibilities for that past's future, of which our present was but one. His closing reflections on Rabelais and his contemporaries as embodying at a historical crux or crossroads a now-lost or suspended alternative to the "main road to modernity," the latter the one actually taken and the former a real but unrealized possibility, are then perhaps the best place to close an introduction that, while reproducing a "story," signals an openness to other stories—of literary production, reception, reading—cast in multiple tenses of the imagination.

Introduction (2)

The Frenchness of French Literature

DAVID COWARD

The sixteenth century in France saw the emergence of a generation that for the first time conceived the idea of a national literary culture, open to the lessons of the past and to foreign influences but independent of them.

Of course, nothing comes from nothing. The Renaissance, which began in Italy in the fifteenth century and spread throughout Europe, was built on principles dating from classical antiquity when the territory occupied by imaginative literature was first laid out. The Greeks captured the tragic and comic perspectives on life by giving them a tangible form as actable plays. The rules of prosody provided a settled framework for the many varieties of the poetic impulse. Fables distilled moral lessons from short tales, while long, epic narratives extolled heroic values, denounced treachery, and provided object lessons in humankind's duty to itself, to the collective, and to the gods. Themes and forms, together with the aesthetic principles that supported a hierarchy of disciplined configurations of the creative imagination, combined to enshrine the artistic ideals of truth, beauty, and usefulness in clearly understood ways and defined the best and worst of the human spirit.

The ancient world drifted slowly to a close that was marked finally by the breakup of the Roman Empire in the fifth century. There followed a "dark time" when written culture survived almost exclusively within the institutions of the Church. During this *medium aevum*, or "Middle Age," which separated classical antiquity from modern times, the center of civilization moved slowly from the Mediterranean to northern Europe. After the millennium, a first renaissance in the twelfth century saw an upsurge of secular literary activity that, while reconnecting with modes and practices dimly remembered from older cultures, pursued its own evolving preoccupations against a background of shared ideals: courtly love, chivalric honor, and duty to God, king, and the feudal hierarchy. Lyric poetry, the lives of saints, warrior epics, and, later, theater, poetry, and magical romances slowly combined to define the vocation of literature, which is to tell us about human nature and the world we live in. By the end of the fifteenth century, literary forms had been, in broad terms, set. And ever since, each generation has inherited evolving codes and conventions that have given the word "literature" a moveable content and shaped the craft of writing. Poets inherited established poetic meters, storytellers learned lessons from epic and romance, and each generation of playwrights added something to the traditions of theater.

The modern age, marked by the introduction of printing, began around 1500. It did not signal a clean break with the past: it was merely a moment in the continuum of history. Yet it did mark a turning point, for it met a number of the preconditions essential to the very idea of a literature that was different from that of other nations and distinctively French.

The first of these is the Frenchness of France. During the Middle Ages, the patchwork of duchies, courts, and regions of what had been Gaul were brought under the authority of the area now known as the Ile de France. With time, France expanded to its "natural," that is, more or less physical boundaries. But already, by the time Henri IV added Navarre to the kingdom in 1589, France had long had a strong sense of national identity. A leading European power, it was also *mère des arts* and in time grew confident enough to conceive the spread of French culture as a *mission civilisatrice*, its unique contribution to human progress.

That culture was shaped over time by the historical process. The French Church, alert to unorthodox tendencies, eliminated the Cathar heretics, resisted the Protestant Reformation, and remained, through its pastoral message and educational role, a conservative power that few French authors entirely escaped. The absolutist French state, validated by the Church's support for the divine right of kings, also achieved a high degree of influence over cultural evolution. National unification had been rooted in the centralization of power, which, save for the brief prominence of Louis XIV's Versailles, ensured that the nation's affairs have been directed from Paris. This strong centripetal tradition has set much of the nation's literary agenda. Decisions made in Paris by official institutions (notably the various French academies) together with the many passing *querelles*, *affaires*, *guerres*, schools, movements and "isms" that began in the capital and spread outward, aimed to make French culture as one and indivisible as the Revolution of 1789 set out to be.

Catholicism and the centralizing principle are defining features of Frenchness that have done much to shape the French psyche, language, and cultural assumptions in ways that have at times made France both highly civilized and insular. The public life of France has been rooted in the regularity, clarity, and harmony of its structures. French gardens, French thought, French town planning, French music and art reflect the orderliness of the French mind. Where the Anglo-Saxon tradition is drawn to empiricism, the French have an in-built taste for abstract thinking, that distillation of general ideas from the chaos of experience. It is this primacy of reason that has given the literature of France its philosophical cast, from the "universal" rules of classicism and the program of the Enlightenment to the committed writings of the existentialists and the theories of the New Criticism of the twentieth century.

But if France has exported French taste and values to the world, so French cultural ambitions have been both challenged and enriched by foreign influences. The example of Italy in the sixteenth century, Spain in the seventeenth, and Britain in the eighteenth enthused French minds. After 1789, the reaction against ancien régime values led to a relaxation of classical strictness. Yet the democratic forces released by nineteenth-century Romanticism and positivism never completely overlaid French formalism, which still remains the default position of French public life and culture. Further contact with foreign influences—English, German, and, in the twentieth century, the United States—has diluted but not overlaid the ideals of clear thinking and clear expression, though the impact of commercialism and the information culture have in recent times provided a serious challenge to old ways.

The second requirement for a national literature was a national language. In 1500, many dialects, patois, and distinct languages like Breton or Occitan were spoken in France. But linguistic unification was implicit in the process of centralization: to be fully "France," the nation needed to speak a common language, which was to be *le français de Paris*. The policy was officially confirmed in 1539 by François I in the Ordonnances de Villers-Cotterêts, which decreed that henceforth all court proceedings throughout the kingdom would be recorded "en langage maternel François et non autrement." In 1549, Joachim du Bellay published *La défense et illustration de la langue française*, which made the case for French, then regarded by scholars as an inferior mode of expression, to be recognized as a proper vehicle for poetry. Enriched by modern technical terms and a vocabulary renewed by interpenetration with Greek and Latin, French could compete with the languages of the ancient world and modern Italy. Though in the 1580s, Montaigne considered French to be still a fragile tongue, literary French was accepted by the court, the ultimate source of preferment and honors. In 1635, the newly founded French Academy was charged with producing a dictionary that would fix the meaning of words for all to understand. Boileau endorsed the new linguistic rules, which made written and spoken expression precise, orderly, and elegant. By the 1780s, Rivarol could proclaim the victory of *la clarté française*.

The claim was both partial and premature. The vast majority of the king's subjects—and in due course the children of the French Revolution—were illiterate and strangers to books. In 1794, the Abbé Grégoire put the number of citizens who spoke no French at six million, about a quarter of the population. Parisians traveling through the provinces continued to encounter communication problems. In the nineteenth century, railways, cheap newspapers, and the introduction of universal primary education after 1880 accelerated the spread of French. Yet as late as 1900, interpreters were still available in Norman law courts to defendants with little or no French. By then, the Third Republic's elementary schools were actively discouraging the use of local "jargons" that prevented citizens from participating fully in the life of the republic and impeded progress. This policy was resisted by regionalists at the time (the defense of Provençal had already been undertaken by the poet Mistral) and subsequently criticized as cultural vandalism. Its objective was achieved, however, and literacy rates rose. In 1827, Victor Hugo had sworn, as he later expressed it, to jam "a red bonnet on the old dictionary." But the spread of primary education would prove, in due course, a more effective means of making French accessible to all.

In practice, however, *la clarté* remained the preserve of the educated elite. *Le beau parler* is still valued, but the percentage of nonstandard French remains high among the general population, and France continues to possess a richer tilth of argot than most European languages. The old exclusiveness has long since been weakened by the rise of democracy, a process that quickened in the twentieth century, and particularly after 1945. The authority of Academy-authorized French has been challenged by the adoption by both popular and serious writers of words, coinages, expressions, and relaxed grammar drawn from regional, American, popular, youth, and immigrant cultures. Du Bellay would have been pleased, but not Boileau.

The spread of literacy and the liberalization of culture have undermined the status of "official" French for writers inside France and in francophone countries as well. For them, French has a particular status not only as an official language of international organizations but also as the language of revolution, the rights of man, freedom, and equality. As such it is now used as the medium of communication between francophone nations in international negotiations, even those in which France has no interest and at which no French officials are present. On the other hand, the growing confidence of some francophone cultures has led writers to hesitate about whether to continue using French or revert to vernacular languages. Some, notably in Quebec, would reject the French Academy's prescriptive authority and adopt a freer, less metropolitan vehicle for their work. The formality of French at home and abroad has thus been undermined, and new linguistic registers have become available. It is also the case that different categories of writing call for different modes of expression, so that authors' choices are often made for them.

For authors are both individuals and members of a society that shapes their outlook according to their place in it. They are products of religion, education, language, economic system, and political regime and, within their individualism, share common traits. In France, few escape the distinctive respect for reason, abstraction and generalization; elegance of style and form; and, not least, the judgments of Paris. Aspiring authors everywhere gravitate toward capital cities in search of fame and fortune. But *la montée à Paris* means aiming at the literary center, being caught up in movements, coteries, and *cénacles* that have leaders, followers, and, inevitably, breakaway renegades. French authors pride themselves on their independence, yet they also treasure collective programs that are cultural extensions of the centralizing principle. They issue *arts poétiques* and manifestoes and expel dissidents.

There were no authors as such in the Middle Ages. Writings were almost invariably the product of many hands, not least of copyists and performers. Names attached to a work designated personas (Marie de France, for example) rather than persons. Later in the period authors were sometimes named, but they remain shadowy figures for the most part. Relatively little is known about even the most celebrated of them, François Villon.

Since there was no significant market for manuscripts, authors depended for their living on employment in Church or royal and ducal courts. After 1500, the printing revolution was too modest in scope to pay a living wage, and writing was almost exclusively an occupation for persons of leisure and, increasingly, of both sexes. Marguerite de Navarre, who was sister to François I, and Rabelais, a doctor of medicine, did not depend on their sales. Montaigne, in his château, was keen not to be mistaken for an author who wrote for money.

After 1600, the theater began offering playwrights modest returns that eventually enabled a few, like Corneille or Molière, to pay their way. But the number of theatergoers was small and book-buyers too few to make writing a viable profession. Moreover, authors' copyrights were unprotected by law, a situation from which only publishers benefited. Authors continued to look to the court and Church for sinecures and sought the private patronage of royal and aristocratic personages. In this they were supported by the crown, which saw the advantage to national prestige of a thriving literary culture. By the 1630s, writers were appearing in a more favorable light, and rewards were given to those who served the right causes. A generation later, Louis XIV regarded the artist as a jewel in his crown and was suitably generous to those who blew his trumpet for him. Aristocrats and a new breed of financiers anxious to *vivre noblement* followed the royal example, and the literary salons turned approved authors into celebrities. The award of royal pensions and gratifications was institutionalized in 1663 and, together with an increase in court appointments (as secretary, royal historiographer, and so on), they supplemented earnings from authorship but also enhanced authorship itself. Even so, the distinction between the rich man who wrote for his own amusement and the author who did it for a living was strictly maintained. Racine was ennobled, but he remained a superior kind of domestic servant. Boileau, the voice of classicism, was thrashed by footpads hired by his betters, whom he had displeased.

But patronage ran the risk of creating a literature written to order, designed to please—and not offend—a paymaster. Royal patronage posed an even greater threat, that of making literature an arm of government. Soon, strengthening its grip on pens, the state set in place an administrative machinery that vetted manuscripts, limited the number of authorized printers, and practiced strict censorship. After 1718, a license to print was required, unlicensed books were burned, and authors and publishers faced stiff penalties. In the event, few were seriously inconvenienced, though Voltaire and Rousseau fled the country to avoid arrest and Diderot was briefly jailed. But the threat of retribution made many uneasy, so that self-censorship was added to that practiced by official censors, whose numbers grew as the publishing industry expanded. With the rise of a middle class eager for information, culture, and entertainment, there were new opportunities for writers who became journalists and produced dictionaries, encyclopedias, and compilations of many sorts. Some also looked to the theater, where a run of fifteen performances could bring a round sum. But no one before 1750, and few after that date, lived by his or her pen. Even Voltaire's fortune came from shrewd investments, not from his writings.

Yet by the 1770s, writers were finding a new outlet for their wares: the book-buying public. The old dependency on patronage was replaced by the money to be earned from the prospering book trade, which could sustain the first professional authors. Nevertheless, authors were still vulnerable to the sharp practice of publishers and exposed to the depredations of pirates at home and abroad. The rights of authors were asserted by the Revolution in 1793 and were restated at intervals over the next century. But a fair system of royalty payments had to wait until the 1880s, and not until 1886 did the Berne copyright convention protect French authors against international piracy.

But by then, the day of the professional writer had arrived. At the start of the nineteenth century, more than two thousand copies were rarely printed of works of fiction, though popular novelists like Pigault-Lebrun and dramatists like Pixéricourt were made rich by their overactive pens. By the 1840s, technological advances in the printing trades and the growth of the reading public hiked print runs for reasonably successful novels to five thousand, and sales of poetry and theater tickets were more than healthy. But the largest rewards went to the *roman feuilleton* of Eugène Sue or Dumas *père* when the new age of cheap newspapers earned brand-loyalty for their titles by publishing sensational serials. The audience for mainstream boulevard theater grew rapidly after the 1860s, and in 1897, Rostand's *Cyrano de Bergerac* ran for eighteen months at the Porte-Saint Martin. Fiction was now routinely first published in newspapers before being reissued in volume form, the most popular titles in editions of thirty thousand copies. Cheap collections, vigorously promoted, gave financial independence to the growing number of professional authors who set out to please literature's new master: the paying public.

Serious writers fared less well—Balzac was famously short of money—and many looked first to court patronage, revived by Napoleon, and later to government ministries that offered small pensions, minor posts, and even sinecures to suitable candidates. Others in the second half of the century supplemented their incomes with journalism. The rise of the popular press gave them opportunities to sell stories, poems, and articles and make their names. Both Zola and Maupassant graduated to literature through journalism.

There were, however, other rewards in the form of status. In the seventeenth century, authors pleased but also instructed according to classical precept. They provided lessons in private and public virtues and were leaders of taste and ideas. During the Enlightenment, their stock rose. Reason gave them a new authority to advise monarchs, devise constitutions, and direct society; they were visionaries with a crusading zeal to shape the future of civilization. Romantics like Musset, who accused the Enlightenment of depriving humankind of its certainties without replacing them with new values, denounced reason and set about teaching people to think with their feelings and imagination. One result was to generate sympathy for the poor and support for the new socialist principles. Hugo is the clearest example of the poet-as-prophet, but the invasion of literature by progressive, political, liberal ideas was widespread. Some, like Chateaubriand or Lamartine, held high political office. Poets publicized causes and initiated practical, sometimes revolutionary action. But there were also outsiderly artists who rejected the world, convention, and restrictive bourgeois values, and some, like Rimbaud or Mallarmé, adopted "difficult" modes of expression that most readers found obscure. The Jules Vernes and Paul Févals wrote for money or fame or both. But in growing numbers, socially conscious, positivist-minded authors served progress and science and sought to move the world on from the order defined by monarchism and the Church. By the 1890s, novelists in particular were beginning to fill the ranks of what, after 1898, would be called "intellectuals." Free of patronage, authors were no longer content to be judged by public opinion: they set out to shape it. Henceforward, the contestatory role of literature would expand until it grew into a form of extraparliamentary opposition to established power.

Since 1900, writing has been a full-time occupation for only a small minority, despite the proliferation of literary prizes and occasional government attempts to improve copyright arrangements or set up schemes to support struggling authors. In 1968, a publishers' report set the number of active authors in France at forty thousand, of which only a handful lived by their pens. Those who venture into film or television may fare better, and star performers in popular fictional genres are richly rewarded. But writing as a career remains precarious and unpredictable, and in particular the status of the literary author has declined dramatically. Poets, playwrights, and novelists once commanded respect as teachers, sages, and prophets. But their role has been overtaken by the experimental and human sciences that explain human nature in quantifiable terms, just as specialists in many disciplines—sociology, politics, economics, psychiatry—account with greater authority for the tensions within the self and the ways the self is shaped by modern urban environments. In the 1960s, the New Criticism claimed that books were written by the zeitgeist, the socioeconomic forces of which authors were the unwitting mouthpieces. Playwrights were demoted by the *création collective* movement for political reasons, and writers were shackled to large, profit-driven publishing corporations that discouraged experiment and, against new writing, backed winning formulas. If writing had become a trade, publishing was a production line.

Authors have largely stopped standing above their readers, whose uncertainties they share. One exception is provided by those who set out to raise and redirect the consciousness of women. In the Middle Ages, the idealization of women promoted by courtly love and the code of chivalry competed with the traditional gross satire of the *malices des femmes*. During the first of many *querelles des femmes* sparked by the *Le roman de la rose* in the thirteenth century, Christine de Pizan defended the right of women to be heard in terms echoed in the 1540s, as part of the *querelle des amyes*, by Louise Labé, who asserted that they were capable of competing with men in artistic endeavors. Cultivated women writers emerged around the Pléiade, and the association between women and the arts was asserted by aristocratic ladies who played a central role in the nation's cultural life until the end of the ancien régime. They helped to define taste and consolidate classicism in the seventeenth century; in the eighteenth, the Enlightenment found a home in their salons, which offered a platform for the *philosophes* and intellectual debate. But women were not simply literary impresarios; they were poets, letter writers, and participants in the wider intellectual conversation. They also ceased to be the inspiration of poets and the reward of the warrior. Mlle de Scudéry wrested the long, mythological romance from the heroic male tradition and turned it inward, to sentiment. In her wake, Mme de Lafayette and Mme de Villedieu developed the short *nouvelle*, which would steer fiction toward the psychology of character in contemporary situations. By the 1690s, women were writing history and short tales and took part in the religious debate over quietism and the *Querelle des anciens et des modernes*. Many achieved eminence. After 1700, Mme Dacier was France's most famous Hellenist, and by the 1740s, Voltaire's mistress, Mme du Châtelet, had become widely respected as a mathematician. Mme de Staal-Launay's *Mémoires* (1755) pioneered the interest in the private lives of individuals and, after 1750, among the many novelists of both sexes, Mme Riccoboni's elegant character studies stood out by their quality and insight. At a time when literature was starting to move out of the aristocratic sphere and express the concerns of the middle class—the noble salon hostesses of the first half of the eighteenth century became *grandes bourgeoises* in the second—women authors also began to turn to the paying public: Mme du Châtelet was a marquise, but Mme Riccoboni was an actress before trying to live by her pen. During the Enlightenment, women carved out a space, both social and discursive, in philosophic circles, and their input as readers and authors, especially of novels, directed attention in special ways to forms of what the eighteenth century understood as "sensibility." Their case for the right to be heard was stated many times, and they won male supporters. In 1772, Louis Thomas said that they were "slaves" in a patriarchal society, and Laclos believed it would take a "revolution" to make them free.

The revolution he had in mind was not that of 1789, which granted rights to men but not to women. Women like Olympe de Gouges protested vociferously to no avail. The misogyny, which was even stronger during the Revolution than it had been during the ancien régime, was aggravated by Napoleon whose Civil Code (1806) restricted women to the same legal rights as those accorded to minors and mad persons. The same battle was rejoined in the 1830s by Flora Tristan and George Sand. But the progress made during the Revolution of 1848 was rolled back by the reactionary Second Empire. Meanwhile, from the queens of the *cabinets de lecture* of 1810 to the franker, racier writings of Gyp, Rachides, and Colette, women authors continued to advance against largely hostile public opinion. There were victories. In 1910, Marguerite Audoux, a beneficiary of the introduction of universal primary education, won the Prix Goncourt and gave working-class women a modern voice. Yet poetry and fiction, theater and the new medium of cinema remained predominantly male domains. Between the two world wars, no female writer won the Prix Goncourt. But after 1945, women writers emerged in force. Marguerite Yourcenar and Marguerite Duras were major authors of the later twentieth century, which also felt the impact of literary intellectuals like Simone de Beauvoir and Julia Kristeva.

The bulk of women's fiction, like writing generally, has remained faithful to the realistic, naturalistic tradition. It deals with relationships in both historical fiction and the novel of contemporary manners. But libertarian feminism has encouraged more open attitudes to sexuality, franker discussions of the couple and a new self-confidence in readers. *Ecriture féminine*, which means writing in other ways and about other things, has largely dismantled the barriers of the old misogyny.

If authors acquired "Frenchness," so did their readers. Before the advent of printing and for some time afterward, books were not read but heard. They were recited or declaimed in public gatherings. One of the side effects of the printing revolution was to make reading a personal experience. It was an early stage in the long, slow discovery of private life, that part of the self that is lived separately from the communal. But although no two readers have identical tastes, readers taken together constituted the new reading public, which, by creating demand, exerted a strong influence on the direction literature would take.

The reading public is not monolithic but made up of constantly moving parts. It can be divided vertically, that is historically, in time, and horizontally, by constituencies: learned and popular, literary and scientific, and so on. The publishing trade uses broad-brush categories like the old divisions of highbrow, middlebrow, and lowbrow and, more recently, mass-market, trade, library, digital, and others. A French specialty is the *collection* (*Bibliothèque rose, Série noire,* etc.), which targets specific interest groups, while *le best seller* (a term imported from the United States in 1948) applies to cookbooks or celebrity autobiographies, as well as the latest must-have fiction titles. "Literature," a moveable concept regularly redefined, has a stubborn, but now relatively small place in the public's affections.

But demand does not define importance. A small minority of writers have always pleased themselves—the Sades and Rimbauds, pioneers and groundbreakers—but most have been obliged to play tunes called by their pipers: publishers, patrons, and most recently the paying public. The size of this public has always been difficult to assess, though attempts to quantify it have been made using literacy rates, the number of editions of a book, and the size of print runs. Such estimates must be treated with caution. Marx's *Das Kapital* was not a publishing success, yet its influence has been enormous. On the other hand, large sales do not guarantee literary quality. For evidence of what readers thought of what they read, reception theorists look to private journals, letters, and the periodical press.

In the sixteenth century, readers formed a small part of the population, for literacy and leisure were in short supply. Religious works and pamphlets written for and against the Reformation were printed in modest but significant numbers, and during the transition from hand-copied manuscripts to printed books, some medieval works were reissued by the new printer-publishers. But while twenty editions of the popular *Roman de la rose* appeared by 1540, the total number of copies circulating remained small. Before 1500, the average number of printed copies of a book was about two hundred. During the ancien régime, the figure rose in the seventeenth century from about 1,000 or 1,500 to the exceptional 4,000 copies of the first edition of Rousseau's *La nouvelle Héloïse* (1761). Using another measure, the size of the cultured public of Paris in 1700 (of a population of about half a million) has been estimated by combining the total number of seats in the capital's theaters: the figure was somewhere between ten thousand and seventeen thousand. Later estimates by Voltaire and others put the figure at about thirty thousand. These potential buyers did not all purchase literary works. Practical books, like Barrême's *Le livre des comptes faits* (1682), a ready-reckoner, had huge print runs, but serious works of nonfiction averaged 600 to 800 copies, while plays and novels might run to between 1,500 and 2000. Sixteen editions of Laclos's *Liaisons dangereuses* (1782) appeared within eighteen months of the first, and of these fifteen were pirated versions, a clear indication of its commercial popularity. By then, illegally or clandestinely published "seditious" books had a strong share of the market, a sure indication of the growing opposition to the ancien régime.

At first, the reading public was socially homogenous, since it was limited to the educated elite. It was not restricted to the aristocracy (like Louis XIII, many nobles preferred hunting to books), for it had always included elements of the educated middle class. They sought information about distant lands and scientific discoveries, and in the writings of authors with distinctive personalities they discovered insights into other selves and knowledge of the world. By the early seventeenth century, readers gradually adopted the values of *honnêteté*, which stood for taste, discrimination, and conformity to established norms. Social pressures declared works of "low realism," such as Scarron's *Roman comique* (1651–57), which recounted the farcical adventures of a troupe of actors, to be vulgar and beneath the attention of the *honnêtes gens*. But by 1700, when the seat of political power was migrating from Versailles to Paris, the *honnête homme* had ceased to be a courtier and was mutating into an urban *homme d'esprit* and then into the *philosophe* who had emerged from the middle class through the merit that was urged as a better recommendation than birth.

By the time the ancien régime collapsed in 1789, the lower reaches of the *tiers état* were also becoming enthusiastic consumers of journalism and buyers of books. Literacy rates had risen significantly, and in the late eighteenth century half the male population and under a third of women could sign the parish register. But there were probably still fewer than half a million French men and women capable of reading a book. Yet the poor had not been completely deprived. The early seventeenth century saw the appearance of the first printed volumes, illustrated by crude woodcuts and enclosed in distinctive blue paper covers, which were sold not in shops but by itinerant hawkers. The chapbooks of the *Bibliothèque bleue* were aimed at the barely literate and ranged from tales of chivalry and magic to almanacs, practical manuals, medical advice, and a high percentage of works of religious interest, mainly saints' lives and devotional tracts. They were books without authors, the work of men associated with the printing trades at Troyes, Rouen, and Caen, where most were published. Although only about fifty new titles were added each year, old texts were regularly revised and printed in editions of two thousand to five thousand copies, with key volumes related to faith occasionally reaching forty thousand. By the Revolution, a million copies a year were being sold in country areas to impoverished nobles, small farmers, and village schoolmasters, who read them out loud to their families or classes. In towns, where literacy rates were higher and minimum educational attainments were required of apprentices, they were read by skilled workers, barber-surgeons, lawyer's clerks, and servants in wealthy households, who constituted the cultural elite of the lower classes. Slowly, they graduated to the *cabinets de lecture* (subscription libraries), which, beginning in the 1760s, reached their height in the 1820s, when there were five hundred in Paris alone.

The *littérature de colportage* continued to thrive in town and country. At its peak, in 1847, nine million chapbooks were sold by hawkers. But, faced with increasing government controls and competition from cheap books and newspapers, the *Bibliothèque bleue* finally ceased publication in 1863. By then, the new industrial working class constituted a growing market for books. Peasants and peasant life, the plight of the urban poor, and working-class heroes became fashionable subjects for poets and novelists. The *roman feuilleton* took over where the *littérature (de colportage)* ended, and both had a significant role in widening the scope of fiction. The promotion of the lower orders to a position of seriousness in literature is one way of defining the new realism of the midcentury, when the scene was already being set for the explosion of the mass culture of the twentieth century. In the 1880s, state primary schools opened their doors to all, and by 1900, 83 percent of French people could read and write. The literary public changed, too, as society developed more democratic forms and economic progress extended privileges once reserved for the few to the many. Improvements in secondary education proceeded slowly, but after 1945 educational opportunities were widened further and cultural institutions made themselves more accessible, by Jean Vilar's *Théâtre national populaire* movement, for example. One significant consequence was that the "high" art of the elite declined as the buying power of the mass of citizens rose.

The technological printing revolution of the 1830s produced not only more books but more books of more kinds. With each new decade that passed, publishers catered to new subsets of the reading public, and authors supplied the new demand for practical information, knowledge, and rational discussion, but also for fiction aimed at targeted audiences: crime, romance, books for juveniles, science fiction, historical novels, adventure yarns, and so forth. The market—which directed the alliance between publishers and writers—has continued ever since, taking directions that have not always pleased the discerning reader. As the reading public expands, the status of literature may remain high, but the money is elsewhere, with reader-demand and a market that prefers meteors to masterpieces.

For the development of literature cannot be understood by disregarding the great change brought about by the printing revolution and its lasting influence on the attitudes and practices of authors, publishers, and readers. A great disruption began with the arrival of the printing press in Paris in 1470. The first books were works of theology and erudite commentaries, mainly in Latin and Greek. The first best-selling author was Erasmus, who sparked the humanist revolution, which steadily abandoned the classical languages and adopted the vernacular. The Protestant Reformation in France was launched on the back of the French language.

Progressive minds were delighted with Gutenberg's invention and foresaw a time when the free circulation of knowledge would replace the empire of kings by a Europe-wide republic of letters that promised the communion of scholars and human cooperation. There were casualties, from the disappearance of the scrivener's craft to the general undermining of Latin and Greek, both made necessary by the urge to make the new printed books available to as many people as possible. For Renaissance scholars, this was an article of faith. But it was also the creed of the printers who financed the revolution. The drive to make books accessible to many was a business requirement, and printers took steps to accelerate the process by developing practices that made reading print easier for their customers. Regional and local dialects were marginalized, and vocabulary, spelling, and punctuation were standardized. Paragraphs were introduced, as were the apostrophe and acute and grave accents, so that the way texts were displayed on the page made the meaning clear: the Greek New Testament published by Estienne in 1551 divided the chapters into numbered verses, a practice that became standard.

But new kinds of writing were also generated. The first printed books maintained medieval literary categories, but in the decades after 1500, printing helped fix poetic meters, shaped the five-act structure of plays, and oversaw the birth of the novel. From the start, the French book trade was thus marked by the same centralizing tendency and elegance of style that were already expressive of the national temperament. The guiding hand of a series of authoritative scholar-printer-publishers, the most celebrated being the Estienne dynasty, which lasted until 1674, was instrumental in shaping the modern idea of literature.

The authorities were wary, for they could not foresee where the new invention would lead. The unsupervised dissemination of knowledge and opinion was a potential threat to church and state, for Luther's ideas would not have spread so far and so quickly without the printing press. Although François I welcomed printing, the theologians of the Sorbonne were less tolerant. To curb dissent, the Church of Rome instituted a *chambre ardente* in 1547 and two years later the *Index librorum prohibitorum*, the list of banned books that, regularly updated, would last until 1966. Subsequently, measures were taken to reduce the number of printers in Paris and the provinces and particularly to neutralize the importance of Lyons, which the Inquisition identified as a hotbed of Protestantism.

In the seventeenth century, a combination of absolutist political theory and Gallican tendencies within the Church led to the eventual transfer to royal officials of supervision of the book trade, leaving the Sorbonne to root out theological unorthodoxy. Whereas England in the 1690s allowed books to be published and the courts to rule after publication on whether they should be banned or not, France opted for a system of prepublication censorship. A permission to print (*privilège*) was required, manuscripts being vetted by censors who grew in number throughout the eighteenth century. Controls on the number and activities of printers were tightened, and the publication of pirated or banned matter (mainly religious and political unorthodoxy and obscenity) was made a punishable offense. The effect was to make the producers of literature more cautious and to curb freedom of speech, which had once fired hopes of a new republic of letters. After 1750, however, the rules were applied with increasingly laxity as the censors themselves were won over to the aims of the Enlightenment.

But authors and publishers could not afford to provoke the authorities. Consciously or unconsciously, most authors practiced a form of self-censorship (the avoidance or removal of potentially dangerous matter before submission to the authorities), thus blunting what they had to say. To escape detection, others resorted to subterfuge by publishing books under false names and false imprints in the provinces or in Holland. Either way, their freedom to speak their minds was modified by the constraints under which they worked. Some *libraires* lent themselves to such practices, but most could not afford to offend government, churches, schools, institutions, and conservative book-buyers on whose custom they depended. Many considered it safer to avoid controversial matters and restricted themselves to poetry, plays, fiction, and works by recognized authors.

In August 1789, censorship was abolished by the National Assembly's Declaration of the Rights of Man, which stated that "la libre communication des pensées et des opinions est un des droits les plus précieux de l'homme; tout citoyen peut donc parler, écrire, imprimer librement." The new freedom was short-lived, and restrictions— much more draconian than those imposed by the *direction de la librairie* during the ancien régime—were reintroduced and later confirmed and extended by Napoleon who silenced "seditious" authors, closed most newspapers (just four remained in 1811), and allowed only eight theaters to operate in the capital. In 1810, a third of the capital's print shops were closed, and publishers were required to swear an oath of allegiance to state and emperor.

Thereafter, official attitudes to censorship continued to follow the ebb and flow of politics. Liberal after a change of conservative regime, they turned repressive and were often a cause of the next upheaval. The limited freedom allowed by the Charter of 1814 was reduced in 1819; those controls were lifted after the Revolution of 1830 but reimposed in 1835, relaxed again after 1848, but restored by the repressive Second Empire, which prosecuted, among others, Baudelaire and Flaubert in 1857. It was not until 1881 that a law granting the freedom of the press ended the system of state censorship and made alleged offenses against the public interest a matter, not for the state, but for juries in open courts.

From then on, except at times of national crisis, notably the Great War, the German occupation of France after 1940, and the Algerian War, state-directed censorship ceased, and the role of government was limited to enforcing laws concerning public morality, personal privacy, and national security. The occasional prosecutions for obscenity culminated in 1957 with a high-profile action that ended in a fine for the publisher Jean-Jacques Pauvert for issuing a scholarly edition of Sade. The trial opened a debate that was ended not by argument but by the permissive climate of the 1960s, and writers thereafter were rarely troubled, though anti-obscenity curbs were reinstated for a time in the 1970s. The huge expansion of the book trade has made it more difficult to keep a rein on what appears in print. The advent of the Internet has raised a question over what exactly constitutes "publication" and throws doubts on the ability of governments to enforce infringements of laws covering sedition, obscenity, or slander, which have come to loom less large than the new targets of terrorism, industrial espionage, and child abuse.

Although prepublication censorship has been long since abandoned, the literary consciousness still harbors suspicions of authority. For generations, injustice and oppression have been associated with the Church's hold on moral absolutes and the dangers of the Caesarism that motivated Napoléon, Louis-Napoléon, General Boulanger, and, so his critics say, General de Gaulle. The idealistic goals of 1789 have yet to be fully attained, and the autocratic exercise of power of the Terror of 1794 still touches nerves. As a consequence, the default position of progressive authors in the twentieth century has been contestation, of which Sade has been elected the patron saint. Since 1945, with a few exceptions like the "Hussards" of the 1950s or Raymond Picard's rejection in 1965 of the super-liberal New Criticism as a *Nouvelle imposture*, the center of gravity of intellectuals and serious writers has been left of center. Anticapitalist, anti-American, antiglobalist attitudes have replaced the traditional target since the time of Louis-Philippe: the bourgeoisie. Such views are held by a sufficient section of the reading public for the book trade to maintain its now centuries-old role of midwife to literature.

But how is literature to be distinguished from mere words on paper? Dryden observed that "by criticism, as first instituted by Aristotle, was meant a standard of judging well." Trying to decide what "judging well" means has been a central part of the French literary scene since the first *arts poétiques* appeared during the Renaissance. In practice, it has meant, and still means, judging by the yardstick of some external authority. Du Bellay's denunciation of medieval and "Marotic" poetry was summary and polemical rather than doctrinaire, and Montaigne was an impressionistic critic, more in tune with Anglo-Saxon empiricism than the French love of abstract absolutes. But when literary life began to organize in the seventeenth century, criticism gradually turned into a separate discipline. Both authors and critics believed in the existence of an ideal of beauty and that the ancients had achieved it. The writings of Aristotle could be used to yield principles for the guidance of those who wished to excel once more. Identifying and applying those principles proved controversial, however, and disagreements led to high-profile disputes that in venom mimicked the bitter theological disagreements that were all too familiar. The "rules" of literature constituted a code of rigorous dogma that permitted only "regular" works to be set before the sophisticated public of *honnêtes gens*. By 1660, polemical *querelles* had defined the superiority of verse over prose; of the noble and heroic over the pastoral and the satirical; the "hierarchy of genres" (epic, tragedy, exalted forms of lyric poetry, and so on); and the three unities of time, place, and unity without which no play could possibly meet the full requirements of *le bon goût*. Imitation of the ancients was mandatory and good taste essential. *Le goût* was defined by *bienséance* (what is seemly) and by *vraisemblance* (what is true-seeming), both of which sanitized the most indecorous mythological subjects for the modern public.

The result was a literature written largely to order, though this is not to belittle it: writing against constraints has always brought out the best in good writers. They mostly worked within the limits set by self-appointed arbiters of literary excellence and the requirements of the salons. But gradually a new voice asserted itself, that of literary journalism, aided by changes in public mood, which created a reaction against the pedants and purists (half of Molière's plays do not respect the rules) and added *l'art de plaire* to the equation. It was not enough that literature should satisfy the mind: it was also required to please the heart.

The *Querelle des anciens et des modernes*, which broke out in 1687, opened a clear divide between two opposing views. Against the traditionalists, the "moderns" argued that taste, being variable and arbitrary, is no basis on which to found valid literary principles. Reason, being universal and absolute, is to be preferred. The dogmatism of the "ancients" was overturned, and other progressive ideas followed: the relativism of taste and even the admission that posterity is the ultimate judge of literary merit. The consequence was that the old dogmatism, based on the authority of classical theorists, was replaced by a new dogmatism based on the authority of reason.

But striving for the true, the good, and the beautiful, though they remained formal ideals, did not convince all neoclassical authors. Moreover, readers demanded more emotion and more imagination, horrid words for the classical theorists for whom they spelled disorder and chaos. There was a new emphasis on Horace's *utile dulci*, the idea that the best works mix *l'utile et l'agréable*, the useful being interpreted first as intellectual (as in Voltaire's *Contes philosophiques*) and later conferring on literature a moral and social vocation. But Rousseau's influential novel *La nouvelle Héloïse* taught not only France but the whole of Europe the importance of sentiment. It was the beginning of the Romantics' insistence that henceforth writers and readers should feel with their imaginations and think with their feelings.

But classical ideals were not so easily jettisoned. They were revived during the Restoration, by which time the mantle of *législateurs du Parnasse* was being taken over by literary journalists who also argued about how books should be judged. The most influential of them, Sainte-Beuve, discarded monolithic standards of beauty and the sublime and argued that an objective assessment of the life and times of authors should be a factor in any evaluation of their work. For positivists, this was insufficiently rigorous, and they called for more scientific approaches to be adopted. Thus, Hippolyte Taine urged that books be regarded as the product of "la race, le milieu et le moment," while a new generation of university academics devised a methodology that ensured "scientific objectivity" took precedence over personal and impressionistic responses. Critical editions, philology, classification, and bibliography provided the basis for authoritative analysis, a formula that dominated the institutional, academic approach, embodied by Gustave Lanson, until well after the Great War.

In the meantime, writers and groups of writers were fighting battles of their own, adding another voice to the debate. After about 1820, a new age of "movements" and "schools" dawned that laid down new paths to follow. In the 1840s, to counter Romantic excesses, the art for art's sake creed stressed the craft of writing, and then realism decided that the role of literature was to show the world as it is. The naturalists did not think realists went far enough, and symbolism thought both had gone too far. A Niagara of "isms" took the literati (but not the public, which found many of the experiments too "difficult") to the Great War, when literature became understandably jingoistic. But after 1918, it was quickly enrolled under the banners of Freud and Marx, and the surrealists exploited dreams to generate mental states that would force readers to see the world in a different, "revolutionary" light.

For some, the tail of criticism was wagging the dog of literature. Boileau had warned, "Le plaisir de la critique nous ôte celui d'être touché par les belles choses." The thought that there was too much doctrine also alarmed Anatole France, who observed, "La critique est la dernière de toutes les formes de l'art; elle finira par absorber toutes les autres." Literature had been saddled at various times with an educational role, a social conscience, a moral purpose, a civilizing mission, a satirical duty, an aesthetic vocation, and much else besides. But despite the protests, faintly heard, the mill of theory ground on. After 1945, existentialists used novels and plays to publicize the new duty of revolt and revolutionary resistance to fascism and the bourgeois order. Writers were required to "engage" with reality and "commit" to positive action.

By 1960, a new generation of intellectuals began to see literature as the expression of collective forces operating beneath the level of consciousness. Drawing on a range of specialized social sciences—anthropology, linguistics, psychiatry, political ideology, economics—they set out a new agenda for analyzing literary products. The intentions of authors were declared irrelevant, and, since what they wrote is shaped and determined by the deep psyche and socioeconomic climate, it followed that books are written not by individuals but the zeitgeist. Phenomena were surfaces that disguised truth, and everything was a sign of something else. When properly deconstructed, literature was shown to be a force working through society, not a vehicle of the conscious expression of anything. When structuralism and deconstruction had run their course, postmodernists fled certainties and preferred boundaries, margins, and uncertainties. The ideas were new, but the mechanism was the same: a new absolutism had shown its hand, which remobilized the old centralizing tendencies that now, however, were not institutional, but Parisian.

Many of these debates have been too rarefied to compete with the market concept of literature as entertainment aimed at the majority and instead suit professional writers for whom "literature" is a trade, perhaps a craft but no art. But literary authors have worked, as they always have, with or against the new "législateurs du Parnasse." Generations of journalists, cultural institutions, schools, and movements have sought to set limits as rigorous in their own way as those once imposed by church and state. After a half-century of feverish reflection on the nature and purpose of literature, the flow of new, high-profile theories has, since 2000, slowed significantly. This is unlikely to be the end of the story, however. The centralizing principle is not dead, for it survives in the irrepressible glamour of the cultural elites who inhabit the capital where new ideas are forged and new fashions—the most enduring of all prescriptive influences—are promoted.

But past performance cannot be regarded as a sure indicator of future trends. The history of French literature is by tradition marked out by convenient milestones, broadly corresponding to centuries: Renaissance, classicism, the Enlightenment, Romanticism. Thereafter, as the pace quickened after 1830, easy labeling proved unsuitable for the many new catechisms generated by individualism, corporatism, fragmentation, and diversity. Clearer ways of marshaling the characteristics of past centuries have been proposed. Thus, it might be more useful to speak of an initial phase of exploration and experimentation; an era of formal discipline; and then a period of contestation and progress that ended in the Revolution, which freed personal expression and widened democratic participation, which led to the creative turmoil of the late twentieth century. The implication of a remark made by Marcel Pagnol in 1930 was profound: more people, he said, had seen the films of Chaplin in two decades than all the plays of Molière in three hundred years.

The division by centuries is a useful mnemonic, however, for centuries have their own weather. But it fails to bind the phases of the literature of France into an organic force that both directed and reflected human and social development. The Renaissance began the process of detaching humankind from its feudal deference to a divine creator whose laws were to be obeyed without question. In the seventeenth century, awareness of the self was revealed by Descartes, who showed that thinking defined human nature, that we are able to think about our thinking, and that rational thought is a credible tool for solving the mysteries of creation. The Enlightenment identified natural laws that governed individuals and societies, expressed faith in humankind's ability to accept the implications of reason, and, through Rousseau, began to perceived new ways of preserving the self and improving its relationship with the group. More direct action was taken by the French Revolution, which simply jettisoned the religion, absolutist politics, and centuries of tradition and set about, with mixed success, applying natural laws and reason as a way of directing human affairs. Literary history not only tracks the way society has constantly reinvented itself on new principles; it also demonstrates that literature was itself subject to the same evolutionary processes that Montesquieu defined in 1734: human affairs are not directed by Providence but by action and reaction. Literary history, like any other kind of history, is a chain of causes and effects, the dominant view of one age being the effect of the previous age and the cause of the next. It is dependent on political and institutional change, altered conditions of the book trade, new constituencies of readers, changes in taste and—perhaps most influential of all—fashion. But the process, working in reverse, can also skip centuries. The Romantics fell out of love with classical theater because it was actionless and passionless, in which they agreed with Queen Victoria, who found French tragedy "not pleasing and extremely unnatural." But they also discovered the Pléiade poets, dismissed by previous arbiters of taste as unruly and uncouth.

But there are also permanent losses and gains. Poetry has lost its glamour, but the poetic sense lives on. Tragedy as a genre died finally in the 1840s, but the tragic remains. Comedy reached a fork in the road around the time of Molière and divided into openly comic theater and the "serious" play that has been the staple form of dramatic art for the past two hundred years. Fiction has forged ahead, widening its scope and recently acquiring graphic and interactive forms. Autobiography, a latecomer, has flourished. Before the first stirrings of private life around 1750, writing about the self took two forms: it was either a record of public service or a confession of sins intended as a step on the road to salvation. Modern autobiography was invented by Rousseau, Rétif de la Bretonne, and Casanova, who offered readers personalities that were distinctive and secular. Belief in God had ceased to be an adequate guide to living. Instead, exposing their warts to public view, autobiographers hoped to achieve self-knowledge, forge a personal identity, and gain public acceptance of their unique personas. The "hierarchy of genres" is still in force, though now its summits are occupied not by tragedy and the epic but by the novel and—France's latest gift to literature—the cinema.

At the start of the twenty-first century, literature faces serious challenges. For generations, and especially since the introduction of the cheap *livre de poche* format in 1953, publishers have been targeting mass markets where fiction and accounts of real lives, the biggest winners of the Darwinian struggle for literary survival, seem unstoppable. French publishers cater to many carefully differentiated readerships (crime, books for women, juvenile and science fiction, espionage, graphic fiction), though not all aim at the bottom line. Some imprints reflect more serious interests, women's writing, avant-garde fiction, or the poetry issued by small presses, as respect in France for the nation's literary heritage is generally stronger than in Anglo-Saxon countries. Further competition comes from a new area, francophone writing, which also privileges fiction and true lives. French universities still give pride of place to the traditional syllabus, but they face mounting pressure from influences that set a higher value on popular literature than on the canon of great authors. Literature is subject to intense pressures: commercial imperatives are making literature a branch of entertainment, while prominent intellectuals treat it as a suburb of sociology. For the first, quality is measured by sales; for the second, the use of literature is to reveal truths about society at large and in particular the condition of women and the problems of race, immigration, the marginalized, and the troubled youth of the *banlieues*. By this reasoning, a newspaper, a government form, or a piece of pornography can be more revealing about social realities than Proust and no less estimable for that.

Even the term "French literature" is being challenged, for it has become too general to be useful. Alternatives have been suggested. "Histories of French literature" would cast a wider net and include the history of reading: why should sophisticated tastes be more significant than the concerns of readers of the *Bibliothèque bleue* or the *Série noire*? "Literature in European languages" widens the boundaries by focusing on France, Switzerland, and Belgium, while "literature in French" goes further and opens the door to francophone writings that serve local and nontraditional readerships. "French literatures" gives member-state status to cinema (heir to theater), women's fiction, graphic novels, and, leading the charge, crime fiction. Until recently literary history has been the history of elites. The outsiders are now on the inside.

Although the effect is to disperse the notion of "literature," these trends remain a reflection of the centralizing influence of a Paris-based intellectual elite. But if Barthes's observation that literature is "ce qui s'enseigne" is true, then governments will continue to set the official parameters of literature. But that will be as nothing compared with what looms on the horizon.

The introduction of printing in Paris in 1470 set in motion forces that changed the world: it ended the divine right of kings to rule, overcame the feudal system, and delivered a body blow to the Church. The rise of the Internet will have no less far-reaching effects. Our twenty-first-century world is still at the incunabula stage of the new electronic revolution. Literature is set to become information that will be posted and accessed in new ways. "Frenchness," like "Englishness," will be absorbed into a wider human diversity. A cheap device can hold libraries larger than those once owned by the cultured few, and if the ownership of books can be so quickly transformed, what new ways will be found of writing them? Already there are novel forms of automatic writing, bloggers are the new chroniclers of their times, and interventionist fiction allows readers to make up the story they want to read as they read it. Will national literature be subsumed into a global literature? Will language be needed when stories can be told, transnationally, in moving pictures? Publishers will disappear like the scriveners of old, books will persist for a time then acquire new e-forms, programmers will be the new authors, readers will be consumers, and reading itself may be abandoned in favor of some other mode of communication.

What we call literature is a procession, a parade that is constantly on the move. What looms at the beginning of the twenty-first century is what loomed in 1500 and it, too, is also merely the next moment in the continuum. But whatever metamorphoses it undergoes, the literary impulse will continue until humans cease to feel a need to understand themselves and the world around them.

* *

Erasmus and the "First Renaissance" in France

EDWIN M. DUVAL

In 1495, an impoverished Augustinian monk from the Netherlands arrived in Paris, intending to earn a doctorate in theology at the Faculté de Théologie—or "Sorbonne" as it was then known—of the University of Paris. He spent the better part of the next four years in the French capital, returned again in 1502 for two more years, and a third time at the end of 1504 for yet another year or two, with increasingly frequent interludes elsewhere. In all that time he never came close to earning his doctorate, but he was transformed by his experience in Paris from an obscure but ambitious monk into the citizen of the world and the towering intellectual figure we know today as Erasmus of Rotterdam (1467/69–1536).

It must be said that Erasmus was not well suited for the study of divinity as it was taught at Paris. Scholastic theology, the specialty of the Sorbonne, was a kind of rational metaphysics, forged during the twelfth and thirteenth centuries through ingenious efforts to harmonize the doctrines of the medieval Church with the newly discovered logic of Aristotle. Erasmus was by nature and nurture neither a logician nor a metaphysician. Nor could he tolerate the "corrupt" medieval Latin and abstract dialectical forms in which theological arguments were advanced. He valued simple piety over complex doctrine, harmony over disputation, and classical literature over everything else. Instead of studying theology, he spent much of his time in Paris writing Latin poetry, hoping to become famous as a poet. To make ends meet he gave Latin lessons to schoolboys, composing clever Latin dialogues for his students to recite. He also began culling Latin proverbs from his omnivorous readings in Latin literature. In 1500, he published 818 of these, together with his own learned commentaries, under the title *Collectanea*. This was the first of many works of classical erudition to come. He also wrote a Christo-centric moral treatise in classical Latin style, which he published in 1503 under the title *Enchiridion militis christiani*, or *Handbook of the Christian Soldier*, the first of many works of Christian piety to come. Having discovered in Louvain a manuscript of philological annotations on the text of the Greek New Testament by the Italian humanist Lorenzo Valla, he published these too, in 1505, the first of many critical editions to come. And he threw himself heart and soul into the study of ancient Greek, teaching himself so well that in 1506 he could publish his own Latin translations of the comic author Lucian; in 1507, his own Latin translations of Euripides's *Hecuba* and *Iphigenia in Aulis*; and in 1508, a new edition of the *Collectanea*, now titled the *Adagia*, containing four times as many proverbs, a vast number of them Greek.

Virtually all of Erasmus's mature works can be seen as extensions of these Parisian beginnings—his great treatises on education and rhetoric; his moral treatises; his scholarly work on the Greek New Testament (including the first printed edition of the Greek New Testament in 1516); and most important for students of literature, his moral and satirical works: the *Moriae encomium*, or *Praise of Folly* (1511), a coruscating paradoxical encomium inspired by Lucian and directed against the follies and vices of contemporary Europe and its institutions; successive editions of the *Adagia* (1515 and following), in which commentaries on proverbs grew into immense essays on political, moral, and religious topics; and successive editions of the *Colloquia*, or *Conversations* (1518 and following), in which the early language-learning exercises were elaborated into complex Lucianic dialogues satirizing popular superstitions and abuses of the Church. Common to all these diverse works is the ideology that undergirds them: a characteristically Erasmian fusion of classical and biblical learning, of philology and exegesis, and a new kind of theology—an anti-theology, really—which Erasmus himself consistently referred to as the *philosophia Christi* (philosophy of Christ): an ethics founded directly on the words of Jesus as they are recorded in the Greek Testament and interpreted by the earliest Christians from Paul to Augustine, whose essence is peace, brotherly love, and freedom from the ritualistic constraints of both the Old Testament and the modern Church.

If France played a determining role in the making of this Erasmus, Erasmus played an even more determining role in the shaping of the Renaissance in France. It was Erasmus, more than any of the great Italian humanists of the fourteenth and fifteenth centuries, who inspired in the French a belated enthusiasm for antiquity, with the result that the ancient *fontes*, or "sources," to which sixteenth-century French humanists strove to return—in keeping with the Renaissance watchword best formulated by Erasmus himself: "first and foremost you must hasten to the sources themselves, that is, to the Greeks and ancients"—were biblical and patristic as much as they were Greek and Roman. This fact lent a decidedly religious cast to the French Renaissance from the very beginning, and led directly to one of the greatest ideological clashes in French intellectual history. The Erasmian, "Renaissance" fusion of classical learning and the sacred texts of Christianity was radically incompatible with the scholastic, "medieval" fusion of Aristotelian logic and medieval Church doctrine, and from this incompatibility arose a long series of polar oppositions: grammar, rhetoric, and poetry versus dialectical logic; moral philosophy versus scholastic theology; original sources versus tradition; the primitive Church of the first four centuries versus the medieval Church of the twelfth through the fifteenth centuries—and most acutely in France, Christian humanists versus the Faculty of Theology of the University of Paris.

Because he had inspired one of the factions in this clash of opposing ideologies, and because he was the most famous Christian humanist in all of Europe, Erasmus quickly became the common point of reference and of contention in the power struggle that inevitably resulted. He was lavishly praised and promoted as an icon by his fellow humanists in Paris and viciously attacked and censured by the theologians of Paris. Erasmus's copious correspondence contains fascinating firsthand glimpses into this conflict. Of his many French correspondents, two in particular, both exact contemporaries, can be taken as emblematic: Guillaume Budé (1468–1540), a like-minded humanist, author of erudite studies of Roman law and numismatics, and the most accomplished Hellenist in Europe, and Noël Béda (ca. 1470–1537), zealous defender of orthodoxy, master of the notorious Collège de Montaigu where Erasmus had spent his first, most miserable year in Paris, and all-powerful syndic of the very Faculty of Theology where Erasmus had once studied.

Erasmus's correspondence with Budé consists of some forty-eight extant letters in elegant Latin and ancient Greek, exchanged between 1516 and 1528. Most tellingly, Budé tries repeatedly (first in 1517 and again in 1523–24) to entice his counterpart back to Paris to spearhead the humanist movement in France. In practical terms this meant assuming the directorship of Budé's own pet project, a new institution of higher learning that would be devoted to the teaching of classical Latin, ancient Greek, and biblical Hebrew, and to the study of both Greco-Roman and Judeo-Christian antiquity, sheltered by the king of France, François I, from the persecutions of the reactionary Sorbonne. In 1523, the king himself wrote to Erasmus, confirming Budé's invitation and beseeching Erasmus to accept it. If the king of France had had his wish, Erasmus would have returned to Paris for good, not as a doctor of theology but as the inaugural director of the "College of King's Readers," or *Collège Royal*—one of France's most prestigious institutions, which still exists today as the Collège de France. One cannot help but wonder how French literary and cultural history might have evolved differently had this royal plan for humanistic reform been realized.

Erasmus's correspondence with Noël Béda tells the other side of this story. It consists of eleven extant letters exchanged between 1525 and 1527, at a time when the Faculty of Theology and its notorious syndic were out for blood in their relentless pursuit of a new heresy called Lutheranism—a "Lutheran" being anyone whose strict orthodoxy they suspected, Erasmus being easily the most conspicuous of these. In 1523 and again in 1526, the Faculty, acting on Béda's recommendation, had censured several of Erasmus's works. At issue in these letters is Erasmus's edition of the Greek New Testament and what both correspondents refer to as his stated positions on "celibacy of the clergy, monastic vows, fasting and the interdiction against the eating of meat, the observance of feast days, the evangelical counsels, the translation of Holy Scripture into the vernacular, the canonical hours, divorce, the creeds of the church." This catalog of hot-button issues is noteworthy in naming most of the practices that Erasmus consistently referred to as *constitutiones humanae*, or "human institutions": ritual observances invented by the medieval clergy and enforced by the Church under pain of excommunication but for which no biblical or patristic authority exists and from which, moreover, Christ had explicitly liberated his followers: the cult of saints, dietary restrictions like the Lenten fast, monastic orders, the priesthood, canonical hours, fixed liturgies, the Mass. While Erasmus attacked these as sacrilegious vestiges of paganism and "Judaism," Béda defended them as holy practices necessary to salvation, sanctioned and even required by the Church. Their increasingly vitriolic exchange on these subjects was a dialogue of the deaf, turning on two incompatible notions of "orthodoxy" and "authority": on the one hand, conformity with scripture as understood by the educated individual; on the other hand, submission to dogma as determined by theologians and enforced by the Church. Their letters ceased only when their dispute moved to a more public arena, with direct appeals to the Faculty of Theology and to the king of France and the publication of scurrilous pamphlets and ad hominem attacks. Béda eventually went too far by attacking the king's own sister, Marguerite de Navarre. He was banished briefly from Paris in 1533 and exiled for good in 1535, one year before Erasmus's death. But by this time, the dispute had escalated well beyond all individual actors to become a national crisis. The Erasmian dream of an enlightened Christian Renaissance was dead, the battle lines between Calvinists and Catholics were clearly drawn, and the Wars of Religion were looming on the horizon.

∗ ∗ ∗ ∗

It is hardly surprising that a scholar of Erasmus's stature played such an important catalyzing role within the elite, Latinate sphere in which French humanism clashed with the traditionalism of the Sorbonne. Less expected but no less consequential is Erasmus's influence on a whole generation of French writers in the vernacular—a generation that flowered in the 1530s and 1540s and that French literary history often identifies as the "première Renaissance," conveniently represented by three major writers: the great comic author François Rabelais (1483?–1553), the charming court poet Clément Marot (1496–1544), and an authentic royal: Marguerite d'Angoulême (1492–1549), beloved sister of King François I, duchess of Alençon through her marriage in 1509 to Duke Charles, and queen of Navarre through her marriage in 1527 to Henri d'Albret.

This influence is all the more surprising when we consider that Erasmus himself—one of the most prolific writers in an age of astoundingly prolific writers—never wrote a word in any vernacular language: not even his native Dutch, much less a foreign vernacular like French. Nor did he have the slightest interest in any work that was not written in one of the humanists' "three languages": Latin, Greek, or Hebrew. His influence appears more remarkable still when we consider that two of the most salient characteristics of French literature of this period are a systematic recourse to popular medieval literary forms and a predilection for a style that is "vulgar" in all senses of the word—not only vernacular but often popular and sometimes extremely crude. Between Erasmus's elegant, classicizing Latin prose and Rabelais's ribald and often coarse comic epics, or Marot's medieval allegories, or Marguerite's farces and pop songs, there would seem to be no common ground. And yet Erasmus informs all of these in some crucial way. Discerning this influence can help us discover not only the character and meaning of these works but significant differences among them. These three writers, and lesser writers like them, knew one another, supported one another, and on occasion even collaborated with one another, but their works are radically different in some respects—because, one is tempted to say, they are Erasmian to such different degrees and in such different fashions.

As paradoxical as it may seem to the modern reader, rowdy Rabelais was by far the most consciously and enthusiastically Erasmian writer of the three. It would be no exaggeration to say that without Erasmus there would have been no *Gargantua* or *Pantagruel*. Nearly as paradoxical, perhaps, is the fact that the pious and decorous Marguerite was the least Erasmian of the three. Despite many shared values and convictions—belief in the unique authority of the Bible, a radically Christo-centric vision of Christianity, an inward piety, and a loathing for rational theology—she was deeply hostile to everything Erasmus came to represent.

Once again Erasmus's correspondence offers a fascinating glimpse into crucial distinctions and oppositions, this time within the single camp of the Renaissance avant-garde. Near the end of 1532, Rabelais sent a very Erasmian letter to Erasmus, written in elegant Latin interspersed with long passages in Greek, in which he expressed his boundless admiration and gratitude to the great humanist, whom he calls his "most humane father" and more: "I would also call you 'mother,' if by your indulgence that were permitted me. . . . You have given me my education, you have never ceased to feed me with the purest milk of your divine learning; whatever I am, whatever I am good for, it is to you alone that I owe it." This letter is by no means uncharacteristic of its author. As early as 1520 and 1521, Rabelais had written two similar letters, also in elegant Latin and Greek, to Guillaume Budé, and in 1532 he published three scholarly works—one of them the *editio princeps* of two short works by Hippocrates and Galen, in Greek, with Rabelais's own annotations in Latin—all preceded by dedicatory epistles to French humanists written in the same Latin and Greek style. Rabelais, a former monk and self-taught Hellenist like Erasmus, clearly viewed himself as a humanist in the Erasmian mold. Yet in the same year of his first scholarly editions and his letter to Erasmus, he published the first and most popular of his works in the vernacular, *Pantagruel*. The question that arises, then, is not why the author of *Gargantua* and *Pantagruel* would write to Erasmus, but why an Erasmian humanist like Rabelais would write such vulgar works in the vernacular as *Gargantua* and *Pantagruel*? For the moment, it must simply be observed that Erasmus never answered Rabelais's letter. This is perhaps not surprising, because in 1532 Rabelais was completely unknown while Erasmus was the most famous man in Europe, admired by multitudes and loathed by as many, mired in controversies and in failing health, with only four more years to live.

A few years earlier, however, in 1525 and in 1527, Erasmus had written two letters to Rabelais's younger contemporary Marguerite, addressing her first as the recently widowed duchess of Alençon, then as the newly married queen of Navarre. The first is a personal tribute and an expression of condolence for Marguerite's recent losses and calamities; the second is an expression of support for Louis de Berquin, Marguerite's protégé and Erasmus's imprudent French translator, who was then suffering the persecutions of Noël Béda. We know that Marguerite never answered the first letter, and we can safely assume she never answered the second. And yet between 1521 and 1524, Marguerite had pursued a long and intense correspondence with Guillaume Briçonnet, bishop of Meaux—another Christian humanist and victim of Noël Béda—centered on the meaning of the Bible and its implications for a purely interior, personal form of Christian devotion. Marguerite snubbed Erasmus, just as Erasmus, more understandably, would snub Rabelais.

The symmetry of these two unreciprocated epistolary overtures throws into sharp relief some of the paradoxes of Erasmian influence and suggests fault lines within a defining feature of the *première Renaissance* that literary history usually represents as monolithic and identifies, for want of a better term, as "evangelism." By probing these paradoxes and fault lines one can arrive at a fairly complete and nuanced appreciation of French vernacular literature of the 1530s and 1540s. But first we must know how to recognize Erasmus's influence.

One measure of this influence is the force and frequency with which Erasmus's signature themes and ideas are expressed. Another is the use of literary devices and modes that Erasmus was the first to introduce and that for a very long time remained closely associated with him: the paradoxical encomium, the satirical dialogue, and a pervasive irony so mercurial that it is sometimes extremely difficult to pin down. Many of these features can be traced directly to the second-century Greek rhetorician and satirist Lucian of Samosata, whose works Erasmus and his friend Thomas More began publishing in Latin translation in 1506. Anything that looks "Lucianic" is in fact almost certain to be Erasmian. Most of Erasmus's mature *Colloquies* are satirical dialogues in the Lucianic style, in which two or more characters holding opposing views on religious and moral questions work out their differences (or not) in dialectical fashion. In most cases one side quickly emerges as the correct one, the other as untenable and even ridiculous. "The Shipwreck" (1523), for example, presents a powerful case against the traditional practice of making vows to saints. "The Girl with No Interest in Marriage" and "The Repentant Girl " (1523) condemn premature monastic vows and hint at the sordid goings-on in convents. "Julius Excluded from Heaven" (1518), an anonymous dialogue never acknowledged by Erasmus but universally attributed to him, condemns war in the person of the recently deceased "warrior-pope" Julius II, who boasts to Saint Peter—thereby unwittingly indicting himself—of his countless military campaigns against Christian princes in defense of the temporal power of the Church. The dialogue ends as Peter points out the incompatibility of war and the *philosophia Christi* and sends Julius down to his rightful abode in hell.

Other colloquies are more subtle and complex. "A Fish Diet" (1526), for example, stages a long and very learned argument between a fishmonger and a butcher about the legitimacy of Lenten fasting, the former arguing *pro* on the basis of doctrinal discussions he has overheard among Dominican doctors of theology, the latter *contra* on the basis of his own, self-directed readings of the Bible. The butcher seems to come out ahead, as one would expect in Erasmus, but rather than reaching a definitive conclusion, the two agree to leave the issue unresolved and dine together instead, in a characteristically Erasmian spirit of nondogmatic brotherly love.

The work for which Erasmus is best known to modern readers— *The Praise of Folly*, first published in Paris in 1511 and 1512 and expanded in 1514 and 1516—is the best and most complex example of Erasmian irony. What distinguishes this paradoxical encomium from similar works by Lucian and other ancients is that it is also a prosopopoeia, in which the allegorical personification of foolishness itself, Stultitia, does the talking, praising herself (a foolish thing to do, as befits Folly). Since it is not Erasmus but Folly who speaks, we have to interpret her words accordingly. Everything she praises we understand to be either trivial or harmful—except when it is not, as when she extols the "folly of the Cross," expanding on 1 Corinthians 1:17–25 and 3:18–23 (for one can hardly expect Folly to be consistent!). Erasmus takes great pains to point this out in the prologue to the work, reminding his readers not to take offense at anything Folly says because it is not an insult but rather "an honor to be insulted by Folly."

⁙ ⁙ ⁙ ⁙

Rabelais's first work in the vernacular, *The Horrendous and Dreadful Deeds and Acts of Prowess Performed by the Renowned Pantagruel, King of the Dipsodes, Son of the Great Giant Gargantua, Recently Composed by Master Alcofrybas Nasier*—or simply *Pantagruel*, as it came to be known—seems at first glance to inhabit a world far removed from that of Erasmus. Its characters (giants and tricksters), its genre (burlesque, chivalric epic and fabliau), its themes (drinking and fighting), style (rambunctious and ribald), even its typeface (Gothic bastard) are all ostentatiously medieval and popular. But the book also contains strong hints of an Erasmian orientation. One is found in the famous letter sent by Gargantua to his son Pantagruel, who is far from home studying in Paris (chapter 8). The letter is written in a conspicuously decorous style, replete with long Ciceronian periods and learned allusions. It contains the most explicit description in French of the opposition between the calamitous "dark ages" brought about by the "Goths" who invaded the Roman Empire and destroyed all literature and learning, and the modern age of the Renaissance in which all ancient disciplines, works, and languages—not only the humanistic "three languages" (Greek, Latin, Hebrew) but also Aramaic—have been restored to their former honor and luster. And it exhorts Pantagruel to master completely all of these languages, works, and disciplines, so as to become a veritable "abyss of learning," a gigantic embodiment of Renaissance humanism itself. One detail that makes this vision of the Renaissance recognizably Erasmian is the fact that in a review of "all disciplines," theology is replaced by daily reading of the Bible in its original languages. Another is that the stated purpose of all this study is not erudition for its own sake but an exemplary moral life and a perfectly just and peaceful reign under the future king of Utopia. Not only does Gargantua's program of study correspond exactly to those spelled out in Erasmus's various works on pedagogy, but it establishes Pantagruel as Erasmus's ideal Christian prince as set forth in *De principis christiani*.

Another Erasmian passage is the prayer uttered by Pantagruel in the last moments before his decisive single combat with the cannibal giant Loup Garou (Werewolf), champion of the usurping tyrant, King Anarche. In this prayer the hero states that his war against the Dipsodes is not an imperialist war of aggression but a purely defen-

sive war, necessary to preserve home and homeland against an unpro-
voked and treacherous invasion. God himself, says Pantagruel, strictly
forbids all other kinds of war, even wars undertaken for the defense of
the true religion, since faith is the business and the prerogative of
God alone, requiring no helping hand from humans except in the
form of confessions of faith and preaching of the Word. The irenism
of this statement is purely Erasmian. In many places and in many
manners Erasmus stated and restated that war and Christianity are
mutually exclusive. Not only wars between Christian nations but
wars against non-Christian infidels are strictly forbidden.

Several details confirm the Erasmianism of this passage, too. One
is Pantagruel's explicit statement that his "total faith and hope are in
[God] alone," an infallible indicator of evangelism and an implicit
rejection of all works (vows, masses, pilgrimages) and intermediaries
(saints, priests, monks). Another is the vow with which Pantagruel
ends his prayer. Erasmus often condemned vows to saints as a form of
idolatry and paganism. Pantagruel's vow is something entirely different. "If Thou art pleased to come to my aid," he says, speaking directly to God, "I vow to Thee that throughout all lands, both in this
country of Utopia and others, where I have power and authority, I
will have Thy Gospel preached pure, simple, and entire, so that the
abuses of a bunch of hypocrites and false prophets, who, by human
institutions and depraved inventions, have envenomed the whole
world, will be driven forth from around me." The "human institutions" that Pantagruel vows to abolish (*constitutions humaines* in
French) are precisely those *constitutiones humanae* that Erasmus never
tired of condemning as "abuses" and "depraved inventions" that had
so completely corrupted the Church: pilgrimages, vows, the cult of
saints, Lenten fasting, monastic orders, liturgical hours and prayers,
the Mass—so many abrogations of Christian liberty and of Christ's
New Law of love, invented by the "hypocrites" (priests and popish
"papelars") and "false prophets" (theologians). In place of all these
Pantagruel will restore the text of the Gospel by having it read,
preached, and explained in its entirety as a coherent whole (*entière-
ment*), free of interpolations and extraneous interpretations (*simple-
ment*), and purged of all articles of faith invented by scholastic theology (*purement*), in the original text as it has been established by

humanist philology. Pantagruel's vow is answered by a heavenly voice saying: "Do this and you shall vanquish."

These two passages help us perceive even in the foolish passages a meaning that is no less Erasmian. Pantagruel does indeed "vanquish" in the end, by establishing in Utopia a new golden age of peace, love, and convivial joy. What allows him to do this, according to the logic of the narration, is precisely the humanist education that has transformed him from an uncouth and ignorant giant into a wise Solomonic and even Christ-like mediator, capable of resolving the most intractable legal cases and reconciling even the most antagonistic of litigants. Many episodes that first appeared silly or vile begin to look like oblique, good-humored expressions of something crucial to the grand arc of the plot, giving a distinctly Erasmian cast to the form as well as the ideology of the book.

Pantagruel was an instant success and a runaway best seller, to which Rabelais hastened to add a prequel (*Gargantua* in 1534 or 1535), and much later a sequel (*Tiers Livre de Pantagruel* in 1546), followed by a sequel to the sequel (*Quart Livre de Pantagruel* in 1552). These later books tend to be less rambunctious in form and style than the first, and much more obviously learned. The *Tiers Livre*, especially, is a virtual compendium of humanistic erudition and modes of expression, much of it recognizably Erasmian, all in the service of recognizably Erasmian themes. A brilliant paradoxical encomium of debts appears near the beginning, for example; an equally brilliant paradoxical encomium of a plant called "Pantagruelion" at the end; and a dense farrago of adages at the very center. The *Quart Livre* satirizes all the usual enemies of both humanism and humanity in the grotesque inhabitants of islands encountered during a sea voyage inspired by Lucian's *True Story*. *Gargantua* retains much of the popular flavor of *Pantagruel* but offers an obviously Erasmian explanation for this un-Erasmian appearance. In the prologue the narrator presents his books as "Sileni of Alcibiades," borrowing liberally from Erasmus's commentary on that adage to claim—ironically?—that behind their apparent foolishness lies a precious hidden meaning: "very lofty sacraments and horrific mysteries, concerning [not only our religion but] our political state and our domestic life." Whether we take the narrator's claim literally or not, whether we read superficially for hilarious jokes or deeply for hidden messages, we are always led back to same negative view of the obstacles to human well-being: theologians and monks, *constitutiones humanae*, medieval ignorance and acedia, warmongers and egotists, violence, hatred, and entrenched orthodoxies of all kinds. Rabelais's Erasmus is "humanistic" in the modern sense as well as the Renaissance sense of the word: concerned almost exclusively with human relations and human communities—peace, justice, and convivial joy in a redeemed and enlightened world.

∵ ∵ ∵ ∵

Marguerite d'Angoulême was a prolific writer who published almost nothing. As a woman, as a *dévote*, and especially as the sister of the king of France and a duchess and queen by her marriages, she inhabited a social sphere so exclusive and so lofty that "going public" by means of the printing press was virtually unthinkable. Her works were widely circulated and read within the elite circles of royal and ducal courts, however, as large numbers of elegant surviving manuscripts attest. Paradoxically, many of these works are extremely plain and popular in genre, form, and style. Those that are more elevated are either courtly (like the unfinished Decameron published posthumously as a fragment under the spurious title *Heptameron*) or decidedly "medieval" (like the short, early dream-vision titled *Dialogue en forme de vision nocturne* and the long, late allegory of a pilgrim's progress titled *Les prisons*). None of her works is ironic. None is funny. None is learned. In all these respects, Marguerite is a very un-Erasmian writer. She was nevertheless attacked by the same enemies as Erasmus: by the zealously orthodox Béda on one side, and by the equally zealous French reformer Jean Calvin, her former protégé, on the other. To judge by their common adversaries Marguerite and Erasmus would appear to occupy the same middle ground between orthodoxy and reform, where a return to the foundational texts and principles of the primitive Church would occur within the established Church, not in opposition to it. But as Erasmus's two unanswered letters suggest, the "common ground" defined negatively by its opponents was riven by fundamental differences of ideology, of form, and of substance.

The only book that Marguerite voluntarily entrusted to a printer for mass reproduction and public dissemination offers the most revealing glimpse of her character as a writer. This little book, published in Alençon in 1531, contains three long poems in rhymed couplets: *Le miroir de l'âme pécheresse* (*Mirror of the Sinful Soul*), *Discord estant en l'homme par contrarieté de l'esperit et de la chair* (*Discord between the Spirit and the Flesh*), and an *Oraison à nostre seigneur Jesus Christ* (*Prayer to Our Lord Jesus Christ*). All three are intense, prayerful, first-person monologues, inspired by Paul's Epistle to the Romans and addressed to Christ as a personal savior. The *Miroir* is the most characteristic. The first-person speaker is strongly marked feminine, not because it is the voice of Marguerite but because it is the prosopopoeia of an anonymous "soul," represented as an essentially feminine thing by nature as well as by grammatical gender, whether it belongs to a man or a woman. This everyman's soul is tormented by an agonizing awareness not only of its own innate, ineradicable sinfulness, but of its utter powerlessness to redeem itself by means of its own will and actions. It inhabits a radically Pauline world characterized by what Luther and Calvin called the "total depravity" of postlapsarian humankind. The only means to salvation is the free gift of God's unmerited grace. Marguerite illustrates this principle by having the speaking soul pass from utter despair through hope and doubts to complete certainty of its own salvation, progressing only by acknowledging its own vileness and nothingness [*rien*] and thus making itself available for possession by the Everything [*Tout*] that is Christ's forgiveness and love.

To this fundamentally Pauline plot Marguerite adds an intensely personal, affective dimension that is typical of all her writing. Throughout the poem the soul describes its own singular relationship to the singular person of Christ. Precisely because the soul is feminine and because Christ is masculine, this relationship is assimilated at every turn to each of four possible affective relationships between a woman and a man—daughter-father, sister-brother, mother-son, and especially wife-husband—and to a specific biblical story that functions as an analogue, a type, a precedent, and a promise. The biblical model for the wife-husband relationship is the most traditional and most easily exploited. It derives directly from the series of erotic love songs exchanged by a bridegroom and his bride in the Song of Songs, interpreted since the twelfth century as an allegorical expression of the love between Christ and the individual believer. The other biblical models are more original and require more inventive exegetical tweaking: the parable of the prodigal son for daughter and father, Miriam and Moses for sister and brother, the quarrel between two mothers adjudicated by Solomon for mother and son. All of these, interpreted allegorically, tell the story of the soul's unworthiness repaid by Christ's unmerited love, of the soul's betrayal of that love repaid with Christ's even greater love, forgiveness, and joyful reunion. The poem ends with a long, ecstatic monologue in which the soul is consumed by love and yearns for an ever more complete annihilation of its own autonomous being and complete dissolution in infinite, ineffable love of Christ.

The peculiar fusion in this poem of an austere Pauline theology of salvation, on one hand, and a personal, ecstatic, almost solipsistic love between a sinful soul and the person of Christ, on the other, results from the convergence of two independent traditions: a medieval tradition of female mysticism going back to the early thirteenth century and illustrated by figures like Marguerite Porete, Catherine of Sienna, and Marguerite's younger contemporary, Teresa of Avila; and a theological tradition inaugurated by Paul, elaborated by Augustine, and recently made current and controversial thanks to the notorious heretical writings of Martin Luther. Marguerite knew both of these traditions well—the former through works like Porete's *Miroir des âmes simples* (*Mirror of Simple Souls*), a major source of the *Miroir de l'âme pécheresse* and of many later works; the latter through Marguerite's correspondence with Guillaume Briçonnet in the early 1520s and contraband translations of Luther's own works.

Though strange to modern readers, this blend of female mysticism and hard-nosed Lutheranism is a defining feature of virtually all Marguerite's writing—her allegorical monologues from the early *Dialogue en forme de vision nocturne* to the late *Prisons*; her evangelical farces from the early *Malade* and *Inquisiteur* to the late *Comédie de Mont-de-Marsan*; and her *Chansons spirituelles*, pious *contrafacta* composed to be sung to the tune of well-known, often risqué and even mildly obscene popular songs of the late fifteenth century.

❧ ❧ ❧ ❧

Rabelais and Marguerite are both called *évangéliques* by modern scholars, and rightly so, but they clearly represent very different strains of evangelism. Rabelais's is Erasmian and humanistic, Marguerite's anti-Erasmian and mystical. This difference is evident not only in what these two writers wrote, but in their manner of writing. One feature common to both is the use of familiar, popular forms and styles to express meanings that are radically new—a practice that gives rise to works that look today like strange hybrids of "medieval" and "Renaissance" characteristics. But even in this, the differences between Rabelais and Marguerite are striking, and revealing.

Marguerite's use of popular genres and a plain style—so disconcerting at first glance in the work of such a highborn princess—is entirely consistent with her mystico-Lutheran ideology. If salvation depends not on one's own efforts but on recognizing the worthlessness of everything one is and can do, then pretentiousness of any kind—including literary pretentiousness—can only be an obstacle to salvation. Small children, ignorant simple folk, servants, and (in Marguerite's strongly held antifeminist view) women, are always much closer to salvation than are mature adults, learned scholars, nobles, and males, precisely because they are by nature less capable and less self-sufficient, and because they know it. Having fewer illusions of self-worth, they have fewer obstacles to overcome in recognizing their own intrinsic depravity, powerlessness, and dependency on grace. For Marguerite the princess and author, farces, popular songs, and simple, unadorned speech are signs and effects of self-abnegation and self-annihilation—efforts to achieve a kind of *dégré zéro de l'écriture* and a self-inflicted *mort de l'auteur*—which are necessary preconditions for an ecstatic union with Christ.

Rabelais's use of popular forms and styles has a completely different function. For Rabelais, the "popular" is a lowest common social denominator, allowing for a purely human communion of all men, low and high, in which Christ's new law of brotherly love is fully realized here on earth. It is the sign and precondition of a universal evangelical brotherhood. This social dimension of popular culture explains the many Bruegelian scenes of joyful *beuveries* in Rabelais—most notably in *Gargantua*, where we find a bibulous, rustic banquet and a convivial celebration of the anti-monk Frère Jean, and in the prologues to Rabelais's books, where a high-spirited narrator addresses his readers familiarly, with a typically Rabelaisian mixture of popular ribaldry and learned allusions, as members of the same communion, drinkers of the same wine, sitting together around a common table. In all such scenes, wine and "bons mots" are the symbols and the efficacious agents of a nonsacramental communion of unpretentious fellow drinkers.

The fundamental difference between these two functions of popular culture points to two radically opposed kinds of "evangelism." Both are biblical, both are Christ-centered, but Rabelais's is human, social, convivial; Marguerite's is transcendent, individualistic, and ecstatic. In this sense Rabelais and Marguerite can be said to represent two separate axes of Renaissance evangelism, corresponding to two distinct kinds of "communion": horizontal versus vertical, human versus divine, active versus passive. Both are present in Erasmus, but there is no doubt that Rabelais's is more typically "Erasmian"—and more consonant with Erasmus's *philosophia Christi*—than Marguerite's.

Another indication of this difference is the value attached by each of these authors to erudition. For Rabelais, as for Erasmus, humanistic learning is a gift from God, a providential means to the most desirable end of a life lived on earth in peace and harmony, in accordance with God's purpose. For Marguerite, learning is not only unnecessary but actually harmful, constituting one of the most insidious temptations of a sinful world. It encourages the sinful illusion that by one's own efforts one can attain a higher good, thus feeding the ego and thereby cutting oneself off permanently from grace and communion with God. Even philology, which for Erasmus is the essential key to understanding the text of the Bible, is for Marguerite a diabolical lure. In her later works she comes close to suggesting that even reading the Bible, even in translation, is unnecessary because everything it teaches can be apprehended directly from the ultimate source, so to speak, by means of an ecstatic, mystical marriage with Christ.

Marguerite was as conscious of her differences with Erasmus as Rabelais was conscious of his proximity. In two late works she pointedly represented Erasmian humanism in an extremely negative light. One of these is the evangelical farce *Comédie de Mont-de-Marsan*, in which four female allegories interact symbolically. La Mondaine (Worldly) is concerned only with her body and is proud of her physical beauty. La Superstitieuse (Devout) is concerned only with her soul and is proud of her works of piety, certain that she will be saved by mortifying her own flesh. La Sage (Wise) converts and reconciles the first two by offering each a copy of the Bible, promising that if they study this book they will be reborn in humility and virtue, love of God, and love of neighbor. But the play does not end here. The three happy ladies encounter a fourth, a lovesick Bergère (Shepherdess) who seems to care nothing at all for body, soul, or mind, but sings ecstatic love songs about her absent lover. She is identified in the dramatis personae as "ravished by the love of God" (*ravie de l'amour de Dieu*) but, as the three other characters point out, her words contain no indication that her love is spiritual or that her lover is Christ. Are her words meant to be allegorical? We have no way of knowing. All we know is that the Bergère is beyond the reach of reason. She cannot be bothered to read the Bible, much less to study it, less still to join into communion with her sisters. The play ends as the three others leave in disgust, and the shepherdess remains alone on the stage, singing her heart out like a mad Ophelia. However we choose to interpret the play, it clearly represents the defeat of Erasmian humanism.

A similar defeat is represented in Marguerite's greatest work: the long allegorical poem *Les prisons*, which describes three successive stages in a male narrator's life. In the second of these the narrator is seized by a love of the world and all it contains. A cheerful old man named Amateur de Science (the French equivalent of *philo-sophos*) providentially appears to convince him that the "world" he admires is in fact a prison; that the thirst for honor, wealth, and pleasure (the three "concupiscences" condemned in 1 John 2.15–17) are "tyrants" that bind him to a transitory world governed by fickle Fortune; and that learning holds the key to freedom, virtue, and immortality. Inspired by the old sage, the narrator devotes himself entirely to study. He labors tirelessly to master all the humanistic disciplines: philosophy, poetry, law, mathematics, medicine, history, rhetoric, and finally theology, which consists not of abstract metaphysics but of unmediated study of the text of the Bible. Here again we recognize the Erasmian ideal of learning in the service of a Christian life, and here again the Erasmian ideal is shown to fail. Once liberated by liberal studies, the narrator discovers he has once again become a prisoner, this time of the letter of all these texts, and of the capital sin of *cuyder*, or prideful presumption. Laboring on his own to know everything, the narrator has simply repeated the original sin against God and brought about his own fall from grace. Providential grace intervenes, unsolicited, to liberate the self-imprisoning humanist. A sudden manifestation of the Spirit leads to the conflagration of the universal library and all the books it contains. The poem ends with an apocalyptic vision and a long song of ecstasy and praise uttered by a narrator now freed from his own being, reduced to "nothing" and "ravished by Love, transported by joy."

The anti-Erasmianism of these works is so apparent that it is tempting to view La Sage and Amateur de Science as representations of Erasmus himself, and the love songs of the ecstatic Bergère and the mystical transports of the spiritually liberated narrator of *Les prisons* as Marguerite's replies to Erasmus's two unanswered letters. To the eloquent, learned, ennobling Latin prose of the humanist, Marguerite responds with the irrational vernacular ravings of an illuminated ignorant "nothing," innocent of books and even of the Book, and simply "ravished by love." From Marguerite's point of view, Erasmian humanism consists in dead letters and sinful pride. Illumination comes directly from the Spirit, unsought, unearned, unlearned, and incomprehensible to the wise—an extreme case of the "folly of the Cross" that is foolishness to the Greeks seeking wisdom.

❧ ❧ ❧ ❧

In their differences Rabelais and Marguerite define two poles of a continuum along which most of their contemporaries can be situated. The best-known and most interesting of these is Clément Marot, the court poet famously dismissed by Boileau in the next century as a facile versifier. As Marguerite's court poet and secretary, and later as court poet and secretary of the king himself, Marot indeed wrote circumstantial verse that is deft, witty, and charming. But he also wrote works that are very close in spirit to Marguerite's. An obvious example is his relatively late project of translating the biblical psalms into the French vernacular—publishing thirty of them in 1541, another twenty in 1543. These are in fact paraphrases more than translations, similar to Marguerite's *Chansons spirituelles* in that Marot composed them in lyric stanzas designed to be sung as four-part "chansons parisiennes," then very much in vogue. Marot acknowledged this aspect of his translations in the dedicatory poem of the 1543 edition, addressed to the "Ladies of France," where he clearly enunciates the principle of the *Chansons spirituelles*: when the ladies sing these "love songs" with new words written by God himself (the God who *is* love), the Holy Spirit will inhabit and transform their hearts by grace. Marot also contributed directly to some of Marguerite's own works. His very first psalm translation (psalm 6) first appeared in a 1533 edition of Marguerite's *Miroir de l'âme pécheresse*. The joyful, transformative song sung by the blessed children at the very center of Marguerite's farce *L'inquisiteur* is none other than Marot's translation of psalm 3.

At other moments Marot appears closer to Rabelais—by no means as learned but similarly concerned with a more social, human form of evangelism. His most accomplished works are satirical and polemical poems that attack the same carnal, formalistic *constitutiones humanae* that Rabelais satirizes so effectively. Many of these poems are autobiographical: epistolary accounts of the two occasions on which Marot was imprisoned for "eating fat during Lent" and of his flight into exile at a time when Noël Béda's influence was unchallenged and all "Lutherans" were being rounded up and executed. One such work is a mordant allegorical poem titled *L'enfer*, modeled on book 6 of Virgil's *Aeneid*. Another is a verse epistle written in exile in which "la belle Christine," an allegory for the paleo-Christian church, is contrasted with the whore of Babylon, an allegory for the Roman Catholic Church. All of these are brilliant portrayals of the abuses of Church and Parliament and justifications of the poet's own actions on religious and biblical grounds. This vein of satire is unmistakably Rabelaisian, and Erasmian.

Other poems by Marot fall somewhere between these two poles. An early work titled *Le temple de Cupido* (1514), for example, relates an allegorical quest for "Ferme Amour" (constant love), clearly identified as Christ's love for humanity and *agape* among Christians, which the narrator eventually finds simultaneously in his own heart and in the love between François, future king of France, and his new bride Claude de Bretagne. When writing in this "middle ground," Marot is often recognizably Erasmian. Verse translations of two and possibly three of Erasmus's own *Colloquia* on the theme of women and marriage corroborate this orientation. Marot's psalm translations also owe something to Erasmus's idea that all Christians should have direct access to scripture in their own language. The poem in which Marot dedicates these translations to the ladies of France in fact echoes a famous passage of Erasmus's *Paraclesis*, a preface to his edition and Latin translation of the Greek New Testament, which looks forward to a day when not only women, but plowers, artisans, and tradesmen will sing psalms as they toil in their fields and shops and on the road. The juxtaposition of this echo with allusions to Marguerite's idea of conversion through song makes this wonderful little poem an emblematic fusion of the Erasmian and anti-Erasmian strains of sixteenth-century evangelism.

∗∗ ∗∗ ∗∗ ∗∗

Despite their many differences Rabelais, Marguerite, and Marot were attacked by the same enemies, who were also Erasmus's enemies, and like Erasmus they eventually found themselves caught in the cross fire between increasingly antagonistic factions—an entrenched Catholic orthodoxy on one side and emerging Protestant orthodoxies on the other. All three were victims of Erasmus's nemesis, the hyperorthodox Noël Béda. At the same time, Jean Calvin denounced Rabelais as an "atheist" and Marguerite, more obliquely, as a "spiritual libertine." Marot fared somewhat better with this faction at first, finding refuge from Catholic persecution in Calvin's Geneva in 1542, where he contributed his psalm translations to the new Geneva Bible, but Marot's urbane wit eventually proved too worldly for the dour Calvin, and he died in double exile from Catholic France and Protestant Geneva, in Turin, in 1544.

Rabelais's last book, the *Quart Livre*, published in 1552, represents a world wracked by intractable wars and mutually exclusive ideologies, with *Papimanes* (pope maniacs) on one side, and *Papefigues* (those who make obscene gestures at the pope) on the other; the Holy

Roman Emperor Charles V on one side, and the Lutheran German princes on the other; "Matagotz, Cagotz, et Papelars" of the Roman Catholic Church on one side, and "Demoniacles Calvins imposteurs de Geneve" on the other. By this time Erasmus, Marguerite, and Marot were all dead, and Rabelais, first and last of the French Erasmians, had only a year to live. With Rabelais's death in 1553, an era of precarious brilliance came to an end. What both sides of the ideological divide viewed—mistakenly—as a fainthearted middle ground shrank to nonexistence, leaving only hardened and mutually excommunicating orthodoxies in its place. Although some distinctive features of Erasmus's writing can still be found in later years—the Erasmian form of dialogue that survives intact in the feminist dialogues of Catherine Des Roches, for example, and the digressive ruminative style of the *Adagia* that lives on in Montaigne's *Essais*—the humane, ironic, and optimistic Christian humanism that Erasmus had come to represent could not survive the clash of hardened creeds, inquisitions, and martyrdoms. Erasmianism itself was dead.

As a consequence of this demise, literature produced by the next generation of French writers was entirely different from that of the first generation. The characteristic fusions of classical and biblical antiquity, of high and low cultures, of popular simplicity and elite erudition, of comedy and piety, of "medieval" and "Renaissance," disappeared without a trace, giving way to a "purer" literary Renaissance that cultivated classical themes in classical forms, channeled Christian and secular influences into completely separate spheres, and never, ever, treated religion with humor. This was the era of the Pléiade, whose project was to re-create classical poetry in the French vernacular, bestowing on their king, their nation, and themselves all the prestige that Pindar and Homer, Horace and Virgil, had bestowed on Greece and Rome and themselves. This second Renaissance was proclaimed with great fanfare in 1549, through publication of the *Défense et illustration de la langue française*, in which Joachim du Bellay called for a complete break with the literary past and the creation of a completely new French literature. But the seeds of this Renaissance had in fact been sown earlier. The final paradox of a paradoxical generation of French writers is that the first sonnets in French, the first epigrams in French, some of the first elegies and eclogues in French, and the very first translations and imitations of Petrarch, cynosure of the new Renaissance poets, were written not by members of the Pléiade but by that most versatile and mercurial of first-Renaissance poets, Clément Marot.

Works Cited and Recommended Further Reading

The complete works of Erasmus are currently being made available in excellent critical editions, thanks to two ongoing projects, both expertly annotated by large teams of the most prominent Erasmus scholars of the past fifty years. The *Opera omnia Desiderii Erasmi Roterodami* (Amsterdam: North-Holland and Elsevier; Leiden: Brill, 1969–), now almost complete with some forty-three volumes published (but no plans to publish the letters), offers the definitive text of the Latin original. The standard Latin edition of the letters remains the *Opus Epistolarum Desiderii Erasmi Roterodami*, ed. P. S. Allen, 12 vols. (Oxford: Clarendon Press, 1906–58). The *Collected Works of Erasmus* (Toronto: University of Toronto Press, 1974–), progressing nicely with fifty-seven of eighty-six projected volumes now published, offers the most complete collection of English translations. The letters (vols. 1–25) are unfortunately incomplete as of 2016, extending only through July 1530 (vol. 16). Erasmus's correspondence with Noël Béda quoted in this chapter is from letters 1579 and 1581 in *The Correspondence of Erasmus: Letters 1535–1657*, ed. Charles G. Nauert and Alexander Dalzell (Toronto: University of Toronto Press, 1994), identical text in both letters. Until the remaining volumes appear, the reader may consult a French translation of the complete letters, *La correspondance d'Erasme*, ed. Aloïs Gerlo and Paul Foriers, 12 vols. (Paris: Gallimard; Bruxelles: Presses Académiques Européennes, 1968–84). Erasmus's complete correspondence with Guillaume Budé is also available in a French translation by the foremost Budé scholar, Marie-Madeleine de la Garanderie (Paris: Vrin, 1967).

The best-known works of Erasmus are also available individually in English: *The Praise of Folly* in a fine translation with excellent notes by Clarence H. Miller (1979; 2nd ed., New Haven, CT: Yale University Press, 2003); the complete *Colloquia* in Craig R. Thompson's *The Colloquies of Erasmus* (Chicago: University of Chicago Press, 1965); and a good sampling of the *Adagia* with a very helpful introduction by Margaret Mann Phillips, in *The "Adages" of Erasmus: A Study with Translations* (Cambridge: Cambridge University Press, 1964).

Many good critical biographies of Erasmus are available in English. Among them are György Faludy, *Erasmus of Rotterdam* (London: Eyre and Spottiswoode, 1970); Léon-E. Halkin, *Erasmus: A Critical Biography*, trans. John Tonkin (1987; Oxford: Blackwell, 1993); and especially Richard J. Schoeck, *Erasmus of Europe: The Making of a Humanist*, 2 vols. (Edinburgh: Edinburgh University Press, 1990–93). Useful studies of a more analytical nature include Margaret Mann Phillips, *Erasmus and the Northern Renaissance* (1949; rev. ed., Woodbridge, UK: Boydell and Brewer; Totowa, NJ: Rowman and Littlefield, 1981); and Erika Rummel, *Erasmus* (London: Continuum, 2004). Also useful is Erika Rummel, *Erasmus and His Catholic Critics*, 2 vols. (Nieuwkoop: De Graaf, 1989). A very handy encyclopedia is the supplement to the *Collected Works of Erasmus*, titled *Contemporaries of Erasmus: A Biographical Register of the Renaissance and Reformation*, ed. Peter G. Bietenholz and Thomas B. Deutscher, 3 vols. (Toronto: University of Toronto Press, 1985–87).

Two good editions of Marot's complete work exist in French. The *Œuvres complètes*, ed. François Rigolot, 2 vols. (Paris: Editions Flammarion, 2007–9), has the distinct advantage in presenting the poet's works as they appeared in first editions. The *Œuvres poétiques complètes*, ed. Gérard Defaux, Classiques Garnier, 2 vols. (Paris: Bordas, 1990–93) is more erratic in this regard and contains many errors, but is more copiously (perhaps excessively) annotated. There are at present no reliable translations of Marot's most interesting poetry. There are, however, several good studies in English. These include Pauline M. Smith, *Clement Marot: Poet of the French Renaissance* (London: Athlone, 1970); M. A. Screech, *Clément Marot: A Renaissance Poet Discovers the Gospel; Lutheranism, Fabrism and Calvinism in the Royal Courts of France and of Navarre and in the Ducal Court of Ferrara* (Leiden: Brill, 1994); and Dick Wursten, *Clément Marot and Religion: A Reassessment in the Light of His Psalm Paraphrases* (Leiden: Brill, 2010).

For bibliographical details regarding Rabelais and Marguerite de Navarre, see the chapters on both in this volume. Rabelais's letter to Erasmus quoted in this chapter is from *The Complete Works of François Rabelais*, trans. Donald M. Frame (Berkeley: University of California Press, 1999), 746. The passage from *Pantagruel* is from ibid., 227. Marguerite de Navarre's *Comédie de Mont-de-Marsan* can be found in *Œuvres complètes*, vol. 4: *Théâtre*, ed. Geneviève Hasenohr and Olivier Millet (Paris: Honoré Champion, 2002).

∗∗ ∗∗

Rabelais and the Low Road to Modernity

RAYMOND GEUSS

In 1532, or conceivably 1531, a rather old-fashioned-looking volume appeared at the booksellers in Lyons with the title *Pantagruel: Les horribles et espouventables faictz et prouesses du tresrenomé Pantagruel Roy des Dipsodes, filz du grant géant Gargantua* (*Pantagruel: The Horrifying and Dreadful Deeds and Prowesses of the Most Famous Pantagruel, King of the Dipsodes, Son of the Great Giant Gargantua*). It recounts the fantastic adventures of a young giant named Pantagruel and his good friend Panurge in war and peace; the author is given as Maître Alcofrybas Nasier, an anagram of François Rabelais. In 1534, or possibly 1535, a kind of prequel to the story of Pantagruel appeared in the form of a narrative of the adventures of his father Gargantua: *La vie inestimable du grand Gargantua, père de Pantagruel* (*The Inestimable Life of the Great Gargantua, Father of Pantagruel*). The year 1546 saw the publication of a third volume, *Le tiers livre des faicts et dicts heroique du bon Pantagruel* (*The Third Book of the Heroic Deeds and Sayings of the Good Pantagruel*), where the author is openly named as François Rabelais, Doctor of Medicine. *Le quart livre des faicts et dicts heroiques du bon Pantagruel* (*The Fourth Book of the Heroic Deeds and Sayings of the Good Pantagruel*) was published in 1552, the year of Rabelais's death.

What is a contemporary English-speaking reader to make of a series of four books written in an incessantly punning, not yet standardized, sixteenth-century French with lashings of Latin, Greek, Basque, Italian, Gascon, German, Limousin, and several other real—and some imaginary—languages by an absconded monk turned physician, which satirizes archaic social customs, monastic and legal institutions, forms of education and dress, eating habits, and obscure philosophical doctrines and literary genres? Since virtually no one can read these texts unprepared, not even modern francophones, we are all in one way or another dependent on translations and an appended explanatory apparatus.

Translation dependence is, of course, a common characteristic of everyone's access to most of world literature. No single individual can be expected to read *The Tale of Genji*, *The Bhagavadghita*, *The Oresteia*, *Mrs. Dalloway*, *Salammbô*, *The Dream of the Red Chamber*, *Der Mann ohne Eigenschaften*, and *Gilgamesh*, to take a few random examples, *all* in the original. There is, however, a striking difference between reading a translation of *Genji* and reading a translation of Rabelais. It is not just that we need a translation of Rabelais's text, but that the text itself depicts a world in which an irreducible variety of languages and dialects—real or imaginary, rustic or polished, fully understood, half-understood, misinterpreted, not understood at all, or inherently incomprehensible—are constantly rubbing up against each other. It is not insignificant that one of the two very first people Pantagruel encounters (in chapter 9 of *Pantagruel*) when he arrives in Paris is Panurge, who greets him in thirteen different languages, some of which Pantagruel not only does not understand, but cannot even securely identify (unsurprisingly, given that some of them are imaginary languages), but who then turns out to be a native of Touraine. So even if someone addresses you in Dutch, Spanish, or Danish, or all of them successively, you cannot exclude the possibility that he is actually a *landsmann* from the very same region of France from which you hail. Pantagruel's second encounter (in chapter 6 of *Pantagruel*) is with a student who originally speaks to him in a bizarre and barely comprehensible, because hyper-latinate, "French" but eventually lapses into the almost equally obscure patois of his native Limousin. Even if one encounters a "known" language one cannot be sure it will be spoken in anything like its "standard" or "pure" form. In fact the idea of a "standard French" did not exist in the sixteenth century, and this episode might be thought to throw some doubt on the credibility of the whole idea of a "pure" idiom, except to the extent to which this is an artificial sociological construct that is externally imposed on people. "French" in some sense derives from Latin, but adding ever more Latin does not result in a "purer" French; rather, it produces something neither fish nor fowl and easily comprehended by no one.

Language itself is a central concern of *Pantagruel* and the successor volumes. It is an important fact about our world that *different* languages exist and that interpreting them is an unavoidable, ceaseless, and difficult task. That our need for translations is universal and that any translation is uncertain and potentially fallacious may seem rather trivial claims, but much of Western literature presents action in a world that is resolutely monoglottal. In the *Aeneid*, how are Dido and Aeneas represented as conversing? Surely Dido would speak Punic to her sister in book 4, lines 416ff., just as, presumably, Aeneas tells his story in books 2 and 3 in (some dialect of Mycenaean?) Greek, yet Dido's speech to Anna and her *monologue intérieur* in book 4, lines 534ff. are given in the same flawless Latin as Aeneas's tale. For Vergil, speculations about how Dido and Aeneas spoke to each other are as pointless as asking how many children Lady Macbeth had or whether Mrs. Dalloway could speak Italian. For the purposes of the *Aeneid*, the realities of variation between languages *do not matter*. Vergil's Latin is to stand as the fully transparent medium for presenting what Dido and Aeneas are conceived to have "really said and thought."

Issues of translation and "interpretation" were especially pressing in a society like that of sixteenth-century France, which was deeply informed by a "religion of a book." For a long time, the text of The Book had been effectively beyond question: It was the so-called Vulgate, a standardized edition of the Old and New Testaments in Latin produced in the fourth century AD. By Rabelais's time, "Vulgate" had become a misnomer, because although Latin could have been construed, at least notionally, as the "common tongue" of everyday speech (*sermo uulgatus*) in the West when this translation was originally made, by the sixteenth century this was no longer true. Yet the *ipssisima uerba* (the very words themselves) of this text had acquired a veneer of sanctity through long use, and the Catholic Church clung to it tenaciously.

In the sixteenth century, the standing of the Vulgate came under pressure from two sides. If, it was argued, the Vulgate had come into existence as scripture in the then common everyday language of the times, why not do the same for the sixteenth century, when Latin had ceased to be the language of everyday speech, and translate scripture into the various vernaculars? If so, who had the authority and power to say whether or not the translation was "correct"? Given the role of appeals to the scripture in all domains of life, the power to certify a translation or a set of interpretative notes, or (in some cases) to punish those who produced unauthorized or deviant versions was power indeed, and so, understandably enough, the Catholic Church wished to reserve it for itself. The Church hierarchy was hostile to any project of translating scripture into a vernacular. That was one side of the story: the issue of turning the Christian scriptures *into* the vernaculars (or not). The other side of the story was that the Vulgate was itself a translation of an original, so why use *it* as a basis for a rendering of the scriptures into the vernaculars (if one decided to do this)? Why not go back to the Greek originals? What then if it turned out that the Vulgate was mistaken in its rendering of the Greek? Or that the Vulgate reading was only one of a number of different possible translations? Suppose that the Greek text itself turned out not to be self-evidently inviolate and uncorrupted, but to exist in different versions that exhibited variations, so that an editorial decision needed to be made about which of these variants to accept? Given the extent to which certain important doctrinal and organizational issues might be seen to depend on accepting the reading of the Vulgate as the definitive one, one can easily see how even studying Greek—an activity to which Rabelais devoted much time and energy—could come to be seen as a potentially subversive act.

In this highly charged atmosphere where power and authority, religion, politics, and issues of translation and interpretation were deeply intertwined, one can see how the pressure to take a position on hermeneutics and to join one party or another became intense. The "wrong" decision could cause you to end up knifed in the gutter or shackled to the stake awaiting combustion, and there was no safe, recognized, "neutral" position one could adopt *hors de la mêlée*. Even to suggest that such a position was *possible* was itself to make a highly inflammatory contribution to the struggle, because it could be taken to mean that ideological squabbles either did not matter or could not be settled. Those who were perfectly prepared to exterminate their doctrinal opponents physically would not take kindly to the suggestion that their differences did not matter or were not decidable.

Under the circumstances, it is small wonder that language and its proper interpretation loomed so large for Rabelais.

The plurality of human languages, the potential opacity of specifically verbal behavior, and the need for, but uncertainty of, translation and interpretation are merely further instances of a more general phenomenon that is connected with all forms of signification. Verbal signs—language—are not the only forms of meaningfulness, nor the only kind of signs that require "interpretation," and Rabelais explicitly recognizes this. After all, the long chapter 13 of *Pantagruel* is devoted to the description of a debate that is conducted silently, entirely through gestures, and another chapter of *Gargantua* treats the "language" of colors. Finally, in the *Tiers livre* even the lolling of a fool's head can be taken as a sign that is to be interpreted as a clue to how one should act and what the future will hold. The realm of that which requires interpretation is much wider than "language" (in the sense in which we call "Danish" one language and "Greek" another). There is a continuity between trying to make sense of what the speaker of Dutch is saying, knowing what the use of a certain color means, and "reading" the world of signs around us so as to know how to act in it.

That the difficulty here is an omnipresent one becomes especially clear in the *Tiers livre*, where Panurge is trying to get practical advice about whether or not he should marry. This book illustrates the unfeasibility of getting a useful, authoritative answer to questions like this from any external sources *because of* the impossibility of interpreting any of the proposed answers in a way that is unequivocal. Pantagruel and his friends exhaust all the means at their disposal—sortition, consultation with oracles, interpretation of dreams, advice from purported experts (lawyers, theologians, medical doctors, philosophers)—but to no effect. Panurge is left at the end of the book as confused as he was at the beginning. It is not, that is, that any of the oracles they consult simply fails to respond—as happened at the end of the ancient world when the oracles simply stopped operating. Nor is it that anyone raises any particular questions about the authority of the method used, as would increasingly be the case in the period after Descartes, but it is simply that no one can decide what the response has actually been, that is, what exactly it means.

The answers that Panurge gets in response to the question about his marriage fall into three broad categories. First, there are "responses" that are radical non-answers. We are presented with experts who respond with completely irrelevant remarks; deaf-mutes who produce physical gestures that seem to be responses, but the point and meaning of which is anyone's guess; and philosophers who talk around the question in an even more than usually pointless way without coming to any determinate conclusion at all. Second, there are forms of divination that may seem *prima facie* to give a clear answer, but turn out on investigation to be deeply ambiguous and admit of widely divergent and even contradictory readings. The *sortes Vergilianae* operated by opening a copy of Vergil and picking a verse at random. Any given verse by Vergil chosen as a source of advice can be read, however, as it turns out, one way, or another way, often in completely contradictory ways, as chapter 10 of the *Tiers livre* shows with particular clarity.

The third kind of advice to Panurge is given (twice) by Pantagruel, first when in chapter 10 of the *Tiers livre* he asks rhetorically whether Pantagruel does not know his own will, with the implication that knowing his own will would give him the solution to his difficulty. Panurge's problem, however, is not lack of self-knowledge (in anything like the everyday sense of that term). When Pantagruel asks him whether he doesn't know what he wants, the answer to that is that he knows very well what he wants: to get married *while knowing for certain that he will not be cuckolded*. This is on the face of it an odd question in the context of a "serious" concern with the grounds and authority of "knowledge," although it is one of the standard themes of some early modern comedy (in Molière, for instance). Rabelais characteristically blends the comic and the serious. At the level of the "serious" Panurge knows perfectly well that there is something wrong with this volitional state—the certainty he wants is not available. If he did not know this he would not be tormented. So the real problem is generated not by Panurge's desire to marry, but by his pathological fear of being cuckolded. In chapter 29 of the *Tiers livre* Pantagruel states that he stands by the advice he has already given to Panurge, which he now formulates as "every man must be the arbiter of his own thoughts and seek counsel in himself," and attributes Panurge's problem to his *amour de soi*. His desire to have a wife while retaining a certain conception of himself (as a non-cuckold) clouds his judgment and blinds him so much that it skews his reading of what the authorities and oracles tell him. So the question shifts from "Should Panurge marry?" to "Can Panurge get a grip on himself and *change* his state of will, realizing he cannot have certainty about the future and relaxing about it?"

We are left at the end of the *Tiers livre* in a peculiar situation that will be very uncomfortable for a certain kind of mind. It is hard to read the *Tiers livre* through without forming the opinion that in fact *all* the sources of advice consulted, to the extent to which they give any advice at all, say the same thing: namely, that Panurge is fated to be cuckolded. Rabelais goes out of his way to show how Panurge can, and does, take the relevant passages in exactly the opposite way, as recommendations to marry and predictions that his wife will be faithful, loving, and hard-working. Yet it is not at all clear that there is, or could be, a systematic way of proving that Panurge's reading is wrong.

The search for clear, distinct, authoritative answers to questions about how we humans should act is unending. The need for action often imposes on us a binary structure (you either move out of the path of the oncoming lorry or you don't), although human thought is not always organized in this binary way. Given the overwhelming and primary importance of action for humans, though, binary distinctions are salient in all societies. *Divisio* is a fundamental phenomenon. All known human societies make *some* kind of distinction between what may and what may not be said, shown, or done in what context. We call some of these distinctions those between "the forbidden" and "the permitted," "the sacred" and "the profane," "the taboo" and "the utilitarian," "the decent" and "the indecent," "the polite" and "the rude," and this crude list does not in any way exhaust human inventiveness. Individual human societies differ from each other in the nature, importance, and function of *divisio* along a number of dimensions.

Since speaking, writing, and publishing are all actions, some categories of the permitted and the forbidden can naturally apply to literature, too. A poem, play, or novel can be judged decent or indecent; in some countries blasphemy is a crime, that is, subject to potential coercive intervention. In Rabelais's own lifetime the Sorbonne had his books banned, and when, after his death, the Vatican started printing a formal *Index librorum prohibitorum* in 1559, all of his works found a place on it, although we do not know whether this was because they were thought specifically to promote licentiousness, because of some perceived doctrinal deviation, or simply because they exuded an air of unspecified, but general, indecency.

From the idea that there are standards for what may and what may not be published it is but a short step to the idea that there are proper internal standards of appropriateness for particular literary genres. This idea is especially strong in the aesthetic theorizing that was dominant in antiquity, and it became exceedingly influential again when resurrected by "humanist" writers of the Renaissance. Rabelais was in many ways a full-blown and enthusiastic member of the humanist movement. At considerable personal cost, he had himself acquired a firm knowledge of ancient Greek and did extensive reading in "classical" Greco-Roman literature, and he was an avowed admirer of the prince of humanists, Erasmus, whom he addresses in an elegantly turned Latin letter, shot through with phrases in Greek, as "pater mi humanissime" (my most humane father, perhaps with the further connotation: my father, you who are the greatest of the humanists).

"Renaissance humanism" was as complex and internally differentiated a phenomenon as any of the major intellectual and cultural movements in the West. As the name indicates, one of the central ideas was the (re)orientation and refocusing of cultural and spiritual life on "man." The humanists found, primarily in Cicero, what they took to be the irresistibly attractive ideal of the *homo humanus*. One can think of this ideal as constituted by three positive elements, which are designated by the three Greek words *to metron*, *paideia*, and *philanthropia*. *To metron*, "the measure(d)," indicates that humans should in the first place live by an ethic of moderation, rejecting excess of any kind and not aspiring to the impossible. Thus Pindar writes: "Do not, my soul, strive for eternal life, but exhaust the means at your disposal," and the odes of Horace are a nearly inexhaustible source of admonitions to *aurea mediocritas* (the golden mean). Moderation applies also to cognitive claims. People should limit what they claim to "know" to what they—and any human—can clearly and certainly see and understand. Thus, torturing people is clearly a direct visible evil, and one should not embark on it on the basis of opaque, uncertain, or highly controversial religious doctrines. Aesthetically, this implies a preference for what is surveyable by the human senses and well-proportioned, which means commensurate with those human forms of sensation and perception.

Paideia, the second of the three elements, means both "education" in the sense of the process of formation and the state of being a "cultivated" person. The cultivation in question is the art of speaking decorously and well, which is taken to mean clearly and in a way appropriate to the situation. The concept of "clarity" then got connected with notions of purity of diction and avoidance of solecisms, of the dysphonic, the unprecedented or unusual, but also of the demotic, and with a return *ad fontes* (back to the sources) to the especially "pure" Latin of Cicero. Gargantua's letter to his son in chapter 8 of *Pantagruel* formulates some of the goals of the new humanistic education, and Eudemon's speech in chapter 14 of *Gargantua* is a concrete instance of results that could be expected. Finally, *philanthropia* refers to a general attitude of benevolence toward all humans, with perhaps a special emphasis on understanding the limitations of human life and compassionate tolerance of human weakness, foibles, even minor deviancy.

As important as these positive ideals are, the features of their world from which the humanists recoiled in horror are at least as important in understanding them. They summed up these negative ideals by calling them "barbarous," "Gothic," or (eventually) "medieval." The Gothic world was one of obscurantism; immoderate, overheated fantasies; and superstitions—one in which people spoke a language full of plebeian usages, grammatical solecisms, and unheard-of neologisms, and indulged in pointless scholastic logic-chopping. Gothic art was in general disproportioned and misshapen, and in it natural forms were grotesquely distorted.

A moment's reflection will suffice to see that there was a basic tension inherent in "humanism," at any rate, as it presented itself to Christians in the early modern period. Protagoras, who first said that man is the measure of all things, is also on record as saying that we can know nothing certain about the gods. This was not a position that was fully comfortable for any sixteenth-century Christian to take without reservation. Rabelais makes fun of many contemporary Christian institutions, including the papacy, monasticism, the mass, indulgences, fasting, even the scriptures (through parody), but of course this does not mean that he failed to understand himself as a Christian. Rabelais too, then, could be expected to feel some of the discomfort here, because surely Christianity requires a view that is not anthropocentric, but theocentric. Belief in transcendent "truths" that are not clearly expressible in human language and the striving to lead an immortal life, which is so firmly rejected by Pindar, are a constituent part of it. That the Christian scriptures can lay no claim to literary elegance and are written not in high-status "pure" Attic, but in semi-literate Koiné was a problem for educated Christians from the start, but it becomes a special problem for humanists in the Renaissance.

The Renaissance humanists had their own clear version of *divisio*, and this applied also to literary genres. Serious genres, like epic or tragedy, require an appropriately serious form of treatment. They treat "high matters" (peace and war, the deaths of princes, grand politics) through the actions and speech of "high" personages (kings and heroes) who address each other in an appropriately polished, formalized, decorous form of speech. The ancient theorists recognized the existence of genres, such as comedy, that treat of the everyday doings of common folk, and here they permit nonpolished and nondecorous forms of speech and action. Thus, Athenian comedy treated the concerns not of mythic heroes (Herakles, Agamemnon) but of ordinary Attic citizens, even peasants, and tolerated a looseness in meter, a colloquialism in speech, and an avowed proletarianism in attitude and behavior that would have been considered impossible in a genre of greater standing and prestige such as, for instance, tragedy. And, of course, comedy did not just tolerate but gloried in the absurd, the inconsequential, the ridiculous in matters of plot and in forms of speech that were intended to cause the audience to laugh—that is exactly the sort of thing which constitutes the very substance of Rabelais's books.

A lack of dignity and standing compared to epic and tragedy was the price comedy paid for its relaxation of strict standards of decorum. *Divisio* of an extreme form was assumed to exist between tragedy and comedy: in the ancient world there was no known instance of a poet who had written both comedies and tragedies. So Athenians were used to seeing the god Dionysus in one play (Aristophanes's *Frogs*) as a buffoon who beshits himself in fear on stage, asks for a sponge to clean himself up, and appeals to his own priest (seated on a special throne that is still visible today) for protection against one of the other characters, and then seeing him in another play (for instance, Euripides's *Bacchae*) as a terrible and vengeful deity inflicting excruciating punishment on those who fail to worship him. These were, however, not just different plays, but plays in different genres. Their *divisio* took, then, a rather different form from that practiced at the court of Louis XIV or in a late-eighteenth-century salon.

There are some signal difficulties with the received view about the respective "seriousness" of tragedy and comedy. "Serious" is used in two different ways. First, it can refer to a sober, deadpan mode of presentation. It can, however, also be used to refer to that which can, or even must, be taken account of, as opposed to that which can be safely ignored. Jokes, slapstick, and badinage are virtually by definition not "serious" in the first of these senses, but it does not follow that they cannot be "serious" in the second sense. Aristophanes's treatment of the sophistic movement in *Clouds* is exceedingly droll, but it does not follow from that that it has no bearing on actual educational policy, or that it could safely be ignored. If Aristophanes can be construed as having made some "points" in his comedy that really need to be addressed, the fact that they are presented as, or in the form of, "jokes" should not disqualify them from consideration. Plato has Socrates say that the play created a prejudice against him that it was hard to overcome, and this, one might think, is another aspect of comedy should not be brushed off as "just a joke." The authors of the *Index* also seem not to have taken all "comic" works as nugatory and negligible.

In various places, in particular in the prologue to *Gargantua*, Rabelais specifically discusses how seriously his works should be taken. Like everything else in the human world, his book does not, as it were, itself stand in the light of its own transparent intelligibility, but requires an "interpretation." He uses an image taken from Alcibiades's account of Socrates in Plato's *Symposium*. Alcibiades compares Socrates to one of the figures of Silenus, which, he says, one can buy in the Athenian marketplace. These figures were like Russian dolls with a smaller doll inside: the outside was rough and crude, painted "with frivolous, merry figures," but when one opened it, inside there was an attractive image of the god. Similarly, Socrates was (notoriously) physically ugly, gauche, apparently foolish and ridiculous, but, as we would say, his mind or soul, or spirit was beautiful, adroit, deeply serious, and sublime. This too is a kind of *divisio*: an "outside" in strict opposition to a contrary "inside." Rabelais applies this concept to his own work by claiming that the exterior of his books may be grotesque, ridiculous, and uncouth, but they conceals within themselves something that is the exact opposite: hidden meanings and sublime, serious truths. Scarcely, though, has he made this distinction than he immediately undercuts it by saying that perhaps he was drunk when he wrote the book and did not intend any of the profound hidden meanings one might attribute to his work. But then, Rabelais adds in a further twist: Homer did not intend all the sublime, hidden truths later interpreters attribute to his work either. This does not, as it were, simply return us to the original point from which we started— namely, this looks like a trivial and frivolous work, and, in addition, was written while the author was drunk, so it can be ignored. Rabelais is not denying any "serious meaning" to his own work because it is comic but rather rendering problematic the whole original set of distinctions between surface appearance and hidden meaning and between "serious" and "frivolous." It is not that nothing is "really" serious—not even Homer—but that the comic can also be serious.

The above discussion is an instance of the fact that Rabelais is, to say the least, not keen on *divisio* except as a potential object of mockery. In one of the very first chapters of the first book in the series, *Pantagruel*, we are given a list of books in the Library of St. Victor. The individual titles, some in (more or less proper) Latin, some in deeply medieval dog-Latin, some in French, are in themselves mostly absurd, and the whole is an incongruous and disordered juxtaposition of works on completely different topics: books on alchemy, military matters, law, the art of living (one volume is titled *The Art of Farting Discretely in Public*), theology, and cookery all jostle together amicably.

Rabelais also takes aim at one of the central religious institutions of the Middle Ages, the monastery. Monastic life was explicitly founded on the division of the day into standardized parts, each with its own assigned task, and on the absolute obedience of each monk to "the rule" (usually some variant of the "rule" of St. Benedict). These rules are founded in the Christian notion of original sin. If the human will is aboriginally corrupt and thus, to the extent to which it asserts itself independently at all, sinful, then one way forward is blind obedience to a set of established rules. As Benedict himself writes in chapter 7 of his *Rule*: "We are prohibited from doing our own will." The more perfect and more abject my obedience, the closer I can hope to get to a state of complete abrogation of my own will: I read the sixty-sixth psalm at Lauds *because* that is what is prescribed by the Rule, not because I have decided on this. By slavishly following the Rule, it is not (really) I who am acting, rather the Rule is acting (through me).

In stark contrast to this, in Thélème, the utopian "(anti)monastic" community described in *Gargantua*, there is no fixed division of the day into parts for antecedently specified activities, but what activities take place are decided "according to what is fit and opportune." In fact, "their whole life was ordered not by laws, rules and regulations, but according to their own volition and free will," and there are no rules. Or rather, the only rule is the anti-rule "Do as you will"—essentially the advice given by Pantagruel to Panurge in the *Tiers livre*. This trust in the human will *is* perhaps related to certain humanist concerns and themes, but Rabelais's insistence on the inherent indeterminacy of definitive interpretation introduces a skeptical note.

Rabelais, then, shared with the other members of the humanist movement a contempt for scholasticism in all its forms and for medieval educational practices and wanted to replace them with new humanist *paideia*, was deeply suspicious of "superstitions," and valued very highly "philanthropic" benevolence, such as that which is increasingly shown by Gargantua and Pantagruel. On the other hand, his works clearly exhibit an attachment to the Gothic world, which stood on the other side of the line the humanists wished to draw between themselves and the medieval past. One of the first and most obvious ways in which he differed from the humanists was simply that he did not write *Pantagruel* and its successors in Latin (as his admired models Thomas More and Erasmus would probably have done), but in a language that could not even by any stretch of the imagination be called a "pure" vernacular. The language is full not only of individual neologisms of the kind the humanists tried to avoid, but of several fully invented (imaginary) languages. *Pantagruel* and its successors display an enthusiastic engagement with the "medieval" world of wonders, marvels, and fabulous doings, and also with the distorted, disproportioned, and exaggerated. The main story concerns giants, who by their very size are out of proportion to the usual human measure. Also their size keeps changing: are they three meters tall? Five meters? One hundred meters? Their size seems to change to fit the requirements of the episode in question. If chapter 22 of *Pantagruel* is right in describing Pantagruel's tongue as more than two leagues long, then "pissing a full chamber-pot," as he is said to do in chapter 20 of *Gargantua*, is not only unimpressive, but might suggest that he has some problematic physiological condition.

Nor is the exuberance, energy, and celebration of excess, which are such important—and, to modern taste, endearing—features of Gargantua and Pantagruel, humanist virtues. Although certain central, apparently authoritative figures in the text occasionally *preach* moderation and self-restraint, the work itself tells a very different story. In fact the occasional praise of self-control or the "middle way" is presented as just one strand in the polyphonic clatter that constitutes the central reality of the books: sometimes it is more prominent, sometimes less, and sometimes it seems completely absent. Rabelais belongs, then, as much to the "Gothic" period and sensibility as to what is called the "high Renaissance"; even this distinction seems to lose its sharpness when applied to him.

If the Gothic period is the past—albeit a past that deserves perhaps in part to be loved and appreciated—and if the Renaissance—in some sense a call for a return to some of the ideals of a yet deeper past—is Rabelais's present, what of the future? The meaning of "modern" is contextual. The humanism that looked, and was, so "modern" in the 1520s, did not at all look very "modern" in the second half of the twentieth century. So where does "proper" modernity begin for us? Perhaps, following Virginia Woolf, in 1910? Or in 1989? There is of course no absolutely right answer, but for specified purposes some ways of breaking history down can be more useful than others. For the purposes at hand, I wish to suggest that the beginning of "proper modernity" would be the 1960s, both in what it succeeded in doing (initiating a certain relaxation of previously existing cultural and social norms) and in what it failed to do (achieve any kind of significant economic or political change). If, for the purposes of discussion, one accepts this, there are a number of ways in which Rabelais seems "properly" modern, especially with respect to some of the developments that characterize Western history during the four hundred or so years that separate his age from us. It is as if he represented an untraveled, but possible, shortcut from the 1550s to the post-1960s. It would perhaps have been a somewhat muddy and not always completely salubrious path. One need not overlook the dark shadows in Rabelais' work—think of the pervasive misogynist elements in it—but then no one is foolish enough to expect a perfect model for human action in a set of sixteenth-century texts, and many would think it folly to expect it in *any* individual text or set of texts. In any case, the road we actually took through Wars of Religion, royal absolutism, capitalist original accumulation, colonialism, and our record of treatment of women, the poor, and people of color was not itself all that edifying.

The main road to modernity diverges from the shortcut when the very briefly flourishing world of Thomas More, Erasmus, Rabelais, and Montaigne comes to an end. All four of these figures exhibited an ability to accept a relatively high degree of uncertainty and ambiguity in human affairs. They all seemed to cultivate a mildly skeptical ability to distance themselves from, and laugh at, themselves and their own necessities. They all clearly appreciated forms of play in literature (and elsewhere) that are not resolved into seriousness and a grim acceptance of the status quo, and they were all willing to countenance the possibility of a collective human life not structured by an overwhelming centralized agency for using coercive force.

Crudely speaking, one can call all these traits aspects of what Rabelais calls "pantagruelism" which he further defines at the end of *Pantagruel* as "living in peace, joy and health, always enjoying good cheer"; in the *Tiers livre* as "never taking in bad part anything one knows to flow from a good, frank, and loyal heart"; and finally, in

Quart livre, as "a certain merriness of mind pickled in contempt for things fortuitous." As the space within which pantagruelism can flourish is diminished, this whole world gradually withers away. Descartes, the Reformation (and Counter-Reformation), and Hobbes all, each in its own way, mark the transition, and one can see its effects in the more conformist aspects of literary works like Cervantes's *Don Quixote*.

Don Quixote depends on a hearty, down-to-earth, peasant realism. A windmill is a windmill, giants are giants. Windmills are not giants, and anyone who thinks they are is either simply mistaken or mad. Madness, like any defect, is inherently risible. The more persistently someone harms himself by pursuing mad illusions, the more risible he is. Don Quixote instantiates in an especially vivid way a particularly imperious will-to-power of the imagination. He will impose his imaginary reconstruction on reality, in spite of all resistance and no matter what the world's real constitution is. Cervantes presents this as inherently backward-looking—a return to medieval ways of thinking and acting—as completely out of touch with the world, and as ludicrous. His novel also has one of the most dispiriting and disappointing endings in world literature: Alonso Quisano "comes to his senses" and is reinserted into the mundane village life it was his great glory to have escaped—as "Don Quixote"—by the sheer force of his own imagination and will. His reconciliation with and re-submission to the status quo (including the Church) seems a kind of willed conformism imposed from the outside by the author, who is eager to impose his own will on a Quixote who seems almost about to escape his control. Cervantes very forcefully reaffirms that sanity is sanity, madness madness, the Church the Church, and Quisano's actions as "Don Quixote" irredeemably insane. The peasants who laughed were right all along.

Some of Rabelais's humor sometimes approaches this heavy-handed doltishness, but in general he keeps his distance *both* from any glorification of the monomaniacal interventive will *and* from the idea that the only alternative to that is conformity to the status quo. When Pantagruel tells Panurge he should become "arbiter of his own thoughts" that does not mean he should impose his obsessions on whatever he encounters, as Quixote does, and his admonition to

Panurge to know his own will without being deluded by self-love does not mean that he should make up a wholly new identity for himself and expect the world to conform to the will of this new person. Frère Jean's devotion to the pleasures of eating and especially drinking may go "over the measure," but this excessive vitality is also not anything like the Don's willingness to call a windmill a giant in the interests of inventing a challenge for himself and reaffirming a completely delusional self-conception. Exuberance is one thing; an almost transcendentally overweening self-will something completely different. Quixote's invented identity is by no means immoral in itself—the knight errant is a defender of the poor, the weak, the helpless—but there is still something about the kind of "modernity" the Don actually instantiates—the absolute, utterly relentless insistence that the world conform to my will—that cannot help calling to mind Cortez, the desperado who with a mere handful of other ne'er-do-wells obliterated the Aztec Empire in Mexico with exceptionally ruthless brutality.

Rabelais had more recognition and toleration of ambiguity, and of a variety of different points of view between which the choice is not absolutely clear, than anything one can find in Cervantes's novel. Real "play" is possible for Rabelais within the fluid, flexible, open-ended framework of meanings that constitute our life, and this play is rewarding in itself and can sometimes even be subversive of established structures without madness or the use of overt violence. *Pantagruel* began, as has been mentioned, with hermeneutics, an inexact and uncertain human enterprise if any is—What is the student from Limousin saying? How is one to understand the varying intelligible greetings of Panurge?—and the series of Rabelais's books ends in the fourth volume with Panurge beshitting himself with fear, like Dionysus in *Frogs*. Unlike the perhaps foolish and cowardly, but unembarrassable god (being shameless is one of the advantages of being a Greek god) Panurge tries desperately to deny this evident fact. He lists sixteen different terms for "shit," only to deny that any one of them correctly describes what covers his breeches and to claim implausibly that the substance in question is actually "saffron from Ireland." A heroic (but also pathetic) attempt at "reinterpretation." Readers will make up their own minds about this, but the work ends, or at any rate peters out, without anyone, whether another character or the author, making an authoritarian gesture that would impose a decision on the issue.

"Road to modernity" is a metaphor. Nothing wrong with that, but it is worth pointing out that it needs interpretation. In particular it does *not* mean that the present is the ordained end of history, or that the present is "good," or that the present actually realizes to the full the potentialities of pantagruelism, the acceptance of difference and uncertainty, and the possible ludic relaxation of some of the more authoritarian forms of *divisio*. We have not reached the predestined end of any road, but it is now possible perhaps to see that we would all have been—and all would be—better off without the single-mindedly willful ego, relentlessly imposing itself on a potentially flat, monolingual world that is thought to need no interpretation and that is kept in order mainly by the brute force of Leviathan. But then Rabelais would not have needed to be told that.

Works Cited and Recommended Further Reading

The Pléiade edition edited by M. Huchon and F. Moreau (Paris: Gallimard, 1994) contains the French text of Rabelais's works with a series of useful introductions, textual variants, and notes. M. Screech's *Pantagruel and Gargantua* (London: Penguin, 2006) contains a translation of all four of the books that are universally accepted as authentic, presented in the order in which they originally appeared (i.e., *Pantagruel* first, then *Gargantua*) and also of the *Fifth Book of Pantagruel*, which was first published several years after Rabelais's death, and the authenticity of which is unclear. Screech's translation also contains rather full explanatory notes, including detailed accounts of the exceedingly complex history of publication of the various versions of all five books, and translations of some relevant ancillary material. The translation that gives the best sense of the style of the original is that by its seventeenth-century translators, Sir Thomas Urquhart and Peter Anthony Motteux, which has been reprinted many times.

Four authors, two ancient and two "modern," will on most accounts form particularly important nodes in the literary genealogy of Rabelais. The two ancient authors are Aristophanes, who combines verbal pyrotechnics with a highly developed sense of the absurd in the treatment of what are in themselves weighty and serious topics (war, education, sexual politics) in a way that often seems to prefigure Rabelais. See especially *Clouds* (on the sophistic movement, especially Socrates) and *Frogs* (literature and politics).

Rabelais translated several texts by Lucian, a late ancient satirist who was active in a number of genres and in the Renaissance acquired a certain reputation as an "irreligious" writer. The modern reader who is unacquainted with his work might begin with Lucian's "A True History," "Sale of Lives," "Dialogues of the Gods," and "The Fly." Usable bilingual editions of Aristophanes and Lucian are available in the Loeb Library series.

The two modern authors whose work throws the most light on Rabelais are the two slightly older "humanists" Sir Thomas More and Erasmus of Rotterdam. There is a good bilingual edition of More's *Utopia*, ed. Logan, Adams, and Miller (Cambridge: Cambridge University Press, 1995). Rabelais often seems to be drawing on one or another of the short essays by Erasmus in his huge collection of *Adages*. A full translation of the *Adages* by R. Mynors has been published in the context of the *Collected Works* (Toronto: University of Toronto Press, 1982–2006); in his translation of *Pantagruel and Gargantua* (cited above) Screech is very good at drawing the reader's attention to individual references to the *Adages*. The other work by Erasmus that stands in the background of much of Rabelais is *The Praise of Folly*, trans. B. Radice, with an introduction by A. Levi (London: Penguin, 1993).

Three older scholars made contributions that remain of great value to the understanding of Rabelais and his work. L. Febvre's magisterial *The Problem of Unbelief in the 16th Century: The Religion of Rabelais* (originally in French, 1942), trans. R. Gottlieb (Cambridge, MA: Harvard University Press, 1982) is the natural place to start thinking about questions of religion.

Erich Auerbach's famous essay on the world in Pantagruel's mouth (originally in German, 1946) appears in translation as chapter 11 in his *Mimesis*, trans. R. Trask (Princeton, NJ: Princeton University Press, 1953). Mikhail Bakhtin's *Rabelais and His World* (originally in Russian, 1931), trans. H. Iswolsky (Cambridge, MA: MIT Press, 1968) is still a treasure-trove of imaginative reflections on language, high and low culture, laughter, and the grotesque.

Screech's *Rabelais* (London: Duckworth, 1979) gives a rather balanced introduction in English to the life and works, and for two slightly more technical, but general books one might recommend Guy Demerson, *L'esthétique de*

Rabelais (Paris: SEDES, 1996); and E. Duval, *The Design of Rabelais's Pan-tagruel* (New Haven, CT: Yale University Press, 1991). A standard older work on Rabelais's language is L. Sainéan, *La langue de Rabelais*, 2 vols. (Paris: Boccard, 1922–23); slightly more recent is F. Rigolot, *Les langages de Rabelais*, 2nd ed. (Geneva: Droz, 1996). *The Cambridge Companion to Rabelais*, ed. John O'Brien (Cambridge: Cambridge University Press, 2011) contains essays by various hands on different aspects of Rabelais's work and a bibliography of additional works that can usefully be consulted on special topics.

Marguerite de Navarre

Renaissance Woman

W E S   W I L L I A M S

Sometimes described as the "first modern woman," Marguerite de Navarre occupies an extraordinary place in French Renaissance culture. Commonly referred to simply as "Marguerite," in part because of the secondary meaning of the name as "pearl," she was, as well as sister to King François I, a skilled political operator in her own right, working to effect change within the French court and on the wider European stage. At a time when church and state were both inseparable and in conflict, she served as a critical friend to religious reformers, such as Guillaume Briçonnet, the influential bishop of Meaux, and Lefèvre d'Etaples, who published a translation of the Bible into French in 1530. An assiduous letter writer in several languages, she maintained an active correspondence with a wide range of radicals across Europe. The fact that her early modern social network included people who disagreed, often violently, with each other, such as John Calvin and Martin Luther, as well as her fellow-stateswoman-and-poet, Vittoria Colonna, is testament to her ability to sustain civil conversation even in the midst of political and religious turmoil. Her skill in diplomacy was perhaps most spectacularly evident when her brother François lost one of his several wars and Marguerite was sent to Madrid to secure his release from imprisonment and a new treaty with France's more powerful neighbor, Spain. All of these characteristics and achievements have marked her as a person of interest to historians for some long time; but she was also well respected within her own lifetime as a writer, principally as a poet.

A well-placed patron, she protected dissident writers from the forces of cultural conservatism of her day, most notably the Sorbonne, which regularly condemned the works of many of her circle, and her own. Much of Marguerite's writing was published only after her death; even now the full extent of its range—from didactic and mystical poetry, through satirical plays, to the collection of tales known as the *Heptameron*—is little appreciated. In its diversity alone this body of work stands as an exemplary demonstration of what one woman, given the advantages of her station, could, and did, achieve. The poetry and the plays repay close study, and some useful pointers are offered in Edwin Duval's brief treatment of the poetry in this volume. But it is with the *Heptameron* that Marguerite de Navarre secured herself a place in literary and intellectual history, and it is this complex, hybrid collection of stories that most deserves, and rewards, the attention of the contemporary reader. The following introductory outline of the prehistories and critical afterlives of her work has two principal aims. The first is to present curious anglophone readers with inroads into the contexts of its original mid-sixteenth-century appearance in print; the second is to give some sense of the enduring interpretive challenges and pleasures that the *Heptameron* still affords.

∗ ∗ ∗ ∗

Begun perhaps as early as 1520, but probably composed for the most part in the last five years of its author's life, the *Heptameron* was left unfinished and unpublished at her death in 1549. Its title derived from the Greek term for "seven"; the collection has as its heart seventy-two stories, interspersed by a series of often extended discussions between the storytellers themselves. We do not know what title Marguerite intended for her work, nor do we know if she ever planned to publish it herself. A selection of the tales was first printed in 1558 by the scholar and entrepreneur in the (then) fairly new field of vernacular publishing, Pierre Boiastuau. An odd and fascinating character in his own right, Boiastuau was a prolific translator and compiler of accounts of monstrous births, natural disasters, and historically significant characters, and his collections—variously published as "tragic tales" and "prodigious, or marvelous stories"—proved enormously successful. They also served, among other things, as a source-book for Shakespeare's *Romeo and Juliet* and *Hamlet*. Boiastuau's *His-*

toires des amans fortunez, or *Verie Pleasant Discourses of Fortunate Lovers,* as the first, Elizabethan, translation has it, contains just sixty-seven stories, arranged in an order different from that found in any of the later versions of the text. It omits the "frame"—the discussions between the storytellers that are found in the fullest manuscripts—and makes no mention of Marguerite at all. Within the year, a rival Protestant publisher, Pierre Gruget, brought out an "authorized" edition: *L'heptaméron des nouvelles de très illustre et très excellente Princesse Marguerite de Valois, Royne de Navarre* both assigns the text to the (now long dead) queen and claims to have "restored it to its true order." Marguerite's prologue is reinstated, as is the crucial internal framework of discussion between storytellers, with tales distributed over seven days. Gruget further "authorizes" his edition with a fulsome dedication to his patron, Marguerite's daughter, Jeanne d'Albret.

The extensive prologue sets the scene: a group of travelers—five men and five women—are thrown together by natural disaster; stranded, while their servants build bridges back to the world from which they have been cut off, they tell each other stories to pass the time. A hybrid of the philosophical dialogue form and the collection of tales, both of which had been successful modes of vernacular writing in Renaissance Italy, the *Heptameron* makes the most of its author's analytical interest in topics such as love and friendship, marriage and (in)fidelity, and the conflict between personal conviction and established religion. Self-consciously reworking Boccaccio's *Decameron,* the tales are often cautionary in content and tone, expressing either anger or a tragicomic sense of resignation, both at the state of the Catholic Church and at human corruption in general. Some of the storytellers seem motivated by steadfast religious convictions, while others (the majority) play out through their narratives what have been rightly called "restless scenarios of unsatisfied desire." Decadent or abusive priests and monks line up to minister to credulous Christians, whose belief in the efficacy of good works or ritual actions leads to disaster and death. Husbands deceive their wives (and often their chambermaids, too), and wives trick faithful, would-be chivalric suitors into committing not only adultery, but also murder. Rape is more common than consent, and sex is rarely, if ever, fun; incest (even when it is enjoyable) takes place more by mistake than design.

A courtly pastime, Marguerite's collection is also a deliberately provocative transposition of the scenes and themes of Castiglione's urbane (and distinctly urban) *Book of the Courtier* into the oddly determined setting of an abbey in the Pyrenees. Sharing much with its Italian sources (the second of which is already a response to the first), the *Heptameron* also differs from both in important respects. Boccaccio has his characters initially gather at a church before leaving Florence to stay in a villa outside town, thereby escaping the plague. Marguerite's storytellers, by contrast, are all far from home when disaster strikes; pilgrims, patients, or tourists, they were taking the waters in the mountains when the heavens opened and floods made the roads home impassable. Readers of the Bible might already be inferring particular significance from Marguerite's flood; they might begin to see the *Heptameron* as something akin to a set of ransom tales, and imagine that the characters here gathered are somehow exemplary, representatives of a wrongful world, in danger of extinction. They would not be mistaken in so doing, for the survivors themselves wonder what they might have done to deserve such punishment, loss, and temporary exile. Their stories are in part pastime; but they are also penance of a kind.

For the wrongs of Marguerite's world are certainly plentiful. Shaped by a distorted courtly code and by religious conventions that serve principally to mask the abuse of power, her stories evoke a society in which a model of masculinity consisting of conquest and military glory has been transposed into the language of economic and sexual power. In tale after tale, marital fidelity and religious faith are trafficked in exchange for temporary (and, so the argument goes, illusory) reward. The culture evoked is one Marguerite knew well: that of sixteenth-century aristocratic society. But it is also our own, for, as the discussions between the storytellers makes plain, theirs is a world in painful transition, with its values, ethos, and codes being appropriated to its own needs and desires by the increasingly powerful bourgeoisie. The *Heptameron* can be read both as an index of time-bound processes of cultural appropriation and as a timeless inquiry into something called "human (as opposed to bestial, or angelic) nature." The meditation on human frailty it fosters is encouraged both by the religious setting and by the further changes Marguerite makes both to the Italian tradition and to recent French responses to it, such as that of Rabelais, with his utopian (anti)monastery, Thélème (for more on this, see Raymond Geuss's chapter in this volume). After giving her storytellers refuge in an abbey (as opposed to a villa), she further complicates social and spiritual hierarchies by suggesting that narrative, scripture, and discussion might all prove redemptive. First, she places a woman, Oisille, the wisest and the oldest of the survivors, in the role of religious leader of the assembled gathering; she then has Oisille (possibly an anagrammatic representation of Marguerite's own mother, Louise) read aloud each day the scriptures in French, accompanied by a brief analysis of the text she has selected for the day. There are, as noted above, similarities here with Rabelais's *Gargantua*; but the frame in which the *Heptameron*'s stories are told is at once more pious and more radical. With a powerful woman determining the structure of their day, Marguerite's storytellers learn to draw lessons from their collective experience, much as they had from Oisille's reading and exposition of scripture. The local monks, meanwhile, can occasionally be seen hiding behind a hedge, eavesdropping on both the tales and the conversations of their curious visitors.

That an equal number of men and women survived the flood might be taken as a further sign. As Marguerite's characters enter (like animals) the "ark" that is the abbey garden "two by two," romantically minded readers might anticipate their return home as fully-fledged humans: each paired off happily with another. But in fact both gender difference and distinctions between human and bestial love turn out to be conflictual, unresolved themes in these tales. Here again, Marguerite can be seen to be responding critically to her sources. Boccaccio's *Decameron* pitted three women against seven men, and Castiglione's company comprised just four women to ten men, more than one of whom argues that since women are "most imperfect beasts and of little or no worth in respect of men, incapable of performing any virtuous actions in themselves" it is quite right and proper that they "should have a bridle put upon them, creating shame and fear of infamy, such that they may by force be brought to some good." In such a context, the priority given to Oisille and the equality afforded to male and female participants in the narrative exchange staged by the

Heptameron clearly serves to signal polemical opposition to Marguerite's precursors' views on the quality of, and the (supposedly bestial) relations between, the sexes.

The last of the significant differences from her Italianate sources is marked by Marguerite through the figure of Parlamente (a character commonly identified with the author herself). She recalls that when the French court had first thought of reworking the *Decameron*, all present had decided "to exclude those who studied and were men of letters"; the worry was that anyone so trained could not avoid "adding such art and rhetorical ornament to the telling that they would in part falsify the truth of the accounts." Perpetuating this resolutely amateur aesthetic, the *Heptameron*'s storytellers agree to the same constraints: they swear to tell only stories that they know to be true. In so doing, they not only diverge from the Italian tradition, they also lay the foundations of a specifically French mode of philosophical narrative: Montaigne both read and learned from Marguerite's tales, and he echoes the words of the *Heptameron*'s prologue very precisely in his essay "On Cannibals." Marguerite inaugurates, then, a radical truth-telling project, which, although it remained both unpublished and incomplete in her lifetime, endures to this day. As if to signal the fact that the story had only just begun, she leaves us not with the full one hundred tales we might have expected from a French *Decameron*, but just seventy-two and the promise of more to follow. The discussion after the final tale concludes with the following, teasing invitation: "It's about death, and it's about a monk. So please all listen carefully."

⁙ ⁙ ⁙ ⁙

Marguerite's historical situation is crucial to an understanding of her work, destined as she was to a life whose rhythms were set to those of high politics and dynastic scheming. Before examining aspects of the *Heptameron* in detail, it seems useful—given the claims it makes to documentary truthfulness—to explore something of the context both of this remarkable author's life and of her influence on the work of her contemporaries. Born Marguerite d'Angoulême in 1492, the eldest child of one of several heirs presumptive to the throne of France, she died in 1549, queen of Navarre by her second marriage. The half-

century in which she lived saw the world transformed, and her writing bears the traces of the discoveries, innovations, and intrigues of
the time. From Renaissance through Reformation to the New World,
the tales of the *Heptameron* offer insights into the everyday, lived experience that underscores world-historical change on the grand scale.
Despite her being older than her brother, there was never any question that she, as a woman, might reign as queen of France by virtue of
her own qualities or title. But her politically astute mother, Louise de
Savoie, herself only nineteen years old when her husband had died,
nonetheless devoted considerable energy and intelligence to ensuring
that if (or as it turned out, when) the time came—in other words,
when enough other people died, and not enough other boys had been
born—both her children would be ready to assume royal power. Well
educated herself, Louise insisted that the girl be offered the same
humanist education as her brother: Marguerite became proficient in
Latin, Hebrew, Spanish, and Italian, and widely read in philosophy,
natural sciences, and theology. Much of this learning would find its
way into the *Heptameron*, and it informed Marguerite's other writings
to such an extent that in her funeral oration she would be characterized as "perfect in Poetry, learned in Philosophy, and both completed
and consumed by Holy Scripture."

The point of this exceptionally high level of education (at least as
far as Marguerite's mother was concerned) was to make the girl properly marriageable and to compensate for her relatively poor dowry.
For ten years, she was the only French princess on offer on the matrimonial market. As she moved through puberty and adolescence, a
long series of possible matches came and went, among which the
most startling might have been the request, in 1505, by Henry VII of
England for Marguerite's hand either for himself or for his son,
Henry (who would, of course, go on to marry several times). The
then French king Louis (who had other plans for her) blocked the
English match; in retrospect, this looks to have been a lucky escape,
but the alternative was not all that much better. Persuaded by an exceptionally large dowry underwritten by the king himself, one Charles
d'Alençon agreed to marry the girl in 1509; a courtly eyewitness suggests that Marguerite "wept enough tears to hollow out a stone" during the entire ceremony. Though her husband was highborn, he was

also an illiterate oaf, who seems (like many of his noble kind) to have been proud of the fact. People of her station were not expected to marry for love, but this does seem to have been a spectacularly unlovely match.

Not for nothing is marriage, whether dynastically arranged or clandestinely contracted, the subject of several of the *Heptameron*'s tales. Among these, stories 21 and 40, linked by being about different generations of the same noble family, have received much recent critical attention. Detailing the force of desire unconstrained by social convention, they also deal in the (pointless) violence of corrective action undertaken in the name of honor. In the first misbegotten generation, a count imprisons his sister in a castle in the forest and murders her secretly contracted husband, whose status as a lower order of noble had brought shame on the family. A generation later the same count imprisons his own daughter, Rolandine, in the same castle: following the example of her aunt, she too had secretly married an inappropriate suitor (in this case "the bastard son of a good and noble family"). In the discussions that follow both tales, some of the storytellers feel sympathy for Rolandine in particular, but most concur that she had exercised poor judgment in her choice of husband. It is the women in the group who are the most forceful advocates of parental control. Perhaps surprisingly for modern readers, it is they who plead most strongly the case against the legitimacy of clandestine marriages, arguing an experientially determined sense that men who engage in illicit love are unlikely to prove faithful, worthy husbands in the end. And as if to confirm both their specific argument, and the general sense that, morally speaking, things are going from bad to worse, Rolandine's husband (the "bastard") soon forgets his imprisoned bride, proves unfaithful, and dies an inglorious death—all this despite his being "as gallant and worthy as any man of his day" (in other words, hardly, if at all.)

Responding to anagrammatic and other clues in what have been termed the most "fully historical" of all the stories, early readers soon identified the noble line under threat in these twinned tales as the illustrious Rohan family. But recent critics, starting from the observation that both stories stage heated arguments between mothers and their daughters, have also drawn further, persuasive inferences from these paired narratives. After careful analysis both of letters exchanged between family members, and of legal affidavits preserved in court archives, they have shown how the stories (also) rework events from the author's own life. Behind the screen of the names and locations cited in the text, the sorry story of the marriage of Marguerite's own daughter, Jeanne, enforced by François I, before being legally contested and annulled on the grounds of nonconsummation seems to be being played out across these tales. In such contexts, it is striking how "well" the story of Rolandine ends; all she really wanted was a husband, and so once the "bastard" has safely died, her father frees her and is able to secure a new and better (because arranged) match for his daughter. Political expediency is reimagined as desire, and everyone lives happily ever after.

The young Marguerite's own unhappy match, which proved childless, but lasted until d'Alençon's death in 1525, served its dynastic purpose, in that it consolidated the family's position. And when, in late 1514, the French king Louis XII died without a male heir, leaving his cousin François as next in line to accede to the throne, Marguerite was able not only to accompany her mother and brother to court but also to enter into her own, specific, inheritance. As princess, as well as older and clearly more intelligent sister to the king, she assumed the multiple roles for which she had been so assiduously prepared: political operator, patron of the arts, and religious reformer. Given the tenor of the times, many writers sought her protection, and the tone of praise for her character and writings was set early. Erasmus, for instance, wrote to her in the following gently subversive terms: "For many years I have cherished the many excellent gifts that God bestowed upon you; prudence worthy of a philosopher; chastity; moderation; piety; an invincible strength of soul, and a marvelous contempt for all the vanities of this world. Who could keep from admiring, in a great king's sister, such qualities as these, so rare even among the priests and monks?" She resisted his efforts to secure her patronage and allegiance to his views but was more persuadable by Clément Marot, one of a number of poets whom she both promoted and protected, and from whom the now celebrated characterization of Marguerite as someone in possession of "a woman's body, the heart of a man, and the mind of an angel" derives.

The "royal trinity" of mother, brother, and sister was initially receptive to proposals for Reform, even in a context where radical thinkers were held to be dangerous fundamentalists, enemies of the established Christian way of life. Anyone found in possession of officially condemned works was liable to prosecution, but like most such regulations, this was not systematically enforced. Because of her privileged status, Marguerite was able to collect, have translated, and translate for herself a wide range of seditious writings, including several, such as Luther's treatise on monastic vows of celibacy, that are (silently) quoted within the *Heptameron* itself. But the pressure to move against the Reform became impossible to resist after the night of concerted direct action known as the "Affair of the Placards" (October 17–18, 1534), when a group of Swiss radicals posted broadsheets titled "Genuine Articles on the Horrific, Great and Unbearable Abuses of the Papal Mass, Invented Directly Contrary to the Holy Supper of Our Lord, Sole Mediator and Sole Savior Jesus Christ" in towns across France. Because one of the heretical posters had been nailed to the door of the king's own bedchamber, the threat to national security was invoked, and the clampdown began. Both the poet Marot and the young Calvin were among those who sought (and found) temporary refuge at Marguerite's court in Nérac (which lay beyond the jurisdiction of Paris). Over the next ten years, many of Marguerite's other early associates were executed: strangled and burned at the stake like the translator and poet Etienne Dolet, or, like Antoine Augereau, one of her printers, hanged. Others managed to survive, among them François Rabelais, another occasional member of her circle. In dedicating the *Third Book* of his *Gargantua and Pantagruel* to her at a particularly tricky moment in his life, Rabelais invokes Marguerite's "abstracted mind, ravished and ecstatic," and as a physician implores her to pay more attention (perhaps by reading his book) to pleasure and the needs of her body, "the mind's host and domestic dwelling." Evidence suggests she enjoyed Rabelais's work; and, according to rumor and fiction, extending from Marguerite's own time to our own, she was the secret mother of his two children.

Marguerite was, clearly, far more than a marriageable princess, a patron, the subject of anti-Reformist attacks, and the object of male writerly fantasies; she was also, long before the posthumous publication of the *Heptameron*, a published poet. Her work inspired other women to follow her example, as two distinctive instances make clear, each emblematizing the significance and range of Marguerite's influence on early modern European culture. First, the poetry and the politics of religion and of translation: when just eleven years old, Princess Elizabeth of England set about translating into English prose Marguerite's long penitential poem *Le miroir de l'âme pécheresse* (1531), an extended meditation on (among other things) spiritual self-abasement in the context of complex family relations. She offered the manuscript, held together by an embroidered and initialed binding, as a New Year's gift to her stepmother, Katherine Parr. It is unclear how Elizabeth came to own a copy of Marguerite's poem, but it may have been passed on to her by her mother, Anne Boleyn, who had spent several years at the French court as a child. A cleaned-up version, prefaced by the Protestant Reformer John Bale, was published in book form as *The Glasse of the Synnnefull Soule*, and went through several editions (1548, 1568, 1582, and 1590) during Elizabeth's lifetime. Between mother(s) and daughter, France and England, manuscript and print: the poem's complex interweaving of licit and illicit desires and sublimation gained in both religious and political significance with each new move. The early reception of Marguerite's poetic *Mirror* can be read as an emblem of the controversial half-century that followed her death.

The prehistory and the psychology of narrative in French also derive much of their energy from Marguerite's work. If Mme de Lafayette can be said to inaugurate the psychological novel with her *Princesse de Clèves* (1678), it surely matters that she does so by way of homage to her Renaissance precursor. Three salient points suggest Marguerite's power and influence here: first, Lafayette's novel is organized as a number of tales set within a frame; second, its action unfolds very precisely in the year of the *Heptameron*'s publication; third, and most pertinently, the only explicit reference to any other work of history or fiction in the novel is that made to the *Heptameron*, which the Princesse de Clèves is said to have been reading both to pass the time and in an effort to distract herself from her own increasingly anxious situation. These two actual and fictional princesses embody, then, early readings of Marguerite's work, even as they each redefine still further what it meant to be an early modern woman reader, translator, and writer.

❖ ❖ ❖ ❖

Turning away from the text's early reception to focus more closely on matters of structure and theme, it is important to recognize both that there is nothing altogether new about the *Heptameron*, and that this particular set of stories is properly groundbreaking. For it is through such a doubly determined description that the work can best be understood for what it is. A perpetuation of the medieval French tradition of the fictional *fabliaux* and a cutting-edge experiment in truth-telling; an unforgiving account of the intersecting worlds of early modern caste, religion, and sexual politics, disguised as a utopian fantasy about equality; a quasi-Rabelaisian intertwining of oral and written narrative, of text and commentary, debate and dissent; a foundational text in the history of women's writing, and the mother of all realist narrative in French: the *Heptameron* is all of these things, and more. And yet, today, beyond the university, it is too little known, or read.

It is not difficult to see why. For modern anglophone readers, especially those raised on the novel, the *Heptameron* can appear at first sight to be either strange or dull. Clearly more than the sum of its parts, it nonetheless does not really quite hang together; and given the elaborate introduction, what follows seems either inconsistent or incomplete. Similar things might be said of the work of other writers of the European Renaissance; narratives left unfinished, structured in ways that appear to privilege parts over the whole, and peopled by characters whose inner lives are, if not unexplored, then either opaque or inexplicable. But if, unlike the other two properly significant French prose writers of the time, Rabelais and Montaigne, Marguerite is hard to recognize as truly modern, then this is perhaps because she has had (as yet) no direct inheritors or imitators in English. The point here is less about translation than traffic, or trade. Florio, Bacon, and Shakespeare all trafficked in Montaigne, such that he now feels at home in the English language; Swift did the same both for and with Rabelais. Marguerite's *nouvelles* are less transportable, and her legacy is, linguistically speaking, more parochial: her significant imitators have all, with the notable exception of Elizabeth I, been French; and they have all been women.

But the difficulties that the *Heptameron* now presents to "nonprofessional" readers (in other words, precisely the kind of readers for whom it was originally intended) are not all attributable to reception history and the politics of canon formation. Some are inherent to the thing itself, which is to say to its structure, its internal design, or argument. Clearly, the collection is unfinished, since rather than a round hundred, there are just seventy-two stories; but twenty-eight more would not make the defining difference. It's true that it ends well (the seventy-second is one of the best tales of all), but—and this is perhaps the most significantly disenchanting feature of the collection for modern readers—nothing really changes across the course of the book. Similarly disappointing, for many readers, is the minimal attention given to sustained characterization. While the first story makes clear the fact that each narrative is motivated by the personal interests of its narrator, attempts to tease out further, satisfyingly hidden (quasi-Chaucerian) connections between specific tales and their tellers soon prove either unfruitful or unconvincing. None of this has stopped readers from seeing in the *Heptameron* a kind of roman à clef: a disguised, sometimes anagrammatically encoded portrait of Marguerite and her courtly friends. This interpretive tradition was initiated by the court gossip-monger and fabulist Pierre de Brantôme. Trading on secrets passed on by his parents and grandmother, whom he numbers among the storytellers, Brantôme took pleasure in "outing" many of the characters in the tales as well. Given the salience of the theme of rape in the stories, some of Marguerite's more recent biographically inflected feminist readers have (as suggested above) similarly read the collection as a kind of thinly veiled autobiography. Documenting the generally brutal world of dynastic and forced marriage, the *Heptameron* can be shown to record the repeated sexual assaults Marguerite herself suffered from supposedly chivalrous men at court, including (some argue) her own brother. Her characters' repeated insistence that they are telling true stories has, then, consistently been matched by a readerly determination to make of Marguerite's collection, above all, something akin to testimony, part of the historical record.

And yet while the *Heptameron* richly repays such an approach, it also resists it. The prologue places the tales under the dual categories of "pastimes" and "examples": these are not only true stories, but also exemplary fables, which extend—as the discussions between the characters amply demonstrate—beyond their specific, documentary worth and serve as lessons for those astute enough to apply them to their own situations and lives. An understanding of the poetics and the practice of "exemplarity" has been central to much recent literary debate about the *Heptameron*, with close attention paid to its defining terms: testimony and witness; lesson and example; evidence, judgment, and proof. Some critics have pointed out that from the outset—from the very first story onward—these terms are all subject to such different interpretations that any stable, let alone authorially sanctioned understanding of them is undermined. Others insist that the text nonetheless both invites and sustains exemplary readings, as well as supports allegories that have, over time, ranged from the Neoplatonic through the psychoanalytical to the queer, and beyond. From the very first (unauthorized, anonymous, and posthumous) printing of the tales, the reception history of Marguerite's singular text shadows the twinned histories of interpretation and ideas.

Among the printer Pierre Gruget's "improvements" to the text was the prefacing of each of the stories with a short summary, outlining its moral import, and most subsequent editions have preserved and perpetuated this editorializing of Marguerite's *nouvelles*. This last term, included in the title Gruget assigned to the collection, is not readily translated into contemporary English. While it cannot properly mean "news" in any sense (whether *Weekly World*, Fox network, or *Washington Post*), its meaning might reasonably extend from the rather literal "new things" or "novelties," through "short stories" or "novellas," to "the gospels." The fact that the term's elasticity matters, with each of its key elements—innovation, brevity, and gospel truth—held in productive tension, is best grasped by way of further, close consideration of the structural and thematic changes that Marguerite made to the storytelling traditions she inherited.

The first of these innovations is the placing of the narrative exchange within the distinctive, and unsettling, context of extreme physical danger. Like refugees from a Hollywood disaster movie, or those who gather at the borders of contemporary Europe, the characters who share tales in the abbey garden of the *Heptameron* have been radically, often painfully, displaced from their ordinary lives. This point leads to the second, more significant alteration Marguerite makes to her sources: the constitution of the group and the nature of their exchange. As noted above, her Italianate models are reconfigured as an argument in favor of equality, as Marguerite gives voice to an equal number of men and women. What is more, since the characters take what we might call narrative turns in presenting their stories, they learn far more than just how to pass, or bide their time. For, by way of the discussions that intersperse the stories, at times heated, at others respectful, they also learn how to listen, and how to argue with each other. The effect of this arrangement, proposed by Parlamente (whose very name signifies dialogue or negotiation), is to suggest that trading in stories is at once an end in itself and a means to the (temporary, provisional) establishment of more equitable social structures. As each participant in the game nominates a successor once the discussion of his or her own tale is complete, they come to realize that (even more than the interrupted journeys on which they had been engaged) their narrative exchanges are properly boundary-crossing.

Marguerite deliberately calls the reader's attention to this dually determined state of affairs: "We are, in this game, all equals!" declares one of the male characters, his surprise marking the fact that the same cannot be said of the world in which they normally operate: a world from which they have, temporarily, been exiled, but to whose dangers and inequalities they determinedly (even obsessively) return, as each tells a daily tale. This last point is underlined by the third and most significant of Marguerite's innovations to narrative tradition: the group's agreement concerning the matter and the manner of the tales they will share. It is worth recalling the terms of this agreement, as it amounts to a narrative contract and mirrors Marguerite's own mimetic contract with her readers: we will choose only contemporary subjects for our stories; we will exclude all rhetorical flourishes from their telling; and we will narrate only tales that we know for a fact to be true. For the most part, the characters keep to the rules; on the one the occasion when they obviously do not (story 70, based on the thirteenth-century poem the *Châtelaine de Vergy*), the clarity of the reasons set out for and against deviation from the rules of game is striking. Oisille (urged to tell the tale) argues that "there are two reasons why I ought not to. One is that it is a long story, and the other is that it is not a story of our time, and although it is by a reliable author, we have after all sworn not to tell stories from a written source." As Oisille warns, she would be explicitly breaching conditions one and two of the narrative contract, as well as sidestepping the third: the truth-telling condition, which perpetuates the orality of the tales, narrating only events either witnessed by the individual storyteller or *heard* from someone they knew to be truthful. But Parlamente counters that an exception can, in this one instance, be made: "That is true, but if it's the story I think it is, then it's written in such antiquated language, that apart from you and me, there's no one here who will have heard it; so it can be regarded as new." Her argument, a complex combination of old and new, familiar and strange, writing and hearing, public knowledge and truths intimately shared, does more than give permission to Oisille to rework an old story for a new audience; it also underwrites the worth of Marguerite's own enterprise.

This degree of self-consciousness about translation, innovation, and the transition from oral to written narrative (like the peculiar quality of attention given to the tales' anticipated reception) is one of the most intriguing features of the *Heptameron* for modern readers. By way of conclusion, it seems useful to explore one last instance of such reflexive consideration of the conditions of worthwhile narratability, found in an unlikely context. With its multiple incests and unwitting romance, story 30 stretches the limits of credibility. Set in the court of Navarre, it explores the actions and desires of a devout young widow, characterized in the introductory blurb by Gruget as "a remarkable example of human frailty, who tries to conceal her horror, but only goes from bad to worse." Known for her sincere devotion, as evidenced by years of fasting, pilgrimages, and similar acts of piety undertaken since the death of her husband, the widow hears rumors about her fourteen-year-old son's inappropriate (and, it seems to her, wholly unlikely) sexual advances toward one of her servants. To test the truth of these claims the widow resolves to swap beds with the chambermaid, and, before long finds herself unaccountably enjoying sex with her son. Both disturbed and ashamed by what she cannot quite recognize as her own actions, she attempts to make amends by sending her son away to the wars, and, when the time comes, by having the child born of their incest adopted and brought up by her own kindly brother. All this is done with the best of intentions and in the hope that distance from home would ensure that neither child became corrupted by her own clearly baleful presence. In due course (of course) her two children meet and fall in love. As if enjoying the tragic irony of it all, the tale's narrator, Hircan (commonly thought to represent Marguerite's own second husband, Henri d'Albret, king of Navarre), wickedly indulges the tropes of romantic love, cross-fertilized by those of family: "They were very much in love. Never was there such love between husband and wife. For she was his daughter, his sister, his wife. And he was her father, brother and husband." In a society founded on closely contracted dynastic alliances, Hircan slyly suggests, things can't get any better: "They endured for ever in this great love." But the mother knows that for things to really be as they seem, she must both avoid the sight of the true love that they embody and keep her dark secret to herself: "in the extremity of her penitence, she could not see them show their love, but she would withdraw to weep alone."

If the tale's content seems to flout the truth condition the narrators have set themselves, then Hircan's rhetorical embroidery certainly transgresses the collective agreement not to entertain flowery or studied poetic language. And yet story 30, for all that it has woven into its texture multiple echoes from medieval sources, Luther's sermons, and poems inscribed on contemporary tombstones, is included by historians among the twenty or so tales that have been verified by research. More significantly, perhaps, none of the storytellers themselves find it in the least unlikely, nor do any object to Hircan's narrative style. He acknowledges before he begins his story that it is "most piteous and strange," but this is more by way of advertisement than warning. Oisille, for her part, agrees, after hearing it, that "one could not hear a stranger story than that." But as the discussion develops, it becomes clear that there is no reason to doubt the tale's veracity, since everyone recognizes, behind the widow's folly, the truths that this woman's "example" teaches, as well as the real villains of the piece.

The interpretive tone is set by Parlamente: "For sure, the first step man takes trusting in himself alone is a step away from trust in God." The other characters then line up to trade in similarly sententious lessons, all of them redirecting the example away from this particular woman and toward either "man" in general or themselves: "He is a wise man, who recognizes no enemy but himself, and distrusts his own will and counsel, however good and holy they may appear to be," says one; another concurs, adding, "and nothing should induce a woman to risk sharing a bed with a male relative, however close he may be to her." Is Marguerite secretly (as some argue) talking about herself and her doubtful (some say incestuous) relations with her brother? Or is the lesson to be drawn here more general than specific? The text, rather than answering such questions, offers further instruction, this time disguised as an image: "It's not safe to set a naked flame near tinder." The novelty (or otherwise) of this image is not what matters; its function is to inscribe the events of the tale in the register of the proverbially true, the universally known. This is made clear by the last of the group's interpretive glosses, offered by Ennasuite (a character Brantôme identifies as his own mother): "Without doubt [the widow] was one of those foolish, vainglorious women who had had her head filled with nonsense by the Franciscans, and thought she was so saintly that she was incapable of sin, as some of them would persuade us to believe that through our own efforts we actually can be, though this is an extreme error."

The events of this story may well be "most strange," and overdetermined self-assurance is clearly a mistake; but putting faith in mendacious and corrupt priests is, Marguerite suggests, the truly "extreme error." This last point is underscored by a remarkable instance of something like a *mise-en-abîme*—the narrator Hircan's self-conscious reference to monks not only as characters in his story, but also as habitual eavesdroppers on the storytellers' exchanges. The presence of the local monks, hidden listeners to the group, goes all but unremarked, and Hircan's mention of them here is their second (and final) appearance in the *Heptameron*: "But you're not taking notice of what I can see!" he exclaims to his companions, interrupting in the process their devout and rather sententious moralizing of his tale. "While we've been telling our stories, the monks have been listening behind the hedge!" As if to draw attention to the topical parallelism of the monks' position as the true villains metaphorically "behind the story" as well as literally behind the hedge, Hircan adds a satirical sting to his tale, observing that "they didn't even hear the bell for vespers, but now that we've started talking about God, they've run off and they're ringing the second bell." The dually inflected moral of the story—sin manufactures opportunity from which grace alone can redeem us, and the teaching of the Church serves, more often than not, to make matters worse—is clear and compelling. Similarly compelling is the seductive force of this tale *as story*.

The extent of Marguerite de Navarre's writings is still being established. Her significance and influence, already remarkable in her own lifetime, continues to be explored in novel forms. Julia Voznesenskaya's *The Women's Decameron* (1985), for instance, a collection of tales linked by a frame in which ten women confined to a maternity ward in Soviet Leningrad both narrate and discuss their experiences over the course of ten days, owes much to the *Heptameron*, though its author rather obscures the fact. More openly indebted to its precursor is Henriette Chardak's recently published (and as yet untranslated) *La passion secrète d'une reine* (A queen's secret passion). A direct descendant of the *Heptameron* in both structure and theme, it retells Marguerite's story by way of a series of imagined analytical sessions interspersed with a factually based historical account, audaciously presenting Marguerite as a pioneering feminist, free-thinker, social worker, and (here's the secret) lover of Rabelais, mother to their twin daughters, Françoise and Jeanne. From the young Elizabeth I's translation of the *Mirror*, through the novel transpositions represented by *La Princesse de Clèves* and *The Women's Decameron*, right down to the psychoanalytically inspired revelations of *La passion secrète d'une reine*, Marguerite's is a body of work that has proved foundational in the history of women's writing in several languages and cultures. It also urges its readers—whoever and wherever they might be: working in the library, commuting to work on the train, or hiding behind a hedge—to explore further the peculiar imaginative capacities generated by narrative fiction that locates itself within the domain of truth.

That Marguerite herself considered the touchstone of truth to be found in scripture—and more specifically in the gospels—seems clear; relocated in the context of their initial appearance, these *nou-velles* define the queen as (in the terms of her own time) an *evangelical*. Indeed, many contemporary readers took the *Heptameron*'s pessimistic theology of human fallibility, focused as it is on the consequences of the Fall, to be a posthumous declaration of their author's religious affiliation: the queen, they argued, had been Protestant in all but name. Such arguments add a retrospective sheen to the work, and in making of the text an early example of *littérature engagée*, they make of Marguerite a religious rebel with a contemporary cause. And yet, while there is much to be gained from recapturing the particular, polemical energies of a work's original context, it is important that in so doing we do not lose sight of other, similarly determining, truths. For Marguerite's fiction also embodies a further distinctive belief, or habit of mind, which stands in constant tension with its pessimistic Reformist theology and its often brutal, socially situated realism: the idea of the perfectibility of humankind. It is the triangulation of these competing claims (or theories) about what it means to be human that make Marguerite de Navarre's *Heptameron* such a compelling read. And it is her commitment to everyday human experience as the grounds on which all theories can, and must, be tested that makes the "first modern woman" a child of that distinctive cultural moment we call the Renaissance.

Works Cited and Recommended Further Reading

Throughout, I have quoted Marguerite de Navarre from *The Heptameron*, trans. P. A. Chilton (London: Penguin, 2004), which has a fine introduction. As a sampler of recent approaches, *Critical Tales: New Studies of the "Heptameron" and Early Modern Culture*, ed. John D. Lyons and Mary B. McKinley (Philadelphia: University of Pennsylvania Press, 1993) cannot be bettered. The following give a good sense of Marguerite's work in relation to larger backgrounds—political, cultural, and religious: Natalie Zemon Davis, *Society and Culture in Early Modern France* (Stanford, CA: Stanford University Press, 1975); John D. Lyons, *Exemplum: The Rhetoric of Example in Early Modern France and Italy* (Princeton, NJ: Princeton University Press, 1989); Wes Williams, *Pilgrimage and Narrative in the French Renaissance* (Oxford: Clarendon,

1998); Timothy Hampton, *Literature and Nation in the Sixteenth Century: Inventing Renaissance France* (Ithaca, NY: Cornell University Press, 2001); Carla Freccero, "Archives in the Fiction: Marguerite de Navarre's *Heptaméron*," in *Rhetoric and Law in Early Modern Europe*, ed. Victoria Kahn and Lorna Hutson (New Haven, CT: Yale University Press, 2001), 73–94; and Margaret Ferguson, *Dido's Daughters: Literacy, Gender, and Empire in Early Modern England and France* (Chicago: University of Chicago Press, 2003).

A French complete works is under way, published by Champion, in Paris. The most affordable (and best) French version of *L'heptaméron des nouvelles* is that edited by Nicole Cazauran and Sylvie Lefèvre (Paris: Gallimard [Folio], 2000). Renja Salminen's edition of *Le miroir de l'âme pécheresse* (Helsinki: Soumalainen Tiedeakatemia, 1979) includes Elizabeth I's translation. Few of the other poems (or plays) have been translated, but some are included in *Selected Writings: A Bilingual Edition*, ed. and trans. Rouben Cholakian and Mary Skemp (Chicago: University of Chicago Press, 2008). The standard and still very fine critical discussion of the poetry is Robert Cottrell, *The Grammar of Silence* (Washington, DC: Catholic University of America Press, 1986); but see also Paula Sommers, *Celestial Ladders* (Geneva: Droz, 1989); Gary Ferguson, *Mirroring Belief* (Edinburgh: Edinburgh University Press, 1992); and Susan Snyder, "Guilty Sisters: Marguerite de Navarre, Elizabeth of England, and the *Miroir de l'âme pécheresse*," *Renaissance Quarterly* 50, no. 2 (1997): 443–59.

The major French studies of the life and works remain those of Pierre Jourda, *Marguerite d'Angoulême, duchesse d'Alençon, reine de Navarre (1492–1549): Etude biographique et littéraire*. 2 vols. (Paris: Champion, 1930); and Lucien Febvre, *Autour de l'Heptaméron: Amour sacré, amour profane*, 2nd ed. (Paris: Gallimard, 1944). Two useful formally attentive studies in French are Gisèle Mathieu-Castellani, *La conversation conteuse* (Paris: Presses Universitaires de France, 1992); and Philippe Lajarte, "D'une fonction l'autre: Pour une pragmatique de la nouvelle dans *l'Heptaméron* de Marguerite de Navarre," *Cahiers Textuel* 10 (1992). Among the best formally focused studies in English are Marcel Tetel, *Marguerite de Navarre's Heptameron: Themes, Language, and Structure* (Durham, NC: Duke University Press, 1976) and B. J. Davis, *The Storytellers in Marguerite de Navarre's "Heptameron"* (Lexington, KY: French Forum, 1978).

The recent biography by Patricia F. Cholakian and Rouben C. Cholakian, *Marguerite de Navarre: Mother of the Renaissance* (New York: Columbia University Press, 2006) is an excellent, if distinctly partial account; it contextualizes the groundbreaking arguments of Patricia Cholakian's earlier study, *Rape and Writing in the Heptaméron of Marguerite de Navarre* (Carbondale, IL: Southern Illinois University Press, 1991). The best historical accounts of specific aspects of Marguerite's life include Barry Collet, *A Long and Troubled Pilgrimage: The Correspondence of Marguerite d'Angoulême and Vittoria Colonna, 1540–1545* (Princeton, NJ: Princeton University Press, 2000); Carol Thysell, *The Pleasure of Discernment: Marguerite de Navarre as Theologian* (Oxford: Oxford University Press, 2000); and Barbara Stephenson, *The Power and Patronage of Marguerite de Navarre* (Ashgate: Aldershot, 2003).

* *
** **

Ronsard

Poet Laureate, Public Intellectual, Cultural Creator

TIMOTHY J. REISS

By 1555, five years after his first book, Pierre de Ronsard (1524–85) was the principal literary figure of his day, called, roughly in the order of his publications: "the French Pindar," "Horace," "Petrarch," "Homer," "Virgil," "Prince of Poets." He was the prime poet, quantitatively, and maybe qualitatively, writing some of the loveliest lyric poetry of his era and much of the most enduring philosophical and political poetry. He would be a leading public intellectual bridging trouble and tradition, consulted by court and kings, and a (the?) vital player in rethinking the role and power of the French language and its letters, as well as prosody—these last three, vital stakes in the political and ideological response to civil war and in constituting the nation-state. Some think Ronsard's intimate, Joachim du Bellay (1522–60), was the better lyric poet, but in sheer quantity and impact Ronsard, in his own day and long after, far outweighs him. Even if, eighty years later, Ronsard's star had waned, by the 1920s the judgment that he was "the begetter of modern French poetry" was again a critical chestnut.

The poet never doubted. He described himself in the preface to that first book, his *Quatre premiers livres des odes*, as "the first French lyric author, who has led the rest to the path of such honorable labor" ("lyric" meant music, essential to great poetry), and often exulted in creating a golden era in French poetry, routing "the vile monster Ignorance"—said ode 1.3, to Henri II's sister Marguerite—his "lute first / to show the way / to ring out so cleanly" (De sonner si proprement), by recovering the Greek and Latin lyricists. Ten years later (though the earlier preface had acknowledged that Clément Marot was a skilled vernacular poet), he named himself, in *Complainte contre fortune* in his *Second livre des meslanges*, "With great labor quite the first . . . / Who led the Muses from Greece to France, / And first measured their steps to my cadence, / And instead of Latin and Greek / First made them speak French, / Boldly defying the ignorant rabble" (thereby defaming Marot and others). In his 1563 "Reply to the Attacks and Calumnies of Sundry Genevan Preachers and Ministers," the last great civil war thrust of his *Discours des miseres de ce temps*, speaking for himself and his Catholic Church, he scorns his attackers as able to write at all only by his having given them the language to do so: "You cannot deny it: for with my plenty / You all are filled, I am your only study, / You are all issued from my greatness, / You are my subjects, and I am your law. You are my streams, I am your source."

By then, Ronsard really was *Poëte du Roy*, king's poet (as he had long sought); close to the queen mother, Catherine de Médicis; cherished by young Charles IX; and royal "counselor and almoner" from January 1559, before the deaths of Henri II and François II. He was a favored court confidant and spokesman, dicey as such favors were, especially during the ever more vicious civil strife after 1560. So these equal boasts bore unequal weight. In 1549, before the *Odes*, Ronsard was a figure known only to his schoolmates and teachers. His cultural creation was poetic and aesthetic—not yet of philosophic, political, or religious heft. The boast presages the growing layers and arenas of influence, justifying the future cardinal Jacques-Davy du Perron's (1556–1618) claim in his 1586 funeral eulogy, that Ronsard "had always been exposed and formed in the public glare and in acts and words of which France has been so very long the theater." But if the boast's import in the last ode of his novice collection, "To his Muse," was just poetic, even cultural in a narrow sense, it augured more; notably after the *Odes'* success. The poem recasts the mature Horace's famed *Exegi monumentum aere perennius*:

> Plus dur que fer, j'ay finy cest ouvrage,
> Que l'an dispos à demener les pas,
> Que l'eau rongeade, ou des freres la rage,
> Qui rompent tout, ne ru'ront point à bas,
> Le mesme jour que le dernier trespas

M'assoupira d'un somme dur, à l'heure
Sous le tombeau tout Ronsard n'ira pas,
Restant de luy la part qui est meilleure.
Tousjours tousjours, sans que jamais je meure,
Je voleray tout vif par l'Univers,
Eternisant les champs où je demeure
De mes Lauriers honorez et couvers:
Pour avoir joint les deux Harpeurs divers
Au doux babil de ma lyre d'yvoire,
Qui se sont faits Vandomois par mes vers.
Sus donque, Muse, emporte au ciel la gloire
Que j'ay gaignée, annonçant la victoire
Dont à bon droit je me voy jouyssant:
Et de ton fils consacre la mémoire,
Ornant son front d'un Laurier verdissant.

(Harder than iron have I ended this work, / That the year
quick to maim one's steps, / The wasting rain, or brothers'
[the winds'] fury, / That smash all, will not o'erturn. / The
very day that final death / Lulls me into a hard sleep, at that
hour / all Ronsard will not go under the tomb, / The best part
of him remaining./ Forever forever, without my ever dying, /
I shall fly full alive through the Universe, / Eternalizing the
meadows where I dwell, / Honored and covered with my
laurels: / For having joined to the sweet prattle of my ivory
lyre, the two different harpers [Pindar and Horace] / Who
have become Vendômois by my verses. / Up then, Muse, carry
to the heavens the glory / I have won, declaring the victory /
In which by good right I see myself rejoicing: / And of your
son consecrate the memory, / Decorating his brow with laurel
greening.)

The decasyllabic ode flaunts his project. It is praise poetry of his
muse and himself but mostly of king, queen, princes, statesmen, poets,
lovers. It takes from Latin to draw French out of "infancy" (says his
preface). It unites the two great Greek and Roman lyricists, ending a
work whose strident Hellenism hyped new sources and the erudition

to use them. It rejects "medieval" poetic genres for ancient ones, sig-nally, in the *First Book*, Pindar's triads of strophe, antistrophe, and epode, the first two metrically alike, the third different, but all triads alike, letting two tunes set the ode. Very *singable*, in alternating femi-nine (final mute-*e*) and masculine rhymes, it is metrically adept, its decasyllables' latent tedium, their interior breaks, caesuras, all placed as required after four syllables (in French verse, the interior mute-*e* is voiced save before a vowel; the final mute-*e* is silent), offset by a rhyme scheme of plain alternating *rimes croisées* (abab) in paired cou-plets, whose second rhyme gives the first of the next pair: yielding a set of quasi-*rimes embrassées* (abba), ababbcbccd . . . , ending in serial near or actual *rimes léonines* (two or more final homophonous sylla-bles) on *vers, victoire, mémoire*, and joy/fertility (*jouissant/verdissant*). It fuses abstract and figural *topoi* of (poetic) glory, peace, death, immor-tality, memory, with a loved home reality (a usual motif in Ronsard, here the Vendômois fields where his body lies). Finally, ending a first collection by calling it a life's monument relishes its being anything but, and augurs Ronsard's endless reworking, typical of his day's poet-ics, its appeal and beauty.

These formal, topical, and semantic elements—new in French (some were), age-old, the poet says, in the Ancients whose *imitation* he exalts and his public praises—recall that no post-Romantic "origi-nality" is at issue. Far from it: the ideal was to express in French ideas, beliefs, desires, songs that others had uttered before, elsewhere, oth-erwise. Here lay "invention," and the old canons of rhetoric and poet-ics provided the devices, *topoi* (places), and figures realizing *that* "orig-inality." These "fair inventions, descriptions, comparisons" were, said Ronsard's 1565 *Abbregé de l'art poëtique françois* (Breviary of French poetic art), poetry's nerves and pulsing life. His posthumous *Franciade* preface held "figures, schemes, tropes, metaphors, phrases and pe-riphrases" needed most for the "prosy" twelve-syllable alexandrine line—whose novelty this chapter's last third explores. "Invention" and "originality" raise two further unfamiliar elements. A general one is that intellectual activities were less fragmented than now (hence the normalcy of "Renaissance man"). Beside Ronsard's ideal of the poet as *vates*, inspired seer with quasi-divine access to knowledge and wis-dom, that poetry, logic, rhetoric, philosophy, theology, and political action were autonomous was inconceivable. Poetry, passion, politics, and place were imbricate, and none could be but refound or rebuilt. Ronsard and his fellows sought for poetry the depth of act and wisdom, breadth of intellectual address, expressive flexibility, and communicative intelligence they felt Greeks had found in Homer, Romans in Virgil.

No idea fell *ex nihilo*. Poetry was joyous recognition in the endless kaleidoscope of the known. Petrarch's love poetry, ringing changes on Latins and troubadours, had untied one sort of novelty-intradition in Italy, Spain, England, and France, where Marot shared in little, but in whose cultural hub of Lyons, Maurice Scève (1501–64), Louise Labé (1520–66), Pernette du Guillet (1520–45) and others wrote radiant Petrarchan lyric (Scève another of the few unallied poets Ronsard saluted). Du Bellay, with his 1549 *Olive*, soon joined. So did Ronsard, but only after his *Odes* loosed a graver, public, legacy of ancient festivals of city and nation culture invested in great Games and their victors. Pindar's victorious athletes became Ronsard's princes, prelates, patrons, and poets; ancient festival, competition, and panegyric became France's present wars, court grandeurs, prayers for peace and golden-age renewal, beauty of country, future peerless culture, with large room for Hesiodic, Virgilian, and Ovidian myth, amity, banter, and bucolic love—also evoking renewal. So his boast may not be coy. Post-1560 editions alter "ton fils" to "Ronsard," surely because, as the poem tells his immortal soul spanning the universe, these lines easily hinted blasphemous identification with Christ (of which Petrarch too had been accused). Such hubris followed giving poetry such wide mediatory and guiding roles, besides Ronsard's dedicating half of his first printed poems to people of the highest rank and council—after addressing others privately.

These themes and people found him. He first saw Paris in 1533, aged nine, when his father put him in the elite, conservative Collège de Navarre. He benefited little there, except for becoming acquainted with Charles, later cardinal de Guise, and in six months returned to being tutored at the family manor near Vendôme, a hundred miles southwest of Paris. His family were old gentry, keepers for their Vendôme lords of the Gastine forest, whose magic imbued the poet—"*saincte Gastine*" of his first *Amours* (sonnet 132), where beloved Cassandre sang and dreamed (131); his home and constant muse (*Odes*, 2.23); its cutting forlorn augury of men's brutality and discord with nature (*Elégie*, 24). Nature was not just the site of, or cover for, human acts, pastoral, brutal, or amatory, but of its own delights, beauties, and God's presence resounding to spirit and senses. In 1569, he thus addressed his poem "Le chat" (The cat), on nature and its animals, to his friend Rémy Belleau (1528–77): "Dieu est par tout, par tout se mesle Dieu, / Commencement, la fin, & le millieu / De ce qui vit, & dont l'ame est enclose / Par tout, & tient en vigueur toute chose / Come nostre Ame infuse dans noz corps." (God is everywhere, everywhere God mingles, Beginning, end and middle Of whatever lives, and whose soul is enclosed Everywhere, and keeps everything alive Like our soul infused in our bodies.) The artful enjambments of these opening decasyllables make a sentence whose plenitude equals that of its sense and willful ambiguity in ties of life to life and soul to soul in God, nature, and humans. Ronsard fears cats, yet they embody God's guardian presence. Comparison is irresistible to Christopher Smart's "For I will consider my cat Jeoffry. / For he is the servant of the living God." His 1750s poem reads and answers Ronsard. It is not alone.

Ronsard's father, Louis (1479–1544), who began fighting at age fifteen in France's Italian wars, won the highest knightly Order of St. Michael from his field-commander, Louis d'Orléans, and favor from the king when Orléans ascended to the throne as Louis XII. In 1518, Ronsard *père* became *maître d'hôtel* (steward) to François I's dauphin. In 1526, when his own youngest son, Pierre, was two, this meant his attending the two princes, the dauphin François and Henri, to Spain, as hostages for their father's liberty after his capture at the Battle of Pavia (February 24, 1525). There Louis stayed, mostly alone in prison, until all three of them returned to France in 1530. Meantime, Pierre and three older siblings (three others died before his birth) were raised by their mother, Jeanne Chaudrier (ca. 1490–1545), who came from a well-connected, wealthy Poitou family, a social step above her husband when she and Louis wed in 1515.

Maybe this Poitevin link, along with a later adored and much-sung clerical living in Touraine, helped inspire the Poitevin René Descartes's well-known love for his "jardins de Touraine"—and for Ronsard: gardens the poet celebrated, for instance, in the lovely pastoral

Voiage de Tours, added to *Amours* 2 in the 1560 *Oeuvres*, relating a trip made by Ronsard and his younger friend Jean-Antoine de Baïf (1532–89) to a wedding at Ronsard's soon-to-be living on the islet of Saint-Cosme-lès-Tours: "C'estoit en la saison que l'amoureuse Flore / Faisoit pour son amy les florettes esclorre / Par les prés bigarés d'autant d'aimail de fleurs, / Que le grand arc du ciel s'emaille de couleurs . . ." (It was in the season when amorous Flora / Made the buds open for her beloved / Over meadows dappled with as much flowers' enamel / As the great heavenly bow is enameled in colors . . .), and so on, for another 330 alexandrines, the grand line that Ronsard and his friends made standard in French (parallel in ease and feel to English blank verse), flexibly shifting from grandiosity to lighthearted joy in spring and fertility.

Some think Pierre was partly tutored by a paternal uncle, canon of Le Mans cathedral and vicar-general to cardinal-bishop Louis de Bourbon, for this youngest nephew inherited his uncle's library in 1535. A tutor's death could be why his father had him made page in 1536 to the dauphin François, whose Provence campaign he joined on August 4. On the 10th, he witnessed François's death, and the autopsy that was required by suspicion of poisoning. His father now became *maître d'hôtel*, and his second brother almoner, to the new dauphin, Henri, and Pierre became page to Charles, next in line. October saw him shifted to serve their sister, the ailing Madeleine, affianced to Scotland's James V. Married at Notre-Dame in Paris on New Year's Day 1537, they sailed north in May, arriving on the 19th after a stormy trip. The queen's health worsened. Ronsard attended her until she died on July 7, then had to wait as James negotiated marriage with Marie de Lorraine, sister of Ronsard's college associate, Charles de Guise. Marie came to Scotland in June 1538. Like many, Ronsard would idolize her daughter Mary, born in 1542, Queen of Scots at a week old. Not made page to Marie, as his father hoped, he left with Madeleine's last courtiers in August, riding through London and England's southeast to rejoin Charles d'Orléans at Amiens at October's end. In two months, he was on an embassy through Brussels (as courier to his prince's intended, daughter of Emperor Charles V) back to Scotland. A still stormier trip landed them at Queensferry as their ship sank under them.

Back in France in March 1539, he was placed in the *Écurie royale*, the court military school. From May to August 1540, he was in Lazare de Baïf's (1496–1547) embassy to a Diet at Haguenau with imperial princes, seeking allies against the emperor. Ronsard returned very ill, partly deaf, and for two years recuperated at home. His distress was likely as much emotional as physical. Deafness closed any opportunity for a diplomatic or military life. He turned to poetry. In March 1543, he went with his father to Le Mans for the funeral rites of their relative, diplomat and general Guillaume du Bellay. His brother bishop René tonsured Ronsard, making him eligible for church revenues and livings. Ronsard also met the bishop's secretary, Jacques Peletier du Mans (1517–83), learned in mathematics, medicine, grammar, law, and Greek, and a poet who had translated the first French version of Horace's *Art poétique* in 1541 (its printing is a mystery; no copy is known before a 1545 new edition). The two became firm friends, with Peletier acting as quasi–poetry tutor to Ronsard. Later in 1543, Peletier became rector of the Paris Collège de Bayeux. Ronsard returned to his palace school and duties to his prince, spending all his spare time across the river at Baïf's grand house, working with his son Antoine, a Greek and Latin prodigy, and his teachers—above all, Jean Dorat (1508–88), who became the beloved teacher of Ronsard and the whole band of friends, all soon urging a revolution in French letters.

In June 1544 and January 1545, respectively, Ronsard's father and mother died, and he spent ever more time with his literary friends. In September, Charles d'Orléans died of plague, and Ronsard passed into the dauphin Henri's service. In spring 1546, Peletier met Joachim du Bellay in Le Mans or Poitiers, as Ronsard did a year later, legendarily by chance in a country inn. Du Bellay joined their group. The year 1547 also saw the deaths of Lazare de Baïf and, to more urgent sense of change, of François I and Henry VIII. Ronsard and Baïf entered the university, studying at the Collège de Coqueret with Dorat (who was not, contrary to myth, its principal until 1556). From the mid-1540s, Ronsard had been building his odes, the first appearing in print as a jokey ode-*blason* salute to erotic chic in Peletier's 1547 *Œuvres poëtiques*, listing beauties favored in a lover, to which Peletier replied in ensuing verses. Henri's accession apparently freed Ronsard of duties, as he rethought poetry and its creative cultural and political work. And 1548 brought Mary, Queen of Scots, to Henri's court, engaged to the four-year-old dauphin François—as if Ronsard's material and spiritual pasts were fusing in a day, a place, a group. In 1549, he published a skilled Petrarchan pining lover's song and a reworked Petrarchan sonnet, these amorous poems balanced by three "state" poems, each a separate brochure (the last, "Hymn to France," included the two Petrarchan poems).

One is a 1548 epithalamium to his family's lord, Antoine de Bourbon, duc de Vendôme, on marrying Jeanne, Marguerite de Navarre's daughter, François I's niece. In sonnet 172 of the 1552 first *Amours*, tying together love, politics, and spirit of place, Ronsard would celebrate his adored Gastine and their short-lived son Henri's birth, praising his valor and future defeats of Spain. Both poems easily slid to their eponymous next son, who became heir to the French throne a year before Ronsard's death and Henri IV five years later, in 1589. Jeanne was fiercely Huguenot, while Antoine was a Catholic leader, slain at the siege of Rouen in 1562. Ronsard would long hew a middle path, like his future patron, Queen Catherine, whose June 1549 Paris Entry he feted, with Henri II the city's "new God," for a spring of wealth, fertility, victory, and courage. His ode must have been ordered by the festival's grandmaster, Anne de Montmorency, constable of France, brother-in-law to Gaspard and Odet de Coligny, future Huguenot leaders, and Ronsard's beloved patrons all—as the Guises, less loved, were amid Catholics. A 1547 "hymn" sings a France of agricultural, raw, and pastoral wealth; power, harmony, friendship, and peace; of storied heritage and divine legitimacy, its people Hector's progeny (ll.119–20: the epic *Franciade* hinted here, as in the *Odes*); its cities, ports, lovely lands, rivers, industries, arts, mathematics, great princes and "me, thy poet" (l. 217). These poems foretell the diversity and bounty, erudition, linguistic riches, intellectual force, and high ambition of the 1550 *Odes*, boding their variety of rhythm and matter, skill and ease—*sprezzatura*—of touch and tone, dizzying verbal wealth and felicity, music, polemic and philosophy, their paean to kingship and its order, to the French land and nation (hence the *Franciade*), to nature and/as divinity. They echo the high dreams of du Bellay's 1549 *Deffence et illustration de la langue françoise*, his "Petrarchan" *Olive*, and those Ronsard encomia. Ronsard's January 1550 *Odes* are their first great original achievement.

Ronsard and his fellows did create a Western tradition from Homer and Pindar via Virgil and Horace to Petrarch and later Italians, instituted future dominant poetic genres and their prosody, and set the benchmark to follow or reject. Modern French students still learn Nicolas Boileau's (1636–1711) scorn in his 1674 *Art poétique* (refusing Ronsard's call for glad abundance) and, with his "enfin Malherbe vint" (at last came Malherbe [1555–1628]), that poet's fabled erasing of Ronsard's poetry. They do not read Descartes's intimate, Marin Mersenne (1588–1648), who, hailing the creative musician Jacques Mauduit (1557–1627), notably his requiem for Ronsard, lauds "this prodigious Genius of poetry" (in whose verse music is crucial). Nor do they hear the regard of Louis XIV's and Colbert's critical czar Jean Chapelain (1595–1674). Do they see the key topos of Stéphane Mallarmé's later, radical *Coup de dés*, whose speaker says "nothing . . . will have taken place . . . but the place . . . save . . . maybe . . . a constellation," as conjuring the Pléiade, being, like these ancestors, end and beginning?—not least as his earlier well-known "Sonnet in-yx" (one a *Phénix* reborn) evokes a seven-star constellation, is built of standard quatrains and tercets, in the capitalized regular alexandrines normalized by Ronsard, and ends on "Anguish," "deceased nude in the mirror, even / as, in the oblivion enclosed by the frame, it is fixed / By twinklings right upon the septet"? The Pléiade as burden and comfort alike? Will they see the same reference in René Char's self-vision as Orion, whose belt points to the Pleiades? Such allusions can be unlimitedly multiplied.

Ronsard vastly *did* what du Bellay *said* in the *Deffence* (whose writing Ronsard shared). They meant to forge a tradition by translating language, meaning, and culture from great poets of other ages and places (like a bee, said Ronsard, echoing Seneca, and others, flitting among flowers to blend pollens into honey); create an idiom able to *express* and *build on* these vitalities; mold familiarity with poetic genres able to sustain the highest levels of thought and culture; fix prosodic rules that best transmitted these; and fit all to a politics and ideology of the stable state and society that these techniques sought to help establish. Gustave Cohen ended his *Life and Work* by listing nine new/

ancient genres this project entailed: Horatian and Anacreontic "ode-let," Pindaric ode, Virgilian and Theocritan eclogue, Tibullan elegy, political satire, long philosophical poem, Homeric and Virgilian epic, Petrarchan love sonnet, comedy and tragedy. Ronsard excelled at the first eight, initiated the first seven. The project also involved rethinking prosodic forms, notably what *had* been the old heroic decasyllabic line (that Ronsard still used by royal order for the *Franciade*, he said, equivocally *à contre cœur*) and replacing it by the twelve-syllable alexandrine: he perfected the last and rethought the first, as well as octo-syllabics for the *chanson*, penta- and heptasyllabics (Paul Verlaine's touted *vers impair?*).

Ronsard did this in civil war's soon increasingly savage embrace, many of whose key players he knew with some intimacy: a status amplifying his influence on the elites. This was unusual, if not unique. Marot, the major poet just before him, was Marguerite de Navarre's court poet and secretary before being both to her brother François I. At the time of Ronsard's first publications, a laureate role at Henri II's court was held by Mellin de Saint-Gelais (1491–1558), who unwisely attacked Ronsard, only to find himself fast rebuffed by such elite opponents as Marguerite, Henri II's sister, and Michel de l'Hôpital, the king's and Catherine's great chancellor—further brightening Ronsard's star. As he said in a great ode to l'Hôpital on poetry's power (written just after the mid-1550s spat, printed in the *Fifth* and then *First Book*), the more envy tried to sink him, the higher he floated. For Ronsard had entered these circles long before he shone as poet and public intellectual with a cultural role eclipsing that of any court forebear—as his death's impact would show (akin, *mutatis mutandis*, to public passions at those of later icons like Voltaire, Hugo, Valéry, or Sartre).

Here, in addition to earlier glimpses of poetic content, remarks on two famous odes are in order, one printed, both written, in 1550, and later added to the collection. The ode on Henri II's March 1550 peace with England became the first of the *First Book*. Extravagant praise of Henri's moral, cerebral, and martial gifts swiftly yields to the myth of the goddess Peace's defeat of Chaos and the forming of the four elements to create a golden age world. She cannot, though, prevent the discord of Troy—happily, it turns out—for Hector's son Francion will, as Cassandra and Hector's ghost predict, found the French royal dynasty whose latest avatar proves able to bring back Peace and her putative golden age. With Henri's pay, Ronsard will sing this epic and give the king the one sure lasting memorial of "the divine and rare equity in which a king is clothed" (ll. 422–24), against slander, flattery, and poetasters' cackle. He ends with a call for victory now in Italy against Spain and in the "Indies" in the future, but also with serio-comic barter for the king's cash, whose tone makes the most of his early proximity to Henri and his siblings. This ode and the ode to l'Hôpital appeal as much to the same pantheon of poets, Homer, Hesiod, Pindar, Lucretius, Horace, Virgil, Ovid, as to myths of Peace. But the former's ten triads pale beside the latter's twenty-four.

"Wandering through the fields of Grace," the poet gathers flowers to crown the gods' darling who, defending Ronsard, has restored Memory's daughters, the Muses. Seven years after their birth, wanting to meet their father, Jupiter, they fearfully follow Memory to Ocean's undersea palace where the gods are feasting, and where "by Nature are enclosed in the depths of a hundred thousand vessels, the seeds of all things" (ll. 137–39). At Jupiter's wish, they sing of the strife of peace and war (Minerva and Neptune), truth and heresy (gods/titans), culture and ignorance (gods/giants). After three triads, the last, too, is brought to peace by the Muses' "sweet song," ravishing Jupiter and charming Mars, war itself, to sleep. Sung poetry's defeat of war's chaos mirrors Peace's victory over Chaos in the near-concurrent peace ode. So it does Love's victory over Chaos, opening sonnet 42 of the first *Amours*, which prefigures the "rounding of the perfections of my passions' *petitz corps* [those seeds of things]," shaping in love "my soul's sphere"; or sonnet 37's ordering of the same "little bodies, swerving as they fall, cast together by chance blow, [having] composed the world" as love my heart. Both odes were collected in 1552 with the *Amours*: these ties of amity, love, and sociable peace are as willful and important (we shall see), as was Lucretius's paean to Venus's ordering of atomic chaos.

The ode to l'Hôpital is not half over. Jupiter gives the Muses rule over nature's sounds, over seers, poets, prophets, oracles, and universal harmonies. He grants reverence from princes who honor poetry's power and vows poetry's power to eternalize such princes. Poetry is part art (art of arts), mostly virtuous inspiration (rarest gift, he tells du Bellay in ode 1.16), shown so in a history from first *vates* to late "melancholics." Of these he is one, says a 1556 *chanson*, ultimately in *Amours* 2, about how imagination puts all he sees into visions of his beloved: "Et m'esjouys d'estre melancholique / Pour recevoir tant de formes en moy" (And I revel in being melancholic, to receive in me so many shaping fantasies). Aristotle felt that a melancholy disposition defined all those "eminent in philosophy or politics or poetry or the arts" (953a10–12). Antiquity provided not just poetic authority. Philosophy offered poetry grounds for untold intellectual authority. All this, says the ode to l'Hôpital is reborn via its dedicatee and a few others: love, peace and poetry uniting. The *Franciade* is forecast here, too.

Clear by now was that if Dorat was the group's beloved, sensitive mentor and scholarly guide, Ronsard was its inspiring poetic heart. Only he had exultant omnifarious sweep. In his funeral oration, du Perron said that if "past ages have seen men excel in one genre of poetry, none has been seen till now who embraced all facets of poetry at once, as he has. Homer did bear off the palm amid epic poets, Pindar amid lyric, another amid bucolic and so on. But they have split poetry's universal glory between them, and each has taken his bit. Never has there been but one Ronsard who possessed it totally in full and totally whole." The poet's Pléiade editors echo Gérard de Nerval in hearing a maid in Scarron's 1651 *Roman comique* trill an ode of "old Ronsard's" as she does dishes. Actually, street musicians "sing the old air badly," but if all are misrecalling another case, mine is enhanced. This is not, *they* say, "imaginary 'popular' ronsardism," but a jibe like Malherbe's, Balzac's or Boileau's. But Ronsard's appeal *was* wide, and the vignette equally recalls Virgil's mass appeal or Montaigne's report of peasants of both sexes in Florentine fields singing Ariosto to their lutes' tune. Du Perron records a view general during Ronsard's life and after. Scarron (and another?), like Montaigne, is retailing fact, however interpreted. Memoirs and chronicles record not just formal musical performances of Ronsard, but, says Kenneth Jones, "their being sung or hummed by lawyers, soldiers, and ladies accompanying themselves on the lute or guitar" (72).

A perfect such song is another ode(let), to Cassandre, first inserted in the revised 1553 *Amours*, moved to the *First Book* of the *Odes* in 1555: "Mignonne, allon voir si la rose / Qui ce matin avoit desclose / Sa robe de pourpre au soleil / A point perdu, cette vesprée / Les plis de sa robe pourprée / Et son teint au vostre pareil." (Darling, let's see if the rose / That this morning did unclose / Its crimson robe to the sun / Has not wholly lost, this eve / The folds of its crimson sleeve / And its tint to yours akin.) Stirring popular and elite publics, this carpe diem's eighteen octosyllables became anthology fodder, like many of Ronsard's love sonnets: "Que me servent mes vers, & les sons de ma lyre"; "Mignongne, levés-vous, vous estes paresseuse," to Marie in 1555; "Comme on voit sur la branche au mois de May la rose," on her death; or, to Hélène, "Quand vous serez bien vieille, au soir à la chandelle," both 1578. I name these to mark signal prosodic change after the *Odes* and first *Amours*. The 1554 *Bocage* and *Meslanges* assay eight-, ten-, and twelve-syllable lines. The first, notably, accents alexandrines even in its sonnets. Of the next two collections, 1555's *Continuation des amours* (sonnets to Marie) and *Hymnes*, the first uses alexandrines near-exclusively in its sonnets (decasyllables rule his earlier love sonnets); the second in twelve of fifteen hymns: the dedication and all of the longest, most subtitled *vers heroiques* (as are fifty-eight of seventy *Continuation* sonnets) versus three in *vers communs*, the decasyllables of hymns printed earlier. The second book of hymns (1556)—some of them test runs for the *Franciade*, said Ronsard in at least one—uses only alexandrines. He also now added the alexandrine dedications to Henri II for the complete *Odes* and their third book.

Since Corneille, Racine, and Boileau, the alexandrine has been touted as the grand meter of epic French reason, clear and distinct thought, and a generally well-ordered condition, if sadly ancien régime–oriented: "governments change; prosody stays ever intact," Mallarmé ironizes in *La musique et les lettres*. By his day, poets were voicing anguish at the poetic and ideological curbs that they felt this meter coerces. Ronsard's hymns, of Homeric, orphic, Callimachan, and Christian sources, indeed told devotion to monarchy, its values, and its agents' antique and Christian virtues and heroic aura, as well as its, their, and France's accord with nature, seasons, cosmos, and divine reason. All things human yield to vicissitudes of time and temper. Virtue and God right them. The sonnets confuse issues, but for now their and the hymns' subtitles offer alexandrines as *heroic verses* to replace the epic meter of old French *roman*, which was (save *Alexandre*) decasyllabic—and until Ronsard, the only line called "heroic" (as du Bellay said in the *Deffence*, where, indeed, he never so much as mentioned the alexandrine). In the *Abbregé*, equating the alexandrine to the Greco-Latin epic hexameter ("our hexameter . . . hereditary instrument . . . national cadence," says Mallarmé in *Crise de vers*), he details usage of the twelve-syllable line, its "rest" (caesura) *always* on the sixth, and its *rimes plates* (aabbcc: his norm, here only implied) alternating masculine and feminine, for setting to music, "for Poetry without instruments, or without the grace of one or several voices, is not at all enjoyable, any more than instruments without animation by a pleasing voice's melody." "Composition of Alexandrines must be grave, noble and (so to say) high-spoken, the more as they are longer than others and would feel like prose if not composed of select, grave and resonant words and in rhyme rich enough that its richness prevents a prose style, and lingers in the ears until the next line's end." Two years later, he adds that he had wanted to compose the *Franciade* in alexandrines ("that I brought into fashion and honor"), but had to obey, "against my wish," royal orders to do otherwise.

His 1572 preface explains his epic's decasyllables differently. While, thanks to him, Ronsard agrees, alexandrines are now in fashion at court and with the young, and "would have been a hundred times easier to [use] than others, the more as they are longer and so less constrained [*moins sujets*]," he had "the ashamed awareness [*la honteuse conscience*] that they savor too much of prose [*qu'ils sentent trop leur prose*]." His longer, posthumous, 1587 preface opens on the topic. In youth he had "ignorantly" given alexandrines "the rank of our language's heroic meter," as "more suited to mighty tales and the mind's finest ideas than other common verses." Long thought, use, and experience "had disabused" him: "they savor too much of over-facile prose, and are too enervated and flabby," save, he repeats, for translation, where their length eases explanation, or tragedy, where performance alters effect. Alexandrines' rhythm and meter now seem too near the heart of normal French usage (as the Protestant Bible might be in mass explanation). A taut conflict between the two prefaces illuminates this thought. In 1572, Ronsard claims having based his epic "rather on Homer's simple ease [*naïve facilité*] than on Virgil's meticulous care." By 1587, Virgil has taken over, despite Ronsard's knowing that "the envious will cackle on about my stressing Virgil more often than Homer, *his* master and model." Does not Virgil's *curieuse diligence* now resonate with what Ronsard calls the extra *difficulty* of the greater metric constraints of decasyllables?

It is as if Ronsard were afraid and "ashamed" of the alexandrine, which is too "easy" because too close to French's natural rhythms, potentially constraining the language itself by imposing revealed metric bonds that could ultimately constrain its rhythms and therefore its meanings. Poetry and its demands would be not a separate, vatic, or elite practice, but at the very core of language. Mallarmé usefully returns, again in *Crise de vers* reflecting on Victor Hugo's death to the effect that not only he thought "verse is simply itself literature; that you have verse as soon as diction is accentuated, rhythm as soon as style is." This is the other chronological end, as it were, of Ronsard's fear about the alexandrine and its need to be endowed with high tropes and figures (he repeats in the posthumous preface) for its richness to "prevent prose style": a proximity to prose marks the meter as capturing something like an essence of French *langue*. For Ronsard, attaching poetry to music may have been another way to displace that capture; for Mallarmé, quite the contrary: "music rejoins verse to form poetry." For Ronsard this might increase, if not (shameful) nightmare, at least a weight of political and intellectual responsibility that the 1562–63 civil war polemics and attacks unpleasantly typified. If rhythm and meter capture the heart of everyday language, speaking to power is no vatic activity, but targets the core of what enables such power to function at all—which was exactly the point of late-nineteenth-century poets' attack on the alexandrine, as the Jesuit Victor Delaporte's irate 1898 polemic against them, *De la rime française*, makes conspicuous.

This may be why Ronsard's period of emphasizing alexandrines was relatively short, more or less from 1554 to 1565, except for the late sonnet sequence for Hélène (1578). The most important *Discours* on the civil wars are dated 1562–63, the elegies were mostly all written by 1565, and the sixty-four alexandrines closing the late *Franciade* preface may be their own commentary. After 1560, 80 percent of Ronsard's still prolific output was in non-alexandrine meters—not counting the epic's 6,150 decasyllables. What Ronsard *says* about the alexandrine may be one thing; what he *does*, perhaps another. Let us look at a short passage from *Hymne de la Justice* to his old college colleague, Cardinal Charles de Guise:

> DIEU transmit la JUSTICE en l'âge d'or ça bas
> Quand le peuple innocent encor' ne vivait pas
> Comme il fait en peché, et quand le VICE encore
> N'avoit franchi les bords de la boette à Pandore:
> Quand ces mots, *Tien & Mien*, en usage n'estoient,
> Et quand les laboureurs du soc ne tourmentoient
> Par sillons incongneuz les entrailles encloses
> Des champs, qui produisoient, de leur gré, toutes choses . . .

> (God sent Justice to earth in the golden age / When innocent people did not yet live / As they do now in sin, and when Vice / Had not yet crossed the rims of Pandora's box: / When these words, *Yours and Mine*, were not in use, / And when workers of the plough did not torture / Through unknown furrows the closed entrails / Of the fields, that produced, of their own accord, all things.)

The hymn continues with the growing human evils that degrade the golden age (and this garden of Eden) until Justice flees back to heaven, and God/Jupiter threatens not another Flood, but a universal Fire. Temporarily saved by Mercy and Destiny, eventually comes great king Henri II, in whose lieutenant and minister, Charles de Guise, Justice will again come to earth. The twelve-syllable line in successive *rimes plates* tells an inexorable story, whose outcome we know from the title dedication and first lines. These lines' regularity typify the meter for the next three centuries. Each line is halved in hemistiches by a caesura that must fall on a strong sixth syllable/vowel, of a syntactically and lexically strong word or phrase (verb, noun, adjective, adverb, full or nearly so in meaning). The special force of mute-*e* can serve to stretch out that syllable even when it does not count in the meter. In the first line here, the first accent falls on *JusTICE*, even as its mute elongates into the *en*. The next caesural stresses fall on the last syllables of *innoCENT*, *pechÉ*, *BORDS*, *MIEN*, *labourEURS*, *incongNEUZ*, whose meanings for conflicts of sin and innocence, vice and virtue, work and leisure, are clear. Meantime, the stronger stresses of successive rhymes bear the argument/story sternly forward. And, as Jacques Roubaud notes, the paired rhymes work to enlarge the unit from one line to two, providing twenty-four places for potential changes in rhythm rather than twelve (Ronsard's lingering line memory)—indeed, the rhymes being pairs of pairs, the unit grows to forty-eight (I refer especially to chapters 4 and 5 of *Vieillesse d'Alexandre*). For Ronsard, this is what risks making the alexandrine prose. I parse this passage because it also contains so much future philosophical argument (and terms), from Montaigne to Rousseau and indeed Hugo.

Alexandrines were not just this. Du Bellay opened his 1558 *Les regrets* by defying Ronsard's lead, in an alexandrine sonnet no less regular:

> Je ne veux point fouiller au sein de la nature,
> Je ne veux point chercher l'esprit de l'univers,
> Je ne veux point sonder les abîmes ouverts,
> Ni dessiner du ciel la belle architecture.

> (I do *not* want to rummage in nature's breast, / I do *not* want to search the universe's spirit, / I do *not* want to sound the open deeps, / Nor to draw the heavens' lovely architecture.)

The series of denials, the caesural stress on verbs of human hubris, the *rimes embrassées*, the sonnet form, all counter the "heroic" or epic alexandrine; or tragic, says Ronsard. He does likewise. Indeed, in the sequence of sonnets for Marie, he queries his intellectual ambitions and the alexandrine in which he most lately expressed them. He does so by bookending the sequence with a first sonnet that, asking his friend for a solution, opens: "Tyard, everyone said of my beginning / That I was too obscure for the ordinary person: / Today, everyone says the opposite, / And that I betray myself by speaking in too low a manner"; and with a closing sonnet:

> Marie, tout ainsi que vous m'avés tourné
> Mon sens, & ma raison, par vôtre voix subtile,
> Ainsi m'avés tourné mon grave premier style,
> Que pour chanter si bas n'estoit point destiné.

> (Marie, just as you have turned / My sense and my reason, with your gentle voice, / So have you turned my first grave style, / That was not destined for such low song.)

Just as the first poem is in *rimes embrassées*, so is this last (indeed, the abba/abba was usual in all the quatrains of Ronsard's sonnets, alexandrine or decasyllabic). The first caesura is not, this time, on a major syntactical term (*ainSI*), though the others are, and this first line uses, too, a heavy enjambment: . . . *tourné Mon sens*.

Ronsard's love sonnets are typically more rhythmically complicated than the longer forms—odes, hymns, elegies, *discours*. While the first two quatrains usually follow that abba/abba rhyme, the tercets, always intertwined in rhyme, may be ccd/eed, cdc/dcd, ccd/dee. Enjambment is common; caesural stress on a weak syllable, lexically or syntactically, is not unusual. Yet in the main sonnet series to Marie and Hélène, the alexandrine is the preeminent meter. Indeed, in the latter, I think there is one exception in both books (1.16), while even the latter sequence's two *Chansons* are in a meter of twelve- and six-syllable lines: demi-alexandrines. The many such sonnets that are so familiar as to be almost proverbial suggests that their meter does manifest in some fundamental way the rhythms of the language, the thought and emotions it expresses—or have historically come to do so. Here, Cécile Alduy's strong book on the 1550s craze in France for *Amours* lets me take conclusions a bit further. After hesitations over the preferred form (Scève wrote *Délie* in *dizains*), these sequences were invariably sonnets, really modeled after du Bellay's *Olive*. Alduy asks why, in France, against the diversity of Petrarch's *Canzoniere*, most sequences kept to one genre. Ronsard's *Hymne de l'éternité* offers a clue, voicing unity in its capacious epic alexandrines, as parts in concord that describe love sonnet sequences as a genre, as it does their emotional and spiritual drives and goal of their principal images. Alduy also asserts the importance of these sequences in forging a national language, often in "competition" with Italy, despite the seeming *legèreté* of their matter. This makes them sketches and even figures of amity/love (Aristotle's and Cicero's *amicitia*) as essence of the well-ordered society and state (suggesting why love became crucial to the later politics of tragic theater).

Apropos of Ronsard, this brings into view a last set of poems I would like to address, the *Discours des misères de ce temps*, written mostly in 1562–63 (each first in print as a pamphlet), with three from 1560–61; these were gathered in 1567 as a potent defense of Catholic France, but especially of the monarchy and Catherine's efforts at permanent negotiated peace. These were not Ronsard's last foray into political verse. They were his one skirmish in fierce polemic. As such, one wonders how far the 1574–84 Protestant alexandrine epics *Judith* and *Sepmaines* by Guillaume du Bartas (1544–90) and *Les tragiques* (1616) by Agrippa d'Aubigné (1552–1630, a great Ronsard admirer) reply to Ronsard's 1562–63 *Discours* and 1572 nationalist and monarchic epic (in no sense Catholic propaganda, but firmly for Charles IX, his Valois dynasty, and the Christian France he takes them to embody, and that unhappily went on sale two weeks after the Saint-Bartholomew's Day massacre, with evident effects on interpretation). One can ponder, too, the far larger aesthetic (and political) success and influence of these epics, leading in turn back to the *Discours*, whose flexibility of alexandrine is more redolent of the sonnet sequences than of the *Hymnes*, *Elégies*, or even *Franciade*'s decasyllables. I give just one example, taken from what became the opening *Discours*, addressed to Catherine, first printed as a separate *plaquette* after the outbreak of the first War of Religion, begging her to continue piloting her child Charles and France:

Il faut premierement qu'il ait devant les yeux
La crainte d'un seul Dieu: qu'il soit devotieux
Envers la sainte Eglise, & que point il ne change
La foy de ses ayeulz pour en prendre une estrange.

Ainsi que nous voions instruire nostre Roy
Qui par vostre vertu n'a point changé de loy. (ll. 37–42)

(First he must have before his eyes / Fear of one God: [he
must] be reverent / Toward the holy church, and not at all
change / The faith of his ancestors to adopt a foreign one. /
As we see taught our king / Who by your virtue has not at all
changed law.)

This awkward translation tries to catch these lines' layout as well
as their sense. In late 1561, Ronsard had written a verse *Institution* for
young King Charles IX—a short "Education" or "Mirror" (published
alone in 1562, then included in the *Discours* collection)—recalled
here, thus implicitly setting Catherine's right religious education of
Charles against Jeanne d'Albret's wrong, "foreign," training of *her* son
Henri. These six lines work what became a virtual battle cry: "Une
foi, un roi, une loi" (one faith, one king, one law). Ronsard can easily
accent two of the terms as *rimes plates* (ll. 41–42). He cannot do the
same for the third because of the rule of alternating masculine and
feminine pairs. Breaching another rule in repeating a rhyme, he *could*
place *foy* three lines away. His solution is stronger and more interesting. He signals the primacy of the slogan's first term by leading into
it with the full first hemistiches of lines 38 and 39 (fear of God, devotion to the church) and by encasing it in its two negating words at the
feminine rhyme, *change* and *estrange* and, above all, setting it at the
head of line 40 by enjambment: "que point *il ne change la foy* de ses
ayeulz." Using this device, Ronsard breaches the rule that hemistiches, and above all lines, should usually be "whole" in sense. Certainly "que point il ne change" can be called whole. The run-on is
nonetheless strong enough to draw attention to *foy* in its relation to
roy and *loy*.

A few lines later, Ronsard transforms the virtually absolute
hemistich-divisional rhythm of his alexandrines: "Que dira Pharamond! Clodion, & Clovis! / Nos Pepins! nos Martels! nos Charles,
nos Loys . . . ?" (What will say Pharamond! Clodion, and Clovis! Our
Pepins! our Martels! our Charles, our Louis . . . ?) (ll. 57–58). The
first line quite hammers its two six-syllable divisions, its exclamation

at the caesura, "Clodion" fairly flows, as it were, into "Clovis," the second hemistich closed with another exclamation. The next line jerks us into stresses on its third as well as its sixth syllables. We start actually to *feel* the potential dynastic rupture. No conjunction flows from king to king, each and all (*nos . . . nos . . . nos . . . nos*) a separate moment. This is what will happen if Catherine and, through her, Charles, cannot keep control, by negotiation if possible, force if necessary, of religion and the nation, *foi, roi, loi.* Such moments show the alexandrine's power and flexibility, generally visible in the sonnets, which lies (as appears in these fraught *Discours*) in the twelve-syllable meter's provision of more combinatory "places" (Roubaud) for rhythmic variation. It was a power that would live on, as Mallarmé would note. What difference they might have made to *La Franciade* we cannot know. Nor can we ever know which of Ronsard's reasons for *not* writing it in alexandrines was more important.

Royal order and his own tentativeness about "heroic verse" clearly coexisted. But the latter is (perhaps) the more interesting. It shows Ronsard struggling, beyond the superficialities of expanding his language's vocabulary with new words, ever greater use of figures, terms of art, dialect, and so forth (chief objects of later criticism), with the very nature of language in its rhythms and metrics. He knew that these affected *what* it could say as well as *how.* In the *Odes*, the *Elégies*, the *Discours*, the *Hymnes*, and the *Franciade*, at stake were the nation, the state, its principal representatives and leaders, as well as what he referred to as "the most excellent conceptions": the deepest possibilities of thought and action. Experiment in such things was more "safely" committed to sonnets. But there, too, at heart, the issue was the grounds of human relations and that *amicitia, amor,* that from antiquity to Ronsard's own time had been taken as the enabling force of all human society. The *Discours* were especially tensed because the conflicts they feared tore *amicitia,* broke social relations (all too clearly for Ronsard, losing his friend Louis des Masures and Châtillon/Coligny patrons), and forced them potentially to be replaced by something else: maybe a coerced contract that late-nineteenth-century poets would see epitomized in the alexandrine. Perhaps the Valois fell because they insisted on (thinking in) decasyllables.

That may be a joke. But Ronsard's poetic and intellectual grandeur lies not least in his unbroken engagement with what in it is not a joke.

WORKS CITED AND RECOMMENDED FURTHER READING

I cite Ronsard, *Oeuvres complètes*, ed. Paul Laumonier, Raymond Lebègue, and Isidore Silver 20 vols. (Paris: STFM, 1914–75). Ronsard revised non-stop, and this edition alone presents the work chronologically. Its eighteen text volumes are online (not 19 and 20: *Addenda, Errata*, tables, and indexes). The latest Pléiade *Œuvres complètes*, ed. Jean Céard, Daniel Ménager, and Michel Simonin, 2 vols. (Paris: Gallimard, 1994), follows Ronsard's own last edition (1584) with all variants. Du Perron's eulogy is in *Oraison funèbre sur la mort de Monsieur de Ronsard (1586)*, ed. Simonin (Geneva: Droz, 1985). Mauduit's requiem is online (score in Mersenne's 1636–37 *Harmonie universelle*). The first *Life* has two modern digitized editions: *La vie de P. de Ronsard de Claude Binet (1586)*, ed. Laumonier (Paris: Hachette, 1910); and Helene M. Evers, "Critical Edition of the *Discours de la vie de Pierre de Ronsard*" (PhD diss., Bryn Mawr College, 1905).

English translators have belabored the love poetry. Besides various twentieth-century medleys, Humbert Wolfe offers a good bilingual *Sonnets pour Hélène* (London: Eyre & Spottiswoode, 1934); and Morris Bishop provides a beautifully rendered multitude in his romanticized *Ronsard, Prince of Poets* (London: Oxford University Press, 1940). Recently, Malcolm Quainton and Elizabeth Vinestock deliver a wide French *Selected Poems* (London: Penguin, 2002) with English prose crib; Philip John Usher gives a fine *Franciade* (New York: AMS, 2010); and Clive Lawrence a splendid *Cassandra* (Manchester: Carcanet, 2015), hitting tone, rhythm, rhyme, even run-ons—with literal inaccuracies yielding to affective verity.

Of criticism and history, I cite two French works, one among several still key to Ronsard study from the 1910–20s, the second recent: Gustave Cohen, *Ronsard, sa vie et son oeuvre* (1924), new ed. (Paris: Gallimard, 1956); and Cécile Alduy, *Politique des "Amours": Poétique et genèse d'un genre français nouveau (1544–1560)* (Geneva: Droz, 2007). The early group is chiefly Pierre Chamard, Pierre Champion, Paul Laumonier, Pierre de Nolhac, and Marcel Raymond. Their compatriots' later output is giant. On the alexandrine, I note Jacques Roubaud, *La vieillesse d'Alexandre: Essai sur quelques états du vers français récent* (Paris: Maspero, 1978). English books bulk less, perhaps owing to Ronsard's resistance to translation.

The dean is still Isidore Silver, *Ronsard and the Hellenic Renaissance in France*, 4 vols. (St. Louis, MO: Washington University Press; Geneva: Droz, 1961–87); and *The Intellectual Evolution of Ronsard*, 3 vols. (Geneva: Droz, 1969–92). Some monographs need mention: Dudley Wilson, *Ronsard, Poet of Nature* (Manchester: Manchester University Press, 1961); Elizabeth Armstrong, *Ronsard and the Age of Gold* (Cambridge: Cambridge University Press, 1968); Richard A. Katz, *Ronsard's French Critics, 1585–1828* (Geneva: Droz, 1966), which sinks claims of Ronsard's 250-year eclipse; K.R.W. Jones,, *Pierre de Ronsard* (New York: Twayne, 1970), still a sterling introduction; Malcolm Quainton, *Ronsard's Ordered Chaos: Visions of Flux and Stability in the Poetry of Pierre de Ronsard* (Manchester: Manchester University Press, 1980); Ullrich Langer, *Invention, Death, and Self-Definitions in the Poetry of Pierre de Ronsard* (Saratoga, CA: Anma Libri, 1986); Sara Sturm-Maddox, *Ronsard, Petrarch, and the "Amours"* (Gainesville: University Press of Florida, 1999), *the* book in English on Petrarch and Ronsard; Virginia Scott and Sara Sturm-Maddox, *Performance, Poetry, and Politics on the Queen's Day: Catherine de Médicis and Pierre de Ronsard at Fontainebleau* (Aldershot: Ashgate, 2007), which studies a likely 1564 performance; and Carla Zecher, *Sounding Objects: Musical Instruments, Poetry, and Art in Renaissance France* (Toronto: University of Toronto Press, 2007), on Ronsard's music. Terence Cave's chapter in his *Cornucopian Text: Problems of Writing in the French Renaissance* (Oxford: Clarendon, 1979) is basic, and his edited *Ronsard the Poet* (London: Methuen, 1973) is still fruitful critical work. Grahame Castor's *Pléiade Poetics: A Study in Sixteenth-Century Thought and Terminology* (Cambridge: Cambridge University Press, 1964) transformed its topic's study. So, now does *Poétiques de la Renaissance: Le modèle italien, le monde franco-bourguignon et leur héritage en France au XVIe siècle*, ed. Perrine Galand-Hallyn and Fernand Hallyn (Geneva: Droz, 2001). Many musical settings exist, old and new: for example, Arthur Honegger and Darius Milhaud.

Du Bellay and *La deffence et illustration de la langue françoyse*

HASSAN MELEHY

The word "Renaissance," in the sense of a vast rebirth of society, culture, and politics, was not used in sixteenth-century France, when major changes in these areas occurred, but rather, for the first time, in the mid-nineteenth century by historian Jules Michelet. Nonetheless, the idea of a great renewal of literature, by way of a modern rebirth of the culture of Greek and Roman antiquity in close connection with the growing international presence of the French state, is a central concern in Joachim du Bellay's *La deffence et illustration de la langue françoyse* (*The Defense and Illustration of the French Language*). This artfully written text, which appeared in 1549, the very middle of the sixteenth century, stands out among the poetic treatises of the time in a number of ways. Signing the work only with his initials,[1] du Bellay proposes a wholesale revitalization of French poetry as a national literature that will find its place among the other literatures of Europe, with the aim that before long it will surpass them in quality. He speaks on behalf of a group of young writers, commonly known as the Pléiade, who regarded themselves as responsible for inventing a new poetry, distinct from the poetry of the previous several centuries (the period we now call the Middle Ages). Although there is a lot of variety in the work of these poets—who included, among others, Pierre de Ronsard, Jean-Antoine de Baïf, Etienne Jodelle, Rémy Belleau, Pontus de Tyard, Jacques Peletier du Mans, and du Bellay himself—they shared the common mission of renewing poetry, and the *Deffence* is, for the most part, their manifesto.

In the text, du Bellay calls for the renewal of French poetry as an enrichment and glorification of the French language. His proposals to this effect aligned quite well with the recent designation of French as the official language of matters of state: in the Ordinance of Villers-Cotterêts of 1539, François I had declared that French would replace Latin in this function. Du Bellay is supporting and extending this new status of French: by giving poetry the role of promoting the language, he ties the latter to its recent elevation. Hence, he is also contributing to the glorification of the state, which in the sixteenth century was expanding to the point of attaining imperial status. Throughout his treatise, du Bellay speaks of poetry and military action in the same terms: for example, one of the main words in his title, *Deffence*, has strong military connotations; in a key passage, he places the names of ancient Greek and Roman military leaders, including Pericles, Alcibiades, and Caesar, alongside those of Homer and Virgil; and the last chapter is titled "Exhortation to the French to Write in Their Language: With Praises of France." That is, one of the main purposes of poetry is to celebrate the rising status of France and so to participate in its conquests. Also telling in this respect is the name that du Bellay and Ronsard used for their circle, "Brigade," before opting in about 1556 for "Pléiade," in commemoration of a third-century BCE group of Alexandrian poets who wrote in Greek.

The new name, "Pléiade," signals the trait that in the *Deffence* du Bellay claims for the new poetry, the one that makes it part of a renaissance: French poets must write in imitation of their predecessors in Greek and Roman antiquity, with the goal of equaling and eventually surpassing them. Although French poets, as well as those of several other countries of western Europe, had long been aware of and borrowed from the legacy of antiquity, du Bellay's innovation is to place the reverence for ancient poetry at the center of poetic practice. In fact, he goes so far as to say that French poetry is deficient for having so far failed to look to ancient verse as its principal model: he insists that French writers have not yet written outstanding poetry with a few rare exceptions—he names Jean de Meun and Guillaume de Lorris, two "old French poets" who, respectively, began and completed the thirteenth-century *Roman de la rose* (*Romance of the Rose*). As for authors in his own century, du Bellay is particularly hard on Clément Marot, whom he unkindly offers as an exemplar of simplicity and ordinary language. He also omits his predecessor's name, with evident dismissiveness, from a list of three exemplary elegists: Ovid,

Tibullus, and Propertius, all Romans who wrote in Latin. Du Bellay's omission is part and parcel of his refusal to recognize the poetry of his time as equal to that of antiquity.

It was easy for his contemporaries to recognize the absence of Marot's name as du Bellay's response to the *Art poëtique françois* (*The French Art of Poetry*) by Thomas Sébillet, a widely read treatise that makes no bones about the superiority of French verse. Du Bellay's regular belittling of Marot may be explained by this rivalry with Sébillet, which du Bellay carries out by affirming the superiority of his own approach to poetry, that of imitating the ancients. His jibes also stem from his rivalry with the recently deceased Marot himself. Part of du Bellay's program, and also that of his fellow members of the Pléiade, was to make the fourteen-line sonnet the form of choice for French poetry: Marot was the first French popularizer of the sonnet, and he also translated the work of Petrarch, who in the mid-fourteenth century had established the sonnet form. Although du Bellay implicitly criticizes Marot for translating Petrarch (translation is an important topic in the *Deffence*—this subject will be treated more extensively below), du Bellay himself later wrote poems that suggest an interest in and even respect for this aspect of Marot's work.

Indeed, in his very short career as a poet (he was active for about nine years before his untimely death in 1558), du Bellay broke several of the apparently important rules he lays down in the *Deffence*: not only did he translate poetry from Latin but he also wrote verse in Latin, against the principle signaled by the title of book 1, chapter 11: "That It Is Impossible to Equal the Ancients in Their Languages." In addition, instead of following the prescription for the moderate use of archaisms, "a few antique words . . . that we have lost through our negligence," which will adorn the language with a dignity comparable to that of religious relics, du Bellay wrote his poetry in a French that very much belonged to his time. Hence, instead of viewing du Bellay's prescriptions as strict rules to be followed, it would be better to understand the *Deffence* as a positioning, a staking out of territory in the very competitive field of poetry, which in the sixteenth century was encouraged by the French state as an integral part of advancing its political interests both at home and abroad. What marks the *Deffence* from beginning to end is a series of rivalries: with recent and contemporary French poets, with the other national poetries that were taking shape in Europe, namely, in Italy and Spain, and also with the ancients, whose poetry and political status, according to du Bellay, France had a good chance of one day surpassing. The *Deffence* is charged with the notion that poetry goes hand-in-hand with military might and imperial expansion. In light of this close linkage of poetry and conquest, it is easy to understand Greek and Roman antiquity not only literally but also as stand-ins for contemporary political and cultural rivals. Du Bellay's strategy is, first, to put French on an equal footing with the languages with which it is competing, and then to move it to the highest rank through his program of creative borrowing from other languages, which he terms "imitation." That is, this renaissance of French poetry will come about through a confrontation with other national poetic traditions, one that takes from them what it needs in order to defeat them.

Because of du Bellay's apparently self-contradictory position of arguing for the greatness of French poetry by putting down almost all of its current exemplars, the *Deffence* was immediately the target of critics. Among the first was Barthélemy Aneau, professor of rhetoric and principal of the Collège de la Trinité in Lyons (now the Collège-Lycée Ampère), who in 1550 or 1551 anonymously published a full-scale attack on the *Deffence*, the *Quintil horatien* (Horatian Quintilius), named for Quintilius Varus, a censor whom the Roman poet Horace calls a friend in his famous *Ars poetica* (*The Art of Poetry*). Thus invoking a parallel between Sébillet and Horace, Aneau responds as follows to du Bellay's title: "Who accuses or who has accused the French language? Surely no one, at least not in writing." In fact, du Bellay doesn't get very specific about who the accusers are. Following his argumentative claims that all languages are equal in their origin, that French is, at least in its potential, just as good a language for poetry as Greek and Latin, though not yet as rich in its expressive power and turns of phrase as these two, he rather vaguely blames "those ambitious admirers of the Greek and Latin languages" for holding back the enrichment of French in their refusal to recognize its suitability to poetry. To this characterization Aneau replies, "You are one of them," since du Bellay elevates Greek and Latin to such a high status, the threshold that French must attain by becoming like them. "And you call this defense and illustration, rather than offense and denigration?" continues Aneau. "For there is not in your whole book one single chapter, not one single sentence, showing some virtue, luster, ornament, or praise of our French language."

Engaging in aggressive rivalry, Aneau is writing polemically, and like most polemicists he exaggerates. It is not true that French had not been "accused": there were many in sixteenth-century France who insisted on the inherent superiority of the ancient languages, many who wrote poetry only or mainly in Latin, many who dismissed or ignored the thriving and long-standing tradition of writing in French. Du Bellay of course acknowledges this tradition with his praise of the authors of the *Roman de la rose*, as well as of Jean Lemaire de Belges, who, says du Bellay, "seems to me to have been the first to render illustrious both the Gauls and the French language."[2] But Aneau is quite right to signal, as this last sentence from the *Deffence* indicates, du Bellay's generally low regard for the tradition of French vernacular poetry, and also to call into question the younger poet's depiction of French as a language in need of "enrichment."

What du Bellay means by "enrichment" has, since Aneau's remarks, been a subject of controversy among critics. Some have considered the text as also embodying an offensive strategy, especially since it borrows from both legal and military proceedings: du Bellay insists on aggressively confronting the poetry written in other languages and taking the best it has to offer in order to enhance French poetry. That is, he characterizes the French Renaissance as an event that asserts its presence on the international scene of his time, appealing to a standard by which all national literatures may be measured, the writings of antiquity that are the common currency of scholars and writers in Europe. Early in the book, to describe the process of enriching the French language, he offers the example of the Romans, whose language at the outset was, he makes quite clear, in need of enrichment. In his description, du Bellay pursues a rather elaborate agricultural metaphor that suggests domestication, improvement, and increased yield. The Romans, he writes, "like good farmers, first transplanted it [their language] from a wild to a cultivated site. Then, so that it might yield fruit better and more quickly, pruning away the useless branches, they replaced them with fine and cultivated branches, taken in masterly fashion from the Greek language, which were rapidly so well grafted to their trunk and made to resemble it that from that time on they have no longer appeared adopted but natural."

According to this account, the Latin language needed attention, comparable to that which a farmer gives to domesticating plants, in order to be at home in Rome: it needed to be transplanted or moved from one place to another—from the wild place where it was born (as is the case for all languages, du Bellay affirms in his first chapter, "The Origin of Languages") to the growing civilization of ancient Rome. In the terms of this metaphor of cultivation, the language that is original or natural to the Romans is the "trunk" of the tree. Borrowing these "fine and cultivated branches" from Greek models that ostensibly reached a high level of accomplishment, the Romans then graft them to the trunk. But as with any grafting procedure, as du Bellay recognizes, the result is a hybrid, and the original or natural condition of the trunk or language changes into something else, an admixture of elements from different sources. Although the trunk may remain recognizable as a version of what came first, it has changed in joining with the new grafts. It is therefore no longer what it was in its natural state. Its new parts, the grafts, are not part of the plant's essence. Du Bellay suggests as much by saying that the grafts were "made to resemble" the trunk (they do so only through the skill of the cultivators) and that, finally, they "appeared" to be natural rather than adopted.

Du Bellay's prescription is for French poets to follow this example. Hence, he not only locates the major source of French poetry outside France, in Rome, but he also indicates that the cultivation of a language is necessarily a multilingual, transnational process. But the implication is that, in borrowing from poetry in another language and from another culture in order to improve one's own, one diminishes the stature of the poetic source: cutting the very best branches removes them from the place where they once thrived and consequently does damage to the trunks they grow on. That is, in considering a preceding or contemporary literature in another language, a rival literature, as great and thus worthy of serving as a model, the aim is to clear at least some of it away in order both to make room for and to fortify one's own. As he continues his argument, du Bellay includes Greek, along with Latin and French, among the languages that at some point have been in need of cultivation: in order to enrich their language, the Greeks did the same to an unnamed predecessor. In this perspective, the ascendancy of national literatures is a cyclical process, involving poetic traditions that attack and attempt to supplant predecessors, only to undergo the same treatment in return. Of course, in du Bellay's account it is evident that Greek in some fashion lasted through the borrowings that the Romans made from it, and that in the modernity of European humanist learning, in which both Greek and Roman literature are appreciated as relics from the past, they share the field in which they are held in high regard. At the end of book 1, chapter 3, du Bellay looks forward to the day when, in connection with the ascendancy of the French empire, writers in French take their place alongside their Greek and Roman forebears, equaling them.

In keeping with the idea that poetic achievement should come with and bolster military might, in introducing the idea of imitation he suggests that the multilingual, international field of literary achievement is akin to a bloody battlefield. In a strangely mixed metaphor, to describe the Roman imitation of Greek writers, he returns to his agricultural terms and also adds those of cannibalism, which would have been known in his time primarily through accounts, usually fictionalized, of some of the indigenous inhabitants of the Americas, who practiced it as a wartime victory ritual: "By imitating the best Greek authors, transforming themselves into them, devouring them, and, after having thoroughly digested them, converting them into blood and nourishment, selecting, each according to his own nature and the topic he wished to choose, the best author, all of whose rarest and most exquisite strengths they diligently observed and, like shoots, grafted them, as I said earlier, and adapted them to their own language." The grafting that du Bellay with apparent innocence slips in at the end has suddenly become something quite violent in its juxtaposition with the metaphor of cannibalism: according to the latter, authors tear apart and absorb the work of their predecessors, incorporating it into the body of their own. The writings of the earlier authors is not strictly speaking eradicated, since it persists as part of the new flesh that has grown stronger by eating the old—indeed, the new flesh must completely mix itself with the old through the process of transformation that du Bellay mentions.

Again, every rising national literature is a hybrid of the forerunning literatures from which it takes its models. Although du Bellay places particular emphasis on Greece and Rome, he also includes "Italians, Spaniards, and others" in his roster of authors whose work should be regarded as source material. Italy and Spain were rival European countries that were also developing national literatures in tandem with an increasing international presence, and du Bellay presents the new French poetry as in continual, adversarial dialogue with them. Of course, the aim of French poetry, in the defensive strategy that he advocates, is to treat the exchange as a competition to be won. Du Bellay proposes, in effect, that the old and new literatures be known and understood primarily in connection with their contribution to the new French literature. This notion reflects the reality of sixteenth-century France, in which the names of Roman and Greek poets, such as Vergil, Horace, Pindar, and Homer, as well as that of the Italian predecessor whom du Bellay holds in high regard, Petrarch, are most widely and popularly known through the French writers who address and rework them.

The central paradox of the *Deffence*, the notion that in order to become superior, French poetry must account for its own inferiority, leads to the particular character of du Bellay's poetics: opposing treatments such as Sébillet's that regard French poetry in relative isolation from other literature, and consequently rankling their partisans such as Aneau, du Bellay proposes that French poetry distinguish itself precisely by being hybrid, by building itself up on the basis of foreign literatures, and so by establishing itself as a kind of clearing house for them. Du Bellay develops the idea of a polyglot, transnational literature operating in continual dialogue with its counterparts through his notion of imitation. Yet to the frustration of many of his readers, he never provides a comprehensive definition of imitation, instead mentioning in circumstantial fashion several different practices. In addition, his terminological choice may seem odd to readers of the history of poetics: the word "imitation" has long been the standard translation of the Greek μίμησις (*mimesis*—in Latin, *imitatio*), which in Aristotle's *Poetics* is the very function of poetry. However, Aristotelian imitation is not supposed to be that of other poetry, but rather of reality, specifically the behavior of human beings and the depiction of the natural world. That is, as a copy, it has a clearly defined original. But when du Bellay speaks of the imitative function of poetry as bearing on other poetry, the latter in turn developed through imitation, the question arises as to just what the original of poetic imitation is. If poetry is to be judged, according to Aristotelian criteria, by the effectiveness of its imitation, then will a poem in du Bellay's view be an achievement if it successfully imitates its model? What would such imitation involve? Borrowing specific segments of its text—words, phrases, entire passages? Capturing a broad sense of the qualities of an admired poem?

When he begins explaining imitation, du Bellay addresses both these notions. As to the first, he speaks of those writers who, "diverting themselves with the beauty of words, miss the force of things"; hence he suggests that it is ideas and perhaps also more general aspects of a literary work that should serve as a model. It is, however, important to note his constant emphasis on the centrality of language to poetic practice, by which he means something quite material: words, phrases, rhetorical figures, the expression of ideas in language, and the overall fine quality of a literary work. Because of his insistence on rhetorical elegance, he makes clear that imitation is not translation: early in the *Deffence* he states that translating the distinguished poems of Greece and Rome will yield inferior works and not contribute to enriching French as a literary language. Indeed, he goes so far as to lay down the rule that poetry should not be translated, comparing the practice to sacrilege: "O Apollo! O Muses! Thus to profane the sacred remains of antiquity!" (As mentioned above, somewhat later he himself violated this dictum.) He justifies his stance toward translation by saying that it is impossible to render a poem "with the same grace the author put into it," since "each language has an indescribable something that belongs to it alone, so that if you strive to express its inborn quality in another language, abiding by the law of translation, which is never to stray beyond the bounds of the author, your diction will be constrained, cold, and graceless." That is, trying to remain as close as possible to both the letter and meaning of a text only results in placing distance between the original text and the new one, as well as between the language of the new text and the natural quality of the language in which it is written. Imitation, on the other hand, since it involves transformation of one author into another and one text into another, abolishes any such distance. Du Bellay reserves translation for works that primarily convey knowledge, affirming that translators provide a valuable service in offering important learning to those without the resources to become fluent in foreign languages.

Despite this distinction, du Bellay's idea of imitation entails some translation: continuing his remarks about borrowing words from other authors, he writes, "it is no vice, but greatly praiseworthy, to borrow from a foreign language ideas and words and to claim them as one's own." Even if it is primarily the ideas or the overall quality of a text that is the target of imitation, some words will necessarily be involved, as grafts to a newly written text, words translated from the model texts in Greek, Latin, Italian, and Spanish. Imitation would involve taking parts of texts, rearranging them, and placing them in a new context—because of this freedom to move elements around, the law of translation would not apply, and the author of the new text would make choices suitable to her or his own local, present-day situation and thus create a highly effective literary work. Rather than being constrained by the stiffness of diction of the translated phrases, the author could strategically place them so as to challenge and complicate the established conventions of the language in which he or she is writing—in very much the sense du Bellay understands the term, such a practice would be an enrichment of this language.

In the brief conclusion of the *Deffence*, du Bellay suggests just such a use of parts of the literary works of Rome. One passage metaphorically links French imperial expansion to the imitation of works that poets will do in order to glorify France: "Up then, Frenchmen! March courageously on that proud Roman city and from her captured spoils (as you have done more than once) adorn your temples and altars." This affirmation seems to contradict du Bellay's characterization of the translation of poetry as sacrilege, especially in the case of literary works, relics, that are removed from their original location and put to use in the temples of the "religion" of a foreign invader. But what makes this practice different from the sacrilege to which du Bellay refers earlier is that it involves a use of relics in a new version of the old "religion" that in fact does it honor by equaling it, rather than offering the inferior work of translation. This practice achieves such an effect by dismantling the relics—cutting them up for grafts, or cannibalizing them—rather than making empty, falsely pious gestures of preserving the relics intact. The new "religion," the new literature, and the new nation will take the place of the old, in keeping with the cyclical notion of history that du Bellay at times affirms, in which one civilization arises in the wake of another's fall. Under such circumstances, imitation is a process of taking parts of another literature— which, again, may also be a modern one, from a nation in competition with France for imperial primacy—and incorporating them into one's own as the basic part of the latter's enrichment.

This understanding of imitation is in keeping with du Bellay's own process of composing the *Deffence*: he borrows quite heavily from an Italian text of his time, Sperone Speroni's *Dialogo delle lengue* (Dialogue on languages), first published in Venice in 1542 and well known among French humanists. Du Bellay's borrowings from Speroni are so great that they prompted Pierre Villey, the early-twentieth-century scholar who first signaled their extent, to characterize the *Deffence* as a work completely devoid of originality. This judgment of the *Deffence* was more or less the consensus among critics for most of the twentieth century, although interest in the text as the manifesto of the Pléiade remained high. For the past several decades, scholars have contested this view, seeing in the *Deffence* an example, even a model, of the very practice of imitation that du Bellay prescribes for poets. Since the *Deffence* is ostensibly a treatise, not a work of poetry, it might not be obvious that this is what du Bellay is doing. However, the language of the text is quite poetic: it is made up of elaborate, flourishing sentences, heavily marked by rhetorical figures, including many exclamations in the midst of a more coolly persuasive argument. Indeed, Aneau takes him to task for an overuse of metaphors, mixed ones to boot, in a text better suited to "propriety," proper or literal usage—that is, a treatise. But another of du Bellay's innovations in Renaissance France, his challenge to poets, is to bring poetic writing to prose texts, as he does here.

Instead of simply repeating what Speroni's text says, du Bellay strategically borrows passages and redirects their meaning and context in response to his own time and place. The *Dialogo delle lengue* is, in fact, a dialogue, and the six interlocutors say many different things, disagree with each other, and misunderstand each other—no one position emerges as the dominant one. Du Bellay takes parts of the speeches of several of the interlocutors and arranges them into an argument. For example, one of the speakers, Pietro Bembo (based on the historical figure of the same name), argues against the insistence of another, Lazaro Bonamico (also the name of a historical figure), that modern languages will never equal Greek and Latin. Bembo claims that in the Tuscan dialect of Italian, two centuries earlier Petrarch and Giovanni Boccaccio wrote works equaling those of antiquity; however, he also grants that sixteenth-century Italian is weak but may see a revitalization with the growing interest in Tuscan. Unlike du Bellay, he does not stress the contemporary language as the one in which a rebirth of literature will take place but rather looks back to fourteenth-century Tuscan; and this language, rather than Greek and Latin, will offer a model for the present day. So it is less a question of taking works in Greek or Latin as models to imitate than of regarding them as setting a high standard. Although he borrows and translates lengthy passages from the *Dialogo*, du Bellay grafts them to his text in order to yield a new argument.

It is striking that he effectively announces the French literary Renaissance by borrowing so heavily from an Italian text—as though he were devouring it, merging this text with his own. That is, his declaration of a renewed language and literature in French incorporates something foreign as both a source of strength and an obstacle to overcome. He is demonstrating the process of producing the French Renaissance on the basis of foreign elements, the very thing he advocates. Although in his poetic practice he diverges at times considerably from his own prescriptions, in relation to his major Italian source, Petrarch, he adheres closely to this idea of imitation. Moreover, the imitation of Petrarch is at the heart of the French literary Renaissance by way of the prescriptive dominance of the sonnet form: although Marot wrote the first sonnets in French, beginning with du Bellay's *Olive* the Petrarchan sonnet became central to French poetry, not only for the other members of the Pléiade, but also for Louise Labé, who begins her 1555 sequence of sonnets affirming women's equality in erotic relationships with a poem in Italian, unmistakably invoking Petrarch. For centuries the sonnet remained the French poetic form of choice. A brief consideration of du Bellay's most distinct imitation of Petrarch, the sonnet sequence *Songe* (*Dream*), will demonstrate the avenues by which the French literary Renaissance built itself on an Italian forebear. (It is ironic that Petrarch learned the sonnet form from the poetry in Provençal that he read while in southern France, where his father, a lawyer, worked for the exiled papacy in Avignon—so the sonnet comes from a "lesser" Romance language of medieval France, one whose existence du Bellay nowhere acknowledges.)

Among his last writings, *Songe* is an appendix to his sonnet collection *Les antiquitez de Rome* (*The Antiquities of Rome*), which du Bellay published alongside *Les regrets* (*The Regrets*), the other sequence he wrote while in Rome working as secretary to his relative Cardinal Jean du Bellay, the French ambassador to the Vatican. The title page of *Antiquitez* characterizes it as "a general description of her [Rome's] greatness," adding that it is also, antithetically, "a lamentation on her ruin." And to make clear the link between the two very different sequences in the book, the text says, "with a Dream or Vision on the same subject." The lamentation of *Antiquitez* focuses on the grand monuments of ancient Rome, which du Bellay presents as conspicuously absent, even unnamed: "these old palaces, these old arches . . . and these old walls," he writes in sonnet 3, repeating the word "old" in order to underscore the ubiquity of signs of age. He thus recognizes the two meanings of the word "antiquity," venerability and decrepitude. What is most distinct about ancient Rome, celebrated in its heyday as well as in sixteenth-century tourist literature as the Eternal City, is that it fell into ruin—so its eternal status could only ever have been a fiction, and it is subject to the same decay as everything else. Remaining among the ruins is the poetry of Rome, which speaks from the city's ruined tombs. In keeping with the notion of imitation from the *Deffence*, du Bellay's speaker observes the ruin of Rome and its poetry as part of his own composition. The lamentation has an ironic dimension, since the clearing away of Rome that the sonnets of the *Antiquitez* both note and enact allows space for the rise of the French poetry that du Bellay is exemplifying. He builds the new poetic monuments on the ruins of the old.

Songe is quite different because it does describe some of the monuments of Rome, but fantastically, as though in a dream or vision, as the title indicates. Besides the full title, parts of the sequence very clearly rework a text by Petrarch, the *Canzone delle visioni* (*Song of Visions*), poem 323 of the *Canzoniere*, the Italian poet's most widely read collection, through which the sonnet was known in Renaissance France. The *Canzone delle visioni* was widely known in France in Marot's translation from the early 1530s, *Le chant des visions de Petrarque* (Petrarch's Song of Visions). Petrarch's original is not a sonnet or sequence of sonnets, but rather a series of six twelve-line stanzas followed by a tercet; Marot's is the same, except that the final short stanza is a quatrain. Du Bellay's *Songe*, however, is a series of fifteen sonnets—in selecting this form, he further acknowledges Petrarch as a source. The six visions of Petrarch are of ruin and decay, beauty brought down by a destructive force: they have long been understood to constitute an allegory of the emptiness of earthly beauty. The images are of a wild animal that devours a noble creature; a ship decked out with gold, ivory, and ebony that sinks in a sudden storm; a laurel tree struck by lightning; a fountain swallowed up by an earthquake; a phoenix that meets its final death upon discovering the laurel and the fountain; a lady (Petrarch describes the woman about whom he writes many of the poems in the *Canzoniere*, Laura) killed by a snakebite. The concluding tercet is the poet's declaration of the desire for death as the only relief from the loss of worldly beauty.

Of Petrarch's visions, du Bellay borrows the earthquake, which topples a huge crystal monument (sonnet 2); the tree, which becomes an oak, is destroyed by barbarians (sonnet 5); the phoenix, which becomes an eagle that goes down in flames, but is then reborn from the ashes, like a phoenix (sonnet 7); the fountain, whose stream is muddied by a troop of fauns (sonnet 12); and the ship, which also goes down in a storm, but which resurfaces (sonnet 13). Du Bellay explicitly acknowledges Petrarch by saying that this new ship is "richer" than the one that appeared to "the sad Florentine." He also tacitly acknowledges Marot's translation of the *Canzone delle visioni* by reproducing a line from it: he describes the ship and its cargo as "the great wealth, second to none." Although the French phrase, "La grand' richesse à nulle autre seconde," is a straightforward translation of the Italian, "l'alte richezze a null'altre seconde," there are several reasons to believe that the repetition is not coincidental. In sixteenth-century France, poetry was such a serious pursuit that poets tended to be quite familiar with the noted works; also, du Bellay places this ten-syllable line in one of his sonnets of this meter, reproducing Marot's, instead of tailoring it to one of the poems in alexandrine, or twelve-syllable, verse with which he alternates the former in both *Antiquitez* and *Songe*. So in this sonnet he also borrows from Marot, showing just how translation may be used as part of imitation. In the other poems of *Songe*, du Bellay offers a series of calamitous images of ancient Rome, most of which he takes from the Book of Revelation's depiction of the destruction of Babylon/Rome during the Last Judgment. However, rather than coming to the finality of the End Time, each vision of Rome is followed by another in which Rome rises, only to fall. And in sonnets 7 and 13, there is, unlike in Petrarch's *Canzone delle visioni*, a rebirth. That is, du Bellay presents Rome as part of the cycles of rising and falling civilizations—since in his poetic theory he proposes Rome as a model, Rome may, in his poetry, stand in for subsequent empires. The result of the process, though, is that, in the wake of Rome's ruin, he writes his sonnets, monuments to the French literary Renaissance. He does so by borrowing from the visions of creation and destruction in the work of Petrarch, a much more recent model of civilization and literature in Italy—so from the passing of the older poetry, there is revitalization.

Du Bellay thoroughly recognizes an international and multilingual literature that France must face in its efforts to attain foremost status in the linked realms of politics and literature. Looking back to antiquity as a model has the dual effect of acknowledging the international community of humanist scholars and writers who regarded the legacy of Greece and Rome as the greatest source of learning, and of contributing to the establishment of standards according to which the western European political and intellectual centers could compete with each other. Du Bellay does not hide his interest in the rivalries among these political and cultural powers, since he also advocates

borrowing from the poetry of Spain and Italy. In both these countries, the Petrarchan sonnet thrived in the sixteenth century, and it
was soon to do so in England as well. Particular to du Bellay's poetics
is its proclamation of the multilingual and international orientation
of the renewal of French poetry. Although the major writers of the
Italian Renaissance drew heavily on antiquity and also borrowed from
the poetry of other countries, the idea of a direct confrontation with
and appropriation of other contemporary literatures did not find formulation as such. In England, the situation was a bit different, mainly
because of the interest among humanists, chiefly those connected to
Richard Mulcaster, the headmaster of the Merchant Taylors' School
in London, who introduced his pupils to the Pléiade and the *Deffence*.
The most distinguished of them, Edmund Spenser, translated du Bellay at the age of sixteen for inclusion in a Protestant tract, Jan van der
Noot's *Theatre for Worldlings*, and later published revised versions of
this work in *Complaints*, a collection that appeared in the wake of the
success of the first three books of *The Faerie Queene*. The other poems
in *Complaints*, as well as parts of *The Faerie Queene*, are strongly marked
by du Bellay's ideas and language. Among readers of Spenser's du Bellay was Shakespeare, who borrowed phrases from this work for *Sonnets*; some of Shakespeare's plays also show clear signs of his readings
of sixteenth-century French prose writers François Rabelais and Michel de Montaigne. But these French sources tend to be somewhat
hidden in the work of Spenser and Shakespeare; neither they nor any
other English Renaissance writer made a public declaration of the
importance of borrowing from other languages and literatures comparable to du Bellay's. This insistence is what makes the *Deffence* a
unique work of poetics in the European Renaissance.

NOTES

1. He wrote I.D.B.A., for Joachim du Bellay, Angevin: in sixteenth-century
    typography, there was no distinction between the letters "I" and "J," in
    English or French; an "Angevin" is someone from the French region of
    Anjou.
2. In its strict sense, the word "Gaul" designates a member of the ancient

tribes that populated France before and during Roman times. Du Bellay uses it, as did many in the Renaissance, as a synonym for the French.

Works Cited and Recommended Further Reading

Quotations from du Bellay's writings are from *Joachim du Bellay: "The Regrets," with "The Antiquities of Rome," Three Latin Elegies, and "The Defense and Enrichment of the French Language"* (bilingual edition), ed. and trans. Richard Helgerson (Philadelphia: University of Pennsylvania Press, 2006). The recent French edition of choice is du Bellay, *La deffence, et illustration de la langue françoyse*, ed. Jean-Charles Monferran (Geneva: Droz, 2001). The latter volume also includes the complete text of Barthélemy Aneau's *Quintil horatien* (299–361) as well as Claude Gruget's 1551 French translation of Speroni's *Dialogo delle lengue* (193–279), along with the original Italian of the latter in facing-text format. Quotations from Petrarch's *Canzone delle visioni* are from *Petrarch's Lyric Poems: The* Rime Sparse *and Other Lyrics* (bilingual edition), trans. and ed. Robert M. Durling (Cambridge, MA: Harvard University Press, 1976), 502–5. Clément Marot's translation of the *Canzone delle visioni*, "Chant des visions de Petrarque," may be found in Marot, *Oeuvres poétiques*, ed. Gérard Defaux (Paris: Classiques Garnier, 1996), vol. 1, 347–49.

As for scholarship on du Bellay, Pierre Villey's *Les sources italiennes de la "Deffense et illustration de la langue françoise" de Joachim du Bellay* (The Italian sources of Joachim du Bellay's *"Defense and Illustration of the French Language"*) (Paris: Champion, 1908) remains an exceptionally valuable source on du Bellay's poetic treatise, and it is very instructive on the importance of the Italian Renaissance in sixteenth-century France. A scholarly work that initiated a series of reflections on the originality as well as the major importance of the *Deffence* in how French Renaissance writers understood their historical role is Margaret W. Ferguson, "The Exile's Defense: Du Bellay's *La deffence et illustration de la langue françoyse*," *Publications of the Modern Language Association* 93, no. 2 (1978): 275–89; Ferguson followed up on this with her book *Trials of Desire: Renaissance Defenses of Poetry* (New Haven, CT: Yale University Press, 1983). Around this time, Thomas M. Greene discussed the place of the *Deffence* in Renaissance poetic theory: *The Light in Troy: Imitation and Discovery in Renaissance Poetry* (New Haven, CT: Yale University

Press, 1982). Ignacio Navarrete, "Strategies of Appropriation in Speroni and Du Bellay," *Comparative Literature* 41 (1989): 141–54, is a superb demonstration of what du Bellay does with Speroni's *Dialogo delle lengue*. In my own recent *The Poetics of Literary Transfer in Early Modern France and England* (Farnham, UK: Ashgate, 2010), I consider the *Deffence* in close connection with du Bellay's poetry as part of an examination of how English and French national literatures established themselves.

* *

Montaigne

Philosophy before Philosophy

TIMOTHY HAMPTON

"This book is not for you," says Montaigne to his readers at the outset of his *Essays*. "It was written for my family and friends. I am not trying to become famous or admired. . . . Don't waste your time on such a vain and frivolous subject as this." Montaigne's warning that his book is not good for very much is the first of many such pronouncements in the history of French literature, from André Gide's exhortation in *The Fruits of the Earth* to "throw my book away," to Rimbaud's rejection of poetry for life as a trader in East Africa. Yet Montaigne's denigration of his book is not a rejection of literature. It betrays his uncertainty about presenting a work that is so closely allied with a single life. Paradoxically, however, the originality of the book derives precisely from the way in which the author places his "vain and frivolous" concerns at the center of human experience. His book is useful because, like its author, it makes no claims to be exceptional.

Montaigne's *Essays* are a unique instance in European literature of a work of philosophy that makes no claim to truth, to systematic analysis, to the development of concepts, or to the formulation of conclusions. The book touches on issues of crucial importance to the nature of the self, the limits of knowledge, the ethics of personal and political engagement, and the diversity of customs and cultures. Yet whatever authority it enjoys derives from its depiction of the modest, curious, personality of its author. It stands as the last and perhaps greatest philosophical text of the premodern world, offering a meditation steeped in history and in the observation of everyday life. It precedes the invention of modern philosophy by René Descartes in the 1640s, with all of the developments that flow from the onset of the Cartesian method. Yet at the same time, precisely because of its rootedness in the Renaissance, Montaigne's work grows in relevance and importance in the postmodern culture that has emerged since the late twentieth century. Following the work of such figures as Derrida, Deleuze, and Foucault, the colors of the Cartesian tradition have begun to fade, and Montaigne grows in brightness. Montaigne is deeply rooted in the classical culture of the early modern era, yet, precisely because of his passion for exploring the limits of that culture, he emerges as a surprisingly modern—even postmodern—author.

We can best locate Montaigne's work at the intersection of a great intellectual movement and a great political crisis. The intellectual movement is humanism, which was imported from Italy and came to prominence across northern Europe in the early sixteenth century. Steeped in the study of rhetoric and history, obsessed with classical antiquity, humanist culture is devoted to ideals of heroism: military, moral, and intellectual. It blends ideals of virtue and political action with the study of classical languages and training for public service. However the great excitement that accompanied the northward movement of humanism—and which we can read in the generation of Rabelais and Erasmus, fifty years earlier—had begun to wane by the time of Montaigne. The delighted rediscovery of classical authors had given way to an overload of knowledge, which led to a culture of the digest, of the excerpt, and of empty displays of learning for its own sake. Moreover, the political climate had changed. A newly militant Catholic Church, coming off of the reforms of the Council of Trent, was increasingly intolerant of the humanist interest in classical pagan culture, and the Protestantism that had overtaken much of northern Europe had little use for learning that was not theological.

No less important for the *Essays* than the diminished vitality of humanist intellectual life were the terrible wars between Protestants and Catholics that tore France to pieces for more than three decades, between 1560 and the mid-1590s. The Wars of Religion in the sixteenth century are the greatest political crisis in French history before the French Revolution. They decimated the aristocracy, depriving the nation of leaders, and visited unspeakable horrors on the general population. Treaties, truces, and political councils were powerless to slow the bloodshed, as France became the battleground between an international Protestant movement supported by England and the forces of Catholic reaction, backed by Spain. Theological disagreement became the pretext for aristocratic bloodletting, as powerful provincial families developed their own militias. The culmination was the famous Saint Bartholomew's Day Massacre of 1572, in which the Catholic monarchy countenanced the targeted murder of Protestant leaders in Paris, touching off weeks of violence all across France. This political crisis was intimately linked to the intellectual crisis of humanism, mentioned above. For the failure of humanist moderates to counter political fanaticism was an index of the intellectual crisis of the late sixteenth century in France. It provides the backdrop to Montaigne's skeptical attitude toward his own culture.

Like his contemporaries Shakespeare and Cervantes, Montaigne is a transitional figure, looking back ironically and with some melancholy on the classical culture of the Renaissance, even as he shapes the emergence of modern literature and thought. He works from inside the heroic culture of humanism while exposing its limitations. Just as Don Quixote undermines heroic ideals through his adoration of knights of chivalry, and just as Hamlet compares his own hesitations to the decisiveness of classical heroes, so Montaigne is steeped in the ideals of humanism, even as his own exploration of his limitations casts an ironic glance on the heroic figures and forms that shape him. His work gives the first voice to the common experience of a world in which classical heroes and values have lost their unimpeachable authority. Montaigne is often pigeonholed by intellectual history as a "skeptic." But he is much more than that. He is the first of the moderns. He invents a literary personality that discovers value and dignity in its own capacity to doubt himself. This makes him the most accessible and relevant of early French writers.

In the letter to the reader that opens his book, Montaigne describes the *Essays* as a self-portrait. If he lived in the New World, he says, where people go without clothes, "I can assure you I should very gladly have portrayed myself here entire and wholly naked." The book is not an autobiography in the conventional sense of the word. There is no chronology, and very little happens. It consists of 107 chapters on diverse topics, divided into three books. Some of the chapters bear titles suggesting conventional moral themes, such as the essay "Of Moderation." Others are startlingly new, such as "Of Cannibals," which deals with the recent encounters between French settlers and the cultures of Brazil. Still others seem deliberately trivial, such as the very brief essay on thumbs. Some essays barely treat of the topic announced in the title, and certain themes unexpectedly pop up in dramatically different contexts across the book. However, the variety in subject, tone, and size of the different essays (from one page to more than two hundred) is precisely the point. For these pieces give us a picture of Montaigne's response to a whole range of themes and situations. The variety of topics makes the *Essays* not merely a book about philosophy or politics or history, but a book about Montaigne. And because he treats so many different topics, the literary creation "Montaigne" who binds the "vain and frivolous" book together emerges as a figure who is both appealingly modest and endlessly fascinating.

Montaigne began to write in response to two deaths. The first was the death of his father, Pierre Eyquem, in 1568. Pierre had been a devoted admirer of Renaissance humanism, and, in particular, of Erasmus of Rotterdam. He took pains to provide Montaigne with a splendid humanist education. The young boy was taught Latin even before he learned French, thus making him a native speaker of the language of the classics—a kind of "classical Roman" dropped down in the middle of early modern France. His first love, he tells us, was poetry (Virgil, Horace, and especially Ovid). But he was deeply steeped in moral philosophy (Cicero, Seneca, and Plutarch, whom he read in a French translation, knowing no Greek) and in classical history (Livy and Polybius). Among his own contemporaries, he read widely in history in French, Italian, and Latin—Guicciardini's *History of Italy*, Commynes's histories of France, accounts of travel and exploration such as Jean de Léry's 1578 *History of a Voyage to the Land of Brazil*, the political thought of Bodin and Machiavelli, the poetry of Petrarch, du Bellay, and Ronsard. He rarely quotes the Bible or the Church Fathers, drawing instead from Roman and Greek civilization. Aristotle interests him little, and his reading of Plato is biographical rather than philosophical—he is interested in the personality and habits of Socrates. This education destined him, as a member of a recently ennobled family, for a life of public service. The ideals of heroism, of military virtue, and of the exercise of rhetoric in the political world were the cornerstones of his education. The humanist culture that gained popularity among the Renaissance elite aimed to turn the notoriously illiterate and rough French nobility into a cadre of sophisticated and learned men of letters, equipped to serve the monarchy in a newly unified country with imperial ambitions. This was the education that Rabelais had imagined in the 1530s, in *Pantagruel* and *Gargantua*, and the education enjoyed by Ronsard and du Bellay, the poets who reinvented French letters at midcentury. However Montaigne's education left him with both a strong sense of obligation to "the best father who ever was," and a clear sense of inadequacy at his own modest success, lack of ambition, and generally lazy nature. His acceptance of these diverse features of his personality is one of his most affecting features.

Some years later, after Montaigne had begun a somewhat indifferent career as a jurist, his father asked him to translate into French a treatise on natural religion by the Spanish philosopher Raymond Sebondus. Montaigne's longest essay, "The Apology for Raymond Sebond," comes out of this undertaking. It reflects his engagement with the skeptical tradition that informs many of the essays. It displays his interest in the Pyrrhonism of Sextus Empiricus—recently coming back into vogue—for whom the goal of philosophy was to reach a state of absolute uncertainty, or *ataraxia*. It is in the "Apology" that Montaigne despairs of the possibility of humans knowing anything. Instead of promoting an ideal of mastering many fields of knowledge—yet another ideal of humanism—Montaigne notes that knowledge and human perception are inevitably marked by error and illusion. In response to this situation, he offers the question that remains his most famous line, "What do I know?" (Que sçay-je?) This question, which is often taken by commentators as an expression of confusion or extreme doubt, is, in fact, a call to clear the decks of grandiose claims to truth, in favor of a modest but endless program of self-exploration and personal growth.

The second death that shaped Montaigne was the death of his best friend, Etienne de La Boétie, a brilliant humanist writer whom he

met at the parliament in Toulouse in 1557. A political philosopher
and poet in both French and Latin, La Boétie was from Sarlat, not far
from Montaigne's own ancestral home, in the Dordogne region of
southwestern France. Given the generally illiterate and violent tenor
of sixteenth-century life in France, the companionship of a fellow
reader and thinker from his own region must have been an exceptional source of pleasure for Montaigne. Moreover, it placed Montaigne and his friend in a long literary tradition of male friendship,
going back to Seneca's friendship with Lucilius, something that must
have added delight to Montaigne's cultivation of their relationship.
When La Boétie died suddenly, at the age of thirty-three, Montaigne
was devastated. La Boétie had been his soulmate. As he notes mov-
ingly in the essay "Of Friendship," if anyone asked why he loved La
Boétie, he would reply simply, "because it was he, because it was I."
Moreover, to add insult to personal loss (and bind personal experience to political crisis) La Boétie's early philosophical exercise, *Of
Voluntary Servitude*, in which he meditates on the curious fact that the
masses of people allow themselves to be ruled by a single monarch,
was taken up and published by Protestant militants as a justification
for regicide. Demoralized and frustrated, Montaigne abandoned his
legal career and, in February 1571, at the height of the Wars of Religion, inscribed on the wall of his study a Latin phrase announcing
that he was retiring from court and public activities to dedicate his
life "in calm and freedom from all cares" to preparation for death.
The posture of idleness and retirement informs the freedom of reflection that is at the heart of the *Essays*. Yet Montaigne did not "retire" in any monastic sense; he simply turned his back on the pursuit
of a career involving power and prestige. He dedicated himself to
writing and published a first edition of the *Essays* in 1580. Then he
made a journey to Rome, chronicling his impressions in a *Travel Journal* (discovered in the eighteenth century) that offers important information about Italian customs during the late Renaissance and recounts his efforts to keep the *Essays* off of the Vatican's Index of
Prohibited Books. Over time, Montaigne's disinclination for public
life became a strength. He served two terms as the mayor of Bordeaux
at a time of extreme tension between Protestants and Catholics. And

his eminence as a writer so enhanced his reputation as an honest political broker that he was able to serve as a negotiator and adviser for both Catholics and Protestants (including Henri of Navarre, the future King Henri IV) in the religious wars. Thus the *Essays* are both personal and deeply public, since they register the encounter between a specific personality and the customs, events, and personalities that make up his political and cultural world.

Central to any reading of Montaigne's book should be an appreciation for the form of the "essay"—that new literary genre that he seems to have invented. The French word *essayer* means "to try out," or "to test." It connotes both the act of tasting and the practice of weighing things (as in our English notion of an "assayer," who weighs precious metals). Thus an essay is manifestly not a treatise or a systematic exposition of a philosophical problem. It draws in many ways on the tradition of the familiar letter, which Montaigne knew from the writings of Cicero, Seneca, and Erasmus. Indeed, Montaigne points out at one point that, had La Boétie not died, he would have put his energy into an exchange of letters. Thus, in a sense, the *Essays* are a set of letters with no correspondent.

The essay is a mongrel literary form, closely allied with commentary or gloss. Its point of departure is not subjective inspiration or transcendent experience, but the detritus of culture—well-worn topics, clichés, old ideas that it seeks to examine anew. Montaigne's essays are thus best understood as exercises in combining bits of cultural information, rather than as the confessions of a fixed interior "self" desperate for expression. Montaigne works by the logic of juxtaposition; he piles up quotations from classical writers, usually cited in the original Latin, anecdotes from his wide reading in ancient and modern history, pithy moral sayings (often used ironically), and his observations about both the material he has gathered and about his own habits and moods. These essays have no "thesis," and it is often difficult to discern a unifying thread or idea. Instead, we are treated to the spectacle of the essayist "trying out" (essaying, testing) his own opinions and thoughts against the events around him and the received ideas of his culture. The purpose is to test the limits of both—to see how his own opinions compare to what history and society teaches us, and to pass judgment on both himself and the world around him.

This means that the essay might be thought of as a kind of space, inside which the humanist culture that Montaigne inherited is broken up and recombined. Thus, for example, in the delightful essay "Of Idleness," one of the briefest and earliest of his compositions, Montaigne considers the notion that a retirement from active life should lead to a quiet mind. His own experience, he points out, has been precisely the opposite; the less he has to do, the more his mind races from topic to topic. He evokes a series of metaphors about fertility and excess and weaves them around a set of Latin phrases from classical literature—Horace, Lucan, Martial—that all mention the problem of dispersal and of excessive busyness. Read in their contexts, these quotations have nothing to do with each other: one is from a scene of war in epic, another from a poem about what makes good poetry, a third from a satirical epigram. Yet when they are placed together in the space of Montaigne's page, they suddenly begin to speak to each other. They become a set of surfaces against which he bounces his own ideas. Through a technique that prefigures the collage and paste-up poetics of the twentieth century, new meaning is created, and old ideas take on new form.

Because the *Essays* are a forum for testing the writer's judgment, they must necessarily remain open-ended. Montaigne built the process of self-correction into his writing practice. He published several different editions of the *Essays*. After the publication of the first two books, in 1580, a second, expanded edition, including a third book, appeared in 1588. However what is remarkable is that the second edition does not "revise" the first edition by replacing awkward phrases with better ones, tightening arguments, or correcting misquotations—the normal processes that define "revision." Instead, Montaigne took the first version of his book, reread it, and simply added more text to what he had already written. New ideas, quotations, and sometimes entire paragraphs are inserted into the middle of existing sentences, to reflect the state of the essayist's mind at the moment of rereading. This curious and virtually unique writing practice was continued throughout Montaigne's life, and a third major edition was published after his death in 1592.

Modern scholarship has made it possible for us to study the different "layers" of the text. Most editors insert marks (usually a, b, and c) showing where new text was added. In this way we can read the book, not only from left to right, to appreciate the linear rambling of Montaigne's ideas, but also, as it were, archeologically, or "vertically," to watch how he reread a given essay and decided to add a new quotation or introduce a new idea that opens a digression. So, for example, in "Of Idleness" he expands the very brief first version of the essay. He adds, for the second edition, a passage from Virgil's *Aeneid*, where the ideas spinning in the agitated mind of Aeneas are compared to bits of light bouncing off of water in a bronze bowl. This addition both expands scope of the essay, bringing in yet another classical authority, and comments ironically on the writing process, wherein revision scatters ideas about to generate new ideas. As Montaigne continues to write and rewrite the *Essays*, the book grows in all directions, like an amoeba. It becomes coextensive with the life of the author, ending only when his body gives out. As he says in the essay "Of Practice," "What I chiefly portray is my cogitations, a shapeless subject that does not lend itself to expression in actions. . . . My portrait is a cadaver on which the veins, the muscles, and the tendons appear at a glance, each part in its place. One part of what I am was produced by a cough, another by a pallor or a palpitation of the heart—in any case dubiously. It is not my deeds that I write down; it is myself, it is my essence." This linkage of body and text—so startlingly modern—underscores the constantly evolving, metamorphic impulse behind the *Essays*.

The shifting, mutable nature of Montaigne's writing—one part produced by a cough, another by pallor—has wide-ranging moral and even political implications. Because the text is constantly changing, every insight that Montaigne puts forth is open to revision and questioning—either as his wandering argument unfolds or as he returns to reread and revise his text. As he notes in the very first essay, "Man is a marvelously vain, diverse, and undulating object. It is hard to found any constant and uniform judgment on him." Therefore, the establishment of a solid "position" from which to reflect—that gesture that will be so important for the establishment of the Cartesian *cogito* forty years later—is but a temporary tactic. It follows that any claims to absolute standards of judgment or truth are necessarily immediately open to revision. Montaigne's suspicion of his own opinions at any given moment extends to his comments on culture and society. For example, in what may be his most famous meditation on human customs, the essay "Of Cannibals," we find a discussion of the culture of the Tupi in Brazil (known to him principally through his reading of Léry, though he also claims to have met a sailor who had lived there). In his account of the Tupi, Montaigne accepts their customs on their own terms, as evidence of a virtue that his own culture could scarcely comprehend. He points out that, while eating one's enemies might seem savage, it is no less savage than some of the recent spectacles of cruelty that have been seen in France, where mobs of religious zealots have torn apart the live bodies of their "heretical" neighbors. He goes on to admire the courageous cannibals, comparing them to ancient Romans. He contrasts their bravery with the cowardice of the Europeans, and concludes, ironically, "Truly here are real savages by our standards; for either they must be thoroughly so, or we must be; there is an amazing distance between their character and ours." Coming out of his absorption in classical culture, Montaigne presents an image of cultural difference that is strikingly modern. His account of Brazil in "Of Cannibals" helped to found the field of study that we know as anthropology.

However, it is not only in the context of cultural understanding that Montaigne's interest in the contingent, temporary nature of judgment may be seen. Precisely because he recognizes the limits of his knowledge, he demonstrates remarkable tolerance for things beyond his reach. Modesty, flexibility, and an ability to imagine the experience of others counterbalance Montaigne's acute awareness of the limits of what he knows. The *Essays* feature a number of moments at which, through startling leaps of the imagination, Montaigne sketches out strikingly progressive ethical or moral positions barely glimpsed by his contemporaries. Thus, in the essay "Of Cruelty," he condemns torture and acknowledges the obligation humans have to care for nature. In "Of Cripples," he speaks out against the burning of witches. In "Of a Monstrous Child," he interprets the body of a child born with a birth defect as a sign, not of "deformity" or "evil" (as would have been customary in his day) but as evidence of the wondrous variety of nature. "What we call monsters are not so to God," he concludes. "We call contrary to nature what happens contrary to custom." And in the great "Apology for Raymond Sebond," he imagines that his cat may be playing with him as much as he is playing with his cat. Montaigne's sensitivity to the mutability of experience and the limits of knowledge makes him skeptical of pomp and grandeur—among scholars as well as kings.

It is unclear whether we are to understand Montaigne's appealing modesty of judgment as the emanation of a particular personality, expressing itself in print, or whether it is the form of the essay itself that imposes and shapes the essayist's sensibility. Either way, the *Essays* offer a signal instance of a personality deeply imbricated in the twists and turns of language and literary creation. "I have no more made my book than it has made me," says Montaigne in "Of Presumption." And as the *Essays* unfold, the process of self-revision becomes more complicated. The earliest chapters often seem little more than exercises, in which Montaigne takes a classical theme (sadness, virtue), or a famous quotation from a classical author and embroiders upon it. However, by the time we reach the third book of the *Essays*, the individual chapters have become quite long. Montaigne moves beyond an early interest in the Stoic tradition (recently revived by a number of his contemporaries, most notably the great Dutch humanist Justus Lipsius) to a much more flexible ethics based on self-acceptance and suspicion of intellectual authority.

At the same time, as the political situation in France worsens, political and ethical themes emerge as central concerns. Thus, the third book begins with an essay titled "Of the Useful and the Honorable," in which Montaigne contemplates the question of whether one should betray one's own ethics in order to serve one's king or state. These issues, pertinent to anyone who works in an institutional setting, were quite close to Montaigne. He was a traditional Catholic, faithful to king and Church in a time of political strife. Yet he was also a *politique*, a moderate intellectual who believed that France's troubles could only be solved in political, rather than religious terms. His sensitivity to the fragility of human judgment makes him suspicious of any kind of zealotry, and of any authority that would pretend to come from beyond this world through divine commands or mystical transports. Such messages, he realizes, can lead humans to commit terrible violence upon their fellows. His focus instead is on the social and ethical value of conversation, of negotiation, and flexibility. In his moderate insistence on political compromise as a solution to the religious wars, he helps to define the ethical language of modern political culture, as a world of sectarian empires begins to give way to a community of states.

Montaigne's claim that one part of his book is produced by "a cough" and another by his pale complexion underscores the importance of the body in both the arguments and the composition of the *Essays*. Like Rabelais and Shakespeare, Montaigne lives close to the world of the body. Death, sex, violence, and illness come up again and again in his work. Montaigne suffered terribly from kidney stones, and, in the third book, he uses his own discomfort to develop reflections on change and aging. Because the body is subject to decay, and because corporeal experience shapes the act of judgment, the practice of philosophy is understood as a process, not as a set of absolute claims. Montaigne's establishment of the link between bodily change, writing, and judgment runs counter to the tradition of abstract philosophical maxims and aphorisms that would come to characterize much of later French literature from La Rochefoucauld to Cioran. Moreover, his understanding of the mutable body as a source of ever-changing insight reminds us of why Descartes would be so insistent on separating philosophical reflection from bodily experience.

The counterweight to Montaigne's interest in the decline of the body is his great attention to the role of the face, or "countenance." His humanist training made him familiar with the classical tradition of immortalizing great men in sculpture and portraiture. Courtly writers such as Baltasar Castiglione, in his *Book of the Courtier* (1528), had noted the importance of presenting an appealing face to the world. Erasmus, by contrast, had privileged humble figures such as Socrates and Christ, men whose unglamorous bodies concealed inner beauty—like texts to be deciphered. Montaigne stresses the openness and honesty of his own face, which, as he recounts in "Of Physiognomy," has saved him from more than one difficult situation in the civil conflicts of his day. He stresses that his open manner inspires trust in others and has helped him in his work as mayor and mediator.

This comfort with himself is one of Montaigne's most appealing features. It goes hand in hand with his acceptance of his foibles (imperfect education, bad memory, brusqueness, impatience). "I do nothing without gaiety," he says in "Of Books." He presents himself engaged in the social world around him as well as the intellectual world of his favorite authors. He values peasants as teachers of virtue as much as he does philosophers. In his essay on education, he emphasizes the importance of conversation and of associating with people from all walks of life as the key to a well-rounded and virtuous personality. Thus, it is no accident that the very last pages of the final essay—the beautiful meditation "Of Experience"—underscore the importance of humility and social engagement. Montaigne laments the mystical transports of Socrates—the one feature of the great philosopher that he cannot stand—and he notes that grandeur is of little value: "On the loftiest throne in the world we are still sitting only on our own rump." He ends the book by quoting Horace's poem to Apollo, begging the god of health and poetry to grant him long life. Let us dedicate our old age, says Montaigne, to the god of wisdom, "but gay and sociable wisdom." The French word *gaye*, which John Florio's English Renaissance translation usually rendered as "blithe" or "cheerful," implies a kind of lightness of spirit, expressed through a pleasant countenance. In his definition of wisdom as "gay and sociable" Montaigne firmly places philosophy in the social world. Gaiety and conversation, the ability to draw lessons from all walks of life—these are the hallmarks of the sage. Wisdom is gleaned from a philosophy of social engagement—not from the abstractions of mathematical reasoning or logical paradoxes. Montaigne roots the cultivation of virtue and judgment in his own attention to the world around him, in his body, in the course of his common life.

By linking philosophy to the world of the everyday—"without miracle and without eccentricity"—Montaigne lays to rest the Renaissance culture of classical ideals, ideal forms, and monumental lives. Like Cervantes in his celebration of the idealistic but deeply mortal Don Quixote, Montaigne turns the somewhat rigid culture of Renaissance humanism against itself, extracting from its heart a self that is noble and virtuous precisely because it cannot live up to accepted ideals of nobility and virtue. Notwithstanding Montaigne's aristocratic bearing, there is something democratic about this social and gay model of philosophy, since it locates wisdom within the reach of each of us.

Given Montaigne's skeptical engagement in the everyday world, his deep moral focus, his grounding in the study of history, and his creativity as a stylist of French, we should not be surprised that his most devoted readers have themselves been figures on the edge of the disciplines of philosophy and anthropology, straddlers between the world of literary fiction and the study of the self. The two great dogmatic personalities of seventeenth-century France, Blaise Pascal and René Descartes (the first seeking to blend Christianity and philosophical reflection, the second seeking to ground philosophy in rational thought) both suffered anguished relationships toward the easygoing Montaigne, with his cheerful acceptance of ambiguity and change. Yet Francis Bacon drew deeply on the *Essays* in his own philosophical reflections, and William Shakespeare quoted Montaigne on several occasions, most famously in the description of the utopian island world of *The Tempest*. Even more influenced were Jean-Jacques Rousseau, whose *Confessions* and *Rêveries* are deeply indebted to Montaigne, and the novelist Gustave Flaubert, who called him "the nursemaid" of French prose. Ralph Waldo Emerson's blending of practical advice and skeptical reflection makes him Montaigne's greatest American heir. And it is certainly true that the explorations of morality and power that we associate with the names of Friedrich Nietzsche and Michel Foucault can scarcely be imagined without the example of Montaigne. All of these eccentric readers and writers remind us that the *Essays* are both a touchstone for the intersection of philosophy and literature and a lasting guide for the perplexed. Endlessly fertile and suggestive, the *Essays* continue to demonstrate that, despite the disclaimer of their author in his letter to the reader, "This book *is* for you, after all."

Works Cited and Recommended Further Reading

Shakespeare read John Florio's 1603 translation of the *Essays*, which is available online at http://www.luminarium.org/renascence-editions/montaigne.

Also important is Charles Cotten's 1686 version (http://www.gutenberg
.org). *The Complete Works of Montaigne*, trans. Donald Frame (London: Everyman's Library, 2003), which I have used above, is a readable modern version that contains Montaigne's posthumously discovered *Travel Journal*. The
recent Penguin version by Michael Screech, *Michel de Montaigne: Essays*
(London: Penguin, 1993) is also very accessible. James B. Atkinson and
David Sices, *Selected Essays* (Indianapolis, IN: Hackett Classics, 2012) is superb for the main essays.

For Montaigne's historical context, J.H.M. Salmon, *Society in Crisis: France
in the Sixteenth Century* (London: Routledge, 1979) is an excellent guide. A
literary critical account of the crisis of community that shapes the period
may be found in Timothy Hampton, *Literature and Nation in the Sixteenth
Century: Inventing Renaissance France* (Ithaca, NY: Cornell University Press,
2000).

Two biographies in English deal with Montaigne's life from different per-
spectives. Donald Frame, *Montaigne: A Biography* (San Francisco: North
Point Press, 1984) is a deeply historical account. Sara Bakewell, *How to Live:
Or a Life of Montaigne in One Question and Twenty Attempts at an Answer* (New
York: Other Press, 2010) focuses more on Montaigne's philosophical quest.

Hugo Friedrich, *Montaigne* (1949), trans. Dawn Eng (Berkeley: University of California Press, 1991) remains a solid introduction to his humanist
culture. Jean Starobinski, *Montaigne in Motion*, trans. Arthur Goldhammer
(Chicago: University of Chicago Press, 1985) is a general account of the *Essays* by a major European literary critic. David Quint, *Montaigne and the
Quality of Mercy* (Princeton, NJ: Princeton University Press, 1998) explores
Montaigne's engagement with classical moral philosophy and contemporary
politics.

The Cambridge Companion to Montaigne, ed. Ullrich Langer (Cambridge:
Cambridge University Press, 2005) is an excellent collection of scholarly
articles covering many aspects of Montaigne's work. On Montaigne's relationship to the rise of printed books, see George Hoffmann, *Montaigne's
Career* (Oxford: Oxford University Press, 1999). A study of Montaigne that
approaches him from within an Anglo-American philosophical tradition is
Ann Hartle, *Michel de Montaigne: Accidental Philosopher* (Cambridge: Cambridge University Press, 2003). Stephen Toulmin, *Cosmopolis: The Hidden
Agenda of Modernity* (Chicago: University of Chicago Press, 1992) considers
what modern philosophy would have been had it taken shape from Mon-

taigne, instead of Descartes. Lawrence D. Kritzman, *The Fabulous Imagination: On Montaigne's Essays* (New York: Columbia University Press, 2012) offers an account of Montaigne in the context of postmodern theory. Terence Cave, *How to Read Montaigne* (London: Granta, 2007) approaches him through the lens of cognition. Ralph Waldo Emerson's essay, "Montaigne, or the Skeptic," remains a stimulating engagement with his thought, as does Virginia Woolf's brief essay from 1925 in *The Common Reader: First Series*.

Molière, Theater, and Modernity

CHRISTOPHER BRAIDER

The classical tragedians of seventeenth-century France are routinely said to have invented the modern stage. A key element was the three "unities" extrapolated from Aristotle's *Poetics*, demanding that a play's action unfold within a single natural day; be confined to a single, readily identifiable place; and exhibit the logical consistency required to convey an air of internal natural necessity and coherence. However, more even than the unities themselves, the crucial breakthrough lay in the methodized *vraisemblance*, or dramatic verisimilitude, for which they supplied the framework.

As the unity of action demonstrates, the rules French playwrights followed were derived from the principle of immanence underlying the Aristotelian theory of dramatic "imitation," or *mimesis*. The term "immanence" originates in metaphysics, where, in opposition to the transcendence associated with Platonic Ideas or a divine Creator set apart from his Creation, it describes the world as experienced from within its own natural limits, to the exclusion of anything outside, above, or beyond it. Applied to literature, it brings out the fundamental contrast between narrative and theatrical forms of representation. Unlike the epics, myths, histories, or biblical stories in which tragedy sought the plots it set onstage, drama avoids mediating narration in favor of seemingly self-engendered human action. What is seen or heard in theater is no mere verbal *account* of the events involved (Aristotle's *diegesis*) but rather the theoretically indiscernible counterpart of events themselves. Nothing, then, could be shown to happen except as the spontaneous reflex of the passions, perceptions, and interests that determine how characters respond to the actions in which they are embroiled. The result was the perfected "natural illusion" of which classical dramatists were justly proud: the overwhelming sense of visceral reality required to provoke the powerful emotions of pity and fear, hope and doubt, exultation and despair spectators were meant to feel.

To be sure, what period playwrights and audiences took "nature" to be reflected moral as well as dramatic conventions peculiar to the culture of the time. The famous "quarrel" or literary controversy surrounding Pierre Corneille's *Le Cid* (1637) provides a test case. In addition to criticizing Corneille for mounting a series of events (two duels, two trials, a Moorish invasion, and the ensuing pitched battle) that could not conceivably fit within a single natural day, the poet's adversaries lambasted him for creating a heroine whose undying passion for her father's killer was seen to bespeak a whorish hypocrisy no tragic heroine could display and retain that name. The problem, though, was less her passion's "natural" unthinkableness than the way it violated the aesthetic *bienséance*, or "seemliness," involved. After all, everyone was perfectly aware that the actual historical woman on whom Corneille based his heroine did in fact marry her father's murderer. The issue accordingly concerned what convention demanded of convincing tragic heroines if the play was to produce the expected impact.

Still, as evinced by the potentially scandalous character of the historical, legendary, and even biblical events on which playwrights drew for plots, the sense of nature associated with the principle of immanence governing dramatic *vraisemblance* raised metaphysical as well as literary stakes. A commonplace of contemporary theatrical theory and practice was the rigorous avoidance of the *deus ex machina*, or "god from a machine," as a device for resolving dramatic denouements. If the key to a successful action is its internal logical consistency, such that nothing happens that cannot be understood to form a natural effect of equally natural causes, miraculous interventions have to be rigorously proscribed. But what does this entail if not a fundamentally naturalistic picture of the course of events and of the world those events characterize? In this sense seventeenth-century tragedy participated in the same revolutionary disenchantment of sublunary experience witnessed in the contemporary triumphs of early modern natural science, politics, historiography, and philosophy. The poetic principle of immanence was thus a direct literary counterpart of the metaphysics of immanence alluded to a moment ago. The common denominator of Cartesian mechanism, positing a strictly material explanation of physical phenomena independent of divine intervention; of Spinoza's historical critique of holy writ, which interpreted the Bible as the work of human authors struggling to solve equally human problems; or of Hobbes's systematization of Machiavellian political science, portraying government as the rational manipulation of amoral social forces is the elimination of even indirect resort to God in any form. Insofar as dramatists imposed exactly similar constraints on a well-wrought plot, they helped lay the groundwork for our modern world.

Nevertheless, if, in inventing the modern stage, French classical tragedy helped pave the way to the modern world, it fell to the great comic poet Jean-Baptiste Poquelin, known to us by his stage name, Molière, to have created the first truly convincing portrayal of modernity itself. Molière's preeminence in this regard is due in the first place to the fact that he was an actor and director as well as poet—unlike any other leading playwright of the day, he worked onstage even as he wrote for it. The illusionistic *vraisemblance* that was, for his rivals, a matter of poetics was his bread and butter. Beyond composing "regular" comedies whose unfolding plots supplied the basic information audiences needed to understand what was happening, he professionalized every aspect of theatrical performance.

Contemporary observers commented on the unprecedented discipline his company achieved, remarking not only on the elements of Molière's personal performances, and in particular his astonishing *démontages*, changing facial expression in the blink of an eye, but also on his troupe's work as an ensemble. Spectators noted, for instance, the precise timing of exchanges of glances between Molière's actors, and the skillful blocking and painstakingly counted steps that choreographed their physical movements to maximum effect. Above all, there was the growing naturalism of his company's acting style, abandoning the bombastic declamatory mode adopted especially in tragedy in favor of something approaching the tones and postures of everyday life. Molière himself made the point in a series of virtuoso parodies of the day's leading tragic actors in *L'impromptu de Versailles* (*The Versailles Impromptu*) (1663), a one-act comedy that, despite its title, taught a carefully scripted lesson on the art of acting in which, pretending to rehearse a play commissioned by the reigning monarch, Louis XIV, for performance at court, the troupe takes the audience backstage to reveal the mechanics of their trade. Molière's parodies of rival actors lampooned everything from the unrestrained eating habits that made them too fat for their roles to the way the narcissistic meals they made of their lines in pursuit of the "brouhaha" of public approbation impeded dramatic flow.

Molière was aided in all this by the fact that, as author as well as actor and director, he imposed the discipline of a playbook on his company. Molièresque comedy was deeply indebted to the improvisational style of the *commedia dell'arte*: Molière's earliest plays, now lost to us for this very reason, were Italianate scenarios—bare plot lines that left it to the actors to improvise their parts in the course of performance, making up their lines and physical business in accordance with the prefabricated character types in which each specialized. Nevertheless, by the late 1640s, everything Molière's actors said and did was written down for them in a predetermined script, and then rehearsed under the poet's exacting directorial eye. Nothing was left to chance, even though the product was the seeming artlessness of live action.

However, the deepest source of Molière's modernity was his genre, comedy itself. As numberless period theorists asserted in Aristotle's wake, comic drama is rooted in the terms and conditions of ordinary life. Where the heroes and heroines of tragedy are greater than we are in degree if not in kind, being more noble, valorous, and accomplished than the normal run of mortals, their comic counterparts perform at the same level as we do—only, if anything, worse—in that they are as a rule more extravagantly ludicrous than we are quite comfortable in acknowledging of ourselves. Where heroic patterns of character commit tragedy to depicting the world as it ought to be, comedy focuses on the world as it is, whatever lofty ambitions its inhabitants pursue. In the case of comedy, then, realism of the sort Molière's troupe aimed at is a matter of *vraisemblance* in both uses of the word: the sense of natural plausibility required to sustain the dramatic illusion also conforms to the demands of conventional propriety that Corneille's *Le Cid* violated. While it was seen to be improbable for a tragic heroine to divide her heart between her lover and the murdered author of her days, a comic heroine's readiness to sacrifice not only her father but a geriatric husband on the altar of sexual bliss was a stock feature of comic plots. So while tragedy was obliged to rearrange even the facts of history in the service of a grand ideal of human conduct for which ordinary experience provides little warrant, comedy reduces heroic idealism to the flesh-and-blood contingencies of day-to-day affairs.

To use a medical metaphor—which Molière's career-long satirical obsession with medicine recommends—if the springs of tragic action are symptoms of the messy empirical particulars that tragic characters strive to overcome, comedy diagnoses the underlying pathology that defines the world both arts reflect. As Molière puts it in the *Critique de L'école des femmes* (*The Critique of the School for Wives*) (1662), staging a critical conversation about an earlier play that I will turn to shortly, "When you depict heroes, you do what you like. These are portraits painted at pleasure, in which one seeks no resemblance, and you need only follow the promptings of an imagination that takes flight and that often quits the true for the fabulous. But when you depict men, you paint according to nature. People want such portraits to bear a likeness, and you've achieved nothing if you don't make us recognize the people of your age." By contrast with tragedy, comedy is thus a "public mirror" devised to enable audiences to see their own faces, foibles, and flaws—what they really are, whether they like it or not. Molière's plays accordingly not only paint an image of the world the poet and his contemporaries lived in; they offer increasingly critical *soundings* of that world designed to explain, among other things, the low facts of life as comedy depicts them.

Three plays lay out the core of Molière's comic vision: *Tartuffe* (1664–69), *Don Juan, ou le festin de pierre* (*Don Juan, or The Stone Guest*) (1665), and *Le misanthrope* (1666). All three were staged as part of the ferocious public controversy ignited by *L'école des femmes* (*The School for Wives*) (1662), as increasingly sharp rejoinders to the renewed "quarrel of the morality of theater" occasioned by what many in the public decried as the earlier play's combined "obscenities" and "impieties." Charges of immorality had been leveled at theater from the earliest days of Christianity—a peculiar feature of the seventeenth-century version of the debate was in fact the insistence with which it recycled arguments originally articulated by Tertullian and Augustine in the third and fourth centuries CE. Actors were denounced for being professional liars, prostituting themselves in the service of pleasures inimical to Christian virtue. Careful scrutiny of even the noblest tragedy revealed that, far from fostering a spirit of humble worship, theater's fundamental subjects were the passions of ambition, revenge, hatred, and sexual love. A natural outgrowth of these facts was the notorious depravity of players' daily lives, producing scenes of drunkenness and debauchery that spilled over into the public playhouse, where wine and women were purchased at will.

The quarrel had been temporarily suspended with a royal edict of 1643—inspired by Cardinal Richelieu and policed by the Royal Academy that he had created in 1635—which declared the newly polished theatrical productions promoted under state supervision to be exempt of the disorders for which the stage had traditionally been vilified. Even so, by episcopal decree, all actors and actresses in the archdiocese of Paris were subject to automatic excommunication as long as they continued in their profession—a decree so rigidly enforced that, despite his fame and the highly remunerative royal patronage he enjoyed, Molière had to be buried in the middle of the night to avoid a public scandal. The ground was thus laid for a fresh outbreak of hostilities as soon as occasion permitted.

L'école des femmes supplied it. The play tells the story of one Arnolphe—a man predestined for cuckoldry by his very name, which recalls the folkloric patron saint of betrayed husbands, Arnolf de Cornibont. (The historical Arnolf was not in fact a saint; but the connotation of an abundance of *cornes*, or "horns," in the unfortunate toponym he bore proved irresistible.) Despite the unlucky augury of his name, Arnolphe intends to marry. However, having made a twenty-year study of the marital misfortunes of his fellow citizens, he has developed a foolproof plan based on what he calls, in grandiloquent allusion to Descartes, a carefully worked-out "method." Some years past, he purchased an orphan girl, Agnès, whom he has had educated in a convent far from the haunts of men and according to a pedagogical system of his own devising. The aim is to render her *une sotte*, a woman so ignorant of the ways of the world and her own desires as to be incapable of deceiving him. Needless to say, the scheme comes to grief when Arnolphe's bride-to-be meets the handsome (if witless) Horace and falls in love. The result is the hero's feverish struggle to retain the upper hand in the face of Agnès's ever-clearer grasp of her own identity and wishes. "For Love," as Horace puts it in one of many foolish confidences to the man in whom he fails to detect his rival, "is a great teacher: what one never was he teaches us to be; and, often, his lessons change our whole way of life in an instant."

Simple—and even routine—as its plot may be, the play pushed the limits of public propriety. Just as theater's devout enemies would insist, the play's theme is love rather than virtue. Molière then rubs salt in the wound by making it inescapably plain that by "love" here he means sex—and sex in explicit defiance of the pious commonplaces of orthodox morality, trotted out in a hilariously self-defeating sermon Arnolphe delivers on the joyless duties of a properly submissive wife. Further, to a parodic sermon whose satirical force provoked righteous indignation in its own right, the play adds a series of smutty double-entendres that gave great offense: mention of cream tarts in a context that makes obvious scatological allusion to sexual discharges; an explanation of the springs of male jealousy that employs the image of a man sticking his thumb in another man's bowl of soup; and above all, an episode in which, recounting to her captor the circumstances of her first meeting with Horace, a shamefaced Agnès lingers over a dangling definite article (*le* . . .) when describing how the young man took hold of an item of her person. Even though the offending object turns out to be a harmless ribbon, since the relevant definite article is masculine in French (*le ruban*), it could not fail to make both Arnolphe and the audience think of sexual body parts, all of whose names are masculine—*le sein, le tétin, le cul, le con*. The result was as stupendous as it was predictable: a storm of pamphlets, satirical plays, angry homilies, bawdy verses, and even a public outcry in the playhouse itself, pitting the poet's freethinking partisans in the cheap seats against right-minded gentlemen clustered in the loges.

Molière's initial response to the controversy took the form of the two short plays mentioned earlier: the *Critique de L'école des femmes*, staging a mock debate in which we get, in addition to ridicule of lay enemies in high society, the first attested use of the word "obscenity" in French; and the *Impromptu de Versailles*, which takes the fight to the rival theatrical company that had seized on the quarrel to bring Molière down a peg. His first major retort, however, was the original, three-act version of *Tartuffe*, staged at court in 1664.

Tartuffe turns the tables on the poet's high-minded adversaries by portraying them not, as in the *Critique* or the *Impromptu*, as fools or bloated incompetents but as religious hypocrites bent on destroying the hard-won secular pleasures and liberties on which both the authority and well-being of the modern state depends. The specifically political stakes are emphasized by the way the denouement in all versions, from 1664 down to the final one of 1669, incorporates the king himself, Louis XIV, in person.

The action foregrounds the behavior of a bourgeois *père de famille*, Orgon, whose pious mother, Mme Pernelle, opens the play by scolding her son's children and beautiful second wife, Elmire, for indulging in the newfangled worldly delights of the day—fancy clothes, sumptuous dinner parties, flirtatious *galanterie*, and of course, as chief among them, theater. The focus thus falls from the outset on everything that makes modern life worth living. The head of the household deepens the threat. Doubtless under pressure from his mother, Orgon has contracted pious scruples of his own. In search of spiritual guidance, he has become enamored of one Tartuffe—a man whose hypocrisy, though perfectly plain to everyone else in the family, Mme Pernelle excepted, escapes the infatuated father. Worse still, he introduces Tartuffe into his home, where, in addition to stuffing his face, the scoundrel tries to seduce his benefactor's wife even as Orgon decides to marry his daughter to him. By the time the spirited Elmire manages to open his eyes, it is too late. For Orgon has just deeded his house to the interloper, giving him at the same time incriminating papers relating (so the date of the premiere leads us to surmise) to the anti-royalist strife of the Fronde era of 1648–52, when the reigning monarch was still in his minority.

It is at this point that royal officers intervene, ostensibly to evict Orgon and family from their home. However, at the last moment and, given that the play premiered at court, in the presence of the sovereign himself, one of the officers reveals his identity as the king's personal lieutenant, sent by Louis to expose Tartuffe as a criminal on whose fraudulent doings the king's eye has rested all along. Having opened with the arraignment of the worldly blessings that the king's wise conduct of the political economy has showered on his grateful subjects, the play closes with shameless flattery designed not only to praise Louis but also to enlist him in defense of Molière's art:

Remettez-vous, Monsieur, d'une alarme si chaude.
Nous vivons sous un Prince ennemi de la fraude,
Un Prince dont les yeux se font jour dans les cœurs,
Et que ne peut tromper tout l'art des Imposteurs.
D'un fin discernement, sa grande âme pourvue,
Sur les choses toujours jette une droite vue,
Chez elle jamais rien ne surprend trop d'accès,
Et sa ferme raison ne tombe en nul excès.
Il donne aux Gens de bien une gloire immortelle,
Mais sans aveuglement il fait briller ce zèle,
Et l'amour pour les vrais, ne ferme point son cœur
A tout ce que les faux doivent donner d'horreur.

(Sir, all is well; rest easy, and be grateful.
We serve a Prince to whom all sham is hateful,
A Prince who sees into our inmost hearts,
And can't be fooled by any trickster's arts.
His royal soul, though generous and human,
Views all things with discernment and acumen;
His sovereign reason is not lightly swayed,
And all his judgments are discreetly weighed.
He honors righteous men of every kind,
And yet his zeal for virtue is not blind,
Nor does his love of piety numb his wits
And make him tolerant of hypocrites.)

The preceding précis of the play's royalist theme suffices to underline the modernity of the position Molière stakes out for himself as champion not only of the new secular order of which theater serves as both mirror and agent but also of a new vision of political sovereignty. Despite his sacred anointment as God's surrogate, one as capable, on *Tartuffe*'s showing, of seeing into the darkest corners of his subjects' hearts as the Almighty himself, the king Molière portrays is a conspicuously rational figure whose chief duty is no longer the defense of religion but rather that of the secular society of which theater is the flower. But Molière's modernity is also and more profoundly seen in the unmistakable ambiguity of the play's denouement. For though the king does rescue Orgon from the consequences of pious excess and folly, the chances of anything comparable happening in real life are infinitely remote. The *vraisemblance* brought to the portrayal of the comic undoing of the bourgeois household is violated by the means of sparing it the fate it has brought on itself: the kind of *deus ex machina* that period theorists proscribed precisely on the grounds of its utter implausibility. Molière's embarrassingly extravagant encomium of the king is thus undermined by the miraculous character of the event that occasions it, pointing in the process to a much darker vision of the political order it is the monarch's duty to govern.

That there was ample room for doubt is underscored by the fate of the play itself. Though the king reportedly loved it, and professed himself mystified by the fuss the devout party at court made about it, *Tartuffe* was banned from the stage within weeks of its premiere. It subsequently took five years, at least two rewrites, and a string of petitions before Molière's company was allowed to stage it as a regular part of the repertoire. As absolute as Louis XIV's personal rule was taken to be, he apparently felt powerless to intercede at least until the death of his mother, Anne of Austria—a woman whose own late turn to rigorous piety after a gaudy youth recalls Orgon's mother.

That Molière keenly felt the sting of the king's desertion in the *Tartuffe* affair is evinced by the next play in the sequence, *Don Juan*. In act 5, shortly before the arrival of the statue of the murdered commander that sends the title character to hell for his misdeeds, Molière's version of the legendary reprobate takes an unmistakably topical turn. Increasingly beset by angry representatives of every sector of society, from peasants and shopkeepers to sword-bearing nobles, the don announces his intention to wear the mask of religious devotion. He justifies this decision to his horrified valet, Sganarelle, whose role Molière played, by asserting that, despicable as such a course may be, "there is no longer any shame in it; hypocrisy is a fashionable vice, and all fashionable vices pass for virtues. The character of a good man is the best of all roles one can play today, and the profession of a hypocrite has wonderful advantages. It is an art the imposture in which is always respected; and even if you're found out, nobody dares say anything against it. All other human vices are exposed to censure, and everyone is free to rail against them at the top of their voices. But hypocrisy is a privileged vice whose hand shuts everyone's mouth, and peacefully enjoys a sovereign impunity." It is above all in Don Juan's subsequent account of the source of this "sovereign impunity" that we meet the link to *Tartuffe*. For, as he explains, while all other vices involve isolated individuals, each given over to his or her private vice, hypocrites have formed a tight conspiracy, working in concert to shield each other from retribution: "If I were to be discovered, without stirring a finger, I'd see the whole cabal take up my cause, and its members would defend me against one and all. This is, in sum, the true means of doing with impunity everything I want. I'll set myself up as censor of other people's actions, judge ill of everyone, and retain a good opinion only of myself."

The "cabal" Don Juan mentions has an inescapable contemporary reference. It alludes to the "cabal of the devout," a political pressure group whose spearhead was the Company of the Holy Sacrament: a semi-secret, lay-religious association devoted to infiltrating secular society in order to rectify public morals by punishing people its members deemed wicked and by attacking worldly pleasures they judged inimical to Christian life. A prominent figure in the group was Molière's sometime patron, the reformed rakehell, Armand de Bourbon, prince de Conti, in whom scholars have followed period commentators in seeing a model for Molière's don. With *Don Juan*, then, the poet widens the attack launched in *Tartuffe* by targeting not just an isolated hypocrite but the semi-official *party* of hypocrisy of which he saw himself the victim.

However, as broad as this new front in the literary wars that *L'école des femmes* touched off may be, *Don Juan* strikes still deeper. When asked, in act 1, why he continues to serve a master he vehemently denounces as "a madman, a dog, a devil, a Turk, a heretic, who believes in neither heaven nor hell nor werewolves," Sganarelle replies both simply and directly: "a great lord who's a wicked man is a terrible thing. I'm compelled to remain loyal to him, whatever I wish; fear fills in me the office of zeal, bridles my tongue, and very often reduces me to applauding what my soul abhors."

It is impossible to understate this remark's significance, placed as it is in the opening scene of exposition in which the play states the comic *agon*, or "dramatic conflict," it will rehearse. A member of the circle of the "libertine," freethinking atomist, Pierre Gassendi, as well as an habitué of the socially as well as morally marginal world of the stage, Molière was a materialist, committed as such to a systematically naturalistic picture of reality. It was therefore not entirely without reason that one of his adversaries labeled him a "devil incarnate" bent on ridiculing the conventional pieties of the age. Nevertheless, like other libertines of the time—including Thomas Hobbes, author of *The Leviathan* (1651), and the Spinoza of the *Theologico-Political Treatise* (1670), works that sought to found political science on a thoroughly demystified material basis—Molière worried about the consequences of the demoralized vision of human community freethinkers advanced. It is important, then, that, just as in *Tartuffe*, where Orgon's family is rescued from catastrophe by the secular miracle of royal intervention, the core problem *Don Juan* addresses is that, barring something like the arrival of the stone guest, sent by God himself to restore not only justice but the civil order the title character disturbs, there is literally nothing in the world as Molière knew it to protect us from monsters like Don Juan. A grandee as well as an atheist, entitled, as he threatens at one point, to bullwhip his servant for one word of reproach, and protected from paying the price for his sins by the credit his noble father has at court (at least until the son's depredations affect other grandees like himself), Don Juan stands beyond the reach of human justice just as certainly as he proves immune to ordinary moral feeling.

To make matters worse, any attempt to argue otherwise by invoking the higher authority of Church teaching or the inherent nobility of human nature winds up sounding like sentimental nonsense. Whence the play's most brilliant as well as scandalous move, provoking howls of rage in pious quarters. The only consistent spokesperson for justice and morality the play provides is the comic servant, Sganarelle. The defense of the right is accordingly allotted to a clown.

Sganarelle's first attempt to convert his master takes the form of a parody of the Italian humanist Pico della Mirandola's famous *Oration on the Dignity of Man* in which, whirling his body in circles to demonstrate the miraculous power of free will, Sganarelle gets his toe caught in the hem of the doctor's robe he wears as a disguise and falls flat on his face. His second issues in an astonishing anticipation of Lucky's speech in Samuel Beckett's *Waiting for Godot*. The speech needs to be cited at length to convey its full weight. Appalled by his master's plan to escape into the impunity of membership of the cabal of the devout, Sganarelle produces a comic masterpiece of scrambled proverbs and grotesquely garbled literary echoes whose nonsensical associative leaps betray at once the urgency and logical inconsequence of his apology for belief:

> Know, sir, that if you take the crock to the water often enough, it will break; and as that author whose works I don't know put it so well, man, in this world, is like a bird on a branch; the branch is attached to the tree; who attaches himself to the tree obeys good precepts; good precepts are worth more than handsome words; handsome words are found at court; at court are courtiers; courtiers follow fashion; fashion springs from fancy; fancy is a faculty of the soul; the soul is what gives us life; life ends in death; death makes us think of heaven; heaven is above the earth; the earth isn't the sea; the sea is subject to storms; storms torment vessels; vessels need a good pilot; a good pilot has prudence; prudence isn't found in young people; young people owe obedience to the old; the old love riches; riches make rich people; rich people aren't poor; poor people suffer want; want knows no law; who knows no law is a brute beast; and, in consequence, you'll be damned to all the devils.

The amazing thing here is how comic *vraisemblance* inspires delighted laughter even as it measures the extremity of the situation the play sets before us. On one hand, there is no other way for a clownish valet to speak: as Sganarelle confesses, he has had no formal education and, besides, it is his job to make us laugh. Yet, on the other hand, to what would even the most polished and learned apology for belief amount if not to a more plausible yet nonetheless equally helpless appeal to inchoate feeling? It is worth noting that Sganarelle's central argument resembles the one that Blaise Pascal invokes in the apology for Christian religion sketched out in the *Pensées* (first, highly imperfect posthumous edition, 1670). "The heart has reasons reason doesn't know. This is what faith is: God as felt by the heart, not reason." Neither Sganarelle nor Molière has of course any interest in defending religious belief. Still, for all the heartless accuracy of Don Juan's cynicism, feeling clamors that there just *has* to be an alternative if we are not to sink into the state of bestial chaos to which Molière's own materialist leanings seem to condemn us. If Don Juan is so convincing, it is in part because, legendary seducer of women who ought to know better, he is a supreme confidence man. But he is also convincing because he is simply *right* about the way the world works; and if he is right, what is the social order itself if not a confidence trick whose promise of justice is just as empty as the arch-seducer's professions of love?

Given *Don Juan*'s underlying violence, it will come as no surprise that it was shut down after a mere fifteen performances, not to be staged again, or even printed in an unbowdlerized edition, until the nineteenth century. Molière's next move was accordingly in part an act of propitiation—an attempt to lower the temperature by staking out some sort of middle ground between himself and the general public in order to recruit allies against his increasingly virulent enemies. The result was the play the era regarded as his masterpiece, *Le misanthrope*.

Le misanthrope achieves many things, in particular the perfection of the "comedy of character," the genre for which Molière is most famous, and to which the subsequent history of world as well as French theater remains indebted to this day. With only a few exceptions, like the classically based *Amphitryon* (1668), the brooding *George Dandin* (1668), and a late return to knockabout farces, all of the plays he wrote from this time until his death in 1673 are comedies of manners featuring a central character type round whose absurd obsession the action revolves: a miser, a social climbing bourgeois, a bluestocking, or a hypochondriac, set in the bosom of a modern nuclear family whose robust normality invariably triumphs in the end.

Though no family is actually involved in his case, *Le misanthrope*'s Alceste sets the tone. Doubtless a prickly man to start with, Alceste has the misfortune of falling in love with the rich, beautiful, and dangerously witty young widow Célimène. Célimène's merry widowhood is important. The fact that she has already married not only means she is no longer a sexual novice like *L'école des femmes*'s Agnès; it has freed her from the contemporary marriage market. Taken together with her wealth, freedom from the need to marry grants her an independence expressed by the enviable number of suitors drawn to her boudoir by her wit as much as her beauty. She thus presides over a salon one of whose attractions is her gift for drawing satirical word-portraits of the members of her wide acquaintance at court. She thereby embodies everything that is both most glamorous and most frivolous in the Parisian high society of the day—a circumstance that heightens the contrast with her morose lover, Alceste, whose character it is to pose as being the sole honest man in a world of chattering coxcombs and sycophants.

The contrast formed by the lead romantic pair defines the play's *agon*, laid out in the opening dialogue between Alceste and his friend Philinte. In the face of what he portrays as the hollow insincerities of court life, where everyone pretends to be everyone's friend even as they betray each other at every turn, Alceste demands unyielding plainspokenness. Commenting on a recent example of Philinte's shameful pliability, he exclaims:

> Une telle action ne saurait s'excuser,
> Et tout Homme d'honneur s'en doit scandaliser.
> Je vous vois accabler un Homme de caresses,
> Et témoigner, pour lui, les dernières tendresses;
> De protestations, d'offres, et de serments,
> Vous chargez la fureur de vos embrassements:
> Et, quand je vous demande après, quel est cet Homme,
> A peine pouvez-vous dire comme il se nomme,
> Votre chaleur, pour lui, tombe en vous séparant,

Et vous me le traitez, à moi, d'indifférent.
Morbleu, c'est une chose indigne, lâche, infâme,
De s'abaisser ainsi jusqu'à trahir son Âme:
Et si, par un malheur, j'en avais fait autant,
Je m'irais, de regret, pendre tout à l'instant.

(I call your conduct inexcusable, Sir,
And every man of honor will concur.
I see you almost hug a man to death,
Exclaim for joy until you're out of breath,
And supplement these loving demonstrations
With endless offers, vows, and protestations;
Then when I ask you "Who was that?," I find
That you can barely bring his name to mind!
Once the man's back is turned, you cease to love him,
And speak with absolute indifference of him!
By God, I say it's base and scandalous
To falsify the heart's affections thus;
If I caught myself behaving in such a way,
I'd hang myself for shame, without delay.)

Alceste's demand for sincerity is not unconnected with his equally unconditional demand that others—and of course Célimène in particular—single him out in the way he himself does, honoring the attitude of scornful isolation he affects. Yet as the play hilariously demonstrates in pretty much every scene, he is right about the petty hypocrisies of the world in which he lives. The question is whether these hypocrisies are avoidable, or even quite as bad a thing as Alceste asserts.

Whence the thrust of Philinte's rejoinders. He concedes his friend's major point: for all the empty *politesses* they shower on each other, people are, as a rule, every bit as despicable as Alceste says. But it is surely the part of a wise man to accept people as they are without tormenting himself about it, since nothing will change them. Responding to Alceste's indignation at the "phlegm" with which he is content simply to "reason" about human depravity, Philinte resorts to animal imagery of great topical resonance when read against the background of the emergent political science of Hobbes and Spinoza:

> Oui, je vois ces Défauts dont votre âme murmure,
> Comme Vices unis à l'Humaine Nature;
> Et mon esprit, enfin, n'est pas plus offensé,
> De voir un Homme fourbe, injuste, intéressé,
> Que de voir des Vautours affamés de carnage,
> Des Singes malfaisants, et des Loups pleins de rage.

> (Why, no. These faults of which you so complain
> Are part of human nature, I maintain,
> And it's no more a matter for disgust
> That men are knavish, selfish and unjust,
> Than that the vulture dines upon the dead,
> And wolves are furious, and apes ill-bred.)

Echoing Hobbes's notoriously bleak characterization of *homo homini lupus*, or "man as a wolf to other men," Philinte playfully yet unmistakably poses the core question *Don Juan*'s Sganarelle does in response to the problem of what happens when a "great lord" turns out to be a "wicked man." What would the world be like if everyone were indeed "sincere," as true to their inner natures as Alceste demands? Would we in fact be better than we are, or would we descend into a state of anarchy in which human predators openly wage the Hobbist "war of all against all" that the hollow conventions of social hypocrisy at least mitigate even if only by disguising its underlying horrors?

The central issue *Le misanthrope* joins is thus the value of the courtly system of *honnêteté*, which was one of the most distinctive features of contemporary French social conduct. The French upper classes of the day prided themselves on their worldly *savoir faire* and, at its heart, a highly developed art of conversation in which wit, good manners, and the stylish gallantries of polite flirtation enabled people to enjoy each other's company, regardless of their hidden motives. Despite the period name for it, there was nothing honest about *honnêteté*. People continued to scheme, hate, and betray each other, by

Philinte's estimate every bit as much as Alceste's, as they always have and always will. Yet, in conforming to an artificial code of polite good breeding that tamed at least the outward displays of their underlying bestiality, people's behavior was better than their characters—and, in the world that *Tartuffe* and *Don Juan* depict more candidly, if less disarmingly, than *Le misanthrope*, that is a good deal more than nothing.

Needless to say, once the play's action gets in full swing, the emphasis shifts from the deep social questions raised in the opening scene to the comic spectacle of Alceste's defeat at the hands of his own self-contradictory moral intransigence. Though he wants Célimène despite the fact that she is the epitome of everything he claims to despise, he contrives to make union with her impossible even when, disgraced by the public discovery of her double dealings with other men, she finally consents to give her hand. For what he demands at that stage is not merely marriage but joining him in rural seclusion—an exile from social pleasures she rejects, because even public embarrassment is preferable to life in what Alceste calls "the desert" of the countryside. However congenitally predatory human beings may be, they are also social animals incapable of surviving without each other's company.

Where, then, *Don Juan* and, in its more ambiguous way, *Tartuffe* assert Molière's outraged defiance of the prevailing order, *Le misanthrope* counsels the ironical acceptance and moderation Philinte enjoins—yet at significant conscious cost. If it is true that, in the end, we need to learn how to live with each other, we manage to do so only on condition of ceasing to be *honest* with each other in just the way the code of worldly *honnêteté* suggests we should. Accordingly, when Alceste stomps off at the final curtain, we laugh, getting back to the game along with everyone else.

But, especially when we recall that Molière himself played the role, Alceste's huffy departure represents something more. The sunny normativity that, in subsequent denouements, makes the Molièresque comedy of character the progenitor of the modern TV sitcom would not be without its darker moments. *Le bourgeois gentilhomme* (*The Would-be Gentleman*) (1670) and *Le malade imaginaire* (*The Imaginary Invalid*) (1673) would close with spectacles of utter madness in which an Erasmus-like "praise of folly" offers glimpses of true torment and insanity. Nevertheless, Molière would never again attempt anything like what he accomplishes in *Tartuffe* or *Don Juan*. With Alceste's proudly self-defeating exile, Molière in effect agrees to play, in his own person as a man as well as actor, director, and playwright, the role of public scapegoat—but only on condition that the social order in whose behalf he makes this sacrifice acknowledges the duplicity of the culture of good manners in whose name peace is restored.

Works Cited and Recommended Further Reading

The French source for Molière is *Œuvres complètes*, ed. Georges Forestier, 2 vols. (Paris: Gallimard, 2010). All translations are the author's, except for *Tartuffe* and *Le misanthrope*, where Richard Wilbur's wonderful versions are used from the Harcourt Brace paperback edition of 1993. For two excellent accounts of Molière's career, see Larry F. Norman, *The Public Mirror: Molière and the Social Commerce of Depiction* (Chicago: University of Chicago Press, 1995); and Joan De Jean, *The Reinvention of Obscenity: Sex, Lies, and Tabloids in Early Modern France* (Chicago: University of Chicago Press, 2002). On the wider metaphysics, see Christopher Braider, *The Matter of Mind: Reason and Experience in the Age of Descartes* (Toronto: University of Toronto Press, 2012). For a handy biography, see Virginia Scott, *Molière: A Theatrical Life* (Cambridge: Cambridge University Press, 2000).

* *
** **

Racine, *Phèdre*, and the
French Classical Stage

NICHOLAS PAIGE

For English-speaking readers, one tragedy alone has escaped the shipwreck of what is usually called French classicism: Jean Racine's *Phèdre* (1677). The fussy austerity of "classicism" itself, a word that is often made more forbidding still by the addition of the prefix "neo-," may go some way to explaining why we have let the rest of the pro-duction—with a few exceptions—sink. If Racine and the rest of the period's dramatists all signed on to the same stony manifesto, packed with prescriptive rules and a set of rationalized formal constraints—well then, it's hardly any surprise that the works don't speak to a post-Romantic age. *Phèdre* is the tragedy we can keep around, the classical play that gives the lie to classicism by smuggling in, in the breast of its heroine, a desire so monstrous that measure, reason, and rules don't stand a chance.

We keep it around, but even *Phèdre* is not an easy sell nowadays. Anglophones might assume that they are simply on the other side of a cultural and linguistic divide: surely the French instinctively under-stand those "rules" and grasp the arcane and untranslatable beauties of the twelve-syllable rhyming couplets—alexandrine verse—used by dramatists of the time. In fact, the French will tell you as readily as anyone else: Racine, *Phèdre* included, is difficult to stage. And it's not just our postmodern world that's to blame. Already, in the early part of the nineteenth century, far closer to Racine in time than he is to us now, Stendhal was saying much the same thing in his Romantic mani-festo *Racine et Shakespeare*. Racine was a Romantic in his day, claimed Stendhal, but time has made him classical; if he returned to 1820s France, and made use of modern rules, he would have everyone dissolving in tears, locked in delicious illusion, instead of inspiring merely the "rather cold feeling" of admiration.[1]

So *Phèdre* is perennial, but also, maybe for two centuries now, historically estranged. What has happened? Have we simply misplaced the mindset of Racine's contemporaries? Perhaps we moderns lack the "ancient tragic sense of life" that playwrights used to tap into, and that the noted critic George Steiner once saw disappearing after *Phèdre*. Maybe our bourgeois world demands grit and realism, whereas aristocratic audiences of the time expected entertainments more ceremonial, more stylized, disciplined by classical doctrine. Yet Racine's situation is considerably more complicated. Stendhal was right, in that the dramatist was indeed considered modern in his day—an innovator celebrated for the unsurpassed naturalism of his representations of human passion. But somewhat in the manner of religious reformers of the time, he packaged his innovations as a return to a better past.[2] Which is to say that Racine's plays, rather than being manifestations of a coherent and discrete mindset to which we no longer have easy access, are historically heterogeneous, built of materials we sometimes recognize and sometimes do not. Such is their particular challenge: not quite foreign enough to forget about or exoticize, and not quite modern enough to embrace.

⁂ ⁂ ⁂ ⁂

Phèdre opened in Paris on New Year's Day 1677. In retrospect, the play takes on the aura of the capstone, as it turned out to be Racine's last tragedy for the public stage: soon after, Louis XIV named him royal historiographer, a glory that far outshone even the reputation he had earned as France's foremost tragedian. But it's also right to say that even at the time the play was intended as something of a *summum*, a deliberately major literary event. For in the mid-1670s, tragedy was on the defensive. It was hemmed in on the one side by Molière's new brand of urbane comedy, which rejected the stock plots of farce and held instead a mirror to the upper classes, avid for what we would now call relevance. And it was threatened on the other side by the fashion for French opera, the rapidly developing genre of "lyric" tragedy that that relied on song to pull heartstrings and on stagecraft to dazzle the eyes. The twin threats, comedy and opera, explain why in these years Racine started to fish for subject matter with extra tragic gravitas. Turning away from the more or less historical plots that had been tragedy's mainstay since the 1630s, he found what he needed in myth.

And what he needed was gods. In 1674, he adapted the story of Agamemnon's appeasing sacrifice of his daughter Iphigenia; and then it was the turn of Phaedra and Hippolytus, victims of Venus's mischief and Neptune's wrath.[3] Steiner might say that Racine's tapping into the tragic sense of life of the ancients was a last gasp before the unstoppable encroachment of the secular in Western culture spelled "the death of tragedy." But Steiner himself recognized that conjuring the gods did not come naturally to Racine, who bathed in a literary culture that was already secularized. Drama had to be believable: "No belief, no feeling," repeated the period's theorists, who found support for their conviction in the work of Aristotle and Horace; accordingly, the vast majority of the period's tragedies featured historical subject matter. The pagan gods, from such a perspective, could only be problematic subjects: Tragic with a capital T, certainly; but dangerously unmodern, because seventeenth-century Christians did not share the superstitions of the ancients. In *Iphigénie* and *Phèdre*, then, Racine needed to steer a difficult path, tapping the sublime subject matter for an appropriate dose of awe while keeping divine agency thoroughly in check.

So what might appear at first glance as a sensitivity to sacred dread—supposedly now lost to a modern audience—was the result of a calculated choice. Racine was performing a balancing act, turning belief in divine agency into something that his protagonists subscribe to but that his audience need not. Phèdre certainly has a lot to say about the gods. Where is her *raison* (her "senses"), she rhetorically asks her nurse, Oenone, toward the start of her opening scene. She answers her own question: "Je l'ai perdue. Les Dieux m'en ont ravi l'usage." (They are lost: the Gods have spoiled me of their use.) A few lines later, as the avowal of her desire for Hippolyte sticks in her throat, she accuses one goddess in particular of a multigenerational grudge: "O haine de Vénus! O fatale colère! / Dans quels égarements l'amour jeta ma Mère." (O enmity of Venus! Fatal anger! / Into what errors love impelled my mother!) (The reference is to her mother Pasiphae's mating with Zeus in the form of a bull.) Then finally, when the cat's out of the bag, she delivers one of the play's most famous couplets, describing in the historical present the beginnings of her infatuation for her stepson: "Ce n'est plus une ardeur en mes veines cachée / C'est Vénus toute entière à sa proie attachée." (No more an ardor in my veins concealed, / it is Venus, wholly fastened on her prey.) Of course, mythologically speaking, all this is right. Venus *is* all to blame. Such is the plot as given to us by Euripides. There, Aphrodite herself announces at the play's start that she intends to use Phaedra to destroy the hero Hippolytus, for the latter has spurned the goddess of love and chastely dedicated himself to the service of Artemis. But no goddess prefaces Racine's version with claims of responsibility for the coming calamity. And so as far as Venus's enmity is concerned, we have only Phèdre's word to go on. Sacred dread there is, but it is experienced by spectators only through the prism of the heroine and other characters.

Yet how often we hear about the crushing weight of "destiny," with respect both to this particular tragedy and—by extension—to classical tragedy in general. G.W.F. Hegel, no fan of Racine for doubtless many reasons, claimed that his Phaedra made for a bad tragic character because she had no agency, and generations of critics who have not necessarily seconded Hegel's blanket dismissal of the French playwright have been happy to sign on to the idea that human volition has no place in this universe. In a particularly famous reading from the 1950s, descended from Hegel via György Lukács, Lucien Goldmann claimed that Racine's view of the human will followed from his Jansenist upbringing—the Jansenists being the heterodox sect whose main tenet was the inability of believers to advance the cause of their own salvation, which instead depended on divine grace. Tragedy, by this reckoning, became the expression of an entire metaphysical worldview in which individuals could only cower under the gaze of a inscrutable hidden deity. Goldmann's attempt to read Racine's oeuvre through the doctrine and experience of the Jansenists is much more subtle than many accounts of the playwright's so-called fatalism, but it does not square any better with the basic fact that seventeenth-century French tragedy generally tried to steer well clear of deities, hidden or otherwise. It was a genre that was all about human choices. Which is why, moreover, Racine's choice of subject for his 1677 play was such a bold one, as we can see from an analysis published just days after *Phèdre*'s own appearance in print. There, an anonymous critic opined that the heroine's incestuous desire was particularly problematic on the modern stage because audiences could no longer believe that she was tyrannized by a pagan divinity: "attributing vice to the will of the criminal alone, [we moderns] can find no pretext, no mask, and no excuse for this horrible act." The myth of Pheadra was a bad one for a modern tragedy, then, precisely because it did not allow for the free exercise of human will.

Racine recognized the danger, certainly, which is why he constructed the play as he did, cannily allowing us to have our gods and our reason too. On the one hand, the pagan characters believed in their pagan divinities, and their dread suffused the play with a tragic awe. On the other, Racine did all he could to make that belief the very subject of his tragedy. Racine's careful work is particularly evident in the tragic denouement, recounted by the messenger Théramène. The inherited myth runs as follows. Theseus, believing his son to have made incestuous advances on his wife, calls upon Neptune to avenge the insult; immediately thereafter, Hippolytus, trying to escape his father's wrath, is attacked at sea's edge by a monster from the deep; the master horseman is dragged to death by his own coursers. Even Seneca's version, in which the nurse can already be found warning Phaedra that men use the gods as an alibi for their lust, gives us a monster with a divine mission: the beast hotly pursues the hero and his frightened horses, which finally throw their master down. By contrast, Racine's monster has morphed into something more like a public menace, one that happens to frighten off everyone but the hero. Hippolyte alone steps forward to fight, mortally wounding the creature. Unfortunately, the beast's terrific death throes—spurts of fire, blood, smoke—then frighten the team of horses. We wonder: mightn't this be an example of wrong-time-wrong-place coincidence? Of course, the monster does come ashore right after Thésée's imprecations: one must ask if this can only be bad luck. But that's just it: divine agency becomes a question—one that Racine encourages us to entertain with another detail present only in Théramène's description of the uncontrollable horses: "On dit qu'on a vu même en ce désordre affreux / Un Dieu, qui d'aiguillons pressait leur flanc poudreux." (Some say / one could even see, in the dread hurly-burly, / a God stabbing with goads their dusty flanks.) Some say, yes: some always claim to see the supernatural. Racine's is thus a delicate rationalization of the myth, one that leaves us suspended between the world of the characters and a more modern, disenchanted frame of reference.

In the end, this rationalization helps explain why this play is now known as *Phèdre*, and why we think of it as its heroine's tragedy. Euripides didn't write a *Phaedra*; he wrote a *Hippolytus*, whose main tragic action was the destruction of the titular hero. Seneca in his version did a lot to develop the role of Phaedra, so much so that manuscripts come down to us under the titles of both the queen and her stepson; but the Latin poet's imitators in the Renaissance reverted to prioritizing, in their titles, the fate of Hippolytus. Surely there was some difficulty in making Phaedra the center of the play, given what legend provided poets to work with: she was, after all, but a cruelly used tool of a goddess's revenge; the tragic "fault" was Hippolytus's, that is, his public and ill-considered disdain for Aphrodite. But once Aphrodite's overt intervention was removed, the queen herself could become a suitably Aristotelian tragic heroine—"not quite guilty, not quite innocent," says Racine in his preface to the play, and therefore able to excite our compassion and horror in the manner claimed by the *Poetics*.

The playwright points, in this preface, to one of his efforts on Phèdre's behalf: whereas previous versions had her denouncing Hippolytus's advances directly to her husband, Racine spares her such base calumny by attributing it to Oenone's initiative. But beyond this scapegoating of a plebian Machiavel—a common tactic for relieving tragic princesses and princes of responsibility for heinous acts—Racine makes Phèdre herself dramatically interesting through sustained attention to the heroine's attempts to contain or repress her desire. "To speak or not to speak?" This, for Roland Barthes, in his famous book *On Racine*, was the question of *Phèdre*. Indeed, speaking is at the center of this purportedly mythological tragedy, which is at the same time a purely human drama of avowal, of words that cannot be stifled and that once proffered cannot be recalled. Phèdre confesses her desire first to her nurse, then to the man she loves, and finally, after having poisoned herself, to her husband. Only the last of the avowals, the purifying one, is forthrightly executed: "Les moments me sont chers, écoutez-moi, Thésée" (Moments are precious to me. Listen, Theseus), she says, before taking ownership of her actions: "C'est moi qui sur ce fils chaste et respectueux / osai jeter un oeil profane, incestueux" (I myself dared to cast upon that chaste, / respectful son, profane, incestuous eyes). (Ambiguous ownership, perhaps, since she follows the admission with a displacement of guilt toward "heaven" [le Ciel] and Oenone.) The other admissions are oblique, partial insinuations that must be midwifed by interlocutors savvy enough to fill in the words that she cannot pronounce. Her first periphrastic reference to the object of her love is the stuff of anthologies:

OENONE: Aimez-vous?
PHÈDRE: De l'amour j'ai toutes les fureurs.
OENONE: Pour qui?
PHÈDRE: Tu vas ouïr le comble des horreurs.
    J'aime . . . à ce nom fatal je tremble, je frissonne.
    J'aime . . .
OENONE: Qui?
PHÈDRE: Tu connais ce fils de l'Amazone,
    Ce prince si longtemps par moi-même opprimé?
OENONE: Hippolyte? Grands dieux!
PHÈDRE: C'est toi qui l'as nommé.

(OENONE: Are you in love?
PHÈDRE: I have love's total fury.
OENONE: For whom?
PHÈDRE: Now you will hear the peak of horrors.
    I love—at that fatal name, I am cold, I quake—
    I love—
OENONE: Whom?
PHÈDRE: You know that son of the Amazon,
    That prince so long, now, by myself oppressed?

Oenone: Hippolytus? Great Gods!
Phèdre: It was you that named him.)

Racine did not invent this passage: Euripides had already shown his
Phaedra tip-toeing around the feared name in just this way, and the
last hemistich, arguably the most famous six syllables in all of French
classical drama, is in fact lifted verbatim from a French predecessor's
version of the tragedy (Gabriel Gilbert's *Hippolyte*). But Racine takes
what he finds in tradition and spins it into a thematic web. There's
Phèdre's confession to Hippolyte, which starts as a confession of love
for his father—"Oui, Prince, je languis, je brûle pour Thésée" (Yes,
Prince, I am burning, languishing for Theseus)—before veering dis-
turbingly off-track in a way that leaves her interlocutor searching
awkwardly for an innocent interpretation of her words. "Ah! Cruel,
tu m'as trop entendue" (Ah, cruel, you have understood me too well),
she says, making further denial impossible. And we should note that
Hippolyte too struggles to speak of his own love for the pure Aricie—once before his tutor, Théramène; again before Aricie herself;
and a third time before his father. On the whole, he does a more direct job than his stepmother, but like her, he cannot quite come out
with everything that must be said. His last words to his father, who
has just accused him of lust for his stepmother, are a masterpiece of
innuendo.

> Vous me parlez toujours d'inceste et d'adultère?
> Je me tais. Cependant Phèdre sort d'une mère,
> Phèdre est d'un sang, Seigneur, vous le savez trop bien,
> De toutes ces horreurs plus rempli que le mien.

> (You speak still of adultery and incest?
> I will not reply. Yet as her mother's child
> Phaedra is of a blood, you know too well,
> More plentiful in all those horrors than mine.)

Obliquity ends up finding its mark once again, and a furious Thésée is
immediately spurred to request Neptune's intercession. The king's invocation of the god is as confident and spontaneous as the other pro-

tagonists' avowals have been indecisive. But if Thésée is the only one here to speak with authority, it does not buy him anything more than stammering gets the others. The tragedy of speaking is universal.

"Racinian characters are never lower on the scale of human grandeur than when they are moved to make a rational argument," wrote Paul Bénichou in a classic analysis, meaning that their attempts at reasoning with others are usually but thin rationalizations, barely keeping a lid on the craziness boiling underneath. This is in direct contradistinction to the heroes of Racine's elder rival Pierre Corneille—heroes who both know what they want and possess the rhetorical know-how to advocate for it. Corneille's protagonists like to use the first-person pronoun, often coupled with words such as "want" or "must"; their will is in synch with their acts, and it is always and endlessly declared. Corneille's choice was an innovation: resisting his contemporaries' Aristotelian love of so-called recognition plots, where the poet retains crucial bits of information from both characters and audience until the climax (Jocasta is Oedipus's mother!), Corneille reasoned that such bursts of surprise could produce pleasure only once and not on repeat viewings. Instead, it was the sustained dilemma facing characters who evaluate head-on all their irreconcilable options that produced real tragic emotion. The audience participated in this dilemma, and then took pleasure in the hero's resolution of it—a pleasure he termed admiration.

Not knowing just what one should say, or saying more than one intends, clues us into a break with Cornelian heroism and by extension with an entire conception of tragedy. Racine's heroes didn't behave heroically. They were, in a word, "natural." And this word was used very early on to qualify Racine's work—used by the playwright himself, by his supporters, and even by his detractors. Detractors said: legendary heroes had their own nature, they weren't like us; and at any rate, tainting heroic subject matter with more mediocre motivations (such as love) could only, by definition, destroy the elevated dignity that tragedy depended on. Defenders, meanwhile, reasoned that Racine was doing just what he said, which was aiming for the very Aristotelian effects of "horror and pity," produced when bad things happen to decent (but not perfect) people, and that the audience's pleasure depended on a kind of commonality between viewers and characters.

Such insistence on Racine's naturalness may seem strange given what is surely the governing modern commonplace about French classical theater—its extreme artifice, its ascetic devotion to decorum, its elimination of anything that breathes. But it's our modern commonplace that is strange. For their part, seventeenth-century theorists of the stage, who did indeed propose and parse rules for dramatic production, did so to enhance the believability of the spectacle. When one went to the theater, the experience was ideally felt to be that of finding oneself before the actual people portrayed—in our case, Theseus and his unhappy family. Thus theorists continually tried to jettison practices felt to be overly artificial and consequently destructive of the spectator's illusion of experiencing the reality depicted. For example, anyone with a passing knowledge of French classicism recognizes "No blood on stage" as one of its cardinal rules. From there we extrapolate the squeamishness of an upper-class audience unwilling to be shocked by representations of violence, cocooned in their denial of reality itself. In fact, theorists offered a number of sometimes contradictory justifications for the proscription against spilling blood on stage, and a major one, lifted from Italian Renaissance theory, was simply that represented violence was unconvincing and thus ridiculous. Likewise, the three famous "unities"—of time, place, and action—were commonly justified not as tools to stifle the eruption of anything arbitrary or unplanned, but as necessities of illusion: a spectator transported between acts from France to Denmark would be so cognitively disturbed that the dramatic spell would be broken; ideally, some maintained, a play should even be in "real time."

So when words stick in Phèdre's throat, they do so as part of this larger quest for characters we can believe in. The way dramatic characters should be made to speak was the object of considerable thought at the time. The earliest French tragedies, from the second half of the sixteenth century, were made up largely of lamentations—extended feats of eloquence in which characters bemoaned cruel fate. (Not created for the professional stage, which did not exist yet in France, such works obeyed the conventions of poetic practice more than those of drama.) Much critical energy was expended in the following century to distance tragedy from anything that smacked of the rhetorical arts. Speech was pushed to be less flowery and overtly sententious: extended metaphors and comparisons, everywhere in Renaissance tragedies, became unwelcome markers of the poet's voice; and playwrights were warned to instruct through the drama itself, not by filling characters' mouths with maxims. Monologues and asides, meanwhile, needed to be deployed judiciously and motivated by the circumstances of the play, lest we feel their artifice. A common thread runs through these observations and others: poetic eloquence moves us, but it is at the same time the enemy of feeling, because people who are truly in the grip of passion simply don't talk like poets. On the contrary, real emotion may well be anything but wordy: "Often true passions, when really intense, remain mute, or are expressed confusedly."

Such was the observation of Hiliare-Bernard de Longepierre, the first to attempt the soon-to-be-unavoidable comparison between Corneille and Racine. And on the matter of emotional speech, which was for Longepierre the only matter that counted, Racine won hands down. Some brute statistics, drawn from the work of Sabine Chaouche, hint at how this effect was achieved. In Corneille's generation, plays were made up of approximately 86 percent affirmative declarations, 3.5 percent exclamations, and 11 percent questions. In Racine's mature plays (*Andromaque* to *Phèdre*), the numbers are 77 percent, 4.5 percent, and 18.5 percent. Measurably, then, *Phèdre* belongs to a larger family of characters who are not sure of themselves. (One monologue in *Bérénice* [1670] consists of 64 percent interrogations; another, in *Bajazet* [1672], tops out at 73 percent.) Similarly, the playwright uses about three times the number of interjections ("Ah!") as his rival Corneille. And another scholar, Marie-Lynn Flowers, has calculated that Racine's sentences are roughly half as long as those of his contemporaries—both easier to follow, therefore, and less obviously rhetorical constructions. Those sentences, meanwhile, are often left unfinished, as characters trail off or are interrupted. The technical name for the device is aposiopesis, and it is indeed a device, a poetical "figure." But unlike a figure such as reversion—ask not what your country can do for you, but what you can do for your country— it is designed to be self-effacing.

Self-effacing: that is, pointing not to the words, not even to the words' "meaning," but to what the words cannot say, to the hidden passion that cannot talk straight. Words here are not a window onto the soul; they are the emergent part of the human iceberg. It used to be that the period scholars now commonly call early modern (roughly 1500 to 1750) was held to demonstrate the triumph of the individual—a moment in which, in Jacob Burckhardt's pioneering formulation, man was no longer "conscious of himself only as member of a race, people, party, family, or corporation," but became instead "complete," which is to say, cosmopolitan and of universal aspirations. Lately, and in part under the influence of Michel Foucault, scholars have taken to speaking of the early modern constitution of a rather less resplendent being, a "deep" individual whose inner recesses became the object of scrutiny, much of it hostile. For Foucault, sex was at the root of this transformation, that is, sex seen no longer as a practice subject to variation and modification, but as an identity, a secret bent that defines each of us and that we are urged to confess, be it to priest, psychoanalyst, or talk-show host. Racine's theater in particular seems of a piece with such a development: in it, amorous passion, shorn of chivalric and Neoplatonic nobility, becomes something more like an instinct, something that you are not responsible for, that you cannot master, and that gets in the way of everything else you should be doing. And something that, at least in *Phèdre*, as Foucault predicts, you want desperately to confess, so as to, again, "Rend[re] au jour . . . toute sa pureté" (give back to the light . . . its purity).

Of course, all manner of uncontrollable lust had spilled onto the tragic stage before Racine. It was, however, safely quarantined within reprehensible characters—bad examples, or more accurately negative exemplars, whom we could look upon in moral horror, and who in any event had little trouble articulating the evil in their breast. ("How archaic a character like Edmund in *King Lear* sounds, with his unmediated access to his own wickedness," writes the critic Thomas Pavel.) Racine's instinctually driven protagonists, by contrast, and in the parlance of today's undergraduates, are "relatable": even the unalloyed tyrant Nero is depicted, in *Britannicus*, on the cusp of his passage over to the dark side, so that we can still feel his obsessive love for the young Junie as, well, something like love. Surely the power of a character like Phèdre—the way she takes over a myth in which she was originally but one player among many— owes a lot to Racine's ability to let us see things from her point of view. If many readers have come away with the feeling that hostile fate is to blame for Phèdre's woes, only part of this comes from our preconceptions about tragic destiny: the rest is the result of the persuasive intensity the playwright has brought to the case the protagonist makes for her helplessness.

Racine was not alone in seeking to craft characters whose manifest imperfections do not inhibit but in fact encourage the development of what was at the time called pity, compassion, or interest, and what at least resembles—I will come back to this—what we now call identification. Indeed, his tragedies are part of a broader generational shift, and the passage from Corneille to Racine in tragedy resembles what we can observe in the domain of the novel. Madeleine de Scudéry, a contemporary of Corneille, was the most celebrated novelist of the 1640s and 1650s; her episodic, multivolume works, called heroic romances, were full of willful characters whose walk matched their talk. The Comtesse de Lafayette, who came on the literary scene just as this brand of heroic romance was going out of style in the early 1660s, played Racine to Scudéry's Corneille. Lafayette's novels—her enduringly famous *Princesse de Clèves* (*The Princess of Clèves*, 1678) but also her unjustly forgotten *Zayde* (1670–71)—were full of characters struggling, sometimes successfully, often not, to bring their unruly passions into line. Moreover, her readers reported many of the same effects that Racine's commentators described, foremost a particular sort of bonding with beings whose predicaments had some measure of conformity with their own. Even the revolution in comedy wrought by Molière can arguably be understood in this context—as an attempt not only to put contemporary society and its ridicules on stage, but also to invent characters whose comic blindness and obstinacy do not keep us from partially viewing the world through their eyes. (The best example, though not the only one, is *Le misanthrope*'s Alceste, praised by a critic of the time, Donneau de Visé, as a creation that was both "to some extent ridiculous" and yet also able to "say quite sensible things.")

One frequent interpretation of this shift in what was valued in a literary character is loosely sociological: the new breed of unhappy heroes is a sign of the political pessimism of the aristocracy in the 1660s and 1670s. The Fronde, the midcentury revolt against the authority of Louis XIV's regent, Anne d'Autriche, and her minister, Mazarin, had sources in both the new aristocracy of the robe (essentially legal professionals) and the landed aristocracy of the sword; the eventual crushing of the Fronde, and subsequent solidification of Louis XIV's absolutist rule starting with the death of Mazarin in 1661, deprived French nobles of their former independence and importance. Given such context, it is not hard to see why Cornelian heroism, focused on the military exploits of the highest nobility, would be replaced by the heroes of Racine, who have trouble doing much of anything against an increasingly tyrannical royal power, and who instead content themselves with the more mundane matters of the heart. There is probably much truth to this: why indeed would a dramatist bother to craft meditations on the intricacies of governance and war for an essentially disenfranchised audience?

A second explanation for what Bénichou called the "destruction of the hero" finds a cause in Jansenism and its deep spiritual pessimism: for some critics, the doctrine can be detected not only in Racine, who as a child actually attended the famous Jansenist school at Port-Royal, but also in the work of people whose biographical links to the sect are more tenuous—in *La Princesse de Clèves*, but also in the *Maximes* (*Maxims*, 1665) of Lafayette's friend the Duc de La Rochefoucauld. Yet studying what actual readers of the period said they liked in Racine and Lafayette reveals something other than an interest in the condemnation of fallen humankind and its uncontrollable passions. If readers did not want characters to admire, this was because people could not simply do what they decided, for all the right reasons, to do: the human heart was a recess of unknowable desires and motivations, and the writer's task was to open up that interiority. Longepierre thus describes the heart as Racine's true subject, which was putty in his hands: "He manipulates it as he wishes, he unfolds its every crease, he sounds its deepest point; he pierces its twists and turns, and not one corner of this dark and impenetrable labyrinth escapes his penetration." Yet in virtually the same breath, Longepierre expands enthusiastically on the pleasure Racine's audience takes in the display of a heart that is not so much devious and vice-ridden as beatingly alive before us, a swirling locus of emotions—"faintness, ardor, transport, fear, ruse, artifice, anxiety, anger, languor, delicacy, and more." If it was indeed Racine's intention to offer his audience a sour mirror in which to recognize their own sinful nature, he would seem to have failed: notwithstanding its destructiveness, passion here is described as completely seductive. Love, not simply a prime subject of Racine's tragedies, ends up being something like the feeling that passes between audience and characters: "How can a heart that recognizes its own image in these animated and lively portraits not be touched by them? It is thus that [the viewer's heart] has no power to resist." In such phrases, Longepierre goes well beyond the traditional Aristotelian language of pity to stress the identificatory bond between viewer and character.

Identification may be well and good in novels and comedy, one might allow; but how can it be compatible with tragedy—a genre that, like epic, is almost by definition peopled with larger-than-life legends, men and women occupying the highest reaches of political and military power? The objection is sound, at least historically, for it goes back to Racine's detractors at the time. But this was what Racine took as his challenge—to stretch the bounds of tragedy, to open it to the values that someone like Longepierre articulates, while at the same time keeping it truly tragic. And the formula he would exploit was to make passion itself tragic. That is, it was not that the personal and the political were tragically opposed, that heroic aspirations were pitted against the heart's siren call. This was more or less Corneille's formula, one that inevitably made love subordinate to what the dramatist called the "male" passions of ambition and revenge. Racine's approach, by contrast, was to make amorous passion unruly, destructive, something that we might want to call not so much by the noble name of "love" but by the more pathological term "desire." Desire did not stand in a tragic face-off with the masculine political passions; rather, it infected everything, to the point where any action, no matter how rational the alibi, always had it as its secret wellspring. There wasn't hard action on the one hand and soft love on the other—a dialectic that epics from the *Odyssey* and the *Aeneid* to Torquato Tasso's

Jerusalem Delivered (1581) had consecrated by thematizing heroism's resistance to erotic temptation. There was simply this consuming desire, which served as a perverse and universal human motivator. Such was modern tragedy for Racine: a tragedy his audience could relate to.

So what could have happened in the intervening centuries to make these works seem so distant? In the 1820s, as we have seen, all Stendhal could muster for Racine was cool admiration, not the tears earlier audiences had shed. Roland Barthes, surveying postwar productions of *Phèdre*, concluded bleakly: "I am not sure that it is still possible to stage Racine today." Is this state of affairs explainable through anything else besides the truism that time lays all convention bare, and that one season's naturalness is the next's affectation? Barthes's diagnosis was that Racine's theater was an uneasy mixture of the properly tragic—themes of guilt and destiny and the gods—and a distinctly more modern and bourgeois aesthetic in which characters became psychological individuals, motivated by purely human desires. Twentieth-century productions, he found, accentuated this psychological dimension, drawing the work further toward bourgeois drama, further from what it contained of true tragedy. The only possible remedy was to attempt to distance Racine, notably through a type of antipsychological diction that would avoid falling into the trap of assuming that words must be a kind of translation of thought; instead of trying to motivate psychologically each utterance, actors would do better to embrace the rigor imposed by the alexandrine verse. But precisely because Racine's tragedy is at bottom heterogeneous, Barthes did not seem sure that this would work. The problem was not simply that we now project a psychology onto work that is not psychological. It is that Racine is a meeting point where, according to Barthes, "elements of true tragedy mix inharmoniously with the seeds, already growing, of the bourgeois theater of the future." Barthes thinks it is better to estrange the work than to modernize it; but he also recognizes that in fact Racine is every bit as modern as he is archaic.

Barthes's diagnosis was intended as polemical, and as such it contains much that is debatable, sometimes even plain wrong. (For instance, to say that the alexandrine was intended to impose distance directly contradicts what people at the time said—that, on the contrary, it was the form of verse that most resembled ordinary human speech.) But he does grapple seriously with the real question hiding under the truism that "tastes change": why should plays with their contemporary reputation for naturalness be so hard to put on today? For Barthes, the reason lies in the historical hybridity of Racine, who has one foot stuck in true tragedy of the past and the other in a bourgeois drama to come: his modernity is incomplete, and so our efforts to treat him as if he were fully modern can only backfire. But I would suggest two other possibilities.

The first is that Barthes may be overestimating the extent to which Racine's "language of the heart" marks an incursion of specifically bourgeois values into literature. It is understandable why one might want to trace an arrow from Racine (or from a novelist like Lafayette) to the effusive bourgeois sentimentality of the next century, and there is a certain logic in assuming that identificatory relations between character and consumer must be the mark of a bourgeois public, whose ideology is that of the Everyman. Even in the absence of a good history of identification—a reading mode denigrated by professional critics, and thus understudied—it seems dubious to suggest that all discourses of fellow-feeling can be reduced to a common bourgeois cause. In his fifth-century BCE *Defense of Helen*, Gorgias wrote, "Those who hear poetry feel the shudders of fear, the tears of pity, the longings of grief. Through the words, the soul experiences its own reaction to successes and misfortunes in the affairs and persons of others"; surely he could not already have been expressing a "bourgeois" aesthetic. To understand Racine's passions, maybe instead of looking forward we should look *back*—back, say, to Renaissance debates on the proper manner of depicting emotion, debates that can be chased further upstream still, to their various Greco-Roman sources. From this point of view, modern Western literary history would present a series of competing techniques for presenting interiority: the sonnet, the tragic monologue, autobiography, the epistolary novel, free indirect discourse, stream-of-consciousness. The types of plots Racine developed, and the verse he wrote, were part of this long history, rather than a symptom of epochal change.

The second possibility, not unrelated, is that the ideological assumptions underwriting this interiority are in fact many and distinct. It is no doubt true that Racine wanted to craft "relatable" characters; but it is equally true that relatability for him meant something it no longer does. If we follow the critic Raymond Williams, for example, our current view of tragedy is determined by the fact that modern literature is inescapably a literature of the individual: "Our most common received interpretations of life put the highest value and significance on the individual and his development, but it is indeed inescapable that the individual dies. . . . Tragedy, for us, has been mainly the conflict between an individual and the forces that destroy him." As doomed individuals, we relate to the situations represented individuals find themselves in and the emotions that arise out of those situations. "We think of tragedy as what happens *to* the hero," continues Williams, but in much of the Western (Aristotelian) tradition, "the ordinary tragic action is what happens *through* the hero" (my emphasis). Admittedly, *Phèdre*, via the centrality of Phèdre, allows us to read it according to our modern obsession with the individual. Yet we should weigh this against the fact that, as a playwright steeped in the Aristotelian tradition, Racine viewed Hippolyte's death as the tragic action, an action that the poet needed to produce through a concatenation of factors of which Phèdre's desire (like Oenone's counsel) is but one. Her desire is not, to be precise, tragic; it is the means by which the tragic action is precipitated. To see here a meditation on the human condition as such is thus something of an optical illusion, generated by our historically peculiar vantage point.

From the vantage point of Racine's audience, Phèdre acted as a host for the viewers' identification by having passions they could share—quite literally. The job of the dramatist was to bring before that audience passionate heroes; with skill, those passions would be felt by the audience. Variations existed in the way theorists of the time thought about this transfer of emotion; and as they did before and have since, people puzzled over Aristotle's cryptic remarks on catharsis and over the paradox Sir Philip Sidney summed up as "sweet violence" (how do we take pleasure from the representation of sometimes unpleasurable emotions?). Racine himself had given a formulation of that paradox in his introduction to *Bérénice*, where he speaks of "majestic sadness" as being the sought-after product of the tragic poet's art—the "majesty" being the *je ne sais quoi* that distinguished it from just plain sadness, which no one would want. Small differences aside, however, the general opinion did not vary a lot: we did not go to the theater to see meditations on humankind's fate; we went to have our emotions aroused by seeing heroes and heroines who were similarly aroused. (If this sounds a little unsavory, it's because in the wake of the new brand of aesthetic philosophy introduced by Immanuel Kant and Hegel, this type of explanation for the emotions produced by art went downmarket, applying only to supposedly debased genres like horror and pornography.) Moderns might say that we identify with Phèdre because, caught in a no-exit snare, she represents the dilemma of the human condition. But for someone like Longepierre, what is marvelous about Racine is his ability to so accurately represent the labyrinth of human emotions that we are "touched" by them. Arguably, both formulations are types of identification, but they do not describe the same reading experience. In one (Longepierre), you recognize your own feelings in a character; in the other, you imaginatively enter into a character's situation. A small difference, perhaps—but enough to explain why Racine's vaunted naturalness no longer quite comes across.

Such are two explanations for Racine's apparent distance that at least have the advantage of resisting the idea of some crystalline classical aesthetic, now inaccessible. And we should also resist the idea that *Phèdre*'s relatively happy fate—it's still staged and translated, and still on a lot of reading lists and course syllabi—is entirely based on misconceptions. Initially called *Phèdre et Hippolyte* (*Phaedra and Hippolytus*), the tragedy was, after all, rebaptized *Phèdre* by none other than its creator on the occasion of the play's second edition in 1687: this would seem an acknowledgment that in the end it *is* Phèdre's not quite unavowable desire that constitutes the real heart of the tragedy. And if this is so, then surely it can't be too wide of the mark to conclude that when Racine comes upon the formula for making tragedy out of amorous passion gone wrong, he also invents, with the same stroke, a tragic vision of human desire. For us to pronounce Racine difficult to stage, we first have to want to stage him; that is, a play like

Phèdre beckons to us before it pushes us away. Unquestionably, Racine is of a different age; but he is just as unquestionably part of a history from which we are not, in fact, separate. The fact is that French classicism is nearer to us than we usually think, even if it remains a little too far away for total comfort.

NOTES

1. Unless otherwise indicated, translations are my own.
2. This is why the playwright could both be appreciated for his modernity and, in the "battle of the books" that pitted Ancients against Moderns, find himself in the Ancient camp.
3. I use accepted English spellings of figures of ancient myth and history when referring to the figures generally, and French spellings in reference to Racine's own characters.

WORKS CITED AND RECOMMENDED FURTHER READING

Barthes, Roland. *Sur Racine*. Paris: Seuil, 1963.

Burckhardt, Jacob. *The Civilization of Renaissance Italy*. Translated by S.G.C. Middlemore. 1860. Reprint, New York: Albert and Charles Boni, 1935.

Bénichou, Paul. *Morales du grand siècle*. Paris: Gallimard, 1988.

Chaouche, Sabine. *L'art du comédien: Déclamation et jeu scénique en France à l'âge classique (1629–1680)*. Paris: Champion, 2001.

Corneille, Pierre. *Discours de l'utilité et des parties du poème dramatique*. In *Oeuvres complètes III*. Edited by Georges Couton. Paris: Gallimard, 1987.

Dissertation sur les tragédies de Phèdre et Hippolyte (anon.). In Jean Racine, *Oeuvres complètes I: Théâtre-poésie*. Edited by Georges Forestier. Paris: Gallimard, 1999.

Donneau de Visé, Jean. "Lettre écrite sur la comédie du misanthrope." In Molière, *Oeuvres complètes I*. Edited by Georges Forestier. Paris: Gallimard, 2010.

Flowers, Mary Lynn. *Sentence Structure and Characterization in the Tragedies of Jean Racine: A Computer-Assisted Study*. Rutherford, NJ: Fairleigh Dickinson University Press, 1979.

Foucault, Michel. *The History of Sexuality*. Vol. 1: *An Introduction*. Translated by Robert Hurley. New York: Random House, 1978.

Gorgias. *Defense of Helen*. In *Ancient Literary Criticism: The Principal Texts in New Translations*. Edited by D. A. Russell and M. Winterbottom. Oxford: Oxford University Press, 1972.

Longepierre, Hiliare-Bernard de. "Parallèle de M. Corneille et M. Racine." In Adrien Baillet, comp., *Jugement des savants sur les principaux ouvrages des auteurs*. Paris: Charles Motte et al., 1722.

Pavel, Thomas. "Between History and Fiction: On Dorrit Cohn's Poetics of Prose." In *Neverending Stories: Toward a Critical Narratology*. Edited by Ann Fehn, Ingeborg Hoesterey, and Maria Tatar. Princeton, NJ: Princeton University Press, 1992.

Racine, Jean. *Phaedra*. In *Three Plays*. Translated by George Dillon. Chicago: University of Chicago Press, 1961.

Steiner, George. *The Death of Tragedy*. London: Faber and Faber, 1961.

Stendhal. *Racine et Shakespeare: Etudes sur le romantisme* (1828). Expanded ed., Paris: Michel Lévy, 1854.

Williams, Raymond. *Modern Tragedy*. Stanford, CA: Stanford University Press, 1966.

Readers have a number of English translations of *Phèdre* to explore, from the sober Dillon version I quote from here to Richard Wilbur's rhyming couplets (New York: Harcourt Brace Jovanovich, 1986) and Ted Hughes's "amplification"-translation (London: Faber and Faber, 1998). For most purposes, there are no significant differences between available French texts of the plays. Georges Forestier's critical French edition of Racine's works, *Oeuvres complètes I: Théâtre-poésie* (Paris: Gallimard, 1999) is a mine of historical information on the plays and their literary and cultural context.

Balanced introductions to Racine's tragedies are relatively plentiful; Odette de Mourgues, *Racine, or the Triumph of Relevance* (Cambridge: Cambridge University Press, 1967) is a good place to start. R. C. Knight, *Racine: Modern Judgements* (London: Macmillan, 1969) reprints some important older scholarship, including English translations of classic essays by Leo Spitzer, Georges Poulet, and Jean Starobinski. Lucien Goldmann's "Jansenist" interpretation can be found in *The Hidden God* (New York: Humanities Press, 1964); Roland Barthes's structuralist *On Racine* (Berkeley: University of California Press, 1992) remains a tour de force. Erich Auerbach,

Mimesis (Princeton, NJ: Princeton University Press, 1953), sees classical theater (Racine, but also Molière) as a rejection of serious realism. A representative cross-section of more recent criticism can be found in Edric Caldicott and Derval Conroy, eds., *Racine: The Power and the Pleasure* (Dublin: University College Dublin Press, 2001). For a bracing and contrarian tour of scholarship old and new, see John Campbell, *Questioning Racinian Tragedy* (Chapel Hill: University of North Carolina Press, 2005). For wider studies of French classicism, see Christopher Gossip, *An Introduction to French Classical Tragedy* (London: Macmillan, 1981) and John Lyons, *Kingdom of Disorder* (West Lafayette, IN: Purdue University Press, 1999); the latter is the best English-language study of classical "doctrine." And in *The Death of Tragedy* (London: Faber and Faber, 1961), George Steiner situates Racine's work both in the local context of French classicism and with respect to the Western tradition of tragedy in general.

Lafayette

La Princesse de Clèves and the Conversational Culture of Seventeenth-Century Fiction

KATHERINE IBBETT

An anxious husband asks his wife why she has left the court and insists on refusing all social interaction; at first, embarrassed, she tells him only that she longs for the tranquillity of the countryside, and then, as her disbelieving husband presses her further, she announces that she will tell him something no wife has ever told her husband: that she cares for another man, but that nothing has ever taken place between them and that she will not name him.

Little do they know that the countryside retreat in which this painful conversation takes place is not, in fact, a tranquil retreat; indeed, the unnamed man in question is present and listening in to their conversation. The wife does not name the man; the husband is unable to get her to identify him, despite his best efforts; and the man listening in does not know that he is the person of interest. Only the reader is privileged enough to know both the identity of the man and that he is eavesdropping at this most intimate marital moment. We lean in, eager to see what will happen, but uncomfortably aware that as readers we too are engaged in a form of eavesdropping.

This is the central scene of a novel by Marie-Madeleine Pioche de la Vergne, the comtesse de Lafayette (1634–93), known in French as Madame de Lafayette but in Anglo-American scholarship as Lafayette. The novel, *La Princesse de Clèves*, flouted expectations even before its publication, and the history of how it has surprised and sometimes annoyed readers is part of what makes the novel exceptional. *La Princesse de Clèves* was electrifying to French readers on its publication in 1678, and has stayed central to arguments about fiction and its value since then; most recently, its defenders took to the streets against then President Sarkozy, who had questioned the usefulness of studying such a text.

Before even the publication of the novel, its singularity had been touted by another new genre: the newspaper. Donneau de Visé, the proprietor of a circular called the *Mercure Galant*, published a similar story as a teaser; the paper then solicited the opinion of the public on the princess's strange confession, going on to produce three issues of a special supplement and a review all devoted to the novel. An entrenched battle between fans and critics ensued, making this novel into an event, or what the French call a *querelle*, from its initial appearance. To further the debate, two scholars of the novel—one for, one against—went up against one another in lengthy published discussions, which argued again about the propriety or otherwise of the princess's confession. Even the form of this criticism was conversational, since literary criticism had not yet been sequestered in the academy: the critic who attacked the novel, Valincour, framed his assessment as a series of chatty dialogues between imagined readers.

This central eavesdropping scene of the novel, and the reading public's reaction to it, placed the public consumption of private conversation at the heart of this emerging genre. Readers were charmed by an imagined entry into private and hitherto inaccessible conversations: novels were spaces in which readers listened in to conversations between people—especially women—who imagine themselves to be talking in private, and they were also objects about which conversation raged. The novel as a genre pushed private life into the open, and, moreover, told its readers that they should consider private life to be publicly significant.

Before we can take on the significance of that dynamic for both Lafayette's novel and other texts of the period, we'll take a detour through the plot and novelty of the *Princesse*. A beautiful young woman, heiress to a great fortune, is brought to court by her mother, who watches over her with great care. After much negotiation, the daughter is eventually married to the prince de Clèves, a man who loves her even though this is not required of such marriages. Moreover, he wants her love in return; this proves impossible, since she has as yet no idea of what love means. She remains unmoved by her husband, who deeply regrets this. But she then meets a fabled figure, the duc de Nemours, and throughout a series of carefully managed scenes discovers what it means to care for someone, who, events suggest, is also inclined toward her, as the French term puts it. Almost every intimacy is refused by the princess. Eventually, in the scene described above, the princess confesses her feelings for an unnamed other to her husband, without realizing that Nemours is listening in. Later, she hears this story relayed back to her in court gossip, and accuses her husband of having spread the story, not knowing that it is Nemours who is responsible for the gossip. The husband is unable to get over both what he has heard and his wife's suspicion of him; soon he becomes ill and dies. Now, the reader feels, a different novel is beginning, and after a decent interval of mourning we imagine the union of the two lovers. But this does not happen. After much anxious reflection, the princess retreats to the country, rejects Nemours's attempts to intrude on her retreat, and eventually moves into a convent. Some years later, we are told in brief lines at the end of the novel, Nemours's love diminishes. The princess never returns to court; in the abrupt ending of the novel, we learn only that she lives part of the year in a convent, and part quietly at home.

Reading the *Princesse* today, we are often put off by the first pages, which bristle with the complicated relations between various aristocratic families. But for the seventeenth-century reader, tracing these names was part of the pleasure of the text. The *Princesse* is a historical novel, but it provided its original readers with what we might call a history of the present. Written in 1678, but set in 1558, the novel presents a past world that looked very familiar, as though it could be a novel about the elaborate court culture of Versailles under Louis XIV, also a gossipy, factional court where "there reigned . . . a kind of orderly unrest which made life very enjoyable but also very dangerous for a young girl." Indeed, seventeenth-century readers, accustomed to acclaiming Louis's court as the greatest ever, were troubled by the novel's opening line, which seems to suggest that the court of Henri II surpassed that of the Sun King for "courtly magnificence and manners." But Lafayette's strangely familiar court was also a lost world: the names traced in the opening pages are the not-so-distant ancestors of Lafayette's first courtly readers, and those readers would have known that many of those mentioned were soon to come into cataclysmic conflict during the Wars of Religion that from 1562 to 1598 had set Catholics and Protestants in violent opposition to each other.

The novel's particularity was also apparent in its form: compared with the most popular readings of the day, this text looked rather strange. Seventeenth-century readers were familiar with both much longer and much shorter versions of fiction in prose. In the early to midcentury, the most popular texts were lengthy multivolume romances, like Honoré d'Urfé's *Astrée* (1607–27), or Madeleine de Scudéry's *Clélie* (1654–61, translated into English soon thereafter). These books were set in a distant past and featured lovers separated through external forces, like earthquakes or unkind parents (in contrast to Lafayette's novel, in which the lovers are kept apart only through the princess's own objections).

Such novels often began life as conversations in salons, and in reconstituting conversational profusion on the page they would produce a similar effect among their readers. Midcentury novels revolved around endless and often joyful conversations between friends, about the right way to be friends, or whether it is easier to love melancholy or merry women. These conversational set-pieces take place frankly and straightforwardly within the pages of the book, and gave rise to a host of further discussions, imitations, and satires. In a series of debates about the emotions in *Clélie*, for example, the heroine maps "the land of tenderness" in a foldout map that showed readers—and other characters—how to get from a new friendship to a tender one. The map established "tenderness," somewhere between dear friendship and romantic love, as a buzzword of the period, a complex early modern concept that reveals the paucity of our own vocabulary for thinking about friendship and affiliation. Clélie tells her readers that tenderness can be reached through one of three routes: the easiest and fastest is to follow the river of inclination, a key term of the period, which indicated a firm attraction. But one can also reach tenderness along the slower paths toward admiration or recognition, following small villages marked "love letters," "assiduity," "generosity." The paths to tenderness gave the seventeenth century an important vocabulary for negotiating relationships, to be found everywhere in fiction of the period.

In contrast to these meandering tomes, another popular form of prose fiction came in a shorter form: this was known as the *nouvelle historique*. These were shortish stories about more recent historical events—often the religious wars of the sixteenth century—and often featuring characters who, like those in the *Princesse*, were almost titillating in their familiarity to the contemporary reader. Where the multivolume romances featured outlandish adventures and surprises, this shorter form proclaimed its allegiance to a hotly contested category known as *vraisemblance*, or "verisimilitude": according to such strictures, events or conversations portrayed had to be historically allowable even if they did not actually happen. This kind of writing was pioneered and fostered by women writers—including Lafayette herself, whose *Princesse de Montpensier* (1662) is often thought of as the first of the genre—and it allowed readers to watch writers maneuvering in delicate terrain, claiming to show the intimate stories of public figures without overstepping into vulgarity or historical impossibility.

Lafayette, whose family had many literary connections at court and elsewhere, had grown up on the midcentury romances, and the precise parsing of emotions and their vocabulary that we see in the *Princesse de Clèves* certainly owes something to romances like *Clélie*. But where in *Clélie* characters would pause to address explicitly a particular keyword, in the *Princesse* those keywords accrue, slowly refracting so that where initially they seem almost without weight, their careful repetitions nudge us to see how significant they are for the novel: a good example is the word *éclat*, which might be translated as "brilliance," and which characterizes the pale beauty of the princess herself, the wonders of the court, the conversation of its inhabitants, and so on. But one can die of too much dazzle: an *éclat* is also a splinter, and in a scene that seems to insist on the darker side of all these brilliant things upon which to look, the king himself dies of a splinter from a lance that pierces his eye.

And Lafayette's novel is significantly shorter and clearer in plot structure than those unwieldy romances; it looks more like a slightly longer version of the *nouvelle historique*, those historically plausible short stories. But it does something quite distinct and new within that tradition: it fleshes out the historical record by inventing a character who, although she might have existed, never did in the way the other named figures had done. And as if that invention was not enough, Lafayette gives that central character an extraordinary and subtly manipulated form of interiority, brought about through various innovative narrative turns. In this curiously impersonal narrative, featuring a deeply reticent heroine, we see a careful maneuver around the notion of character and depth—like the princess's anxious husband, we strain to see whether the character has hidden depths that she is refusing to show us, or whether she is so restrained that she is entirely constructed from propriety. Lafayette works hard to take us into the princess's private world, but also at times to push us out from it.

That impenetrability or inscrutability is brought to a skillful peak at the ending of the novel, often particularly troubling to modern readers familiar with the marriage plot conventions of nineteenth-century novels, in which difficult courtships are followed by nuptial relief. Here, even as the novel promises an ending we think we might applaud, that ending is foiled by the retreat of the princess, a retreat that is both precisely explained—we know where she is, when, and for how long—and not explained enough—we know little of her emotions or inner life at the end of the novel, and the reader may well feel as stranded as her admirer Nemours, who has the door shut in his face with no further explanation. The novel's closing sentence ("Her life, which was quite short, left inimitable examples of virtue") leaves us wondering quite what an example that cannot be imitated might be, and what we who are left in the novel's wake should make of this heroine we are not able to follow.

If the debates around the novel centered largely on the heroine's propriety (one critic, Bussy-Rabutin, even wondered why she sinks to her knees when speaking to her husband, and what sort of physical abandon that might indicate), they also participated in a larger cultural anxiety about the propriety of women's writing. In this period, women often published their works anonymously, lest the behavior that took place within the text be imagined as an autobiographical transfer of their own life. In this case, Lafayette's text was published anonymously, but there was much talk about the identity of the author: in certain circles it would have been an open secret who the writer was, and easy to identify her. Her other works circulated before publication in the salons where she was well known, and she was not given to denying authorship when accused of it.

Part of the strategic game of anonymous publication can be gauged in what we call the "paratext," the often playful notes and blurbs attached to books. But in English translation, the publisher's note affixed to the opening of the *Princesse* loses something of its provocatively equivocal quality, since in English one has to gender the possessive pronoun, referring to his or her identity when one speaks of the author, whereas French allows more ambiguity; as the Terence Cave translation puts it, "the author has not felt able to declare *his* identity; *he* was afraid that *his* name might diminish the success of his book" (my emphasis). But in this period, it was very often women who chose to publish in such ways, so that their readers might give them as "fine and equitable" a reading as possible. And Lafayette plays games with these questions even within the novel itself: in the lengthy account of a misplaced letter that circulates at court, and the assumptions and blunders made about its author, Lafayette lets us see something of the apprehension that pertained in this period to the question of an author's identity.

Of course, it is one thing to speculate about the author of something that has been launched deliberately into the world. But as the plot of the novel makes clear, it is not only published stories that circulate and fascinate those who hear them. In a painful development after the princess's confession, she has her own words repeated to her by the dauphine, at which point she understands that at court even the most private stories can be set inexorably into public conversation (although she thinks her husband is to blame, rather than Nemours, the eavesdropper). This alarming turn of events might have recalled, for the seventeenth-century reader, a recent furor over the publication of some private love letters written by a woman writer—Marie-Catherine Desjardins, known as Madame de Villedieu—which in 1668 were published against her will and under her own name by her former lover.

Lafayette was a regular at the court of Versailles, where courtiers and king alike engaged in careful surveillance of each other. And her novel is punctuated by a series of scenes of intrusion or surveillance that are suffered and then rebuffed by the princess: most famously the extraordinarily suggestive multiplication of viewing, in which the princess is alone in a room at her country estate gazing at a portrait of Nemours that she has had brought there for that purpose, not knowing that Nemours is spying on her through the window, neither of them knowing that her husband's manservant is watching the both of them.

Like many other moments in the novel, this is a scene that appears to promise a moment of mutual devotion: "To see a woman he adored in the middle of the night, in the most beautiful place in the world, to see her, without her knowing he was there, entirely absorbed in things connected with him and with the passion she was hiding from him— what lover has ever enjoyed or even imagined such delight?" But the princess and Nemours are divided on the significance of her practice: Nemours, hopeful that his moment has finally come, tries to enter her room, but when his scarf is caught in the window, she hears the sound and seems to recognize him, retreating promptly into another room where her companions await her. The princess pays homage to the painting as the sign of her beloved, rather than wanting her devotion to bring about his actual presence.

Nemours, in contrast, acts like a hero of the romances popular earlier in the century; in imagining he can climb through a window and disregard the physical as well as moral barriers that separate the two, he could be in a different kind of text entirely from that of the princess, who scrupulously observes the distance between emotion and action. Stuck on the window, Nemours is figuratively stuck on the edge between two genres, the swashbuckling romance and the plausible novel: the one where you can climb in windows, and the other where such a thing is unthinkable. Indeed in the defense of the novel by the abbé de Charnes, brought out by the same publisher as the book itself, readers teasingly suggested that Nemours's night spying on the princess was the ultimate sign that the text draws on the romance tradition, since only a hero of romance could spend a night wandering outside without coming down with a heavy and unromantic cold. Likewise, the philosopher Fontenelle scoffed that this scene "stank of *Astrée*," that earlier novel about adventurous shepherds and their mostly pliant beloveds. Nemours's inability to understand the new and more austere rules of the game, his propensity to get stuck while doing what comes naturally to a hero of romance, points to quite how far Lafayette had moved from those older prose narratives.

This much-discussed spying scene is only the most extraordinary of a range of narrated encounters that insist on the demarcation of public and private space only to cross its line. Such a structure is central to the plot of the novel and to its strange ending, which is explained according to spatial terms, for the princess chooses to remove herself physically from difficult situations in order to break herself of bad habits, to retreat to her "cabinet" or private room or to her estate at Coulommiers.

Even as it observes the princess's desire for privacy, the novel asks the reader to participate in the intrusion into her space apart. But despite its heavy flagging of spatial structures, the text does not figure a clearly defined private individual who resists an encroaching public surveillance. For the novel also seems to suggest that without the larger world there would be no self, or rather that the princess comes to know who she is and what she thinks only by participating in the cacophonous circulations of public life at the court. Thus the princess comes to consciousness of her desire, that most intimate of feelings, only through rumor: hearing talk of Nemours and the dauphine, she blushes, and shutting herself away then realizes an interest in Nemours that she had not yet admitted to herself. In this version of events, gossip leads not to confusion but to clarity and self-knowledge. A little later, the princess recognizes herself as the unnamed object of gossip when the dauphine tells her that Nemours is in love with someone who won't respond. Lafayette's configuration of events indicates that the self becomes aware of its position only in public circulation.

Lafayette's novel was not the only text of its day that turned around the question of gossip and eavesdropping. Seventeenth-century France was deeply fascinated by the conversation of women, by its virtues and charms and capacity to construct vibrant intellectual and emotional gatherings, but also its potential to wreak social havoc. All kinds of texts sought to listen in to what women had to say: in a rambunctious series that appeared in eight installments throughout 1622, known as the *Caquets de l'accouchée*, a man convalescing from a grave illness is told to listen to women gathered round the bed of a woman who has given birth, on the grounds that listening to this conversation would improve his own health. More refined texts were keen to break into the bedroom and listen to women's conversation, too: the grammarian Claude Favre de Vaugelas's magisterial *Remarques sur la langue française* of 1647 formed some of his reflections on the ideal French speech by hearing the spirited conversations of women in the *salons*, the influential and innovative social institutions of the period. Women's conversational abilities and practices were scrutinized by all who observed them, and those women who could best play the game could adroitly manage their reputation through the deployment of verbal exchange.

The most prominent salon of the period was that of the marquise de Rambouillet, who had arranged her rooms for the express purpose of encouraging conversation, in a series of small spaces in which one could talk easily. She welcomed aristocrats but also writers and other cultural figures, and the conversations that she fostered and directed were central to cultural and political innovation throughout the midcentury: the chief minister, Richelieu, was so concerned about the salon's political significance that he tried to recruit the marquise as a spy.

Lafayette was a regular at the Rambouillet salon, as were writers such as the playwright Pierre Corneille and the novelist Madeleine de Scudéry, whose romance *Clélie* mapped the emotions of the midcentury and who later in life would also publish a series of conversations purportedly stemming from her own salon. The favorites gathered in the marquise's best blue bedroom, the famous *chambre bleue*—a space made for entertaining visitors—and especially in the space between the daybed and the wall, known as the *ruelle*, or "alleyway." Out of these spaces arose much of the literary production of the century, much of it specifically drawing on the figure or form of conversation, as in the dialogic exchanges of *Clélie* or Lafayette's own novelistic attention to conversations promised, overheard, and betrayed. The salons established that the best conversation arose from certain spatial configurations and that people who wanted to know what was happening needed to listen in to women talking. This was a private space with a public significance, directed by a woman.

The lure of women's conversation made itself felt in all kinds of writing during this period. In 1655, a text devoted to eavesdropping (if far removed from the deeply restrained anxieties of Lafayette) for-ever changed the erotic landscape of France. This was the anonymous dialogue *L'école des filles*, soon made available in translation in Resto-ration England, a society avid for such French titillation (Samuel Pepys recounts his reading of it with mingled shame and pleasure). The *Ecole* lets the reader eavesdrop on an extraordinarily intimate conversation between two young women discovering sexual pleasure and intent on fulfillment. Where the *Princesse de Clèves* gives us the conversation of aristocrats, the *Ecole* is resolutely a tale of bourgeois women, but we know it was consumed with as much fervor in court as in town—when in 1687 it was discovered in the room of the ladies who attended to the daughter-in-law of Louis XIV, it caused a great scandal.

This text was certainly written by a man—two men were charged with obscenity for its publication—but it presents men as inarticulate fools and women as skillful verbal strategists. The naive Fanchon is instructed in sexual pleasure by her older cousin Suzanne, and the two of them set out what one needs to know in order to progress in physical pleasure. But in this text, sex cannot be separated from speech: in order to have good sex, one must take up a whole new style of conversation. Fanchon, an eager student, learns important new vo-cabulary with alacrity, and the quick-witted pair of young women mock men's inability to speak articulately during sex, laughing at the ways men yell out without any verbal capacity at all.

The *Ecole* suggests a cultural fascination with and anxiety about what it is that women get up to when they talk among themselves, and about women's abilities to deploy speech to such effective ends. The same anxiety can be seen in the mocking satires of salon conver-sation, like Molière's comedy *Les précieuses ridicules* (*The Pretentious Young Ladies*, 1659) and Antoine Baudeau de Somaize's faux-dictionary of salon speech, *Le grand dictionnaire des précieuses* (1660), both of which tongue-in-cheek texts peddled the notion that salon women used particular and outlandish language, and which encouraged the reading public to ape such vocabulary dismissively. Small wonder, then, that women writers like Lafayette might be particularly concerned to trace the downside of this eavesdropping culture. In giving us a world in which women are worried that their conversations might be overheard, *La Princesse de Clèves* seems to reflect sadly on the cultural obsession with listening in.

Lafayette's reflections on women's private conversation and its pitfalls stage a defense of conversation as what has been called "feminist pedagogy." The novel revolves around a series of digressions that frequently baffle the modern reader. Just as the plot seems to advance tentatively, suddenly it pauses for a character to tell the princess (and by extension the reader) a lengthy historical story, which often seems surprisingly irrelevant to the love story that we today regard as the central business of the text.

These digressions derive from earlier forms of prose fiction, like the romance, which featured multiple storytellers and strange inserted tales that could be imagined as set-pieces but also reflected on the central concerns of the text. Here, even in Lafayette's terser form of fiction, the digression serves a similar purpose, but it is more tautly staged: the princess is told a story she needs to know in order to navigate the court. For as her austere mother puts it, "If you judge by appearances in this place, you will frequently be deceived; what you see is almost never the truth." To know what's what when one arrives in a new place, one must know one's history, and that history is transmitted through conversation, chiefly through conversation between women and about women. So the princess learns from the example of Diane de Poitiers, the mistress of Henri II, whose exceptional political power derives from her intimacy with the king, and in counterpart she also heeds the story of Anne Boleyn, a figure of loathing in Catholic France, whose unfortunate end suggests that the power derived from sexual politicking might not be durable or peaceful. If we judged on appearances, these tales would look like narrative detours. But the painful examples they present will be central to the princess's decision making and thus to the ending of the novel. If the princess retreats from Nemours and from the reader at the close of the text, it is because she does not wish to become a moral tale that could be circulated to future young ladies who need to learn the ways of the court.

The interest in overhearing women's conversation plays out somewhat differently in a genre that appeared at the end of the century:

the fairy tale. A 1677 letter by Madame de Sévigné, an eloquently gossipy aristocrat who is the source for so much of what we know about the seventeenth-century court, tells us that by that date, fairy tales were already told in court circles; they were also told in salons in town, such as that of the marquise de Lambert. The fairy tales that began to appear in printed collections (Charles Perrault, *Contes en vers*, 1695; *Histoires ou contes du temps passé avec des moralités*, 1697; Marie-Catherine d'Aulnoy, *Les contes des fées*, 1697) were perhaps already familiar from oral traditions, but the printed versions made sly intertextual references to other editions: the palace of a charming cat princess in one of d'Aulnoy's tales, for example, has murals showing scenes from "Le chat botté," one of the fairy tales of Charles Perrault. The fairy tale was both an old genre, drawing on a long tradition of female storytellers, and a new one: the term *conte de fée* enters into the language in 1698, the same year that d'Aulnoy's multivolume *Contes nouveaux ou les fées à la mode*, a collection insisting on the new and fashionable status of these tales, was published.

Like the novel, the new genre of the fairy tale was in large part the work of women: not just d'Aulnoy, but also Marie-Jeanne L'Héritier de Villandon and Catherine Bernard. When men published such collections, they worked hard to figure old traditions of female orality in their text: the frontispieces of Charles Perrault's tales featured engravings of Mother Goose characters, decrepit peasant ladies telling tales by the fire, sometimes to entranced listeners whose flamboyant bonnets give them away as members of the court.

Although fairy tales were read avidly, literary critics for the most part steered well clear of the new genre, probably, as Lewis Seifert suggests, because they did not want to elevate it by taking it seriously. But in many ways the seemingly lighthearted fairy tale plays intelligently with literary tropes and philosophical discussions of the most serious kind: the repeated scenes of recognition in which characters recognize, for example, that a cat is really a princess recall Aristotle's discussion of anagnorisis—the moment of transition from ignorance to knowledge—in the *Poetics*, a text central to the most highbrow discussions of tragedy in the seventeenth century. The strange, speaking animals of the fairy tales also recall the seventeenth century's persistent debates about the question of human rationality (most famously that of René Descartes), since they often seem smarter and more thoughtful than the rather doltish humans who surround them, capable of thinking as a human and as an animal all at once: d'Aulnoy's charming white cat serves her courtiers rat stew, but recognizes this might trouble her princely guest so also provides more traditionally human fare for him.

Fairy tales evinced a knowing, courtly nostalgia for fireside tales, allowing courtly readers to recall a collective past they probably never knew. Often they also gestured toward an earlier moment of the court itself. By the late seventeenth century, Louis XIV was elderly. Under the influence of his pious wife, Madame de Maintenon, the court had become deeply conservative; the luxurious and playful aesthetic of Louis's younger years, when the court first moved to Versailles, was long gone, and political optimism had been replaced by gloom. The often hyperbolic descriptions of courtly interiors found in the fairy tales—mirrored walls, porcelain palaces, color, and comfort—nod to an earlier courtly culture that flourished when the marquise de Montespan, Louis's official mistress, set the pleasure-seeking tone for the court in the 1670s.

But by the 1690s, the austerely ultra-Catholic *dévot*, or "pious," culture praised women only in their role as virtuous mothers; as Seifert describes, the fairy tale became a key text in the debates about the proper role of women, offering us characters ranging from Perrault's renewal of the Patient Griseldis, praised for her obedience to her husband, to d'Aulnoy's witty and vigorous White Cat, who governs alone and runs circles around male cats and men alike.

Other stories of the late seventeenth century also uphold worldly pleasure-seeking against the newer and more restrictive gender roles. The writing of the *mondains*, or "worldly figures," showcases all things new and magical. *Mondain* writers shunned the restrictive aesthetic of *vraisemblance* that had held earlier literary forms like tragedy and novels such as *La Princesse de Clèves* hostage and embraced with delight all that was improbable, crazy, and pleasurable. Take the strange "Histoire de la Marquise-Marquis de Banneville," a story traditionally credited to the cross-dressing ambassadorial abbé de Choisy, but possibly coauthored by Marie-Jeanne L'Héritier de Villandon and Charles Perrault, both authors known for their collections of fairy tales.

First published in 1695 in the newspaper *Mercure Galant* (the same paper that had brokered debate around *La Princesse de Clèves*), the text tells the tale of a boy whose mother brings him up as a girl so he can stay home from war. When the little marquise is brought to Paris, she is celebrated everywhere for her beauty and playfulness; eventually she meets a young man and longs to marry him, which makes her mother rather nervous. We await the revelation of bodily truth. The end of the story brings a strange and delightful twist on the trope of recognition. In their marriage bed, in the dark, the two young people reach for one another and discover that each is not as they had imagined: the wife who is really a man is thrilled to discover that her new husband is a biological woman. Each decides to stay within his and her adopted gender identities, and at the end of the story we are told that a child is on the way. On the one hand, the tale of recognition and resolution looks conventional and heteronormative—a man and a woman marry, a child is born—but its surprising variant on a familiar narrative also prompts us to question conventional appearances.

The reader who had learned from *La Princesse de Clèves* that appearances at court can be deceiving might find one particular kind of moral in this text. But the story of the marquise also encourages its readers to revel in the play of appearances: the authors take pains to note just where the marquise shopped for diamond earrings and how her skillful application of cosmetics set off her particular beauty in just the right way. This is a genre that delights in artifice and in all it can offer us. In doing so, it too casts a nostalgic glance to earlier days of courtly behavior: the marquise and her girlfriend bemoan the fact that girls nowadays have to do so much of the flirtatious work themselves, and do not receive the same attention from men that their mothers would have decades before. Women today, they sigh, no longer receive the same attentions from men: the little cares, the kindnesses. The characters are mourning a lost culture of *galanterie*, the highly coded practices of flirtatious behavior that had governed relations between men and women earlier in the century. But they do so by drawing on the terms Madeleine de Scudéry had used in setting out her *Carte de Tendre*, the map of tenderness. One novel's conversation inspires another.

The centrality of conversation to this burgeoning of prose fiction in the seventeenth century points to the appropriative flexibility of these new genres: borrowing from oral traditions and salon games, writers—especially female writers—crafted a market for literature that was both titillating and educational, and in so doing positioned themselves as authors about whom people at court and in the city and even other fictional characters could not stop talking.

Works Cited and Recommended Further Reading

French editions: Madame de Lafayette, *La Princesse de Clèves*, ed. Bernard Pingaud (Paris: Gallimard, 2000); Honoré d'Urfé, *L'Astrée, première partie*, ed. Delphine Denis (Paris: Champion Classiques, 2011); Madeleine de Scudéry, *Clélie*, ed. Delphine Denis (Paris: Gallimard, 2006); anonymous, *Recueil général des Caquets de l'accouchée*, ed. Georges Bourgeuil (Albi: Passage du Nord-Ouest, 2012); anonymous, *L'école des filles ou la philosophie des dames* (Paris: Allia, 2012); Marie-Catherine d'Aulnoy, *Les contes de fées*, ed. Constance Cagnat-Duboeuf (Paris: Gallimard, 2008); and François-Timoléon de Choisy, Marie-Jeanne L'Héritier, and Charles Perrault, "Histoire de la Marquise-Marquise de Banneville," ed. Joan DeJean (New York: MLA Texts and Translations, 2004).

The most useful English translation of Lafayette's court novels (and the one that I have used here for quotations from *La Princesse de Clèves*) is *The Princess of Cleves, The Princess of Montpensier, The Countess of Tende*, trans. Terence Cave, Oxford World's Classics (Oxford: Oxford University Press, 2008). For translations of other texts mentioned, see Honoré d'Urfé, *Astrea*, trans. Steven Rendell (Binghamton, NY: Medieval and Renaissance Texts and Studies, 1995); Marie-Catherine d'Aulnoy, *The Tales of the Fairies, Compleat* (New York: Garland, 1977); and François-Timoléon de Choisy, Marie-Jeanne L'Héritier, and Charles Perrault, "The Story of the Marquise-Marquis de Banneville," trans. Steven Rendell (New York: MLA Texts and Translations, 2004).

A thorough account of seventeenth-century conversation and its significance for women writers can be found in Elizabeth Goldsmith, *Exclusive Conversations: The Art of Interaction in Seventeenth-Century France* (Philadel-

phia: University of Pennsylvania Press, 1988). On salon culture and its significance, see especially Faith Beasley, *Salons, History and the Creation of
Seventeenth-Century France* (Farnham, UK: Ashgate, 2006). On women and
the seventeenth-century novel more broadly, see Joan DeJean, *Tender Geographies: Women and the Origins of the Novel in France* (New York: Columbia
University Press, 1993). On the question of the princess's plausibility, see
especially Nancy K. Miller, "Emphasis Added: Plots and Plausibilities in
Women's Fiction," *PMLA* 96, no. 1 (1981). On the strangeness of Lafayette's
novel and its status in literary history, see Nicholas Paige, "Lafayette's Impossible Princess: On (Not) Making Literary History," *PMLA* 125, no. 4
(2010). On fairy tales, see especially Lewis Seifert, *Fairy Tales, Sexuality, and
Gender in France, 1690–1715: Nostalgic Utopias* (Cambridge: Cambridge University Press, 1996); on the marquise-marquis, see also Seifert, *Manning the
Margins: Masculinity and Writing in Seventeenth-Century France* (Ann Arbor:
University of Michigan Press, 2009).

From Moralists to Libertines

ERIC MÉCHOULAN

The French seventeenth century has often been labeled, in admiring tones, "the century of moralists." In a widely known study, Paul Bénichou even claimed, "if today we still consider the classical centuries great, it is because in those centuries a moral philosophy developed that gave humanity a true sense of its own value." Yet at the same time, the seventeenth century also saw the emergence of what was to be called "libertinage" (also known as "freethinking"), a movement that questioned—and, in the eyes of some, cynically undermined—the very basis of moral and religious belief. Moralists and libertines—a strange pairing of apparent opposites. And yet the pair belong together as siblings in a new literary family. Together they initiated new forms of thought and writing that embodied a largely secular outlook on the major questions of human nature and the moral life and that are also intended for a lay, as well as an erudite, reader. Ancient forms such as the fable, fairy tale, dialogue, aphorism, or "characters" are adapted and transformed to essentially "modern" purposes, while new ones, such as the portrait, maxim, letters, short stories, travel writings, and utopias, were increasingly favored by a rapidly expanding reading public. The rise of moralist and libertine writing is directly linked to the spread of literacy in the seventeenth century and fueled a growing taste for texts on practical ways of life as well as for fictional representations.

It was natural that, in a Christian environment, freethinkers and libertine writers would be viewed with suspicion as subversive. But, as Nietzsche (a great admirer of the moralists) was later to propose, this was also the case with "moralists." He claimed (in *The Will to Power*) that the moralist was the opposite of a "preacher" and was rather someone who sees "morality" as suspect, open to skeptical inspection, and who thereby becomes himself suspect. By the beginning of the eighteenth century, the word *moraliste* entered the French language, and a celebrated trio of moralists was established: La Rochefoucauld, Pascal, and La Bruyère, whose perspectives, styles, and references are nevertheless very different from each other. La Rochefoucauld belonged to the highest nobility, and his *Maximes* are devoted to disclosing and anatomizing the hidden dynamic of the "vices" that underlie people's actions and attitudes. Pascal, the son of a lawyer and tax assessor, inventor of a sophisticated computing machine, designer of a public transportation system in Paris, physicist, and mathematician, was also a fascinating theological controversialist who advocated a more rigorous faith in God and showed the paradoxical behavior human beings display in the world when caught between the richness of thought and the poverty of greed. La Bruyère, born in a Parisian middle-class family, was called to the bar; became the secretary of the prince de Condé, a prominent nobleman; and demonstrated in his *Caractères* an ability to decipher the social absurdities and individual obsessions concealed in the most everyday forms of behavior.

It is harder to say exactly who the libertines were: this was above all a polemical category, which therefore needs to be used with care. In the seventeenth century, Montaigne was sometimes considered to be one of the first libertine writers, because of his tone, his way of showing off his ego, and his use of skepticism or even Epicureanism. But it was with the denunciations of freethinking and sodomy in the 1620s, and the trial of the courtly poet Théophile de Viau for atheism and homosexuality that the category of "libertinage" really came into use. This was part of a Catholic Counter-Reformation strategic tactic to link sodomy and atheism. Epicurean and skeptic philosophies fueled new ways of thinking. For example, Cyrano de Bergerac (1619–59) is one of the more challenging and inventive authors cited as an example of freethinking. He received a good education in Paris, was a soldier during the Thirty Years' War, and was part of Gassendi's circle (Gassendi's ambition was to reconcile Epicurean naturalism with Christian principles). Cyrano tried to pursue a career as dramatist and novelist. His contemporary, La Fontaine (1621–95), who wrote fables and short stories, was perceived as both a moralist and a libertine writer, but he was obliged to officially repudiate his licentious stories in order to secure his later election to the Académie française. Coming from a good middle-class provincial family, he took over his father's government position and became a successful man of letters in Parisian aristocratic circles.

Libertines dealt with excesses, be they sexual or skeptical. And contrary to the legend of classicism (which is supposed to promote a sense of haughty balance), moralists also dealt with excesses in a manner that was itself often excessive and certainly radical. (That is probably what charmed Nietzsche.) The moralists did not simply denounce particular and personal lifestyles; they investigated the common habits of human beings. More precisely, they tracked the multiple social stances that excessive self-love can take. *Amour-propre* is the founding category and the central focus of both moralist and libertine thought in the seventeenth century, and its analysis crucially involves a notion of excess, a human self that, in the expression of its interests, passions, and vices, disrupts and overflows itself.[1]

This new focus on the self involved a kind of early modern Copernican revolution: God was no longer imagined as being at the center of the universe, and instead every human being began to feel himself or herself to be the real center. So the doctrine of original sin was revisited and revised: it came to define a space punctuated with objects of a vain and self-centered desire, around which we propel ourselves in obedience to our passions, looking for more possession of goods or greater domination over people. Having lost confidence in the traditional theocentric cosmology, the modern world looked as if perpetually dislodged from its axis. This displacement is what the libertine writer, Cyrano de Bergerac enacts when his hero travels to the moon and discovers speaking birds who think of the earth as their moon. Not only is outer space the only place for freethinkers. In addition, everything is inscribed in a system of relativity. In sending his hero to the moon, Cyrano gives him the same kind of distant and literally detached position from the human world.

The scientific fantasy of a trip to the moon is also a moral discovery of a new vantage point from which we can look at human ways of being. The correct calculus begins to be of paramount importance. When La Fontaine attacks superstition, he also values sense perception as analyzed by reason. The fable "An Animal in the Moon" shows, for example, how to control accuracy in sense perception:

Mais aussi si l'on rectifie
L'image de l'objet sur son éloignement,
Sur le milieu qui l'environne,
Sur l'organe et sur l'instrument,
Les sens ne tromperont personne.

(One rectifies the image of an object according to its distance /
to the medium that surrounds it / to the organ and the
instrument.)

Moralists consider the world as a theater: from a distance that is sufficiently great to allow detachment, they observe a scene in which
different social groups interact, in competitive fashion, driven sometimes by imitation, sometimes by rejection. So they have to investigate what it is that fundamentally moves people.

The view according to which human beings are driven by the
search for their individual pleasures was in fact a view shared by libertine writers and moralists alike. With Pascal's *De l'esprit géométrique*,
however, it is taken in a very particular direction: as yet one more
proof of human frailty manifested by the lack of any stability in one's
own pleasures. Pleasures are different for everyone and vary within
each person—so diverse indeed that persons are as different from
themselves at different periods as they are from other people.

In the general quest for a stability that should theoretically come
from the fact of possession or domination, self-love plays a game of
hide-and-seek: it cannot show too much of itself, but at the same time
it definitely needs to be acknowledged and admired: as La Rochefoucauld puts it, "Self-love is the greatest of all flatterers" or "Self-love is
subtler than the subtlest man of the world." In this way, the "self"
acquires a new autonomy. Moralists tell, and libertines advocate, the
story of the self's autonomous actions, its perilous adventures in the
mobile world. These writers do not define good and evil; instead,
they question how those terms are understood and defined. They
posit a program of knowledge based on the operations of autonomous reason in interpreting human experience. Cartesianism made
human consciousness the ground of knowledge: the moralists and
libertines explore the nature of that ground.

Previously, moral doctrine was closely linked to theological and political power, which prescribed manners and behaviors for anybody who wanted to appear as a "good" man or woman. Yet, with the advent of Europe's civil and religious wars in the sixteenth century, action in the name of moral "conscience" became a source of conflict and massacre rather than of peace and social harmony; hence, morality could no longer be sustained by specific religious or traditional communities. Before the Renaissance, morality rested on Christian beliefs, but from the Renaissance onward, in order to be a good Christian, belief on its own was insufficient; behavior, the display of moral conduct became paramount. In the seventeenth century, however, moral discourse shifted from fastidious prescription of rules to a form of deconstructing description; it offered ways of reading appearances rather than the prescribing of forms of behavior. The writer Saint-Evremond, who could himself be considered a moralist, compares the two great dramatists, Corneille and Racine. According to Saint-Evremond, Corneille depicts people as they should be, and Racine as they are: this reflects the shift from prescriptive education to critical anatomy. In the last edition of his *Maxims*, La Rochefoucauld chooses to begin with a bitter denunciation: "Our virtues are nothing but vices in disguise." The form of the inaugural maxim itself is quite telling: "nothing but" reflects, in exemplary fashion, by the force its own example, the required movement of thought. The reader needs to experience this reductive movement from the exterior carapace of apparent virtues to what lies beneath it: the pulpy mass of vices. The "nothing but" invites and performs a stripping away of the "disguise," the mask that enables humans to think of themselves as virtuous beings.

Increased social mobility had also encouraged some to step out of inherited roles, leading to a redefinition of the individual: less "Who am I?" than "Who could I become?" Vices and virtues that were supposed to be firmly opposed began to look like the results of a personal or social dynamic. As Pascal would to put it, "We do not keep ourselves virtuous by our own power, but by the counterbalance of two opposing vices, just as we stay upright between two contrary winds. Take one of these vices away and we fall into the other."

There was a literary correlative to these new kinds of interest in the human self. Treatises inspired by philosophers such as Aristotle or theologians such as Thomas of Aquinas were gradually replaced by a diversity of genres no longer subject to the authority of scholars: maxims, portraits, short essays, fairy tales, fables, letters written by men and women sharing the pleasures of society. Another difference consisted in the moralists' interest in the small truths (and illusions) of living instead of the great truth of Life, in everyday sensible questions more than in a metaphysical search for the underlying logic of reasoning. Historians of print culture have shown how the rise of books devoted to urbane moral doctrine took place at the expense of scholarly treatises in the second half of the seventeenth century. Instead of long and elaborate dissertations full of quotations and references, readers turned to short forms, without reverence for previous authorities. This in turn instituted a new type of cultural "authority," which was shared by both moralists and libertines; even erudition was now at the service of polite society and urbane circles.

For such a society, it was not enough to perform one's moral duty. One had to take pleasure in the very exercise of virtue: politeness was a social skill that made the virtues enjoyable. This engendered a *social utility of pleasure*, which would eventually permit the elaboration of what the eighteenth century would call "aesthetics." It has sometimes been said that after the sixteenth century, an "aestheticizing" of social conduct increasingly prized grace, elegance, and style as the defining elements of social behavior, as can be seen in the various seventeenth-century treatises on civility (Faret's *L'honnête homme*, 1630, or Courtin's *Nouveau traité de la civilité*, 1671). But the formula needs to be reversed: what would eventually be named "aesthetics" was, in the early modern period, shaped by the moral code of apparent disinterestedness and the social pleasure of politeness. In other words, it is important to understand the relation of the seventeenth century to what followed, that what was later to be called "aesthetic" was determined by the social, and not the other way round. The relevant code involved a kind of theatricalized stylistics of behavior designed to avoid blind submission to the power of self-interest: sometimes it can even take the shape of disinterestedness. "Self-interest speaks all manner of tongues and plays all manner of parts, even that of disinterestedness," writes La Rochefoucauld. It is a question of social position and behavior: we can use our self-love if we know ourselves well enough to behave properly according to our social standing and that of the persons we are meeting, and thereby to make a good impression on others. The *expression* of my self must make the right *impression* on others: they are both elements of a kind of "social physics."

If everyone is motivated only by self-interest and self-love, how is it still possible to live together? There are of course reciprocal needs. But that would not be enough to convince people who are always limited and constrained by all the other persons' interests. According to moralists and libertine writers, there are two operations that allow for the constitution of a "community": illusions about oneself, and the power of imagination. The kind of self-knowledge that, according to Descartes, was supposed to anchor our relation to the world is dismantled and even destroyed beyond repair by self-flattery and self-deception. As the author of tales of animality, La Fontaine could argue in favor of the existence of souls of animals against the division Descartes introduced between animal machines and human thought. This is a way of returning humans back to their animal nature, but also of depriving them of the illusory glory of their assumed superiority. Human consciousness is both necessary and inaccessible, as La Rochefoucauld claims in the maxim that headed the first edition of his book: "Self-love: we cannot sound the depths or pierce the darkness of its chasms. . . . There it is often invisible to itself." In order to preserve our interests, we need to disguise ourselves; but "we are so used to disguising ourselves from others that we end by disguising ourselves from ourselves." Pascal puts it even more bluntly: in order not to see what seems annoying, "we agreeably gouge out our own eyes," and he adds further on: "We are nothing but lies, duplicity, contradiction, and we hide and disguise ourselves from ourselves."

La Bruyère portrays people so obsessed with their *idées fixes* that they simply do not notice around them the disgust, contempt, and rejection of others. For example, in *Les caractères*, he writes: "Gnathon lives for no one but himself, and the rest of the world are to him as if they did not exist. He is not satisfied with occupying the best seat at table, but he must take the seats of two other guests, and forgets that the dinner was not provided for him alone, but for the company as well. . . . At table his hands serve for a knife and fork; he paws the meat over and over again, and tears it to pieces, so that if the other guests wish to dine, it must be on his leavings. He does not spare them any of those filthy and disgusting habits which are enough to spoil the appetite of the most hungry; the gravy and sauce run over his chin and beard; if he takes part of a stew out of a dish, he spills it by the way over another dish and on the cloth, so you may distinguish him by his track."

We can also run into the opposite obsession: people are so eager to be admired that they are ready to act, for example, as cowards if it means that they are in fact considered courageous, or even to lose their lives in order to live more completely in other people's memory: "We even die gladly provided people talk about it," Pascal claims. It means that everyone behaves according to reputation and flattery, like the crow that the fox fawns over in order to get to the cheese in La Fontaine's famous fable. In this way of understanding the world, people are so keen on reputation that they feel and think according to collective constructions; hence, for instance, "some people would have never fallen in love if they had never heard of love." This implies that self-interest opens up two contradictory paths: we deal only with our own pleasure as if nobody else really exists, or we find our own pleasure in recognition by others. This second path creates the possibility of reciprocal bonds: "Self-interest, blamed for all our misdeeds, often deserves credit for our good actions."

Moralists disclose the fundamental contradiction of human beings: infatuated with one self, everyone desires to enforce an absolute power on others, but no self can really dispense with other people. Therefore, the establishment of a social and political order is necessary in order to adjust the disorder generated by original sin (but not address its root and real cause). In loving oneself with that infinite love that was destined only for God, human beings do not love anybody else. Yet self-love forges links between us in spite of our mutual hostility: we do not love other people because they are naturally loveable, we love other people *so that* they love us. Meanwhile, everyone has an interest in constituting a civil society that can work despite inequalities, since everyone is so vain as to enjoy even the slightest form of recognition and glory: "Such is our vanity that the good opinion of half a dozen of the people around us gives us pleasure and satisfaction."

This leads Pascal and the moralists to attribute a fundamental psychological and social energy to imagination: "Imagination decides everything: it creates beauty, justice and happiness, which is the world's supreme good." Imagination fools reason, but it is also able to provide illusory satisfactions. Since an imaginary satisfaction is still a satisfaction, people at once enjoy it and yet blind themselves with its pitiful outcome. "The bonds securing men's mutual respect . . . are bonds of imagination." For these writers, imagination is granted a special standing among the human faculties. It means that it is also a way, for Pascal, to persuade people. He appeals to his readers' imaginations with fictive experiences that constitute analogical examples on which to meditate: "Put it to the test: leave a king entirely alone . . . with complete leisure to think about himself, and you will see that a king without diversion is a very wretched man." Just as Pascal the physicist proved the existence of a vacuum by testing the atmospheric pressure at the bottom and at the top of a mountain, Pascal the moralist shows the presence of the human void in evaluating the social pressure at the top and at the lowest point of diversion.

Cyrano de Bergerac wrote one of the first great science-fiction novels, a demonstration of his own powers of imagination. He actually insists himself on the power of imagination in one episode that presents an allegory: the narrator discovers that a tree of gold, emeralds, and pearls under which he was resting produces, as a fruit, a little man who tells him that he is a king and that the tree is composed of his people. And to prove it on the spot, the tree falls apart into little dancing men around him. Then the king and his people dance together so that "the dancers became confused with a much more rapid and more imperceptible motions; it seemed that the object of the ballet was to represent an enormous giant; for as they drew nearer each other and redoubled the swiftness of their movement they became so closely mingled that I perceived nothing but a great, open and almost transparent colossus. . . . The most agile of our little dancers leaped up with a flourish to the height and into the position needed to form a head, others hotter and not so loose formed the heart; and others much heavier only supplied the bones, the flesh and the plumpness." Who are these little people who can form a complete body? Cyrano plays on what Descartes called "esprits animaux": the little king claims that they are spirits, but not at all immaterial, they are animals just as human beings are animals. He also plays with the very idea of the *body politic*, as in Hobbes's *Leviathan* frontispiece, where the sovereign's body is composed of all his people. Who are these *esprits animaux*? Since they were born in the sun, explains the king, "where the principle of matter is action, our imagination is necessarily much more active than that of the inhabitants of the opaque regions and the substance of our bodies is also much finer. Granted this, it inevitably follows that since our imagination meets no obstacle in the matter as it desires and since it is mistress of our whole mass, it causes this mass to pass, by moving all its particles, into the order necessary to create on a large scale the thing it has formed in little." In the libertine way of thinking, the relation between being and appearance, between body and soul, deals with imagination and the speed it confers on matter. There is no stability of being, but only operations of provisory stabilization. We could say the same with the notion of "self": the self characterizes what I think of as "me," but its definition and its recognition depends on others. This is why reputation matters so much to us: we live in the mirror of others; we exist as an image in the imagination of others.

Various short forms of writing (maxims, characters, fables, portraits) exemplify this kind of operation. It is largely here—in the formal varieties of brevity—that we can locate the importance of the moralists for a history of modern French literature. Differences of perspective are proffered in these fragments of thought. It is even possible, from one fragment to the other, to offer contradictory principles. La Fontaine provides a good example of this fluid, contradictory dialectic. In his dedicatory epistle to the king's son, La Fontaine emphasizes the power of language and, relatedly, the central issue of his own writing as ethical in nature:

> Je chante les héros dont Ésope est le père,
> Troupe de qui l'histoire, encore que mensongère,
> Contient des verites qui servent de leçons.
> Tout parle en mon ouvrage, et même les poisons.
> Ce qu'ils dissent s'adresse à tous tant que nous sommes.
> Je me sers d'animaux pour instruire les hommes.

(I sing those heroes, Aesop's progeny, / Whose tales, fictitious
though indeed they be, / Contain much truth. Herein,
endowed with speech— / Even the fish!—will all my creatures
teach / With human voice; for animals I choose / To proffer
lessons that we all might use.)

Yet there is perceptible irony in the way La Fontaine plays with
both the legacy of the ancients and the conventions of the authoritative voice. Speaking animals (even the obvious dumb ones, like fish)
are able to give moral lessons, as natural history can be both full of
lies and full of truths. Yet some of the fables show how bad it is to
speak. Language is a malediction for the crow or the tortoise, because
for them speech is above all a matter of vainglory: "She'd have done
better/ To go her ways without speaking. . . . Imprudence, vanity and
babble have all the same paternity" ("The Tortoise and the Two
Ducks"). Or in "The Arbitrator, the Hospital Visitor, and the Hermit," despite the witty jests, communication is deceptive and even
fatal: "It is good to talk, and better to keep quiet." The fable as a literary genre lends itself to this kind of instability of perspective, and is
very much part of its point for La Fontaine; it is what above all makes
his use of this ancient form seem modern.

Very often, such writing stages a problematization of the self insofar as the question of the "self" implicates language as well. Cyrano's
narrator speaks directly to the readers: it is one of the first novels to
use a first-person narrator. Nevertheless, since the story narrates a
reversal of perspective, the speaking "I" is itself put into question,
rendered incorrigibly unstable. The moralists also acknowledged the
power of imagination, for creating the possibility of a point of view
that is both from above and from inside. But the moralists themselves
also belong to the very community they are describing from an apparently exterior position; they are inside as well as above, the Olym-
pian position thus relativized to a purely human scale; this is part of
the recognition of what it is to be "modern," constrained, fragile, and
contingent. As Pascal puts it in respect to the freethinker who imagines he could be unconditionally free to think what he, by himself,
wants to think: "we are embarked" in the world. For him, all human
beings are in a boat that drifts them through the social tempests to an

ineluctable and fatal wreckage—if they do not wake up and consider the necessity of a God.

Such a position is also emphasized by La Fontaine at the end of his fable "The Power of Fables." Despite its social illegitimacy, the power of diversion of the fable reveals a useful political power:

> A ce reproche l'assemblée,
> Par l'apologue reveille,
> Se donne entière à l'Orateur:
> un trait de fable en eut l'honneur.
> Nous sommes tous d'Athènes en ce point, et moi-même
> Au moment que je fais cette moralité,
> Si Peau d'âne m'était conté,
> J'y prendrais un plaisir extreme.
> Le monde est vieux, dit-on, je le crois; cependant,
> Il le faut amuser encore comme un enfant.

> (Chastened, the popular, agog, is wakened by his apologue:
> His lowly fable sets them all abuzz.
> In this, we are Athenians, all of us.
> And if, even as I am writing thus,
> "The Ass's skin," this very minute
> Were told me, I should revel in it.
> Though old our world, however one construes us,
> Still, often, like a child must one amuse us.)

We are Athenians all, but now stripped of the dignity of the citizen of the Athenian polis, driven back regressively, via the exposure of frailty and vulnerability, to the condition of childish behaviors. It is a vision both comic and bleak of what it is to be human. At the same time, notwithstanding this belittling of human beings, the power accorded to imagination seems to have resulted in a remarkable invention of forms of writing. That is why ancient forms receive new impetus and development, while new ones were increasingly favored by a growing reading public. They fueled the taste of a larger reading public for writing on practical ways of life as well as for fictional representations.

In questioning traditional social structures and imagining new models of behavior, they launched a program of investigation that would be taken further by the writers of the Enlightenment. They also assigned a new, largely social, function to "literature": literature was now seen as a social means of shaping individual and collective life stories. The ancient question of how to live had become the question for literature, not only to ask but also to answer, model, and regulate.

There was however one great exception, or complicating case: Blaise Pascal. Pascal wrote neither to make a career, nor for pleasure. His appearance in the public sphere was motivated primarily by a sense of indignation. An angry man, Pascal raged against atheists, libertines, and even those whose faith in God was, in his opinion, too weak (Montaigne, for example, with his "me" displayed so conspicuously) or impertinent (Descartes, for example, whom he deemed "vague" and "useless"). His anger, however, was also directed against priests who upheld theological interpretations that he considered unacceptable (the Jesuit priests in particular). Although anger is counted among the human vices, indignation is nevertheless a necessary aspect of Christian behavior, at least insofar as it aims to correct those it criticizes. Indeed *saeva indignatio* (savage indignation) was a term of both ethics and rhetoric, and in its latter guise was often seen to underlie certain forms of literary writing, above all the genre of satire, of which Pascal would prove himself a major practitioner, crucially in the *Lettres provinciales*.[2] It is with this work that Pascal first entered the public sphere. He wanted to bring to the attention of a larger audience (one that was not restricted to theologians or priests) attacks that were being made against proponents of a strict interpretation of the Bible and the Church Fathers (particularly Saint Augustine). In doing so, Pascal came to the defense of Antoine Arnauld, who was at risk of being condemned by the theology faculty at the Sorbonne. Rather than compose a densely erudite treatise addressing debates on topics such as divine grace and the salvation of humankind, he wrote short epistles. These letters, published immediately after having been composed, one after another, treated laborious theological questions like divine grace or salvation in a clear and concise manner. Published anonymously, and without any mention of the publisher's name or the place where they were printed, the letters would later be collected in book form, under a false publisher's address. The police were never able to stop their printing and diffusion.

In order to elicit his reader's interest, Pascal feigned a position of ignorance in relation to these theological debates, the position of one seeking to inform himself of the views and arguments of the disputing parties, and sending the results to a friend living far from Paris (hence the complete title: *Lettres à un provincial de ses amis*, abridged as *Lettres provinciales*). In a sense, he invented the genre of investigative journalism, albeit a type of journalism that was concerned with transcendental questions. But it was of course more than simply an inquiry. It was a performance, animated by a ferocity of purpose contained and controlled by a scintillating irony, leading him to the conclusion that "these are disputes of theologians, not of theology."

These theological debates have lost much of their appeal today, but that is not in any case why we read the *Lettres provinciales*. We do so because they constitute a landmark in the history of French literature, specifically the history of French literary prose. The great French critic, Sainte-Beuve, claimed (controversially) that prose was the natural medium of French literature, and that Pascal was the greatest of its prose artists. Let us see how, for example, he stages the beginning of his third letter, after having shown us an answer from his provincial friend in which his correspondent refers to the public success of the first two letters and the praise they received from a member of the French Academy: "I have received your letter; and, at the same time, there was brought me a manuscript copy of the censure. I find that I am as well treated in the former, as M. Arnauld is ill-treated in the latter. I am afraid there is some extravagance in both cases, and that neither of us is sufficiently well known by our judges. Sure I am, that were we better known, M. Arnauld would merit the approval of the Sorbonne, and I the censure of the Academy. Thus our interests are quite a variance with each other. It is his interest to make himself known, to vindicate his innocence; whereas it is mine to remain in the dark, for fear of forfeiting my reputation." The elegant and witty binary plays on an inversion of values and social positions, where the author in an ironical demonstration of modesty actually stages Arnauld's innocence. Pascal does not play only the angry tune of the quarrel or the serious tone of theological inquiry, he also draws on a subtle and playful humor, and he captures his audience by this quick movement from one tone to the other. We see this at work when he publishes the supposed reply of his provincial friend, quoting a lady (probably Madeleine de Scudéry, a famous writer) and in so doing allowing himself a moment of self-publicity: "it is so very ingenious, and so nicely written. It narrates, and yet it is not a narrative; it clears up the most intricate and involved of all possible matters; its raillery is exquisite; it enlightens those who know little about the subject, and imparts double delight to those who understand it."

Pascal's letters successfully create a new reading public. But he does not simply smash his opponents by his sarcastic wit; rather, as a good man of science, he regularly gives rules of argumentation while he is making a point: for example, "I never quarrel about a term, provided that I am apprized of the sense in which it is understood," which permits him a moment later to say to the father he is interrogating: "this is merely playing with words, to say that you are agreed as to the common terms which you employ, while you differ with them as to the meaning of these terms." Or later, accused of scoffing at religious matters, he replies with a lesson on Christian and charitable mockery and its use by the Church Fathers. He gives a new fashion to the classical rhetorical use of *delectare* (pleasing) and *docere* (instructing), with the aim of *movere* (touching) the reading public in these serious theological and political issues.

The *Lettres* are also of note in that through them Pascal effectively invented a type of public intervention new to the period. In the seventeenth century, anyone who spoke publicly had to be authorized to do so. If one did not have the kind of social position that authorized a public voice, one was expected to speak only on behalf of a recognized body or institution. Under the cover of anonymity, Pascal asserted the contrary: "It is not very likely, standing as I do, alone, without power or any human defence against such a large body, and having no support but truth and integrity, that I would expose myself to lose everything by laying myself open to being convicted of imposture." Thus, he claimed to speak truth precisely because he was a lone voice, without institutional warrant. By contrast, the Jesuits formed a corporate body, exercised power, and were guilty of imposture. Pascal's claim, thus, is that of an engaged intellectual who, alone, did not hesitate to denounce the established powers. In France, the invention of this sort of public figure is generally understood to belong to Voltaire or even Zola, but it is clear that, structurally, Pascal was already on the way to "composing" such a figure. "Composing," literally, because Pascal's writing was indebted to manuscript files supplied by his friends, Antoine Arnauld and Pierre Nicole. In this sense, he was far from alone in his endeavors. However, it is important to recognize the originality of Pascal's writing posture, which serves to reinforce a posteriori a reading of his work as that of an engaged intellectual who was already integrated into the semiautonomous world of literature.

In the last years of his life (he was thirty-nine when he died, always having suffered from poor health), he collected a series of reflections ("thoughts") that were intended as an apologia for the Christian religion. So as to convince those who did not believe, or believed but with reservations, in God, he did not undertake to prove the existence of God nor to impress his readers with the beauty of the celestial machinery. In an innovative manner, he attempted to start from the standpoint of a strictly human anthropology, distanced from any transcendence, in order to better demonstrate its limitations. Thus he outlined a profoundly contradictory feature of human beings, seen both as the masters of the world thanks to their reason and as the slaves of their infinite desire for power and goods. His aim was to make others aware of these contradictions and thereby elicit a deeper interrogation in all with regard to their existence in the world and of themselves. Such a contradiction was supposed to be the proof of the remnants of their original nature and of their fall into a second and miserable nature. With such knowledge, perhaps it would be easier to turn to God. Pascal also used a very unusual mathematical argument, based on a probability calculus: if you wager that God does not exist, and you are right, you risk a finite life against nothing, but if you wager that God exists, and you win, you bet a finite life on earth against an infinite life in paradise. Since libertines are supposed to be rationalists, it is then their rational interest to wager that God exists.

In this way, he sketched a portrait of libertines and skeptics by strategically adopting their postures. By assuming their logic, he hoped to better convert their souls. However, their conversion did not depend solely on rationality. One cannot simply go from the order of reason to the order of charity and belief in God. This can only be accomplished by a radical leap enabled by divine grace. One can, however, prepare the ground rationally (by showing the logical contradictions and constant paradoxes that constitute our way of life) and understand that such a leap is necessary.

These many reflections were written on sheets of paper, some highly worked and well-written, others consisting of only brief notes in the register of the aphorism or the remark. Pascal himself gathered some of the reflections into bundles to which he gave names or headings (Vanity, Wretchedness, Boredom, Contradictions, etc.), or simply left them in disordered form, to be collected in a work still to come, according to a plan he explained in Port-Royal to a few of his friends. But he died before he was able to accomplish this.

In the seventeenth century, it was virtually inconceivable to value shapeless drafts to the point of making them public (it was not until Rousseau and especially Chateaubriand that this would become legitimate). The overall sense of organization that would form a work was its determining feature. But Blaise Pascal was an exception. His writings on mathematics and physics were shown very early on to be those of a child prodigy. His family's adoration of him and his friends' immense respect meant that his papers were fastidiously preserved, carefully recopied in the same state he had left them in. In the end, it was agreed that the reflections that seemed useful should be published, even if some needed to be rewritten. Antoine Arnauld (whom Pascal had helped defend) and Pierre Nicole (who also helped with this defense) agreed to take on this task. But it was impossible to turn it into a continuous text. Therefore, its fragmentary state was preserved under a general, vague title, *Pensées*, and the various elements were reclassified according to themes. This is how the fragments appeared in all editions until those that were published after the Second World War. In these later, modern editions of *Pensées*, the fragments were presented in the same order in which they had been originally copied, without modification, a presentation that was more legitimate from a philological point of view, in the sense of offering the material to be read as it had been originally written. At the same time, the compositional history does also raise the question of the spirit in which the modern reader is to read them as "fragments," given the new understandings and valuations of the fragment that arose as part of the legacy of Romantic thought and literature.

But there were two different copies made after Pascal's death, and editors today choose one or the other, which does not change the text itself but does change the order of presentation and the numbering of the fragments.

One could say that this is unimportant. But let us take one example of what it changes, where Pascal describes the origin of politics:

> The bonds securing men's mutual respect are generally bonds of necessity, for there must be differences of degree, since all men want to be on top and all cannot be, but some can.
>
> Imagine, then, that we can see them beginning to take shape. It is quite certain that men will fight until the stronger oppresses the weaker, and there is finally one party on top. But, once this has been settled, then the masters, who do not want the war to go on, ordain that the power which is in their hands shall pass down by whatever means they like; some entrust it to popular suffrage, others to hereditary succession, etc.
>
> And that is where imagination begins to play its part. Until then pure power did it, now it is power, maintained by imagination in a certain faction, in France the nobles, in Switzerland commoners, etc.
>
> So these bonds securing respect for a particular person are bonds of imagination. (Pascal, *Pensées*, 828)

The English translator follows here the numbering of Lafuma's edition, published in the 1960s. But the problem is that on the page left by Pascal, a few sentences were added at the end, after Pascal had drawn a line across the page. Lafuma and the English translator both assumed that this demarcated another fragment, giving it the number 829: "These great mental efforts on which the soul occasionally lights are not things on which it dwells; it only jumps there, for a moment, not for ever, as on the throne." In contrast, recent editors like Michel Le Guern, Philippe Sellier, and Gérard Ferreyrolles think that there is a kind of continuity between the fragments and keep them together. Sellier and Ferreyrolles show the little drawn line, Le Guern only a blank space. The choice matters.

It is striking that the fable of the origin of politics that Pascal imagines takes place without any reference to God, as if the destiny of humanity was played on a pure immanent ground, far from any transcendental plan or divine power. It is only a matter of "rapports de force," and following from that of illusion fueled by the imagination. Contrary to what apologists do, Pascal does not seem to put humanity's fate in God's hands. Once he makes the observation that men are drawn by their desire, and in particular by their desire for domination, everything else logically follows.

So it seems perfectly understandable that the first editors of Pascal's *Pensées* decided to keep only the last section as a separate fragment (what Lafuma called fragment 829), but put aside the first. It was only in the 1779 edition that the first section appeared, but placed very far away from the second section because of the classification of the text into different "themes." Lafuma, following the order of the first copy, moves them closer, but not together. It can seem difficult to see any continuity of thinking between the two. But the editorial decision makes it even more difficult. The choice of bringing them together opens up a new understanding of Pascal's work: the allusion to the "throne" still keeps a reference to the order of politics, while the enigmatic beginning points toward a specific operation of the soul. It is highly probable that what Pascal has in mind here is what grace can do: when human beings, by a great mental effort against their immediate desire for domination, humbly accept their state of misery, the light of divine grace can illuminate them. But grace can always recede, and it is difficult to be able to stay in its light.

Thus, if we adopt the philological insight into a continuity between the fragments, or even a possible jump symbolized by the little line drawn between the immanent order of domination and the transcendental illumination of grace, we can see how Pascal adopts a libertine perspective on politics, even more radical than the Hobbesian version of *homo homini lupus*, since, for Pascal, there is no rational calculus leading to a social contract, only *rapports de force* and blindness. But Pascal also offers us another line of thought, if we are able to forget our desire for domination. If we decide to read them as two different fragments, one on political order, the other on grace, we emphasize the impossible jump from politics to grace. A philological issue reveals here two different understandings of one crucial theological problem.

While the duc de La Rochefoucauld's 1665 work, *Réflexions ou sentences et maximes morales*, voluntarily assumed a fragmentary nature, the same cannot then be said of Pascal's project. But the huge success of Rochefoucauld's *Maximes* legitimated the fragmentary style that *Pensées*, as it appeared in public, would further develop. The publication of La Bruyère's *Caractères* in 1687 would definitively secure this fragmentary style within the pantheon of moral literature. It was from this point on that one could speak of the "moralists." Instead of writing scholarly treatises, they adopted a worldly point of view, despite the fact that their challenge was, above all, to convince others of the absurdity of the world and the true existence of life after death. This is a strange twist in the history of humanity: how a patchwork apology that aimed to deconstruct human vanity became a glorious moment in French literature.

NOTES

1. *Amour-propre* covers a range of meanings (self-love, self-interest, vanity, conceit, self-respect, self-esteem, and so forth). The one term that conveys most of these in English is "self-love."
2. The expression *saeva indignatio* is often associated with that other great satirist, Jonathan Swift, most notably in W. B. Yeats's translation of Swift's epitaph poem.

WORKS CITED AND RECOMMENDED FURTHER READING

All quotations in the text are cited from the translations included below.

Baird, A.W.S. *Studies in Pascal's Ethics*. The Hague: Martinus Nijhoff, 1975.
Bénichou, Paul. *Man and Ethics: Studies in French Classicism*. Translated by Elizabeth Hughes. New York: Anchor Books, 1971.

Cyrano de Bergerac. *L'autre monde*. Edited by M. Alcover. Paris: Champion, 2001.

———. *Voyages to the Moon and the Sun*. Translated by Richard Aldington. London: Routledge, 1980.

Hammond, Nicholas, ed. *The Cambridge Companion to Pascal*. Cambridge: Cambridge University Press, 2003.

Hodgson, Richard G. *Falsehood Disguised: Unmasking the Truth in La Roche-foucauld*. West Lafayette, IN: Purdue University Press, 1995.

Koppisch, Michael. *The Dissolution of Character: Changing Perspectives in La Bruyère's "Caractères."* Lexington, KY: French Forum, 1981.

La Bruyère, Jean de. *Caractères*. Edited by R. Garapon. Paris: Classiques Garnier, 1962.

———. *Characters*. Translated by H. Van Laun. London: Routledge, 1929.

La Fontaine, Jean de. *Fables*. Edited by J.-C. Darmon. Paris: Le Livre de Poche, 1998.

———. *The Complete Fables*. Translated by Norman R. Shapiro. Urbana: University of Illinois Press, 2007.

La Rochefoucauld, François de. *Réflexions ou sentences et maximes morales*. Edited by L. Plazenet. Paris: Champion, 2002.

———. *Maxims*. Translated by Leonard Tancock. London: Penguin, 1959.

Moriarty, Michael. *Fallen Natures, Fallen Selves: Early Modern French Thought II*. Oxford: Oxford University Press, 2006.

Pascal, Blaise. *Lettres provinciales*. Edited by M. Le Guern. Paris: Gallimard, 1990.

———. *The Provincial Letters*. Translated by T. M'Crie. London: J. M. Dent, 1904. See also eBooks@Adelaide, http://ebooks.adelaide.edu.au/p/pascal/blaise/p27pr.

———. *Pensées*. Edited by M. Le Guern. Paris: Gallimard, 1988.

———. *Pensées*. Edited by G. Ferreyrolles and P. Sellier. Paris: Le Livre de Poche, 2000.

———. *Pensées*. Translated by A. J. Kreilsheimer. London: Penguin, 1995.

* *

Travel Narratives in the Seventeenth Century

La Fontaine and Cyrano de Bergerac

JUDITH SRIBNAI

> Ambulo ergo sum.
>
> —GASSENDI, IN RESPONSE TO DESCARTES

Ambulo ergo sum (I walk therefore I am). This phrase could be used as a maxim by seventeenth-century travelers and storytellers alike and, in a broader sense, it speaks to a certain way of being and existing in the world. In this chapter, I consider what that meant in relation to the production of certain genres of travel writing, what broadly we can call the "informative" and the "playful." The playful can be understood as an ironic commentary on the informative, often in terms that implicitly ironize an entire tradition running all the way back to antiquity, but most especially to the Renaissance. The latter was the moment when the early modern period was imagined as a flowering of "the age of discovery," when travel, trade, conquest, scientific exploration, and cultural encounter created new forms of European "curiosity." Two particularly apt examples of this trend are the writings of Savinien de Cyrano de Bergerac and Jean de La Fontaine (famed for his *Fables* but less well known as a travel writer, of sorts).[1]

The expression *ambulo ergo sum* in fact originates in a debate of the 1640s between René Descartes and Pierre Gassendi, two philosophers who were almost entirely opposed. Descartes saw "I think therefore I am" (*cogito ergo sum*) as a first principle. He contended that this certainty, upon which we can build further metaphysical truths, proceeds from our existence as a thinking thing, the "I" grasping itself in its activity of reflection. Among other things, Gassendi reproaches Descartes for overlooking what this "I"—which thinks, doubts, affirms, and negates—truly *is*. To say that we are thinking things does not, according to Gassendi, say anything about our nature and wholly dismisses our corporeal existence. In short, Gassendi sees *ambulo ergo sum* as no less true than *cogito ergo sum*. The positions of the two philosophers become all the more irreconcilable when we take into account the way in which Gassendi gives sensory experience an indispensable role in accessing knowledge. What we see, touch, taste, our physical existence, is inseparable from us, from what we are, and constitutes our first and fundamental access to the world and to knowledge.

Descartes traveled for a time across Europe but preferred the solitude and comfort of his stove-heated room (*son poêle*) to think in peace. Gassendi, who was more sedentary, moved between Provence and Paris, passing his nights outside gazing at the stars and observing Mercury. The seventeenth century is often, for better or for worse, assumed to be driven by the Cartesian standpoint, which gave birth to modern science. Examining the seventeenth century through travelogues allows us, in some respects, to see it apart from Descartes and Cartesianism. Wanderers and explorers are often required to investigate who they are and what they thought, until then, to be immutable and unquestionable: Are they different from those they encounter? What defines or legitimates their customs and habits? Do animals also have souls? Are time and space always and everywhere measured in the same way? Are understanding, knowledge, and what we consider true universal? The questions that Gassendi poses to Descartes are, in many ways, those that preoccupy other travelers and witnesses in a century that was more complex and less sure of itself than we often think. This is nicely demonstrated by the two authors considered here: Cyrano de Bergerac and La Fontaine—both of them detractors of Descartes, if not readers of Gassendi—appear to be very different, but in reality they share certain doubts and hesitations

Cyrano de Bergerac (1619–55) and La Fontaine (1621–95) have, on the face of it, seemingly little in common. The former, often associated with "the Libertines," was fairly close to the Baroque aesthetic, an author who had a few successes during his lifetime and was rather quickly forgotten after his death. He was rediscovered only in the nineteenth century (by Charles Nodier and Théophile Gautier), before becoming the legendary character that we know today, thanks to Edmond Rostand's 1897 play, *Cyrano de Bergerac*. In contrast, La Fontaine was close to power, elected to the Académie française in 1684, celebrated while alive for his *Fables*, and quickly became an emblematic figure of seventeenth-century poetry and French literature in general. These differences are reflected in their texts and are of interest perhaps above all as illustrations of the highly varied character of the works subsumed under the general—and generic—heading of "travel literature."

Cyrano's travel novel, in fact, consists of two texts: *L'autre monde* (*The Other World*) or *Les Etats et Empires de la Lune* (*The States and Empires of the Moon*) and *Les Etats et Empires du Soleil* (*The States and Empires of the Sun*). They were published posthumously, the first in 1657 and the second in 1662. The character-narrator, who is sometimes known by the name Dyrcona, a play on the name of the author, Cyrano, one night takes a walk with friends while "the moon was full": "The various thoughts provoked in us by the sight of that globe of saffron diverted us on the road." Carried away by his enthusiasm, he proclaims: "For my part, said I, I am desirous to add my fancies to yours and without amusing myself with the witty notions you use to tickle time to make it run the faster, I think the Moon is a world like this and that our world is their Moon. . . . Perhaps in the same way, said I, at this moment in the Moon they jest at someone who there maintains that this globe is a world." It is this double recourse to imagination (What if the moon was a world?) and reversal (What if we are the moon of the moon?) that launches the story. The narrator, stung by "these feverish outbursts," attaches to himself "a number of little bottles filled with dew," which the sun's heat attracts. His first stop is New France, where he builds a machine that takes him to an earthly paradise and then to the moon, where he encounters the daimon of Socrates. An Ethiopian, who seemingly appears from nowhere, then brings the narrator safely back to earth. *Les Etats et Empires du Soleil* begins with the narrator's arrival in Toulouse, where he is quickly thrown in prison because of the publication of the account of his voyage to the moon. He escapes thanks to his ability to construct an icosahedra and flies to a macula, "one of those little Worlds that fly around the Sun," and from there makes his way to the sun. The story ends abruptly when the main character, guided by Tommaso Campanella, visits the Province of the Philosophers and waits impatiently for Descartes, who has just arrived, to take the floor.

In these two novels, we see that fiction and imagination play an essential role. It is often the imagination of the narrator that triggers the journey or invention that makes possible the discovery. The "Why not?" is, as a result, a recurrent engine of action that allows the narrator to convert fantasy into possibility: Why not visit the moon? What if the world were infinite? What if youth had authority over their elders? What if trees could speak? Cyranian fiction becomes then a place to explore unproven hypotheses that were important subjects of debate in the seventeenth century: the infinitude of the universe, heliocentrism, the existence of the void. In the course of his voyages, the narrator meets a number of characters, some drawn from literature and mythology, others from the philosophical or scientific tradition. On the moon, as we have seen, he meets the daimon of Socrates; on the sun, Campanella, Italian philosopher and author of the utopian dialogue, relevantly titled, *La cité du soleil* (*The City of the Sun*, 1623), is his interlocutor. On the sun, the descendants of the oaks of Dodone, trees that were used to build Jason and the Argonauts' boat, speak Greek and recount the love stories of Orestes and Pylades, of Narcissus or Hermaphrodite. The governor of Montmagny, the wise men of the moon, the little man of the macula, the prophet Elijah, each expound their theories concerning the generation of children, the materiality of the soul, the movement of the earth, or the birth of erotic passions. The story buzzes with all these voices that, though at times contradictory, always amusingly disturb our habits and conventions of thought.

These two texts by Cyrano represent the topoi of travel literature: the encounter with "otherness" forces the main character to relativize his convictions, whether they be theological, scientific, or ethical. Using the principle of reversal, Cyrano holds a mirror to his readers, showing them their inconsistencies and their fragility. However, the burlesque tone, the comic displacement, and the play with language prevent us from seeing clearly the novel's actual thesis. Perhaps the earth turns because the damned, who are imprisoned in its center with the fire of hell and are "flying from the heat of the fire to avoid it, clamber upwards and thus make the Earth turn, as a dog makes a wheel turn when he runs round inside it?" The polyphonic aspect of the two novels, along with the proliferation of theories and foolish explanations that are often subversive, thus endow the texts with a remarkable heterogeneity and make it very difficult to place them in a genre: are they "comic novels," precursors of science fiction, "epistemic novels," or utopian visions? The voyage is, precisely, the opportunity for us to encounter these genres and tones. *Ambulo ergo sum*: the more the narrator walks around and visits these worlds, the more the identity of the novels blurs, the more the identities of the characters become uncertain. The narrator is taken for a man, an animal, a monkey, a creature of God, an aggregate of atoms. In the end, neither he nor the reader can decide what he is. The more the narrator walks, the more the worlds, the theories, and the genres seem to multiply without necessarily excluding each other.

The *Lettres à sa femme* (*Letters to Madame de La Fontaine*), which Jean de La Fontaine addresses to his wife, Marie Héricart, between August 23 and September 19, 1663, does not fall within the category of extraordinary journeys. Published posthumously, they are subtitled *Voyage de Paris en Limousin*, the only voyage that the author accomplished. It is an epistolary narrative comprising a mix of prose and verse (what technically is known as "prosimetrum"), composed of six letters written by La Fontaine while in exile. As the faithful protégé of Nicolas Fouquet, superintendent of finances who was condemned and imprisoned on the order of King Louis XIV, La Fontaine left Paris, it would seem, out of loyalty to his patron. In his fourth letter, he refers to the incarceration of Fouquet at Amboise: "All of this poor Monsieur Foucquet could never, during his stay, enjoy for a single moment; they had closed up all the windows of his room, leaving only a hole up above." During his voyage, La Fontaine is accompanied by M. Jannart, uncle of his wife, who has also gone into exile because of Fouquet. We see that the referential anchor, the genre, and the scope of the voyage are very different from those we find in Cyrano. Although coerced into leaving, La Fontaine transforms necessity into choice by deciding to make curiosity the cause of his trip: "The fancy of traveling had entered my mind some time before, as if I had had presentiments of the King's order. It had been more than a fortnight since I spoke of nothing else, than to go soon to Saint-Cloud, soon to Charonne, and I was ashamed of having lived so long without seeing anything. I shall no longer be reproached for that, thank heavens! We were told, among other marvels, that many of the Limousin women of the highest bourgeoisie wear hoods of sharp-pink cloth over caps of black velvet. If I find one of these hoods covering a pretty head, I will be able to amuse myself in passing, but only through curiosity."

The desire to explore; the drive of "fantasy," which in the seventeenth century belongs to both imagination and caprice; and the excitement of "wonder"—in short, the "curiosity" that incites one to lift the veil of the secret of Limousines[2]—all these elements parody the beginning of a travel narrative. Each letter recounts the steps of the convoy: from Meudon to Clamart (1), from Clamart to Orléans (2), from Orléans to Amboise (3), from Amboise to Richelieu (4), and finally, from Richelieu to Limoges (6). Only the fifth letter is entirely devoted to the description of Richelieu's château. Elsewhere, the narrator decides a priori what will capture his attention. Between Châtres (Arpajon) and the threatening valley of Tréfou (in fact Torfou, in the Maine-et-Loire), he unceremoniously avoids several landmarks: "After the meal, we again saw many châteaux on the right and left; I will not say a word, as it would be an infinite labour."[3] Certain places, like Tréfou, are but an occasion for inward reflection: "For as long as the road continued, I didn't talk about anything else but the advantages of war." At other moments, the travelers pass their time debating religious subjects or by recounting local amorous anecdotes or by going for a stroll.

La Fontaine's judgment is generally determined by an aesthetic principle and the pleasure it awakens: things, landmarks, towns, and their inhabitants are either beautiful or ugly. Thus, the young woman from Poitou is not beautiful enough. When he sees the Maid of Orléans it brings him no pleasure: "I found in her neither the appearance, the stature, nor the face of an Amazon"; Amboise is "pleasant and diverting"; Blois, "very beautiful"; the shores of the Loire are a "fine countryside" and one cannot say "enough of its marvels";

Poitiers is a *"villace"* (a city of no interest); and Billac is, at first sight, "vexatious," with "its mean streets, its badly accommodated and badly proportioned houses." In sum, La Fontaine has little recourse to explanation or description. For example, in speaking of Montléry, a fortress built by the English, he explains: "As for the fortress, it is demolished, but not by the years; that which remains, which is a very high tower, has not fallen into ruin, although they destroyed one side of it. There is still a stair remaining, and two rooms where English paintings are seen, which is a proof of the antiquity and singularity of the place. Such is what I learned from your uncle, who says that he entered the rooms; as for me, I saw nothing. The coachman only wanted to stop at Châtres."

In many ways, the narrator of *Voyage de Paris en Limousin*, this "child of sleep and laziness" who complains of his lack of memory and assures us that "this journey would be a fine thing if one didn't have to get up so early in the morning," is an anti-traveler. His letters, like *Les états et empires* of Cyrano, can be read as a critical parody of the narratives of great travelers that, having met with a certain amount of success, flourished and were well known in France, although travel writing did not yet exist as a formally codified literary genre after the manner of drama and poetry

The second half of the sixteenth century in Europe was marked by the politics of conquest and territorial expansion, leading several sovereigns to sponsor major expeditions. These expeditions were, in turn, recounted by explorers in travelogues. They were not, however, just official reports; they would quickly captivate the European imagination. Beginning in 1534, Jacques Cartier, at the expense of King François I, led three expeditions to North America. These were detailed by Cartier in his *Relations*, a travelogue that was subsequently translated into both English and Italian. This was followed by Samuel de Champlain's *Les voyages de la Nouvelle France occidentale, dicte Canada* (*Voyages to New France*), which was published between 1603 and 1632. In 1578, the Protestant Jean de Léry came back from "France Antarctique"—today's Rio de Janeiro, where he was sent by Calvin— and published his *Histoire d'un voyage fait en terre de Brésil* (*History of a Voyage to the Land of Brazil*). The French explorers and sailors competed with the colonizing enterprises of Spain and Portugal, whose political and economic influence extended into Africa, India, and South America. These expeditions and the resulting accounts made a lasting impression on European readers, who were brought through the medium of writing to parts of the world whose natural riches, climate, and geography were unexpectedly novel, and, at the cultural level, into an encounter with other customs and mores. At all levels, these experiences and accounts of conquest, domination, and encounter strongly influenced the European imagination.

In the late sixteenth century, Montaigne, in the famous essay that was to become a canonical instance of its kind, "Des cannibales," examined and explored the concept of the "savage" as mediated by these accounts of what was then called the "Nouveau Monde." Montaigne poses the following questions, ones that will themselves travel throughout Western thought and literature, down through the eighteenth century into the Romantic period, and on into the twentieth century. Should we not situate, interpret, and understand what we call the savages' "barbarism" in the context of their own society—which is, in fact, one that we know nothing about? Are we not obliged to consider the moral and religious beliefs that we thought universal to be relative? Are we not perhaps, in their eyes, the barbarians and savages by virtue of our own habits, beliefs, and customs? While appealing to the myth of the "noble savage" (judged to be closer to a "natural" condition that we have lost and forgotten), Montaigne already deploys the strategy of thought-provoking inversion that Cyrano would take up in his own way.

In addition to these expedition narratives, there were the accounts of missionaries, in particular the Jesuits, which also played a fundamental role in the representation of the "Other" in the seventeenth century. From the Crusades onward, territorial annexation and religious conversion became inseparable. The work of converting infidels was constantly invoked as an argument for expansion. In the context of the Protestant Reformation, sustaining the role of Catholic missionaries became a central concern for the Church. Jesuit accounts, in reports that appear in France between 1632 and 1672, contributed to the diffusion of knowledge about the Americas and the Near East, in addition to arousing interest in distant lands among the learned and ordinary public alike.

Cyrano and La Fontaine, who were both the inheritors and contemporaries of these accounts, enjoyed negotiating the conventions of the genre. They were mindful of three problems that recur among explorer narratives: the problem of memory and its reliability (one must remember, note, and report); the problem of vision (one must see, bear direct witness); and the problem of the transmission of knowledge (one must represent that which is unknown to the reader and that for which the narrator, at times, has no words).

As he prepares to describe Richelieu's château, La Fontaine confesses: "I promised you by the last post the description of the château Richelieu; rather cursorily in order not to tell you untruths, and without taking into consideration my slight memory or the trouble that this enterprise was bound to give me." The poet often refers to his faulty memory. He who extols the beauty of Vaux-le-Vicomte has sudden amnesia when trying to evoke the riches of Richelieu. La Fontaine tells us that it is a place that is exceptionally spacious but admits: "I do not quite recall its shape," and "neither do I remember of what the base court, fore court, and subsidiary courts are composed of, nor the number of pavilions and *corps-de-logis* of the château, still less of their structure. These details have escaped." In addition to this implied criticism of Richelieu (to which I will later return), La Fontaine frees himself from the obligation of the traveler to precisely report what he has seen. In doing so, he undercuts his authority and legitimacy as a narrator: there is no longer the promise of authenticity, totality, or objectivity. Cyrano employs the same device. In *Le soleil*, the narrator encounters a tiny man who lives on the macula and who assures him: "I will reveal to you . . . secrets which are not known in your climate." The author goes on to explain that the meeting concludes with ". . . a still more private conversation, in which he revealed to me very hidden secrets (on part of which I shall keep silent, while the rest has escaped my memory)." How do we know what a narrator may or may not have said, what he remembers, and what he invents? Even though this extraordinary voyage does not rest on a referential agreement, Cyrano plays with the genre while, at the same time, underlining the kinship it has with his own fiction.

The traveler is a person for whom sight is primordial: he or she witnesses and reports what is seen. However, La Fontaine is not con-

cerned with what he misses or does not capture his interest: in Am-
broise, he chooses not to visit the room of the prince and, of the fortress of Montléry, we are told that he "saw nothing." In contrast, the
narrator of *Etats et empires* is attentive to what he sees and seeks explanations for it. Cyrano indicates his satirical intent when the main
character tries to justify the plausibility and possibility of the most
fantastic facts. Upon his return to earth, he insists that he is an eye-
witness to the mores and customs of the Selenites, imitating the kinds
of justification supplied by the genre of the travelogue: at the behest
of his friend M. de Colignac, so we are told, he provides an account
of the "extraordinary things" that he has seen, and on that basis publishes the book *Etats et Empires de la Lune*. There is of course a joke
here, as fiction is allowed to justify fiction, once again blurring the
line between true and invented narratives. Cyrano here questions the
assumptions of travel narratives: the authority of the narrator, the
validity of subjective judgment, and the legitimacy of eyewitness accounts, which are always infused with the dreams, desires, and prejudices of their author.

In the end, and largely because of its pedagogical functions, travel
literature often appears to be a hybrid genre, combining stories, descriptions, and commentaries. It aims to transmit knowledge to readers who, a priori, know nothing of and share nothing with, the world
that is being explored. The first letter of La Fontaine immediately
calls into question this supposed virtue of the genre. His wife, he
confirms, devours the light reading of chivalric novels, which she
knows by heart. La Fontaine plays on this to justify the interest of his
letters: "Consider, if you please, how useful this would be for you, if,
in fun, I had accustomed you to history, either of places or persons.
You would have the wherewithal with which to divert yourself your
whole life, provided that this was without the intention of remembering anything, still less of citing anything. It is not a good quality in a
woman to be learned, and it is a very bad one to affect appearing as
such."

Pleasure and banter, that which is opposed to erudition and learn-
ing, guide the traveler and his readers. Moreover, on the road, La
Fontaine refuses to adopt the role of the masterful knowing subject.
Concerning the town of Montléry, for example, he asks: "Does one

say Montlhéry or Montléhry? It's Montlehéry when the verse is too short, and Montlhéry when it's too long. Montlhéry therefore or Montlehéry, as you wish." It is poetry, the art of rhyme, and aesthetic balance which take precedence over knowledge. The pleasure of the bon mot allows fiction and literature to find a place alongside erudite and scholarly texts. Again, from this perspective, Cyrano and La Fontaine are close despite their many differences. *La Lune* and *Le Soleil* resemble the expositions of scholars and philosophers on subjects as diverse as the movement of the earth, the plurality of worlds, the corruptibility of the sun, the arrival of the apostle John in paradise, the affective life of plants, or the immortality of the soul. All these theories and hypotheses are bundled together. Put another way, the practice and sharing of knowledge is seen as consisting in the capacity to invent and generate fiction. Science is not only the practice of seeing, experimenting, and explaining perceptible phenomena. It is also a manifestation of the capacity to imagine. The main character makes his way to the sun because he is transported by a "burning of fever," a joy that animates his will and allows him to see that which remains invisible to "the most obstinate." This is the same principle that would arouse the enthusiasm of the scholar. Science nourishes fiction, and fiction, in its turn, stretches the limits of science.

In the cases of both La Fontaine and Cyrano, the reader is deliberately drawn into a world of satire and critique directed at an increasingly popular genre. The political, religious, or scholarly functions of travel stories are strongly undermined and discredited. On the other hand, imitation equally confers legitimacy on the pleasant and extraordinary accounts of both La Fontaine and Cyrano. Similarly, the hybridization of genres and themes found in both texts, in addition to the prestige given to the imagination and fiction, accord to pleasure and dreams the same importance that is conferred on science or scholarship.

To occupy his fellow travelers, Socrates's daimon offers the narrator "a miraculous book without pages or letters; in fine, it is a book to learn from which eyes are useless, only ears are needed." By turning the key of the book, "immediately, as if from a man's mouth or a musical instrument, this machine gives out all the distinct and different sounds which serve as the expression of speech between the noble

Moon-dwellers." The narrator describes it as miraculous, explaining: "[Y]ou have continually about you all great men, living or dead, and you hear them *viva voce*." In a certain sense, this is how we experience Cyrano's two texts. *L'autre monde* is the distant descendant of Lucian's *True Story*. The Roman voyager (who also finds himself on the moon) assures us that he has "no truth to put on record, having lived a very humdrum life." He adopts, that is, the liar's paradox: "I now make the only true statement you are to expect—that I am a liar." Cyrano was greatly influenced by Lucian's game playing and borrowed several episodes for his own work.

Cyrano's two texts are, in fact, saturated with references to earlier works: *The Man in the Moon*, by the Englishman Francis Godwin; *The City of the Sun*, by the Italian monk Campanella; *The Metamorphoses* by Ovid; and, of course, Homer's Odysseus, a character in whom storytelling and travel merge. The Socratic love banquet raises questions about the tales of anthropophagy worthy of Léry. The materialist thesis of the Epicureans is explored by the Selenite philosophers or the birds of the sun. The episode of the narrator as beggar in Toulouse is a gesture to the comic novels that came from Spain and from which *La lune* borrows several of its formal aspects. It would be impossible to cite all the literary references and allusions. The point that matters concerns their radically heterogeneous character: philosophical dialogues, satirical works, ancient travel narratives, contemporary accounts of utopias. These literary journeys unfold on several planes: the intervention of real-life people (Descartes) or well-known fictional characters (the daimon of Socrates); the reappropriation of topoi from the ancient odysseys or the early modern picaresque novels; and the staging of a familiar thesis in amplified, deformed, or caricatured fashion. Cyrano thus practices his own particular brand of scholarship. *Ambulo ergo sum*: the story exists as a complex weaving of these perspectives, genres, and voices, among which we can wander as we please.

La Fontaine's work is equally inscribed in a literary tradition in a manner demonstratively marked in the writing. He owes the very form of "galant" travel writing (which is directly opposed to scientific accounts) to *Voyage d'Encausse* by the poets Chapelle (1626–86) and Bachaumont (1624–1702). In this work, the two travelers are looking to escape their Parisian excesses but end up dedicating their expedition to the procuring and enjoyment of good food. Furthermore, while evoking the novels of the Knights of the Round Table that his wife so adored, La Fontaine does not hesitate to pastiche their style: "Supper time having arrived, knights and ladies were seated at their rather poorly spread tables, and afterward went to bed immediately, as one might imagine; and with that the chronicler brings the present chapter to a close." Later on, to describe the Loire, the poet both recalls and dismisses a reference to Ovid: "Que dirons-nous que fut la Loire / Avant que d'être ce qu'elle est? / Car vous savez qu'en son histoire / Notre bon Ovide s'en tait." (What say we the Loire was / Before being what it is? / For you know that concerning its history / Our good Ovid is silent.) It is thus left to La Fontaine to make up for this lacuna, which he does while simultaneously insisting that the Loire has no mythical allure ("Et disons ici, s'il vous plaît, / Que la Loire étoit ce qu'elle est / Dès le commencement des choses." (And let us say here, if you please / That the Loire was what it is / Since the beginning of things.) Rivaling the ancients, La Fontaine confers on his voyage the quality of a literary divertissement, offering his readers variations on well-known poetic themes. We find, for example, the topos of *locus terribilis* (frightening place), when he crosses the valley of Tréfou, "République de loups, asile de brigands" (Republic of wolves, sanctuary of brigands), a motif that occasions a more general reflection on human ills: "En combien de façons, hélas! le genre humain / Se fait à soi-même la guerre!" (In how many ways, alas, does mankind / Make war upon itself!).

It is important to emphasize that in both *Voyage de Paris en Limousin* and La Fontaine's *Lettres*, the narrator is an exiled or rejected character. As previously remarked, La Fontaine recalls the conditions under which he goes into exile, along with the sadness aroused in him by the prison in which Fouquet was confined. In Cyrano's novels, even though the main character leaves voluntarily to explore the moon, he is thereafter hunted, imprisoned, or threatened with death. For example, an inappropriate remark provokes the anger of the prophet Elijah, who then casts him out of the earthly paradise. On the moon, he is taken for an animal, caged with a character from a Godwin novel, and summoned before a tribunal. When he returns to earth, the publication of his account gains him the wrath of those "most obstinate," and he is once again pursued and imprisoned. On the sun, it is the birds who this time accuse him of being a human and put him on trial. Mistreated and often cast in the role of the Other, pursued because he is misunderstood, the main character is forced to flee, a fate that causes him to leave most of the places he visits. The worlds described are imprinted with a remarkable violence. War, death sentences, incarceration, and cannibalism are common ills. The inversion that the accounts provide does not, thus, propose a better world. On the moon, a young man explains that, in their community, the young have authority over the old and that "the old render every deference and honour to the young." The reversal of the customs of the narrator and his readers is striking; the young man obliges us to question what we consider evident. However, in the end, the young Selenites treat the oldest badly, viciously whipping them if necessary. The stateless and foreign status of the narrator allows him to accurately illustrate this commonplace violence.

Despite their burlesque and satirical tone, the works of La Fontaine and Cyrano provide a reflection on the cruelty and savagery of politics—a politics that, at the same time, refers to the sovereign power but also to the community, to the difficulty of living together. Both La Fontaine and Cyrano lived through the Fronde (1648–53), a violent civil war that divided France. The revolts, which began while Louis XIV was still a child, sought to oppose the establishment of an absolute monarchy (the concentration of power in the hands of the king). Richelieu, in particular, who was then minister to the king, greatly contributed to the preservation and consolidation of the monarch's power. When Louis XIV came of age, he continued to assert his power over the nobility. A way of controlling the nobles was to incorporate them into his court. It is in this context that Louis XIV thought it prudent to imprison the rich and influential minister Fouquet.

La Fontaine alludes to these unsettling events during his comical voyage. For instance, when he wishes to leave Richelieu, he finds the doors locked: "There was a rumor that some gentlemen of the province had formed a plot to save certain prisoners, suspected of the murder of the Marquis de Faure." Upon arriving at Etampes, he notices "some vestiges of our wars, . . . the work of Mars, worthless mason if ever there was one," and recalls the wounds left by the Fronde: "Beaucoup de sang françois fut alors répandu: / On perd des deux côtés dans la guerre civile; / Notre prince eût toujours perdu, / Quand même il eût gagné la ville." (Much French blood was then spilled; / Both sides lost in the civil war. / Our prince would have always lost, / Even if he had won the city.)[4] Once again, the poet provides a glimpse of both the danger of power (those who decide, who can declare war and impose exile) and its vulnerability (the most powerful can, in an instant, fall). He also underscores vanity of authority, inscribed in a version of *vanitas vanitatum*. At the Richelieu estate, when in the queen's room, La Fontaine remarks, "There is so much gold that in the end I was bored. Consider what the great lords can do, and what misery it is to be rich: it was necessary to invent rooms of stucco, where magnificence hides itself under the appearance of simplicity." Through oxymoron (the misery or poverty of being rich), if he wishes, the poet can, in one line, sweep away all the grandeur of the world. It is he who decides whether or not to offer a literary legacy to great men. The poet also can take up his own place in this creation of historical and literary memory, which in seventeenth-century thought and culture was characteristically a response to the transience and vanity of existence. In sum, La Fontaine, as later in the *Fables*, constructs a poetic realm, a lyrical garden that is similar to but also contrasts with the gardens where the kings flaunt their power.

As we have seen, Cyrano also questions everyday oppression. Although *Etats et empires* cannot be considered descriptions of utopias in our normal understanding of the genre (they propose no ideal social model), certain passages can be read as "great escapes." For instance, on the moon, one can offer poems for the payment of dues; thus, "no one dies of hunger except the blockheads, and men of wit live in perpetual good cheer." It is the dream of a society where writers are never penniless or dependent on rich patrons to survive, and where spirit is valued over wealth and worldly power. When, on the sun, the oaks of Dodone recount the mythological love stories of Hermaphrodite, Narcissus, or the young prince Artaxerxes to the main character, the stories take the form of a eulogy to forbidden love. These passages stage all possible affective relations. It is this utopian dimension of the "possible" that opens up a new horizon in the text: where we can love someone of the same sex, where nothing prevents us from falling in love with an animal or a tree. For instance, Artaxerxes, because he was nourished by the fruit of Orestes, falls in love with a plane tree: "It was even noticed that the tree jealously ranged and pressed its leaves together for fear lest the rays of daylight as they glided through should also kiss him. The king for his part placed not limits to his love. He caused his bed to be made at the foot of the plane-tree and the plane-tree, not knowing how to repay such a friendship, gave the most precious thing trees have—honey and dew—which it distilled every morning upon him."

If these loves are possible, it is because Cyrano imagines a world where matter circulates so freely that identities, genres, and categories blur. Trees, flowers, cabbages, humans, monkeys, and daimons appear to be living, changing from one form into another, coming together to make other things and other beings. The main character, in his travels, is continuously transformed under the influence of the sun, moon, or heat. He is rejuvenated, loses his hair, is famished, satisfied, made transparent or opaque. The text provides the loose map of another, a "possible," world, where movement and transformation permit escape from categorization and from all forms of power. In this context, friendship plays an essential role and, in a certain way, provides an alternative space. The main character is saved from death, suffering, or persecution by his friends, whether they be human, magpie, or daimon. In Toulouse, he takes refuge at the home of his friend Colignac, and the two of them spend their time with the marquis of Cussan. This episode provides a brief narrative respite, because although the main character is persecuted for his novel, the domain of Colignac becomes a refuge and pretext for the protagonist to celebrate another realm: "In one word we enjoyed, so to speak, both ourselves and all that is most agreeably produced by Nature for our use; we placed no limits to our desires save those of reason." Concisely stated, this extraordinary voyage is, at the same time, the experience of belonging to nowhere and freedom to cultivate places other than those to which nature, history, and culture typically confine us.

The travel literature of La Fontaine and Cyrano dramatizes a number of pregnant seventeenth-century questions: the relativity of customs and beliefs, the relationship between political power and art, the modes of constituting a literary history, the particularity of the human soul, and the place of humans in creation. Through many different kinds of reflection in many different registers—moral, political, historical, rhetorical, epistemological, and metaphysical— travelogues, by playing with points of view and reversals, find an entertaining way of inviting readers to deal with some of these questions by, in turn, questioning their own beliefs, opinions, and prejudices. Generic hybridity and polyphony are symptomatic of this experience of decentring and displacement. The "decentred" and the "displaced" are modes of experience and representation we tend to associate with our own time, but, in their own specific ways, they are also a feature of the landscape of the seventeenth century. Walking, wandering, and continual movement are signs of a vitality that creates the conditions for an encounter with the Other, but also the life of a spirit that meanders from one idea to another, from one pleasure to another. La Fontaine and Cyrano can be read as adhering to the axiom *ambulo ergo sum* because their characters are ever-changing and protean. In a certain way, it is in traveling or walking that they better perform this complex, plural identity. We are here far from the "modern subject" in that other sense of "modern," a subject sure of its own existence and nature with which we often associate the seventeenth century.

Notes

1. I would like to sincerely thank Julian Menezes for translating this text. I also thank Eglantine Morvant and Karina Cahill for their help and suggestions.
2. The "hood" is, as indicated by the context, made of velour and worn on a woman's head. When La Fontaine wrote his text, this accessory was no longer in style. The poet thus dreams of visiting this strange country where time has stopped, where clothing is so outdated that it is no longer known in Paris.
3. Here I have changed the translation to better reflect the original.
4. Here again I have changed the translation to more closely reflect the grammatical construction of the original.

Works Cited and Recommended Further Reading

Campanella, Tommaso. *The City of the Sun: A Poetical Dialogue*. Translated by Daniel J. Donno. Berkeley: University of California Press, 1981.

Cartier, Jacques. *Voyages of Jacques Cartier*. Translated by Ramsay Cook. Toronto: University of Toronto Press, 1993.

Champlain, Samuel de. *Voyages to New France*. Translated by Michael Macklem. Ottawa: Oberon Press, 1977.

Chapelle, Claude Emmanuel Lhuillier, and François Le Coigneux de Bachaumont. *Voyage d'Encausse* (1665). Edited by Y. Giraud. Paris: H. Champion (Sources classiques), 2007.

Cyrano de Bergerac, Savinien de. *Les Etats et Empires de la Lune*. Paris: Flammarion, 1984.

———. *Les Etats et Empires du Soleil*. Paris: Flammarion, 2003.

———. *Other Worlds: The Comical History of the States and Empires of the Moon and the Sun*. Translated by Geoffrey Strachan. London: Oxford University Press, 1965.

Descartes, René. *Discourse on the Method of Rightly Conducting the Reason, and Seeking Truth in the Sciences*. Translated by John Cottingham, Robert Stoothoff, and Dugald Murdoch. Cambridge: Cambridge University Press, 1985.

———. *Meditations on First Philosophy*. In *The Philosophical Writings of Descartes*. Translated by John Cottingham, Robert Stoothoff, and Dugald Murdoch. Cambridge: Cambridge University Press, 1985.

Gassendi, Pierre. *Recherches métaphysiques, ou doutes et instances contre la métaphysique de R. Descartes et ses réponses*. Translated by Bernard Rochot. Paris: Vrin, 1962.

Godwin, Francis. *The Man in the Moone*. Edited by William Poole. Peterborough: Broadview Press, 2009.

La Fontaine, Jean de. *Lettres à sa femme: Voyage de Paris en Limousin*. Paris: Valmonde, 1995.

———. *Journey from Paris to Limousin: Letters to Madame de La Fontaine*. Translated by Robert W. Berger. Madison, NJ: Fairleigh Dickinson University Press, 2008.

———. *Le songe de Vaux*. Paris: Droz, 1967.

Léry, Jean de. *History of a Voyage to the Land of Brazil*. Translated by Jeanet Whatley. Berkeley: University of California Press, 1993.

Lucian of Samosata. *True Story*. Translated by Charles Whibley and Francis Hickes. N.p: Nabu Press, 2010.

Montaigne, Michel de. *The Complete Essays*. Translated by M. A. Screech. London: Penguin Classics, 1993.

Ovid. *Metamorphoses*. Translated by David Raeburn. London: Penguin, 2004.

The critical literature on La Fontaine is vast, but there is relatively little on the *Voyage*. The articles by Jean-Pierre Collinet and Madeleine Defrenne in *La découverte de la France au XVIIe siècle* (Paris: Centre National de la Recherche Scientifique, 1980) introduce the reader to many of the issues raised by the text. Patrick Dandrey, *La Fontaine ou les métamorphoses d'Orphée* (Paris: Gallimard, 2008) offers an overall view of his life, works, and poetics. On the political context of La Fontaine's writings and its relation to power, the classic study remains Marc Fumaroli, *The Poet and the King: Jean de La Fontaine and His Century* (Notre Dame, IN: University of Notre Dame Press, 2002). Cyrano has regained a degree of popularity over the past few years. Two works are good introductions to the complexities of *L'autre monde* and to the different approaches to it: Bérengère Parmentier, ed., *Lectures de Cyrano de Bergerac* (Rennes: Presses Universitaires de Rennes, 2004); and Michèle Rosellini and Catherine Constantin, *Cyrano de Bergerac: Les états et empires de la lune et du soleil* (Neuilly: Atlande, 2005). The work of Mary Jo Muratore, *Mimesis and Metatextuality in the French Neo-classical Text: Reflexive Readings of La Fontaine, Molière, Racine, Guilleragues, Madame de La Fayette, Scarron, Cyrano de Bergerac and Perrault* (Paris: Droz, 1994) situates the fictional approach of Cyrano in relation to his contemporaries.

More general studies of the travel fiction genre in seventeenth-century France include Norman Doiron, *L'art de voyager* (Paris: Klincksieck, 1995); and Marie-Christine Pioffet, *Ecrire des récits de voyage* (Quebec: Presses de l'Université Laval, 2008). Ellen R. Welch, *The Taste for the Foreign: Worldly Knowledge and Literary Pleasure in Early Modern French Fiction* (Newark: University of Delaware Press, 2011) places the genre within the contemporary scientific context.

The Quarrel of the Ancients and the Moderns

LARRY F. NORMAN

In the second half of the seventeenth century, at the height of the reign of Louis XIV, it is hardly surprising that France indulged in some exuberant triumphalism. Abroad, its predominance on the Continent naturally proved a powerful stimulant to self-esteem. On the domestic front, the systematic reorganization of power by a centralized monarchy was extolled for eradicating the vestiges of feudal disorder and superstitions. A new epoch had arrived, and they called it the age of Louis le Grand, the Sun King. And there was yet more reason for satisfaction. Beyond national confines, France applauded a wider set of advances. The achievements of the natural sciences and rationalist philosophy, forged decades earlier by figures such as Galileo and Descartes, were recognized as having now exponentially increased not only knowledge of the universe, but also the basic human capacity for acquiring such knowledge through innovative empirical and deductive methods. They called it the age of philosophy. Daily life too appeared happily transformed. The vast refinement of manners and sociability, first disseminated from Italian courts, was hailed as the hallmark of a sophisticated civilization cleansed of the barbarity that sullied past centuries. They called it the age of politeness.

In short, the period understood itself as uniquely new, or more precisely as modern, as fundamentally different from—and better than—the past. The old Renaissance dream of remodeling the present age by emulating the glories of the classical past was fast losing pertinence. Why admire antiquity? Had not the prestige of Louis eclipsed that of Augustus? Had not critical reason exposed the absurdity of ancient philosophy and cosmology? Had not the graciousness and gallantry of Paris and Versailles surpassed Athenian elegance or Roman urbanity?

The answer, almost all seemed to agree, was affirmative. Or, more precisely, most accepted the evidence of progress in most arenas. For there remained this nagging question: might not certain domains of human activity progress at different rhythms than others, or not progress at all? Indeed might not progress in some spheres inevitably entail decay in others? It is here that what we call literature posed some vexing problems. Does national power produce poetic excellence? Are the rigors of methodical reason conducive to the flights of creative imagination? Can refined manners coexist with fiery genius?

These are the fundamental questions concerning the very nature of literature and the arts that fed a long-running debate called the Quarrel of the Ancients and Moderns. Under consideration was the relation of literature to the political, moral, and philosophical good; whether the two cohered or conflicted; and whether poetry and the arts progressed in lockstep with other human endeavors or instead marched to their own peculiar beat.

The debate was officially inaugurated in 1687 with the public reading at the hallowed Académie française of a poem, "Le siècle de Louis le Grand" (The century of Louis the Great) that argued that the splendors of the current regime also signaled the superiority of modern French literature over Greek and Roman classics. The author of the panegyric, Charles Perrault, was a man of letters who had been instrumental in the regime's propaganda efforts but who would become better known to posterity for publishing the first French literary fairy tales, including "Cinderella" and "Little Red Riding Hood." In reaction to what was perceived as a provocative attack on classical antiquity, the most prominent literary critic and satirist of the day, Nicolas Boileau, was according to all reports visibly and audibly scandalized. But the fracas was hardly surprising. The two were long spoiling for a fight. They and their allies had been skirmishing for well over a decade, debating for example the relative merits of the newly fashioned art of French opera (with Perrault championing as modern innovators its first great composer and librettist team, Lully and Quinault) as opposed to those of classical verse tragedy (with

Boileau lauding Racine's proclaimed fidelity to Greek and Roman sources). Now the skirmishes became a battle, indeed a decades-long polemical war, immediately known as the *Querelle* and dividing the literary world into opposing "parties" supporting the two respective chiefs. Among the "ancient" partisans were many of the writers who were later fixed in the firmament of the French canon and who supported Boileau, sometimes relatively quietly or tactfully (Racine or La Fontaine), sometimes forcefully (La Bruyère). Perrault, on his side, could count among the "moderns" one of the great rising stars of the world of letters, Bernard Le Bovier de Fontenelle, whose popularization of the new sciences and whose irreverent wit would later provide a potent model for Enlightenment *philosophes*.

The quarrel produced an explosion of printed texts aimed at the general reading public, ranging from Perrault's four-volume modern-party manifesto in dialogue form, the *Parallèle des anciens et des modernes* (Parallel of the ancients and moderns, 1688–97) to a massive array of shorter essays, poems, and polemical prefaces. After a lull in the first decade of the eighteenth century, the debate was reignited when Anne Dacier's earlier translation and vigorous defense of Homer's *Iliad* was pitted in 1714 against Houdar de La Motte's avowedly modernizing adaptation, which condensed the Greek epic into a trimly decorous tale suitable to contemporary tastes. Another set of writers entered the fray, with a literary lion like Fénelon taking up Homer's defense in his 1714 "Lettre à l'Académie française" (Letter to the French Academy), while on the other side the relative newcomer Marivaux mocked the Greek poet with the bitingly parodic verse of his 1716 *L'Homère travesti* (Homer travestied).

At a time when France largely set the terms for literary debate in Europe, the quarrel naturally spread abroad. Its influence was particularly powerful in Britain, where it made a deep impact on writers such as Alexander Pope, whose landmark 1715 translation of the *Iliad* borrowed substantially from Anne Dacier and other French critics engaged in the debate. Jonathan Swift, while slyly skewing his humor in favor of the ancient cause, famously satirized the whole affair in 1704 with his mock-epic *The Battle of the Books*. Swift's title became synonymous in the English-speaking world with the whole conflict, but his caustic derision of some of the quarrel's polemical excesses should not lead us to underestimate its considerable sway throughout the eighteenth century. The most substantive arguments elaborated by Boileau, Perrault, and their allies and heirs proved an inescapable reference, indeed often a fundamental groundwork, for the literary and aesthetic thought of Montesquieu, Voltaire, Diderot, Rousseau, and, beyond France, Vico and Hume.

To understand the enduring hold of the quarrel on the literary imagination, one must appreciate the seriousness of the stakes. First, the conflict engaged the most fundamental and complex issues concerning the relationship of literature to history. This complexity is unfortunately belied by the reductive dichotomy evoked by the quarrel's own name, which conjures up the kind of trivial rivalry associated with a beauty contest. In this case, it would be one where each of the two contestants, Greco-Roman antiquity and modern Europe, awaits its crowning as something like Western civilization's best overall epoch. But if one scratches the surface, the chronological paradigms under debate suggest a much more nuanced and fertile vision of cultural history.

Indeed, a surprisingly rich historical consciousness was at play even among those most enamored of modern times. Ironically enough, it was often their very admiration for the present that caused them to seriously reflect on the intricacies of the past. Modern partisans, impressed by recent political, scientific, and social advances, developed a theory of human progress that, though it attained perfection only in the present age, began in antiquity itself. They configured the past as a series of dynamic stages: classical Athens presented a leap of progress over the primitive Homeric world, just as imperial Rome presented yet another advance over the ages of Pericles or Alexander. They of course scorned the Middle Ages (as did the classical-loving ancient partisans) as a temporary regression. But whereas the defenders of antiquity hailed the advent of the Renaissance as a restitution of previous glory, modern partisans tended to leapfrog over the humanist recovery of pagan classics directly to the current century's unprecedented achievements, heralded by the arrival of Descartes.

This vision of progress led to some powerful paradoxes. The modern apologists, despite the apparent interests of their party, often heaped praise on classical Rome, now seen as the most advanced stage in the evolution of antiquity. This surprising praise could admittedly serve their purposes, for it allowed them to better decry the primitiveness of Rome's predecessor, Greece, now viewed as what Perrault called the "most ancient among the ancients." But something deeper was also at work. If the key indications of progress were, as Perrault argued, to be found in methodical reason, moral propriety, and exactitude of linguistic expression, then it follows that Virgil could truly be counted a "modern" before his time. Or rather a modern very much of his time, of that first modernity constituted by Augustan Rome. So Perrault affirmed in the *Parallèle*: "I find a great difference between the works of Homer and those of Virgil. To the same degree that the first, though admirable in certain spots, seem full of vulgarity, puerility, and foolishness, so the second seem to me filled with refinement, seriousness, and reason; all of which is explained by the different time periods in which they wrote, and that Virgil is more modern than Homer by eight or nine hundred years."

As Perrault's comparison shows, modernity proved to be a fundamentally relative term in the quarrel. First, it was historically or chronologically relative: eight centuries of progress made imperial Rome quite "modern" in comparison with Homeric Greece. But the term also entailed a relation of values as well as of eras: it implied a judgment concerning comparative degrees of rationality, methodical order, and sophisticated elegance. Given the impossibility of entirely dismissing the classical past—it was after all still the basis under Louis XIV for elite education and cultural production—the champions of French superiority made the most of a state of affairs that they could not, and perhaps did not entirely wish, to change. They thus promoted their own preferred brand of antiquity. Seen from this angle, the whole affair was a conflict between two wings of a global Ancient party, where the Modern party was the Roman party, or Augustan party, hailing the first apex of reason and refinement and the literary values of clarity and decorum it incarnated.

The ancient partisans in turn naturally had their own preferred antiquity. As the name of their cause would seem to require, it was precisely the "most ancient among the ancients" that they embraced: antiquity in the superlative. The choice was bold. Rather than cling to the pillar of Latin authority, rather than cut their losses and abandon their most vulnerable flank, that distant epoch Perrault dubbed as "full of vulgarity, puerility, and foolishness," Boileau and his allies instead doubled down, and celebrated above all the most remote antiquity, that of Homer and the Greeks. Boileau drives the point home in a 1701 letter to Perrault, where he fashions his own parallel between Augustan Rome and modern France. Here the Ancient party leader, despite his admiration for certain Latin poets, shows astonishingly little mercy in his disparagement of classical Rome. The irony, however, lies only on the surface. For frequently the first beneficiary of Boileau's parallel between Latin and French culture is an even more ancient one, that of Greece. Boileau had already made clear a quarter century earlier his preference for the primordial. In the 1674 *Art poétique*, for example, he decisively confers "to the Greeks this divine elevation / Which Latin frailty never attained" (chez les Grecs cette hauteur divine / Où jamais n'atteignit la faiblesse latine).

Boileau's letter to Perrault expands considerably on this cutting couplet by cataloging the "frailties" of a derivative Augustan culture. When snubbing imperial Rome, Boileau sometimes gives the prize to an earlier, more inventive Latin literature of less "modern" times: under Augustus, Boileau claims, "there was not a single comic playwright whose name is worth remembering: the Plautuses, Ceciliuses and Terences were dead a century before." The rebuke is revelatory. Unlike Perrault, Boileau chooses not to equate military and political grandeur (which he too concedes to Augustus) with literary excellence: sometimes poetry and drama peek before a nation's power does. Even here, the earlier Greek source no doubt lurks in Boileau's mind, and he might have cited his ally, Longepierre, who claimed in his 1687 *Discours sur les anciens* (Discourse on the ancients) that Terence himself is "nothing but a shadow and weak copy" of the Athenian playwright Menander, thereby affirming the Ancient party's principle that "the shadow is less than the body," the imitator less than the inventor. So too, for Boileau, the Greek past is always ready to emerge from the shadows as the true source of creativity. When, for example, he turns to the visual arts, Boileau cannot resist remarking that the only successful artists under Augustus were imported from the Hellenized east; they were "the Greeks of Europe and Asia, who came to Rome to practice the arts that the Romans, so to speak, did not know."

Taken as a whole, the two parties' wide-ranging debate over the relative value of Homeric originality and Virgilian refinement has deep implications for the evolving understanding of cultural and literary history. The stark divisions that emerge during the quarrel between Greek and Roman epochs (and between their subtler chronological subdivisions) demonstrate the extent to which any idealization of a Greco-Roman synthetic whole largely dissolved during the debate. In this sense, the whole conflict represents a crisis, and a certain collapse, of Renaissance humanism. As the eighteenth century progressed, this Greco-Roman divide would widen, with German neoclassicism and the later Romantics firmly handing the prize to the Hellenophiles (or at least doing so in the literary and aesthetic realm, while Roman models continue to hold considerable sway in the political domain, as the revolutionary and Napoleonic periods would later so abundantly illustrate). And the quarrel, with its interest not only in classical Greece, but more important, with the preclassical world of the Homeric age—what Fontenelle called in his essay "Sur la poésie en général" (On poetry in general) "the most ancient Greeks, still savage"—also opens the path for the various primitivisms and "noble savages" of the Enlightenment.

Turning from the evolving conceptions of the past to those concerning the present day, Boileau's letter to Perrault holds yet another lesson. If Augustan Rome proves at times too "modern" for the ancients' apologist, he is nevertheless at pains to demonstrate that there is in fact a certain modernity, indeed a French modernity, that he not only respects but frankly admires. Just as we have seen the Modern party embrace its own preferred antiquity, so too did the Ancient party laud its own favored modernity. On this point, Boileau's concession to Perrault is stunning: "You and I are not so far apart in our thinking as you think. . . . Your intention is to show that . . . the Age of Louis XIV [le Grand] is not only comparable but also superior to all the most illustrious ages of antiquity and even to the Age of Augustus. You'll be quite surprised when I tell you that I am entirely of your opinion on this matter."

Just how "modern" was the champion of the ancients? In terms of political history, Boileau readily accepts the advantage of Louis XIV, affirming that the original Augustus could not defeat the modern monarch whom he applauds as the "French Augustus." But Boileau goes considerably further. He eagerly extols the advances of modern sciences, proclaiming himself delighted to join in the moderns' self-congratulation and to "triumph with Perrault" over the defeated ancients. He likewise agrees on the superiority of contemporary philosophy, elevating far above the Romans both Descartes and Gassendi. There should be no surprise here. Boileau had long displayed an enlightened scorn concerning the reactionary neo-Aristotelianism of the hidebound Sorbonne, even penning a satire lampooning its benighted rejection of Harvey's discovery of the circulation of blood.

But for Boileau the sciences are one thing, and literature and the arts entirely another. Though he willingly grants the best modern French writers an edge over the ancients in certain genres, he still refuses to tightly join literary progress to that of the sciences or philosophy. From this angle, the quarrel is one of the first great tremors to rip asunder what C. P. Snow would later call "the two cultures." Indeed, Boileau suspected at times that the advancing reach of rationalist and scientific inquiry might perhaps not only be irrelevant, but even detrimental, to poetic inspiration and creativity. Thus while he praised Descartes for his mathematical and deductive achievements, Boileau was concerned, according to his friend Jean-Baptiste Rousseau (not to be confused with the later and more illustrious Jean-Jacques), about what he feared was the philosopher's baleful effect on the vitality of literature: "I have often heard M. Despréaux [Boileau] say that the philosophy of Descartes had cut poetry's throat; and it is certain that what poetry has borrowed from mathematics has desiccated its spirit and accustomed it to a concrete or material precision that has nothing to do with what might be called the properly metaphysical precision of poets and orators. Geometry and poetry have their separate and distinct rules, and those who wish to judge Homer by Euclid are no less impertinent than those who wish to judge Euclid by Homer."

By the final phase of the quarrel, the modern partisan Jean Terrasson affirmed in his 1715 *Dissertation critique sur l'Iliade d'Homère* (*Critical Dissertation on Homer's "Iliad"*) that the rancorous divorce between the humanities and the sciences seemed irrevocable: "We see that those learned in different sorts of knowledge believe each other useless to society. Let them burn all the poets and all the historians, exclaims a physicist or a geometer, but let us keep all the books of geometry and physics! The sentiment is reciprocated by the poet and the historian, who use the same terms against the works of geometry and physics." From a more global perspective, the whole debate may be seen here as yet another battle in an enduring struggle between rational philosophy and imaginative literature, dating back at least to Plato's denunciation of Homer in *The Republic* and to what Ernst Robert Curtius aptly termed the "rebellion of Logos against Myth— but also against poetry."

Or at least "against" a certain definition of "poetry," one whose perimeters open another key set of issues at stake in the quarrel. How, in the age of triumphant reason and scientific revolution, was one to understand the peculiar nature and function of imaginative literature, huddled here on the sidelines together with its sister arts? Along with the questioning of literary and cultural history, the interrogation of aesthetic values thus emerged with equal vigor. The term "aesthetics" might admittedly appear in this context somewhat anachronistic: it was after all a creation of the mid-eighteenth century. Yet that new conceptualization arose seamlessly out of the reflection undertaken during the quarrel concerning the necessity of a separate category for creative works whose secretive appeal to the senses and imagination profoundly distinguished them from the purely rational and cognitive pursuits associated with other branches of human knowledge and endeavor.

On the modern side, Perrault eagerly tackled the problem. As a sensitive critic of both literature and the visual arts (he composed in 1668 a verse treatise on painting, *La peinture*), and furthermore as a poet himself, he was quite aware of the sensuous and imaginative charms that defined aesthetic beauty. But he consistently placed such verbal and visual attractions under the stern tutelage of rigorous reason. The hierarchy of disciplines, he affirmed in the *Parallèle*, is clear: "it is up to the philosopher to lead the poet, not the poet to lead the philosopher." It was a maxim his allies and heirs would repeatedly trumpet. Rather than two cultures, the new age was to have only one,

that of philosophy (understood at the time to include all logical investigation, including the sciences). To its empire all others were naturally to submit. As Fontenelle phrased it in "Sur la poésie en
général":

> There is no doubt that philosophy has now attained new de-
> grees of perfection. It has thus shed a light that is not limited to
> the domain of philosophy alone, but that instead gains new ter-
> ritory every day, and ultimately spreads over the entire world of
> letters. Order, clarity, correctness, which were once qualities
> rare even among the best writers, are now much more com-
> mon. . . . Will poetry take pride in the glorious privilege of
> being exempt from this improvement? Ancient philosophers
> were more poets than philosophers. They reasoned very little,
> and they taught whatever they wanted with complete freedom.
> When modern poets prove to be more philosophers than poets,
> we can say that each side has its own turn.

"Order, clarity, correctness" are also the watchwords of Perrault's
literary criticism. And the *Parallèle*, despite its conversational framework, sets out a surprisingly systematic modern rationalist aesthetics
based on these principles. The system is grounded in a tripartite hierarchy of the faculties deployed in the arts, ascending in value from
the bodily senses to the emotions of the heart and ultimately to the
crowning gift of human reason. In a section of the first volume dedicated to the visual arts, Perrault's spokesperson in the *Parallèle*, the
Abbé, first lays out this hierarchy, which he will later apply to literature. He does so by distinguishing three principal elements in a canvas. First is the use of colors, which appeals to the visual senses. Second is the portrayal of various emotions through the depicted
subjects' expressions and gestures, which touches the viewer's heart.
And finally there is the careful arrangement of all the parts of the
composition, whose deliberate design is appreciated by the mind
alone. This last element represents for Perrault the highest aspect of
art. The "overall plan and . . . the attractive order of a composition
that is judiciously organized" constitute the only aspect of painting
that "pleases our reason, and makes us feel a joy that is admittedly

less intense, but more intellectual and spiritual, and thus more worthy of man."

Perrault proceeds to apply this same tripartite hierarchy to the other arts. In music, the tone of a beautiful voice delights the ears; variation in movements touch the heart; and, most important, the "admirable economy" of a complex musical arrangement pleases the intellect. Likewise, in poetry and eloquence, the sound of words gratifies the audience's senses; the swelling figures of rhetoric stir the passions; while finally, and much more edifyingly, the "beautiful economy of a discourse's design rises to the highest part of the soul and gives it a completely intellectual and spiritual joy."

It is important to appreciate here the abstract, immaterial character of literature's highest function: sensorial and emotional pleasures have their place in Perrault's system, but the stylistic virtuosity that produces them is always subordinated to intellectual design. Indeed, Perrault goes so far in his favoring of conceptual precision over seductive form as to proclaim his preference for clarifying translations over the suggestive but hazy ambiguities of works in their original language. "Modern languages are more clear and less prone to foolish nonsense than ancient ones." It is only in recent times, of course, that writers have attained the linguistic, narrative, and intellectual instruments necessary for this kind of unerring exactitude. At the base of these instruments' success, the Abbé explains in the second volume, is the perfection of what he heralds as modern "method." "Clear, precise [*nette*], and methodical" literary expression, so absent in antiquity and so universal in the present day, owes its triumph to recent mathematical and logical innovations, Perrault affirms, crediting above all Descartes. Although the Modern party leader contested some of the specific philosophic positions of the author of the *Discours de la méthode* (*Discourse on Method*), Perrault believed that Descartes's construction of that method, so securely based in geometric principles, had rightly revolutionized literature. Deductive rigor now trumped mere talent or instinct. It is no surprise that Perrault's Modern party followers would soon be known as the "geometers." Houdar de La Motte would go so far in his *Réflexions sur la critique* (Reflections on criticism) as to describe poetry in these Euclidian terms: "The geometric approach is certainly quite as valuable as that of literary commentary. . . . The art of poetry has its own axioms, its own theorems, corollaries, and demonstrations; and though its forms and terms may appear in a different guise, it is always fundamentally the same steps of reasoning, the same method, however adorned they be, that result in true proofs."

But what exactly, in the realm of imaginative literature, is being proved or demonstrated? Here we come to the final element of Perrault's aesthetics: its didacticism. Conceptual design and methodical execution both ultimately serve, he affirms, the reader's instruction. For Perrault, the utility of literature is, we have seen, "intellectual" and "spiritual." But more important, especially in the domain of fiction—whether dramatic or narrative, verse or prose—it is fundamentally moral. Precision and economy are simply tools to effectively deliver a carefully formulated lesson. The position may seem banal, but the repercussions are critical. Valuing above all moral clarity, Perrault casts serious doubts, for example, on the merits of Aristotelian pathos, whose effects of "pity and fear" depend in part on the imperfections of a virtuous yet flawed hero. To this moral murkiness, Perrault prefers characters painted in black and white. Indeed, in the preface to the first volume of the *Parallèle*, he decries translations of morally suspect ancient poetry as a menace to public's well-being. The dissemination of such Greek works, he asserts in language recalling Plato's *Republic*, goes "against the political good." In contrast, he hails modern works such as Jean Chapelain's recent epic poem about Joan of Arc, *La Pucelle*, for their stark "contrast" between an impeccably "perfect hero" and an unambiguously evil ("très méchant") villain. Only such absolute and edifying dichotomies can "furnish a morality which the masters of art demand from such works so as to make them useful to the entire public."

As Perrault's censure of classical literature's moral ambiguities suggests, the demands of contemporary propriety required breaking some ancient idols. Old artistic forms needed serious revision. Indeed, new genres needed to be created. In terms of the dramatic arts, this translated into support for the innovative libretti of the very first French operas. For poetry, it meant embracing the edification of Christian verse epic, as opposed to the pagan Homeric model backed by partisans of the ancients. Perrault himself penned such a religious epic, a *Saint Paulin* that proved as largely overlooked as Chapelain's *Pucelle*. But another of Perrault's modernizing creations would not be so soon forgotten. In an effort to provide a French response to (and replacement for) the lurid tales of pagan mythology, Perrault crafted his own fictions filled with magical marvels more fitting modern morals. Starting in the mid-1690s with verse tales such as "Peau d'âne" ("Donkey Skin"), followed by the 1697 prose *Contes* (*Tales*) that introduced in print such figures as La belle au bois dormant (Sleeping Beauty) and Cendrillon (Cinderella), Perrault published the first versions of these fairy tales, an event whose impact would be felt throughout Europe. Ironically enough, their success owed much to their playfully irreverent and often ambiguous moral messages. This should not be surprising. Perrault was after all a writer whose genius could resist his own theoretical demands (the same might be said of his opponent, Boileau). But whatever sly indulgences he permitted himself, Perrault insisted that he was strictly guided by his literary principles, and in his preface he proudly proclaimed that his fairy tales, unlike scandalous Greek myths, consistently promoted "good morals" and contained nothing that "might offend either modesty or decorum."

What did Boileau and his allies make of these modern literary and aesthetic principles? It must first be admitted that they hardly rejected them in totality. Boileau was a man of his day, and just like Perrault, he is well known for praising clarity, reason, and moral propriety. In retrospect, both men (and both parties) reveal themselves to be champions of neoclassicism. Although the term was not yet in currency, it can help to illuminate the conflict. The Modern party might be said to put the "neo-" in neoclassicism: they updated and indeed fortified the classical ideals of luminous intelligibility and flawless decorum through the favorable reinforcements of contemporary rationalism and politeness. Boileau and his allies, in contrast, kept the "classic" in neoclassicism—"classic" taken here in the sense (current in the seventeenth century) of a long-admired author who served as an exemplary model for a genre. In other words, while the defenders of antiquity did not fail to promote their own abstract principles, they nevertheless privileged above all the concretely individual works from whose irreducible artistry these principles were presumably culled. They furthermore attributed the enduring allure of these classics not only to their demonstrable (if not geometric) coherence and concision, but also to the more obscure operations of creative genius and the mysterious effects of language that transcended, they argued, mere rational method. And these primordial qualities, flourishing in simpler times, were often resistant to the historical trajectories of ameliorative progress on which glided other human pursuits. In this sense, they constituted a truly "ancient" party rather than a merely classicizing one. Indeed, their use of antiquity might prove disturbing to any notion of classicism or neoclassicism identified solely with order, lucidity, and reason.

Boileau staked out his position well before the quarrel officially commenced, most notably with two critical works published together in 1674. The first was his celebrated literary treatise in verse form, the *Art poétique*, which offered an elegant variation on the basic principles of poetic unity and decorum inherited from Aristotle and Horace and refined by earlier Renaissance humanists. Appealing to the common sense of the leisured reading public, the poem presents a carefully modulated form of neoclassicism. Its opening lines, for example, equitably balance the requirements of reason and regularity with enthusiastic praise for the mysteries of Parnassian inspiration and instinctual genius. The beginning of its third canto likewise mitigates the demands of decorum and didacticism by extolling the fierce passions of tragedy, including the thrill afforded by such "horrendous" (*affreux*) spectacles as those of a "blood-soaked Oedipus" and a "parricidal Orestes." Through this balancing act, the *Art poétique* constitutes an effort to claim the center ground in literary debates, cautiously containing—without rejecting—the contemporary dictates of rationalism and propriety.

Boileau's sensible centrism, however, proved wobbly. With his second great work of 1674, the translation from ancient Greek of Longinus's treatise *On the Sublime*, he adopted a considerably more pointed position. Turning from the mainstream tradition of Horatian and Aristotelian criticism to the more neglected Longinus, Boileau entered into an audacious defense of the apparently unmethodical, even inexplicable, aspects of ancient literature. He did so by turning the traditional reading of Longinus's work—that of a pedagogic manual for the orator—on its head. In his preface, Boileau crucially defines the sublime not as a mere (albeit the highest) register of rhetoric, but instead as something very different: as the ineffable power of language that escapes the logical mechanics of rhetorical production and analysis. The sublime becomes in Boileau's hands a type of supernatural force vested in poetry, "the marvel inside language" (*le merveilleux dans le discours*). It adds to the common use of words an indefinable supplement. This intangible dimension of language produces in the reader not a comforting pleasure but a violent movement: the sublime, Boileau famously exults, "carries away, ravishes, transports" (*enlève, ravit, transporte*) the reader.

Boileau's embrace of Longinus so defined the Ancient party that it was sometimes called the party (or, more polemically, the "cabal") of the Sublime. It is thus fitting that Boileau's most sustained responses to Perrault, begun in 1692, are contained in his twelve *Réflexions critiques sur quelques passages du rhéteur Longin* (*Critical Reflections on Some Passages from the Rhetor Longinus*), the last three of which were published only in the years after his death in 1711. Although more impassioned in tone and less systematic in approach than Perrault, Boileau nevertheless offers here a counteraesthetic to the one elaborated by the Modern party leader. In place of Perrault's emphasis on denotative exactitude, Boileau's explication of the mysteries of the sublime lead him to praise what appears to be the opposite of transparent precision: a certain shadowy power in words that he calls a "majestic and elegant obscurity." As the qualifiers "majestic" and "elegant" make clear, the "obscurity" in question does not result from just any poetic gibberish. Boileau was after all as rigorous in his own way as Perrault. Nevertheless, by lauding obscurity, Boileau has consciously picked fighting words. He has asserted that great literature depends on something other than the light of reason alone. "The sublime," he explains, "is not, properly speaking, a thing that can be proved or demonstrated; instead . . . it is a wonder that seizes, strikes, makes itself felt."

Boileau is taking aim not just at the intellectualism of Perrault's approach, but also at the abstract quality of that intellectualism. The literary force that "seizes, strikes, makes itself felt" arises for Boileau not so much from the immaterial and conceptual design lauded by his modern opponent, but instead from the irreducible concreteness of the words themselves and their sonorous and connotative effects. Boileau takes on here Perrault's preference for the corrective translation over the suggestive original. Despite his own enthusiasm for translating classics, Boileau proves to be something of a theoretician of the untranslatable. The auditory and associative networks of each language are fundamentally unique, he claims, and words that are "noble and sweet to the ear in their original language, would be base and gross once translated into French." Whereas Perrault firmly subordinates the musicality of language to "the purely intellectual and spiritual joy" of its carefully constructed meaning, Boileau privileges instead a "power" and "beauty" that "consists primarily in the number, arrangement, and magnificence of the words."

It is furthermore a beauty, according to Boileau, that "method" alone cannot produce. Boileau rallies to the notion of an unmethodical "beautiful disorder" (*beau désordre*) that he earlier adopted in his *Art poétique*. In opposition to Perrault's maxim dictating that poets be guided by their inner philosopher, the Ancient party leader promotes elusive intuition as a crucial source of the sublime. In another work aimed directly at Perrault, the 1693 *Discours sur l'ode* (Discourse on the ode), Boileau exuberantly claims that "beautiful disorder" can result from an "impetuous" talent that succeeds by "sometimes disregarding the rules," and even by surrendering to the arbitrary inspiration of "chance" itself. He puts genius before method. In retrospect, Boileau, for all his praise elsewhere for measure and restraint, might strike us as more Romantic than neoclassical, particularly when extolling, as here, the "movements and transports where the mind appears to be led more by the demon of poetry than guided by reason."

Boileau's "demon of poetry" could be quite diabolical indeed. Not just poetically, but also morally. This brings us to a final aspect of Boileau's sublime, its prudent but unmistakable resistance to the Modern party's emphasis on didacticism. Just as the sublime asks readers to temporarily abandon the cognitive norms of their reasoning intellect, so too they must sometimes set aside, however briefly, the moral norms of their age and nation. Of course, there are for Boileau strict limits to this literary license. He could, after all, attack what he deplored as "lubricious" modern novels and operas with a zeal at least equaling Perrault's denunciation of what he, for his part, labeled ancient "filth." Boileau nevertheless positioned himself early as a critic who sought to clearly distinguish a work's emotional impact from its moral influence. When commenting in the *Art poétique* on the passions of Virgil's Dido, for example, he insists that the reader may "condemn her fault while partaking in her tears." The ethical gray area of tragic pathos, which we have seen treated with skepticism by Perrault, requires for Boileau the reader's nuanced leniency.

The pleasures of the sublime demand equal permissiveness. Thus, in the tenth of his *Réflexions* he elevates as a great exemplar of the modern sublime the mad egoistical cry of Pierre Corneille's Médée (Medea), who when asked what might guarantee the success of her murderous revenge plot, exclaims "Moi / Moi, dis-je, et c'est assez!" (Me / Me, I say, and that's enough!). The horror of the infanticide here foreshadowed forced Corneille himself, despite his claims that he had no need to excuse his heroine's infamous crime, to defend himself in his later dedicatory preface to the 1635 play by asserting that tragic characters need not be virtuous, but simply accurately depicted. When explaining the verse's power, Boileau goes a step further by not even bothering with such justifications; he simply dodges all moral considerations as apparently irrelevant. "Can one deny that in this monosyllabic Me there is the Sublime, and the highest Sublime? What strikes us in this passage if not the audacious pride of this magician, and the confidence she has in her art?"

Boileau's defense, hesitant though it often was, of a certain moral autonomy for literature became one of the most consequential arguments adopted by the future champions of antiquity. Anne Dacier, for example, could divorce literature from morality in the starkest terms: "The aim of poetry is to imitate," she states in her preface to Homer's *Iliad*, "and its imitation can be [as] vicious in regard to good politics, as it is excellent in regard to good poetry." Others went further and suggested that literary value and the political good were not only frequently independent of each other, but that they could even bear an inverse relation. Such was the gist of Fénelon's defense of Homer when he claimed, "The more the [pagan] religion was monstrous and ridiculous, the more one must admire [Homer] for having raised it up with so many magnificent images. The cruder the morals and manners were, the more stirring it is to see that he lent such power to what is so irregular, so absurd, so shocking." Faced with his own conflicted admiration for Homer, Fénelon urges the reader to develop a kind of double consciousness: a philosophical and moral one that disapproves and an aesthetic one that takes delight.

The vexing relation between literature and philosophy would prove to be one of the great questions stimulating thinkers throughout the rest of the eighteenth century. Ancient literature continued to be a crucial battleground, and the arguments of the quarrel resonated powerfully in the Enlightenment. But after the storm of the conflict finally began to quiet, the partisan divisions—always, as we have seen, intricate and nuanced—proved even more paradoxical. The progressive and freethinking Diderot, for example, was in many ways an heir of the Modern party. Yet when it came to literature and the arts, he embraced precisely the primitive sublimity that Perrault denounced. In antiquity he found an antidote to the stifling constraints of modern decorum. These refinements might serve societal happiness, but they proved deadly to imaginative genius. Thus, after enumerating in his 1758 essay "De la poésie dramatique" ("On Dramatic Poetry") a lurid catalog of the barbarous ancient customs that produced terrifying tragedies and sublime epics, he observes, "I do not say such customs are good, only that they are poetic," explaining, "the more a people are civilized and polite, the less their manners and morals are poetical."

Jean-Jacques Rousseau was, in a very different manner, equally conflicted. Indeed, he might be called a one-man quarrel of the ancients and moderns. The ancient partisan in him reserved a special disdain for the moderns' celebration of progress and refinement, for which he blamed the prevailing vices of artificiality and inequality. He admired the simplicity of Homer, even arguing in his posthumous "Essai sur l'origine des langues" ("Essay on the Origin of Languages") that the primitive orality of his epics was vastly superior to the vain sophistication of more advanced literate societies. Yet when it came to the moral and political function of literature, he proved in many ways an heir to the same modern partisans he elsewhere scorned. Beginning in 1750 with what is called his *First Discourse* (*Discours sur les sciences et les arts*), he unflinchingly denounced the continuing sway of Greco-Roman paganism in poetry and the arts, castigating the "images of all the waylaying distractions of the heart and reason, carefully drawn from ancient mythology." His 1758 *Lettre à d'Alembert* went considerably further, condemning with a zeal worthy of Perrault the immorality of classical tragedy, attacking its flawed heroes and heroines, and endorsing in the name of "public rectitude" the banning of all such works' performance. He thus adopts the solution proposed by Plato in *The Republic* and seconded by modern partisans: discarding the old, the contemporary world must craft new forms of art aimed at inculcating what Rousseau called "useful lessons" for the public good.

Finally, the quarrel owes its enduring influence not only to the substance of its arguments, such as those evoked by Diderot and Rousseau, but also to the manner and the context in which those arguments were originally made. The word "quarrel" (*querelle*) is instructive here. The great literary and theatrical *querelles* that preceded it, those, for example, around Corneille's *Le Cid* (1637), and Molière's *L'école des femmes* (*School for Wives*, 1662–63) and *Tartuffe* (1664–69), had begun to establish the terrain for debates engaging the reading (or viewing) public. Lasting decades rather than only a few months or years, the quarrel of the ancients and moderns vastly expanded the field for such discussions from a single topic to the entire gamut of cultural production across the ages, and to the full array of issues at stake concerning literary value and the progress of the arts. It also continued to broaden the audience for these debates. It is crucial to note here that the Ancient party, as much as the Modern one, wrote in approachable and elegant French, avoiding neo-Latin learning and pedantic terminology. More important, Boileau and his allies joined their opponents in generally rejecting arguments based on authority, whether it was scholarly, religious, or institutional. Recourse to such extraneous support was, they understood, risible to the leisured and cultivated readers whom they targeted. Ancient as well as modern champions thus appealed to the pride this audience took in its independent reason and innate good taste. The parties argued through graceful verse, witty dialogues, and seductive prose. Perhaps more significant, they published compelling translations (and free adaptations) of classics into modern French, opening these newly accessible texts up to a broader public.

It is in that spirit that by the early eighteenth century the quarrel naturally migrated, as Montesquieu satirically notes in *Les Lettres persanes* (*The Persian Letters*), to the first cafés to be opened in Paris, where the boisterous exchange of ideas helped to produce the increasingly powerful notion of public opinion. Literature and the arts, which were carving out their own distinct sphere in the quarrel, were now fully open to freewheeling public debate. Both parties had prepared the terrain. Modern partisans had ruthlessly exposed hallowed masterpieces to critical reason and to the new forms of unfettered research that would occupy the coming century; the defenders of antiquity, for their part, had boldly reinvigorated old ideas concerning the primeval and intuitive nature of poetry and the arts that would feed Enlightenment and Romantic interest in artistic genius, aesthetic experience, primitivism, and the sublime. Furthermore, such literary and aesthetic discussions could easily slide into the political and societal issues raised by the ancient works under consideration— including the paganism, republicanism, and sexual license so troubling to modern Christian monarchies—and thus allow a side entrance into those more regulated (and censored) domains. Thus did a debate that reconfigured our understanding of literature's past also reshape its future prospects.

Works Cited and Recommended Further Reading

Note: All translations of passages quoted in this chapter are my own.

Boileau, Nicolas [Boileau-Despréaux]. *Œuvres complètes*. Edited by Françoise Escal. Paris: Gallimard (Bibliothèque de la Pléiade), 1966.

Corneille, Pierre. *Œuvres complètes*. Edited by Georges Couton. 3 vols. Paris: Gallimard (Bibliothèque de la Pléiade), 1980–87.

Curtius, Ernst Robert. *European Literature and the Latin Middle Ages*. Translated by W. R. Trask. New York: Pantheon (Bollingen), 1953.

Dacier, Anne Lefebvre. *L'Iliade d'Homère traduite en français, avec des remarques*. 3 vols. Paris: Rigaud, 1711.

Diderot, Denis. *Œuvres esthétiques*. Edited by Paul Vernière. Paris: Classiques Garnier, 1994.

Fénelon, François de Pons de Salignac de La Motte. *Œuvres*. Edited by Jacques Le Brun. 2 vols. Paris: Gallimard (Bibliothèque de la Pléiade), 1983–97.

Fontenelle, Bernard Le Bovier de. *Œuvres complètes*. Edited by Alain Niderst. 9 vols. Paris: Fayard, 1990–2001.

La Motte, Antoine Houdar de. *Textes critiques*. Edited by Françoise Gevrey and Béatrice Guion. Paris: Champion, 2002.

Longepierre, Hilaire-Bernard de. *Discours sur les anciens*. Paris: Abouin, 1687.

Marivaux. *Œuvres de jeunesse*. Edited by Frédéric Deloffre. Paris: Gallimard (Bibliothèque de la Pléiade), 1972.

Montesquieu. *Œuvres complètes*. Edited by Roger Caillois. 2 vols. Paris: Gallimard (Bibliothèque de la Pléiade), 1949.

Perrault, Charles. *Parallèle des anciens et des modernes, en ce qui regarde les arts et les sciences* (1688–97). Reprint, with introduction by H. R. Jauss. Munich: Eidos Verlag, 1964.

Rousseau, Jean-Baptiste. *Correspondance de J.-B. Rousseau et Brossette*. Edited by P. Bonnefon. 2 vols. Paris: Cornély, 1910–11.

Rousseau, Jean-Jacques. *Œuvres complètes*. Edited by Bernard Gagnebin, Marcel Raymond, et al. 5 vols. Paris: Gallimard (Bibliothèque de la Pléiade), 1959–95.

Snow, C. P. *The Two Cultures and the Scientific Revolution*. Cambridge: Cambridge University Press, 1960.

Swift, Jonathan. *A Tale of the Tub [and] The Battle of the Books*. Oxford: Clarendon Press, 1958.

For a rich historical account of the quarrel in France and Britain, see Joseph M. Levine, *The Battle of the Books: History and Literature in the Augustan Age* (Ithaca, NY: Cornell University Press, 1991); for a briefer introduction, consult Douglas L. Patey, "Ancients and Moderns," in *The Cambridge History of Literary Criticism*, vol. 4 (Cambridge: Cambridge University Press, 1989). Joan DeJean considers the quarrel in the broader context of recurring cultural wars in *Ancients against Moderns* (Chicago: University of Chicago Press, 1997); Sara E. Melzer examines the relation between ancient Roman and early modern French imperial ambitions in *Colonizer or Colonized: The Hidden Stories of Early Modern French Culture* (Philadelphia: University of Pennsylvania Press, 2012). For an excellent introduction to the contradictory pulls of French neoclassical aesthetics, see E.B.O. Borgerhoff, *The Freedom of*

French Classicism (Princeton, NJ: Princeton University Press, 1950). To pursue further development of the themes highlighted here, see Larry F. Norman, *The Shock of the Ancient: Literature and History in Early Modern France* (Chicago: University of Chicago Press, 2011).

Concerning the continuing influence of the quarrel in the Enlightenment, see Peter Gay, *Enlightenment: An Interpretation; The Rise of Modern Paganism*, vol. 1 (New York: W. W. Norton, 1966) and, more recently, Elena Russo, *Styles of Enlightenment: Taste, Politics, and Authorship in Eighteenth-Century France* (Baltimore, MD: Johns Hopkins University Press, 2007) and Dan Edelstein, *The Enlightenment: A Genealogy* (Chicago: University of Chicago Press, 2010). For Boileau and the sublime, see Nicholas Cronk, *The Classical Sublime: French Neoclassicism and the Language of Literature* (Charlottesville, VA: Rookwood Press, 2002) and Emma Gilby, *Sublime Worlds: Early Modern French Literature* (London: Legenda, 2006). On Perrault's modernism, consult Jeanne Morgan Zarucchi, *Perrault's Morals for Moderns* (Frankfurt: Peter Lang, 1984).

Among the important works in French must be noted Marc Fumaroli's extensive introductory essay to the anthology *La querelle des anciens et des modernes* (Paris: Gallimard, 2001), as well as François Hartog, *Anciens, modernes, sauvages* (Paris: Galaade, 2005) and Levent Yilmaz, *Le temps moderne: Variations sur les anciens et les contemporains* (Paris: Gallimard, 2004).

* *

Voltaire's *Candide*

Lessons of Enlightenment and the Search for Truth

NICHOLAS CRONK

The appearance of *Candide* in early 1759 was a publishing sensation, what we would now call a "media event." Following the first edition in Geneva, others instantly sprang up all over Europe, in Paris, London, Liège. Would-be censors protested in vain; the book was everywhere and unstoppable. Voltaire's short novel, never since out of print, has gone through countless editions and been translated into every imaginable language. In what is the sure sign of a classic, the book has left a mark on the language we speak. One celebrated rejoinder, "Let's eat some Jesuit!" (mangeons du Jésuite!), became an instant catchphrase in French, while other expressions from the book, such as "Panglossian" and "pour encourager les autres" (to encourage the others), have entered English usage. The book continues to have a vital place in English-speaking culture. In 1932, Bernard Shaw published an imitation of *Candide* titled *The Adventures of the Black Girl in Her Search for God*; the short novel was instantly banned in the Irish Free State on account of its criticism of the Church. Leonard Bernstein's musical *Candide*, composed to a libretto by Lilian Hellman, opened on Broadway in 1956 and continues to be widely performed on both sides of the Atlantic. Mark Ravenhill's *Candide* (2013), written for the Royal Shakespeare Company, is a modern response to Voltaire's novel, exploring our contemporary obsession with positive (Panglossian?) thinking that encourages us to rationalize evil out of existence. In preparation for the play's opening, the playwright "translated" Voltaire's entire novel into a series of 140-character episodes, which were tweeted eight times a day over a period of two months. There are many ways for modern readers to discover *Candide*.

If we look at the title page of an early edition, we can see how early readers came to know the novel (see fig. 1). *Candide, ou l'optimisme*: the term *optimisme*, as we shall see, refers to a particular philosophical view, but the word itself, an import from German, was then a new coinage in the French language, so its presence in the title of a novel was potentially pretentious or comic. The work is said to be "translated from the German of Dr. Ralph," an old device that would have deceived no one, especially as the alleged German translator has an incongruously English name. Voltaire's name appears nowhere—and of course, his celebrity was such that everyone knew the book was by him. The year of publication, 1759, is correctly stated on the title page, but no place of publication is given, and no publisher is named— these are the hallmarks of a clandestine printing. In fact, in the course of 1759, there were no fewer than seventeen different printings: the one illustrated here was published in London by John Nourse, and it appeared very shortly after the first edition in Geneva, so quickly in fact that it seems that Voltaire must have slipped Nourse the manuscript even before the Genevan edition had appeared, no doubt as a precaution, should the Swiss edition be seized by police.

The eighteenth-century book market was an international one, and French editions published in London found their way to the Continent; but this London edition also reminds us that in mid-eighteenth-century London, there were educated printers able to publish books in French, and educated Englishmen wanting to read novels in French—and in the case of the copy illustrated here, we can see, from his signature on the title page, that one later eighteenth-century reader was presumably George Canning (1770–1827), the future prime minister. And for those English readers who could not read French, there were translations galore: no fewer than three different English versions, one of them published by Nourse, appeared in London in the course of 1759; and all three had to be reprinted in the course of that same year: the public appetite for *Candide* was insatiable.

Candide remains one of the most widely read novels of the eighteenth century, and for many readers it provides an introduction not just to the writing of Voltaire but to the thought of the age of the Enlightenment. Voltaire (1694–1778) was born and died in Paris, but spent most of his long and restless life away from the capital. He trav-

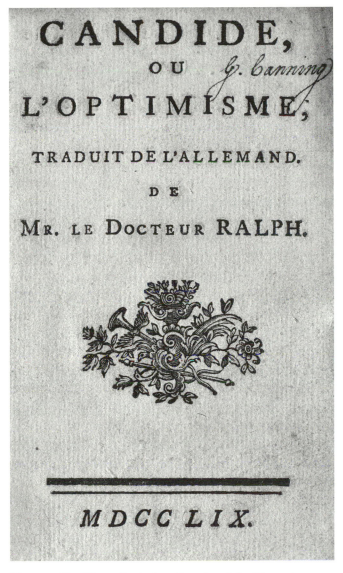

CANDIDE,

OU

L'OPTIMISME,

TRADUIT DE L'ALLEMAND.

DE

Mr. le Docteur RALPH.

MDCC LIX.

Figure 1. *Candide, ou l'optimisme* [London: John Nourse], 1759.
Private collection.

eled to England in the 1720s, where he was an enthusiastic student of English culture, and to Berlin in the early 1750s, where he was the guest of Frederick the Great. He moved to a house, Les Délices, on the outskirts of Geneva in 1755, and finally settled, in the late 1750s, at the Château de Ferney, a grand residence situated near Geneva, but on French soil. Voltaire, now the most famous living author in Europe, was dubbed "the patriarch of Ferney," and works continued to pour from his pen until his death at the age of eighty-four. Today, he is remembered for *Candide* and a handful of other short fictions, like *Micromégas*, *Zadig*, or *L'ingénu*, and for the *Lettres philosophiques*, published after his visit to England.

In fact these works represent only a tiny fraction of his writings: the *Complete Works of Voltaire* currently being published by the Voltaire Foundation in Oxford will number well more than two hundred volumes when it is completed, in a few years' time. Voltaire was prolific and wrote in every known genre, from the most prestigious, like epic poetry and classical tragedy, down to the most ephemeral, like articles for the press or occasional verse. The other *philosophes*, Montesquieu, Diderot, Jean-Jacques Rousseau, are remembered for important individual works; Voltaire is remembered for being Voltaire. In whatever genre he was writing, he used his trademark irony to express skepticism about dogmatic belief, in particular about entrenched religious belief. The name Voltaire is itself an invention (he was born François-Marie Arouet), and in some ways it is his greatest literary creation: more a label than a name, it has come to represent a way of looking at the world. And *Candide* expresses that Voltairean take on the world perhaps better than any of his other books.

❖ ❖ ❖ ❖

When the English novelist Aldous Huxley reread *Candide* in the years after the First World War, his first response was to remark on how modern the book seemed: "Read the book today; you feel yourself entirely at home in its pages. It is like reading a record of the facts and opinions of 1922; nothing was ever more applicable, more completely to the point. The world in which we live is recognizably the world of Candide and Cunégonde, of Martin and the Old Woman who was a

Pope's daughter and the betrothed of the sovereign Prince of Massa-Carrara. The only difference is that the horrors crowd rather more thickly on the world of 1922 than they did on Candide's world."

Candide tells the story of a journey, albeit in a surreal and comic vein. In the eighteenth century, fictional writers increasingly used the idea of travel as a metaphor: travelers (usually men, but sometimes women) no longer simply discover the delights of new lands, they look abroad to learn more about themselves and their own culture, so that travel becomes a means for acquiring understanding. The English philosopher Locke is a key figure here. In his *Essay Concerning Human Understanding* (1689), Locke argued for an empirical theory of knowledge, against those who believed in a priori reasoning or in revelation. The human mind, said Locke, is a tabula rasa, a blank tablet, on which are written in the course of a human life the experiences derived from sense impressions. The key tenet of scientific method is that truth is discovered through experiment and observation of the natural world, and not by reliance on innate ideas and assumptions. Voltaire wrote about these ideas in *Lettres philosophiques* (1734), first published in London, in English, as *Letters concerning the English nation* (1733), and this work played a key role in the 1730s in beginning to popularize Locke's ideas in France and the rest of Europe.

The principles of empirical thinking came increasingly to shape novel writing in the Enlightenment. The French word *expérience* means both "experience" and "experiment," so that the experiences of a fictional hero or heroine became, quite literally, experiments in how to acquire knowledge. Candide's name—*candidus* means "white" in Latin—is a deliberate nod to Locke's blank tablet. Montesquieu's *Lettres persanes* (1721) describe the reactions of two ingenuous Persian visitors who struggle to learn from their experiences, while Françoise de Graffigny's *Lettres d'une péruvienne* (1747) give a feminist twist to the model, describing the struggles of a Peruvian woman to come to terms with French culture (and men). This use of a foreign culture to relativize one's own could easily become mechanical, but Diderot gives the device sophisticated treatment in his *Supplément au voyage de Bougainville* (written in 1772): in this encounter between the very different sexual mores of France and Tahiti, we are no longer quite sure who is learning what from whom.

Candide, like other novels of the period, presents us then with a hero traveling in search of truth. But this is a comic novel, and in his hectic journeys to so many different countries, Candide is confronted by extraordinary events that flash by at bewildering and implausible speed: for the reader, it is like watching the speeded-up action of an old black-and-white film, with predictably comic results. How can we be expected to learn from our experiences, when there are just so many of them? And what is particular about this story is the way in which Candide is subjected to a crash course in evil: moral evil, the evil that humans inflict on their fellows (war, cruelty, violence); and metaphysical evil, those inexplicable and seemingly random events that God inflicts on humanity (earthquakes, plagues).

So the central philosophical question raised by the novel is this problem of evil: if, as Christians believe, God exists and he is good, why does he permit evil to exist on earth? This is hardly a new problem—think of the Book of Job—but each age has come up with a different way of approaching it. The eighteenth century explored a new answer: what seems evil to human beings appears so only because of their limited perspective; from God's point of view, the world we inhabit is actually the "best of all possible worlds"—in other words, evil does not really exist, when viewed in the larger context. This response to the problem of evil—which in the eighteenth century goes under the misleading name of "optimism"—derives from the German philosopher Leibniz, and a somewhat simplified version of the philosophy is associated with the English poet Alexander Pope, whose *Essay on Man* (1734) was widely read across Europe:

> All Nature is but Art, unknown to thee;
> All chance, direction, which thou canst not see
> All discord, harmony not understood,
> All partial evil, universal good:
> And, spite of pride, in erring reason's spite,
> One truth is clear, whatever is, is right.

In other words, there is nothing random or accidental in God's creation: it is up to each of us to discern the underlying order of divine Providence. It was common in the eighteenth century to suggest that this latent sense of structure was proof of God's existence. In the spirit of this so-called argument from design, Voltaire liked to refer to "God the watchmaker": when you look inside a watch, you know that the machinery was designed and assembled by the intelligence of a watchmaker. Thus the design or harmonious shape of the universe is "proof" of a divine designer or creator. This idea (refuted robustly by David Hume in the mid-eighteenth century) lingers on, and "intelligent design" is a phrase much in circulation since a key US Supreme Court ruling of 1987 concerning the teaching of "creationism" in American schools. According to the static worldview of Leibnizian optimism (which has no place for any notion of change or evolution), there is a providential order in the universe, God is in his place, and, conveniently, evil seems not to exist.

These ideas acquired new urgency in November 1755, as news spread of a calamitous earthquake in Lisbon that killed many tens of thousands. The beautiful city lay in ruins, and public opinion across Europe became preoccupied with this flagrant example of gratuitous evil so close to home. Of course, there were theologians aplenty prepared to argue that this was God's divine judgment on the good citizens of Lisbon; and these theologians in turn became the target of Enlightened rationalist philosophers who were quick to ridicule such notions of providential intervention. Voltaire's response was predictable and immediate: his long philosophical poem rejecting belief in Providence, "Poème sur le désastre de Lisbonne" ("Poem on the Lisbon Disaster," 1756), was circulating widely within a matter of weeks. Candide, a few years later, is an eye-witness to the earthquake and a victim of the vicious theological intolerance it unleashed (chapters 4–6): eighteenth-century readers of the novel would certainly have linked this episode to the controversy aroused by the earlier "Poem on the Lisbon Disaster."

The Leibnizian worldview might seem a somewhat simplistic view of creation, or at least an overoptimistic one (to use the word "optimism" in its modern sense)—that was certainly what Voltaire thought. Dr. Pangloss—his name means "all tongues"—is a German philosopher who has a simple, one-size-fits-all solution to the problem of evil: "Everything is for the best." Whatever disaster befalls him, to the very end of the novel, he repeats endlessly the same mantra. The idea that this work should be read as a satirical attack on the philosophy of Leibniz and his solution to the age-old problem of evil seems evident, and this is certainly how the book was understood in the eighteenth century.

Here is James Boswell, in his *Life of Samuel Johnson*: "Voltaire's *Candide*, written to refute the system of Optimism, which it has accomplished with brilliant success, is wonderfully similar in its plan and conduct to Johnson's *Rasselas*; insomuch, that I have heard Johnson say, that if they had not been published so closely one after the other that there was not time for imitation, it would have been in vain to deny that the scheme of that which came latest was taken from the other." A case, then, of great minds thinking alike—except that Boswell is clearly uncomfortable with Voltaire's famously secular view of the world: "Though the proposition illustrated by both these works was the same, namely, that in our present state there is more evil than good, the intention of the writers was very different. Voltaire, I am afraid, meant only by wanton profaneness to obtain a sportive victory over religion, and to discredit the belief of a superintending Providence: Johnson meant, by showing the unsatisfactory nature of things temporal, to direct the hopes of man to things eternal." So in Boswell's view, Voltaire's prime aim, beyond discrediting Leibnizian optimism, was to destabilize blind belief in Providence, to make us suspicious of the metaphysical. As the historian Daniel Roche writes, "The appeal of *Candide* lay in its representation of a key idea of the Enlightenment: the embrace of the concrete, the idea that the spiritual does not exist apart from its manifestations."

❖ ❖ ❖ ❖

The characters in this novel mostly accept Providence with a shrug and submit to whatever befalls them, but their attitude is not exactly one of simple resignation. The narrative conveys a strong sense of anxiety, and in this topsy-turvy world, nothing is comfortably in its right place. The traditional reading of *Candide* as a satire on Leibnizian optimism is not altogether wrong, but it is insufficient. The narrative is not preoccupied solely with the problem of evil, and the novel, even though its action is anything but realistic, does also reflect aspects of the "real" world.

In chapter 26, Candide and Martin dine with six dispossessed kings who compare their respective tales of woe: the tone might be that of a fairy tale, but the characters and their stories are all real. War is depicted with particular brutality in chapter 3, a forceful example of gratuitous evil in general. At the same time, this description also reflects a contemporary political situation: in the mid-eighteenth century, a series of wars was fought in Europe, North America, West Africa, and India, which collectively we now call the Seven Years' War (1756–63). This was a world conflict, more extensive by far than anything that had been seen in Europe during the previous century, and the casualties were well in excess of one million. In 1761, when Voltaire revised *Candide*, he extended the title to make the reference to this war explicit: *Candide . . . Together with the Addenda Which Were Found in the Doctor's Pocket When He Died at Minden in the Year of Grace 1759*. Minden is in Westphalia, the very province where Candide's journey begins, and in 1759 it was the scene of a bloody battle in which sixty thousand French troops were defeated by the Hanoverians, allies of the British. The scenes of brutal carnage depicted in chapter 3 are more than just a generalized exemplification of evil; they document precisely the slaughter then taking place on battlefields in Germany.

Voltaire attacks war in general, while also giving voice to specifically French fears about the war currently being fought. At the root of the Seven Years' War was the struggle between Britain and France to expand their trading empires in such places as Quebec and India. By the end of the war, in 1763, Britain would emerge as the dominant colonial power, and references in *Candide* speak to French anguish about the eventual outcome of this global conflict. One notable early British setback had been the loss of Minorca to the French in 1756, as a result of which the English Admiral Byng was court-martialed and executed. Voltaire has fun with this in chapter 23:

"And why kill this admiral?"
"Because he didn't kill enough people," Candide was told.

"He gave battle to a French admiral, and it has been found that he wasn't close enough."

"But," said Candide, "the French admiral was just as far away from the English admiral as he was from him!"

"Unquestionably," came the reply. "But in this country it is considered a good thing to kill an admiral from time to time so as to encourage the others [pour encourager les autres]."

But this was a rare French victory, and in this same chapter, there is an overt reference to the war in North America between France and Britain: "As you know, the two countries are at war over a few acres of snow across in Canada, and they're spending more on this war than the whole of Canada is worth" (a remark that the French-speaking population of Quebec has still not forgiven Voltaire). In the course of 1759, only months after the first appearance of *Candide*, the French planned to invade Great Britain, but two major defeats at sea left the British navy more dominant than before. This political context was difficult for Voltaire: he had made his name in the 1730s as an enthusiastic proponent of English philosophy and literature, holding up English culture as a model for the French. Now he felt obliged to nuance his position, so it is not surprising that when, in chapter 23, the Dutch ship in which Candide and Martin are traveling docks at Portsmouth, Candide refuses to step ashore: Candide travels across the world, yet still does not, quite, set foot in England. Even in a surreal comedy, there are limits.

Connected with this anxiety about colonial wars is a contemporary preoccupation with slavery. In 1758, Voltaire read in Helvétius's *De l'esprit*, a stinging attack on the practice of slavery: "You must agree that every barrel of sugar that arrives in Europe is tainted with human blood." Voltaire responded by adding a scene to chapter 19, in which Candide and Cacambo, as they are about to arrive in Surinam, meet a slave (described as "a Negro") with only one arm and one leg: "When we're working at the sugar mill and catch our finger in the grinding-wheel, they cut off our hand. When we try to run away, they cut off a leg. I have been in both these situations. This is the price you pay for the sugar you eat in Europe." It is often said that Candide is a puppetlike automaton who shows no emotion, but this is not entirely true: the pathetic spectacle of the slave prompts Candide to shed tears, and Voltaire to shed his irony. This is the only occasion in the novel that the word "optimism" is uttered:

> "O Pangloss!" cried Candide, "this is one abomination you never thought of. That does it. I shall finally have to renounce your Optimism."
>
> "What's Optimism?" asked Cacambo.
>
> "I'm afraid to say," said Candide, "that it's a mania for insisting that all is well when things are going badly."
>
> And he began to weep as he gazed at his Negro, and he entered Surinam in tears.

The trade in sugar referred to here is of course just a small part of the international trade fostered by the warring commercial empires of France and Britain, and this trade was supporting a boom in consumerism in western Europe, the like of which had never been seen. Eighteenth-century Parisian culture in particular attained in this period a level of exquisite refinement unequaled before or since: whether we are thinking of the quality and range of fare available, or the refinement of the porcelain on which it was served, or the beauty of the silk dresses worn by the ladies at table, French culture had reached a level of luxury that was a legitimate source of national pride but also a subject of concern. A debate simmered about the ethics of luxury, and Voltaire himself had previously contributed to this discussion, with his poem "The Man of the World" ("Le mondain," 1736). The description of the German baron's château in chapter 1—"his castle had a door and windows. His great hall was even adorned with a tapestry"—is of course a snobbish Parisian put-down of crude German taste; but the description of Eldorado, in the chapters placed at the heart of the novel, can equally be read as a parody (and potential critique) of Parisian hypersophistication. The roads in Eldorado are "covered, or rather adorned, with conveyances of the most lustrous form and substance, bearing men and women of singular beauty, and drawn at great speed" (chapter 17), clearly a reference to the eighteenth-century French obsession with fine coaches; while the food offered at a simple inn—"four different soups, each garnished with a couple of parrots, . . . two excellent roast monkeys . . . another platter of six hundred humming-birds" (chapter 17) is an over-the-top parody of luxurious French gastronomy.

Candide creates a fictional world of pure comic fantasy, but this remains an uneasy and anguished world, and the anxieties of ancien régime France—war with England and the status of France as a world power, the questions of slavery and the colonies, the problem of luxury and consumerism—impinge on the narrative. In an essay introducing *Candide*, the French critic Roland Barthes famously wrote that Voltaire was "the last of the happy writers." Like Aldous Huxley, he seems to think that the ills and misfortunes of the eighteenth century were minor in comparison with our own, and that Voltaire's fast-moving, witty style would no longer be possible or appropriate for a modern writer in the post-Holocaust world. This underestimates the atrocities of eighteenth-century warfare, and more important, it misunderstands Voltaire's polemical style, where the seemingly superficial treatment of profound horror is a deliberate shock tactic.

Modern readers will also find in Voltaire's novel reflections of eighteenth-century society that disturb us, even if they do not seem to have troubled Voltaire's contemporaries. The accusation is often made that Voltaire was anti-Semitic, and while that may be unjust, the passing remark that Candide "was swindled so many times by the Jews" (chapter 30) makes us uncomfortable. *Candide*'s comic world is a very macho one, and women occupy in it a prominent but distinctly limited role as the objects of male lust. In what seems to be the glorious conclusion of the final chapter, the women take responsibility for cooking, sewing, and washing—hardly a blow for women's liberation. The best that can be said for the women in this novel is that they are at least given full rein to enjoy their sexual appetites, including those women in chapter 16 whose taste runs to monkeys rather than men. This remains a resolutely male-centred world, and the one gay character, Cunégonde's brother, the young baron, is written off as a foolish, unfeeling snob. Although severely punished when he is discovered swimming naked with a handsome young Muslim (chapter

29)—he too gets to enjoy his sexual appetites—this experience fails to teach him tolerance toward others, and he remains implacably opposed to Candide's ambitions to marry his sister, because of what he perceives to be Candide's inferior social status. In the resolution of the final chapter, all the characters come together in some sort of harmony—all, that is, apart from the baron, whom the others collectively pack off in a galley. In its depictions of women and homosexuals, *Candide* reflects the opinions and literary stereotypes of its period more than it challenges them. Voltaire urges us in this novel to challenge received thinking, and in applying his lesson, it is right that modern readers will sometimes want to challenge Voltaire's own worldview.

❧ ❧ ❧ ❧

An understanding of the philosophical and historical context of the novel enriches our reading, but it is important to remember that many (most?) modern readers enjoy *Candide* without any of this background knowledge. The novel must clearly appeal to us at another level. Voltaire has written a novel, not a philosophical treatise, and a novel invites us not just to think about ideas in the abstract but to reflect on how characters deal with and live out those ideas; it is not uncommon, for example, for novels to show us characters who live their lives in contradiction with their stated beliefs. In a typical eighteenth-century bildungsroman, the hero learns empirically from the experiences of life, and the novel charts the hero's steadily growing maturity. But does Candide really learn anything from his experiences? As one disaster after another crashes about his head, he continues blithely repeating the lessons taught him by Pangloss. Arguably, he comes to learn something in the final chapter in the garden—a scene to which we shall return. But at the very least, one would have to say he is a slow learner. Candide starts off with Locke's tabula rasa but appears to defy Locke by learning next to nothing: so should we take him seriously? And if Candide is slow to learn, Pangloss appears to learn nothing at all:

> "Now then, my dear Pangloss!" Candide said to him. "When you were being hanged, and dissected, and beaten, and made to

row in a galley, did you continue to think that things were turning out for the best?"

"I still feel now as I did at the outset," replied Pangloss. "I am
a philosopher after all. It wouldn't do for me to go back on what
I said before." (chapter 28)

By his own admission, Pangloss is unable to learn from experience.
But Voltaire's satire here seems less directed at Leibnizian optimism
than at dogmatic and unbending philosophers, who are unable ever
to change their way of thinking. Voltaire is giving us a practical lesson
in skepticism and freethinking.

More than that, the experience of reading this novel reminds us
how human beings reinvent the world to fit in with their precon-
ceived ideas and prejudices. Here is how, in the opening chapter, Pangloss explains how all is right with the (or at least his) universe:

> "It is demonstrably true," he would say, "that things cannot be
> other than as they are. For, everything having been made for a
> purpose, everything is necessarily for the best purpose. Observe
> how noses were made to bear spectacles, and so we have spec-
> tacles. Legs are evidently devised to be clad in breeches, and
> breeches we have. Stones were formed in such a way that they
> can be hewn and made into castles, and so His Lordship has a
> very beautiful castle. The greatest baron in the province must
> be the best lodged. And since pigs were made to be eaten, we eat
> pork all the year round. Consequently, those who have argued
> that all is well have been talking nonsense. They should have
> said that all is for the best."

Here is Voltaire making fun of the argument from design. To say that
"the nose has been formed to bear spectacles" is funny because of the
upside-down Alice-in-Wonderland logic. But does that mean that
Voltaire is dismissing the argument from design? Not necessarily,
since we know from other writings that he has a certain sympathy for
the idea. As this example shows, Voltaire can poke fun at bad logic,
even (perhaps especially) when it leads to a conclusion he agrees with.
Pangloss may have persuaded himself that he is arguing from a gen-

eral and disinterested standpoint, but the reader can see otherwise. Look at the choice of examples here: spectacles, breeches, stones (for building a castle), and roast pork: this is a portrait of the old baron sitting down to dinner at home. Pangloss's mental universe extends no further than his physical domain—and both are rather limited. No philosophical example is innocent, and the give-away here is "Pigs were made to be eaten." The pork-eating German baron, wearing his spectacles and stockings and sitting complacently in his castle, doesn't seem to know about Jews or Muslims: why didn't God design the world for them too?

The argument from design is intended to prove the existence of God: here it proves only the existence of German barons. Is the satire really aimed at Leibnizian optimism? Or at dogmatic philosophers whose sole purpose is to prop up the status quo? Voltaire's writing in *Candide* is steeped in irony, and irony is a complex and corrosive tool. Textbooks explain that irony involves saying one thing while meaning something else: the baron's castle in chapter 1 is described as "the most beautiful of castles," so we know it is not. But this is a slippery slope: once a writer begins to use irony repeatedly, the reader has to pay very close attention. Can we believe anything we read? And can the author even control the irony he has unleashed? *Candide* is so suffused with irony that it is sometimes hard to know quite where it stops, or what Voltaire really means.

Candide might seem an "easy" novel to read: it is funny, the sentences are concise, the action moves at lightning speed; but this is also a novel that makes the reader work. Let us take as an example the final chapter, titled, conveniently, "Conclusion." If we are trying to understand the "meaning" of the work, then this would seem a good place to start—unless, of course, the title is ironic? Their crazy adventures at an end, the characters of the novel finally reassemble, and we experience something of that sense of resolution we enjoy at the end of a Shakespearean comedy. All the characters come together, except for the homosexual baron whom they drive out—already there is a slight shadow cast over the garden. They encounter a wise man, the dervish, "who passed for the greatest philosopher in Turkey," and Candide and Pangloss quiz him about the existence of evil in the world. "What does it matter whether there's evil or there's good," says the dervish. "When His Highness sends a ship to Egypt, does he worry whether the mice on board are comfortable or not?" Pangloss presses on relentlessly with his Leibnizian jabber about "the best of all possible worlds" and "preestablished harmony," to which the wise man responds decisively: "The dervish, at these words, slammed the door in their faces." In other words, faced by apparently insoluble problems, best to say nothing and just get on with life. Martin seems suddenly to be cured of his earlier dogmatism: "Let's get down to work and stop all this philosophizing. . . . It's the only way to make life bearable." This philosophy is crystallized in one of the most famous sound bites of the novel: "I also know," said Candide, "that we must cultivate our garden." And the novel ends—concludes?—with these memorable words: "We must cultivate our garden."

The curtain comes down, and we are left with this highly quotable phrase ringing in our ears. Is this really Voltaire's final word on the subject, the "conclusion" promised by the chapter's title? For what it's worth, Voltaire in his own life did not act like his characters in *Candide*, in fact he continued worrying about the question of Providence until his dying day. He most certainly hated dogmatism and intolerance, but he never argued that faced by a difficult problem, one should just give up. And when we look more carefully at the characters in this garden, there is surely something worrying about their desire to cut themselves off from the rest of society and to keep their heads down. If, while cultivating the garden, they were to raise their heads, "They would often see boats passing beneath the windows of the farmhouse laden with effendis, pashas, and cadis, who were being exiled to Lemnos or Mytilene or Erzerum. They would see more cadis, more pashas, and more effendis coming to take the place of those who had been expelled, and being themselves in their turn expelled. They would see heads duly stuffed with straw being taken for display before the Sublime Porte." In other words, they would see the repeated evidence of systematic and cruel political persecution, the Ottoman Empire being as corrupt as all the other countries they have visited. Is it really the conclusion of the novel that happiness is to be found by selfishly concentrating on one's own work and ignoring the plight of others? This would seem an oddly anticlimactic conclusion to draw.

But if "cultivating the garden" is not the true conclusion of the novel, what is?

One clue might lie in the actual image of gardening: it seems mundane enough, but every eighteenth-century reader was steeped in the Bible, and sure to recognize in "cultivating the garden" an echo of "I am the true vine, and my Father is the gardener" (John 15:1). And if chapter 30 "concludes" with this nod to the New Testament, it is clear that chapter 1 contains an overt parody of the Old Testament: when Candide is kicked out of the castle by the old baron after kissing Cunégonde, we are clearly meant to recall God expelling Adam and Eve from the Garden of Eden after the Fall: "Therefore the Lord God sent him forth from the Garden of Eden *to till the ground* from whence he was taken" (Gen. 3:23, my emphasis). So the idea of cultivating the garden, mentioned explicitly only at the end of the novel, is already anticipated in the opening chapter, by means of these transparent biblical references.

Voltaire is not exactly making fun of the Bible here; he is using narratives that are intimately familiar to his readers to play with the narrative process itself, and the Bible is an obvious place to start. There is a similar effect in chapter 19 when Candide, on his return from Eldorado, loses most of his precious red sheep: impossible here not to see a playful nod in the direction of the Parable of the Lost Sheep as told in the gospels of Matthew and Luke. Other moments in the narrative contain blatant allusions to the best-known contemporary novels. In the very first paragraph, for example, Candide's genealogy is explained as follows: "The older servants of the household suspected that he was the son of the Baron's sister by a kind and upright gentleman of the neighbourhood." Any reader in 1759, English or French, would immediately have recognized this as a reworking of the plot of Fielding's hugely popular *Tom Jones*, which first appeared in 1749 (and in French translation the following year). Having once recognized the imitation, we are given a clue to the future course of the action: Candide, like Tom, is presented as the bastard son of his protector's sister, and we can already guess that following an amorous liaison, Candide, like Tom, will be expelled from his protector's house, and so launched into the world. Voltaire mimics a contemporary English novel at the same time as he mimics the book of Genesis, and this narrative game is all the more amusing and unsettling because a modern novel and the Bible are placed on an equal footing.

Beyond this parody of specific texts, *Candide* is brimming with allusions to what one might call fictional prototypes. Modern readers, necessarily less familiar than were Voltaire's first readers with the earlier traditions of prose fiction, may not be so immediately sensitive to this phenomenon, but it is something that we can sense in the tone of the narration. The shipwrecks, chance meetings, and amazing coincidences are all spoofs of earlier adventure novels, indeed the very structure of the journey is in some sense a reworking of the archetypal journey of Odysseus in Homer's epic. The parody of medieval chivalric epic, by Ariosto in verse (*Orlando furioso*) and later by Cervantes in prose (*Don Quixote*), is often seen as the catalyst of "modern" fiction, and this process continues in *Candide*. True to this tradition, Voltaire's hero (or antihero) is driven mad by love; when, in chapter 19, "Candide, quite carried away, carved the name of Cunégonde on trees as he passed," he acts like the crazed lovers in Ariosto or Shakespeare. Candide embarks on a journey in search of his beloved accompanied by a more down-to-earth male servant, and the assonance between the names Cacambo and Sancho, Don Quixote's companion, speaks for itself. It would be too simple to say that Voltaire is making fun of chivalric romance. Rather, he is exploiting our familiarity with these canonical narrative plots to play with our expectations about the shape of the story.

We began by examining Leibniz's view that, despite appearances, there is a divine order that gives shape to the world. Voltaire counters this metaphysical position by imagining a burlesque fiction where order is absent and where chance alone rules. In this order-less (Godless?) world, the God-as-watchmaker argument becomes irrelevant: the order that might prove God's existence simply does not exist. And how do we, as readers, find order in the world, or even in the novel, in the face of such willful randomness? Perhaps our familiarity with the standard plots of other novels gives us some ability to make sense of *Candide* and to impose our own order on this otherwise disordered universe. And perhaps, in the end, all any of us can do is to create meaning by telling stories, so as to impose some sort of shape on the chaos that surrounds us. The one order that does exist in *Candide* is the order of fiction, and reading to uncover order is in all senses a liberating experience.

Voltaire feels the challenge of Leibniz's ideas, and, like all Enlightenment thinkers, he is troubled by the question of evil. But in *Candide* Voltaire is doing more than just attacking Leibnizian philosophy. He is writing a work of fiction, not philosophy, and he uses the form of the novel to explore different and contradictory ideas, and to encourage his readers to do the same. *Candide* is an extraordinary and liberating work of the imagination, a novel that challenges us to rethink our assumptions about the order of our familiar world. If readers today continue to enjoy *Candide*, it is because we respond instinctively to this hymn to the absurd. Leibnizian optimism may no longer seem immediately relevant to modern-day concerns, but Voltaire's militant call to treat dogma with skepticism certainly does: this lesson never loses its relevance. The caustic black humor of the film *Dr. Strangelove, or How I Learned to Stop Worrying and Love the Bomb* (1964) bears a distinctly Voltairean imprint, not surprisingly because Terry Southern, one of its cowriters, had earlier coauthored with Mason Hoffenberg the novel *Candy* (1958), a provocative rewriting of *Candide*. Voltaire's novel is one we continue to read, and to rewrite.

The "same" book can look very different depending on how and for whom it is printed, and covers can tell us a great deal, even before we reach page one. We began with an edition of *Candide* printed in French in London in 1759, and we finish with a translation by Walter J. Fultz, a mass-market paperback published in the United States in 1952, in a popular series called Lion Books, which sold in drugstores for twenty-five cents (see fig. 2). The cover illustration attempts to rewrite the novel as a 1950s B-movie, while a convenient summary of the plot explains that Candide "chased a virtuous maiden through Europe's most bawdy age." Perhaps the greatest originality of Voltaire's *Candide* is its daring rewriting of the popular fictions of its day; so it was only to be expected that after two hundred years *Candide* itself would be rewritten as pulp fiction.

Figure 2. *Candide*, translated by Walter J. Fultz (New York: Lion Books, 1952). Private collection.

WORKS CITED AND RECOMMENDED FURTHER READING

Throughout this chapter, I have quoted *Candide* in the excellent modern translation, *Candide and Other Stories*, trans. Roger Pearson, Oxford World's Classics (1990; Oxford: Oxford University Press, 2006). Readers may also like to sample one of the early English translations: Eric Palmer's edition of *Candide* (Peterborough, ON: Broadview, 2009) uses the translation published by John Nourse in London in 1759, *Candide, or All for the Best*. There is a fascinating online exhibition titled "Voltaire's *Candide*" (2010) on the website of the New York Public Library (http://candide.nypl.org). The best English-language biography of Voltaire is Roger Pearson's *Voltaire Almighty: A Life in the Pursuit of Freedom* (London: Bloomsbury, 2005); and there is a delightful biographical essay by Richard Holmes, "Voltaire's Grin," first published in *The New York Review of Books* (1995), and reprinted in his collection *Sidetracks: Explorations of a Romantic Biographer* (London: Flamingo, 2000), 343–63. Roger Pearson, *The Fables of Reason: A Study of Voltaire's "Contes philosophiques"* (Oxford: Oxford University Press, 1993) contains a chapter on *Candide*; see also Jean Starobinski, "On the Philosophical Style of *Candide*," in *Blessings in Disguise; or, The Morality of Evil*, trans. Arthur Goldhammer (Cambridge: Polity Press, 1993), 84–100. On Voltaire more generally, *The Cambridge Companion to Voltaire*, ed. Nicholas Cronk (Cambridge: Cambridge University Press, 2009), provides an overview of modern readings. On the historical and cultural background, see Anthony Pagden, *The Enlightenment and Why It Still Matters* (Oxford: Oxford University Press, 2013); Daniel Roche, *France in the Enlightenment*, trans. Arthur Goldhammer (Cambridge, MA: Harvard University Press, 1998); and Charissa Bremer-David, ed., *Paris: Life and Luxury in the Eighteenth Century* (Los Angeles: Getty Publications, 2011). See also Aldous Huxley, "On Re-reading *Candide*," in *On the Margin* (London: Chatto and Windus, 1923), 12–17.

Readers with knowledge of French should download the app "Candide, l'édition enrichie," freely available at the Apple iStore, a joint production of the Bibliothèque Nationale de France and the Voltaire Foundation in Oxford. This contains the full text in French, with a range of annotations and other resources to provide context; it also allows you to listen to the text, read by the French actor Denis Podalydès. A recent collection of essays on *Candide*, incorporating a wide range of approaches, is *Les 250 ans de "Candide": Lectures et relectures*, ed. Nicholas Cronk and Nathalie Ferrand (Louvain: Peeters, 2013).

Disclosures of the Boudoir

The Novel in the Eighteenth Century

PIERRE SAINT-AMAND

The eighteenth-century novel was written in a variety of forms over the course of the century: the picaresque novel, the first-person novel, the epistolary novel. These forms evolved in parallel, each with its highs and lows. There is, however, one feature that is common to all these forms. I shall call it "interiorization." The latter is one way of naming a broader social and cultural development: alongside the eighteenth-century preoccupation with public space and the qualities of "public man" (at the heart of the idea of the "citizen" that was to play such an important role in the French Revolution), there is also a growing focus on private spaces and experiences. One of the most striking manifestations of this set of interests is the representation in the novel of a particular space: that of the aristocratic boudoir. The latter figures extensively in both the eighteenth- and nineteenth-century novel. The former, however, does not always supply the richness of architectural and decorative detail that distinguishes the depiction of the boudoir in the latter, where it becomes integral to novelistic discourse (Théophile Gautier's *Mademoiselle de Maupin* and Honoré de Balzac's *La fille aux yeux d'or* come to mind).

In the earlier novels, often just a handful of descriptive specifics are provided; a few strategically chosen pieces of furniture suffice to highlight the significance of the setting. This economy of descriptive detail is not a disadvantage. It throws the structural function of the site into even sharper relief and thus provides an indication of why this particular topos is more than just a particular, but also, so to speak, a narrative door opening onto a central and defining pattern of eighteenth-century French fiction. The plots of novels unfold in time of course, but space too can become an important element of plot, in addition to its descriptive functions. Often announced as a plot element, the boudoir in the eighteenth-century novel becomes the territory where emotions take shape ("interiorization" hence understood as both physical and psychological "interiors") in accordance with broadly three narrative types. The libertine novel places the boudoir in the domain of scandal; the Rousseauist novel transforms it and accords it a moral dimension; finally, Sade instrumentalizes it as a locus not only of pleasures but of philosophical experience.

There is a celebrated description of the boudoir by the architect Nicolas Le Camus de Mézières. In his treatise *The Genius of Architecture; or the Analogy of That Art with Our Sensations* (1780), the boudoir is defined as the quintessence of rococo aesthetics. The architect registers the term's evolution from its original designation of a simple dressing room in which a woman may find solitude, to its evocation of a woman's temple, where all is purposed to the perfection of her image and to the pursuit of love, the place where the mystery of the bed is choreographed: "The boudoir is regarded as the abode of delight; here she seems to reflect on her designs and to yield to her inclinations. With such thoughts in mind, dictated as they are by the manners of our age, spare no pains to make the room as pleasing as you can. All is to be subordinate to luxury, comfort, and taste. . . . This delightful retreat must arouse none but the sweetest emotions; it must confer serenity upon the soul and delight upon all the senses. It must aim for the ultimate perfection: let desire be satisfied without impairing enjoyment."

Le Camus de Mézières takes pains to evoke certain selected aspects of the decor of this haven—the details of lighting (candles), furniture (a daybed; an ottoman), colors (white and blue). The room itself adopts the contours of the female form, a circularity that pays homage to Venus: "Consider a beautiful woman. Her outlines are gentle and well rounded; the muscles are not pronounced; the whole is governed by a simple, natural sweetness, whose effect we can recognize better than we can express it." Yet "expressing it" is one of the self-appointed tasks of the eighteenth-century novel, employing and deploying the imaginary resources of this place of secret and mystery in ways that highlight the newfound importance of private moments for the individual. Here I shall focus on five examples by five different authors: Marivaux, Crébillon fils, Laclos, Rousseau, and Sade.

Le paysan parvenu, 1734–35 (*Up from the Country*) by Pierre Carlet de Marivaux belongs to the genre of the memoir-novel, a form of first-person narrative that flourished in the eighteenth century. It might well have become a picaresque novel: Marivaux's conveyor of wine, a peasant from Champagne, has all the makings of the adventurer that populates the century's early fiction. He might have taken to the open road of the novel, but Marivaux suspends his character, parking his wine cart and settling him in Paris. Jacob's journey is cut short when he enters into service with his new masters. We leave behind the surprises of highways and byways, their chance encounters, for adventures of a more interior sort. *Le paysan parvenu* is actually a novel of transition: in it we are never far from the street; carriages are placed at the service of love's traffickings, the fixing of rendezvous. The master's house quickly becomes Jacob's experimental laboratory. In particular he discovers, to his enchantment, a series of feminine places: first of all, the mistress's bedroom, where his character is put to the test. Here we find ourselves squarely in the realm of the psychological novel. Jacob marvels up close at these new interiors that exude an air of the fabulous. The peasant meets the inflamed gaze of the lady at her toilette, with the gulf of social class between them. It is as if his vision is transformed by this artifice of flirtation: "At that she went back to her dressing and I took myself off, still turning back to look at her. But she didn't miss anything I did, and her eyes followed me to the door."

Once this space has been breached, in a sense transgressed, Jacob de la Vallée will show less naïveté. Later in the novel, when he winds up in a wardrobe used by Mme de Ferval, he is prepared for the scene that awaits him, able to negotiate the secret moment, the private exchange: "Could there be some servant in there listening?" Jacob makes the most of the moment, quickly kissing her hand. Later, in the boudoir of the very same Madame de Ferval, the peasant redoubles his efforts at seduction. He enters the bedroom of his "goddess" as if stepping into a period painting. Marivaux has set the scene to perfection: stretched out on a sofa with a book, the lady is in a state of dishabille. The novelist delivers Ferval's body by degrees: the foot, the leg, the unknown masterpiece; in short, Jacob confronts an unfamiliar vision, at the outer limits of the possible. His senses instantly awaken, and he discovers the feminine, the other sex: "it was the first time in my life that I really appreciated the value of a woman's foot and leg . . . having seen only women's faces and figures. But now I found out that they were women all over." Marivaux surveys the novelty of the female body in stages, dividing it into a series of moments of pleasure: "Look at that arm, that beautiful form, eyes the like of which I have never seen in anyone else." The peasant must also learn the muted eloquence that secrecy demands: "Speak softly . . . my maid might be in there (pointing to the anteroom)." These scenes show how the character's intensity has been displaced: no longer fueling the energy of the picaresque journey, it is now interiorized in emotions, in the curiosity indulged by the unveiling of bodies, the surprise of love.

In parallel, Marivaux also offers his hero the convenience of bourgeois interiority, in the form of married life. The domestic interior escapes from libertine exchange. By contrast, it is rife with irony, with mockery of religious fervor (the image of Jacob takes the place of the devotional image in his wife's chapel). The marriage bed grows quickly cold; accommodating the husband replete with repeated infidelities, with daily flirtations, Madame de la Vallée still entreats him: "Let's go to bed, my dear, it's late." At home, Jacob is not the seducer, the pseudo-gentleman who seeks to impress with his borrowed clothes. Marivaux shows rather the husband in his "dressing-gown and slippers." In a moment of furtive introspection, Jacob sees himself as master of the house, his image reflected in the mirror of a book: "At about three in the afternoon the bells rang for vespers and my wife went to church while I read some serious book that I didn't understand much of . . . which I amused myself with merely to imitate the behaviour of a gentleman in his home."

Another memoir-novel employs a different strategy: in *Les égarements du cœur et de l'esprit* (*The Wayward Head and Heart*, 1735–38), which inaugurates the libertine novel, Claude-Prosper Jolyot de Crébillon lets his characters evolve in highly social settings (sitting rooms, dining rooms, public gardens). The lovers have difficulty finding private space. They must fend off the public, wait for the crowds to disperse. The word *boudoir* never actually makes an appearance in this novel. Private space is pried from social space, carved out when others have taken their leave. Crébillon's positioning of private space betrays the fragile interiorization of the characters, poised between the opinions of others and their own self-knowledge. Thus Crébillon shows the young Monsieur de Meilcour's panic at unwonted intimacy when he finds himself alone with a woman. Such are the circumstances that condition the narrator's declaration to Madame de Lursay. The aristocratic salon becomes an enclosed space, confining the couple in this liminal moment so opportune for their tête-à-tête: "Our part of the drawing-room was deserted, everyone was occupied." For Meilcour's first rendezvous with his new mistress, the surroundings are similarly propitious, down to the furniture. Canapé and armchair become the props of desire for the occasion, but only after a seemingly interminable supper has ended: "I no sooner found myself alone with her than I was seized by the most horrible fright I have ever been in in my life. . . . I did not dare to look at Madame de Lursay. She easily perceived my difficulty, and told me, but in the sweetest tone imaginable, to come and sit beside her on the sofa where she had placed herself." Night falls on the boudoir and sets the scene. The mistress of the house has seen to all the requisite details of her person: negligee, disarranged hair. Then the scene of seduction can take place: "She half reclined there, her head against the cushions, and amused herself idly and as if abstractedly by tying bows in her ribbons. From time to time she turned her eyes languishingly on me, upon which I would at once respectfully lower my own." Crébillon fills in all the essential elements of the tableau: the kneeling lover, furtive caresses, hand-kissing, declarations of love.

At the end of the novel, a similar scene is repeated, after another seemingly endless meal. Meilcour must await the departure of the guests, including an inopportune marquis whom Crébillon perversely introduces, before he can finally find Madame de Lursay alone: "I found Madame de Lursay reclining on a couch, musing. In spite of the boldness with which I had armed myself, I no sooner found myself alone with her than I was sorry I had got myself into this situation, and would have been glad never to have had the idea that I had so much to say to her." Then their bodies draw close and the much-desired fatal moment can at last arrive: "It was as if my transports increased her beauty, and made all her graces more touching. . . . I was too young not to believe that I loved in return. The work of my senses appeared to me the work of my heart. I abandoned myself to all the intoxication of that fatal moment."

The young Meilcour also makes his entrance into the sacred precincts of the boudoir. A rendezvous leads him to a new conquest, in fact straight to the dressing room of Madame de Senanges. In the coquette's mirror, Meilcour undergoes the trial of seduction by this woman of experience: "She uttered a cry of delight when she saw me. 'Ah, you!' she said in a familiar tone. 'How charming of you to keep your word.'" With this encounter, Meilcour makes another conquest: in Madame de Senanges's dressing room, he also meets his future mistress, Madame de Mongennes. The two women seek to draw out the inexperienced young man: "Is it not so, Madam? One sees very few faces like his. People admire faces all day long that do not come anywhere near it."

The aristocratic interiors depicted in *Le paysan parvenu*—boudoirs, dressing rooms—reappear in the century's most celebrated novel, *Les liaisons dangereuses* (*Dangerous Liaisons*, 1782). Despite the scattered effect evoked by the epistolary novel's crisscrossing of letters, Pierre Choderlos de Laclos's novel, a masterpiece of epistolary fiction, benefits from being read as a novel of space. The claustrophobia of the places in which the characters evolve is strategically employed by the libertines who lead the dance of manipulation in the text. These interiors, which often mimic the intimate space of the letter, reveal the characters in their psychological dimension, as creatures of secrecy with mysterious individual motivations that must be decoded. Here we see the true substance of these paper characters. They are obsessed with plotting.

In one of the major plot lines of the novel, the orders that Valmont receives from Madame de Merteuil entail exploiting the locale by using a deliberately spatial tactic: "[H]er daughter must be seduced. . . . She must be ruined too," Merteuil instructs Valmont with regard to Cécile de Volanges (part 1, letter 44). Letter 96 recounts Valmont's success in this endeavor. In his quest to violate the girl's intimate space, the libertine meticulously studies the chateau's premises. The bedroom that protected the naive heroine who is engaged to be married becomes the site of sexual experimentation, of her first lessons in love. The libertine has foreseen everything: from ways to preserve the hush of the night, to the duplicate keys that leave the room open to compromising intrusion. He also supplies writing materials for the forbidden correspondence: paper, pens, and ink (part 2, letter 73).

Cécile's sleep will never be the same again. Moreover, the young girl wakes up transformed by the incursion, as her mirror reveals the following dawn: "When I woke this morning and looked at myself in the mirror, I frightened myself, I was so changed" (part 3, letter 97). Here Laclos reverses the tableau of female seduction. Appearing in the stark light of day, the stigmata of the sexual act disfigure the heroine. The libertine takes delight in this "mien of the morning after," where the brand of disgrace stamps itself like an indelible tattoo (part 3, letter 96).

The novel's central plot, Valmont's seduction of Madame (Présidente) de Tourvel, also entails the conquest of a private universe, a veritable fortress. Laclos multiplies the occasions on which the space of the pious Présidente is violated. Letter 99, which announces Tourvel's "fall," is not only the declaration of an inveterate libertine, but also that of a clever architectural strategist. In order to carry out his "plan," the libertine studies Madame de Tourvel's apartment in minute detail. Valmont adopts this approach quite early in the novel, in letter 23, when he describes watching the Présidente through a keyhole: Madame de Tourvel reveals herself on the other side as a portrait of devotion and of misery (part 1, letter 23).

Before his conquest of Tourvel in her husband's chateau, Valmont engages in rigorous observation. The vicomte doubles his gaze by employing as a spy his valet, Azolan, who enters the home in lieu of his master to misdirect letters to unintended recipients. Throughout the day, the Présidente can be observed in the details of her routine, her every move minutely watched. "On their arrival Madame went to bed"; "In the afternoon Madame the Présidente went into the library, and removed two books which she carried to her boudoir"; "then she came home, took breakfast, and afterwards began writing, continuing until nearly one o'clock" (part 3, letter 107). The narrative of the famous scene that occurs on "Thursday the twenty-eighth, the day chosen and stipulated" is a paragon of the genre, using all the clichés of military conquest and heroic strategy: "But so as to lose not a moment of time that was precious to me, I carefully examined the locale, and there and then marked down the theatre of my victory. I couldn't have chosen a more convenient one, for there was an ottoman in the room. But I observed that, facing it, hung a portrait of the husband, and I was afraid, I admit, that with so extraordinary a woman, a single look directed by chance in his direction might in a moment destroy the work of so much time and trouble" (part 4, letter 125). The room becomes the stage for Valmont's possession of the Présidente: first an ocular prison (she is surrounded by his gaze), it becomes a chamber of crises and convulsions, and finally a witness to the transgressive pleasure.

Matching this scene in its meticulous preparation is the rendezvous between Madame de Merteuil and Prévan (part 2, letter 85). The marquise receives the officer in her boudoir, but she has transformed the entire house into an impregnable fortress, with a trained guard dog, servants on the lookout, alarm bells. The seduction reverses into an attack, and Prévan is trapped at the very moment when he was about to emerge victorious. This tableau inverts the roles depicted in Jean-Honoré Fragonard's celebrated painting *Le verrou*, which depicts a woman trapped in a bedroom with a sexual champion. The only element common to the two scenes is the "disordered bed" (part 2, letter 85). From Merteuil's apartment Prévan goes straight to prison. Earlier in the novel, the boudoir in the marquise's country house proved more hospitable, when she set out to educate the Chevalier de Danceny. In fact, she tells us, the room is even "in its full splendour" (part 1, letter 10).

Les liaisons dangereuses also enlists the genius of architecture in situations that smack of comedy, in contrast to the scenes of cruelty discussed above. Letter 71 recounts such a story: how the vicomte "disinterred an old affair" with the vicomtesse of M. Here Valmont exploits the proximity of their bedrooms, which are "directly opposite," allowing him to orchestrate a party of four: both the husband of the vicomtesse and her lover, Vressac, are in turn tricked in this masterful scene. By cover of night, doors are discreetly opened and closed. And this is where things become interesting. The vicomtesse, who is in Valmont's bedroom and wishes to return to her own, must be saved in the nick of time: "I obtained the Vicomtesse's consent to giving loud shrieks of alarm such as 'Thief! Murder!' etc., etc.; and it was agreed that, at the first shriek, I should break open the door whereupon she would run to her bed. . . . The door gave way at my first kick" (part 2, letter 71). For the time being, the secret remains under wraps, and appearances are saved before the story can spread.

Another epistolary novel would follow a very different path, opening the way to the sentimental novel with its moralistic treatment of familiar places. This is the best seller of the eighteenth century, Jean-Jacques Rousseau's *Julie ou la nouvelle Héloïse* (*Julie, or the New Heloise*, 1761). Here the author offers a different approach to intimacy; the libertine strategy is abandoned in favor of a radical conversion of the characters. This transformation is reflected in the spaces of the novel: Rousseau leaves behind the familiar sites of seduction for private spaces devoted to the rituals of marriage and family that Rousseau introduces into literature, providing them with robust ideological support.

La nouvelle Héloïse can be seen as the end of the boudoir novel. Rousseau's lovers abandon secret spaces. The confinement that favors all sorts of transgressions becomes suspect: love must instead be revealed in the light of day, it must submit to the world's transparency. We see here the pressure on private space of Rousseau's "republican" convictions and his belief in the "public" virtues, as against aristocratic codes of "secrecy." Letter 54 (part 1), written by Saint-Preux, Julie's lover, describes a scene that will not be repeated, when the wayward lover ends up "in his Mistress's wardrobe," as Rousseau phrases it in the title he gives this letter. This narrative of folly, of fetishistic perversion, of imaginary decadence par excellence, shows the distracted lover pursuing substitutes for the object of his desire in the exalting obscurity that cloaks her personal effects: "Julie! Here I am in your dressing room, here I am in the sanctuary of all my heart worships. The torch of love guided my steps." As he explores the room, Saint-Preux imprints his desire on all the objects he encounters. The absent lover is multiplied in all these enticing fetishes that seduce the intruder. A sort of Pygmalion, Saint-Preux reconstructs this feminine universe in a sort of undress *without* the body, enacting the sensual pleasure of possession without the resistance of the other sex. All the elements of the rococo erotic tableau are present (negligee, mules, neckerchief), as if in an interior painted by Boucher. His epistolary ode to her accoutrements serves as a metaphor for desire, a substitute that compensates for emotion in an exchange that is at once cathartic and erotic:

> How enchanting is this mysterious abode? Everything here flatters and feeds the ardor that devours me. O Julie! It is filled with you, and the flame of my desire spreads to your every vestige. Aye, all my senses are intoxicated at once. Some almost imperceptible fragrance, sweeter than the rose, and lighter than the iris is breathed forth from all over this place. I fancy I hear the flattering sound of your voice. All the scattered pieces of your raiment present to my ardent imagination those of your person which they secrete. This light bonnet which is graced by long blond hair it affects to cover: this happy neckerchief of which at least once I shall not have to complain; this elegant and simple dishabille which so well states the taste of her who wears it; these dainty slippers which fit easily on your lithe feet; this slender corset which touches and enfolds. . . . what an enchanting shape. . . . two slight curves in front. . . . oh voluptuous spectacle. . . . the whalebone has yielded to the form pressed into it. . . . delightful imprints, let me kiss you a thousand times! . . . Ye gods! ye gods! What will it be when . . . ah, I think I already feel that tender heart beating under a happy hand! Julie! my charming Julie! I see you, I feel you everywhere, I breathe you with the air you have breathed; you permeate my whole substance; how your abode is burning and painful for me! It is terrible on my impatience. Oh come, fly to me, or I shall die. (part 1, letter 54)

Saint-Preux will have to flee Julie and the Etange house. He can regain the intimacy of her circle only under the newfound protection of Julie's husband, Monsieur de Wolmar. The lover is domesticated as a friend; only thus can he be received in the household. Rousseau arranges interior scenes—unprecedented in the eighteenth century—

to show the family tableau centered on the mother and mistress of the house. The cabinet of dreams is a thing of the past: Saint-Preux has graduated to the seduction of new sites. One of these is the salon, but it is no longer the aristocratic salon where people mill about in a sea of artifice. Here Julie reigns amid her children: "I saw her surrounded by her Husband and children; this awed me" (part 4, letter 6). The famous Clarens house is now dedicated to the cult of the family, to a strict domestic economy. The house formally banishes the rococo aristocratic space that was dedicated to spectacle and ostentation. It is carefully reconceived by its owners: "Since the masters of this house have established their home here, they have put to their use everything that served only as ornament; it is no longer a house made to be seen, but to be lived in" (part 4, letter 10).

Rousseau provides the keys to this new architecture, in the simplification of space and the condensation of ceremonial areas into more intimate spaces. The bourgeois house is born, enfolding its residents upon themselves in a hygienic confinement: "They have walled up long rows of rooms to change doors that were awkwardly situated, they have divided rooms that were too large so as to have lodgings better laid out. They have replaced oldfashioned and sumptuous pieces of furniture with simple and convenient ones. Everything here is agreeable and cheerful; everything bespeaks plenty and elegance, nothing reeks of wealth and luxury" (part 4, letter 10). Later Rousseau will explain this architecture by praising its *rationalism*: palatial grandeur gives way to an abode of utility and convenience. Domestic space is recalled to order, aligned with nature. It offers a new political image, that of the community reunited in self-sufficiency and transparency. The house enforces a generalized morality of behaviors: "But the sight of this house and of the uniform and simple life of its inhabitants imparts to the soul of onlookers a secret charm that grows and grows. A small number of gentle and peaceable people, united by mutual needs and reciprocal beneficence, here work together through various tasks toward a common goal" (part 5, letter 2).

La nouvelle Héloïse marks the birth of a mythical place, the salon of Apollo, a familiar space but invested with the sacrality of ritual and initiation, the ceremony of intimacy. In reality a simple dining room, in the novel this room becomes the concentrated nexus of the house, the ideal room that sums up the household by absorbing all of its qualities. This is where Julie engages in communitarian experiments conceived as rituals: "it is the inviolable sanctuary of trust, friendship, freedom. The companionship of hearts there binds the table companions; it is a sort of initiation to intimacy, and never are assembled there any but people who would wish never again to be separated." Rousseau writes that the house is inseparable from life; in a sense it gives form to life through a complex magic that explains the teleology of the place, not by enforcing arbitrary rules but rather by conforming to the "example" of life: "If I had to say concisely what they do in this house to be happy, I think I would have answered rightly in saying that *they know the art of living*," explains Saint-Preux (part 5, letter 2).

Above all, it must be said, Rousseau leads his characters "outside," into nature (part 4, letter 11). This is the significance of the Elysée, Julie's orchard where the mistress and mother of house and family can intermittently withdraw. Saint-Preux is impressed with this miniature Eden nestled between garden and forest: "I was struck by a pleasantly cool sensation which dark shade, bright and lively greenery, flowers scattered on every side, the bubbling of flowing water, and the songs of a thousand birds impressed on my imagination at least as much as my senses; but at the same time I thought I was looking at the wildest, most solitary place in nature, and it seemed to me I was the first mortal who ever had set foot in this wilderness." A surprising taxonomy opens his eyes to the discovery of the local plants and a variety of fruits.

This letter, however, inscribes Saint-Preux's curiosity as the inverse of that manifested at his penetration of her dressing room. Natural objects, handled by Julie, are the only ones that arouse the ecstasy of her former lover. During a solitary visit to the garden, fetishizing eroticism sets out again in search of imaginary substitutes: "I shall see nothing that her hand has not touched; I shall kiss flowers on which her feet have trodden; I shall breathe with the dew an air she has breathed; the taste displayed in her diversions will make all her charms present to me, and I shall find her everywhere as she is deep in my heart." But the stroll leads to a radical conversion of the former lover's gaze: "I imagined I was seeing the image of virtue where I was seeking that of pleasure. This image merged in my mind with the features of Madame de Wolmar, and for the first time since my return I saw Julie in her absence, not such as she was for me and as I still like to picture her, but such as she appears every day before my eyes." Thus this outdoor asylum where artificial nature has worked so many miracles again reverts to a metaphor for the interior. L'Elysée becomes one with Julie herself: "Even that very name Elysium called to order the aberrations of my imagination, and brought to my soul a calm preferable to the agitation of the most seductive passions. It depicted for me in some sense the inner thoughts of her who had found it."

Rousseau also abolishes the libertine bed; he dethrones it. This erstwhile site of secrets, intrigues, ravishings, deceits, and traps (as in *Les liaisons dangereuses*) is no more than a tomb. The site of pleasure has been converted to the consecration of matrimonial virtues. Familial ideology arranges Julie's family around her bed in her final moments. It is Julie's husband who draws us into the intimacy of her deathbed. The family scene that he describes, uniting the expiring Julie with those she most cherishes, echoes that of the salon of Apollo.

In his novel *Histoire de Juliette* (*Juliette*, 1799), the Marquis Donatien Alphonse François de Sade does send his heroine out wayfaring, in a late resurgence of the picaresque novel. But what is most memorable about this text is the confinement that encloses horror. Sade continues the emphasis on interior space: secret alcoves, hidden closets. However, their purpose is transformed. Such spaces, similarly employed, had been the exclusive setting of his *La philosophie dans le boudoir* (*Philosophy in the Bedroom*, 1795), a novel consisting entirely of dialogue. Private space is instrumentalized as a site of instruction, of advanced sexual experimentation. Sade distributes masters and student throughout so as to maximize the offerings of the location.

Indeed, Eugénie de Mistival tells Madame de Saint-Ange: "I came hither to be instructed, and will not go till I am informed." Her escape from these two days of captivity will come only after she is once and for all "a doomed girl." Showing off the "delightful boudoir," the hostess reassures the pupil about the imperviousness of the space, which she guarantees secure from the outside world: "[W]e will be more at our ease. I have already spoken to the servants. You may be certain no one shall take it into his head to interrupt us."

Madame de Saint-Ange's boudoir foregrounds the commanding bed, the "niche" of all pleasures; the whole room will be used to further the lesson, reinforcing the actors in their various roles. The furniture and accessories complete and supplement the characters' actions. Madame de Saint-Ange explains the functions of the mirrors thus: "By repeating our attitudes and postures in a thousand different ways, they infinitely multiply those same pleasures for the persons seated here upon this ottoman. Thus everything is visible, no part of the body can remain hidden: everything must be seen; these images are so many groups disposed around those enchained by love." The room is transformed into an optical machine, or rather into a pleasure factory that transforms the projected images of bodies into a surplus of energy. Thus Sade stages tableaux that promote the fluidity of desires, the efficiency of pleasures, through fleeting arrangements orchestrated for an ephemeral profit. Dolmancé is constantly arranging these scenes, reordering the bodies in a perverse choreography: "[L]et's get on with the scene I proposed and, the three of us, let's be plunged into the most voluptuous drunkenness." Elsewhere, he directs: "One moment, while I arrange this pleasure bout in a sufficiently lustful manner. . . . Augustin, lie down on the bed; Eugénie, do you recline in his arms."

With Sade, above all, philosophy insinuates itself into the boudoir not merely in the form of risqué lessons in anatomy administered to the pupil; the master-philosopher Dolmancé also develops a set of materialist theories concerning God, the imagination, nature, and education. Disquisitions on a variety of subjects fill up the lesson time. In the Fifth Dialogue, the boudoir raises the curtain on a historical scene: the revolutionary pamphlet *Yet Another Effort, Frenchmen, if You Would Become Republicans* will be read there in order to cap off the political discussion already begun by the participants. Dolmancé, who bought the tract in the public square (outside the Palace of Equality), even concludes at the end of the reading: "Indeed my thinking does correspond with some part of these reflections, and my discourses—they've proven it to you—even lend to what has just been read to us the appearance of a repetition."

In a biting parody of *La nouvelle Héloïse*, Sade's *Philosophie dans le boudoir* ends with a communal bed that is radically different in spirit from the one in Rousseau's novel. Sade's bed is a far cry from Julie's sacred ceremonial bed, which the dying woman offers to share with her cousin Claire d'Orbe: "[M]y illness is not catching, you do not find me repulsive, sleep in my bed," she pleads (part 6, letter 11). Dolmancé invites his fellow libertines to share the *same* bed, but for the purpose of lecherous pursuits: "[G]ood friends, let's to dinner, and afterward the four of us will retire for the night... in the same bed.... I never dine so heartily, I never sleep so soundly as when I have, during the day, sufficiently befouled myself with what our fools call crimes."

But the dissolution of familial ideology culminates in the ordeal of Eugénie's mother, Madame de Mistival, whose own husband hands her over to the libertines' violence. She suffers endless torments and humiliations (including pincers and the wheel), up to the death sentence that Dolmancé imposes on her: inoculation with smallpox, which will forever destroy her "exceptionally healthy" state, which he finds unacceptable. She is expelled from Madame de Saint-Ange's boudoir on the verge of death. With the mother's sacrifice, the text completes the young girl's lesson in the conquest of liberty: the libertine educational project is accomplished. "And now all's been said," Dolmancé concludes with satisfaction. Mme de Mistival is stricken by the same punishment Mme de Merteuil receives at the end of *Les liaisons dangereuses*. Indeed, Merteuil's beauty is destroyed by smallpox, a disease that serves to "unmask" her, when the novelist offers the reader the public face of her schemes (part 4, letter 169).

The rococo boudoir flourishes in the libertine novel, as seen in a number of minor works. This place is devoted to two enigmas: that of love and that of the woman. A small architectural box that sets the stage for scenes of intimacy, it seeks to make the reader complicit in secrecy as well as in the mechanical unveiling of the ineffable. For these reasons, it would experience a resurgence in the novel of the nineteenth century, in homage to the aesthetics and erotics, and to the reigning taste, of the previous century. Thus Baudelaire, Balzac, and Zola will each in turn restore some of the boudoir's lost luster and mystery. It remains an evocative site of imaginary memory, a space of all possible fantasies, a palimpsest of limitless rewritings. But as well as anticipating a future set of literary developments, it is also something distinctively eighteenth century. It demonstrated the quest for interiority by an aristocratic culture, the libertine arts of dissimulation in the desperate search for secrets, and the hypocritical covering up of sexuality on the part of a society that excelled in compartmentalizing the public and the private. *La philosophie dans le boudoir* illustrates this conundrum eloquently. The republican pamphlet that figures in the latter is crucial here in marking a new social geography of private and public. In delineating new sexual codes and mores alongside the laws of nature, a more open society is brought into the boudoir from the public sphere of opinion, ironically envisioning "houses of debauchery" for women and men regulated by the state. There is nothing secret in these houses; on the contrary, the exploits of lust are now to be recounted publicly, in the banality of everyday discourse.

There is one further development, a twist to the eighteenth-century tale of boudoir and bedroom. Breaking from the shadow of their male counterparts and from the struggle of (bad) education, the women writers of the eighteenth century would respond with their own brand of the novel, in a genre already especially decried when practiced by them. They would answer in a sentimental mode that would leave its marks, define a genre that accounts for their difference, and allow for an alternative opening to the canon. Rousseau and the epistolary novel, *La nouvelle Héloïse* itself, would act as the countermodel from which they would draw their inspiration. Imagining another plot, they would denounce the bedroom of seduction that served often as place of entrapment for the woman and her desire. Two examples: Isabelle de Charrière (1740–1805) in *Lettres de Mistriss Henley* (*Letters of Mistress Henley*, 1784) would turn this place of intimacy and interiority into a locus of estrangement and uncanniness, as she suffers despair and discontent in her marriage (second letter). In fact, the bedroom in this novel appears interchangeable, and it passes without ceremony from the first wife to the new one. Françoise de Graffigny (1695–1758) would go further in *Lettres d'une péruvienne* (*Letters from a Peruvian Woman*, 1747) and take her heroine out of the bedroom altogether. Seeking to provide Zilia a place of her own, of autonomy, Graffigny reserves her the library as the most enchanting room (indeed, when she visits her new house, she skips most of the other apartments). There she cultivates herself, away from the torment of hurtful passions, living what she herself calls her "independent life." Here is literature making a new bid for autonomy that will have a long, if problem-beset, literary afterlife.

Works Cited and Recommended Further Reading

I have concentrated on the following novels, which span the century: Pierre Carlet de Chamblain de Marivaux, *Up from the Country*, trans. Leonard Tancock (Harmondsworth, UK: Penguin, 1980); Claude-Prosper Jolyot de Crébillon, *The Wayward Head and Heart*, trans. Barbara Bray (Westport, CT: Greenwood Press, 1978); Pierre Choderlos de Laclos, *Dangerous Liaisons*, trans. P.W.K. Stone (London: Penguin, 1961); Jean-Jacques Rousseau, *Julie, or the New Heloise*, trans. Philip Stewart and Jean Vaché, in vol. 6 of *The Collected Writings of Rousseau*, ed. Roger D. Masters and Christopher Kelly (Hanover, NH: University Press of New England, 1997); and Marquis de Sade, *Philosophy in the Bedroom*, in *"Justine," "Philosophy in the Bedroom," and Other Writings*, trans. Richard Seaver and Austin Wainhouse (New York: Grove Weidenfeld, 1965).

Two studies I found particularly useful appear in the monumental *A History of Private Life*, vol. 3 (on the Renaissance through the Enlightenment), ed. Roger Chartier, trans. Arthur Goldhammer (Cambridge, MA: Harvard University Press, 1989): these are the essays by Orest Ranum, "The Refuges of Intimacy," 207–63, and by Jean-Marie Goulemot, whose title leaves no doubt as to its relevance: "Literary Practices: Publicizing the Private," 363–95. An impressively rich contribution to this history of the private, with a particular emphasis on rooms, is Michèle Perrot, *Histoire de chambres* (Paris: Editions du Seuil, 2009). On the way in which the eighteenth-century novel reflects the architecture of intimacy and space in general, the reader is referred to the groundbreaking works by Henri Lafon, *Espaces romanesques du XVIIIe siècle, 1670–1820* (Paris: Presses Universitaires de France, 1997) and *Les décors et les choses dans le roman français du dix-huitième siècle de Prévost à Sade* (Oxford: Voltaire Foundation, 1992). Christophe Martin pursues these lines of inquiry in his extensive study *Espaces du féminin dans le roman français du dix-huitième siècle* (Oxford: Voltaire Foundation, 2004). The boudoir, the unifying thread of my chapter, is the focus of Michel Delon, *L'invention du boudoir* (Cadeilhan: Zulma, 1999) and of his *Le savoir-vivre libertin* (Paris: Hachette, 2000), chapter 6, "Lieux et décors." Other essays from which I have drawn inspiration include the pioneering article by Rémy Saisselin, "The Space of Seduction in the Eighteenth-Century French Novel and Architecture," *Studies on Voltaire and the Eighteenth Century* 319 (1994): 417–31. Extending into the field of architecture, it might be said that everything begins with Nicolas Le Camus de Mézières, *The Genius of Architecture; or the Analogy of That Art with Our Sensations* (1780), trans. David Britt (Santa Monica, CA: Getty Center for the History of Art and the Humanities, 1992). The architecture of the boudoir also has its historians. The reader is referred above all to Ed Lilley, "The Name of the Boudoir," *Journal of the Society of Architectural Historians* 53, no. 2 (1994): 193–98. An indispensable source on rococo aesthetics and the eighteenth-century boudoir is Jean Starobinski, "Rococo and Neoclassicism," in *Revolution in Fashion: European Clothing, 1715–1815* (Kyoto: Kyoto Costume Institute, 1989), 10–16. Finally, for an overall history of the eighteenth-century novel, the reader may consult the exhaustive study by René Démoris, *Le roman à la première personne* (Paris: Colin, 1975); and on novels written by women, I recommend Martine Reid, *Des femmes en littérature* (Paris: Belin, 2010).

—Translated from the French by Jennifer Curtiss Gage

Women's Voices in Enlightenment France

CATRIONA SETH

One of the highlights of the collection of paintings housed in the Musée des Beaux-Arts in Lyons is a large oil (256 × 277 cm) by François Gérard titled *Corinne au Cap Misène* (*Corinne at Cape Misenum*). In the foreground to the right, her eyes raised to the heavens, the poetess, dressed much like an antique muse, clutches a lyre in her left hand. Her audience is gathered around her, from the dashing young Scotsman, Oswald Nelvil, to mariners and, in the middle, two young women whose rapt attention is obvious to the beholder. One has to believe that the main character's poetic improvisation has just ended and that all are feeling awe and wonder at what they have heard. Commissioned by Prince Augustus of Prussia for the celebrated salon hostess Juliette Récamier as a memorial to the late Germaine de Staël (1766–1817), the picture in some ways represents the culmination of an ever-increasing, but often challenged, recognition of the power and authority of the female voice in eighteenth- and early-nineteenth-century France.

The eponymous heroine of Staël's 1807 novel *Corinne, ou l'Italie* at once fascinated and repelled her contemporaries. She struck a chord for many as she provided a link between spontaneous creation and literary culture—the character's frequent references to mythology and to antiquity, as well as to more modern writers in her improvisations illustrate this aspect of her approach—but also between modernity and tradition, between north and south (she is half-British and half-Italian), between history's great moments and a possible future for Europe after the revolutionary upheaval. She appeared to offer a long sought-after role model, that of a brilliant and eloquent speaker, a talented and sensitive individual, a cultured and tender woman, as passionate as she is clever, as generous as she is unique. She has secrets to reveal and promises to keep; she is bound at once by her moral rectitude and by a past in which the previous generation has plotted her future with a careful eye to social norms, making her gender and the expression of desire irreconcilable.

As her story shows—she loses both her talent and the opportunity to marry the British nobleman who is in many ways her soulmate—the world might not have been ready for her or her type. Her death is that of a virtuous woman who looks to the heavens for her only possible reward, like Isabelle de Charrière's Caliste. (The latter, as Joan Hinde Stewart remarks in *A New History of French Literature*, gives up the ghost to the strains of Pergolesi's *Stabat Mater* "not . . . because she has engaged in illicit sex; instead, she withers away for lack of it.") Delving a little deeper, we can add that Miss Edgermond was eliminated by the elder Lord Nelvil as a possible wife for his son when, as a young woman, in the privacy of her home, she struck him as something of an extrovert in her behavior. Male prejudice meant he felt threatened by the idea that his heirs could be borne by someone who might metaphorically or literally put on a show. We never learn the heroine's full name: when living as a celebrated poet and improviser, she bears only the pseudonym "Corinne." The elder Miss Edgermond, her first name never mentioned in a symbolic rejection of her individuality, was written out of history by a fictitious death announcement circulated by her stepmother. In much the same way as posthumous publications were sometimes envisaged by those who could not conceive of their texts being published during their lifetimes, symbolic deaths, like changes of names, could release bridled creativity.

When Gérard accepted the order for his celebrated painting of one of the major scenes of the novel—after an initial project by Jacques-Louis David was abandoned—he considered giving the main character the features of her recently deceased creator. Had he done so, he would have been following in Elisabeth Vigée-Le Brun's footsteps: she portrayed Staël as Corinne, with the Sibyl's temple in Tivoli in the background (Geneva, Musée d'Art et d'Histoire) when she stayed with the author on the shores of Lake Geneva in 1807. This small picture of a great woman writer by a great woman painter ended up satisfying neither the artist nor her model, though both initially set great store by the project. The identification of Staël with the fictitious Corinne, a sibyl for modern times, was one made by many of her readers, including some of her closest friends: she seemed, in the world of postrevolutionary France, to be the very embodiment of the independent woman who wished, to the displeasure of many, including Napoleon, to express herself on matters both artistic and political.

Staël started life as the daughter of a remarkable Swiss Protestant couple established in Paris. Her talented Mother, née Suzanne Curchod, who had something of a reputation as a charming bluestocking and gifted amateur actress and who had been courted by Edward Gibbon, had given up writing—or at least any hope of publishing—on marrying Jacques Necker, a wily financier who was to become one of France's most renowned ancien régime ministers and felt that a woman should aim to be a good wife and to further her husband's career. Suzanne Necker took this to heart and ran a successful salon that greatly contributed to his ambitions and prestige. Their only daughter was raised by doting parents in a loving household in which stimulating conversations among the foremost thinkers of the day were the norm. Her initial venture into print was unusual: she published a set of critical essays on Rousseau and his works in 1788, ten years after his death, when his place in the canon was being hotly contested. This shows her to have been taking a keen interest in the republic of letters, in questions regarding the intellectual's place in the public sphere as well as in more directly aesthetic matters. She would later write two seminal treatises that changed the way people thought about literary culture, *De la littérature* (*On Literature*) in 1800, which promotes the Ossianic model and the idea of northern melancholy as essential markers of modernity, and *De l'Allemagne* (*On Germany*) in 1813, which opened French eyes to the Romantic movement flourishing on the other side of the Rhine.

Though born in Paris and deeply attached to the culture and literature of France, Staël, to her dismay, never held French nationality and, in the second part of her life, Napoleon used this against her, repeatedly exiling her from the land in which she had been brought up. Staël's "headquarters" was the castle at Coppet by the banks of Lake Geneva, which has given its name to a loosely defined set of thinkers. The *groupe de Coppet* also included authors like Benjamin

Constant and J.C.L. Simonde de Sismondi, who displayed a truly European spirit at work in the early years of the nineteenth century. It is probably in part because of the form of exclusion they underwent that people like Staël had such a perceptive vision of why French society assumed a remarkable part in the Enlightenment's virtual state, the "Republic of Letters," in which boundaries were only there to be crossed and ideas to be challenged, tested, and promoted. Although it is hyperbolic, the saying "There are three great powers in Europe: Britain, Russia, and Mme de Staël" indicates that even in her contemporaries' eyes, and despite the opposition she had to face, the author of *Corinne* managed to play an important role that far exceeded what was expected of any individual at the time. Her posthumous *Considérations sur les principaux événements de la Révolution française* (*Considerations on the Principal Events of the French Revolution*) (1818) is a groundbreaking work in liberal thinking and had wide-ranging influence on political debates in the early nineteenth century.

Passions were often at the center of Staël's reflections, as several of her works show, possibly most notably her 1796 treatise, *De l'influence des passions sur le bonheur de l'individu et des nations* (*On the Influence of Passions on the Happiness of Individuals and Nations*). One that was written a little earlier, during the French Revolution, displays her consciousness of the reprobation reserved to women's participation in public debates. Called *Réflexions sur le procès de la reine* (*Thoughts on the Queen's Trial*), and published in haste in August 1793, it is a small brochure that constitutes a brave attempt to intervene in Marie Antoinette's fate as she languished in prison after her husband, the king, had been executed on January 21 of that year. Signed simply *Par une femme* (by a woman), it added that the author's name should remain unknown, as it would be of no use. Staël wished to emphasize her sex but not rely on her reputation and high profile: she writes as a woman, about a woman's fate and, in part, for women, hoping that their expressions of feeling might generate an emotional currency to offset the virile models promoted by a republic that was particularly harsh on the late king's wife: she was a foreigner, known disparagingly as *l'Autrichienne* (the Austrian woman). Staël shows considerable political acumen in noting that as a mere consort, crowned but not anointed, the deposed queen of France had no official powers vested in her and had played no direct role in government but that, were she to be put to death, she would become a martyr-figure—"en l'immolant, vous la consacrez à jamais" (to sacrifice her is to grant her eternal consecration). The current "Toinettomania," from Tokyo to Trianon, and of which Sofia Coppola's film is an example, suggests she was right. Staël was taking a courageous stance in her appeal to the republican values of the revolutionaries and in her emotional address to women. Her voice was not to be heard, and the identity of the pamphlet's author having been guessed, the diplomatic quarters of her husband, the Swedish ambassador, were given an unprecedented ransacking.

The Revolution led to an improvement in the rights of blacks or slaves. Women hoped to benefit from the new climate. Olympe de Gouges had already displayed great sensitivity to inequality by writing a play on slavery, *Zamore et Mirza*, which the Comédie-Française accepted in 1785 and put on (unsuccessfully) in 1789 under the title *L'esclavage des nègres* (The slavery of negroes). She also opened her 1788 novel, *Mémoire de Madame de Valmont*, with a "Préface pour les dames ou le portrait des femmes" (Preface for ladies or the portrait of women) in which she defends their right to write but also implores their support for each other. She was a prolific though not particularly esteemed pamphleteer, novelist, and dramatist when, in 1791, she drew up what is now her most famous work, the *Déclaration des droits de la femme et de la citoyenne* (Declaration of the Rights of Woman and the Female Citizen), as a female equivalent to the Declaration of the Rights of Man, and dedicated it to the queen. It was turned down by the National Assembly. Its most famous disposition states, "Woman has the right to mount the scaffold; she must also have that to mount the rostrum." It is an indication of how little the message was heeded that the text was only edited fully by Benoîte Groult in 1986—though Gouges herself was executed in 1793.

Gouges—who is thought to have been the illegitimate daughter of a reactionary nobleman famous for his religious verse, the marquis de Pompignan—was one of the most vocal defenders of women's rights. Another was Théroigne de Méricourt (1765–1817), who, in 1792, called upon her sex to rise up and form a regiment of amazons to defeat the opponents of liberty, a value, she claimed, possibly more cherished by women than by men, because they had been so severely oppressed. Some of her rousing public addresses were published during her lifetime. She wanted female fighters on the front lines and took an active part in energetic protests before being committed to a madhouse, where she died twenty-three years later.

"Liberty, equality, fraternity" might have been the order of the day, but although the Revolution helped free the theatrical and media monopolies and led to the organization of public lectures and classes, women were not expected to be stakeholders in this new cultural economy. A clear illustration can be found in an account of life in Paris in 1801 by the admittedly reactionary émigré, Jean-Gabriel Peltier. The Lycée des Arts's second session of the year gave him occasion to vent his spleen, because a woman had been audacious enough to give a public reading. She was Constance Pipelet, "unknown amongst the unknown" according to the journalist, and was hell-bent on emancipating her sex—her *Epître aux femmes* (Epistle to women) indeed calls on women to rise up and act as the equals of men. She read her own poems on men and on marriage. Peltier considered it irrelevant to pass a literary judgment on her texts but instead stressed the scandal of a newly divorced woman making public jibes at matrimony, drinking in applause, crossing the boundaries between the sexes, and making a show of herself. This was, for him, beyond ridicule: it was obviously indecent. There was a clear equivalence between women who dared to say all, to reveal all in their novels, to expose all in their poems, and those who cast off their clothes in public. In spite of such negative comments—and numerous male authors like Rousseau, a couple of decades earlier, had also vehemently denounced any foray by women into print—many successful books were written and published by them in the long eighteenth century.

One field in which women's intervention in literature caused less of a stir than public readings was that of pedagogical texts. One of the century's best-selling authors was Marie Leprince de Beaumont. Born in Rouen, she spent some time in the duchies of Lorraine and Savoy but became famous as a French educator to the English upper classes. She published more than a hundred volumes in various genres but is most famous for her "Magasins," a series of dialogues first launched in the late 1750s. They include short stories, condensed histories, and biblical readings and purport to be the transcription of an educational program undertaken by young girls who progress in age, manners, and wisdom under the guidance of a governess who owes many of her characteristics to her creator. The different books that make up the series are tailored to suit the pupils' ages. The Magasins were translated into most European languages (Greek, Hungarian, Swedish, Dutch, Russian, German, Spanish, English, and Czech, among others) and used widely for educational purposes well into the middle of the nineteenth century. They include the best-loved version of "Beauty and the Beast" (originally a more risqué tale by another woman writer, Gabrielle-Suzanne de Villeneuve). The success of the story tends to suggest that it tapped into deep-rooted concerns about love and happiness as well as, perhaps, more primeval fears—there have been Freudian readings of the tale which center on loss of virginity as an implicit motif. Leprince de Beaumont's text is the one on which countless storybooks, Cocteau's film, and the subsequent Disney cartoon were based. Although a man, Charles Perrault (1628–1703), penned some of the most celebrated *contes de fées* (fairy tales) to come out of France, like "Red Riding Hood" and "Cinderella," he called them *Contes de ma mère l'oye* (*Mother Goose's Tales*), and women managed to a certain extent to carve out a niche for themselves in fairy tales. The magical episodes, links to an oral tradition, and overall lack of verisimilitude meant that they were seen to be on the margins of literature proper, and the dismissive references to "old wives' tales" show that such prejudice lasted over the decades.

Although, on the whole, Leprince de Beaumont sets out in her Magasins to educate the perfect Roman Catholic wife and mother, her books also encourage girls to think for themselves and demonstrate an interest in fields like geography or science as well as Bible studies or morality. Alongside the fairy tales that her fictional governess tells the younger girls, there are episodes from real life or drawn from mythological and religious *exempla*. She uses Enlightenment vocabulary, referring to the fact that children can be taught to cultivate their intellect and become *philosophes* by using reason and critical judgment, allowing them to speak up though hoping also to school them in not speaking out of turn. They are to be moral, but also, through acceptance of their role, they will be able to express themselves within the private sphere, to do good to those around them, and to make the world a better place. There is something of a Christian utopianism at work in Leprince de Beaumont's vision of the positive effects of women's acceptance of their status and function. She also published dialogues aimed at those who could be entrusted with schooling servants and the poor in the country and displayed a strong belief in the value of education for all ages and social strata.

Le triomphe de la vérité ou histoire de M. de La Villete (*The Triumph of Truth, or Memoirs of Mr de La Villete*), Leprince de Beaumont's 1748 debut novel, deals with a case of what in Rousseauist terms is referred to as "negative education," in which a young man is left to discover the Catholic faith through his own feelings and reasoning rather than by having it drummed into him. One of his adversaries in a theological discussion spouts large chunks of text that are not flagged in any way but quote directly from the *Pensées philosophiques*, which Diderot had published anonymously two years earlier. Leprince de Beaumont was clearly well versed in contemporary literature, even of the most scandalous nature. Her huge influence has often been discounted because historiography has neglected women writers as a whole and the very concept of religious Enlightenment sits ill with the traditional anticlerical vision of the French "Lumières." By reconsidering texts by authors like her, scholars are currently revising the canon and attempting to produce a less monolithic vision of eighteenth-century life and letters.

Other women writers who produced important works on education include Louise d'Epinay (1726–83)—whose *Conversations d'Emilie*, largely based on her experience of bringing up her granddaughter, won the 1782 Prix Montoyon, then a newly created prize awarded by the Académie française for the most useful recent publication in moral terms—and the prolific writer Félicité de Genlis. Celebrated in her childhood as an exceptionally talented harpist, Genlis would go on to write numerous texts, from novels—including the best-selling *Adèle et Théodore* (*Adelaide and Theodore, or Letters on Education*), published to great acclaim in 1782, the same year as Laclos's scandalous *Liaisons dangereuses*, which it outsold)—to conduct books, short stories (like the charming "Mademoiselle de Clermont"), and highly successful plays for child participants on amateur stages, through which they could learn about virtuous conduct by acting out little moral tales. Like Staël, Genlis was often reviled in the gutter press and scurrilous brochures. Her private life—she was mistress to the king's cousin, the future "Philippe Egalité," and governor (the masculine title was used exceptionally in her case) to his children, the Orléans princes—was used to discredit her and her writings. Her books, which number more than a hundred volumes, were widely read, translated, and circulated in many European countries.

Thanks to the various publications on female education, with women at the vanguard, the subject became one of widespread concern in the years before the Revolution—as is attested by several academic competitions, including one at Besançon (1777), in which Bernardin de Saint-Pierre and "Manon" Roland took part, and one at Châlons-sur-Marne (1783), for which Laclos prepared drafts.

If, on the whole, the idea that women could be entrusted with bringing up girls and writing about their education did not create too much controversy, particularly as they tended to stress the moral aspect of pedagogy, another field for which they were considered to have literary gifts was letter writing. Two posthumous volumes published during the eighteenth century contributed to this: the marquise de Sévigné's seventeenth-century letters to her daughter, which give a spirited account of events, first came out clandestinely in 1725, and Englishwoman Lady Mary Wortley Montagu's *Turkish Letters* were translated into French in 1763. Both were widely read and much appreciated by men and women alike; both are at a form of crossroads at once opening onto usually forbidden worlds (the royal court and Turkish life) and documenting the mundane concerns of private individuals. Letter writing was seen as the textual form closest to a conversation: it does not obey rules like a sonnet or a *tragédie classique*. As their rediscovered correspondences (published long after their deaths) show, many important women authors like Charrière or Staël—or the scientist Emilie du Châtelet, whose influence in disseminating Newtonian ideas in France was of huge importance— were consummate letter writers.

While these women's cosmopolitan education and frequent travels go some way to explaining this, material conditions for letter writing improved greatly in France in the eighteenth century: mail coaches were given regular schedules, road surfaces were improved, and literacy rates increased. Some great letter writers did not compose plays or novels but were at the center of networks of correspondents from different geographical areas and walks of life. Several women exchanged hundreds of letters with Voltaire before his death in 1778. They include his niece—and sometime mistress—Marie-Louise Denis (1712–90) and the famous salon hostess Marie du Deffand (1697–1780). The latter, who also corresponded with Walpole, was a keen observer of human foibles, a marchioness who dictated to secretaries after she went blind in her mid-fifties. Her letters display wry reactions to snippets of news that came her way and trace admirable character sketches of her guests. She was lucid about herself and about others, and her affectionate skepticism often gives way to true melancholy. According to the influential nineteenth-century critic Charles-Augustin Sainte-Beuve, "Mme du Deffand est avec Voltaire, dans la prose, le classique le plus pur de cette époque, sans même en excepter aucun des grands écrivains" (Mme du Deffand is, with Voltaire, the most pure of the classics in prose of her time, excepting none, even among the great writers).

Julie de Lespinasse, a close friend of the encyclopedists—she is a major character in Diderot's 1769 *Le rêve de D'Alembert* (*D'Alembert's Dream*)—was initially employed by Marie du Deffand to read for her. They quarreled when the "marquise" discovered that her young protégée—who was in fact her brother's illegitimate daughter—was having private conversations with her salon guests. Julie de Lespinasse moved out and started organizing her own regular receptions. Many of Lespinasse's letters were preserved because she was so closely involved in the daily life of the *philosophes* in Paris. Myriads of other witty and clever women also doubtless penned missives, but these either lie dormant in archives or have been destroyed. Increased interest in private life over the past few decades has led to the uncovering of family correspondences in which women played a prime part, and new corpuses will doubtless become available in the future.

Letter writers speak of their own lives. A field that has drawn recent interest from specialists is that of diaries and journals. While Rousseau provided the impulse for the development of autobiography as we know it, throughout the eighteenth century, others committed their feelings and ideas to paper. Many women, once literate, kept commonplace books in which they jotted down recipes, useful facts for the household, or accounts and so on, but sometimes they actually spelled out their hopes or fears, told of their experiences, and took possible readers—often just their immediate family—into account. A spirited early autobiographical text is the *Mémoires* of Marguerite-Jeanne de Staal-Delaunay (1684–1750), which gives greater scope to introspection and character analysis than most contemporary writings. Brought up in a convent in Rouen—her mother had fallen on hard times—Staal-Delaunay became a lady of the bedchamber and then confidante to the duchesse du Maine, who plotted against Philippe d'Orléans, the regent, and held a sort of parallel court in Sceaux, just outside Paris. Witty and self-deprecating, the memoirist recounts different episodes of her life from her childhood onward, remembers her adolescent crushes, and details some of her struggles, including the time she spent in the Bastille as one of the conspirators in the duchesse's shady political dealings. She describes prison as a curiously liberating experience: though behind bars, she was free to do what she wanted with her time and not subject to her employer's whims. She also recounts how, although she married a baron, she was never treated completely as a noblewoman by the duchesse, and she adds that original sin may be wiped out by baptism, but not the indelible stain of having been a chambermaid by the sacrament of marriage! Staal-Delaunay's writings were printed posthumously. She clearly did not feel it possible for them to be published during her lifetime.

Jeanne-Marie Phlipon (1754–93) also lived at the intersection between public and private spheres. A reader of Rousseau, she was the only daughter of a Parisian goldsmith and his wife. They brought up young "Manon" as a sensitive soul, taking her on excursions to the countryside and providing a loving environment. She married an older man, Jean-Marie Roland de la Platière, and seems to have played a part in composing his speeches and official letters when he became minister for the interior under the Girondin government (1792–93). She wrote her memoirs in prison after the fall of the regime. She knew she was unlikely to escape the death penalty and wanted to leave her daughter something to live on after her death. Her *Mé-*

moires particuliers, which include the account of a scene in which an apprentice in her father's workshop fondled her inappropriately, are only one wing of the diptych. The other is made up of her political memoirs and shows how closely involved she was in major events during the revolutionary years. A picture thought to be of her, by a talented woman painter, Adélaïde Labille-Guiard (Quimper, Musée des Beaux-Arts), portrays the sitter, elegantly clad in pearly white, with a powdered wig and lace cap, at a desk, pen in hand, staring out at the spectator as though interrupted as she writes. Whether or not it represents "Manon" Roland, it corresponds to the idea of an engaging modern person who is both an intellectual and a woman of fashion—one who knows her own mind whether drafting a pamphlet or choosing a dress.

In her professional capacity, Félicité de Genlis used diaries and reports to control the Orléans princes whose education she supervised. She encouraged mothers to keep notes about their children's upbringing. Many appear to have done so, within the upper-middle classes. Their texts are precious illustrations of the way family life was evolving. The age of reason witnessed the blossoming of expressions of feeling that were considered legitimate per se and did not require any informative value to serve as an excuse. Such documents were kept to be read and reread within the family circle. Women and children when traveling, whether with a father or husband who had business overseas or as tourists visiting Rome, for instance, were sometimes encouraged to keep a journal. Anne-Marie Du Bocage (1710–1802), who wrote an epic about the bringing of Catholicism to the Americas—*La Colombiade ou la foi portée au Nouveau Monde* (The Columbiad or faith brought to the New World)—and a relatively unsuccessful play called *Les amazones*, published travel letters ostensibly to her sister as a literary text. The frontispiece of her complete works is a portrait with the caption *Forma Venus, arte Minerva* (She has the looks of Venus and the art of Minerva) as though only by hyperbolic comparisons with Greco-Latin divinities could one salute the exceptional talents of a woman who composed works in the most noble and challenging of genres: epic poetry and tragedy. Du Bocage's chatty letters from Holland or Britain were considered less impressive achievements than her more serious works, but they were probably more widely read.

The letter was also popular as a vehicle for novels during the eighteenth century. Letter and memoir forms made fiction seem closer to authentic documents. Fictional letter writers could express subjective feelings, and the women characters, though often unlucky in love, still have depth and color and are given at least as much place as their male counterparts: the individuals who hold the pen are trying to find themselves and discover how their interactions with others affect the balance of their relationships. Many epistolary novels were written by successful women writers. "Beauty and the Beast" author Leprince de Beaumont penned several, which address questions of education and social issues like breastfeeding or illegitimacy. Her *Nouvelle Clarice* (1767) shows the extent to which Richardson's *Clarissa* influenced writers throughout Europe. The title emphasizes the importance of the heroine, like that of Staël's first novel, *Delphine*, published in 1802. Its epistolary polyphony charts a doomed love story that unfolds with the French Revolution as its backdrop. It is a moving presentation of how generosity can get one into trouble and the dilemmas that social pressure, prejudice, but also a man's lack of moral courage can put on a woman. In some ways, its reverse reflection is Tencin's 1736 *Mémoires du comte de Comminge* in which the anonymous author—mother of an illegitimate son who became famous under the name of d'Alembert—takes on a male voice and recounts how his shortcomings led to him losing his beloved Adélaïde not once, but twice.

Other important novelists who chose the epistolary genre include Marie-Jeanne Riccoboni (1713–92) and Isabelle de Charrière (1740–1805). Most of Riccoboni's novels tell of unhappy romances, often set entirely or partly in Britain, where her correspondents David Garrick and David Hume lived, and some, though original, pretended to be translated from English—this was a commercial ploy as "Anglomania" struck the Continent. Their titles betray the author's shaky command of the language, as in her successful 1757 *Lettres de mistriss Fanni Butlerd à milord Charles Alfred de Caitombridge, comte de Plisinthe, duc de Raftingh*, which contemporaries initially believed to be a true correspondence, in part thanks to a journalistic hoax in which a letter purportedly from an abandoned woman called Fanni to her seducer Milord Charles C., duke of R., was published as authentic. We only have the woman's letters. They show that in the love story that they chart, her emotional investment is greater than his. She starts by idealizing him, and her lucid discovery that he is not what she believed and hoped him to be gives the volume tragic overtones. Many women novelists, in depicting such relationships, were showing that public perceptions of affairs of the heart compounded inequalities between the sexes: a woman's reputation could be lost and her lover's enhanced if news of the liaison circulated. Society, in Riccoboni's novels, allows men to avail themselves of unfair perspectives: they exploit situations that leave their sensitive mistresses facing the consequences of their actions. The stories center on individual relationships but also show how such ties play out in public. There is implicit social criticism in Riccoboni's writing. Like many female novelists, whose tales often take place in the provinces, she does not resort to complicated plots, and the shipwrecks or duels that are ten a penny in certain authors' works are disregarded in favor of moral weakness or inconsistency and the havoc they wreak on everyday existences.

Riccoboni's fiction was translated into different languages, and her books were reprinted several times well into the next century. From the outset, they were popular, particularly among women readers— Sainte-Beuve makes an unverifiable claim that Marie Antoinette had them bound like a prayer book to read during mass. Although this is probably untrue, it is a way of indicating their success—particularly as the queen of France was not an avid reader. Because they were generally set in modern times, the stories allowed contemporaries to identify with the adventures. Such books, which display an acute consciousness of social conventions as they affect both sexes, are often intimate works, with a handful of characters. The epistolary form encourages such closed circuits. It gives unparalleled and unmediated access to the letter writer's moods, like reading over someone's shoulder. Riccoboni is also famous nowadays because of a private correspondence with Laclos after the publication, in 1782, of *Les liaisons dangereuses*. She was concerned with the immorality of the marquise de Merteuil and the question of verisimilitude in the depiction.

While Riccoboni—the illegitimate daughter of a bigamous father—was a Parisian from her birth to her death, Isabelle de Charrière was a cosmopolitan like Staël. She was born in the Netherlands, had married a Swiss nobleman, lived near Neuchâtel, and wrote in French. She is, as Caroline Warman, who published the first English translations of several of her works pithily puts it: "the French, Swiss and Dutch Jane Austen all rolled into one." Charrière's first published text, the 1763 novella *Le noble*, put her on a collision course with her family: it tells of a young aristocrat whose father forbids her to marry the man she loves: he is not quite noble enough. The feisty girl, who wants nothing more than to be in her suitor's arms, elopes. She crosses the castle moat by using the portraits of her ancestors as stepping stones. The author's horrified family attempted to buy up the whole of the print run even though their as yet unmarried daughter's name was not on the title page.

In her subsequent works, which include novels, pamphlets, and twenty-six plays, Charrière often deals with political issues. Twists in her storyline involve societal questions like what to do with illegitimate children and whether boys and girls or the rich and the poor should be brought up differently. In the *Lettres trouvées dans des portefeuilles d'émigrés* (*Emigré Letters*, 1793), there are ideological and class differences between the heroes' families, and we do not know to what extent revolutionary affairs as well as social pressure may influence the shape of things to come: the Terror offers unexpected and dramatic twists in the storyline—like in Staël's later *Delphine*—and shows that by writing truly contemporary fiction, the novelist put herself and her readers on the razor's edge, implicitly admitting that it was impossible to know where the world was heading. Not only does Charrière go far beyond the traditional marriage plot, but one of the characteristics of her fiction is to eschew traditional happy endings— or indeed tragic ones.

Often pessimistic about women's condition in society and never afraid to illustrate the tedium of domesticity, Charrière sets out individuals' choices but leaves the resolution hanging in the balance for the reader to decide or work out. Such choices constitute a refusal to take things for granted or to cede to facility, and they proved particularly interesting at a time of social and political upheaval. Charrière writes with acuity of hope and despair and clearly wants to get readers thinking about societal questions. She uses a medium that allows her to do so by creating engaging and varied figures and putting them in awkward situations. In her 1784 *Lettres neuchâteloises* (*Letters from Neuchâtel*), the heroine has to forgive her beloved Henri who has fathered an illegitimate son with a seamstress (one of several important working-class women in Charrière's works) and make provisions for his upbringing—far away from them all. On the whole, she is much more decisive and savvy than her well-intentioned but somewhat hapless fiancé.

We may never know the extent to which women took up their pens in eighteenth-century France. Many did not write texts to publish them, or if they did allow them to go into print, did not sign them; or, they confided their ideas to a man who would then develop them on paper—a case in point is that of Elisabeth Ferrand (1700–1752), to whom Condillac dedicated his *Traité des sensations*, recognizing her invaluable intellectual input and crediting her with inventing the conceit of the statue coming to life as its senses receive external stimulation. Had he not included profuse thanks in his prefatory text, we would know nothing about her. Though she was in close contact with Charles-Edward Stuart, Clairaut, d'Alembert and others, we have only sketchy biographical details about her and a splendid pastel by La Tour of an elegant woman with a large volume of Newton's works (Munich, Alte Pinakothek). Condillac's statue, who learns through the experience of the senses, building on such cognitive channels for reason to play its part, is in some ways emblematic of the emotional economy of women's writing.

Fear of reprisals for particularly scandalous texts led some men to circulate them anonymously or in manuscript form—think of a major Enlightenment figure like Diderot. In women's cases, social prejudice rather than the nature of their writings is at play. Women were often seen as intellectually inferior. Their productions could be deemed negligible by definition. Some feared for their reputation were they to step into the limelight as authors—the talented Franco-Swiss translator Aimée Steck-Guichelin (1776–1821) resisted friends' encouragements to publish her poems: she was quite happy being an anonymous channel to convert someone else's (a man's) prose into another language for it to circulate, but to see her own verse out in the open would be, she said, like walking down the street clad only in undergarments.

Even among women who did hope to see their works published, there were economic implications of admitting to being a female author: one would get paid less and could, on the whole, expect biased reviews. Françoise de Graffigny (1695–1758), a scion of the minor nobility of Lorraine, is a case in point. Her marriage was an unhappy one, and she left her violent husband. In Paris, she was part of a circle of intellectuals. She sent copious letters to François "Panpan" Devaux about literary life, her health, her conversations. She wrote an epistolary novel about a Peruvian princess, Zilia. Seized from the Temple of the Sun by Spanish invaders, the heroine ends up in eighteenth-century France, under the wing of a tolerant Frenchman, Déterville, who falls in love with her. Zilia, though, considers herself to be pledged to the "Son of the Sun," the heir to the Inca throne, and even when it becomes clear that he has abandoned her, she opts for a single and contented life, accepting friendship but not marriage from her French suitor. The novel is remarkable in that it writes the male voice largely out of the story: we have only Zilia's letters, to her fiancé Aza and her friend Déterville, along with one note from the latter in which he hands over gold treasure from the ransacked Incan temple that will allow the Peruvian princess to live an independent life. After Aza's betrayal, Zilia will grant men space only on her own terms. Her letters offer a tantalizing dissenting option that might hardly have been practical for Graffigny's contemporaries but at least afforded a glimpse of wider horizons.

Like the characters in Montesquieu's *Lettres persanes*, Zilia details European life, in her letters to Aza, with an impartial eye—all the more so because she has had to learn to read and write in French, having run out of *quipos*, Incan knotted cords that initially allowed her to record her life. She depicts Westerners as taken in by appearances and artifice, whereas the culture from which she hails is portrayed by her as virtuous and simple: in an iconic scene, when she has just arrived in Europe, she glimpses a young woman dressed like herself in the costume of the Virgins of the Sun. She rushes toward her and discovers something unknown in Peru: a mirror reflecting her own image. While writing her novel, Graffigny took advice, in person and by letter. When it came to finding a publisher in 1747, she got a male friend to submit it, believing he would get a better deal than she would. The book, which came out anonymously, was a runaway success—more than forty editions were published before 1800; it was translated into five languages; and it served as the basis of a popular method for Italians to learn French and vice-versa. Graffigny admitted to being the author and basked in the glory it brought her. She had a revised edition published in 1752 and included extra passages, in particular a letter purportedly written from a convent in which young girls are educated, as a way of criticizing the poor deal they got. By choosing to make her heroine a Peruvian princess who learns to speak and write French, Graffigny was showing that to many of her contemporaries women were like foreigners.

It is interesting that both Staël (in *Zulma*, for instance) and Charrière (with her unfinished *Constance*) include cases of black women or slaves whose condition serves as a way of addressing all manner of economic and social prejudice, exploitation, and inequalities. A later novella with a similar premise is the highly sensitive *Ourika* (1823), by Claire de Duras (1777–1828), in which a dying black woman tells her tale to a doctor, much as one might to a psychoanalyst: she was brought over from Africa and treated like a trophy, cherished in her childhood, but, once she reached womanhood, excluded from the very society that had lavished attention on her—she could never be the equal of those who had welcomed her as an object of wonder and delight; she could never hope to marry the white nobleman she loved.

While female characters in eighteenth-century women's fiction often get a raw deal, they usually make their case to be heard eloquently and with feeling. Their remarks or behavior can be unsettling: they sometimes challenge or subvert a social order in which they were, like Victorian children, expected to be seen, rather than heard. They thus serve implicitly to show their authors' aspirations. Although many people considered the rise of the novel to be a marker of the decline of highbrow culture—and its frequent association with women only served to underline this—the readership showed its support, and fiction came to occupy an increasingly important place in periodical reviews and private libraries. Even the most exceptional writers, like Charrière and Staël, whose birth and upbringing set them far above most of their contemporaries, remained in some ways on the margins, emblematic of the fact that to many, at the time—and in spite of Poullain de La Barre's assertion in his aptly titled 1673 work *L'égalité des deux sexes* (*The Equality of Both Sexes*), that the mind was not gendered ("l'esprit n'a pas de sexe") or Jaucourt's claim in the *Encyclopédie*'s entry for the word *femme* that natural law could offer no basis for inequality between the sexes—women were by definition outsiders in the intellectual world or, at very least, in the public sphere.

WORKS CITED AND RECOMMENDED FURTHER READING

Women have traditionally been quasi-absent from the canon in French eighteenth-century literature, as publications like the Lagarde et Michard series, used until recently for teaching purposes, illustrate. The impulse for change was in part due to the influence of Anglo-American gender studies. As far as texts go, in France, Chantal Desjonquères's series of eighteenth-century texts put writers like Charrière, Lespinasse, Riccoboni, and Tencin back on the map. Raymond Trousson, ed., *Romans de femmes du XVIIIe siècle*, Bouquins ed. (Paris: Laffont, 2000) includes works by Tencin, Graffigny, Riccoboni, Charrière, Gouges, Souza, Cottin, Genlis, Krüdener, and Duras.

The MLA Texts and Translations series offers English versions of works by several eighteenth-century women writers: Charrière's *Three Women* (trans. Emma Roksby, 2007); Duras's *Ourika* (trans. John Fowles, 1995); Graffigny's *Letters from a Peruvian Woman* (trans. David Kornacker, 1993); and Riccoboni's *Letters of Mistress Henley Published by Her Friend* (trans. Philip Stewart and Jean Vaché, 1993) and *The Story of Ernestine* (trans. Joan Hinde Stewart and Philip Stewart, 1998).

Charrière has been well served by Caroline Warman's translation of several of her works, *The Nobleman and Other Romances* (London: Penguin Books, 2012), and the enthusiastic and knowledgeable introduction to the edition is a joy to read. For context, Cecil Courtney, *Isabelle de Charrière (Belle de Zuylen), a Biography* (Oxford: Voltaire Foundation 1993) is the obvious starting point. Genlis's *Adelaide and Theodore* has been edited by Gillian Dow (London: Pickering and Chatto, 2007). On educationalists, Nadine Bérenguier, *Conduct Books for Girls in Enlightenment France* (Farnham, UK: Ashgate, 2011) is useful. See also *The Memoirs of Madame Roland*, trans. Evelyn Shuckburgh (New York: Moyer Bell, 1990).

Staël's novels are available in modern translations: *Delphine*, trans. Avriel Goldberger (De Kalb: Northern Illinois University Press, 1995); *Corinne, or Italy*, trans. Sylvia Raphael, Oxford World's Classics (Oxford: Oxford University Press, 2009); *Corinne, or Italy*, trans. Avriel Goldberger (New Brunswick, NJ: Rutgers University Press, 1987). A revised version of the 1818 translation of her *Considerations on the Principal Events of the French Revolution* was edited by Aurelian Craiutu (Indianapolis, IN: Liberty Fund, 2008). There are selections of her work in Vivian Folkenflik, ed., *An Extraordinary Woman: Selected Writings of Germaine de Staël* (New York: Columbia University Press, 1995); and Dorish Kadish and Françoise Massardier-Kenney, eds., *Translating Slavery: Gender and Race in French Women's Writing, 1783–1823* (Kent, OH: Kent State University Press, 1994). Staël has been the object of much attention, but biographies of her are of an uneven quality. Maria Fairweather, *Madame de Staël* (London: Constable and Robinson, 2005) is worth reading.

Denis Hollier, ed., *A New History of French Literature* (Cambridge, MA: Harvard University Press, 1989) contains short, pithy essays with bibliographical data on authors including Charrière, du Deffand, Duras, Genlis, Graffigny, Lespinasse, Riccoboni, Roland, Staël, and Tencin. I would also recommend Jean Bloch and Martin Hall's chapters in Sonya Stephens, ed., *A History of Women's Writing in France* (Cambridge: Cambridge University Press, 2000). Another staging point might be Eva Martin Sartori and Dorothy Wynne Zimmerman, eds., *French Women Writers* (Lincoln: University of Nebraska Press, 1994). See also the following titles:

Bongie, Laurence. *Diderot's femme savante*. Oxford: Voltaire Foundation, 1977 (on Ferrand).

Goodman, Dena. *Becoming a Woman in the Age of Letters*. Ithaca, NY: Cornell University Press, 2009.

DeJean, Joan. *Tender Geographies: Women and the Origins of the Novel in France*. New York: Columbia University Press, 1991.

Dijk, Suzan van, Lia van Gemert, and Sheila Ottway, eds. *Writing the History of Women's Writing: Toward an International Approach*. Amsterdam: K.N.A.W, 2001.

Gutwirth, Madelyn. *The Twilight of the Goddesses: Women and Representation in the French Revolutionary Era*. New Brunswick, NJ: Rutgers University Press, 1992.

Hesse, Carla. *The Other Enlightenment: How French Women Became Modern*. Princeton, NJ: Princeton University Press, 2001.

Lokke, Kari E. *Tracing Women's Romanticism: Gender, History and Transcendence*. Oxford: Routledge, 2004.

Stewart, Joan Hinde. *The Enlightenment of Age: Women, Letters and Growing Old in Eighteenth-Century France*. Oxford: Voltaire Foundation, 2010.

———. *Gynographs: French Novels by Women of the Late Eighteenth Century*. Lincoln: University of Nebraska Press, 1993.

Comedy in the Age of Reason

SUSAN MASLAN

The French eighteenth century is known as the age of reason (L'âge des lumières). Writers urged readers to rely on their own use of reason, rather than heeding superstition or unthinkingly following tradition or authority. Writing and "philosophy" became indistinguishable: best sellers investigated the foundation of the social order and the legitimacy of the political order. New discoveries in the natural sciences captivated imaginations. Isaac Newton's announcement that a knowable, definable set of laws governed the physical world led many thinkers to believe that society was likewise subject to a set of universally valid laws: if they could only determine what those laws were, scientists could reform political, economic, legal, religious, and social institutions and, finally, make people happy. What on earth is funny about all of that? How could the age of reason produce comedy?

Comedy was already a tricky business. Molière, the great founder of the French dramatic comedy, commented ruefully, "It is a strange enterprise to make respectable people laugh." By "respectable people," he meant those who could afford to go to the theater and those who were the arbiters of taste; comedy on the fringes of society—at the fairs and on the boulevards—might be easier to pull off because it could make use of traditional farce, physical comedy, and low humor. But those who wrote plays for the major theaters of Paris, where the prestige and the money were, faced myriad constraints. To make people laugh meant making them laugh at something. But many subjects that might make respectable people laugh were taboo. The Crown's censors and the Church's were always on the lookout, always ready to forbid a performance or even jail an author if a play seemed to make an allusion to contemporary political affairs, to important persons, or to ecclesiastical authority.

So, on the one hand, eighteenth-century writers, readers, and spectators were more invested than ever before in the twin projects of critique and reform, in the effort to lay bare the irrationalities, contradictions, and injustices of their society in order to improve it; and on the other, the institutions that governed the theater sought to retain a tight grip over what could be represented on the stage. Moreover, the idea of art for art's sake, that is, the argument that the aesthetic pleasure and value of art was the only important, true justification for its existence, was not yet accepted. Theater, like literature more generally, had to defend itself against claims that it promoted immorality or subversion of rightful authority. Literature's standard line of defense was that it "amused while instructing" and comedy's traditional self-justification was that it held up a mirror to vices so that they might be corrected. Comedy, in other words, was supposed to make faults and even immorality visible and, more important, the subject of ridicule. No one wants to be ridiculous, not even the wicked.

So, with all these limitations and constraints, how could anyone write a funny play? Despite the moral and didactic functions assigned to comedy by theorists and critics, despite the taboos that limited what dramatists could stage and how they could stage it, Pierre Carlet de Chamblain de Marivaux (1688–1763) and Pierre-Augustin Caron de Beaumarchais (1732–99) wrote intensely funny, aesthetically important, and socially conscious plays: they did it by exploiting the best of the traditions they inherited from Molière and from the Italian commedia dell'arte even as they broke new, indeed revolutionary, ground in subject matter and language.

The comedies of Marivaux and Beaumarchais are structured around the relationship between servants and masters. Their plots may develop stories of love and marriage, stories that explore the tensions between obligations to family and authority and the desire for personal autonomy and self-determination, but the place those tensions are discussed and debated is less in the dialogues between lovers than in the conversations between devoted servants and their masters or among the servants who act as witnesses to these struggles. Indeed, just in terms of the number of lines, dialogue between servants and masters and among servants dominates the plays. In Molière's comedies, the prominence of servant characters varied. Some plays, such as *Dom Juan*, feature servants in prominent roles; in others, servants provide bits of farcical or physical humor. But even when servants are important figures in Molière, even when they speak a good deal and advise the master characters with great intelligence and wit—as does the wonderful Dorine in *Tartuffe*—they always serve the master's story, not their own. Molière's servants help or hinder their masters' quests for love or money. The play's plot is the unfolding of the master's quest. Prior to Marivaux and Beaumarchais, servants simply did not have a story of their own.

Why is the role of servants and their relations to their masters important? The theater, and more specifically comedy, was the most important, most influential, and most popular artistic form available for portraying and reflecting on identity, social status, social relations, and even on hierarchy itself. Novels, so important today, still lacked the prestige enjoyed by the theater. In the French theater, servants essentially stood for all members of the lower classes, or, put another way, they stood for everyone who had to work for a living. And in the eighteenth century, the lower classes made up the overwhelming majority of the population. France was still an agrarian society. Of course there was the great city of Paris and the glittering court at Versailles, but most French people, indeed at least 90 percent of them, were peasants who lived in the countryside and made their very meager living by cultivating the land. Historians estimate that 90 percent of the peasantry lived just at or under the level of subsistence. Servants came overwhelmingly from the ranks of the peasantry. They were younger sons for whom there was no soil to till; they were daughters for whom there were no resources available for the dowry that was still an absolute necessity in order to marry. Indeed, some of the poorer provinces became so well known for the steady and abundant stream of servants they sent to towns and cities that employers disregarded their servants' given names and simply called them by their supposed province of origin. We can see a satirical reflection on this practice in Marivaux's play *La fausse suivante* (*The False Lady's Maid*, 1724). When the eponymous protagonist (a rich young lady in double disguise as a man and as her own maidservant) asks Trivelin, who after years of living as a vagabond has finally accepted his fate to live as a domestic servant, a seemingly straightforward question: "What is your name?," Trivelin responds, "As you wish, sir," suggesting a varied list of provinces from which to choose, "Burgundian, Champagne, Poitevin, Picard. It's all the same to me; the name under which I will have the honor to serve you will be the handsomest in the world" (act 1, scene 5).

Although Trivelin's seeming lack of interest in a name, and hence a kind of dispossession of an identity or even what we might today call a personhood of his own, along with his overly fulsome flattery, might seem to indicate that the playwright intended to represent servants as the mere ciphers of the masters, nothing could be farther from the truth. For in that very scene between the would-be mistress disguised as a chevalier and the-soon-to-be servant, there is so much verbal sparring, so many attempts to understand and grasp the meaning of the other (the puzzled employer wonders, "Is he making fun of me?" and asks, "are you laughing?"), so much specific and idiosyncratic speech on the part of Trivelin—his rejection of the term "valet" ("his valet! What a harsh term. Will we never purge such names from our language?")—that we realize Trivelin retains a full, distinct sense of self and that he forces his new employer to recognize him as an individual whose will is not dominated by his master. When the false "chevalier" tries to reject Trivelin's services, Trivelin simply refuses to be rejected, saying, "Let's not bandy about; time is passing and we haven't decided anything yet."

This scene underscores the degree to which Marivaux's servants and masters act as each other's comrades, confidants (for Trivelin knows that his employer is a woman dressed as a man and certainly intends to keep her secret), and allies. Indeed, while Marivaux's servants are utterly capable of pursuing their own distinct desires, whether for money or love of their own, their trajectories never conflict with those of their masters. Sometimes, their emotional lives resemble those of their masters so uncannily they seem more like twins than foils to the upper-class characters. In the first *Surprise of Love* (1722; Marivaux wrote two plays with this title), Lélio, a nobleman, and his servant Harlequin, have sworn to themselves and to each other to live a retired life in the countryside because they are both consumed by melancholy after having been betrayed by the women they loved. They act as each other's companions and as each other's support through emotional trials. As Lélio explains in the play's second scene, "Yes, my friend; I love you; you have good sense, although a bit crude. Your lover's unfaithfulness made love repellent to you; my lover's betrayal did the same for me. You followed me into this solitary life with courage and you have become dear to me because of the correspondence of our spirits and the resemblance of our adventures" (act 1, scene 2). So when Harlequin falls in love with Columbine, maid to the countess who lives nearby, he works with Columbine to make his master Lélio's life adventure continue to resemble his own: the two servants successfully manipulate their employers so that they too fall in love and decide to marry, despite their professed horror of the opposite sex.

The world of Marivaux's characters is based to an extraordinary degree on the tight bond between servants and masters. In typical comedy, and certainly in Molière for the most part, the protagonists have important family relationships that inform and shape the plot: this usually means that the young lovers live under the authority of fathers, uncles, or guardians, and sometimes even mothers, who intend to dictate the course of the young person's life. Often the authoritarian figure insists that the son, daughter, or ward, marry a person of the parent's or guardian's choosing despite his or her love for another. Much of the force of the comedy in such plays comes from the cleverness and stratagems, and even dumb luck by which those who are weak—because they are legally minors and have no right to decide for themselves, because they have no access to economic resources which are monopolized by the father, because they lack moral justification in a society that granted near omnipotence to fathers and endlessly repeated children's duty to obey—triumph over the obstacles put in their way by those who, ostensibly, are strong. Since most comedies were built around the joyful release of laughter that accompanied the upsetting of what was considered the divinely ordained social order, church and state authorities regularly condemned comedies, authors, and actors. Because in Molière wives regularly overcame their husbands and sons and daughters defeated their would-be tyrant fathers, and because spectators in the audiences could not help but side with the young lovers against the old, unappealing figures of repression, comedy was often viewed as vindicating disorder and turning the world upside down. Love in comedies meant love, but it also stood for the right to make decisions for oneself, for autonomy, for freedom.

Evaluating Marivaux against such a backdrop illuminates just how unusual he is. Most of his characters lack any defining social qualifications other than the bare minimum indicated by their names: they often are called simply the countess, the marquis, the chevalier. We know therefore that they are members of the nobility, but that is all we learn. When the noble characters do have names, they are stock comedic first names (Lélio, for instance, is one of Marivaux's faorites) rather than names that convey a distinct individuality. The servants, for their part, are identified as servants by names such as Harlequin and Columbine, which come straight from the Italian commedia dell'arte repertory. These names indicate types rather than persons. And yet, Marivaux manages to enrich these stock figures; he makes them into developed personalities though their extensive and highly particularized use of language.

Perhaps what is most startling about the world that Marivaux's characters inhabit is how bare of social context and how devoid of family it is. In the first and the second *Surprise of Love*, the central female protagonist is a young widow. No mother, father, or siblings have any role in the plot. Widows were especially interesting and useful figures in early modern French literature because of their idiosyncratic status. Among all women, only widows had the legal, and often financial, capacity for self-determination in ancien régime France. They could live on their own, make their own decisions, and spend their own money. Indeed, only widows could rightly be said to have their own money. Married women had the status of legal minors: they could neither sign contracts nor dispose of their money. Widows were clearly literary favorites; they were sought after in marriage plots because their late husband's money came along with them and because they were self-determining. Indeed, the marquise in the second *Surprise of Love* is so free of family interference that her maid, Lisette, takes it upon herself to arrange the marquise's remarriage. She knows that the chevalier would make a good husband for her mistress, and, of equal importance, she herself wishes to marry the chevalier's valet; so she manipulates the chevalier (himself suffering from a failed love affair) into realizing that he loves the marquise by displaying a rival, the count, before him: "I am attached to my mistress, more than I could ever say. And I am desolate to see that she does not want to be consoled, that she cries and sighs. . . . Look, here is the Count; he loves her. You know him; he is one of your friends. Madame the marquise doesn't find him repugnant. It would be a marriage that would be good for her; I am working to make it happen. Do your part to help us" (act 1, scene 10).

All of Marivaux's female characters appear to be self-determining, regardless of their marital status. In *The False Lady's Maid*, the main female protagonist, whom we know only as the chevalier, is a young, rich, unmarried girl. She travels the countryside disguised as a man, hires her own servants, and makes new acquaintances, all in order to decide for herself whether a young man who has been proposed as a potential husband for her is suitable: she learns conclusively that he is not. He is an unscrupulous, cruel, fortune hunter who idiotically reveals his intentions to the cross-dressed protagonist. Marivaux does not feel the need to explain how his rich young lady can manage such independence: she simply does. Her family is absent from the stage; a brother-in-law has proposed the marriage with the dishonorable Lélio, but he does not appear to have either the means or the inclination to force such a marriage. Neither mother nor father is mentioned; we presume they have died. In any case, she is on her own with only her newly hired servant Trivelin for companion and only herself for guide. Critics offer differing accounts of Marivaux's social views: is he an egalitarian *avant la lettre*? Is he a conservative who believes deeply in the need for social hierarchy and social order? One thing is certain: gender hierarchy is utterly absent from his plays. Women are in every way the equals of men.

Even in *The Game of Love and Chance* (1730), Marivaux's most conventional comedy (today his best-known and best-loved play), the heroine, Silvia, is unusually independent and autonomous. She lives in the paternal home, she has a brother, and her father has selected as her future husband the son of a dear friend. All this sounds typical. But what distinguishes this comedy from those of other playwrights is that Silvia's father leaves the decision to marry entirely in her hands.

Her decision will be made based on her own observation of the intended, on the facts that she uncovers. And so, like so many other heroines of Marivaux, she disguises herself. She trades places with her maidservant, Lisette, so that she can observe her intended, Dorante, from a safe, neutral position. Husbands often lead double lives, Silvia reasons. Outside the home, in the world of social relations, they may be witty, attentive, kind, and pleasant company, while at home they may show another, a truer, self that is morose, critical, or even tyrannical. But her suitor would have no motive to adopt a false demeanor before a servant, Silvia believes. Taking on the role of servant is a way to see what lurks beneath social masks. Of course Silvia does not know that Dorante has had the very same idea; he arrives at her house in the guise of his own valet.

Exchanging roles with her maid and disguising her class position is meant to offer Silvia freedom to learn the truth, just as the heroine of *The False Lady's Maid* was able to uncover the nasty reality about her intended by gender and class cross-dressing. Of course it does not quite work out this way, since Dorante has taken the same course of action; indeed, the fact that they have come up with the same plan demonstrates their likeness and suitability for one another. But they do not know this: Instead, the two upper-class characters find themselves mysteriously and inexplicably drawn to what they believe to be lower-class love objects. This predicament causes Silvia and Dorante to question their understanding of social rank as a fixed, real indicator of personal worth. At the play's outset, Silvia's brother Mario, who knows that both protagonists will be disguised as servants speculates: "Maybe Dorante will take a liking to my sister even as a maid; let's see if their hearts reveal to each of them what the other is really worth." Silvia believes that her true social station will somehow, inevitably, make itself felt. She has no concerns that, despite her maid's attire, Dorante's valet will make advances—exactly the scenario that occurs in each of Marivaux's comedies. "I do not fear his love-lorn sighs," announces Silvia, "there is something in my physiognomy that will inspire more respect than love in that jackanapes" (act 1, scene 5).

And the play does seem to bear out Silvia's prediction: the master and the mistress, despite the fact that they each believe the other to be a servant, and therefore that their union would constitute a mésalliance of the greatest order, fall in love. Dorante's buffoonish valet shows no interest in Silvia (disguised as Lisette) but heads straight toward Lisette (the "real servant"). The ramifications for an understanding of class, identity, and individual value appear so radical to the two master characters that Dorante attempts to naturalize his love for a woman he believes to be of the servant class: perhaps she is secretly an illegitimate child of a nobleman, he suggests. The two servants, each thinking the other a master and therefore a great catch, feel no need to delve into the matter further.

The play at once seems to suggest the fluidity and flexibility of class identity—servants and masters change places as easily as they exchange clothing—and to reaffirm the solidity and inescapability of class position. Class cross-dressing allows the two upper-class characters to speak to each more openly than they would have been able to had they been in their rightful social roles; the ritualistic, shell-like language of polite society can be bypassed. Indeed, Dorante and Silvia immediately employ the familiar pronoun *tu*, the pronoun of lovers, with each other, an impossibility were they not in disguise. Yet, the play seems ultimately to be conservative: it closes with the recognition of the rightful ordering of lovers and of society. Does the fact that Dorante believes throughout the play, at least until the denouement, that a servant girl is worthy of his love, and that likewise, Silvia thinks that a valet is infinitely more worthy than his master, offer reader and spectator a chance to question social hierarchy? Does the play offer an interlude in which something like equality is thinkable?

Marivaux directly addresses the questions of class and gender equality in two nonromantic comedies: *Slave Island* (1725), which has recently been revived and performed in important new productions in English as well as in French, and *The Colony* (1750). These are both what we might think of as speculative, utopian comedies; they both try to imagine what it would be like to start a brand new society from the beginning. How or why would some command and some obey? Why and how would some be subjected to others? Is hierarchy natural or inevitable?

In *Slave Island*, two men, a master and servant, and two women, a mistress and maid, find themselves on an island after a shipwreck. It turns out to be Slave Island, an egalitarian society run by the descendants of escaped slaves. Any slave who lands there is immediately freed, and his or her master is forced to serve the former slave for a term of three years. Masters and slaves exchange clothes and names, just as in *The Game of Love and Chance*. But here there is no love story, or rather if there is, the problem the play poses resembles a screwball comedy of remarriage: how can the master-slave couple be put back together once there has been an open avowal that the masters are no better, indeed are much worse morally, than their servants? The play relentlessly reveals the masters to be vicious, physically brutal, utterly self-absorbed, and intellectual vapid. The servants, on the other hand, are represented as, above all, "human," that is, capable of entering into the feelings others and inclined to pity those who suffer. The master-slave hierarchy has no basis other than sheer power: no belief system, no ideology (religious, monarchist, or other) legitimates the servants' subjection or the masters' mastery. Ironically, these master-servant relations are utterly unlike those based on mutual devotion that appear in the romantic comedies. So how can the relationship be reestablished in light of this now open knowledge?

The play seems to offer a conservative answer; emotion compensates for freedom. The master-slave relationship will be reestablished simply out of the goodness of the slave's heart. The two servants accept their subaltern position of their own free will because they hate to see their (former) masters suffer. They consent to their own subordination. What cements the four at the end of the play is ostensibly a bond of sentiment, of shared feeling that the masters recognize and are shamed into adopting. But despite the supposed reconciliation at the end, it is clear that nothing really has changed. Moreover, spectators and readers witness the rejection of every explanation offered for social hierarchy. Crying at the end cannot erase what came before. We are left with a harrowing vision of society: social inequality must persist simply because some must command and some must obey. No morality justifies the system of social relations; necessity simply requires it.

In Marivaux's plays, the obstacles to love and to marriage are not objective, external ones. They are not tyrannical fathers or guardians and certainly not lack of money. They are nearly always internal, psychological, emotional barriers. And this fact contributes to what feels like Marivaux's modernity. In each of his plays we find characters examining and discovering their own feelings—ones they usually did not know they had. And the risks they run are not the typical risks of early modern theater and fiction: to be forced into a hateful marriage or to be forced into a convent. The risks are purely emotional. They are the risks inherent in love: vulnerability, the loss of self, the loss of the perfect autonomy that seems to distinguish Marivaux's unmarried characters as they begin to discover that they do in fact depend on another, not for money or protection, but for happiness. Marivaux's plays have long been distinguished for the subtlety of their language, especially for their language of emotions. Indeed, compared with Molière or Beaumarchais, Marivaux offers little action. The action is talking, and talking—whether to oneself or another—is a path toward the discovery of the self.

If the terrain of Marivaux's comedies is the heart and the psyche, Beaumarchais's great plays take us back to the traditional comic ground of families, tricksters, and the obstacles that power puts in the way of love. Pierre-Augustin Caron de Beaumarchais (1732–99) is himself one of the great characters of the eighteenth century. Born in Paris to a family of watchmakers, he belonged to the artisanal class that would produce great writers and thinkers such as Denis Diderot and Jean-Jacques Rousseau. His own family was a happy and talented one; his beloved sisters were gifted musicians. Beaumarchais was a genius as a watchmaker; he invented a mechanism that improved watches' accuracy while allowing them to become more compact. His invention won the approval of the Académie des sciences and, more important for his future, came to the attention of the court at Versailles. It is a sign of Beaumarchais's ingenuity, charm, and brilliance that he soon landed himself the position of harp instructor to Louis XV's daughters. From there to writer was but a small step. Given this kind of mobility and adaptability, it should not be surprising to learn that later in life he worked as a royal spy and, later still, as a revolutionary overseeing the demolition of the Bastille.

But we remember Beaumarchais today because we identify him with his great character, the equally mobile and talented Figaro. Beaumarchais began his career writing for the stage with two dramas, but he became an enormous success with his first comedy *The Barber of Seville* (1775). The play may be best known to many of us now through Rossini's wonderfully infectious opera, for which it formed the basis, but in the last quarter of the eighteenth century, *The Barber of Seville* made Beaumarchais a literary celebrity and a rich man. The eponymous barber Figaro is a former servant of the extremely rich and powerful Count Almaviva. Figaro and the count bump into each other in Seville, where Almaviva is languishing in his love for Rosine, a young girl who lives with her autocratic old guardian who plans to marry her himself. The count wants Rosine to love him for his merits and not for his rank and wealth; he also wants to get her away from Bartholo, her watchful, oppressive guardian. Figaro devises a plan that will allow Almaviva to accomplish both his aims by disguising him as a soldier and sneaking him into Bartholo's house. Figaro's role is traditional in some respects, innovative in others: his actions seek to help his master by promoting the love and happiness of the upper-class character; this much seems fairly standard. Yet, Figaro stands out for his independence of spirit, his desire to pursue his own ambitions for career and money, and for his ingenuity. When the play opens, Figaro is an independent operator in Seville. Figaro directs the count, not the reverse; Figaro concocts the plan that the count follows. Figaro is intelligent, and his intelligence is made manifest by his sophisticated, often ironic, and always swift tongue.

The Barber of Seville was so successful and earned so much money for the troupe of the Comédie-Française, that the actors begged for a sequel. Beaumarchais obliged, and with what would turn out to be the second play of the Figaro trilogy, *The Marriage of Figaro, or the Mad Day*, he stepped into literary and political history. Beaumarchais finished the play by 1778, and passed his manuscript along to the actors at the Comédie. The actors, as a group, decided which plays they would accept into their repertory, and since only the Comédie-Française had official royal permission to perform tragedy and high comedy, every author with any ambition submitted his or her work to the troupe. The actors wanted to perform *Figaro*; audiences wanted to see *Figaro*, yet Beaumarchais struggled for six years to see his play brought to the stage. The battle ultimately ended in a victory for Beaumarchais and for *Figaro* and a defeat for the king of France, Louis XVI.

First came the struggles with the censors, whose approval was required before any play could go into production in the eighteenth century. Royal censors saw immediately that the work was too inflammatory to be allowed on the stage. Beaumarchais rewrote, cut, and resubmitted. A different censor was called upon to make a decision: he approved the play with only a few more changes. Now the royal court, always desirous of novelty and amusement, got wind of the show. The play was very funny; Beaumarchais had been reading scenes aloud in private houses, and everyone wanted to see it—Marie-Antoinette as much as anyone. Then the play was read to the king. He did not think it was funny. "This play mocks all that ought to be respected!" the king exclaimed, "the Bastille would have to be destroyed for this play to be performed!"

The king was perhaps no great genius, but he saw what his wife and many of the bored nobles in his court missed. *Figaro* was an attack on the central values of the ancien régime. It denied that those who occupied lofty positions were superior to ordinary people; it attacked the very idea of ascribed status. Monarchical French society was a closed caste system based on the idea that aristocratic "blood" was different from that of the common people. Some even believed that the aristocracy was descended from the conquering Franks and that commoners were descendants of the vanquished Gauls. On this account, they were two separate peoples living a thousand-year-old cold war. Figaro was having none of it. The great nobles were neither great nor good men, he asserted unhesitatingly. They had no intrinsic superiority. As Figaro puts it in his famous monologue, the noble Count Almaviva, who rules his territories with absolute authority, simply "took the trouble to be born, and nothing else! As for the rest—a rather ordinary man!"

Not only did *The Marriage of Figaro* attack the nobility (as a political and social institution); it openly criticized so many aspects of the ancien régime that it is hard to keep count. Only the Church was spared. The play also explicitly attacked censorship. It not only allegorized its own history; it also alluded to the ramping up of censorship more broadly in the second half of the eighteenth century (Figaro writes plays and economic treatises only to see them officially burned by the government and to find himself thrown in the Bastille).

It raises the problem of male sexual hypocrisy and the lack of economic opportunity for women, and in Marceline's subplot, it forces men to confront their own injustice ("My God, she's right," the men confess when faced with Marceline's unassailable logic in act 3). It directly takes up the notion of meritocracy, which under the slogan "careers open to talent," was a burning issue in the years leading up to the French Revolution, as careers in the army, for example, were increasingly restricted to those who could prove several generations of noble ancestry. Figaro himself seemed to incarnate the revolutionary, bourgeois idea that positions and responsibilities should be awarded to those with the talents and skills to carry them out, rather than on the basis of birth. Count Almaviva is not very intelligent; he seems slow and dull in comparison with Figaro, whose mind and tongue are nimble and razor sharp. Figaro and his friends invent plot after plot to thwart the count. The count invents nothing; he merely reacts.

In addition, *Figaro* attacks the judicial system: why is it that the unscrupulous count and his handpicked doltish judge have been chosen to administer justice? After all his own unhappy run-ins with courts and judges, it seems that Beaumarchais could not resist representing the utter corruption, venality, and stupidity of ancien régime justice. And Figaro's stint in the Bastille raised one of the central issues of the prerevolutionary years: arbitrary imprisonment without due process. (The word "Bastille" was ultimately suppressed by the censor, but the revised evocation of the "castle's drawbridge being lowered for me, and as I entered, [I] abandoned any hope and freedom" was immediately clear to readers and spectators.)

Pressure for the play mounted. Public opinion, a new and far from fully understood force at this time, backed Beaumarchais and *Figaro*. The king granted permission for the play to be performed only to suddenly withdraw it. He looked weak and indecisive; it seemed that if the public pressed a demand, the monarchy might have to respond. The play was finally performed on April 27, 1784. Crowds burst past the ticket windows and swamped the theater. Every seat was filled, and spectators stood everywhere they could fit. The play ran for sixty-eight consecutive performances after its premiere; it earned more in ticket sales than any other play of the century. But immediately after the play's rapturous reception, the king decided to have Beaumarchais arrested and thrown, not into the Bastille, but into the humiliating Saint-Lazare prison, where those accused of sexual crimes were immured. Everyone was laughing, except Louis XVI. The Saint-Lazare prison was meant to be more sensational and more shaming than the usual dungeon. But public reaction was swift—in the form of anonymous pamphlets, complaints from many of Beaumarchais's highly placed friends and from the supporters of the Comédie-Française's troupe, as well as just plain ordinary resentment against the king's ham-handed and capricious action. Once again, the king capitulated; his authoritarian gesture failed. Beaumarchais was released.

Perhaps Louis XVI could not see something that we see clearly today: the work succeeded not because of its pointed critiques, but because it is a great and very funny play. Beaumarchais showed that a play could be absolutely timely, deeply connected to the circumstances of its creation, and yet remain alive, touching, and meaningful. He accomplished this feat, in part, by drawing on comedic tradition—the play relies on class and gender cross-dressing and a good deal of physical comedy—and infusing it with modern sensibility. *The Marriage of Figaro*, like Marivaux's comedies, has the relation between master and servant at its core. But if Marivaux's masters and servants were tied to each other with what seemed to be an existential bond—so much so that they were often each other's only real social bond—Beaumarchais's *Figaro* shows the bond utterly betrayed, without ethical or moral content, hanging by a thread. Nor is the servant's primary bond with his master; Figaro makes his own bonds with the woman he loves, with friends, and with allies.

Of course, the title immediately announces one central revolutionary aspect of the play. For the first time, the marriage at the heart of the play is the servant's, not the master's. The servant's life takes center stage. *The Marriage of Figaro* asked spectators for something unheard of: that they identify with and root for a servant against his master. For the obstacle to Figaro's marriage and to his happiness is none other than the count. The count is so morally bankrupt and his lust so insatiable that despite the fact that Figaro helped him in his own quest for marriage, he seeks to ruin Figaro's. The count, because he alone is the ruler, imagines himself outside of and above all bonds of fidelity or reciprocity: he owes nothing to Figaro (who believes himself to be the count's friend), just as he has no obligation to his wife.

The Marriage of Figaro tells a sort of early modern sexual harassment story. The count, long unfaithful to his sad, betrayed wife, the former Rosine, desires Figaro's fiancée, Suzanne. As far as the count is concerned, he has a kind of property right in the body of every woman who lives in his domain. The name for this so-called right is the "droit de seigneur." And although the droit de seigneur may have been mythical (this point is uncertain), by referring to this particular "right," Beaumarchais manages to bring the whole complex system of "seigneurial rights" up for scrutiny. Seigneurial rights were very much in force at the end of the ancien régime in France: they were the principal means by which the nobility extracted their income from the countryside. These were the small, everyday obligations and taxes that peasants paid to the lord. For example, in some domains, peasants were required to bake their bread in an oven owned by the seigneur, and of course to pay for the privilege; they often owed the lord a certain number of days of unpaid labor; they might owe their lord a percentage of their harvest; and some peasants were required to pay a fee to the lord upon the death of the tenant-farmer so that the land could be transferred to a member of the family. All these were profit sources for the nobility, but they were also a means by which the lord symbolically asserted his power over the lives of the peasants who lived in his territory. In exposing the count's sexual predation, *Figaro* exposes the nobility as exploiters rather than protectors of ordinary people.

But the play is remarkable too in that Suzanne is not simply an occasion for rebellion. She is a central participant. From the play's very first scene, we see Figaro and Suzanne's shared happiness: they talk, they share confidences, they worry, they laugh. Suzanne takes the intelligent course of confiding to the countess the count's attempts to coerce her into sex. In so doing, Suzanne rightly counts on the countess's solidarity, and they, with Figaro, form the nucleus of what will be a formidable team that will work in concert to foil the count's plan. Another important member of the team is added when Figaro, who had been kidnapped as a child, discovers that the countess's seemingly disagreeable former governess, Marceline, is in fact his mother. Marceline, who up to that point had been a bitter, disappointed woman, immediately becomes a loving, supportive mother. She takes Suzanne into her affections as well, displaying how important female solidarity is in a world in which men make the rules.

Marceline's subplot helps lend the play its feminist hue. In the past, we learn, she had been seduced and betrayed by Bartholo (Rosine's curmudgeonly former guardian); Figaro is their long-lost son. But instead of accepting shame as her lot when her status as unmarried mother is revealed, Marceline grows in dignity as her former seducer, Bartholo grows ever more ridiculous. More important, Marceline becomes the advocate for a crucial new value—personal happiness— that, she argues, is more meaningful than socially imposed norms. Bartholo refuses to marry Marceline, despite his former promises to do so should their son ever be found, because of her "deplorable youth": that is, because of her sexual indiscretion with him thirty years earlier. "What do the refusals of an unjust man mean to us, my son?" she announces, "Your origin is not important, it is where you are going that matters to each of us. . . . Live among a tender wife and mother who will cherish you, be indulgent toward them, happy for yourself, light-hearted, free, and good to everyone." Figaro immediately perceives Marceline's wisdom: "[Y]our words are priceless, mama" (act 3, scene 16). Figaro, Suzanne, and Marceline together embody a new, sentimental model of the family that trumps the formal, sterile, aristocratic family of the childless and miserable count and countess.

Just as Figaro winds up assembling an unlikely but happy family, so too he assembles a seemingly unwieldy, yet effective team to oppose the power of the count. It includes the protean page Cherubin, Suzanne's startlingly sexually precocious cousin Fanchette, and wittingly or not, all the peasants who often crowd the stage without speaking a word. Suzanne and Figaro are wed. Suzanne manages to collect several dowries along the way. The count is humiliated before his wife and forced to admit his wrongs. But there is no reason at the play's close to believe that the count's beliefs or habits will change. Indeed, he has lost to his own subjects only because of their great intelligence and their mutual devotion. The count is an absolute ruler; the other characters cannot oppose him openly. They must scheme, devise, and plot. The powerless act indirectly, because the count possesses all the real power. He has the monopoly on economic resources; he embodies judicial and sovereign authority; he can refuse to allow Figaro and Suzanne to marry; he can consign his wife to a convent.

On the one hand, *Figaro* shows the triumph of feeling and fidelity over official power, but it also shows that Figaro, like his creator Beaumarchais, has an inkling that despite its utter lack of official status, there might be a form of power that could be effectively opposed to that of the count: the power of public opinion. At the end of each of the play's acts, Figaro (and the countess) force a concession out of the count: they make him beg his wife's pardon, they trick him into a symbolic approval of Figaro and Suzanne's wedding, and more. Each time, the count lets the audience know that does not intend to keep his word and that he makes his acknowledgment grudgingly. Yet each time, Figaro arranges to have the stage crowded with peasant and servant characters who, each one an insignificant person, together act as a sort of witnessing public to the count's words and actions. What does it matter to the count if a shepherd or shepherdess knows he is a liar? Gathered together as a community, they serve as a kind of moral authority—a force before which the count does not wish to be shamed. And so he, regretfully, accedes to his subjects' desires. Figaro, the wily stage manager who is also sensitive to the pulse of the community, forces the count into such concessions over and over again and in so doing points to a new direction for politics.

At the end of the eighteenth century, *Figaro* shows a world in which the notion of duty and faithfulness between master and servant, between superior and subordinate, is worn out and empty. The lower classes now have their own desires, their own kin, their own loves. They might even, as in the case of Figaro, have a lot more wit than the powerful but bumbling superiors. Writing about the relation between masters and servants was always a way to write about the composition and logic of society itself. It was a way to explore what the social bond is, how we are related to one another and what our mutual obligations should be. In the trajectory from Marivaux to Beaumarchais, from Harlequin to Figaro, we see the emergence of the individual and the beginnings of the triumph of the middle class. But

Beaumarchais's brilliance was to make a group of misfits—a valet; a spurned countess; an unwed, middle-aged housekeeper; a drunken gardener's niece—the sympathetic voices of a new world of wit, love, and even a new notion of honor.

Works Cited and Recommended Further Reading

All translations of passages quoted in this chapter are my own, although excellent English translations of both Beaumarchais and Marivaux are available in the following editions: *The Barber of Seville* and *The Marriage of Figaro*, in *The Figaro Trilogy*, trans. David Coward, Oxford World's Classics (Oxford: Oxford University Press, 2008); and *Marivaux Plays*, trans. John Bowen, Michael Sadler, John Walters, Donald Watson, and Nicholas Wright (London: Bloomsbury Methuen Drama), 2004. Before suggesting further reading, I would recommend further listening and viewing. *Le Nozze di Figaro* (1786), Mozart's adaptation of Beaumarchais's *Mariage de Figaro*, is spectacularly successful in expressing the joyousness that is at the heart of the play. The opera's libretto was even more heavily censored than was the play, yet all the elements—the celebration of love rather than power, and the privileging of sentiment rather than hierarchy and of community in the place of the exalted ego of the individual—are fully present. Abdellatif Kechiche's film *L'esquive* (2004), which appeared in US cinemas under the title *Games of Love and Chance*, is a fascinating reflection on the role of classical French culture in today's society. The movie depicts a group of high school students, living in a dreary exurban Parisian housing project, who rehearse and ultimately perform Marivaux's eponymous play. Kechiche explained that he was drawn to Marivaux both for his linguistic virtuosity (which he sees paralleled in the adolescents' mastery of their idiosyncratic language), and for his unusual attention to and sympathy with characters from the lower social classes.

For further reading about theater, theatricality, and the relationship among theater, painting, and the novel, see the important studies by Michael Fried, *Absorption and Theatricality: Painting and Beholder in the Age of Diderot* (Chicago: University of Chicago Press, 1988); and David Marshall, *The Surprising Effects of Sympathy: Marivaux, Diderot, Rousseau, and Mary Shelley* (Chicago: University of Chicago Press, 1988). To learn more about servants and masters, see Sarah Maza, *Servants and Masters in Eighteenth-Century*

France: The Uses of Loyalty (Princeton, NJ: Princeton University Press, 1984). Maza has also written a wonderful book that explores the importance of private lives, and specifically private scandals, to public, political life in eighteenth-century France; Beaumarchais is an important figure in her analysis: see *Private Lives and Public Affairs: The Causes Célèbres of Prerevolutionary France* (Berkeley: University of California Press, 1993).

* **

Diderot, *Le neveu de Rameau*, and the Figure of the *Philosophe* in Eighteenth-Century Paris

KATE E. TUNSTALL

Diderot is the central figure of the Enlightenment. True, he is not as well known as either the older Voltaire or his exact contemporary, Rousseau, both of whose self-promotional strategies made them into public figures and causes célèbres. However, insofar as he edited, with the mathematician and physicist, d'Alembert, the single most ambitious publishing enterprise of the period, the *Encyclopédie, ou Dictionnaire raisonné des arts, des sciences et des métiers* (Encyclopedia, or Reasoned dictionary of the arts, sciences and crafts, 1751–72), and, moreover, given that when d'Alembert left the partnership in 1759, he continued to edit that work single-handedly, there can be no question but that Diderot played the crucial role in shaping and disseminating Enlightenment ideas and values. The *Encyclopédie*, it should be noted, comprises twenty-eight folio volumes, seventeen of which are text, and eleven of illustrations. It contains seventy-four thousand entries, written by more than 130 contributors, including Voltaire and Rousseau; Diderot, in addition to his editorial responsibilities, wrote more than five thousand of the entries himself.

This alone accounts for the importance of Diderot in the French and European Enlightenment. In his lifetime, it was for this work that he was primarily known to the public, and not for the works of literature that we read today—*La religieuse* (*The Nun*, 1760), *Le neveu de Rameau* (*Rameau's Nephew*, 1761– or 1772–74), *Le rêve de d'Alembert* (*D'Alembert's Dream*, 1769), and *Jacques le fataliste* (*Jacques the Fatalist*, 1778–80). The latter were only published posthumously. One explanation for this is that Diderot could not afford to repeat the experience of the summer of 1749, when, following the anonymous publication of his *Lettre sur les aveugles* (*Letter on the Blind*, 1749), he was arrested and then imprisoned for three months. The *Lettre* was not his first publication, and, in fact, he had already acquired something of a reputation: the Paris Parlement (the supreme court) had condemned his *Pensées philosophiques* (*Philosophical Thoughts*, 1746) almost as soon as it was published, also anonymously, and decreed that it be "shredded and burned," while at a more local level, his parish priest had been secretly informing on him to the police, reporting that, in addition to the atheistic *Lettre sur les aveugles*, he was also the author of the teasingly erotic *Les bijoux indiscrets* (*The Indiscreet Jewels*, 1748), a tale in which female genitalia are endowed with the power of speech. And so, during the period of unrest in Paris in 1748–49, following the unsatisfactory outcome of the peace negotiations after the end of the War of Austrian Succession (1740–48), Diderot found himself included in a general roundup of known subversives and thrown in prison at Vincennes—the Bastille, it seems, was full.

A few years earlier, in 1746, when the *libraires* (the term covers both booksellers and publishers) had first approached Diderot about their encyclopedia, which, at that stage, was to be a rather more modest enterprise, a simple translation of Ephraim Chambers's two-volume *Cyclopædia* (1728), it had been because he was known to them not as a subversive writer but rather in the more modest guise of translator of such works as Shaftesbury's *Inquiry Concerning Virtue and Merit* (1699; French translation 1745) and, more important for their purposes, Robert James's three-volume *Medical Dictionary* (1743–45; French translation 1746–48). Though it is not impossible that, as their project evolved, the *libraires* were moved to offer Diderot the more notable editorial position owing to the *succès de scandale* of *Pensées philosophiques*, there can be no doubt that they were very far from predicting his incarceration. It seriously jeopardized a project that represented a significant commercial investment on the part of the *libraires*, who wasted no time putting that case, along with that of the indispensable nature of Diderot's editorship, to the comte d'Argenson, minister of state and directeur de la librairie (a kind of minister for censorship, responsible for the publishing and distribution of books in France).

After three and a half months, Diderot was finally let out, though not without having sworn that he would never again publish anything contrary to religion or morality. It was an oath that, strictly speaking, he cannot be said to have kept—*Pensées sur l'Interprétation de la nature* (*Thoughts on the Interpretation of Nature*, 1753), though no doubt rather technical for many readers, and perhaps deliberately so, none-theless made the atheist implications of some recent scientific theory perfectly clear. However, it cannot be denied that he did not publish many of his manuscripts, notably his attack on convent life that is *La religieuse*, a first-person narrative in which the eponymous heroine recounts how she was forced against her will to take the veil, or his comic novel, much of it in dialogue, *Le neveu de Rameau*, which offers, among other things, a devastatingly hilarious and rather disconcert-ing image of the social, political, and cultural affairs of mid-eighteenth-century Paris.

Diderot was known, then, to his contemporaries as the main editor of the most ambitious work of the age, and one of the most presti-gious to boot—the work had obtained the approval of the royal cen-sor (a *privilège*) and would attract more than four thousand fully paid-up subscribers (who, incidentally, thought they had signed up for a mere twelve volumes). Yet the ambition and the prestige of the work did nothing to place him and it beyond controversy. On the contrary, the ambition and prestige pretty much guaranteed it, not least from the Jesuits, commercial rivals in the publishing business, who were keen to quash any competition for their own *Dictionnaire universel* (*Universal Dictionary*, 1704). Moreover, the *Encyclopédie* was some-thing of a Trojan horse; apparently an innocuous compendium of knowledge about the arts, sciences, and technology, it also contained many highly unorthodox views, and furthermore, it stimulated free-thinking by presenting the many and often contradictory views avail-able on any subject, particularly metaphysical ones, and encouraging readers not only to weigh the evidence for themselves but also to enjoy the ironies created by the juxtaposition of so many differing views. Such a spirit of independent, rational inquiry, particularly when applied to questions of faith, could not fail to be incendiary, not least when the cross-references suggested to readers that they might, for instance, go from an article on cannibals or "Anthropophagists" to one on the Eucharist.

As a result, the *Encyclopédie* came under fire not only from the Jesuits but from other Catholic apologists too. Such attacks did not, however, land Diderot back in jail, and though they certainly made life difficult, the volumes continued to appear. In 1752, shortly after the publication of the second volume, the royal council decreed that the first two should be suppressed. The government, however, discreetly authorized the editors to continue their work, thanks in no small measure to the support of both Madame de Pompadour—who is to be seen seated next to several volumes of the *Encyclopédie* in her 1755 portrait by La Tour—and Malesherbes, the new directeur de la librairie, who is thought to have gone so far as to hide Diderot's papers in his own father's house to prevent them from being seized by the authorities. Certainly the extent to which the *Encyclopédie* smuggled in claims that were seditious and/or heretical was a major part of the battle, but there were accusations of literary crimes too. In some cases, these were no doubt a kind of *pis aller*—in 1756, Malesherbes made it clear that the journal *Année littéraire* (Literary year), edited by Elie Fréron who had powerful connections in the devout Catholic sections of the European aristocracy, had no more business declaring a work to be seditious, heretical, or morally offensive than the Parlement would have declaring one to be dull or ungrammatical, with the result that Fréron and others, notably Charles Palissot, accused the *Encyclopédie* of *lèse-littérature*, notably plagiarism, jargon, and sermonizing.

By the end of the 1750s, governmental support for the project was less forthcoming. The political climate had changed: early in 1757, an assassination attempt was made on Louis XV, and as the Seven Years' War (1756–63) went on, the *Encyclopédie* became a useful scapegoat, a way of diverting public attention away from the country's military and political difficulties—as Friedrich Melchior Grimm, the editor of *Correspondance littéraire* (Literary correspondence), observed in 1760: "You'd think that what led to defeat at the battles of Rosbach and

Minden, and to the loss and destruction of our fleet was perfectly straightforward and obvious, but if you ask at Court, you'll be told that such misfortunes are to be blamed on the new philosophy." Indeed, in 1759, the *Encyclopédie* had its *privilège* revoked, and the work was banned, though when all ten remaining volumes nonetheless appeared in France six years later, Malesherbes seems to have turned a blind eye to the illegality of the publication, which the *libraries*, by contrast, playfully acknowledged on the title page, announcing the publisher as one "Samuel Fauche," which is (nearly) to admit that his name was "False."

This was the major *querelle* or culture war of the eighteenth century, and Diderot was firmly at the center of it. Moreover, it made a significant and lasting contribution to French culture by forging a new figure in the social, political, and cultural landscape—one that remains to this day central to French intellectual life or, more accurately, to the French and, most particularly, Parisian cultural imagination: the *philosophe*.

❖ ❖ ❖ ❖

Philosophe is a term that is not, in fact, best translated as "philosopher," if by it we mean someone engaged in the solitary pursuit of knowledge and truth by rational means. Today, *philosophe* is commonly taken to refer to the figure that was triumphantly consecrated by the French Revolution, and which we find illustrated in the following description from Diderot's comic novel, *Jacques le fataliste*: "[P]hilosophes are a breed who are anathema to powerful men to whom they refuse to kneel. They are anathema to magistrates, the licensed defenders of the very abuses *philosophes* attack; anathema to priests, who rarely see them bow their heads at their altars; anathema to poets, those unprincipled men who stupidly regard *philosophie* as taking a hammer to art, not to mention the ones who engage in the odious practice of satire and have therefore never been anything but vile flatterers; anathema to the people who are permanently enslaved by the tyrants who oppress them, the rogues who cheat them, and the jesters who keep them amused." The *philosophe* is presented here as one who speaks truth to power in the name of equality, justice, and freedom, and is easily recognizable as the not-so-distant avatar of the modern figure of the engaged intellectual, who makes public interventions in social and political debates.

It is an image that stands in contrast to the following, taken from the entry "Philosophe" (1765) in the *Encyclopédie*:

> The philosophical spirit is . . . one concerned to observe and be accurate, one that brings everything back to its true principles, but it is not only his spirit that the *philosophe* cultivates; his care and attention go further. . . . Reason . . . requires him to know, study and work at acquiring sociable qualities.
>
> Our *philosophe* does not think he is in exile in the world; he does not believe he is in hostile terrain; he wishes to enjoy wisely and in moderation the fruits that nature affords him, to take pleasure in others and, in order to take any, he must give it in return. Thus he seeks to be agreeable to those with whom either chance or choice has led him to live, and at the same time, he finds in them what agrees with him. He is a civilized gentleman [*honnête homme*] who wishes to please and to make himself useful to others.

The contrast is striking: the article is certainly keen to ensure that the *philosophe* is not thought of as a philosopher engaged in the solitary pursuit of knowledge, but it is also no less keen to present him as a sociable figure, and so, whereas in *Jacques le fataliste*, the *philosophe* disagrees with—and is disagreeable to—pretty much everyone in his reforming zeal, here he is anathema to conflict, fundamentally agreeable to all those around him. And yet this image of the *philosophe* was one that itself generated a good deal of polemic, not least because it presents him as an *honnête homme*, a term that is notoriously hard to translate but which designates a figure that men of letters had fashioned for themselves so as to gain access to the protections afforded by the court and the aristocracy. And so the *Encyclopédie* defines the *philosophe* as one who is agreeable to those very same "powerful men" to whom he is said in the passage from *Jacques* to be outspokenly disagreeable and hostile. There would seem to be some kind of a contradiction here. If so, how are we to understand it?

Certainly the image of the *philosophe* as moving in high society has come to seem problematic to us today, and that is perhaps as much owing to the proto-republican image consecrated by the Revolution as it is to that projected by Rousseau, who made a great show of refusing royal protection and aristocratic patronage on the grounds that it was, precisely, patronizing, and who cultivated in public and in print, notably in his *Confessions* (1782), a counterfigure of the outsider—he was Swiss, not French—whose sincerity was guaranteed by his lack of connections to the rich and powerful, and by his status, which would come to be known as "bohemian." The success of the Rousseauian figure may have made it hard for us to see how relations with aristocratic protectors could be anything other than compromising, but, in fact, autonomy was very far from being the desired goal of most men of letters in the period. Indeed, a new elite space had emerged in the seventeenth and eighteenth centuries, the salon, which was not so much a mini republic of letters, independent of political power and in which writer-citizens freely debated ideas, as a kingdom of culture, in which the man of letters could make his fortune, both symbolic and economic, by means of his sparkling conversation and his learning, provided it was very lightly worn. Moreover, he might do so without ever doing anything so vulgar as addressing the public in print. As Voltaire puts it in the *Encyclopédie* entry "Men of Letters," "There are many men of letters who are not authors, and they are probably the happiest."

By the mid-eighteenth century, the relationship between men of letters in the guise of *honnêtes hommes* and the aristocracy was well established, but the extent to which they should aim to please, as the *Encyclopédie* entry "Philosophe" says they do, began to be called into question. Diderot's coeditor, d'Alembert, imagined how the man of letters might be excused from such a duty in his *Essai sur la société des gens de lettres avec les grands* (Essay on men of letters in high society, 1753). Certainly there is no question of the man of letters avoiding society completely—he is no antisocial misanthrope, and indeed, insofar as society is where he finds the material for his imaginative productions, it is necessary for him. Moreover, if he must pay court, as sometimes he must, d'Alembert's man of letters goes along in good spirit and "laughs at the persona he is thereby obliged to adopt, without feeling any anger or scorn toward him," but there is no need for him to prostrate himself to aristocrats, whose superiority is not innate, all men being naturally equal, and rests merely on birth and fortune, and not on talent. Moreover, he should be wary of patrons, who may appear generous but whose gifts actually involve taking possession of the man of letters, who is then required to be grateful, which he sometimes fails sufficiently to be, leading to what d'Alembert says are the often painful breakdowns in relationships between men of letters and patrons. And in any case, the man of letters should not fear poverty, and d'Alembert proposes the slogan, "Liberty, Equality, Poverty." Indeed, he might even dare to be disagreeable in society; of his own work, d'Alembert says: "However careful I have been ... to speak the truth in the least offensive way I can and without tempering it, I doubt it will have the good fortune of pleasing everyone," and he later asserts: "Every age, and ours above all, could do with a Diogenes; the difficulty is finding men brave enough to do it, and others brave enough to put up with up with it." So rather than being agreeable to his social superiors and supplying clever and witty conversation in return for real and symbolic riches, d'Alembert reconfigures the relationship between men of letters and the aristocracy such that the man of letters might earn those things by being borderline offensive, for, in protecting and supporting him, high society could appear suitably brave and unself-interested, and the man of letters, by virtue of his seeming bravely not to speak in such a way that was calculated to please, could have his authority guaranteed. The *philosophe* was just such a man of letters. And so whereas Kant would later sum up the Enlightenment in the motto *Sapere aude* (Dare to know), d'Alembert promoted "Dare to offend" with, as its crucial counterpart, "Dare not to be offended."

It was a delicate, discursive balancing act, and if Rousseau would break with the *philosophes* in part because of their social elitism, then other opponents of the *Encyclopédie*, who were no less opposed to Rousseau, attacked both *philosophes* and their protectors for indulging in what they saw as a game of smoke and (halls of) mirrors. In his *Petites lettres sur des grands philosophes* (Little letters on great philosophers, 1757), Palissot speaks of the patrons of the *philosophes* as "aristocrats who enjoy slumming it," and he famously likens them to

"Muscovite wives who can only love the men who beat them," adding that the "strategy has worked, and some aristocrats have accorded [the *philosophes*] some consideration precisely because [the *philosophes*] refused to accord it to them, which just goes to prove the ancient maxim which says that to succeed in high society, impudence is as good as flattery." Moreover, for all the *philosophes*' claims to be uninterested in power and glory, they have, Palissot says, set themselves up on "a kind of literary throne" from which they despotically anoint some and not others, and pompously decree, quoting Armande, one of "the learned ladies" in Molière's play of the same name (1672), "None shall have wit save us and our friends." The *philosophes* and their supporters are thus figured as a kind of sado-masochistic clique, trying to lord it over everyone else, monopolizing the public sphere, and claiming, to boot, that everyone is against them and that they are the very embodiment of "merit persecuted."

A similar picture emerges in another text of the same year, *Nouveaux mémoires pour servir à l'histoire des Cacouacs* (New memoirs for use in the history of the Cacouacs, 1757) by Jacob-Nicolas Moreau, who worked in the legal department of the Ministry for Foreign Affairs. "Cacouac" is a neologism that echoes the Greek *kakos* meaning "nasty" or "horrid," and is used in the text—a fictional travel narrative—to designate a hitherto undiscovered race of people with shiny costumes and silver tongues who lure unsuspecting Frenchmen away from their decent Catholic, patriotic values with their incantatory scientific jargon and their nasty cosmopolitan, atheistic ways. Moreau strengthens his accusation about the undermining of French national identity by reference to an earlier culture war, known as the *querelle des bouffons* (1752–54), which had pitted Italian music against French, and in which some prominent collaborators on the *Encyclopédie* had made the case for the Italians. In his *Lettre sur la musique française* (*Letter on French Music*, 1753), Rousseau had gone so far as to say that "the French do not and cannot have music, or if ever they were to, they'd be sorry," to which Moreau replies by having Cacouac music "instill terror" in his narrator. In the end, he manages somehow to escape and return home to France only to discover that the Cacouacs have overrun the country where they are known as . . . *philosophes*.

Such polemic circulated in printed pamphlets, but a new phase began when Palissot took the battle to the most significant cultural institution in Paris, the theater. Diderot had, in fact, already attempted to use the stage to defend the *Encyclopédie* (and was perhaps trying his hand at writing for the theater in case the *Encyclopédie* did go under). In his play, *Le fils naturel* (The natural son, 1757)—one line from which, "consult [your heart], and it will tell you that the decent man lives in society, and that only the wicked man is alone," seems to have been what finally ended the friendship between Rousseau and Diderot—one of the female characters, Constance, speaks of "those men that the nation honors and the government must now protect more than ever." Palissot's play, *Les philosophes* (1760), is a riposte, and though it recycles much of the substance of the earlier attacks, its performance on the capital's most prestigious stage, the Comédie-Française, suggested the anti-*philosophes* were gaining ground. It takes aim at precisely those men said to be honored by the nation and at their governmental protectors by drawing again on Molière, this time *Tartuffe* (1664), as well as *Les femmes savantes* (*The Learned Ladies*), and presenting the *philosophes* as impostors—hypocritical, self-interested, money-grabbing flatterers, whose gullible victim is a woman who has allowed them into her home where she hosts a salon. Moreover, the play crossed a line, and was allowed to so with impunity, in that it satirized individuals by name or, at least, by anagram: "Dorditius" barely disguises Diderot, who is the play's main target, though it is perhaps most memorable for the behavior of the character of Crispin, who crawled around on all fours, munching lettuce (obviously supposed to be Rousseau gone back to nature, as his critics claimed his *Discours sur les origines et les fondements de l'inégalité parmi les hommes* (*Discourse on the Origins and Foundations of Inequality among Men*, 1755) had proposed). Another pamphlet war followed, as did another play, this one by Voltaire, who had not been mentioned by Palissot and was no doubt just as irritated at having been left out—all publicity being good publicity in Voltaire's book—as he was moved by a sense of solidarity with those whom it was now starting to become an insult to call *philosophes*.

A conterfigure emerged here, one who would become known not only by the prosaic compound term "anti-*philosophe*" but also by the more memorable phrase, *un pauvre diable*. In the context of Voltaire's play, *Le café ou l'Ecossaise* (The café, or The Scots lass, 1760), "poor devil" would be a rather overly sympathetic translation; "miserable scum" would come closer to capturing the character of Voltaire's "Frélon," his name a clear echo of "Fréron" but also of *frelon* meaning "hornet," and of *félon*, meaning "traitor," who makes up in obsequiousness, self-delusion, and bile what he lacks in social graces, connections, and talent. He is a creature whose natural habitat is not the private elite space of an aristocratic salon, but a London café, that characteristically bohemian space, where he is heard complaining bitterly that others have obtained grace and favor while he has not, and touting his services as a hired pen, specializing in stinging satire, flattery, and slander, for which he charges by the paragraph. In contrast to the man of letters, who plays down his writing and publishing activities, the *pauvre diable* is very much the scribbler, scraping a living. However, insofar as he lacks social graces and connections, such a figure is, from Voltaire's perspective, not very far removed from the Rousseauian outsider. Certainly Rousseau's down-and-out cultivates a deliberate disregard for such things, and he refuses to use his real talent to allow him to move in high society, but to Voltaire, this is as unacceptable as the talentless sycophancy of the *pauvre diable*, and he brands the citizen of Geneva a *gueux* or "beggar," as well as "Diogenes' ape." Of course, from the perspective of the Rousseauian *gueux*, sycophancy is what characterizes the behavior of the *philosophes* in high society, and the *pauvre* (poor) in *pauvre diable* is not only a quality not to be feared, it is also to be positively championed.

What defines the *philosophe* and his various nemeses, then, is as much the positions they adopt in society as those they adopt on religion or politics. One highly original engagement with the conflicted constructions of the figures of the *philosophe*, the *gueux*, and the *pauvre diable* is to be found in Diderot's *Le neveu de Rameau*. Not the least of its originality is that, unlike the works of Voltaire, Rousseau, Palissot, Fréron, and Moreau, it is a work that would be read only by posterity.

⁂ ⁂ ⁂ ⁂

Le neveu de Rameau nearly didn't survive at all. Many of Diderot's works were unpublished in his lifetime, but they were nonetheless available to a select group of elite readers, including Frederick the

Great and Catherine the Great, who subscribed to Grimm's manu-script journal, *Correspondence littéraire*, and who made up a kind of virtual salon. *Le neveu de Rameau*, by contrast, seems not to have cir-culated at all. Indeed, its very existence seems to have been a secret: there is no reference to it in Diderot's correspondence, no evidence that it was read in a real salon (such as d'Holbach's, of which Diderot was a member), and although Diderot's friend and literary executor, Naigeon, does seem to have had a copy in his possession, he chose not to include it in his posthumous edition of Diderot's "complete" works (1798). That posterity had access to it, which it did, finally, in 1891, involves a tale that would not be out of place in a picaresque novel, involving as it does journeys crisscrossing Europe, forgery, a pair of bastardizing translators, a censorious son-in-law, and manuscripts that pop up and disappear again without a trace.

The story, in brief, is as follows: In Paris in 1821, a work titled *Le neveu de Rameau* was published, claiming to be a newly discovered and hitherto unknown work by Diderot. It was not, however, quite what it seemed, and the publisher was certainly protesting too much when he said he would "pursue any forgers using the full force of the law." The work was itself a kind of forgery; it was not by Diderot, or, at least, not by him in any straightforward sense. It was, instead, a trans-lation or, more accurately, a retranslation back into French—and a rather spiced-up one at that—of a German translation from French that had appeared in Leipzig in 1805, rendered by none other than Johann Wolfgang von Goethe. His *Rameaus Neffe* was, by contrast, no forgery; it was based on a manuscript that had been handed to him by Friedrich Schiller, whose brother-in-law had acquired it from a Ger-man army officer and dramatist by the name of Klinger, who had himself obtained it while posted in St. Petersburg, which is where a large number of Diderot's papers had been sent from Paris after his death in 1784 because Catherine the Great had advance-purchased them in 1765, thereby ensuring him an income following the comple-tion of the *Encyclopédie* and, most important, ensuring herself a per-manent association with a *philosophe* (she would also buy Voltaire's library).

Goethe's translation completed, the manuscript vanished. Nearly twenty years later, back in Paris, the spiced-up French retranslation was quickly denounced as a fraud, and in 1823, another *Neveu de Rameau* appeared, this one based on another manuscript that was in the possession of Diderot's daughter, whose husband had been so offended by his father-in-law's writing that he had taken it upon himself to tone down the manuscript, with the result that the text's second outing in French was not much less of a travesty than the first. Perhaps it is fitting that a work, the central character of which is described not in terms of the direct paternal line but instead in those of the sideways offshoot that is a nephew, would itself produce such lateral literary offspring. Yet in 1890, more than one hundred years after the author's death, and by which time Goethe's *Neffe* had had a formative effect on no less a figure than G.W.F. Hegel, and the 1823 edition had been read and admired by Karl Marx, who also sent a copy to Friedrich Engels, an autograph copy appeared. It was found by the librarian of the Comédie-Française, Georges Monval, not in a library but, as if by chance, in a Parisian bookstall on the Quai Voltaire. Moreover, it was not called *Le neveu de Rameau*; instead, and intriguingly, it bore the title of *Satire seconde* (Second satire). Diderot may not make use anywhere in his work of the standard literary trope of the lost-and-found manuscript, but the story of his own manuscript easily surpasses even the most elaborate example of it.

So what can posterity read in this work? There is no simple answer to this question. That is in part because of the complexity of the work, which is far greater than any of those mentioned so far, and which is the result of its generic indeterminacy and dynamic structure. The novel is tricksy, like all of Diderot's unpublished works, which is not to say that the published ones are perfectly straightforward, far from it, but the unpublished ones, in addition to being more risqué in content (some of the jokes in *Le neveu de Rameau* may be obscene, but *Le rêve de d'Alembert* contains a discussion of the benefits of sex with goats) are also formally and stylistically more intricate. *Le neveu de Rameau* has elements of all of the following but is not consistently any of them: a novel, a philosophical dialogue (which is what Goethe called it) and a play; it also contains a series of descriptions of mimes, not dissimilar in their ekphrastic quality to some of Diderot's art criticism, which requires the reader to imagine paintings no less difficult to realize on canvas than the mimes in *Le neveu de Rameau* would be for any actor to perform, the latter involving as they do such things as "birds falling silent as the sun sets, a brook babbling in a cool, isolated spot, or a waterfall crashing down from the mountains." And although the autograph manuscript calls it a "satire," that may be as much owing to this formal heterogeneity as to its content, which does savage by name any number of historical individuals—and we should note that Rameau really did have a nephew. Certainly the work exacts a delayed revenge on Palissot and his cronies, showing them as vain, vulgar, and venal, and it does so in an exposé supplied, in a deliciously malicious twist, by a former member of their own team, a *pauvre diable*, the nephew of the famous French baroque composer. Yet *Le neveu de Rameau* also works more discreetly, and perhaps thereby more successfully, to sabotage the figure of the *philosophe*, who turns out to be not quite as different and distanced from the *pauvre diable* as one might think. Indeed, it is as much an intervention in the debate between Voltaire and Rousseau over the social codes to be obeyed by the man of letters, as it is Diderot's belated (and today rather unnecessary) revenge on Palissot. As Goethe put it, the work "exploded like a bomb at the heart of French literature, and you have to really concentrate to work out what it hits, and how."

❖ ❖ ❖ ❖

Le neveu de Rameau has been the subject of any number of biographical and autobiographical readings, none of which is satisfactory, and which will be set aside here in favor of an analysis of the ways in which the characters position and reposition themselves in relation to each other and society. The work opens with a framing narrative, in which an unnamed first-person narrator presents himself to the reader as a dependable creature of habit and common sense in a changing world that contains many bizarre individuals, and one in particular, whom the narrator claims to observe from a suitably detached perspective:

> He's a mixture of the lofty and the sordid, of good sense and unreason. The notions of what's decent and what's indecent must be strangely mixed up in his head since he displays the

good qualities that nature has given him unostentatiously and the bad ones shamelessly. . . . I have no respect for such odd-balls. Other people make close acquaintances out of them, even friends. But they do stop me in my tracks once a year when I meet them because their character is so unlike other people's: they disrupt that annoying uniformity which our education, so-cial conventions, and codes of conduct have inculcated in us. If such a man is present in a group, he acts like a pinch of yeast, fermenting and giving a portion of each person's natural indi-viduality back to them. He stirs things up, shakes them about, provokes approval or blame; he makes the truth come out; he reveals who's genuinely good, he unmasks villains; and that's when a man of good sense pricks up his ears and sees the world for what it is.

The narrator's project of exploiting this unnamed oddball for his own heuristic purposes, a project not dissimilar to that announced in the prefaces of many eighteenth-century novels—the Abbé Prévost's *Manon Lescaut* (1731), for instance—will, however, soon be under-mined, for he is unable to contain him within the narrative frame. Not only does the oddball's name escape the narrator's lips while he was trying to withhold it, but he escapes the frame and addresses the narrator directly. Ironically, it is while he is telling the story of how the oddball was only invited to dinner parties on the strict condition that he would not say anything, that the narrator lets his name slip: "If ever he got it into his head to break the agreement and open his mouth, no sooner had he uttered a word than everyone round the table would shout: Oh Rameau! . . . You were curious to know the man's name, and now you do. He's the nephew of that famous musi-cian." Surely this suggests that "Rameau's nephew" cannot have been Diderot's intended title, as it would give away the name-game too soon. And shortly afterward, Rameau's nephew himself upsets the narrative frame by interjecting, "Aha! There you are Monsieur le Philosophe"—a direct apostrophe that turns the tables on the narra-tor, positioning and framing him in what is now the observational field of the nephew, who applies the label *philosophe* to the narrator in a rather mocking fashion, as if to suggest he had overheard what had been said about him.

Such framing and counterframing continues in the ensuing exchange, in which the two men are designated by the narrator using the relational pronouns, "Him" and "Me," and which is conducted in a café, a space the connotations of which we know from Voltaire's play (the *Encyclopédie* entry, "Café," says that cafés are "wit factories, some good, some bad"):

> Aha! There you are, Mister Philosopher, and what are you doing hanging around here with this bunch of layabouts? Don't tell me you too are wasting your time pushing pawns about a board? (That's what people mockingly call playing chess or draughts.)
>
> ME.—No, but when I've got nothing better to do, I enjoy spending a few moments watching people doing a good job of it.
>
> HIM.—In that case, you don't enjoy yourself very often; apart from Legal and Philidor, the rest of them don't have a clue.

Such an exchange is typical: "Him" is forever putting "Me" on the back foot, pulling the rug from under his feet. Here, when "Him" says that "Me" "do[es]n't enjoy [him]self very often," "Me" might have thought (as might we) he was suggesting that "Me" would usually have far better things to do, what with his being a *philosophe*; but it soon turns out that "Him" was referring instead to the scarcity of good chess players, with the implication that "Me" is indeed wasting his time after all, that he might therefore be what "Him" said he was, namely, a layabout. Moreover, since the nephew is in the café too, that makes two time-wasters, and so the distance and opposition that the narrator wished to establish between himself and the oddball as the necessary condition for his detached observations and moralizing interpretations collapses, and it will keep collapsing.

So once "Him" has a voice, how does he present himself to the narrator-"Me," whom he designates as a *philosophe*? He is, by his own admission, a failed musician and, consequently, a hanger-on, parasite, *pauvre diable*, and consummate social actor or hypocrite, who has found himself some protection in the household of Monsieur Bertin and Mademoiselle Hus, known collectively as "Bertinhus"—she an overweight, talentless actress, whom it is the nephew's role to flatter and applaud, closing his eyes and pretending to be "dumbfounded, as if he had heard the voice of an angel," and he a humorless, hypochondriac financier, whom the nephew is tasked with distracting by generally playing the fool and by vilifying the Great and the Good, among them Voltaire, Buffon, Montesquieu, d'Alembert, and Diderot. Bertinhus is thus clearly an anti-*philosophe* stronghold, and indeed "Him" claims that it was there that Palissot's play was conceived, and, moreover, that he was himself responsible for a scene in which "Me" was attacked along with the other *philosophes*. In return for being agreeable and useful to his masters, "Him" is fed, watered, and generally spoiled, "like a pig in clover," as he puts it to "Me," who modestly replies to the mention of the attack on him in Palissot's play by saying, "Good! . . . I'd be mortified if those people who say bad things about so many clever and honourable men took it upon themselves to say good things about me."

However, the nephew is now in a café instead of the Bertinhus anti-*philosophe* anti-salon because his pig-in-clover days are over. One of his dinner-table jokes backfired: acting the host, he had explained to a newcomer, named as the Abbé de la Porte (a journalist), that although the parvenu had been given the "honour" of being seated at the head of the table, where other sycophants were also seated, he would soon be dislodged from that position, and eventually relegated to the bottom of the table, where he would find himself, like the nephew, sitting "como un maestoso cazzo fra duoi coglioni," that is to say (the Italian dialect both masking the obscenity of the phrase and drawing attention to it) "a majestic dick between two balls." Everyone fell about laughing at his vulgar witticism, except Bertin, who was furious and dismissed him, with the result that the nephew has nothing better to do and is reduced to hanging out in the Café de la Régence with the other layabouts, wondering where his next meal is coming from.

Le neveu de Rameau thus unsettles and multiplies the positions available: the nephew seems to be an anti-anti-*philosophe* or, rather, the anti-*philosophes* are also opponents of the nephew. And "Me" advises him to go back and apologize, or, as the nephew puts it, "kiss arse." This is a suggestion that is rather surprising from a man labeled a *philosophe*, unless, of course, arse-kissing is, as the anti-*philosophes* believe, precisely what a *philosophe* does. By contrast, the nephew's refusal to kiss arse (though he does perform a hilarious mime of it) suggests that he, a *pauvre diable*, perhaps now a Rousseauian outsider, is the one behaving as the *philosophes* claim a *philosophe* does, that is to say, with some dignity. "Him" explains: "Should people be able to say to me: Crawl, and I should have to crawl? That's what worms do, it's what I do, and it's what we both do when we're left to our own devices, but we rear up when people step on our tails. And I have had my tail stepped on, and so I shall rear up." Of course, the nephew has already asserted his dignity and reared up—but as a *maestoso cazzo*. So "Him" constantly pulls "Me" into his orbit, undermining the *philosophe*'s attempts to distance himself.

There are some things on which "Him" and "Me" agree, if only briefly, the most important of which is that all the world's a stage on which a "vile pantomime" is acted out, with everyone playing a part in accordance with his or her own self-interest in order to try and get ahead—everyone except the king, or so the upwardly aspirational (if downwardly mobile) nephew asserts, a claim that "Me" disputes, reserving such a distinction for the *philosophe*, on the grounds that he alone depends on nothing and no one. Yet "Me"'s counterclaim will have some unfortunate consequences for the image of the *philosophe*: "Him" backs "Me" into a corner in the ensuing discussion, from which the *philosophe* emerges as neither the Rousseauian *gueux* nor as d'Alembert's Diogenes, the daringly critical socialite, but instead as the outrageously lewd anti-socialite Diogenes of antiquity, alone in his barrel, indulging in a bit of solitary pleasure. And moreover, the counterclaim itself contradicts the narrator's own presentation of the nephew as the oddball by showing that from the nephew's point of view, the real oddball is Monsieur le Philosophe, or "Me."

Moreover, insofar as "Me" might self-identify as a *philosophe*, his claim to be autonomous is rather undercut by his self-designation as "Me," a relational pronoun that depends for its meaning on the existence of a "You" or, more problematically in this case, of course, a "Him." And, furthermore, it is not absolutely clear that "Me" has not, from the nephew's perspective, stepped into the shoes of Bertin, for although the nephew tells his story as one of failure, the story is also a great success when told to "Me," who buys the nephew a drink, and in so doing, repays him for being entertaining, flattering "Me" by satirizing others, and providing useful material for "Me"'s narrative. As "Him" puts it: "There's no better role to play in the company of great men than the fool. The title of King's Fool was in existence for a long time, you know, whereas the title King's Wise Man never was. I myself am Bertin's fool, and lots of other people's fool too, maybe yours at the moment"—although, as is characteristic of this work that never stays still, he immediately adds, "or perhaps you're mine."

❖ ❖ ❖ ❖

It would be a mistake then to read *Le neveu de Rameau* simply as piece of localized polemic directed at the anti-*philosophes*, not least because the *philosophe* does not himself emerge entirely unscathed; and it would be reductive to read the work in purely biographical, autobiographical, or confessional terms. Yet there can be little doubt that the text's dynamics, in which every position is liable at any moment to slip or flip, offer a vision of the complexity and the competitive nature of the socioeconomic, moral, political, and cultural milieu of mid-eighteenth-century Paris, and of the precarious nature of any actor's constructions and projections of both himself and his opponents within it. And the satirical energies of that vision have afforded the text a complex afterlife, not least by way of Hegel, who read the work in Goethe's translation and incorporated parts of it into the very fabric of the *Phenomenology of Spirit* (1807), thereby ensuring its importance to Marx, Foucault, Alasdair MacIntyre, and beyond.

So, the manuscript of *Le neveu de Rameau* may now safely have come to rest in the Pierpont Morgan Library in New York, but the narrator, "Me," "Him," the *philosophe*, the *pauvre diable*, and the *gueux* are still very much on the move. Diderot's exploration of a power dynamic, his comic demonstration of a dynamics of power, has lost nothing of its ability to unsettle. Indeed, perhaps the most important things unsettled by this work of the major figure of the French Enlightenment are the cherished claims, self-representations, and myths of the Enlightenment itself.

Works Cited and Recommended Further Reading

Note: All translations of passages quoted in this chapter are my own.

d'Alembert, Jean Le Rond. *Essai sur la société des gens de lettres avec les grands*. In vol. 4 of *Œuvres*. 5 vols. Paris, 1821–22.

Chambers, Ephraim. *Cyclopædia: An Universal Dictionary of Arts and Sciences*. 2 vols. London: James and John Knapton et al., 1728.

Dictionnaire universel françois et latin. Trévoux, 1721.

Diderot, Denis. *Les bijoux indiscrets*. Edited by Antoine Adam. Paris: Gallimard, 1993.

———. *Le fils naturel*. Edited by Jean Goldzink. Paris: Flammarion, 2005.

———. *Jacques le fataliste*. Edited by Yves Belaval. Paris: Gallimard, 2006.

———. *Jacques the Fatalist*. Translated with an introduction and notes by David Coward. Oxford: Oxford University Press, 2008.

———. *Lettre sur les aveugles*. Edited by Marian Hobson and Simon Harvey. Paris: Flammarion, 2000.

———. *Letter on the Blind*. In Kate E. Tunstall, *Blindness and Enlightenment: An Essay, with New Translations of Diderot's "Letter on the Blind" and La Mothe Le Vayer's "Of a Blind Man."* New York: Continuum, 2011.

———. *Le neveu de Rameau*. Edited by Marian Hobson. Geneva: Droz, 2013.

———. *Rameau's Nephew*. Translated by Kate E. Tunstall and Caroline Warman. Cambridge: Open Books, 2014.

———. *Pensées philosophiques*. Edited by Jean-Claude Bourdin. Paris: Flammarion, 2007.

———. *Pensées sur l'Interprétation de la nature*. Edited by Colas Duflo. Paris: Flammarion, 2005.

———. *La religieuse*. Edited by Florence Lotterie. Paris: Flammarion, 2009.

———. *The Nun*. Translated with an introduction and notes by Russell Goulbourne. Oxford: Oxford University Press, 2008.

———. *Le rêve de d'Alembert*. Edited by Colas Duflo. Paris: Flammarion, 2003.

———. *D'Alembert's Dream*. In *"Rameau's Nephew" and "D'Alembert's Dream."* Translated with introductions by Leonard Tancock. London: Penguin, 1976.

Diderot, Denis, and Jean Le Rond d'Alembert, eds. *Encyclopédie ou dictionnaire raisonné des arts, des sciences et des métiers*. 28 vols. Paris: Briasson,

David l'aîné, Le Breton, and Durand, 1751–72. Available at ARTFL Encyclopédie Project, http://encyclopedie.uchicago.edu.

Foucault, Michel. *History of Madness*. Edited by Jean Khalfa. Translated by Jonathan Murphy. New York: Routledge, 2006.

Goethe, Johann Wolfgang von. *Rameaus Neffe*. Stuttgart: Reclam, 1967.

Grimm, Friedrich Melchior, and Denis Diderot. *Correspondance littéraire, philosophique et critique*. Paris: Garnier, 1877–82.

Hegel, G.W.F. *Phenomenology of Spirit*. Translated by A. V. Miller, with an analysis of the text and foreword by J. N. Findlay. Oxford: Oxford University Press, 1977.

James, Robert, *A Medicinal Dictionary*. 3 vols. London: Printed for T. Osborne and sold by J. Roberts, 1743–45.

MacIntyre, Alasdair. *After Virtue*. Bristol: Bristol Classical Press, 1981.

Molière. *Les femmes savantes*. In vol. 2 of *Œuvres*. Edited by Georges Forestier and Claude Bourqui. 2 vols. Paris: Gallimard, 2010.

———. *Tartuffe*. In vol. 2 of *Œuvres*. Edited by Georges Forestier and Claude Bourqui. 2 vols. Paris: Gallimard, 2010.

Moreau, Jacob-Nicolas. *Nouveaux mémoires pour servir à l'histoire des Cacouacs*. In *L'affaire des cacouacs: Trois pamphlets contre les philosophes des lumières*, edited by Gerhardt Stenger. Saint Etienne: Publications de l'Université de Saint Etienne, 2004.

Palissot, Charles. *Petites lettres sur de grands philosophes*. N.p., 1757.

———. *Les philosophes*. In *"La comédie des philosophes" et autres textes*, edited by Olivier Ferret. Saint Etienne: Publications de l'Université de Saint Etienne, 2002.

Prévost, Abbé. *Manon Lescaut*. Edited by Jean Sgard. Paris: Flammarion, 1995.

———. *Manon Lescaut*. Translated with an introduction and notes by Angela Scholar. Oxford: Oxford University Press, 2004.

Rousseau, Jean-Jacques. *Les Confessions*. Edited by Bernard Gagnebin, Raymond Marcel, and J.-B. Pontalis. Paris: Folio, 2009.

———. *Confessions*. Translated by Angela Scholar, with an introduction and notes by Patrick Coleman. Oxford: Oxford University Press, 2008.

———. *Discours sur les origines et les fondements de l'inégalité parmi les hommes*. Edited by Blaise Bachofen and Bruno Bernardi. Paris: Gallimard, 1964.

Shaftesbury, Anthony Ashley Cooper, Third Earl of. *An Inquiry concerning*

Virtue and Merit. In *Characteristics of Men, Manners, Opinions, Times*, edited by Philip Ayres. Oxford: Oxford University Press, 1999.

Voltaire. *Le café ou l'Ecossaise*. In *Zaïre; Le fanatisme ou Mahomet le prophète; Nanine ou l'Homme sans préjugé; Le café ou l'Ecossaise*, edited by Jean Goldzink. Paris: Flammarion, 2004.

Important studies of the sociocultural landscape of eighteenth-century Paris include Robert Darnton, *The Literary Underground of the Old Regime* (Cambridge, MA: Harvard University Press, 1982); Didier Masseau, *Les ennemis des philosophes: L'anti-philosophie au temps des lumières* (Paris: Albin Michel, 2000); Antoine Lilti, *Le monde des salons: Sociabilité et mondanité à Paris au XVIIIe siècle* (Paris: Fayard, 2005); Geoffrey Turnovsky, *The Literary Market: Authorship and Modernity in the Old Regime* (Philadelphia: University of Pennsylvania Press, 2010); and Louise Shea, *The Enlightenment Cynic: Diogenes in the Salon* (Baltimore, MD: Johns Hopkins University Press, 2010). For Darnton's critics, see Haydn T. Mason, ed., *The Darnton Debate* (Oxford: Voltaire Foundation, 1999); and for the view of the salons that Lilti is criticizing, see Dena Goodman, *The Republic of Letters: A Cultural History of the French Enlightenment* (Ithaca, NY: Cornell University Press, 1996). On the continuing debates over Enlightenment ideas and values, see Kate E. Tunstall, ed., *Self-Evident Truths? Human Rights and the Enlightenment* (New York: Continuum, 2012).

Stimulating and useful work on Diderot and the Enlightenment, and on *Rameau's Nephew* in particular, includes Jean Starobinski, *Diderot: Un diable de ramage* (Paris: Gallimard, 2012); Marian Hobson, *Diderot and Rousseau: Networks of Enlightenment*, trans. Kate E. Tunstall and Caroline Warman (Oxford: Voltaire Foundation, 2011); Kate E. Tunstall, *Blindness and Enlightenment: An Essay* (New York: Continuum, 2011); Colas Duflo, *Diderot philosophe* (Paris: Champion, 2003); Pierre Hartmann, *Diderot: Les figurations du philosophe* (Paris: José Corti, 2003); Walter E. Rex, *Diderot's Counterpoints: The Dynamics of Contrariety in His Major Works* (Oxford: Voltaire Foundation, 1998); and Wilda Anderson, *Diderot's Dream* (Baltimore, MD: Johns Hopkins University Press, 1998). For the Marxist tradition of reading Diderot, see Julia Simon, *Mass Enlightenment: Critical Studies in Rousseau and Diderot* (Albany: State University of New York Press, 1995). There are two journals devoted to Diderot scholarship, *Diderot Studies* (1949–) and *Recherches sur Diderot et l'Encyclopédie* (1986–). For a recent *état présent* of Diderot scholarship in both French and English, see *French Studies*, 67, no. 3 (2013).

Rousseau's First Person

JOANNA STALNAKER

There is a certain irony in the fact that Jean-Jacques Rousseau is celebrated as the inventor of modern autobiography. Like many Enlightenment thinkers, Rousseau was obsessed with origins, and he offered in his *Discours sur l'origine et les fondements de l'inégalité parmi les hommes* (*Discourse on the Origin and Foundations of Inequality among Men*) one of the most influential accounts of natural man ever written. But he was acutely aware that the search for origins is illusory and that the state of nature as he described it was a fiction, "more suited to illuminating the nature of things than to showing their true origin." His attitude toward the originary status of his autobiography was equally ambiguous. It is no accident that he borrowed his title, the *Confessions*, from Saint Augustine's tale of sin and redemption and that he took his metaphor of self-portraiture from Montaigne's *Essais*. Yet even as he evoked these famous models, he proclaimed the uniqueness of his work: "Here is the only portrait of a man, painted exactly after nature and in all its truth, that exists and will probably ever exist." As he presented it, the *Confessions* was neither an imitation of prior models nor a point of origin for future works, but a singular creation, an "enterprise that had no example and whose execution will have no imitators." At the same time, it was a "first article of comparison for the study of men," a work that laid the groundwork for the study of human nature Rousseau had called for in his *Discours sur l'inégalité*. As readers, we are thus faced with an enigma: how can a unique portrait of a man unlike any other provide the basis for a comparative science of man in the Enlightenment tradition? This enigma lies at the heart of Rousseau's literary and philosophical project, whose coherence depends on the articulation of two different figures of the first person: Jean-Jacques and natural man.

Rousseau's place in the history of modern literature has always been complicated by his dual association with Enlightenment universalism and the emergence of the modern self. His natural man has been understood in the context of Enlightenment conjectural histories tracing the passage from the state of nature to civil society. The first person of Rousseau's autobiographical writings, in contrast, has been identified with the earliest stirrings of Romanticism in France, despite the fact that these writings predate the radical break in historical and political consciousness created by the French Revolution. Rousseau's sensitive descriptions of nature, his portrayal of himself as a solitary figure proscribed by society, and his corresponding insistence on the singularity of his perspective have all been taken as evidence that his autobiographical writings look forward to the Romantics far more than they belong to the philosophy of their day.

But to understand Rousseau's contribution to modern literature, we must move beyond this artificial split between Enlightenment philosophy and pre-Romantic literature. The modern self he depicts in the three works of his autobiographical corpus is in fact deeply rooted in the Enlightenment tradition of conjectural histories of natural man. Rousseau insists on this link in his autobiographical dialogues, *Rousseau juge de Jean-Jacques* (*Rousseau Judge of Jean-Jacques*), when the Frenchman defends the vilified author Jean-Jacques by explaining that the latter took his model for nature from his own heart: "Where can the painter and apologist of nature, today so disfigured and maligned, have drawn his model, if not from his own heart? He described nature as he felt himself to be." What this means is that Rousseau's self-depiction is inseparable from his philosophical account of humans in the state of nature. Jean-Jacques and natural man are two figures of Rousseau's first person, both of whom are called on to illustrate his "great principle that nature made man happy and good but that society depraves him and makes him miserable." If Rousseau is central to the history of modern literature, it is because he invented a modern self that was fundamentally divided against itself. This self longed for a lost nature that would connect it to other people and to its original goodness, but it nonetheless remained fully aware that its only hope would come not from a return to the state of nature but from the transformation of corrupt social practices, central among which was literature itself.

Rousseau probably had no inkling of his great autobiographical project when, in 1753, he answered the Dijon Academy's question about the origins of inequality among men. He had already made a name for himself as the prize-winning author of the *Discours sur les sciences et les arts* (*Discourse on the Sciences and Arts*), in which he defied his friends the encyclopedists by asserting that the sciences and arts corrupt morals. But as a Genevan autodidact of obscure social origins, he was in no position to assume he would one day become an international celebrity whose autobiography would capture the public imagination. It is nonetheless striking to see the same themes of self-knowledge that animate his autobiographical corpus appear in the opening pages of the *Discours sur l'inégalité*. Rousseau opens his preface with the famous inscription at the Temple of Delphi, "know thyself," insisting that we must look within before we can hope to understand the origin of social ills. In a savvy rhetorical move, he quotes the renowned naturalist Georges Louis Leclerc de Buffon to lend authority to his claim that self-knowledge is the only true basis for the science of man. Buffon was an empiricist who devoted the many volumes of his best-selling *Histoire naturelle* (*Natural History*) to the precise description of everything under the sun, from quadrupeds to human racial varieties to minerals. But he shared Rousseau's belief that our tendency to view nature as something outside of ourselves poses a serious obstacle to the study of man. In Buffon's view, if our knowledge about man is lacking, it is because we "rarely make use of that inner sense that reduces us to our true dimensions and separates from us everything that is not ourselves." By quoting these lines, Rousseau situates his inquiry in the tradition of Enlightenment natural history, while also underlining the special problem posed by the study of man. He did not eschew empiricist description in his effort to uncover our original human nature: the lengthy footnotes of the *Discours sur l'inégalité* are stuffed with European travelers' descriptions of "primitive" peoples in support of his claims. But at a time when anthropology did not yet exist as a scientific discipline, he insisted that introspection must serve as the primary basis for the study of man. It was this aspect of his work that would lead the structuralist anthropologist Claude Lévi-Strauss to recognize Rousseau as the founder of the human sciences.

To look within and find the original human nature is no simple task, however. Rousseau captures the challenge with an image borrowed from Plato's *Republic*, that of Glaucus, whose original mortal image was disfigured by his years spent under the sea after he was transformed into an immortal sea-god. Socrates uses this image to convey the difficulty of perceiving the beauty of the human soul, "marred by communion with the body and other miseries," whereas Rousseau uses it to convey the difficulty of perceiving natural man disfigured by society. But Rousseau introduces a crucial change in the image: unlike Plato, he refers not to Glaucus himself but to his statue, as if to suggest that what we are after is an *image* of natural man rather than the thing itself. This is consistent with Rousseau's acknowledgment that the state of nature may never have existed at all: "For it is no small undertaking to untangle what is original and what is artificial in the current nature of man, and to know well a state that no longer exists, may never have existed, will probably never exist, and of which it is nonetheless necessary to have accurate notions in order to judge properly our current state." Paradoxically, Rousseau insists that even if the state of nature never existed, we must still gain an accurate picture of it to judge our current social ills. He criticizes natural law theorists such as Thomas Hobbes and John Locke for failing to reach the "true" state of nature and for applying "ideas to the state of nature that they took from society." Curiously, it is the fictionality of Rousseau's state of nature that guarantees its distance from society and hence its accuracy. But what is the basis for such a fiction, and how can it be considered accurate if the state of nature never existed in the first place?

There is no easy answer to this question. One way to understand Rousseau's state of nature is as a thought experiment, designed not to uncover the past but to illuminate and transform the present. Rousseau himself is entirely explicit about the hypothetical nature of the history he proposes: "Let us begin then by setting aside all the facts, for they have no bearing on the question. We must not take the inquiries into which we enter on this subject for historical truths, but only for hypothetical and conditional arguments; more suited to elucidating the nature of things than to showing their true origin, and resembling those that our physicists make every day on the formation of the world." In telling a conjectural history (or story) of man's passage from nature to society, Rousseau is less interested in our actual past than in our present state. Above all, he seeks to effect a change in his readers' feelings about their present condition by instilling in them a nostalgic desire for an irrecoverable past: "There is, I sense, an age at which the individual man would like to stop; you will search for the age at which you would wish that your species had stopped. Discontented with your present state, for reasons that announce even greater discontentments to your unhappy posterity, perhaps you would like to be able to retrograde." Many of Rousseau's readers have taken this to mean that he was a primitivist. As Voltaire wrote in a letter to Rousseau following the publication of the *Discours sur l'inégalité*, "one is overcome by the desire to walk on all fours when reading your work. But since I have been out of the habit for over sixty years, I feel that unfortunately it is impossible for me to pick it up again, and I will leave this natural attitude to those more worthy of it than you or me." A few years later, a popular antiphilosophical play by Charles Palissot depicted Rousseau walking on all fours and chomping on lettuce as he advocated a return to the state of nature.

Yet for Rousseau, this primitivist reading was a grave misunderstanding of his work. As the Frenchman observes in outlining Jean-Jacques's philosophy, "human nature never retrogrades and we can never go back to times of innocence and equality once we have moved away from them; this is one of the principles he most insisted on." The term *rétrograder* was unusual in the eighteenth century, and readers of the *Discours sur l'inégalité* may well have recalled Rousseau addressing them with "Perhaps you would like to be able to retrograde." What the Frenchman makes clear is that Rousseau never intended this phrase as an invitation to his readers to return to the state of nature. Rather, he sought to instill in them a *desire* for the state of nature that would serve as an impetus toward forward-looking domestic and political reform. In these two discourses, Rousseau sought to "destroy the illusory prestige" of civilized society, and cultivating readers' desires for the state of nature was essential to that initial, destructive phase of his philosophical project. But in *Emile* and the *Contrat social* (*The Social Contract*), he offered constructive programs for domestic education and political life that were intended to preserve humans' natural freedom in society rather than returning them to the state of nature.

Rousseau did nonetheless insist that he alone among men had maintained a deep connection to the original human nature. According to the Frenchman, it was Jean-Jacques's solitary life, his taste for reverie, and his habit of introspection that had allowed him to access the original features of natural man: "Only a retiring and solitary life, a keen taste for reverie and contemplation, the habit of withdrawing into himself and searching within in the calm of passions for those first features [*traits*] that have disappeared for the multitude could allow him to recover them. In a word, it was necessary that a man paint himself to show us primitive man in this way, and if the Author hadn't been just as singular as his books, he never would have written them." In an implicit allusion to the statue of Glaucus, the Frenchman suggests that Jean-Jacques may only have recovered an image of natural man rather than the thing itself, an ambiguity nicely captured by the term *traits*, which means both "features" and "traces." He also makes it clear that the process of recovery involves not just introspection but also self-portraiture, an act of writing that is necessarily rooted in humanity's corrupt social state. But his formulation is curious: "it was necessary that *a* man paint himself to show us primitive man in this way." Does this mean that any man could have done so, but that Jean-Jacques was simply the first? Or is the Frenchman right to insist on the uniqueness of Jean-Jacques and his books? In either case, it is clear that literature, and specifically self-depiction, has an essential role to play in allowing us to access a lost nature that will become the basis for future social transformations.

Rousseau began writing an account of his life in response to a request from his editor, Marc-Michel Rey, for a memoir to preface his complete works in 1761. But he did not conceive of the *Confessions* as we know it until 1764, when Voltaire revealed in an anonymous pamphlet that the author of *Emile* had abandoned his five newborn children to a foundling hospital. Rousseau's autobiography was thus first and foremost a response to a public accusation of immorality, all the more damning for an author whose greatest work, in his own eyes, was a treatise on the education of children. The *Confessions* was written in the aftermath of the condemnation of *Emile* and the *Contrat social* in Geneva and Paris and the ensuing warrant for the author's arrest. These were the darkest years of Rousseau's life; years of exile and wandering took him from various places in Switzerland (Môtiers, where the villagers threw stones at his windows, and the Island of Saint-Pierre, where he experienced idyllic reveries) to England, where an initially effusive friendship with the Scottish philosopher David Hume degenerated into a violent and publicly aired quarrel. Rousseau suffered from acute bouts of paranoia during these years, believing that his former friends the encyclopedists were engaged in an international conspiracy to destroy his reputation and falsify his life's works. For all these reasons, the *Confessions* has rightly been read as a work of personal justification in the face of genuine and imagined persecution.

But Rousseau's autobiography can also be read as an illustration of the central tenet of his philosophical system: that "nature made man happy and good but that society depraves him and makes him miserable." If *Emile* is "a treatise on the original goodness of man, designed to show how vice and error, foreign to his constitution, introduce themselves into it from the outside and alter it imperceptibly," the *Confessions* traces the same process of corruption in the author's own life. In "the first and most painful step in the obscure and filthy labyrinth of my confessions," Rousseau reveals that a childhood spanking at the hands of his caregiver, Mlle Lambercier, gave him a lifetime predilection for sexual humiliation and corporal correction. He holds up this episode as a cautionary tale for would-be educators: "How one would change methods with Youth if one saw more clearly the distant effect of this method that is always used indiscriminately and often indiscreetly!" The same corrupting effects of corporal punishment can be seen in the following episode, when the young Rousseau finds himself unjustly accused of breaking a comb and receives a much more brutal (and less desirable) beating at the hands of his uncle Bernard. This injustice marks the end of what Rousseau describes as an idyllic childhood (despite the death of his mother in childbirth and the exile of his father from Geneva), coloring his relationship with his benevolent caregivers and encouraging him and his cousin to engage in rebellious and vicious behavior. As vice enters these previously innocent children from without, even the beauties of nature are obscured:

> That was the term of my childhood serenity. From that moment I ceased to enjoy pure happiness, and I feel even today that the memory of the charms of my childhood ends there. We stayed in Bossey a few more months. We were there as one pictures the first man still in the terrestrial paradise but having ceased to enjoy it. It was in appearance the same situation, and in fact a whole different manner of being. Attachment, respect, intimacy, confidence no longer tied the pupils to their guides; we no longer saw them as Gods who read in our hearts: we were less ashamed to act badly, and more afraid of being accused: we began to hide, to rebel and to lie. All the vices of our age corrupted our innocence and made our games ugly. The countryside itself lost to our eyes the appeal of sweetness and simplicity that goes straight to the heart. It seemed to us deserted and obscure; it was as if covered with a veil that hid its beauties from us.

This account of Rousseau's corruption is the reverse image of Emile's ideal education, which is designed to preserve the natural goodness and freedom of the child while also preparing him for his entry into social life. Unlike Emile's governor, Rousseau's caregivers have allowed all the inequities and vices of society to enter his world and person. It is striking that Rousseau does not blame his caregivers for their injustice—the comb was indeed broken, and all appearances pointed to his guilt—even as he uses the episode to illustrate how quickly social injustice can destroy a child's natural goodness. In a parallel episode, Rousseau unjustly accuses a young servant girl named Marion of stealing a ribbon that he himself in fact stole, allowing his readers to witness the aftereffects of his corruption.

The theme of unjust accusation that crystallizes in the broken comb and stolen ribbon episodes is inseparable from Voltaire's public attack on Rousseau for his abandonment of his children. Voltaire wrote his pamphlet, *Le sentiment des citoyens* (*The Sentiment of the Citizens*), in the voice of the Genevan citizens to accuse a man who had worn his Genevan citizenship as a badge of moral purity and republican political independence. Voltaire's citizens do not mince words in accusing Rousseau of the most grotesque hypocrisy and immorality for failing to raise his own children: "We admit with pain and in blushing that this is a man who still bears the fatal marks of his debauchery and who, disguised as an acrobat, drags along with him from village to village and from mountain to mountain the unhappy woman whose mother he brought to her death and whose children he abandoned on the doorstep of a hospice, rejecting the care of a charitable person who wanted to have them, and repudiating all the sentiments of nature just as he despoils those of honor and religion."

Voltaire's most damning charge was that Rousseau had repudiated the natural feelings of a father in neglecting to care for his children. Rousseau had in fact opened himself to this charge by asserting in *Emile* that all fathers had a sacred moral duty to raise their own children. In the very same passage, he implicitly acknowledged the deep suffering that his abandonment of his children had caused him: "The man who cannot perform the duties of a father has no right to become one. There is neither poverty nor work nor human respect that dispenses him from feeding his children and raising them himself. Readers, you can believe me about that. I predict to anyone who has a soul [*des entrailles*] and neglects such sacred duties that he will long shed bitter tears on his fault and will never be consoled for it."

To those in Rousseau's intimate circle who knew the secret of his abandoned children, these lines must have appeared as a clear avowal of his guilt and anguish. But in response to Voltaire's public attack, Rousseau struck an entirely different tone in the *Confessions*. Far from seeking to atone for his guilt (as he did in the stolen ribbon episode), he justified his decision to abandon his children as one made with their best interests at heart. In describing his relationship with their mother, an illiterate laundress named Thérèse Levasseur, he claimed that he could not run the risk of allowing them to be raised by her poorly educated family: "This is how in a sincere and mutual attachment where I had placed all the tenderness of my heart, its emptiness was still never filled. The children, by whom it would have been, arrived; that was even worse. I shuddered at the thought of giving them over to this poorly educated family for them to be even more poorly educated. The risks of an education in the foundling hospital were far fewer."

This passage has been read as hypocritical and self-serving by modern readers troubled by Rousseau's abandonment of his children. The statistics for infant mortality were dire in ancien régime France: Buffon wrote in his popular *Histoire naturelle* that one-third of infants died within their first year. But survival rates were much worse in foundling hospitals, where the number of deaths was closer to 70 percent. Rousseau was undoubtedly aware of these risks; in *Emile*, he urged mothers to nurse their infants themselves rather than sending them to wet nurses in the countryside, a practice that in his eyes exemplified social corruption and contributed to the high rate of infant mortality. In the same work, he insisted that it was a father's sacred duty to educate his own children rather than putting them in the care of a preceptor. How then could he have abandoned his children and forced their mother to go along with his choice? This question has haunted Rousseau's readers, and it continued to haunt his works until the end of his life, when he again took up the abandonment of his children in the penultimate chapter of the *Rêveries du promeneur solitaire* (*Reveries of the Solitary Walker*). However we judge his moral choice, the terms in which he justifies it in the *Confessions* are significant, for they mirror his authorial choice to erase Emile's parents from his narrative and replace them with himself as preceptor. In both cases, the emphasis is on protecting children from the influences of a corrupting education at whatever cost.

The public did not read Rousseau's response to Voltaire until after both of their deaths in 1778: the first part of the *Confessions* was published posthumously in 1782, and the second part appeared only in 1789, the year of the French Revolution. But the work was anxiously awaited across Europe during Rousseau's lifetime, not just for its personal revelations but also for the damaging secrets it might divulge about his former friends the encyclopedists. In an episode frowned on by literary history, Denis Diderot, Friedrich Melchior Grimm, and Louise d'Epinay edited d'Epinay's fictionalized memoirs to darken the portrayal of Rousseau, in a preemptive counterattack against the

Confessions. During the same years, Rousseau returned to Paris from his years of exile and held readings of the *Confessions* at the homes of various Parisian notables. D'Epinay was sufficiently well-connected to have the readings stopped by the police, but Rousseau found a way to keep them alive by inscribing them into the work itself.

The *Confessions* is in fact structured around two parallel scenes of reading that serve as bookends to the work. Rousseau opens his autobiography with the famous scene in which he presents himself to God on Judgment Day with his book in hand. If the book at first seems strangely superfluous—since God should be able to judge his soul without the intervention of human language—its presence is soon explained when Rousseau imagines a circle of listeners surrounding him for a public reading of the *Confessions*: "Eternal being, gather around me the innumerable crowd of my fellow men [*semblables*]: let them listen to my confessions, let them moan at my indignities, let them blush at my miseries. Let each one of them uncover in turn his heart at the foot of your throne with the same sincerity; and then let a single one say to you, if he dares: *I was better than that man.*" As many readers have observed, it is Rousseau, not God, who stands at the center of this scene, and it is his listeners, not God, who are invited to issue a judgment after hearing his confessions. The scene rewrites John's parable of Jesus and the adulteress, but in a way that underscores the *Confessions*' function as a "first article of comparison for the study of men." The key term *semblables* highlights the motif of comparison and raises the question of whether Rousseau in fact resembles other men. If nature broke the mold after forming him, as he claims in his preface, does he have any *semblables* at all? At the end of his life, when he wrote the *Rêveries du promeneur solitaire*, Rousseau no longer claimed to bear any resemblance to the machinelike beings surrounding him. But in the *Confessions*, he calls on his fellow men to mirror his act of self-revelation in order to bear witness to his essential goodness. In other words, he challenges them to write their own version of the *Confessions*, lending to his work the originary status he claimed it would never have.

The motif of public reading resurfaces on the very last page of the *Confessions*. Once again Rousseau is surrounded by his fellow men, and once again he challenges them to bear witness to his essential goodness. But this time, he recounts an actual reading that took place in Paris in 1771, just before d'Epinay went to the police. In this case, there is no divine presence to sanction the truth of the portrait, and the author's challenge to his audience has become distinctly threatening:

> I have told the truth. If someone knows things that are contrary to what I have just exposed, were they to be proved a thousand times, he knows lies and impostures, and if he refuses to go into more depth and to elucidate them with me while I am still alive he loves neither justice nor truth. As for myself, I declare openly and without fear: Whoever, even without reading my writings, will examine with his own eyes my nature, my character, my mores, my penchants, my pleasures, my habits and can believe me a dishonest man, is himself a man to be suffocated.
>
> I completed my reading thus and everyone was quiet. Madame d'Egmont was the only one who seemed to me to be moved; she trembled visibly; but she composed herself quite quickly and kept the silence along with the whole company. Such was the fruit that I drew from this reading and my declaration.

This conclusion brings the *Confessions* full circle, giving concrete form to the imagined scene of reading that opens the work. But it unsettles far more than it concludes, ending the work on a failure to vindicate Rousseau and a resounding silence on the part of his audience. It is a silence that threatens not just Rousseau's personal reputation but his entire philosophical system, raising the question of whether the goodness he perceives in himself is communicable to others and applicable to mankind as a whole. This haunting question fuels the next work of his autobiographical triptych, *Rousseau juge de Jean-Jacques*, or the *Dialogues*.

The silence of Rousseau's audience at the end of the *Confessions* sets the stage for the "profound, universal ... terrifying and terrible silence" that surrounds him in his most tortured work, *Rousseau juge de Jean-Jacques*. This is the silence of those who have engineered an all-encompassing plot to destroy his reputation, who secretly accuse him of monstrous moral crimes but deny him, through their silence, any chance to learn the charges or clear his name. Unlike the *Confessions*, *Rousseau juge de Jean-Jacques* makes for painful reading. In his preface, Rousseau acknowledges that its "tedious passages, repetitions, verbiage and disorder" reflect a degree of mental anguish that made it impossible for him to undertake necessary revisions. The work has accordingly long been neglected or read merely as a symptom of Rousseau's acute paranoia in the last decade of his life. But in recent years, it has emerged as a key to understanding his negative appraisal of the "new world" created by Enlightenment philosophy—a nightmarish vision that prefigures the famous critique of the Enlightenment by the Frankfurt school theorists Theodor Adorno and Max Horkheimer—and the stakes of his opposing philosophical project. *Rousseau juge de Jean-Jacques* is also essential reading for anyone who wishes to understand the deep connections between Rousseau's autobiographical corpus and his philosophy of nature, between Jean-Jacques and natural man.

The work is composed of a preface and postscript, which Rousseau writes in his own name, and three dialogues in which he stages a debate between a Rousseau figure and an unnamed Frenchman about the moral character and works of a vilified author named Jean-Jacques. In his preface, Rousseau explains this bizarre apparatus as a necessary response to his situation as victim of the plot. Since the accusations against him are cloaked in silence, his only recourse has been to imagine the worst possible case against him and say "with what eye, if I were another, I would see a man such as I am." This exteriorization of Rousseau's judgment of himself reminds us that the first-person justification of the *Confessions* has failed, making it imperative that someone other than the author defend his good name. Yet the Rousseau figure seems curiously unsuited to this task, given his uncanny resemblance to Jean-Jacques: it turns out that he too is a victim of social persecution who has retreated to a life of solitude in communion with nature. To the extent that he and Jean-Jacques appear as two figures of the same person, the Frenchman must be called on to provide external confirmation of Jean-Jacques's goodness.

Yet there is more at stake in the dialogues than clearing Jean-Jacques's name. This is because, as the Frenchman reveals in the third dialogue, the author took his model for natural man from his own heart. To vindicate him is thus to confirm the natural goodness of man that serves as the basis for Rousseau's philosophical system. More broadly, Rousseau makes it clear in his preface that it is not just Jean-Jacques but mankind itself that stands trial in the dialogues. The plot has forced him "to think badly of everyone surrounding [him]," because he views his contemporaries' mistreatment of him as a repudiation of their humanity. They lack pity, an essential quality of humans in the state of nature, and fail to recognize their own nature in Jean-Jacques. If mankind is to be absolved, Rousseau must thus find at least one reader who is sympathetic to Jean-Jacques's plight: "In whatever hands [the heavens] make these pages fall, if among those who read them there is still one heart of a man, that suffices for me, and I will never despise the human race enough to not find in this idea any subject of confidence and hope." Without such a reader, Rousseau will be forced to draw the conclusion he eventually reaches in the *Rêveries du promeneur solitaire*, that he is the sole remaining incarnation of man's original nature in a world inhabited by automatons.

Within the space of the dialogues, Rousseau continually tests the possibility for a sympathetic reading that would connect the reader to Jean-Jacques and to man's original nature. In the first dialogue, the Rousseau figure describes his experience of reading Jean-Jacques's works as one of self-recognition: "I felt in them such a connection to my own disposition that he alone among all the authors I had read was the painter of nature and the historian of the human heart. I recognized in his writings the man I found in myself." Of course, this evocation of self-recognition is highly ironic, given how closely the two figures of Rousseau's split authorial persona resemble each other. This makes it all the more imperative that the Frenchman be convinced to read the works, which he eventually does in the space between the second and third dialogues. When he in turn describes his experience of reading Jean-Jacques's works, he takes their transformative effect on his soul as a means of gauging the author's internal disposition when he wrote them: "consulting myself during and after those readings, I examined as you had wanted in what situation of the soul they placed me and left me, believing like you that this was the best way to perceive the Author's disposition in writing them and the effect he sought to produce." By looking within, the Frenchman has perceived not just the transformation of his own soul, but the resemblance between his transformed soul and that of the author.

The dialogues thus end in communion, with the Rousseau figure and the Frenchman agreeing to accept the "precious deposit" of Jean-Jacques's writings and to form an intimate society with him. The plot has been destroyed, not by a public reparation of Jean-Jacques's reputation (a possibility explicitly rejected by the Frenchman), but by the recognition of a shared human nature within this small social group. The Rousseau figure concludes the dialogue with a peaceful evocation of Jean-Jacques's coming death, an image that tempers the terrifying earlier evocations of him being buried alive by his enemies: "let us prepare this consolation for his final hour that his eyes be closed by friendly hands." And yet the tranquillity of this ending is almost immediately destroyed by an autobiographical postscript in which Rousseau stages his desperate and ultimately failed search for a sympathetic reader for his book. His initial attempt to deposit the manuscript on the altar at Notre Dame is foiled by a locked gate surrounding the altar, an unhappy circumstance he interprets as a sign from God. He then entrusts the manuscript to several acquaintances—including the philosopher Etienne Bonnot de Condillac and the Englishman Brooke Boothby—who quickly prove themselves unworthy of his trust. Finally, he is reduced to handing out pamphlets titled "To Any Frenchman Who Still Loves Justice and Truth" to passersby on public promenades, in the hope that they will be able to reveal the mysteries of the plot to him.

These increasingly desperate attempts to find a sympathetic reader who can confirm Rousseau's innocence can be read as symptoms of an acute mental crisis. But they also give concrete literary expression to the central question that haunts his autobiographical project: how can he be sure that the nature he perceives within himself is shared by other people? In the dialogues, Rousseau stages sympathetic readings that bridge the gap between Jean-Jacques and his readers and result in mutual recognition and harmony. But in his postscript, he portrays himself as repeatedly encountering the same wall of hostile silence he faced in the last scene of the *Confessions*. *Rousseau juge de Jean-Jacques* thus ends not on a note of social harmony but with Rousseau's "final resolution" to renounce further self-justification and accept his fate at the hands of his enemies: "Let men do whatever they want from now on; after having done myself what I had to do, they can torment my life as much as they want, they won't prevent me from dying in peace." Once again, Rousseau evokes a peaceful death for himself, but this time it is a solitary one, with no friendly hands to close his eyes.

Rousseau spent the last two years of his life writing the *Rêveries du promeneur solitaire*, a work many consider his masterpiece. Unlike his previous autobiographical works, the *Rêveries* is neither a narrative account of his life nor an attempt at self-justification. It is a fragmentary collection of ten walks, or reveries, in which he poses the problem of self-knowledge from an intimate perspective and in isolation from other human beings: "But me, detached from them and from everything, what am I myself? Here is what remains for me to find out." For the first time, a writer whose concept of authorship was marked by an ethics of public responsibility claims to write for himself alone: "I am making the same enterprise as Montaigne but with a goal entirely contrary to his: for he wrote his essays only for others, and I write my reveries only for myself." In fact, the choice to write for the self follows directly from Rousseau's failed quest to find a sympathetic reader in the postscript to *Rousseau juge de Jean-Jacques*. He underlines this continuity by placing the word *donc* (thus or so) in the famous opening sentence of the *Rêveries*: "So here I am, alone on the earth, no longer having any brother, kin, friend, society but myself." In this way, the solitude of the *Rêveries* appears as the necessary consequence of the final resolution taken at the end of *Rousseau juge de Jean-Jacques*. And yet even as Rousseau binds the *Rêveries* to the work preceding it, his renunciation of public authorship creates an unbridgeable gap between his last two works, setting the *Rêveries* apart from the rest of his corpus.

The difference is palpable in the luminous, meditative style of the *Rêveries* and in Rousseau's newfound modesty concerning self-knowledge. No longer do we find the brash assertions of intrinsic goodness and innocence so characteristic of his earlier autobiographical works. In the fourth walk, Rousseau begins a meditation on his lifelong devotion to truth by acknowledging that "the *know thyself* of the Temple at Delphi was not such an easy maxim to follow as I had believed in my *Confessions*." In the sixth walk, he goes so far as to question his earlier view of himself as a virtuous man: "Here is what altered quite a bit the opinion I long held of my own virtue; for there is no virtue in following one's penchants and in giving oneself the pleasure of doing good when they lead us in that direction."

Each walk brings a new occasion to "presume less of the self." Self-exploration is a daily activity that must be constantly renewed, a lived practice of philosophy that Rousseau likens to an empirical science: "I will do on myself in a certain respect the operations that physicists do on air to know its daily state. I will apply the barometer to my soul, and these operations if well conducted and long repeated will be able to provide me with results just as certain as theirs. But I don't extend my endeavor that far. I will content myself with keeping the register of the operations without seeking to reduce them to a system." In *Rousseau juge de Jean-Jacques*, the Frenchman had insisted on the rigorous coherence of Jean-Jacques's philosophical system, based on the principle of man's natural goodness. Here, Rousseau limits himself to a daily register of the states of his soul without seeking to reduce his empirical findings to a system. He is no longer compelled to offer his portrait as the basis for a comparative science of mankind, as he had done in the *Confessions*, or as an illustration of man's natural goodness, as he had done in *Rousseau juge de Jean-Jacques*. The work stands on its own as a record of the daily exercises of the body and soul, a "formless journal" of Rousseau's reveries and botanical expeditions.

The rejection of systematic philosophy also means that Rousseau's anguished search for a reader who can confirm his own natural goodness has come to an end. After years of adopting the posture of the Cynic philosopher Diogenes, he has finally extinguished his lantern and given up his search: "When after having searched in vain ten years for a man it was necessary that I at last extinguish my lantern and cry out to myself, there aren't any more. So I began to see myself alone on the earth and I understood that my contemporaries were nothing in relation to me but mechanical beings that only acted on outside impulses and whose actions I could only calculate according to the laws of movement." With subtle irony, Rousseau defines his contemporaries according to the popular materialist philosophy of his day, referring implicitly to Julien Offray de la Mettrie's man-machine and to his former friend Diderot's materialist determinism. His own intimate science of man no longer needs to concern itself with such mechanistic creatures, but simply accepts the strangeness and solitude of the self and turns its attention within.

But the *Rêveries* is not merely a solipsistic record of Rousseau's inner life. It is also an intimate communion with nature, a register of his daily walks and the plants he studied as a passionate amateur botanist. Rousseau compares the work to his herbarium, a "journal of botanical expeditions that allows me to begin them once again with a new charm and produces the effect of an optical device that paints them again before my eyes." Botany was the most popular of eighteenth-century sciences, and Carolus Linnaeus's system of classification had made it more widely accessible than ever before. Rousseau treats this eighteenth-century fad with gentle irony in his fifth promenade, when he depicts himself traversing the island of Saint-Pierre with a volume of Linnaeus tucked under his arm, intent on describing "all the plants on the Island without omitting a single one in sufficient detail to occupy me for the rest of my days."

But in other passages he evokes his passion for botany in more serious terms, transforming this Enlightenment science into an intimate means of discovering the self in nature. His botanical expeditions often lead directly into the reveries he experiences in nature, an overlap he signals by referring interchangeably to the ten chapters of the *Rêveries* as walks and reveries. In the fifth walk, the tongue-in-cheek account of his descriptive ambitions gives way to a lyrical description of the reveries he experienced by the water: "When the evening was approaching I descended the summits of the Island and gladly went to sit down at the shore of the lake in some hidden refuge; there the sound of the waves and the agitation of the water fixing my senses and driving from my soul all other agitation plunged it into a delicious reverie where nighttime often surprised me without my having noticed it. The ebb and flow of the water, its sound continuous but swelling at intervals striking my ear and my eyes ceaselessly took the place of the internal movements the reverie extinguished in me and sufficed to make me feel with pleasure my existence, without taking the trouble to think." In the experience of reverie, the communion between selves anxiously pursued in Rousseau's earlier autobiographical works is abandoned in favor of a communion between self and nature. Rousseau may no longer recognize himself in the machinelike beings surrounding him, but he recognizes himself in nature, experiencing the sentiment of his existence as an expression of his natural place in the cosmos. It is this sentiment, paradoxically, that he most effectively communicated to his readers in a work intended for the self alone.

Modern literature has not been able to dispense with the divided self created by Rousseau. This self was rooted in the Enlightenment attempt to reach the state of nature through conjectural history and has been linked to the foundation of the modern social sciences. But it was also a radically idiosyncratic self, whose shared nature with other humans could never be taken for granted or fully confirmed. The pathos of Rousseau's autobiographical corpus comes from the deep internal divisions to which this self is subject: it perceives its original nature but knows that social corruption makes any return to the state of nature impossible. It seeks communion with other selves but constantly questions the possibility for sympathetic identification. Literature in Rousseau's view cannot resolve these divisions, indeed it incarnates them as a practice rooted in humanity's corrupt social state. But it is also the means of creating fictions of nature, and fictions of the self, which may provide the only possible basis for future social transformations. In this sense, the solitary walker traces a path forward for literature, and it is one we have been following ever since.

Works Cited and Recommended Further Reading

Note: All translations of passages quoted in this chapter are my own, from the editions of Rousseau and Voltaire listed below.

Buffon, Georges Louis Leclerc de. *Oeuvres*. Edited by Stéphane Schmitt. Paris: Gallimard, 2007.

Epinay, Louise d'. *Histoire de Madame de Montbrillant: Les pseudo-mémoires de Madame d'Epinay*. Paris: Gallimard, 1951.

Horkheimer, Max, and Theodor W. Adorno. *Dialectic of Enlightenment: Philosophical Fragments*. Stanford, CA: Stanford University Press, 2002.

Lévi-Strauss, Claude. "Jean-Jacques Rousseau, fondateur des sciences de l'homme." In *Jean-Jacques Rousseau*, 239–48. Neuchâtel: Editions de la Baconnière, 1962.

Palissot, Charles. *Les philosophes*. Paris: Duchesne, 1760.

Plato. *Republic*. Translated by Robin Waterfield. Oxford: Oxford University Press, 1993.

Rousseau, Jean-Jacques. *Oeuvres complètes*. Edited by Bernard Gagnebin and Marcel Raymond. 5 vols. Pléiade. Paris: Gallimard, 1959–95.

Voltaire. *Sentiment des citoyens*. Edited by Frédéric Eigeldinger. Paris: Honoré Champion, 1997.

Rousseau's complete translated works, including the first English translation of *Rousseau juge de Jean-Jacques*, are available in an excellent critical series in thirteen volumes, *The Collected Writings of Rousseau*, edited by Christopher Kelly and Roger Masters (Hanover, NH: University Press of New England, 1990–2010). Among several paperback editions of the *Confessions*, Angela Scholar's translation (Oxford: Oxford University Press, 2000) is both readable and scrupulous in its attention to detail. The most accurate and harmonious translation of the *Rêveries* is by Russell Goulbourne (Oxford: Oxford University Press, 2011), but those of Peter France (London: Penguin, 1979) and Charles Butterworth (Indianapolis, IN: Hackett, 1992) are worth consulting as well.

Although Rousseau's *Confessions* is the best introduction to his life, readers seeking more objective accounts will profit from Leo Damrosch, *Jean-Jacques Rousseau: Restless Genius* (New York: Houghton Mifflin, 2005); and the outstanding critical biography by Maurice Cranston, in three volumes: *Jean-Jacques: The Early Life and Works of Jean-Jacques Rousseau, 1712–1754* (Chicago: University of Chicago Press, 1982), *The Noble Savage: Jean-Jacques Rousseau, 1754–1762* (Chicago: University of Chicago Press, 1991), and *The Solitary Self: Jean-Jacques Rousseau in Exile and Adversity* (Chicago: University of Chicago Press, 1997).

The most influential interpretation of Rousseau's writings, with an emphasis on the deep psychic structures of his personality, remains Jean Starobinski, *Jean-Jacques Rousseau: Transparency and Obstruction*, trans. Arthur Goldhammer (Chicago: University of Chicago Press, 1988). Christopher Kelly, *Rousseau's Exemplary Life* (Ithaca, NY: Cornell University Press, 1987) interprets Rousseau's autobiography in terms of his political philosophy, while his *Rousseau as Author* (Chicago: University of Chicago Press, 1983) sheds light on Rousseau's idiosyncratic conception of authorship. On the vexed question of Rousseau's relationship to the Enlightenment, the most nuanced study is Mark Hulliung, *The Autocritique of Enlightenment* (Cambridge, MA: Harvard University Press, 1994). Arthur Melzer provides a cogent overview of Rousseau's philosophical system in *The Natural Goodness of Man* (Chicago: University of Chicago Press, 1990). Readers interested in the cultural context surrounding Rousseau's celebrity will profit from Robert Darnton's classic article "Readers Respond to Rousseau," in *The Great Cat Massacre* (New York: Vintage, 1985). Dena Goodman offers a bracing feminist critique of Darnton and other historians of the Enlightenment who echo Rousseau's denigration of Enlightenment salon culture in *The Republic of Letters* (Ithaca, NY: Cornell University Press, 1994).

Realism, the Bildungsroman, and the Art of Self-Invention

Stendhal and Balzac

ALEKSANDAR STEVIĆ

At the end of Honoré de Balzac's *Le père Goriot* (*Père Goriot*, 1835) the novel's hero, Eugène de Rastignac, stands at the summit of the Père Lachaise cemetery on the outskirts of Paris, gazing at the city that lies below. An ambitious but impoverished nobleman from the provinces, Eugène had arrived in the capital to study law. Instead, over the course of some three hundred pages, he is treated to a very different kind of education, learning about the intricate rules that govern aristocratic salons and witnessing the steady stream of petty intrigues, personal betrayals, and elaborate conspiracies that permeate fashionable society. In a word, he has learned what it takes to succeed in Paris. And just now, Rastignac has witnessed a particularly sordid episode of Parisian life, the funeral of the novel's eponymous hero, Jean-Joachim Goriot.

Once a wealthy industrialist, Goriot has died a desolate old man, his fortune drained to provide a comfortable future for his two daughters who have now forgotten him. Having secured their places at the heart of the fashionable world by marrying wealthy noblemen, Delphine de Nucingen and Anastasie de Restaud ignore their father even in death, leaving it to Rastignac, a penniless student, to arrange his funeral. While this melodramatic finale clearly suggests that the attainment of wealth and fame in Paris is an exercise in heartless indifference and shameless egotism, it nonetheless fails to dissuade the young provincial from attempting precisely such a feat. Now that he knows the stakes, now that he has seen the depravity, the intrigues, the callousness that seem to pervade high society, he looks down on Paris with a mixture of disgust and desire, as if he is literally about to devour the city: "Rastignac, now all alone, walked a few paces to the higher part of the cemetery, and saw Paris spread out along the winding banks of Seine, where the lights were beginning to shine. His eyes fastened almost hungrily on the area between the column in the place Vendôme and the dome of the Invalides, home to that fashionable society to which he had sought to gain admission. He gave this murmuring hive a look which seemed already to savour the sweetness to be sucked from it, and pronounced the epic challenge: 'It's between the two of us now!'"

Rastignac's successful social ascent and his conquest of the Parisian landscape in *Goriot* is often seen as the paradigmatic event of *La comédie humaine*, the massive series of interlinked novels in which Balzac sought to capture various aspects of contemporary society. The novel brings to the stage not only the young parvenu and the figure of his aristocratic protectress, but also Vautrin, the master criminal who unsuccessfully tries to drag Rastignac into a murder plot as a way to get rich and make his fortune in Paris. And yet, in so many ways *Goriot* follows a pattern obsessively rehearsed by the major bildungsromans of French realism, including Stendhal's *Le rouge et le noir* (*The Red and the Black*, 1830) and Balzac's own *Illusions perdues* (*Lost Illusions*, 1837–43) and *Splendeurs et misères des courtisanes* (*A Harlot High and Low*, 1838–47).[1]

An ambitious young provincial, with little money and even less social capital, emerges on the Parisian social scene. His aspirations may vary: political career, literary fame, vast fortune, lucrative marriage, noble title, a place in the fashionable salons, perhaps all of it. However he defines success, it goes without saying that greatness can be achieved in Paris, and in Paris only. As one of Balzac's heroines puts it in *Illusions perdues*, "no honor, no distinction, comes to seek out the talent that perishes for lack of light in a little town; tell me, if you can, the name of any great work of art executed in the provinces!" For Stendhal, Paris is a "modern Babylon" and "the stage of great events." For Balzac, it is a "labyrinth," a "galaxy," and "an Eldorado." As he writes in *Goriot*, "Paris is a veritable ocean; take as many soundings as you like, you will never know how deep it is. Travel round it, describe it, but no matter how systematic your travels or your description, how numerous and eager explorers of that sea, there will always be some place untouched, some cave unknown, flowers, pearls, monsters, something unheard of, forgotten by literary divers." A self-contained universe harboring untold secrets, separate from the rest of France and subject to its own laws, customs, and linguistic codes, Paris is both the exclusive site of social triumph and an opaque object of youthful fantasies.

To conquer Paris is, then, the central ambition of French realism. But doing so will require a tremendous effort. Rastignac in *Goriot*, Julien Sorel in *Le rouge et le noir*, and Lucien de Rubempré in *Illusions perdues* all reach Paris thoroughly unprepared, struggling to grasp the intricate rules of high-society etiquette. Invariably, their speech, their manners, and their gestures betray them. They say things that shouldn't be said in polite company. They gesticulate too much. They dress badly. Upon arrival in Paris, neither Julien Sorel nor Lucien de Rubempré realize that there is a difference between morning and evening wardrobe. On his first appearance at the Opera, Julien is politely advised that he should come regularly, not in order to see the performances, but in order to observe the fashionable gentlemen and learn from them how to look like a proper Parisian. In *Illusions perdues*, Lucien fares much worse: having appeared at the Opera looking "positively pitiable," he is quickly banished from the circle of Parisian aristocrats to which he desperately wants to belong.

Of course, the young hero is not discouraged by such setbacks. After all, the conquest of Paris is an arduous process during which blunders are inevitable. This is why, only moments after the disastrous showing at the Opera, Lucien appears as determined as ever: "'this is my kingdom,' he thought to himself. 'This is the world that I must conquer.'" Resolve is another shared property. As Stendhal writes of Julien, "who could have guessed that this face, as pale and as gentle as a girl's, hid the unshakable determination to risk a thousand deaths rather than to fail to make his fortune!" Balzac is more succinct: "I shall succeed," cries Rastignac; "I will triumph," repeats Lucien. However, the young protagonist will have to show more than just determination in order to succeed: he will have to demonstrate an utter lack of scruples. For each of the three heroes, the path to success will entail a series of audacious gestures, some of them just shameless, and some outright criminal. In *Goriot*, Rastignac drains his family of their last savings in order to fund the conquest of fashionable salons. In *Le rouge et le noir*, the only way for Julien Sorel to move up the social ladder is to live in a state of perpetual dissimulation: because the elites are dominated by reactionaries—the clergy and the conservative aristocracy—he decides to play the role of a devoted Catholic and a royalist, while he is in fact a liberal and an admirer of Napoleon Bonaparte and despises the very world he seeks to penetrate. In *Illusions perdues* and *Splendeurs*, Lucien de Rubempré goes even further: he cheats, gambles, joins various conspiracies, engages in financial speculation, embezzles funds, uses his journalistic career to destroy reputations, forges checks, prostitutes his lover, and, it would appear, exchanges sexual favors for the guidance of the criminal mastermind Vautrin.

Success, however, doesn't come easily. In fact, it usually doesn't come at all. Among Balzac's and Stendhal's young parvenus, only Rastignac triumphs. He becomes a man of great wealth and excellent connections, a fixture of prestigious salons, a government minister, a duke, and a peer of France. However, after declaring war on Paris at the end of *Goriot*, Rastignac is reduced to a reoccurring minor character. Bits and pieces of his life story are revealed in Balzac's subsequent novels, most notably in *La maison Nucingen* (*The Firm of Nucingen*, 1837), but he will never again take center stage. And while Rastignac's meteoric rise is reduced to a piece of gossip, the dismal failure of Balzac's other young parvenu, Lucien de Rubempré, occupies not one but two large novels. In fact, both Balzac and Stendhal appear to be more interested in the mechanisms of *not* making it. Having dragged Lucien and Julien through the jungle of Parisian intrigues, they orchestrate their protagonists' defeats just as they are about to cement a place in fashionable society by marrying wealthy noble heiresses. A strange asymmetry thus pervades the French realist bildungsroman: on the one hand, a veritable obsession with ambitious young men trying to succeed in Paris; on the other, a curious desire to have them crushed to pieces. What is it that makes a meteoric rise such powerful fantasy, intensely seductive, yet impossible to fulfill?

The answers to this question have traditionally focused on the economic reality that the realist novel sought to depict. According to this line of interpretation, young parvenus are both attracted to and destroyed by the unruly forces of early capitalism. As the critic Georg Lukács insisted, the fundamental problem that Balzac's novels explore is the commodification of all aspects of life. Everything is for sale: not just real estate, industrial products, and stocks and bonds, but also literature, ideas, and reputations. This is certainly a viable description of Balzac's universe, particularly given the fact that so many of his heroes make (and more often lose) their fortunes by engaging in risky financial transactions, speculating on anything from wheat to books. As one of Balzac's professional speculators notes in *La maison Nucingen*, "we live in an age of greed in which no one cares about the value of a thing, as long as he can earn something on it and pass it on to his neighbor."

And yet, although the spirit of speculation animates so much in Balzac, the reality is that the young parvenus of French realism have little interest in becoming captains of the financial industry. They are certainly eager to exploit capitalist modes of acquiring money and influence, including industrial advances and financial speculation, but these are primarily tools for fulfilling other ambitions. What they really want is to be received in the prestigious salons, to be counted among the selected few who make up *le beau monde*, to be famous, to be someone. But what does it mean to be someone, a success, a person of consequence in France, circa 1820? On the one hand, the novels of Stendhal and Balzac eagerly offer startling examples of self-made men and their meteoric rise from humble beginnings: "Bernard Palissy, Louis XI, Fox, Napoleon, Christopher Columbus, and Julius Caesar, all these famous gamblers began their lives crushed by debt or destitute," we are told in *Illusions perdues*. On the other hand, the notions of success and social prestige were still tied to an essentially aristocratic set of values: to be someone is to have a proper pedigree, an illustrious name, and a noble title conferred by the royal patent. It is this tension that gives rise to the central problem of the realist bildungsroman: how do you become someone in a society that was of two minds about what it was to be "someone"?

The sources of this tension lie in the vicissitudes of French political history. Beginning with the Revolution of 1789, France was embroiled in a persistent political crisis. As the historian Roger Magraw points out, "France's unique volatility and instability stemmed from the lack of consensus about political legitimacy. Each successive regime suffered a legitimacy deficit. In eight decades [between the 1790s and 1870s] France had twelve constitutions, and passed through three monarchies, two Empires and three Republics!" In the 1830s and 1840s, when Balzac and Stendhal were writing their novels, many of these political dramas had already taken place. The Revolution of 1789 had uprooted the ancien régime, an absolutist monarchical order dominated by Catholic clergy and the aristocracy, abolishing in the process the very institution of nobility. As the 1789 Declaration of the Rights of Man and of the Citizen specified, because everyone is equal before the law, everyone will be "equally eligible to all high offices, public positions and employments, according to their ability, and without other distinction than that of their virtues and talents." Although the early years of the Revolution were marked by extreme violence, it nonetheless introduced a powerful republican, egalitarian, and meritocratic political ideal in the place of the ancien régime's reliance on inherited privilege: individual abilities instead of illustrious names and noble titles.

Not for long, however. In 1799, a young general named Napoleon Bonaparte executed a coup d'état. While still committed to many key republican values, including legal equality, the abolition of inherited privilege, and meritocratic civil service, Napoleon also established a powerful cult of personality. By 1804, he had created an imperial throne for himself and installed a hereditary dynasty, establishing his relatives as princes of France and his brothers as kings of the countries he conquered. By 1808, this former republican of undistinguished origin was creating his own nobility. The irony was not lost on his enemies. As one contemporary commentator observed, "can the arch-commoner Bonaparte give what he himself doesn't have?"

But there are further twists to be noted. In 1815, with Napoleon overthrown, a conservative monarchy was in place, once again led by the same Bourbon dynasty that was ousted during the Revolution.

During this period, known as the Restoration, the old nobility was also restored. And yet, the legitimists had little choice but to acknowledge the existence of a new imperial aristocracy. France now had two coexisting nobilities—one created during the centuries of the ancien régime and one created out of thin air by the "arch-commoner Bonaparte." Mme de Staël, one of the most prominent literary figures of the period, offers a particularly eloquent account of this state of confusion: "after the Restoration," she writes, "we met in all directions with counts and barons created by Bonaparte, by the court, and sometimes by themselves."

It was this unusually complex moment of French political and social history that attracted the attention of the realist bildungsroman. Rastignac arrives in Paris in 1819, Lucien in 1821, and Julien Sorel toward the end of the same decade. And although the world in which they try to succeed is still rife with feudal notions about wealth and social standing as inherited rather than acquired, recent French history offered a powerful demonstration that a pedigree is not just something to be inherited: rather, it is a thing that can be constructed, a much sought-after commodity, and, finally, something you can just invent for yourself as needed. In a society continuously suspended between competing visions of political legitimacy, a society that has witnessed successive disappearances and resurrections of various elites, in which yesterday's nobility is wiped out only to reappear tomorrow, and in which a republican general has managed to reinvent himself as an emperor with an aristocracy of his own making, the apparently simple question of *who is who*, becomes unusually vexed.

How is one to navigate the path up the social ladder in a society plagued by such overwhelming ideological tensions? One obvious solution was to closely follow the great Napoleonic example. As Maurice Samuels argues, "The French were obsessed with Napoleonic history in the early nineteenth century. Hungry for details about the great man, the post-Revolutionary public devoured the historical representations of the Napoleonic period in all forms." For several generations, he offered the archetypal tale of a man from the margin who rose to a position of unprecedented prominence. Born in Corsica in 1869, shortly after the Mediterranean island came under French government, he could hardly have come from a place more obscure. And although his family was a part of Corsican nobility, this was hardly a sufficient recommendation for a brilliant career in metropolitan France. As Frank McLynn observes, "Corsican 'nobles' were as common as 'princes' in Czarist Russia." The family background was, however, good enough to secure Napoleon a place at the Ecole de Brienne, a military school in France. Once commissioned as an officer, he advanced quickly. At age sixteen, he was a second lieutenant. At twenty-four, he was a brigadier general. At thirty, he was the first consul, effectively ruling France, despite being an outsider whose command of the French language had always been shaky. At thirty-five, he was the emperor of the French and was soon in control of most of continental Europe. By the age of forty-six, he was defeated and exiled. At fifty-one, he died a prisoner on an island far more remote than the one he came from, a symbolically significant fact that will require further consideration.

Unsurprisingly, Stendhal, who served under Napoleon and wrote a biography of the deposed emperor, created a hero simultaneously endowed with Napoleonic psychology and infatuated with the Napoleonic example. Julien Sorel, the protagonist of *Le rouge et le noir*, is an outsider par excellence: a carpenter's son, he has the distinct disadvantage of being born in the remote town of Verrières on France's eastern border. Like everyone else, he dreams of Paris: "[H]e imagined with rapture that one day he would be introduced to the pretty women of Paris, and would succeed in drawing himself to their attention by some glorious deed. Why shouldn't he be adored by one of them, just as Bonaparte, still penniless, had been adored by the dazzling Mme. de Beauharnais?" Despite unexceptional beginnings, he is mentored by the local priest, Abbé Pirard, and manages to learn Latin. This proves to be a vital piece of cultural capital that will open the way to further advances. He first becomes a tutor in the family of Monsieur de Rênal, the town's mayor and a provincial aristocrat whose wife he seduces, and then, realizing that the path to success leads through the Church, he goes on to a Catholic seminary. Recognized as a promising young talent, he leaves for Paris to become a private secretary to the highly distinguished and deeply conservative Marquis de la Mole. Although disdainful of this aristocratic world, he gradually learns its rules, manages to transform himself into "a real dandy," and becomes the lover of the marquis's capricious daughter Mathilde.

Julien's trajectory—from a sawmill on the outskirts of Verrières to Hôtel de la Mole, one of the best-regarded houses in France—embodies the sharp upward movement associated in the collective imagination with Napoleon's triumph. But the analogies run deeper than that. To begin with, Julien's education in the seminary carries an uncanny resemblance to Napoleon's years in Ecole de Brienne. A school report described the young Bonaparte as "quiet, fond of solitude, capricious, conceited, extremely egotistical, speaking little, energetic in his responses, quick and serious in his replies, very much in love with himself, ambitious and aspirant above all." The same image of solitude and conceit emerges in Stendhal's own *Vie de Napoleon* (*Life of Napoleon*, 1817–18): "[H]e spent his years in solitude and silence. He never took part in the games his mates played; he never addressed them with a single word." Twelve years later, as he is writing *Le rouge et le noir*, Stendhal describes Julien's arrival at the seminary in almost identical terms: "Recreation time came round. Julien became an object of general curiosity. But his only response was reserve and silence. In accordance with the maxims he had drawn up for himself, he considered his three hundred and twenty-one fellow students as enemies."

If it is sometimes difficult to distinguish between Stendhal's descriptions of the solitary yet frightfully ambitious Bonaparte and his descriptions of the solitary yet frightfully ambitious Sorel, that has a lot to do with the fact that Julien obsessively emulates the Napoleonic example. At eighteen, he is an expert in the history of Napoleonic campaigns and an avid reader of Emmanuel de Las Cases's *Le mémorial de Sainte-Hélène* (*The Memorial of Saint Helena*), which chronicles the author's conversations with the deposed emperor and reflects on various aspects of Napoleon's military career and political legacy. More than that, Julien measures his every step through the comparison with Napoleon: "for years now, Julien had never let an hour of his life pass without telling himself that Bonaparte, an obscure lieutenant without fortune, had made himself master of the globe with his sword." And if Napoleon could do it, why couldn't he do the same?

The difficulty is that, although the Napoleonic example looms large in the popular imagination, Julien begins his conquest in a decisively anti-Napoleonic era, in which power resides with the conservatives for whom Napoleon is hardly more than a usurper. Julien will have to adapt: "[W]hen Bonaparte first made a name for himself, France was afraid of being invaded; military prowess was necessary and in fashion. Nowadays you find priests of forty earning a hundred thousand francs, in other words three times as much as the famous generals in Napoleon's army. . . . The answer is to be a priest." Given that in Restoration France the path to success goes through the Catholic Church, he must be able to impress with the strength of his religious devotion. He begins by memorizing the whole New Testament in Latin and then goes on to develop a convincing acting routine: "[W]hat endless trouble he took to attain that facial expression of fervent and blind faith, ready to believe and suffer anything, that is so often encountered in monasteries in Italy, and of which Guercino has left us laymen such perfect models in his church paintings." The look in his eyes, the position of his hands as he walks—those are the signs of faith, and those he must meticulously practice if he wants to get anywhere.

But applying Napoleonic lessons in this world hostile to Napoleonic legacy inevitably leads to an internal conflict. In Julien's eyes, Napoleon is not simply an exceptionally successful parvenu who has managed to rise to the top of the pyramid of power, but rather a man who has managed to impose his own revolutionary social vision on France and on Europe. A stark contradiction therefore defines Julien's project: he relies on the revolutionary figure of Napoleon, whom he adores, in order to secure a place among the reactionary elites whom he despises. To do so, he will have to dissociate ambition from inward belief and become something of a professional hypocrite, a fact underscored by the narrator's constant reminders that he has learned by heart the title role from Molière's comedy *Tartuffe, or The Impostor*.

However, we are not in Balzac's universe just yet. In Balzac's works, principles mean nothing: in *Illusions perdues* and *Splendeurs*, both personal and ideological loyalties are easily discarded in the name of success. In Stendhal's, we can still register what Franco Moretti describes as "a sensation of being bound, despite lies and compromises, to one's 'laws of the heart.'" The dramatic opposition between inward beliefs and outward appearances still requires a resolution, and Stendhal hints at one by offering Julien the opportunity to bring his fantasies of upward movement closer to the Napoleonic model that he cherishes.

Toward the end of the novel, he is preparing to marry Mathilde de la Mole, who now carries his child. In order to avoid the embarrassment of giving his daughter's hand to a carpenter's son, the marquis provides Julien with a false noble identity: from now on he is to be known as Monsieur le Chevalier Julien Sorel de La Vernaye. Julien immediately interiorizes the character that the marquis hastily invented for his use: "[C]ould it really be possible, he wondered, that I might be the natural son of some great lord driven into exile in our mountains by the terrible Napoleon? This idea seemed less improbable to him with every passing moment. . . . My hatred for my father would be proof of it. . . . I shouldn't be a monster any more!" What attracts him even more is the fact that his title comes with an officer's rank. Although he has no military experience—he has only recently learned how to ride a horse—Julien immediately begins to fantasize about military achievements: "[H]e was hardly a lieutenant, promoted through favouritism a mere two days ago, and he was already calculating that to be a commander-in-chief at thirty at the very latest, like all great generals, it was essential at twenty-three to be more than a lieutenant. He thought of nothing but glory, and his son." As Julien begins to think of himself as a great military leader in waiting, the reader is tempted to conclude that he is losing his mind and that dissimulation has started to verge on delusion. And yet, this is a moment of symbolic fulfilment: a young lieutenant, he is precisely where Napoleon was at the beginning of his career, which means that he is finally able to imagine his own ascent in properly Napoleonic terms. He is not just successful, but on the way to greatness.

Unfortunately, not for very long. Just as Julien begins to indulge the fantasy of becoming a heroic figure, the novel takes a sharp melodramatic turn: his prospects are ruined by a scathing letter from the former lover, Mme de Rênal, which exposes Julien as a shameless hypocrite who will stop at nothing in his desire "to acquire status and to turn himself into a somebody." Denounced to the marquis in such a way, he attempts a very theatrical murder of Mme de Rênal in a crowded church. Even though he fails, and even though the woman he has tried to murder forgives him and becomes his most ardent defender, Julien is executed.

Paradoxically, it is in this defeat that Julien gets to embody the Napoleonic example most fully. Among many other things, Napoleon was also a man who rose to a position of highest prominence, disturbing the traditional order of things throughout the Continent, only to be declared an outlaw and exiled to a godforsaken island by an unprecedented coalition of old European monarchies. In March 1815, as he was mounting his final attempt to reconquer Paris, his efforts were denounced by the leading European powers as a "last attempt of criminal and impotent delirium." The Declaration of Vienna, signed by the representatives of Britain, Russia, Austria, Sweden, Portugal, Prussia, and Spain states that "Napoleon Bonaparte has placed himself without the pale of civil and social relations; and that, as an enemy and disturber of the tranquility of the world, he has rendered himself liable to public vengeance." Speaking in the name of "all the Sovereigns of Europe," the Declaration really speaks for the old monarchical order that the French Revolution and Napoleon's emergence disrupted; it is in many ways a statement of rejection through which the exclusive club of the great European royal houses refuses the attempt of the usurper Bonaparte to claim his place among them, despite the fact that he was by then married to the daughter of the Austrian emperor.

It is precisely this sense of exclusion from a world to which one unsuccessfully tries to belong that colors the ending of *Le rouge et le noir*. Without denying the murder charge laid against him, Julien insists that he is really persecuted for his ambition: "I see around me men who have no time for any pity that my youth might deserve, and who will wish to punish in me and for ever discourage this generation of young men who, being born into an inferior class and in some sense ground down by poverty, have the good fortune to get themselves a decent education, and the audacity to mingle in what the rich in their arrogance call society." As with Napoleon, the underlying crime is that he has tried to upset the established order of things.

The reasons for Julien's demise are structural: as Maurice Samuels has argued, in the universe of *Le rouge et le noir*, the Restoration is a suffocating era of rigid political control that offers no place for the great ambitions and grand achievements that marked the Napoleonic period. To the novel's central question—how does a man of humble origin become someone in Restoration France?—Stendhal offers the obvious answer: he doesn't. What is more difficult to fathom, however, is Julien's willingness to embrace his own defeat in the wake of Mme de Rênal's damning letter. Critics have long been puzzled by the fact that he makes no attempt to undo the damage and continue his conquest. Quite to the contrary, he appears to relish the sudden loss of control. Following the almost instinctive shooting of Mme de Rênal, Julien refuses to mount any kind of meaningful defense during his trial and begins to look less like a disciplined social climber and more like a defeated Romantic rebel, intermittently resigned and emotionally exuberant, self-destructive, and melancholy. This split can be explained by the fact that *Le rouge et le noir* stands at an important ideological and aesthetic threshold. On the one hand, it professes a commitment to a realist aesthetics—Stendhal's narrator famously compares the novel to a mirror carried along the road to reflect various aspects of reality—while on the other, it refuses to fully let go of an essentially idealized, heroic image of social conquest, rooted simultaneously in the historical example of Napoleon and the literary legacy of Romanticism.

⁂ ⁂ ⁂ ⁂

Balzac leaves little space for such ambiguities. In his mature novels, the commitment to analytical rigor seems absolute. As he writes in the 1842 introduction to *La comédie humaine*, "[S]ocial species have always existed, and will always exist, just as there are zoological species. If Buffon could produce a magnificent work by attempting to represent in a book the whole realm of zoology, was there not room for a work of the same kind on society?" While by no means averse to chance and melodrama, Balzac wants a system; he wants the laws of society clearly expounded and social types classified. In many ways, this is precisely what he delivers: a uniquely comprehensive vision of French society as a complex system in which the interaction between a variety of social groups—from bankers to journalists and from idealist writers to petty merchants—is described in painstaking detail. And yet, Balzac's project seems to transcend its own analytical assumptions: as he works to describe an ordered system, Balzac discovers an equivocal social universe whose laws are many and inconsistent, a universe full of economic and political uncertainty, riddled with innumerable intrigues, and one in which upward social movement is no longer a uniquely audacious endeavor, but everyone's fantasy. At the heart of this complex world, we find Lucien de Rubempré.

Like Julien Sorel before him, Lucien is young, ambitious, poor, and buried deep in the provinces, where he fantasizes about future glory: "[S]ooner or later his genius would shine, like that of so many other men, his predecessors who have triumphed over society." For Balzac too, the source of such fantasies is the Napoleonic example, which, "unfortunately for the nineteenth century, inspired great ambitions in so many mediocre men." And while Napoleon will continue to be a key reference point in both *Illusions perdues* and *Splendeurs*— Lucien's failures are compared with Napoleon's withdrawal from Russia and his defeat at Waterloo—history is present in the novel in a more intricate way, a fact reflected in Lucien's family background. Lucien's father, Monsieur Chardon, was a republican military surgeon turned provincial chemist. Lucien's mother, the last living member of the noble family de Rubempré, has miraculously survived the mass beheadings of 1793, soon thereafter becoming Madame Chardon. And in a further step down the social ladder after the sudden death of her husband, the woman who once bore the illustrious name de Rubempré became the village nurse, known simply as Madame Charlotte. Given this family history, Lucien can perhaps claim a connection to a noble house, but not more than that. The transition of titles generally follows the male line, and for all intents and purposes he is the chemist's son, Lucien Chardon. To claim otherwise is to commit a punishable offense, in theory at least.

But theory seldom applies. Although Lucien's narrative, like Julien's, takes place during the Restoration, at the time when royal prerogatives—among them the right to dispense noble titles—are taken seriously, no one can quite forget that the genie was let out of the bottle, that just a few years earlier a new nobility was created, and that Napoleon generously gave away the titles of barons and dukes. In fact, one of these new nobles, a certain Baron du Châtelet, will be the first to introduce Lucien to the world of aristocratic salons. In a sense, du Châtelet is self-invention embodied. Born simply Sixte Châtelet, and without any actual aristocratic pedigree, he had added the particle *du*, which indicates nobility, before his last name during the early days of the empire. Soon, he started to rise through the ranks of imperial bureaucracy, receiving from Napoleon the title of baron. After the fall of the empire, we find him in a self-imposed exile, but he is soon back to become a part of the Parisian high society that Lucien seeks to penetrate. More than that, by the end of *Illusions perdues*, the Napoleonic baron is made a duke by a royal patent. No doubt, Châtelet is meant to embody a paradigmatic destiny: a usurper turned into a baron by the greater usurper Bonaparte, then turned into a count under the restored monarchy. And if du Châtelet can do it, why shouldn't Lucien?

It is not entirely surprising, then, that Lucien is incited to follow du Châtelet's example. As his protectress, Louise de Bargeton, tells him early on in *Illusions perdues*, the sooner he begins the process by taking his mother's family name, the sooner he can hope to have his decision legitimized by royal patent. The logic, it soon becomes clear, goes something like this: a noble name is a tremendous source of social capital; along with Lucien's beauty, his poetic talent, his status as a protégé of a fashionable lady, this should be enough to secure him a place in high society. Louise further elaborates: "You cannot imagine how helpful it is to young talent to be placed in the limelight of high society! I will get an introduction for you to Mme d'Espard; no one has ever found it easy to get an entrée into her drawing room, where you will meet all the great: ministers, ambassadors, orators of the Chamber, the most influential peers, wealthy and famous people of every kind." Somewhere along the way, as Lucien's fame grows, the king will officially sanction the use of the name de Rubempré. And once he earns the royal stamp of approval, becoming a "proper" rather than a self-made nobleman, new opportunities will arise. He could certainly count on a rich marriage, perhaps even a position in the king's court. And after that—who knows? Even the unapproachable Mme d'Espard seems to support a version of this doctrine: "[I]f you announce at a reception where there are English girls worth millions, or wealthy heiresses, "M. Chardon," that is one thing, but "M. le Comte de Rubempré" is quite another matter. If he is in debt, a count finds everyone willing to help him, and his good looks are brought out like a diamond in a rich setting. We have not invented these ideas, we found them in force everywhere, even among the middle classes." Self-invention, it seems, is the way of the world.

In the universe inhabited by so many self-made noblemen, a single powerful assumption preoccupies the heroes of the French realist bildungsroman: you are not who you are, you are who you appear to be. After all, if a Corsican lieutenant was able to call himself the emperor of the French, why shouldn't a son of a chemist call himself de Rubempré? Stendhal's Julien Sorel had already mastered the art of appearance when he managed to get himself noticed by assuming the pose of religious devotion. Balzac's heroes follow his lead. In *Goriot*, Rastignac quickly abandons his law studies, understanding full well that what he needs to master in order to make a career is not the penal code but the code of conduct in fashionable salons. In *Illusions perdues*, Lucien repeatedly puts all of his efforts (and all of his money) into looking like a man who belongs in fashionable society. To strike the right pose, to speak in the proper idiom, to wear the appropriate clothes, in a word, to look like you belong there: those are the keys to Parisian high society.

Lucien will spend most of *Illusions perdues* and *Splendeurs* attempting to achieve this alchemical transformation of nothing into something, and of something into something more. His first steps are rather unpersuasive. Introduced to the illustrious Mme d'Espard and her circle, he is quickly recognized for what he is: an ambitious provincial with no understanding of proper etiquette. As Mme d'Espard tells Louise de Bargeton, who brought Lucien to Paris, "[Y]ou must wait until the son of a chemist is really a celebrity before you take him up." Forced to withdraw from the Parisian stage, Lucien tries to reenter it through the back door of journalism: he will attempt to make his name as a newspaper critic and a political commentator, accumulate a certain amount of social power, and try to use his influence to regain a place in the world that banished him. Perhaps then he will be enough of a celebrity to procure the royal patent and legally call himself de Rubempré. And yet, after much nasty scheming he has achieved precisely nothing, squandering in the process an extravagant amount of money, most of it not his own. Exiled back to the provinces, at the end of the novel he can only try to repeat the initial trick: dress well, go into a salon, and hope for the best. Once again, to no avail.

Perhaps Lucien has been a bit too hasty, and perhaps he has taken things too literally, but is he fundamentally wrong in assuming that he can get hold of his mother's name and carve for himself a niche in the Parisian salons? It will take Balzac another voluminous novel to answer that question. At the beginning of *Splendeurs*, Lucien emerges as a protégé of Vautrin, the mysterious criminal who had unsuccessfully tried, in *Goriot*, to enlist Rastignac as his apprentice. In *Splendeurs*, this man, whom Lucien describes as worse than the devil, hides under the guise of a Catholic priest, Abbé Carlos Herrera, and engages in intricate criminal schemes that put Lucien's own inept journalistic intrigues to shame: he steals, forges, blackmails, and organizes abductions. The push to turn Lucien into a member of the Parisian elite is now a large-scale criminal operation that stops at nothing: the bulk of funds needed to sustain Lucien's lifestyle comes from effectively prostituting Lucien's lover Esther Gosbeck to the rich Baron de Nucingen. But in the eyes of Vautrin, these are trifling matters. As he notes, "[H]ow many generals died in the prime of their life for the Emperor Napoleon?"

The sacrifices, it would appear, begin to pay off. Lucien is granted the name de Rubempré by the king and is finally considered a serious candidate for a spot in high society. With his new name and a new lifestyle, financed by Vautrin's scheming, Lucien will attain a social status that will allow him to marry the rich, aristocratic heiress Mademoiselle de Grandlieu. And given the financial gain and family connections such a marriage entails, his social standing as a legitimate member of the aristocratic elite will become unassailable: he is likely to be given the title of marquis and a prestigious diplomatic post. Such, at least, is the plan.

However, despite the noble name granted by the king and despite the tremendous amount of money Vautrin has amassed for him, Lucien still has to account for himself: "not only was Lucien's situation insufficiently clear, and the words: 'What does he live on?' which everybody asked as he rose in the world, still in need of a reply." Before he is allowed to marry Mademoiselle de Grandlieu, Lucien is faced with further tasks—to account for the sources of his money and to repurchase the historic Rubempré estate. The second task is entirely feasible; the first is, of course, impossible. With the dubious sources of his wealth exposed, the fiction of legitimacy cannot be sustained. Like Julien Sorel, Balzac's hero is stopped in his tracks only one step away from success. Instead of a promising career and a lucrative marriage, Lucien ends up in prison, where he hangs himself, exhausted by the years of struggle to enter the Parisian *beau monde*. Fittingly, he is buried at the same Père Lachaise cemetery from which Rastignac observed the city before starting his conquest.

First Julien, now Lucien: what are we to make of these persistent failures? With Stendhal it is at least possible to argue that the defeat of Julien Sorel constitutes an unambiguous if deplorable triumph of the reactionary forces. Is it possible that a similar mechanism is at work in *Illusions perdues* and *Splendeurs*? The doctrine of self-invention, reiterated in countless forms throughout the two novels, may be wrong after all: ambitious provincials cannot just miraculously turn into noblemen; the sons of chemists cannot really conquer Paris; you cannot just reinvent yourself at will; nobility is not just a convenient fiction; and you cannot become someone just by pretending that you are someone. And yet, Balzac's world is full of living examples of the contrary. Sixte Châtelet successfully becomes Duke du Châtelet. Rastignac, who was still living in a squalid boarding house in *Goriot*, now emerges as a dandy, a millionaire, and a prominent member of the club of fashionable young men that Lucien is desperately trying to enter. Even Vautrin, an escaped convict with a long and sordid criminal history, manages to reinvent himself as the chief of Parisian police, a post from which he will retire after fifteen years of service.

Why is it that in this world full of pretenders only Lucien can't make it? The simple answer would be that he is just not good enough. The novel offers plenty of support for such a view, repeatedly underscoring his lack of strength and discipline. As Lucien himself admits to Vautrin in his suicide letter, "[Y]ou tried to make [me] a greater figure than I had it in me to be." But if this is the case, why would a writer otherwise obsessed with the dynamics of social mobility spend two voluminous novels following the fate of a lackluster hero? According to Moretti, one of the main functions of the nineteenth-century bildungsroman was that it "contained the unpredictability of social change, representing it through the fiction of youth: a turbulent segment of life, no doubt, but with a clear beginning and unmistakable end." As he adds elsewhere, the function of a literary form like the bildungsroman is that it "reduces and 'binds' the tensions and disequilibrium of everyday experience." Balzac thus portrays the rebellious youth; he indulges high hopes and unchecked ambitions; articulates audacious assumptions about social mobility; and even offers examples of self-invention working perfectly well in practice. Yet in the central example, the one that matters, the desire to become someone is denied, and the doctrine of self-invention is refuted.

But perhaps a simpler solution might be in order. What if failure is about failure, period? That is to say, the defeat of Lucien de Rubempré in spite of all the efforts, and in spite of Vautrin's mentorship, signals precisely the impossibility of 'binding' the tensions that pervade the world of post-Napoleonic France. As Balzac persistently demonstrates, we are dealing with a society whose elites were in constant flux, dissolved and recreated every few years, committed to aristocratic ideals of continuity and inherited privilege, yet inevitably confronted with captivating fantasies of upward movement. It is only natural that a social universe built around these contrary propositions would prove unnavigable.

The power of the "disequilibrium"—to use Moretti's term—that pervaded nineteenth-century France is perhaps best felt in the way in which history intervened in the process of novel writing and publication. In the case of *Le Rouge et le noir*, history was quicker than Stendhal's publisher. At the end of the novel, whose action takes place in 1830 and coincides with the moment of writing, Mme de Rênal wants to ask King Charles X to spare Julien's life. The trouble is that by the time the novel was published, Charles X was no longer in power: in late July 1830, just as Stendhal was correcting the proofs of the already completed book, a revolution took place. Within days, the reactionary regime of the Bourbon Restoration was replaced with the liberal constitutional monarchy under the reign of Louis Philippe, the so-called Citizen King. The very context of Julien's rise and fall became obsolete before the novel was published. And given Stendhal's own biography, one cannot but wonder what this regime change would have meant for Julien. A former Napoleonic civil servant, Stendhal was a "notorious liberal" and stood no chance of reentering government service during the Restoration. Yet by the fall of 1830, he was on his way to Italy to take up an appointment as a consul.

The period during which Balzac wrote *Illusions perdues* and *Splendeurs* was not quite so eventful. He managed to complete the story of Lucien de Rubempré—which he developed from mid-1830s to 1847—without experiencing revolutionary turmoil, though just barely. In 1848, a year after he completed *Splendeurs*, a revolution occurred yet again, reestablishing France as a republic. Just a few years later, in a particularly ironic historical reversal that took place in 1852—and which Balzac would surely have appreciated had he not died in August 1850—the president of this new republic, who happened to be Napoleon's nephew, was crowned as the emperor of the French. Since 1789, France has been a republic, an empire, a monarchy, a liberal monarchy, a republic yet again, and another empire under the rule of a Bonaparte. Who can blame poor Lucien de Rubempré for constantly trying to reinvent himself in such an erratic world, and who can blame him for failing?

Note

1. Richard Terdiman adduces a succinct description of the bildungsroman (literally, "novel of formation" or "novel of education") as a genre "that investigated how individuals approached and entered what their culture designated as adulthood." While the history of this genre and the term itself (*bildung* meaning "formation" in German) is extremely complex, in current Anglo-American usage the term is applied to any novel that chronicles the processes of individual development and socialization of a young protagonist, however successful or unsuccessful such processes may be. Major European examples include Charles Dickens's *David Copperfield* and *Great Expectations*, Charlotte Brontë's *Jane Eyre*, Gustave Flaubert's *Sentimental Education*, James Joyce's *A Portrait of the Artist as a*

Young Man, and Thomas Mann's *The Magic Mountain*, among many others.

WORKS CITED AND RECOMMENDED FURTHER READING

Alter, Robert, and Carol Cosman. *Stendhal: A Biography*. London: Allen & Unwin, 1980.

Balzac, Honoré de. *A Harlot High and Low*. Translated by Rayner Happenstall. London: Penguin, 1970.

———. *Illusions perdues*. Paris: Gallimard, 2004.

———. *Lost Illusions*. Translated by Kathleen Raine. New York: Modern Library, 1997.

———. *La maison Nucingen—Melmoth réconcilié*. Edited by Anne-Marie Meininger. Paris: Gallimard, 1989.

———. *Le Père Goriot*. Paris: Gallimard, 1999.

———. *Père Goriot*. Translated by A. J. Krailsheimer. Oxford: Oxford University Press, 1999.

———. *The Works of Honoré de Balzac*. Vol. 1. Translated by Ellen Marriage. Philadelphia: Avil Publishing Co., 1901.

Declaration of the Rights of Man and Citizen. Reprinted in *The Human Rights Reader*. Edited by Micheline Ishay. London: Routledge, 1997.

Iung, Théodore. *Bonaparte et son temps, 1769–1799: D'après les documents inédits*. Vol. 1. Paris: Charpentier, 1880.

Lukács, Georg. *Studies in European Realism*. Translated by Edith Bone. London: Hillway Publishing Co., 1950.

Magraw, Roger. *France 1800–1914: A Social History*. London: Longman, 2002.

McLynn, Frank. *Napoleon: A Biography*. London: Jonathan Cape, 1997.

Moretti, Franco. *The Way of the World: The Bildungsroman in European Culture*. Translated by Albert Sbraglia. London: Verso, 2000.

Pettiteau, Natalie. *Elites et mobilités: La noblesse d'empire au XIXe siècle (1808–1914)*. Paris: La Boutique de l'Histoire, 1997.

Samuels, Maurice. *The Spectacular Past: Popular History and the Novel in Nineteenth-Century France*. Ithaca, NY: Cornell University Press, 2004.

Scott, Walter. *The Life of Napoleon Bonaparte, the Emperor of the French, with a Preliminary View of the French Revolution*. Paris: Galignani, 1828.

Staël, Germaine de. *Considerations on the Principal Events of the French Revolu-tion*. Edited by Aurelian Craiut. Indianapolis, IN: Liberty Fund, 2008.

Stendhal. *The Red and the Black: A Chronicle of the Nineteenth Century*. Trans-lated by Catherine Slater. Oxford: Oxford University Press, 1991.

———.*Vie de Napoléon*. Edited by Henri Martineau. Paris: Le Divan, 1930.

Terdiman, Richard. *Discourse/Counter-Discourse: The Theory and Practice of Symbolic Resistance in Nineteenth-Century France*. Ithaca, NY: Cornell University Press, 1985.

In *The Way of the World*, Franco Moretti (see above) offers the most conse-quential account yet of Balzac and Stendhal in relation to both the history of the European bildungsroman and the history of capitalism. Compelling interpretations of *Le rouge et le noir* can be found in Erich Auerbach, *Mimesis* (Princeton, NJ: Princeton University Press, 1953); and Peter Brooks, *Read-ing for the Plot* (New York: A. A. Knopf, 1984). In *The Spectacular Past*, Mau-rice Samuels (see above) offers an extensive discussion of Julien Sorel's rela-tionship to the Napoleonic model, as well as, more broadly, of the significance and the representations of Napoleon in the nineteenth century. Readers interested in the relationship between realism and capitalism should consult Georg Lukács's pioneering *Studies in European Realism* (see above), as well as the chapter on Balzac in Christopher Prendergast, *The Order of Mimesis* (Cambridge: Cambridge University Press, 1986). Although a work of eco-nomic rather than literary history, Thomas Picketty, *Capital in the 21st Cen-tury* (Cambridge, MA: Harvard University Press, 2014) offers a penetrating analysis of economic relations in Balzac's novels. Readers interested in *Go-riot* might want to consult the Norton Critical Edition, edited by Peter Brooks, for a wide selection of twentieth-century scholarship on the novel. Among the numerous discussions of *Illusions* and *Splendeurs*, and the figure of Lucien de Rubempré in particular, it is worth noting those in D. A. Miller, *The Novel and the Police* (Berkeley: University of California Press, 1988); and Peter Brooks, *The Realist Vision* (New Haven, CT: Yale University Press, 2005); as well as A. S. Byatt, "The Death of Lucien de Rubempré," in *The Novel*, ed. Franco Moretti (Princeton, NJ: Princeton University Press, 2007), vol. 2. The most significant contemporary treatment of forms of sex-uality in Balzac, including the relationship between Lucien and Vautrin, is Michael Lucey, *The Misfit of the Family* (Durham, NC: Duke University Press, 2003).

Hugo and Romantic Drama

The (K)night of the Red

SARAH ROCHEVILLE AND
ETIENNE BEAULIEU

On February 25, 1830, France's greatest monument of neoclassical culture, the Comédie-Française, was stormed by a mob of young, bearded, shaggy eccentrics, who entered the theater a few hours before the start of the scheduled performance, a tragedy by Victor Hugo titled *Hernani*, despite opposition from the police and from the theater staff, who threw garbage and refuse at the protesters as a deterrent. An apocryphal legend even relates how the young Honoré de Balzac was struck by a cabbage stalk square on the head. The artists, students, and composers who made up this group included Théophile Gautier, Gérard de Nerval, and Hector Berlioz. But within their ranks were several hundred figures less well known today, such as Petrus Borel and the sculptor Dusseigneur (whose workshop served as a meeting place for the Romantics of the Petit Cénacle), as well as a crowd that a year later, in 1831, an article in *Le Figaro* would christen the "Young France," whose names history has for the most part forgotten. Confined within the dark auditorium for four hours, this Romantic contingent was forced to eat, drink, urinate, and defecate in the boxes of the fourth floor, while their leader, Victor Hugo, watched through the peephole cut in the stage curtain. It was prelude to a spectacle that would be of paramount importance a few months later, when on July 25, the authority of Charles X would be rejected during the following "Three Glorious Days," as political power passed to the Orléans branch of the royal family in the person of Louis-Philippe, who ascended the throne at the beginning of the July Monarchy as king of the French, and no longer king of France, as the Bourbons had proclaimed themselves.

A veritable dress rehearsal for the revolution of 1830, the battle of *Hernani* lasted four months and gave rise to a general uproar throughout Paris at each of its performances. As with all plays in the nineteenth century, the whole shebang started with what was then called the "claque," which is to say the more or less homogeneous group of spectators who were paid to gather in the theater in order to honor a play with a loud welcome upon the arrival of the actors and to applaud the heroics—or, on the other hand, to jeer at the playwright's inappropriate language or the actors' lack of ability. (It should be noted that in the nineteenth century, the role of "director" of theatrical works had not yet been developed, and it was often the playwright or a seasoned and popular stage actor who supervised the presentation of the performance.) Sometimes fights (in the literal sense of the term) also broke out within the claque—as occurred during the performance on March 10, when the police had to intervene—or between rival gangs who sought to outdo one another in making noise and in drawing the opinion of the hall over to its side, for or against the show.

This method of manipulating artistic opinion, albeit very common in the Romantic period and almost always favorable to the neoclassical writers, figures importantly in Balzac's novel *Illusions perdues* (*Lost Illusions*, 1837), when Lucien de Rubempré attends an evening at the theater, an episode that was strongly inspired by the battle of *Hernani*. A wonder-struck Lucien goes backstage and, dumbfounded, discovers that the theatrical performance is extended into the audience by the claque, which consists of bribed applauders who must laugh and cheer at the right times, and, conversely, that the stage itself mirrors the auditorium, in that the very dialogue of the play is crafted to court favorable reviews from the "spin doctors"—the critics who shape public opinion.

During the battles over *Hernani*, the claque was infiltrated by supporters of Hugo's Romantic dramas, who were opposed to the neoclassical tragedies of playwrights like Jean Galbert de Campistron and liberal critics like Armand Carrel (the latter of whom wrote four articles against *Hernani*). The Romantics gave loud support to the performance while holding small red cards on which were printed the Spanish word *hierro* (iron), and they dressed in the most vivid colors, like the famous red jacket worn by Théophile Gautier, which literary history has elevated to the level of myth (as it was really a pink-poppy doublet). This was intended to create a striking visual contrast with the attire of the bourgeoisie, who were all dressed in black, as was proper according to the dress code of the time. In his history of Romanticism, Théophile Gautier notes the deep opposition, both sociological and historical, that is revealed by *Hernani*:

> For us, the world was divided into flamboyants and graybeards, the former the object of our love, the latter of our aversion. We wanted life, light, movement, boldness of thought and execution, the return to the beautiful times of the Renaissance and true antiquity. And we rejected faded colors, lean and dry design, compositions resembling groups of mannequins, what the Empire bequeathed to the Restoration. Graybeard also had literary meanings in our thinking: Diderot was a flamboyant, Voltaire a graybeard, same as Poussin and Rubens. But we also had a distinctive taste: adoration of the red. We loved this noble color, now disgraced by political fury—the purple. Red is blood, life, light, heat, and it blends so well with gold and marble. It was a real sorrow for us to see it disappear from modern life, even from painting. Before 1789, you could wear a scarlet coat with gold stripes, but now to see some examples of this forbidden color we were reduced to watching the Swiss Guard take up position, or to viewing the red outfits of the English fox-hunters on display in printsellers' windows. Is Hernani not a sublime opportunity to reinstate the red within the place it never should have ceased to occupy? And is it not proper for a young art student with the heart of a lion to be made the Knight of the Red and to come shaking the blazing color, odious to the graybeards, on this heap of classics which is every bit as much the enemy of the splendors of poetry? These cattle will see the red and will hear the lines of Hugo.

Affirmation of the red against the black, romantic youth against the neoclassical age, artistic passion against the "established" mentality of the Restoration—these are also among the interpretations of the title of Stendhal's novel *Le rouge et le noir. Chronique de 1830* (*The Red and the Black: Chronicle of 1830*), which would be published eight months later in November 1830. The red is intended to be the color of Romantic thought itself, that scarlet red that appears, for example, in the allegorical painting by Eugène Delacroix, *La liberté guidant le peuple* (*Liberty Leading the People*). The scene is of a barricade (in October 1830); featured prominently in the center of the canvas, Marianne holds in her hand a windswept French flag on which we see the red of the blue-white-red tricolor flag replacing the white of the monarchy. A historian of colors (following the research of the medievalist Michel Pastoureau, among others) could easily show that the color of the era is red—a bright, blood red that recalls the beating heart of society, the passion and enthusiasm of youth, and also the carnage of the Napoleonic battlefields found in the historical paintings of Delacroix, such as *La mort de Sardanapale* (*The Death of Sardanapalus*, 1827, inspired by Lord Byron), which is largely covered with blood red, but also with a refined red tending toward ocher, as in Sardanapalus's bedspread.

Similarly, the long hair and poorly cut beards of the Romantics are certainly intended to convey the defiance of youth against the thinning hair of seniors who now wear wigs, whose obsolete appearance, outdated and misplaced in the ongoing century, the Romantics will be all too happy to point out. Without being much mistaken, one could boil Romanticism down to a question of hairstyle, contrasting the fashion of the wigs of the ancien régime with the vivid and natural colors of the Romantics, which would change during the following generation into the artificial colors embraced by dandies like Baudelaire, who dyed his hair green or red in order to shock the bourgeoisie. But the length of the Romantics' hair is also important insofar as it points to a revival of Roman and medieval culture, while dismissing the dominance of the classical centuries. To have long hair in the Paris of 1830 and to dress in bright colors somehow was to declare sensationally, in the manner of Walter Scott, that one is in love with the culture of the Middle Ages—slightly barbaric but alive, and whose true story we only begin to understand with Romanticism—and that one has become attached to ruins, as was made fashionable by Volney in his work, *Les ruines ou méditations sur la révolution des empires* (1791). For this reason, subjects drawn from medieval history would be popular throughout the Romantic era, whether they concerned the resurrection of medieval tales, such as that of *Tristan et Iseut* (an object of increasingly intense research throughout the century, culminating in Joseph Bédier's version of 1900), or simply made-up legends, such as Hugo's *Notre-Dame de Paris* (1831), or reworked historical events drawn from chronicles, such as the one George Sand (Aurore Dudevant) titled *Une conspiration en 1537*, which she excerpts from Benedetto Varchi's *Storia fiorentina* to give to her lover Alfred de Musset, who in turn used it as the basis of his play *Lorenzaccio* (1834).

Much more than a mere fight among rivals for literary recognition, as a key moment of the artistic history of the nineteenth century, the battle of *Hernani* is a literary and political watershed, as much between one generation and the next as between the First Romanticism (the era of Jean-Jacques Rousseau, Chateaubriand, Mme de Staël, Benjamin Constant, Senancour, Joseph Joubert, and some others) and the Second Romanticism, which literary history often labels Romanticism as such, starting with Alphonse de Lamartine's *Méditations poétiques* in 1820 and ending with the failure of Hugo's *Burgraves* in 1843. Of course, *Hernani* is first and foremost an esthetic and dramatic confrontation following the "quarrels" of the ancien régime (the most famous of which remains that between the ancients and the moderns), and preceding by a few decades the "struggles" of the twentieth-century avant-garde (surrealism, cubism, and so forth).

In the Romantic age, literary confrontations readily assumed an epic shape and are preferably called "battles," given the aura of Napoleonic symbolism still ubiquitous, despite the emperor's exile and death on Saint Helena in 1821. Emmanuel de Las Cases's account of Napoleon's death fascinated the entire Romantic generation, which read *Mémorial de Sainte-Hélène* (1822) avidly. Such is the case with Julien Sorel, the protagonist of *Le rouge et le noir*, who keeps with him hidden under his pillow a copy of this veritable Romantic vade mecum, even when he succeeds in entering the house of the noble Mme de Reynal. Several Romantic authors take Bonaparte as a model—an inimitable one to be sure, and one whose epic had truly ended with the Restoration. But they believe he can be resurrected in another field, at once literary and political. Take, for example, the symbolic Napoleonic pose of certain authors like Balzac, or the hand-in-waistcoat pose that Hugo also adopts on occasion, as in 1879, when he was portrayed by Léon Bonnat, a painter who is today unfairly ignored. These Romantics, who reached adulthood in 1830, are thus either sons of Bonaparte's soldiers, like Hugo himself, or they simply have nostalgia for the Grande Armée, about which they had been lulled with legends since their childhood, which was nurtured by the *Bulletins of the Grande Armée*, as would be the case with Musset in *La confession d'un enfant du siècle* (*Confession of a Child of the Century*, 1836).

These reports of battles and of deeds and actions at the military front, drafted and published for the benefit of civilians, were devised through Bonaparte's genius of propaganda, which greatly altered reality to his advantage. We may think, for example, of his success in passing off as a victory the Battle of Eylau, which was disastrous in all respects, notably because of the number of dead, which was in the tens of thousands. The full apocalyptic extent of this disaster is given by Balzac in *Colonel Chabert* (1832), which tells of the fictitious life of an Empire colonel who had miraculously survived the mass grave of Eylau to come back and haunt his wife, now remarried to a Peer of France under the Restoration. As one may note, compared with the lives of their fathers, the existences of the authors of the Romantic generation seem quite pale and orderly, almost bourgeois (to use an insult of the time, which enflamed the passions of artists who sought adamantly to distinguish themselves from those whom Rimbaud called, a few decades later, "those who sit"). In the nineteenth century, art conceived itself as opposed to society, or at least opposed to the bourgeois world of finance and commerce. According to the legend, Guizot, who became minister under the July Monarchy, supposedly said, "Get rich!"—to which Baudelaire responds in one of his prose poems from *Le spleen de Paris* (1869), "Get drunk!"

Thus, during the first months of 1830, the Romantic mob kept this military imagery in mind, which must be taken into account in order to understand the Romantics' agitation when they attacked the Comédie-Française, then simply called the "Française," as opposed to the "Boulevard." The latter was the theater at the Porte-Saint-Martin, where, for the most part, the performances were melodrama, a genre derived from mime and crime scenes, hence the nickname of "Boulevard du Crime." (The filmmaker Marcel Carné depicts this theater with great detail, care, and poetry in his masterpiece, *Les enfants du paradis* [*The Children of Paradise*, 1945], scripted by the poet Jacques Prévert.) For the Romantics, attacking the Comédie-Française somehow amounts to replaying in their own way the storming of the Bastille (which their fathers actually experienced), but this time as an artistic and dramatic imitation. In many respects, French Romanticism transposes the military energy of the previous generation into the conquest of artistic freedom and of new genres such as the drama and the novel, but also poetry: "J'ai mis un bonnet rouge au vieux dictionnaire" (I put a red cap on the old dictionary), claims Hugo in *Les contemplations* ("Reply to an Act of Impeachment"), in reference to the famous Phrygian cap adopted by the revolutionaries of 1789 as a symbol of the new order.

But despite the legend invented by Théophile Gautier, the bold formal novelties were not so shocking to the bourgeois and neoclassical audience, already used to the flexibility of the bourgeois drama from the eighteenth century (Nivelle de la Chaussée, Beaumarchais, Diderot), because enjambment—the romantic versification device par excellence—was already almost inaudible to the audience, which no longer appreciated the quality of the verse and diction, unlike under the ancien régime when the audience went to the theater to listen to verse. Rather, what shocked the audience was the absence of periphrasis and use of the proper term, such as the famous "handkerchief" that the actress Mlle Mars refused to pronounce in view of all the impertinent suggestions that the word induces, and that she ultimately would say only reluctantly and at the insistence of Hugo himself.

The presence of characters from the middle or low social classes also shocked the audience, because this contrasted greatly with the classical rules inherited from Aristotle in the second chapter of the *Poetics*, where he explains, "Comedy aims at representing men as worse, Tragedy better than in actual life." The third chapter adds a second criterion of differentiation—the formal dimension: "For the medium being the same, and the objects the same, the poet may imitate by narration . . . or he may present all his characters as living and moving before us." The Aristotelian typology is derived from these two criteria. The typology divides literary forms into two categories, namely, noble and base imitation, which can be narrated or acted; in combination, these criteria identify comedy as a base and acted imitation, tragedy as a noble and acted imitation, epic as a noble and narrated imitation, and finally historical prose as a base and narrated imitation. This zone of anomie, located at the double crossroads of the noble and the base, of the narrated and the acted, and, according to Aristotle, of verse and prose, gave rise to Corneille's tragicomedy, then to the bourgeois drama, and finally to the Romantic drama, which finishes the dislocation of the Aristotelian system by presenting, for instance, the story of a queen in love with a servant as a topic of comic and even tragic drama, as in Hugo's masterpiece, *Ruy Blas* (1838). What is more, the neoclassical audience perceived as a blunt attack the introduction of elements that were claimed by modern theater as early as 1827 in the preface of Hugo's *Cromwell*, namely, the juxtaposition of opposites such as the sublime and the grotesque within the same play, which literally deconstructs the ancient contrasts inherited from Aristotle.

Behind these revolutions is hidden a profound transformation of artistic and social mores that is revealed especially in the story of the censorship of the play. It was Baron Taylor, royal commissioner of the Comédie-Française in 1830—himself well disposed toward Romanticism—who allowed Hugo to present his play there. But the preliminary censorship inherited from the ancien régime, based as it was on the system of royal privilege that grants the right to print to those above, while refusing distribution to those below, still retained some control over the agenda of the theaters and bookstores. Charles Briffaut was fairly well known in literary history for being ridiculed for censuring Hugo's play *Marion Delorme* two years earlier, and, facing the new threat posed by *Hernani*, he did not want to repeat the same mistake; so he decided rather to let the public assess the aberration it represents. The censor Briffaut therefore predicted, and literally planned the battle of *Hernani*, even before its performance, thus making the play the occasion of a strange transfer of powers of which his contemporaries seem to have been only half aware. The battle fought in the auditorium symbolizes what was at stake in all of French society at the time: the revolt of youth in conflict with the gerontocracy of the Restoration, which does not realize that a profound change of mores is already in progress. Thus, on March 3, 1830, the sculptor Auguste Préault shouted at the old men before him in the hall: "À la guillotine, les genoux!" By recalling that the play of *Hernani* itself tells the story of the condemnation of the pure love of two young people by an old man, Préault uses baldness (the head is smooth as a knee) to refer to the old age of the adversaries of Romanticism, the neoclassics, who are frightened by the impropriety of recalling revolutionary imagery, which was often painful for the survivors of the Revolution and of the Empire. The survivors often had a family member, a close friend, or at least an acquaintance who had gone through what was called "the black widow," namely, the guillotine.

Several years before *Hernani*, Stendhal had already set the stage for this confrontation when the watchword "Romanticism" had then been in use only a few years. In 1824, for example, in *Racine et Shakespeare*, Stendhal still speaks of *romanticisme*, a term he translates directly from English. Indeed, Stendhal notes the generational divide when he declares that "never before in human history has a people experienced, in its manners and pleasures, a change more rapid and complete than during the period of 1780 to 1823; and yet we are told that we should always have the same literature!" The revolutionary split results, among other things, in a passing from an aesthetic of habit ("to be able still to read in one's own heart so that the veil of habit can be torn apart") to one of experience, culminating in the lively forces of the youth ("to be able to put ourselves in the experience for the moments of perfect illusion of which we speak, one's soul must be capable of vivid impressions; one cannot be forty"). Experience pierces the fabric of the experience that comes with age; it makes it obsolete. It is thus not only a question of age (although it is also one), but especially of historic and aesthetic regime change.

In his properly historical conception of laughter, Stendhal challenges, for instance, the notion of classical imitation with which he contrasts imagination: "All the subjects of Louis XIV prided themselves on imitating a certain model in order to be elegant and fashionable, and Louis XIV himself was the god of this religion.... A man, in comedy or in real life, who took to following the impulses of a wild imagination freely without considering anything else, rather than amuse the society of 1670, would have passed for a madman!" So, the habit of imitation on the one hand, and the experience of imagination on the other: (neo)classical aesthetics (or rather, what Stendhal acknowledged as such for the sake of polemics, without regard to the discussion of the idea of imitation by the classics themselves, particularly in the quarrel of the ancients and the moderns) versus a vision of things referred to as "Romanticism" in the *Racine et Shakespeare* of 1825. One way to understand this term would be as a rejection of the mediation of prior models, benchmarks, preunderstanding, and prejudice.

At least this is what Stendhal declares, but of course many passages of his works show the contrary, namely, a passionate attachment to a form of tradition—for instance, that of medieval Italy, the myth of which develops as early as *Histoire de la peinture en Italie* (*The History of Painting in Italy*, 1817), and also the paradox of a plagiaristic rewriting that extols the tradition of freedom stemming from the Italian republics of the Middle Ages. This is where the most tenuous strands of Stendhal's thought and of Romanticism are formed. These strands nonetheless make a knot of such strength that the avant-gardes of the following decades were only able to repeat its manner of distinguishing, quite skillfully, within the Romantic present, what pertains to the current and the contemporary: "Romanticism is the art of presenting to the nations the literary works which, in the current state of their habits and of their beliefs, are susceptible to giving them the most pleasure." A question of habits and beliefs, of mores, of nascent anthropology and history, the Romanticism that is still looking for its name has nevertheless found its formula: it is the work that coincides with the public's horizon of expectation, that touches the heart of the collective concerns of the author and the readers.

But by no means does it strive to be current, in the sense of the political present, for example—Stendhal is very clear on this point: "The newspapers, bearing witness to what happened in the elections of 1824, exclaimed over and over again, 'What lovelier subject for comedy than the candidate!' Hey! No, gentlemen, he is worthless. . . ." A "gunshot in the middle of a concert," the current breaks the frame of the work and misses the contemporaneity that is aimed for. In his desire to "give his contemporaries precisely the kind of tragedy they need," Stendhal is not trying to overtake the present, but rather to find the foundation of his time, to excavate its archeology, because the contemporary, as the Italian philosopher Giorgio Agamben emphasizes, is the archaic: "Contemporaneity is in fact inscribed within the present, marking it primarily as archaic; only he who sees the indications or the signature of archaism in the most modern and recent things can be a contemporary. Archaic means close to the *archē*, which is to say the origin. . . . It is in this sense that we can say that the route of access to the present necessarily takes the shape of an archeology." The pleasure evoked by Stendhal, whose requirement of compatibility between a work and the needs of an era is only the occasion, then becomes the sign of a much more intense ripple than the simple laughter of courtiers: it reveals the agreement between obscure powers or secret movements of the soul, and what takes place on stage or in the broad theater of desire that is the true foundation of Romanticism.

The seismic shock of *Hernani* is thus not an isolated event without consequence: it was prepared for by numerous other factors and resulted in a wide movement that took into account—in Paris as well as in European society in general—the promotion of the present that Stendhal describes and that could in itself summarize what Romanticism is. Studying this Romantic breakdown of the times, the historian François Hartog distinguishes three levels of historicity: the ancient (turned toward the past), the modern (turned toward the future), and that of the last decades of the twentieth century (turned toward the present), which he calls "presentism." Relying especially on the works of Chateaubriand and Tocqueville, Hartog considers the Romantic moment to be that of the separation of the times that came before and the times that came after the event at which the semantics necessary for the implementation of the notion of progress was put in place. Or, at the very least, it is the idea according to which time, that great sculptor, gives shape to its substance by means of the future, and no longer the past, as Chateaubriand's René puts it so eloquently: "But what had I learned so far with so much effort? Nothing certain among the ancients, nothing beautiful among the moderns. The past and present are two unfinished statues: the one has been withdrawn all mutilated from the ruins of the ages, while the other has not yet received its perfection from the future."

At the very beginning of the nineteenth century, perfection was not so much achieved by the return to antiquity, but rather by appealing to the transformative power of the future: it is the future, and no longer the past, that becomes the reference as power of perfectibility. The present, no longer held back by a constant comparison with the distant past (the ancients versus the moderns), finds itself propelled on a time line that resembles an acceleration track for a train of history that is already on the move and that is literally on the way to getting off the ground by the end of the century, with the advent of aviation. This process is analyzed by the sociologists of acceleration as well as by the historians of speed—mindful of the passage of a world that is structured (if we are to believe the words of Chateaubriand) by a "strange harmony between the rotation of the planets, the kicking of the feet, and the intimate vibrations," a world conceived and perceived in relation to the slowness of walking, where the only speed remains that of the horse throughout the duration of equestrian civilization, until the end of this millennial agreement between the human body and the toil that is physical movement.

However, let us now slow down the conceptual race car for a moment and reread Chateaubriand's words, while wondering whether the speaker has already let himself be drawn in by the general movement of the century or, to the contrary, whether he is keeping his balance and, as it were, has become dizzy at seeing the temporal abyss in front of him. If, for Chateaubriand/René, the past remains an "incomplete statue" and the future is a "perfection" that will soon give its shape to the present, Chateaubriand, that swimmer between two shores, nonetheless still remains in between these two moments of history: in a strange present that is neither formatted by the ancient conception of historicity, nor yet integrated with the modern conception. It is a kind of present implied from the discourse, slightly stagnant—a viscous time, to use the recent terminology of a historian of the Middle Ages, a time that sticks unnoticed to that of the enunciation, and that may well be the slow tempo of Romanticism (in Patrice

Loraux's sense of the term), one in which the narrator of Alfred de Musset's *Confession d'un enfant du siècle* seems to get bogged down.

> The life offered to the youths of that time was made up of three elements: behind them was a past that was never destroyed and which still stirred about its ruins, with all the fossils of the centuries of absolutism; in front of them was the dawn of a vast horizon, the first light of the future; and in between these two worlds . . . something similar to the Ocean which divides the old continent from the young America, something vague and floating, a stormy sea full of shipwrecks, crossed from time to time by some white sail or by some ship blowing heavy steam. In other words, the present century, which separates the past from the future, which is neither one nor the other and which resembles both at once, where one does not know, at every step, whether he is walking on a seed or on remains.

This "something vague and floating" that enables Musset to extend the oceanic metaphor gives shape to a fluid present, which is vast and somewhat viscous, like a terrible infinity in which thought stays stuck in a time that is becoming, where nothing is definite yet, neither past nor future, neither seed nor remains, a time that is in limbo, so to speak, suspended, waiting for some kind of status—in brief, it is a time in need, which is all potential and restraint before it transitions into action. It is this suspended time that gives rise to the Romantic movement and its search for the foundation of things beyond the classical rules.

Works Cited and Recommended Further Reading

Agamben, Giorgio. *Qu'est-ce que le contemporain?* Translated from Italian by Maxime Rovere. Paris: Rivages, 2008.

Aristotle. *Poetics*. Translated and edited by S. H. Butcher as *Aristotle's Theory of Poetry and Fine Art*. London: St. Martin's Press, 1894; rev. ed., 1911.

Balzac, Honoré de. *Le colonel Chabert*. Paris: Gallimard, 1994.

———. *Illusions perdues*. Paris: Gallimard, 1974.

Barnett, Marva A., ed. *Victor Hugo on Things That Matter: A Reader*. New Haven, CT: Yale University Press, 2009.

Barthélémy, Dominique. *Nouvelle histoire des Capétiens*. Paris: Seuil, 2012.

Baudelaire, Charles. *Le spleen de Paris*. Paris: Gallimard, 1994.

Chateaubriand, François-René de. *"Atala" et "René."* Montreal: Beauchemin, 2012.

Gautier, Théophile. *Histoire du romantisme*, followed by *Notices romantiques* and by a study on *Le progrès de la poésie française depuis 1830* (1874). Paris: Ressouvenances, 2007.

Halsall, A. W., et al. *Victor Hugo and the Romantic Drama*. Toronto: University of Toronto Press, 1998.

Hartog, François. *Régimes d'historicité: Présentisme et expériences du présent*. Paris: Seuil, 2003.

Hugo, Victor. *Les contemplations*. Paris: Gallimard, 1973.

———. *Hernani*. London: Grant & Cutler, 1982.

———. *Notre-Dame de Paris*. Paris: Livre de Poche, 1988.

———. *Oeuvres complètes*. Vol. 1: *Cromwell. Amy Robsart. Hernani. Marion de Lorme. Le roi s'amuse. Lucrèce Borgia. Marie Tudor. Angelo, tyran de Padoue. La Esmeralda*. Edited by Anne Ubersfeld. Paris: Robert Laffon, 1985.

———. Vol. 2: *Ruy Blas. Les Burgraves. Torquemada. Théâtre en liberté. Les jumeaux. Mille francs de récompense. L'intervention*. Edited by Arnaud Laster. Paris: Robert Laffon, 1985.

Lamartine, Alphonse de. *Méditations poétiques*. Paris: Livre de Poche, 1969.

Las Cases, Emmanuel de. *Mémorial de Sainte-Hélène*. Paris: Seuil, 1968.

Maurois, André. *Victor Hugo and His World*. London: Thames and Hudson, 1966.

Musset, Alfred de. *Les caprices de Marianne—On ne badine pas avec l'amour—Lorenzaccio—Le chandelier—Il ne faut jurer de rien*. Paris: GF Flammarion, 1988.

———. *La confession d'un enfant du siècle*. Paris: Gallimard, 1973.

Robb, Graham. *Victor Hugo: A Biography*. New York: W. W. Norton, 1997.

Roche, Daniel. *La culture équestre de l'Occident XVIe–XIXe siècle*. 3 vols. Paris: Fayard, 2008.

Rosa, Hartmut. *Acceleration: Une critique sociale du temps*. Translated from German by D. Renault. Paris: La Découverte, 2010.

Stendhal. *Histoire de la peinture en Italie*. Paris: Gallimard, 1996.

———. *Racine et Shakespeare*. Paris: Kimé, 2005.

―――. *Le rouge et le noir: Chronique de 1830*. Paris: Gallimard, 2002.

Studeny, Cristophe. *L'invention de la vitesse: France, XVIIIe–XXe siècle*. Bibliothèques des histoires. Paris: Gallimard, 1995.

Ubersfeld, Anne. *Le drame romantique*. Paris: Belin, 1993.

Volney. *Les ruines ou méditations sur la révolution des empires*. Plassan: Desenne, 1791.

Flaubert and *Madame Bovary*

PETER BROOKS

Madame Bovary is the only true "realist novel" of the French nineteenth century. By the time the novel was published, in 1857, "realism" was a much-discussed concept, still controversial. A number of novels would claim the label. Yet many novelists we may think of as the greatest realists, especially the earlier Balzac and the later Zola, tend as well toward the mythic and the allegorical—tendencies that Flaubert robustly resists. There's a paradox here, since Flaubert disliked the label "realist" and found "the real" itself mostly boring when not downright nauseating. But when he chose to leave the more exotic subjects and locales of some of his other fiction, when he set out to situate his story resolutely in "life in provincial France," to paraphrase the subtitle of *Madame Bovary*, he fought things out within the realm of the real more completely than anyone else. His act of representation is firmly anchored in the things of reality.

This claim for Flaubert's realism is grounded in three qualities of *Madame Bovary*: the novelist's choice of impersonality and impassivity, that is, his refusal to announce a position or pass a judgment in his own voice; the patient accumulation of detail that largely constitutes the narrative; and the very thematics of the novel, which show Emma Bovary's dreams in their conflict with the real, and their defeat by it.

When T. S. Eliot said that "all great art is impersonal," that it involves "an extinction of personality," he demonstrated that he had absorbed the lesson of Flaubert, as indeed nearly all the great modernists did. Flaubert pronounced on this impersonality in a number of his letters (he never wrote literary criticism or other essays), and these statements were later made famous by the writers of the twentieth century, who saw in him the master craftsman who made the novel a serious art form. Many of these pronouncements in fact came during the writing of *Madame Bovary*. "The artist in his work must be like God in his creation, invisible and all-powerful: let him be every-where felt but nowhere seen." What does this mean? It is not a pre-scription for a kind of simple phenomenological description of the world but rather a plea to make dramatized characters and situations carry the burden of meaning without explicit authorial intervention of the kind that Balzac was famous for ("Here is why Lucien was un-able . . ."; "To understand what Rastignac felt . . ."). The dramatized life of the novel should be allowed to speak for itself—to show us, not tell us, in a distinction that is now familiar to every student of narra-tive writing.

The impersonality and impassivity of the novelist do not mean his lack of involvement, but rather his investment of his own self into his created worlds. In another letter, Flaubert wrote of the pleasures of being no longer oneself but rather free "to move around in the whole of one's creation. Today, for instance, as both man and woman, at the same time lover and mistress, I rode horseback in a forest on an au-tumn afternoon under the yellow leaves, and I was the horses, the leaves, the wind, the words my people uttered, and the red sun that made them almost close their love-drowned eyes." This must be one of the best descriptions ever of the process of novel writing: the sink-ing of one's own self into others, the capacity to subdue the ego into other persons and animals and things. Flaubert's whole philosophy of creation is captured in this comment. It explains his stylistic choices—for instance, why he makes such large use of free, indirect discourse, staying within the consciousnesses, the sensations, and the language of his characters rather than speaking in his own voice—and also why *Madame Bovary* was such a radically new creation and why it created a scandal, such that Flaubert was put on trial for outrage to public morality. The absence of authorial censure of Emma, the studied re-fusal to make normative judgments, was deeply disturbing. It explains also the apparent contradiction of the exclamation by this exponent of authorial impersonality, "Madame Bovary, c'est moi!": she is me, I am her, because he has sunk himself into her experience of the world.

That experience seems to take place first of all at the level of the detail, for the reader as well as the heroine. Implicitly, Flaubert seems to say that reality comes to us as a kind of noticing of things, often small things, and also a bumping into them. We as readers first meet

Emma Bovary when her future husband goes to treat her father's broken leg. Pause for a moment to note this curious feature of the novel, which starts us off with Charles Bovary, an initially ridiculous figure who manages to become a country doctor. He has been married already and widowed. In fact, Emma is the third "Madame Bovary" mentioned in the novel, after Charles's mother and his first wife, which in retrospect may seem ominous. So we come to meet Emma only as an apparently ancillary figure, Charles's patient's daughter, through Charles's noticings of her. As they stand at the door of her father's house waiting for the doctor's horse, "the fresh air surrounded her, lifting in disarray the stray wisps of hair on the nape of her neck or tossing her apron strings so that they snaked like banners about her hips." When she drinks from a glass that is nearly empty, "the tip of her tongue, passing between her delicate teeth, licked with little stabs at the bottom of the glass." Our picture of Emma seems to be largely constructed from such minute details: the whiteness of her fingernails, her pink cheeks, the tip of her ear emerging from under her hair, the sound of her clogs on the scrubbed farmhouse floor, the little drops of sweat on her bare shoulders. We are not given any full-length portrait of her, as a whole. The world, Flaubert seems to say, must be described. That is the most honest approach to representing it. And honest description focuses on the visible detail, the thing as it meets our senses.

Description of detail can capture the beauty of a moment and a corner of reality. During a winter thaw, Emma goes to get her parasol: "The parasol, of dove-gray iridescent silk, with the sun shining through it, cast moving glimmers of light over the white skin of her face. She was smiling beneath it in the mild warmth; and they could hear the drops of water, one by one, falling on the taut moiré." This is the kind of descriptive moment that made Henry James comment about *Madame Bovary* that "expression is creation, that it *makes* the reality . . . the image is thus always superior to the thing itself." James perceives that the ordinariness of the everyday detail is both that and something more when it becomes language, something fixed in another, enduring medium.

But the descriptive detail can be more disturbing as well. Charles, infatuated following their marriage, "could not refrain from constantly touching her comb, her rings, her scarf." Or, when Emma has become Rodolphe's mistress: "It was for him that she would file her nails with the care of an engraver, and that there was never enough cold cream on her skin, nor patchouli on her handkerchiefs. She would load herself with bracelets, rings, necklaces." This accessorizing of herself suggests something artificial, factitious in her self-definition, as in her affair. Such a conclusion becomes hard to avoid when we reach her second lover, Léon: "He admired the sublimity of her soul and the lace on her petticoat."

This last example, linking sublime soul and lace petticoat, raises problems. The perception is ascribed to Léon, and one can say that the limitations in the way Emma is seen have to do with the limited perceptive powers of her lovers. Charles, Rodolphe, and Léon are all mediocre people. Their love for Emma can go no further than their own narrow capacities. In this sense, the limitations to the reader's perceptions of Emma, seemingly an assemblage of details rather than a coherent whole, are part of the novel's realism. We know her as she becomes an object of desire to others in her world, and it's a narrow world. Consider the stable boy Justin's fascination with Emma's undergarments, which the maid is ironing: "he would stare avidly at all these women's things spread out around him: the dimity petticoats, the fichus, the collars, and the drawstring pantalets, vast at the hips and narrowing lower down." Justin is then sent to clean Emma's boots, enhancing our sense that articles of her clothing are invested with an erotic charge, that they are fetishes. The eros created around Emma makes the details by which we know her something like fetishes. In another example: as Rodolphe follows her into the woods for their first sexual encounter, she lifts her skirt and he gazes "at her delicate white stocking, which showed between the black cloth and the little black boot and seemed to him a part of her naked flesh."

Yet the details by which her lovers know her may also constitute the way she knows herself, and as well the way we readers come to know her, almost exclusively—and perhaps even the sole way her creator knows the world. What I mean to suggest here is that Flaubert's vision of the world tends to come to rest on perspicuous details, things that become invested with the desire and the meaning that we might expect rather to inhere in her person or character. And here is one of the great reasons that *Madame Bovary* seems to us so modern, so fresh after more than a century and a half. Emma is not wholly known, not a fully upholstered character of the sort we associate with nineteenth-century fiction. She is a bundle of details, perceptions, feelings barely held together, not so much a self as someone in search of what a self might be. Something of this comes through in Flaubert's title as well: not *Emma Bovary*, but *Madame Bovary*. She from the outset seems to be deprived of the requisites of selfhood, to be defined by the husband and society from which she is alienated. Her definition as "wife" is set against her search to become, though what is as unclear to her as it is to us.

When we learn at the time of her marriage to Charles that she "would have liked to be married at midnight, by torchlight," we may, like her father, find that idea incomprehensible. But its sources become clear as we read on—past the wedding itself, with its plenitude of Norman eating and drinking—to learn of her reading. Chapter 6 of part 1 details her literary education, from the romantic idyll of *Paul et Virginie* through Christian tracts to Walter Scott. It's the same problem that we encounter in *Don Quixote*: reading matter that produces a distorted view of reality, one that sets Emma up for constant disappointment. Her second attempt at a grand passion, following Rodolphe's treachery, takes shape during a performance of Donizetti's opera *Lucia di Lammermoor*, based on a Walter Scott novel, a drama of heightened emotion that gives her a momentary high that exalts her above sordid reality.

That reality comes to us, as to Emma, piece by piece, especially in an iterative form, as the habitual, the routine that never changes. Flaubert's descriptive use of the imperfect tense, the tense of habitual, repeated action, notably gives us a feeling of inescapable and nauseating depression. One example among many, the object of a commentary in Erich Auerbach's celebrated study of the representation of reality in literature, *Mimesis*, records her mealtimes with Charles: "But it was most of all at mealtimes that she could not bear it any longer, in that little room on the ground floor, with the stove that smoked, the door that squeaked, the walls that seeped, the damp flagstones, all the bitterness of life seemed to be served up on her plate, and, with the steam from the boiled meat, there rose from the depths of her soul other gusts of revulsion." And the passage continues in that vein. Those who want to judge Emma as shallow and self-deluding cite such moments as examples of her false expectations of life, her demand for a romance that exists in books but not in reality.

That is true enough, and many a critic has diagnosed Emma's problem as a romantic distortion of the real and noted that her fate reflects Flaubert's judgment on the delusions inculcated by romance novels, and by the Romantic generation of writers that preceded his own more disabused generation. That's true, too: Emma is indeed deluded and self-deluding. But we should note as well that what makes Emma self-deluding is also what makes her interesting and worthy of our sympathetic attention. Following her initial sense of deception after her marriage, just before we learn of her reading, we are told that since the happiness that should have resulted from love had not come, "she thought she must have been mistaken. And Emma tried to find out just what was meant, in life, by the words 'bliss,' 'passion,' and 'intoxication,' which had seemed to her so beautiful in books." The cynical or world-weary reader may want to respond that those are merely words, and that striving to find their meaning will offer no guidance to real life, but on the contrary only illusions that must be painfully shattered. Nonetheless, Emma's meditation on the meaning of these abstractions, and on their fit with reality, makes her superior to other characters (including Charles) who never examine language or the world at all. Of Charles we learn that his conversation is "flat as a sidewalk." In terms of the Socratic principle that the unexamined life is not worth living, most of the characters in *Madame Bovary* are brain dead, whereas Emma seeks to discover what it all means. We can criticize her for going about it in the wrong way. But she gains our troubled sympathy for trying to change life.

Here again, language is both the apparent escape ladder and the trap. For instance, she wonders about the discrepancy of her life as a newlywed and the traditional discourse of the honeymoon:

> She sometimes imagined that these were, nevertheless, the most beautiful days of her life—the honeymoon, as it was called. To savor its sweetness, she would doubtless have had to go off to one of those lands with melodious names, where the days fol-

lowing a wedding have a softer indolence! In a post chaise, under curtains of blue silk, you climb the steep roads at a walk, listening to the postilion's song as it echoes through the mountains, mingling with the bells of the goats and the muffled sound of a waterfall. As the sun goes down, you stand together on the shore of some bay, inhaling the fragrance of the lemon trees; then, at night, alone on the terrace of the villa, your fingers intertwined, you gaze at the stars and make plans. It seemed to her that certain places on earth must produce happiness, like a plant that was peculiar to that soil and grew poorly in any other spot. If only she could have leaned on her elbows on the balcony of a Swiss chalet or locked away her sadness in a cottage in Scotland, with a husband dressed in a long-skirted black velvet coat, soft boots, a pointed hat, and ruffles at his wrist!

One can read this passage with an ironic smirk or with tears in one's eyes, depending on temperament or simply current mood. It is pathetic and self-delusive, of course, imagined in the language that makes us sign up for cruises to tropical islands, but it is also the stuff of everyone's dreams. If you think that everyone has the right to a certain modicum of happiness in life, Emma's reverie is a place of true pathos. If you think rather that we all are doomed to the discovery of the fundamental discrepancy between desire and fulfillment, then Emma's longings are unpersuasive. Such a passage can thus take on different colorations. It is both touching and pathetic, absurd and meaningful. Emma's daydreams are inauthentic, the stuff of travel brochures, yet they make her also a kind of proto-poet, someone whose imagination recasts the world. "Madame Bovary, c'est moi." Aren't we all daydreamers, inflating our egotistic wish-fulfillments in the realm of fantasy even while we may recognize their falsity?

Language deludes us. It conjures up worlds that have no local habitation for us on earth. There are moments when Emma thinks she is on the verge of an experience that would match the books she has read. Notably, there is the ball at the château of La Vaubyessard that she and Charles are invited to, an episode that will create a "hole" in her existence by making momentarily real a world just dreamed of. It's a world of orchestras playing and a dizzying waltz with a *vicomte*, of maraschino ices, and of the host's father-in-law, a decrepit remnant of the ancien régime: "He had lived at Court and slept in the beds of queens!" Early in the morning, Emma looks out from the window of her guest room in the château: "The first light of dawn appeared. She looked at the windows of the château for a long time, trying to guess which were the rooms of all those people she had observed the night before. She would have liked to know all about their lives, to enter into them, to become part of them." Windows in novels of a realist ambition tend to be frames for observing the world, for the presentation of landscapes and scenes. Here there are two windows. But if Emma can look out of one, she is frustrated in looking in the other, on the lives she would like to know. More than know: to enter, to become part of ("*y pénétrer, s'y confondre*"). Long after the visit to La Vaubyessard, she will ache for a repetition, but this never comes.

What she is left with is the green silk cigar case that Charles finds in the road on their way home the next day. This emblem of a more glamorous existence becomes for Emma the most important object of her existence, one that she takes from the cupboard and fondles when Charles is out. Like so many of the things in the novel, it is both a physical object and more, something endowed with emotion, a fetish. She assumes it belonged to the *vicomte*. "Perhaps it was a gift from his mistress. It had been embroidered on some rosewood frame. . . . A breath of love had passed among the stitches of the canvas; each stroke of the needle had fastened into it a hope or a memory, and all those interlaced threads of silk were merely an extension of the same silent passion." A fetishized object is one that has become meaningful, itself a kind of language. Things and words can change places, as when her reverie over the silk cigar case evokes its probable context, Paris: "The name itself was so vast! She would repeat it to herself softly, to give herself pleasure; it would resound in her ears like the great bell of a cathedral." She buys herself a map of Paris, in order to imagine the word as a visitable place.

Things and words are both subject to wearing out, becoming that flat sidewalk of Charles's speech, or the worn coin whose denomination is no longer evident. When her affair with Rodolphe reaches what she sees as a climactic decision to elope together, Rodolphe decides the time has come to break with her. He begins to rummage in the old biscuit tin in which he has preserved her letters, along with those from past mistresses, and other keepsakes: "some bouquets, a garter, a black mask, pins, and hair—hair!—brown, blond, some of which, even, caught on the iron fittings of the box and broke when it was opened." Opening the box releases "a smell of damp dust and withered roses." When he starts to write his letter of rupture, it has the same withered and generic qualities as these souvenirs. He judges his clichés to be "in excellent taste," and sends them off to Emma, who will nearly throw herself from the attic window after reading them. Such is the gap between the sending and the reading of messages. Clichés can be lethal.

Rodolphe's sense of tedium in his liaison with Emma provokes a reflection on language that seems to speak to Flaubert's own deepest preoccupations as a writer, though as usual without offering us a clear insight into his position. It is worth an extended quotation:

> He had heard these things said to him so often that for him there was nothing original about them. Emma was like all other mistresses; and the charm of novelty, slipping off gradually like a piece of clothing, revealed in its nakedness the eternal monotony of passion, which always assumes the same forms and uses the same language. He could not perceive—this man of such broad experience—the difference in feelings that might underlie similarities of expression. Because licentious or venal lips had murmured the same words to him, he had little faith in their truthfulness; one had to discount, he thought, exaggerated speeches that concealed mediocre affections; as if the fullness of the soul did not sometimes overflow in the emptiest of metaphors, since none of us can ever express the exact measure of our needs, or our ideas, or our sorrows, and human speech is like a cracked kettle on which we beat out tunes for bears to dance to, when we long to move the stars to pity.

This passage appears to carry us beyond Rodolphe's limited capacity to understand the quality of Emma's passion—because the language in which it is expressed has been worn out by prior use—to Flaubert's more general reflection on the limits of language. But we may be left uncertain as to what it is about language that makes it inadequate to the expression of our needs, our ideas, and our desires. Is it simply that we can't find the right words? Or is language itself inherently limited? And perhaps also limiting: we cannot, as Nietzsche said, think outside the prison house of our language. Indeed, our thinking, our feeling, our wanting may themselves be determined by what language allows us to think, feel, desire. We are to that extent creations of language as much as users of language. We cannot find an outside of language, a breakout from the prison.

If that is what Flaubert suggests here, it points a fundamental paradox of his stance as a writer. He worked incessantly to perfect the language of what he was writing. He could spend days on a single paragraph, pacing his study overlooking the River Seine in the Norman town of Croisset, outside Rouen, bellowing his sentences aloud to judge their cadence and their beauty. He was a self-described hermit in the service of art. Yet he was haunted by the suspicion that all language was in the final analysis like Rodolphe's letter: nothing but commonplaces, places where people could gather with a sense of communicating with one another that was limited if not false. In his last novel, *Bouvard and Pécuchet*, left unfinished at his death, Flaubert experiments with the creative possibilities of the commonplace and the cliché, with the idea of a book made up exclusively of the words of others, so arranged that readers would have no idea whether they were to take it ironically or straight.

Already in *Madame Bovary*, Monsieur Homais, the pharmacist-philosopher, is presented as a kind of compendium of clichés, pompous, self-inflated, ultimately as limited in his "freethinking" as the priest Bournisien in his Catholic orthodoxy. The novel also foregrounds the speech of the herdlike collectivity, of the French pronoun *on*—one, no one in particular, everyone. As if to dramatize that the language of commonplace is at the very center of his representation of reality, Flaubert gives a full dramatic representation of its public role in the scene of the *comices agricoles*, the agricultural fair much anticipated by the residents of Yonville-l'Abbaye, the background against which Rodolphe undertakes his seduction of Emma. In the judging arena, the animals are described in loving detail. The judges on the other hand are "*des messieurs*": indistinguishable frock-coated gentlemen who thereafter are referred to as *on*. The speeches of the local notables are labored and cliché-ridden. In counterpoint, Rodolphe's caressing language of flattery shows up as equally banal, second-hand, expressive of nothing but a commonplace notion of seduction. Rodolphe has been claiming a natural affinity that has brought him and Emma together:

> And he grasped her hand; she did not withdraw it.
> "For all-around farming!—" cried the chairman.
> "A few days ago, for example, when I came to your house . . ."
> "To Monsieur Bizet, of Quincampoix—"
> "Did I know that I would be coming here with you?"
> "Seventy francs!"
> "A hundred times I've tried to leave you, and yet I've followed you, stayed with you."
> "For manures—"

This carefully orchestrated counterpoint continues, until we reach:

> "No! I will—won't I—have a place in your thoughts, in your life?"
> "Porcine breed, prize *ex aequo*: to Messieurs Lehérissé and Cullembourg, sixty francs!"
> Rodolphe squeezed her hand, and he felt it warm and trembling like a captive dove trying to fly away again . . .

Henry James described *Madame Bovary* as a world saved by style. That is right insofar as Flaubert's style makes everything, even a tedious small-town agricultural fair, engaging. But it perhaps not so much that the world is "saved" by style than that it is grasped as style, as a kind of oratorio of voices whose interplay and agon make the banal interesting. It is a linguistic medium that shows up Rodolphe's predictability and superficiality—as in his inability to understand the nuances of passion, in which, as noted above, he finds only an "eternal monotony"—and Emma's limitations as a reader of language that she wishes to see as sincere and transparent, when it is isn't that at all. Strikingly, the agricultural fair also produces one of the few characters in the novel who seems beyond our ironic reaction: Catherine Leroux, who receives a prize for "fifty-four years of servitude on the same farm." When the crowd pushes her forward to receive her prize, Catherine Leroux is nearly deaf and dumb. "Living so much among animals, she had taken on their muteness and placidity." Flaubert will develop this brief sketch of a long-suffering farm servant, limited in intelligence and sensibility yet also dignified, in his late novella *Un coeur simple* (*A Simple Heart*) written, he claimed, to show his dear friend the novelist George Sand that he could write something devoid of irony, something that demonstrated what she always said of him: that despite appearances, he had a good heart. Beyond irony lies a life of simple sensation, like that of animals.

Emma attempts to escape from the confines of her existence through her passion for Rodolphe, and then briefly in an effort to aggrandize her husband, Charles, when he undertakes an operation on Hippolyte's clubfoot, an excruciating failure; then, when Rodolphe drops her, she undergoes a brief experience of religious devotion, and then begins a new affair with Léon in the local capital, Rouen. But passion by its very nature seems unsustainable. Emma comes to each new tryst with Léon full of hope for extraordinary sensations, but more and more feels disappointed. Her attempts to resuscitate eros fail. And Flaubert writes this chilling summary aphorism: "Emma was rediscovering in adultery all the platitudes of marriage" (Emma retrouvait dans l'adultère toutes les platitudes du mariage). It is not surprising that the imperial prosecutor at Flaubert's trial was outraged by this sentence, which doubles the matter-of-fact reference to adultery (as itself something banal) with the claim that marriage itself is platitudinous—using in "platitude" a word we normally apply to language (like Charles's speech, "flat like a sidewalk"). Adultery, marriage: all part of the same set of clichés. In the former you find the same boredom as in the latter.

As her affair with Léon is reaching this impasse, Emma is also facing an accumulating mountain of debt. She has been borrowing from the merchant Lheureux, who supplies her with the luxury articles she needs to fulfill her idea of the glamorous life. She gives her lovers expensive accessories—Rodolphe gets a whip with an enameled handle, a signet, a scarf, a cigar case like the *vicomte*'s—and she adorns herself. It is important to her that her world be embellished by pretty things. But to define yourself in terms of expensive accessories becomes costly. Her attempts to borrow money fail. She is declared bankrupt, and the bailiffs come to inventory her possessions: "They examined her dresses, the linen, the dressing room; and her life itself, down to its most private recesses, was spread out at full length, like a cadaver being autopsied, under the eyes of these three men." Losing those things that have defined you presages a loss of self. Emma turns to suicide, by arsenic stolen from the pharmacist's store.

Here Flaubert's realism bears down—as realism often does—on the gruesome, perhaps in a kind of demonstration that to be honest and faithful to the real requires a detailing of the body in pain and sickness. Flaubert was a stickler for exactitude, and he researched carefully the effects of arsenic poisoning before writing Emma's death scene, with its convulsions, sweat, and vomitings. Death itself comes under the guise of the leprous blind beggar and his smutty song, "the hideous face of the wretched man looming like terror itself in the darkness of eternity." Just before the final convulsion that ends in her nothingness, the priest is summoned to administer last rites:

> Then he recited the *Misereatur* and the *Indulgentiam*, dipped his right thumb in the oil, and began the unctions: first on eyes, which had so coveted all earthly splendors; then on the nostrils, so greedy for mild breezes and the smells of love; then on the mouth, which had opened to utter lies, which had moaned with pride and cried out in lust; then on the hands, which had so delighted in the touch of smooth material; and lastly on the soles of the feet, which had once been so quick when she hastened to satiate her desires and which now would never walk again.

This is another passage, not surprisingly, that outraged the imperial prosecutor. This farewell to Emma's body uses the ancient rituals of the Church to remind us of the sensual uses of the bodily parts. Emma at the last is less a coherent self than a physiological bundle, a set of bodily sensations. And that might be the last word of realism.

The bleak aftermath of Emma's death cannot in any manner be seen as redemptive. Charles finds the cache of her love letters. Strangely, he comes to envy Rodolphe, to wish to be him, and when he encounters him sums up what has happened with supreme banality: "Fate is to blame!" (In French, it's more delectable: C'est la faute de la fatalité!) Charles's own death is followed by utter destitution, and Berthe—his and Emma's child, about whom we've heard very little in the novel—is sent off to work in a cotton mill, a bitter end to Emma's dreams of luxury. And the detestable Homais, in the last sentence of the novel, receives France's highest decoration, the Legion of Honor.

Like many nineteenth-century novels, *Madame Bovary* was published first in serial form, in six installments from October through December 1856, in the *Revue de Paris*, which took the liberty of deleting, without the author's permission, some passages that the editors found too risky. Flaubert was furious. The editors were not mistaken in their estimate of the risk, yet their deletions merely attracted the attention of the censors, who wanted to know what went on in what wasn't there. Characteristic here was the scene in which Léon seduces Emma during a long ride in a cab, its curtains closed, that wanders for hours through Rouen. We as readers see nothing of what is going on in the cab. Near the end of its perambulations, a "bare hand" emerges and scatters fragments of paper: the letter of rupture that Emma had prepared for Léon, now useless. But that "bare hand" (*une main nue*) was judged scandalous. Somehow that one small body part ("naked," because a proper woman would be wearing gloves) was more suggestive, more erotic than a full view through the cab windows. By censoring the scene, the editors of the *Revue de Paris* reinforced the fetishistic investment in the detail that suggests the absent whole.

So in January 1857, Flaubert was hauled into court, to listen to Maître Pinard denounce his work for outrage to public and religious morality. The prosecutor's tactic, following his plot summary of the novel, was largely to read selected passages, then to exclaim over their evident immorality. He provided in this manner something of a literary commentary, a reader's response to the effects produced by the novel. He lingered over the scene of Emma's seduction by Rodolphe, predictably; he was especially outraged by the passage describing Emma's beautification by adultery, the paragraph that begins: "Never had Madame Bovary been as lovely as she was during this time." It continues:

Her desires, her sorrows, her experience of pleasure, and her ever-youthful illusions had had the same effect as manure, rain, wind, and sun on a flower, developing her by degrees, and she was at last blooming in the fullness of her nature. Her eyelids seemed shaped expressly for those long, loving glances in which her pupils would disappear, while a heavy sigh would widen her delicate nostrils and lift the fleshy corners of her lips, shadowed, in the light, by a little dark down. Some artist skilled in depravity might have arranged the coil of her hair over the nape of her neck; it was looped in a heavy mass, carelessly, according to the chance dictates of her adulterous affair, which loosened it every day.

And it goes on from there. This makes adultery merely good fertilizer for a woman's beauty, the inevitable matter in which nature will do its work. The "artist skilled in depravity" seemed to stand in for Emma's creator, who gives this passage a final whiplash by ending with the bewitched gaze of the deceived husband: "Charles, as in the early days of his marriage, found her delicious and quite irresistible." The prosecutor indeed recognized the skill with which the depraved artist works: his portraits were "admirable so far as talent," but "execrable from a moral standpoint." Concerning Flaubert, he continued, there is "no covering, no veils, it's nature in all her crudity!"

That was something of a salute to Flaubert's realism—but in a context in which "realism" was still problematic. The court acquitted Flaubert, and his publishers, but not without a short sermon on the goals and the limits of novelistic representation: "the mission of literature should be to embellish and restore the spirit in uplifting intelligence and in purifying manners, more than imprinting disgust in offering a picture of the disorders that may exist in society." The judges considered themselves fully qualified to pronounce on "systems" of literature, ways of going about it. The pretext of painting characters and settings does not permit one to "reproduce" the errors of the chosen characters. Such a system applied to literary works and to painting "would lead to a realism which would be the negation of the beautiful and the good." Flaubert was guilty of "a vulgar and often shocking realism."

The court's judgment on *Madame Bovary* indicates how radical a concept realism still was in 1857. Though we now tend to extend the term backward—and Auerbach's *Mimesis* demonstrates the various ways in which reality has been represented since antiquity—the term really came into use in the 1850s. Balzac, for instance, who died in 1850, began to be called "a realist" around 1853. Then came the decisive contribution (which Flaubert's judge had in mind) of the painter Gustave Courbet, who at the time of the Exposition Universelle of 1855, designed to showcase Napoleon III's Second Empire, set up his own exhibit in what he labeled the Pavillon du Réalisme. His cause was taken up by the short-lived journal *Réalisme*, edited by Edmond Duranty, and his collaborator Champfleury (Jules Husson), whose article on Courbet in 1855 (later a book chapter) became the manifesto of a new movement. Courbet's paintings in his "House of Realism" do at times seem to be pictorial counterparts of *Madame Bovary*, especially his *Burial at Ornans* (fig. 1), which uses the size and scale of heroic history painting to portray a bedraggled group of bourgeois and peasants at a country funeral, pictured in an uneven line next to a hole in the ground that stands directly before the viewer of the canvas. Ugly, was the prime reaction to the *Burial*. Courbet's painting was faulted on three grounds at once: its subject matter was vulgar, ugly, inappropriate; its manner of representation was inept, unharmonious, poorly composed and executed; and its very choice of what painting should be used for was unacceptable: what claim to attention can this outsized painting make on us? Courbet's realism was a scandal, and so was Flaubert's.

Flaubert's later novels in the realist mode (setting aside his works on "exotic" subjects, such as ancient Carthage in *Salammbô* or the various early Christian sects and heresies of *The Temptation of Saint Anthony*) are less perfect in their outcome than *Madame Bovary*, though equally challenging. *Sentimental Education*, which he described as the history of his own generation, pushes Flaubert's impersonality and impassivity further still. Life, experience, and history (the novel takes on a major historical event, the Revolution of 1848) are grasped more and more by way of the language that various actors use. Flaubert's indirect discourse becomes so pervasive that everything asserted in the novel seems to be ascribed to someone—or no

Figure 1. Gustave Courbet, *A Burial at Ornans* (1849). Musée d'Orsay; photo credit: Erich Lessing / Art Resource, New York.

one: to that generalized *on*. It is often difficult to say who is responsible for any given utterance. Who speaks here? The reaction to the novel was largely negative and, especially, baffled. Readers wanted a clearer statement of the author's intentions. By the time of *Bouvard and Pécuchet*, language itself seems to have become the protagonist. The two copyists at the center of the novel take language with excessive literalism, attempting to realize its indications in reality, always with dismal results. That Flaubert apparently planned to make his *sottisier*—his collection of clichés that became known as the *Dictionary of Received Ideas*—part of the second volume of the novel reinforces our sense that it is not so much the world itself as the world as it is spoken that is now the prime object of Flaubert's realism. That, of course, was already on the way in *Madame Bovary*. "Emma was rediscovering in adultery all the platitudes of marriage." Marriage is conceived as a platitude, that is, a banal way of saying things, a cliché, a flatness of speech that then becomes the thing itself.

The scandal of Flaubert's realism continues to have force today because the language in which he creates it is so perfect to the task. I have often taught *Madame Bovary* to students and found that it remains fresh, radical, and unsettling today. We don't read *Madame Bovary* in the same context as Flaubert's contemporaries; the world has changed in so many ways since. And yet Emma's predicament remains astonishingly of our moment. The lessons of feminism have made her aspirations and frustrations only the more pertinent, her fate only the more disquieting. The court wanted Flaubert to show life, love, religion, and morality enhanced by more decorous lighting. We have been disillusioned of that enhancement (though we still yearn for glamor), forced to accept as true much of what Flaubert was the first to demonstrate. We are all, women and men, Emma Bovary.

WORKS CITED AND RECOMMENDED FURTHER READING

Note: Speeches of the prosecutor, defense attorney, and judge at Flaubert's trial are in almost all French editions of the novel, but not in the English translations. I cite these passages from the French edition, my translations.

Auerbach, Erich. *Mimesis: The Representation of Reality in Western Literature*. Translated by Willard R. Trask. Princeton, NJ: Princeton University Press, 1953.

Eliot, T. S. "Tradition and the Individual Talent." In *The Sacred Wood*. London: Methuen, 1920.

Flaubert, Gustave. *Correspondance*. Edited by Jean Bruneau and Yvan Leclerc. 5 vols. Bibliothèque de la Pléiade. Paris: Gallimard, 1973–2007.

———. *Letters of Gustave Flaubert*. Translated by Francis Steegmuller. 2 vols. London: Picador, 2001. (Quoted are letters to Mlle Leroyer de Chantepie, March 18, 1857; and to Louise Colet, December 23, 1853.)

———. *Madame Bovary*. Paris: Folio Classique, 2001.

———. *Madame Bovary*. Translated by Lydia Davis. New York: Viking, 2010.

Gaillard, Françoise. "Gustave Courbet et le réalisme: Anatomie de la reception critique d'une oeuvre; 'Un Enterrement à Ornans.'" *Revue d'Histoire Littéraire de la France* 6 (1980): 978–96.

James, Henry. "Gustave Flaubert" (introduction to *Madame Bovary*, 1902). In James, *Literary Criticism*, vol. 2. New York: Library of America, 1984.

Madame Bovary in the original French is available in a number of paperback editions, including Folio and Garnier/Flammarion. The best English translation is the latest, by Lydia Davis, used here, though that by Geoffrey Wall (for Penguin) is also fine.

The best way to extend acquaintance with Flaubert is through his wonderful letters, which contain most of his comments on his craft: see the two-volume selection of letters in English translation by Francis Steegmuller, *The Letters of Flaubert* (see above). See also Steegmuller, *Flaubert and Madame Bovary: A Double Portrait* (New York: Farrar, Straus and Giroux, 1966). A recent biography is Frederick Brown, *Flaubert* (New York: Little, Brown, 2006). The best biography is Michel Winock, *Flaubert* (Paris: Gallimard, 2013), still untranslated. A classic study of realism in *Madame Bovary* can be found in Erich Auerbach, *Mimesis* (see above). Also pertinent is Peter Brooks, *Realist Vision* (New Haven, CT: Yale University Press, 2005), 54–70. Among the most important books on Flaubert in English (and offering radically opposed views of him) are Victor Brombert, *The Novels of Flaubert* (Princeton, NJ: Princeton University Press, 1966); and Jonathan Culler, *Flaubert: The Uses of Uncertainty* (Ithaca, NY: Cornell University Press, 1974). An interesting study of the trial that followed publication is Dominick LaCapra, *Madame Bovary on Trial* (Ithaca, NY: Cornell University Press, 1982). An important study in social theory of the novel as defined by Flaubert is Pierre Bourdieu, *The Rules of Art* (Stanford, CA: Stanford University Press, 1996). See also Hugh Kenner, *Flaubert, Joyce and Beckett: The Stoic Comedians* (Boston: Beacon Press, 1962); Naomi Schor, *Reading in Detail: Aesthetics and the Feminine* (New York: Methuen, 1987); and Christopher Prendergast, *The Order of Mimesis: Balzac, Stendhal, Nerval and Flaubert* (Cambridge: Cambridge University Press, 1988).

Baudelaire, Verlaine, Rimbaud

Poetry, Consciousness, and Modernity

CLIVE SCOTT

History creates its own anxieties, creates a need to recognize evolutions and locate turning points. It is comforting to be able to identify Charles Baudelaire (1821–67) as the essential pivot between a Romantic past and an emergent modernism, and then to propose that Verlaine and Rimbaud consolidated his initiatives. In his notes on Baudelaire, Jules Laforgue, a poet celebrated for his adoption by Pound and Eliot, obligingly uses the phrase "[He was] the first [who] [to] ..." eight times. If the revolution of 1848, in which Baudelaire briefly took part, failed to establish republicanism, it shifted the sense in which poetry itself might be revolutionary: not as an incendiary vehicle of moral indignation or exhortation, but as the linguistic engineer of a revolution in being and consciousness. Baudelaire was the diagnostician of a new existential condition, which might principally be traced to displacements in urban mentality, in a Paris undergoing radical change at the hands of Napoleon III's prefect of the Seine, Georges Haussmann. This condition was animated and tormented by inner contradiction, by moral unsteadiness, by sudden temperamental shifts between cruelty and apathy (spleen),[1] by spiritual aspiration and dyspeptic cynicism, by mysticism and critical lucidity in creation (note the influence of Poe on Baudelaire's compositional thinking), by selflessness and hypocrisy, by impulsiveness and addiction, and by an irony that was as much a lifeline as a rite of self-laceration. Irony is one of the weapons of dandyism, that "cult of the self" and of the will, that "pleasure of shocking and proud satisfaction in never being shocked," which Baudelaire cultivated as a necessary defensive carapace. Correspondingly, the poet's relationship with his reader is fundamentally changed: "Hypocrite lecteur, mon semblable, mon frère" (Hypocrite reader, my fellow creature, my brother) ("Au lecteur" / "To the Reader"). With the possibility of mutual contempt, the old contract of complicity between poet and audience turns to distrust, and the nagging fear of reciprocal indictment promotes nervous suspicion and unease.

These are some of the respects and senses in which we can identify Baudelaire as the first of the "modernists." But this condition, and the new relationship with the reader it entailed, might not only be expressed, it might also be transformed, by the power of language. Language, for Baudelaire, also has the capacity to found a new inclusivity, to create "correspondences" and morphings between the senses (synesthesia), between the natural and the *surnaturel*,[2] between the material and spiritual worlds, by the device of what Laforgue calls his "immense comparisons," by universal analogy, and indeed by the appropriation of suggestive triggers from the world of women (perfume, hair, deportment, jewelry). Thus, just as Baudelaire takes possession of himself, concentrates the human condition in his own self-consciousness, so equally he cultivates a multiplication of self, a dissolution of self into other kinds of consciousness. Sometimes this free migration of consciousness relates to the *surnaturel*, an expansion and intensification of the perceptual capacity, often associated with the "artificial paradises" of drugs, but by no means dependent on them:

> Edgar Poe says ... that the effect of opium on the senses is to endow the whole of nature with a "supernatural" interest that gives every object a deeper, more willed, more despotic meaning. Even without resorting to opium, who has not known these admirable hours, ... when the sky, of a more transparent blue, opens up depths like an abyss more infinite still, where sounds have musical resonances, where colors speak, where perfumes tell of worlds of ideas? Well, Delacroix's painting seems to me the translation of these fine days of the spirit.... Like nature perceived by ultrasensitive nerves, it reveals *surnaturalisme*.

At other times, however, this self-multiplication has a social orientation and becomes what in the prose poem "Les Foules" ("Crowds") is called "un bain de multitude" (immersion in the multitude), a "universelle communion" (universal communion), a "sainte prostitution de l'âme" (sacred prostitution of the soul), or, more specifically, the pride "d'avoir vécu et souffert dans d'autres que moi-même" (of having lived and suffered in individuals other than myself) ("Les Fenêtres" / "Windows"). Writing itself, almost by its very nature, is the encounter of the prostitute and the dandy, where being spoken by language, and surrendering to it, is an indivisible partner of linguistic mastery and self-control: "Of the evaporation and centralization of the *Self.* That phrase says everything," as Baudelaire puts it in his intimate journal *Mon cœur mis à nu* (*My Heart Laid Bare*).

Barbey d'Aurevilly's article on Baudelaire's *Les fleurs du mal* (*The Flowers of Evil*) of July 1857, designed to add weight to the poet's case in answering the charge of offending public morals, attributes to the collection "a secret architecture." In December 1861, in a letter to Vigny, Baudelaire declares that the only praise he looks for in relation to *Les fleurs du mal* is that it should be recognized not "purely as an album" but as a properly framed structure, with beginning and end. Many studies have devoted themselves to revealing this architecture, picking out the intricate thematic weave and tracing the existential progress of an unquiet mind. I want briefly to suggest the foundations of an architecture more secret still, Baudelaire's writerly metabolism, the operations of his linguistic psyche, the drives of his creative organism, to which he himself refers when he speaks of rhetorics and prosodies as "a collection of rules necessitated by the very organization of the spiritual being." This acute sense that the forms of poetic language have psycho-existential origins, that these forms are not sublimations of drives, nor achievements of self-transcendence, but descents into the instinctive self, is a watershed in the history of poetic writing. Not only does it compel us to recast formal conventions as profound expressive needs, it also alerts us to the reconfiguring of consciousness in the invention of new forms. Over the coming pages, some of the indices of these psycho-existential connections will be traced, in all three of this chapter's poets, in the details of punctuational habits, syntactic and rhythmic propensities, and lexical and acoustic choices.

We might begin by considering Baudelaire's attraction to the exclamation mark and his deep mistrust of enumeration. For Baudelaire, the exclamation mark is not just that sign of vocal amplitude that accompanies apostrophe, or the imperative, or indeed the exclamatory; it is also part of a neurotic condition and a hyperbolic imagination, with other modal values: for example, the urgently revelatory:

> Et l'obscur Ennemi qui nous ronge le cœur
> Du sang que nous perdons croît et se fortifie!
>
> ("L'ennemi")

> (And the shadowy Enemy who gnaws at our hearts
> Thrives and grows strong on the blood we shed!)
>
> ("The Enemy")

the optative:

> Afin qu'à mon désir tu ne sois jamais sourde!
>
> ("La chevelure")

> (So that you are never deaf to my desire!)
>
> ("The Head of Hair")

the resigned, or desperate:

> Et mon âme dansait, dansait, vieille gabarre
> Sans mâts, sur une mer monstrueuse et sans bords!
>
> ("Les sept vieillards")

> (And my soul, an aging, mastless barge,
> Danced, danced on a monstrous and limitless sea!)
>
> ("The Seven Old Men")

Through the exclamation mark we reach for the imperiousness of certain drives in Baudelaire's temperament, an imperiousness he would impose on us in our turn; we remember those words from an earlier quotation: "a deeper, more willed, more despotic meaning." But this gives a converse poignancy, or quiet assurance, or tight-lipped control, or vocal lassitude, to those poems without exclamation marks: for example, "La vie antérieure" ("The Previous Life"), "Parfum exotique" ("Exotic Perfume"), the four "Spleen" poems (only one exclamation mark between them), "Remords posthume" ("Posthumous Remorse").

Most instances of the exclamation mark endorse Baudelaire's more general susceptibility to the amplified and expressionistic, to be found equally in the capital letter of the personified abstraction (allegory), in his love of caricature, in his defense of makeup, and indeed in the heightened consciousness of *surnaturalisme*. As he himself acknowledges, "As far as art is concerned, I confess that I am no hater of excess; moderation has never seemed to me the sign of a vigorous artistic nature." If we think of Baudelaire as a melodramatic writer, then the melodrama lies not only in his pressing need to identify, to name, the motors of moral activity, but also in his need to break bounds, in his exasperated pursuit of truths and experiences hidden from us.

In "Le peintre de la vie moderne" ("The Painter of Modern Life"), Baudelaire addresses the fear of being overwhelmed by detail. If "pêle-mêle" is one term that captures this anarchic assault, "bric-à-brac confus" (jumbled bric-à-brac) ("Le cygne" / "The Swan") is another, and enumeration is its characteristic linguistic manifestation. But the existential threat carried by enumeration is not confined to detail:[3]

> Mais parmi les chacals, la panthères, les lices,
> Les singes, les scorpions, les vautours, les serpents,
> Les monstres glapissants, hurlants, grognants,
>   rampants,   [2>4 // 2>2>2]
> Dans la ménagerie infâme de nos vices, . . .

> (But among the jackals, the panthers, the bitch-hounds,
> The monkeys, the scorpions, the vultures, the snakes,
> The yelping, howling, grunting, crawling monsters,
> In the squalid menagerie of our vices, . . .)

Enumeration extended beyond discursive control, as here in "Au lecteur," ousts the poet from his own text and undoes structure (hierarchy, subordination): the third line in this stanza, for example, begins to sound unaccountably long and breaks the alexandrine's characteristic four-measure shape; if the present participial form is the sustain pedal, then the poet's voice is literally drowned out.

And if we find Baudelaire difficult to define as a political animal, partly because his views are temperamental rather than ideological, then his changeable attitude to the urban crowd is a significant feature of our uncertainty: he may, like Constantin Guys (1805–92), the journalistic graphic artist who is the subject of "Le peintre de la vie moderne," have the vocation to "*marry the crowd*," but the enumerative assault of detail is an analogue of crowd mentality: "An artist with a perfect sense of form, but used to exercising his memory and imagination above all, then finds himself as if assailed by a riot of details, all demanding justice with the fury of a crowd in love with absolute justice." The art of writing, it seems, is in itself an indictment of "absolute equality." Memory and imagination need a site other than the street to reaffirm their powers, and that site is the poet's/artist's lamplit room/studio, to which Guys each evening withdraws: "Now whilst others are sleeping, [Guys] is bent over his table, darting at a sheet of paper the same look that, shortly before, he darted at objects, fencing with his pencil, his pen, his brush, splashing water from the glass up to the ceiling, wiping his pen on his shirt, hurried, violent, busied, as if afraid that the image might elude him, quarrelsome though alone, and falling over himself." Baudelaire assures us that Guys achieves the distilled order and harmony he is looking for. But two troubling factors persist: this creative process is still haunted by breathless enumeration; and Guys is working with the feverish speed of a *plein-air* artist. The street is beginning to invade the room.

The room, then, instead of acting as an aesthetic refuge, may become a place of archaizing self-delusion ("Paysage" / "Landscape"); it may be powerless to undo the frightening hallucination of the street ("Les sept vieillards"); it may surrender its promise of a timeless "supreme life" to Time and its "démoniaque cortège de Souvenirs, de Regrets, de Spasmes, de Peurs, d'Angoisses, de Cauchemars, de Colères et de Névroses" (diabolical procession of Memories, Regrets,

Convulsions, Fears, Agonies, Nightmares, Rages, Neuroses)—that is, to lawless Enumeration personified ("La chambre double" / "The Double Room"). Reading through the totality of Baudelaire's oeuvre, one might conclude that as the room becomes increasingly subject to the street, so the imagination and the memory become increasingly subject to the nerves and to temperament. Proposing this shift of emphasis suggests that capacities of mind shift toward psychophysiological responses, that the exercise of faculties shifts to the "sursauts" (sudden jolts) of susceptibility and consciousness, that continuities of memory shift to the discontinuities of passing sensation, that character traits shift to drives, intensities, nervous disorder. But even in these shifts, Baudelaire clings to older values.

If Baudelaire found the "recueillement" (quiet self-collection) of the room more difficult to indulge—reflecting perhaps his own nomadic existence, as a perpetual fugitive from creditors—and the street an increasingly necessary habitat, what kind of street is it? The first line of "Les petites vieilles" ("The Little Old Women"), "Dans les plis sinueux des vieilles capitales" (In the sinuous folds of old capital cities), gives us a glimpse of the old Paris of narrow, winding alleys, the multicursal labyrinth that confirms the city's "inner" femininity, its secret anatomy, its unencompassable variousness. This is a medieval city in tune with Baudelaire's allegorical and melodramatic propensities. This is the Paris that Haussmann had not entirely eradicated in his masculinist enterprise of penetrative street-planning, panoptic possession, and easy arterial access. Haussmann's limited range of classicizing building models did not manage to expunge architectural heterogeneity; but his newly spacious Paris seemed to generate crowds, noise ("A une passante" / "To a Woman Passing By"), traffic volume ("Perte d'auréole" / "Loss of Halo" and "Le crépuscule du soir" / "Evening Twilight"), and the kaleidoscopic sensation and perceptual acceleration we see in Guys's work. Existentially, Baudelaire is caught in between, on a building site as it were ("Le cygne"), not in a new Paris, but in a Paris in metamorphosis, and this "in between" serves only to mobilize and agitate the polarizations to which he is subject. The formal and generic uncertainties of the prose poems in *Le spleen de Paris*, published posthumously in 1869, express something of this agitation.

In the prose poems, the artistic heroisms of Balzac and Delacroix give way to the mock-heroics of *croquis parisiens* (Parisian sketches). Just as he numbers Guys among the minor poets—and perhaps he feels the same about Manet—so the Baudelaire of *Le spleen de Paris* seems to cast himself in a similar role. The prose poem dislocates canonic forms, acts dysfunctionally in relation to literary norms, and has no clear audience, despite a striking sociopolitical immediacy; its very generic multiplicity, the perverse instability of its streetwise morality, and its rootless and variational relation to life mark it out as a new art of intersections. In rejecting rhyme and metrical measure, the prose poem rejects mnemonicity; it does not ask to be remembered, but rather puts the reader under the pressure of immediate comprehension and consumption, the pressure to be coincident with itself in the moment of reading. Rhythm in the prose poem does not, like meter in verse, map out the way in which the poem delivers itself and is to be digested. Instead it improvises itself in the reader's mind, questions itself, interrupts its own continuities, interrogates its own impulses, is the ever-changing flux of the individual voice and of the crowd. There are no longer prosodic rules, but only performative choices (choices of tempo, pausing, phrasing, accentuation, tone, intonation), a whole theater of available dictions.

It is tempting to see the later Baudelaire as a proto-impressionist: in his insistence that beauty has within it an element of the transient and time-specific; in his sensitivity to the molecular dialogue of colors under changing conditions; in his celebration of the poetry of the street; in his flirtation with telegraphic and notational styles; in his championing of the "minor" art of Guys and his friendship with Manet. But he is just as much a proto-symbolist: in his pursuit of heightened consciousness, of *surnaturalisme*; in his cultivation of synesthesia and universal analogy; in his sense of the constant trafficking between the conscious, the unconscious, the prenatal, the archetypal; in his vision of reality as a palimpsest of sedimented memories and existences (Baudelaire rediscovered himself in Poe and Wagner), and as an elasticated temporality. Or he is just as much a proto-decadent: in his dandyism; in his conflicted need for, and ironic self-dissociation from, his audience; in his temperamental veering between febrility and neurasthenia; in his strategies of outrage and shock; in his inability to surmount the Fall, and the clock of mortality, by the pursuit of immediate sensation and the erasure of memory. But Baudelaire is as much modern(ist) in his irresolutions as he is in his anticipations.

❖ ❖ ❖ ❖

Paul Verlaine (1844–96), in his suite of articles for *L'Art* (November–December 1865), already had the measure of Baudelaire's modernity, describing him as "modern man with his sharpened and vibrant senses, his painfully subtle mind . . . in a word the *bilio-nervous* type par excellence, as H[ippolyte] Taine would say." Further on, he notes that if, in Baudelaire, "the nerves from time to time derange the intellect, increasing tenfold the action of the senses," there is always the countervailing pull toward order. Verlaine in many senses conforms to the same type. But if Baudelaire occupies a space of polarizations, Verlaine's preferred habitat is that of indeterminacy. Baudelaire presents a poet pushed to the periphery, at home among outcasts, an urban beachcomber working alongside the rag-picker; but he takes strength from his defiant aristocracy of spirit (dandyism). Verlaine has no such consolation; his is a position of purer self-deprecation, of self-pity without an immediately visible cause. His poetry generates no social context; poems such as "La soupe du soir" ("Evening Soup") in *Jadis et naguère* (*Long Ago and Not So Long Ago*, 1884–85) are exceptional. For that reason, Verlaine's poems often seem to come into existence ex nihilo, summoned but unmotivated, and thus, however firm their structure, never quite knowing what their agenda is or how they might resolve themselves.

Much is made, justifiably, of Verlaine's cultivation of the *vers impair*, the line with an uneven number of syllables:[4]

De la musique avant toute chose,	4 // 3>2
Et pour cela préfère l'Impair	4 // 2>3
Plus vague et plus soluble dans l'air,	2>4>3
Sans rien en lui qui pèse ou qui pose.	4 // 2>3

("Art poétique," *Jadis et naguère*)

(Music, above all else,
And for that prefer the uneven line

Vaguer and more evanescent in the air,
With nothing in it which weighs or stays.)

("The Art of Poetry," *Jadis et naguère*)

Baudelaire had made occasional use of the *impair*—for example, in "L'invitation au voyage" ("Invitation to Travel") (5/7); "Le poison" ("Poison") (12/7); "Chanson d'après-midi" ("Afternoon Song") (7); and "La musique" ("Music") (12/5)—but principally either to allude to its connections with the *chanson*, or to create discordant relationships with the alexandrine or octosyllable.

In Verlaine's hands, its expressivity derives much more from its inherent capacity for rhythmic uncertainty. While the line of an even number of syllables either balances equal measures against each other (3>3, 4>4) or leaves between measures a clear-cut, two-syllable (or more) differentiation (2>4, 3>5, 5>1), the *impair* acts against equilibrium of measures and allows consecutive use of measures with only one syllable's difference (2>3, 4>3, 4>5). In such circumstances, the poem is likely to become a rhythmic mirage, where the reader strains to hear the rhythmical contours, a design, or a controlling authority. Not only that, but we tend to half-hear, or wish to hear, the parisyllabic neighbors on either side of the imparisyllabic line: the enneasyllables of "Art poétique" make us think predominantly of slightly down-at-heel, innumerate decasyllables (with the caesura at the fourth syllable); but occasionally, as here in the third line, we may also hear, thanks to the absence of caesura, an octosyllable—but a miscalculated octosyllable, embarrassed by a slight syllabic surplus. The eleven-syllable lines of "Ariettes oubliées IV" ("Forgotten Ariettas IV") in *Romances sans paroles* (*Songs without Words*, 1874), with their 5//6 divisions, suggest alexandrines with insufficient initial momentum:

Soyons deux enfants, // soyons deux jeunes filles
Éprises de rien//et de tout étonnées

(Let us be two children, let us be two young girls
Smitten with nothing and dazzled by everything)

The *impair* can produce a rhythmic equivalent of the *glissando*, or of microtonal variation, whose slippages and slidings demand the keenest ear.

But we are straining to detect small tonal shifts as much in vocal quality as in rhythm; and qualities of voice are to be found as much in impersonal, nonhuman agencies, as in human ones, often without any apparent enunciatory source:

Ô le frêle et frais murmure!	3>2>2
Cela gazouille et susurre,	4>3
Cela ressemble au cri doux	4>3
Que l'herbe agitée expire . . .	2>3>2

("Ariettes oubliées I")

(O the frail and fresh murmur!
It warbles and whispers,
It resembles the soft cry
Exhaled by the buffeted grass . . .)

This experimentation with vocal quality is also apparent in Verlaine's cultivation of poems with only one rhyme-gender (for example, "Mandoline" ["Mandolin"], "En sourdine" ["Muted"], Ariettes oubliées II, IV, VIII, IX) or with gender alternating between stanzas rather than, as is the rule, between consecutive rhyme-pairs (for example, "L'amour par terre" ["Love Thrown Down"], "Chevaux de bois" ["Roundabout Horses"], "Birds in the Night"). Feminine rhymes, where the rhyme-word ends with an uncounted mute "e" syllable, will tend to be closed syllables (vowel + consonant [+ e])—*brises/grises, plaine/incertaine, langoureuse/amoureuse*—and thus, it is argued, more prolonged, dying or reverberative, more poignant, more tender. Masculine rhymes, on the other hand, tend to be open syllables (consonant + vowel)—*vent/souvent* (/vã/, /suvã/), *jaloux/fous* (/ʒalu/, /fu/), *tombera/chantera*—and are thus reckoned to be more abrupt, harder on the ear, more uncompromising. Rhyme gender may generate sexist interpretations, but it allows Verlaine to explore the homosexual and the transsexual and all the ambiguities of gender.

But this cultivation of fine-grained rhythmic and tonal variation should not mask an equal and opposite effect:

Rien de plus cher que la chanson grise
Où l'Indécis au Précis se joint

("Art poétique")

(Nothing more prized than the ambiguous song
In which the indecisive and the precise conjoin)

What is this "Précis"? Among those elements that contribute to it, one might mention the dislocated, or dissociated, adjective. "Après trois ans" ("Three Years After") in *Poèmes saturniens* (*Poems under Saturn*, 1866), in which the poet revisits the garden of his childhood, ends:

Même j'ai retrouvé // debout la Velléda
Dont le plâtre s'écaille // au bout de l'avenue,
    —Grêle, parmi l'odeur // fade du réséda.

(I even found the Velleda still standing
Its plaster flaking at the end of the avenue,
    —Fragile, amidst the sickly smell of mignonette.)

Here "Grêle" is pushed into isolation, its antecedent peculiarly uncertain; were it not for the dash, one would naturally associate it with "avenue." It is almost as if this last line refers to the poet himself. Verlaine uses both the line break and the caesura to generate these dislocations, these *rejets*, these words pushed out on a limb, so that, as Jean-Pierre Richard puts it, "Their charm is precisely to be free of this origin . . . and to enjoy an autonomous existence, shorn of all ties, a life which is theirs alone." So here, too, the adverb "debout" is thrust from "retrouvé" by the caesura, just as "fade" is thrust from "odeur." In all instances we find ourselves poised between the suspension prior to the break (line-ending or caesura) and the intensified encounter with the *rejet*, as it seemingly enters into a more distilled, more sovereign version of itself. In "Le paysage dans le cadre des portières" ("The Landscape in the Frames of the Carriage-Doors"), the train creates a whirlwind, which pushes the adjectives ("mince," "étrange") into momentary and stark relief:

Où tombent les poteaux // minces du télégraphe
Dont les fils ont l'allure // étrange d'un paraphe.

(Where fall the slender telegraph poles
Whose wires have the strange movement of a [calligraphic]
     flourish.)

But, more frequently, the precise and the imprecise are not so easily differentiated.

There are two further elements to be extracted from the lines of "Après trois ans." First, the sonority in /ɛ/ ("Grêle"). This unrounded, low-mid, half-open front vowel seems to activate, to summon up, a significant strain in the Verlainian lexicon: "frêle" (frail), "frais" (fresh), "faible" (weak), "blême" (pale), "incertaine" (uncertain), "verser" (pour), "bercer" (lull/rock/cradle), "se plaignent" (complain), "aigre" (sour/shrill/bitter), "maigre" (thin), "détresse" (distress), "cruel." To listen to the music of this verse is not only to listen for the acoustic susceptibilities of a particular psycho-affective organism, but also to hear the processes of acoustic modulation and sedimentation. Sounds act as agents of permeability, ineluctably drifting across the whole genealogy of their relations:

Je *fai*s souvent ce rêve étrange et pénétrant
D'une femme inconnue, et que j'*ai*me, et qui m'*ai*me
                              ("Mon rêve familier")

(I often have this strange and penetrating dream
Of an unknown woman, whom I love, and who loves me)
                              ("My Familiar Dream")

This suffusive influence of sound summons questions of tone, tempo, timbre, intonation, and all those other features of voice that for Verlaine constitute inflexion and that, for him, listening anxiously to the voices in his own poetry, are a constant, nervous preoccupation. What does all this "music" resolve itself into: "plainte" (lament), "murmure" (murmur), "romance" ([love-]song), "chant" (singing/melody), "antienne" (antiphon), "cri" (cry), "gémissement" (moaning), "refrain," "voix lointaine, et calme, et grave" (distant voice, both calm and grave), "voix douce et sonore, au frais timbre angélique" (soft and sonorous voice, with a fresh, angelic timbre), "musique fine" (delicate music)? On his answer, his happiness and destiny may depend.

The other element here is Verlaine's favoring of the preposition "parmi." How can "parmi" be used with a singular noun?

> C'est tous les frissons des bois
> Parmi l'étreinte des brises
>
> ("Ariettes oubliées I")

> (It is all the tremors of the woods
> Amidst the tight embrace of breezes)

And how can one be "parmi" experiences as intangible or generalized as "odeur" and "étreinte"? The simple answer is that "parmi" is not just a passive (unlocatable) position; it actively projects multiplicity or multifacetedness into the singular and invests the intangible with proximity and palpability. The poet-subject may often seem to be "parmi" the sense of his own words.

Is it useful to think of Verlaine as an impressionist? Yes, because of the tension he creates between sensation and mood, between the individual word thrown into relief and the evanescent (musical) envelope, between the individual brushstroke and the overall blendings. Not only has Verlaine radically shifted attention from the object, the percept, to the perceiving consciousness, but this perceiving consciousness relates neither to a unified identity nor to an autobiographical narrative—it floats free, no longer sure of its anchorages or points of reference. If one thinks of Verlaine's verse music as the equivalent of impressionist light, then one might say that it distributes and nuances verbal coloration; not that verbal meaning is cancelled, but its importance lies less in its representational capacity than in its communication of perceptual tonalities. If the Baudelairian street-artist is propelled by the speed necessary to the gathering of visual information, the dynamics of Verlainian utterance derive from the volatility of atmospheric conditions. About his symbolism, on the other hand, we might be less certain. While he has many of the symptoms (the inhabitation of dream, synesthesia, the cultivation of silence and its suggestibility), his verse lacks a metaphysical extension, wrapped around in mysticity though it may be.

Commentators tend to confine Verlaine's poetic achievements to his collections up to and including *Jadis et naguère* (1884–85), with some misgivings about the quality of the poems of anticipated marriage to Mathilde Mauté (*La bonne chanson* [*The Good Song*], 1870) and those of his Catholic conversion while in prison in Belgium (1873–75), principally at Mons, after wounding Rimbaud (*Sagesse* [*Wisdom*], 1880). There are certainly voices, among both critics and translators, that argue persuasively against the wholesale abandonment of the later collections; but there is still a case to be made that, by the later 1880s, Verlaine's poetic vein had been worked out. By this time, he had exhausted the liberties (*vers libéré*) he wished to take with regular versification, liberties that stopped well short of free verse (*vers libre*). Even after the emergence of *vers libre* in 1886, he wrote, in August 1887, to Gustave Kahn, one of the pioneers of *vers libre*, along with Laforgue, that while he applauded the flouting of overpunctilious rhyming and syllable-counting, "I am nonetheless in favor of very flexible rules, but rules even so." Those existential patterns that we come to recognize as characteristic of Verlaine could only be repeated: an emotional dependency countervailed by an urge to freedom (from all responsibility) that could not, however, be sustained; a plaintive self-pity without clearly visible causes; a resistance to the developmental in the interests of the dispersively enumerative; failures of identification in the face of the dubitative and the evanescent; the surfacing of memories that the poet does not particularly want to remember, or has no particular reason to remember. Yet it is Verlaine's ability to capture the ripplings of consciousness at its lower levels, the kinetics of the psyche, the flickering modulations of affective reaction in a subjectivity without a subject, in a sentience divorced from a sentient being, that constitutes his poetic distinction.

∗ ∗ ∗ ∗

There are, broadly speaking, two ways of thinking about the *excessive* expressive force by which poetry seeks to empower language: either it projects language beyond itself, infralinguistically or ultralinguistically; or it increases the intensity, the interiority, of language itself. The latter way naturally preoccupies itself with the recovery of identity through language's own recovery of identity. The former is concerned with the adventures of consciousness prior to, or after, identity. Verlaine might be seen as a poet of infralinguistic projection, a poet of preverbal sounds (murmurings, rustlings, whisperings, pure vocality) and emotions (semiconscious, affective states), whose Catholic conversion constitutes an unconvincing flirtation with the ultralinguistic.

Arthur Rimbaud (1854–91), on the other hand, may seem a hunter after the ultralinguistic, not so much in a metaphysical sense—his hells and paradises are more immanent—as among alternative consciousnesses:

Il n'aimait pas Dieu; mais les hommes, qu'au soir fauve,
Noirs, en blouse, il voyait rentrer dans le faubourg
("Les poètes de sept ans")

(He did not love God; but the men he saw, in the tawny
    evenings,
Dark-faced, in overalls, coming home to the faubourg)
(Seven-Year-Old Poets)

But Rimbaud is not only still shackled by the pull of autobiographical identity (even if fictional), by virtue of which he is a rebel, a social outlaw, one of the colonized, *and* a master of creative ceremonies, but his divorce from himself ("Car Je est un autre" [Because I is an other], letter to Paul Demeny, May 15, 1871) is also both a transformation of self into other *and* a transformation of self into its own capacities ("If brass—wakes up as bugle, it's not its fault. That's clear enough to me: I am present at the flowering of my own thought," letter to Demeny). Grafting oneself onto other perceptual consciousnesses and cultivating the consciousness of self look like variations on the Baudelairean duality of the "evaporation" and "centralization of the *Self.*" But, for Rimbaud, Baudelaire, despite being the "first seer," is still constrained by an "over-artistic milieu" and by a form that is "mean-spirited" (letter to Demeny). Both poets use the word "charité" to describe their prostitutions of the soul, but Rimbaud's is more monstrous, more self-deformative—was this a motive in his stormy relationship with Verlaine?—and his monitoring of his own consciousness does not have the ironic poise of dandyism in view, but rather the development of multisensory thought-in-language as the key to a universal language that "will be of the soul for the soul, synthesizing everything [*tout*], perfumes, sounds, colors, thought latching onto thought and tugging" (letter to Demeny). Different forms of "tout" recur like a mantra in the Rimbaldian enterprise: totality is a presupposition of all phenomena, and the "unknown" he invokes is both a sharing of consciousness and the sense of the infinite extendability of all experience. This is all a thoroughly symbolist project. Perhaps the poet will be able to outflank his own existential contradictions in the very inclusivity (the *tout* perspective) of his perceptual range.

Une saison en enfer (*A Season in Hell*, 1873) addresses this persistent quandary. Rimbaud seems, at one and the same time, to be subject to a kind of creative megalomania ("seer") or control freakdom ("J'ai seul la clef de cette parade sauvage" [I alone have the key to this barbarous sideshow] ["Parade" / "Sideshow"]; "Je réservais la traduction" [I reserved the rights to translation] ["Délires II: Alchimie du verbe" / "Deliriums II: Verbal Alchemy"]); a childlike wonder in face of the universe's capacity so variegatedly to animate itself despite him; and an unscrupulous kidnapper of alien consciousnesses: "A chaque être, plusieurs *autres* vie me semblaient dues" (To each being, several *other* lives seemed to me due) ("Délires II: Alchimie du verbe"). These inner contradictions are perhaps expressed in the desperate paradox of his creative enterprise: "un long, immense et raisonné *dérèglement* de *tous les sens*" (a long, immense and reasoned *disordering* of *all the senses*) (letter to Demeny).

What makes Rimbaud exhilarating reading is his pursuit of recklessness, by which we might understand four things: (1) a readiness to start from scratch without obligations and limitations; (2) the adoption of values without reflection, with the consequence that abstractions/concepts, for example, come directly into being as living forces rather than being merely called upon as moral points of reference:

> Sur les routes, par les nuits d'hiver, sans gîte, sans habits, sans pain, une voix étreignait mon cœur gelé: Faiblesse ou force: te voilà, c'est la force. Tu ne sais ni où tu vas ni pourquoi tu vas, entre partout, réponds à tout. ("Mauvais sang")

> (On the highways, on winter nights, without resting-place, or clothing, or bread, a voice squeezed my frozen heart: Weakness or strength: here you are, that's strength. You know neither where you are going nor why, enter everywhere, respond to everything. ["Bad Blood"];

(3) being unreliable and, above all, at odds with himself, but as a mode of assertive independence; (4) the cultivation of the dislocative and the interruptive. Looking back over these qualities, one might add that the readiness to start from scratch reveals itself in the shifting emphasis of his titles: while the 1869–71 poems are largely generated out of specific occasions or a will to (satiric) portraiture, retrospective and summarizing, the *Illuminations* (composed 1873–75?) are like leaps into differing kinds of experience, unprejudiced, uncompromising, with unpredictable outcomes: "Mystique" ("Mystical"), "Aube" ("Dawn"), "Barbare" ("Barbaric"). The unreflective harnessing of embodied concepts—"Derrière l'arête de droite la ligne des orients, des progrès" (Behind the ridge to the right the line of orients, of advances) ("Mystique")—means that the passage between categories (abstract/concrete, common/proper) is always open, that this is a world of sudden adjustments of dimension, or of perceptual and existential capacity. But if it is unreflectiveness that allows these channels, these possibilities, to remain open, then any falling back into reflection, into stock-taking, may bring it all to nothing, to an artifice, to a system, to an exercise of will, to a hypocrisy. This is the labyrinthine territory that *Une saison en enfer* explores, the territory of the apologist and testamentary writer. This is the territory where being at odds with oneself is most clearly enacted: defiance, self-justification, scorn,

self-derision, indignation, cut through by sudden bouts of frustrated impatience. But the *Illuminations*, it seems, provide a way out of this impasse: being at odds with oneself might resolve itself into a fruitful diversity, into cross-categorial and cross-generic nomadism, a condition in which different states of consciousness might not, after all, be reciprocally disqualifying.

The fourth element of this recklessness—the dislocative and the interruptive—takes us in another direction. In Rimbaud's revisions of *Une saison en enfer* one finds, among other things, a change in the punctuation, with an increase in the incidence of the dash. Rimbaud's use of the dash has received consistent critical attention and has significance not as a tool to fulfill specific syntactical purposes, but rather as a signifier for the presiding mentality of whole texts. The dash has a dislocative function, inasmuch as it suggests sudden ruptures in psychic or perceptual levels or perspectives, inasmuch as it turns smooth discursive surfaces into faceted ones, inasmuch as, by its intimation of speed, it indicates unpredictable veerings of thought, or a will to get to a point. It does not necessarily interrupt the syntax of an ongoing sentence—it sometimes appears with other punctuation, sometimes not—but it does interrupt in the sense that it is a perceptual eruption that cannot be postponed or withstood:

> Une matinée couverte, en Juillet. Un goût de cendres vole dans l'air;—une odeur de bois suant dans l'âtre,—les fleurs rouies—le saccage des promenades—la bruine des canaux par les champs— pourquoi pas déjà les joujoux et l'encens? ("Phrases")

> (An overcast morning, in July. A taste of ashes is borne on the air;—a smell of wood sweating in the hearth,—the retted flowers—the devastation of the walks—the misty drizzle of the canals across the fields—why not toys and incense indeed?) ("Phrases")

The dash, then, is like something injected into a text whose syntax would work perfectly well without it. And this something is like a vocal pressure, the writer's bodily invasion of his own text, a manhandling of the written by the spoken, the insertion of a level of articulatory tension that the written is unaccustomed to. This articulatory tension is evidenced, too, in habits of ellipsis, in deictic words, in exclamation marks. Correspondingly, readers will feel that they are reading dangerously, by fissures and infills, reading a text whose significance is to be measured as much by its activity as its meaning.

But if we respond to a strong oral presence in these texts, we must be careful not to make the wrong assumptions. In speaking of the pressures brought to bear by the speaker, we might assume that Rimbaud's is a vocative world. Although these texts are not without their occasional second-person orientations, it would be truer to say that the second person is an outmoded poetic posture, waiting to be superseded by the third-person accusativity of the prose poem. This development is nowhere more apparent than in Rimbaud's continuing use of the apostrophe. Apostrophe, as we find it in the poems of 1869–71 and 1872, perpetuates its rhetorical role of vocative invocation:

—Ô buffet du vieux temps, tu sais bien des histoires

("Le Buffet")

(—O sideboard of the olden days, you have plenty of tales to tell)

("The Sideboard")

In the *Illuminations*, the apostrophic "Ô" of vocative address (Ô + noun) is still to be found. But this form of the apostrophe is always aspiring to accusative structures (Ô + definite article/possessive adjective/demonstrative adjective + noun): "Ô la face cendrée, l'écusson de crin, les bras de cristal!" (O the ashen face, the escutcheon of horsehair, the arms of crystal!) ("Ô la face cendrée . . ."); "Ô ses souffles, ses têtes, ses courses" (O his breaths, his heads, his careerings) ("Génie" / "Genie"); "Ô cette chaude matinée de février" (O this warm February morning) ("Ouvriers" / "Workers"). "Ô" expresses a self that wishes itself *inside* experience, not to assimilate and confine it, but to bathe in it, as an independent (accusative) force. "Ô" has a projective aspect, is a desire for a sentient fullness, looking for future fulfillment.

In a world such as this, it is difficult to know whether the adoption of prose is a defiant act of slumming it, a refusal of the bourgeois standard (poetry), or precisely the embrace of a medium that allows the miracle of the ultralinguistic to emerge from banality (brass that wakes up a bugle). In other words, is prose an assertion of identity (revolt) or an assertion of nonidentity (nonaffiliation, unformedness, despite forebears in the prose poem like Aloysius Bertrand and Baudelaire), or, above all, a recovered innocence? But in what senses an innocence? As the medium of a new language, a language unimpaired by the rhetorics, the aesthetics, the ideologies of verse making, a language permeated by a kind of unguardedness, a recklessness of the kind already described: "entre partout, réponds à tout" (enter everywhere, respond to everything) ("Mauvais sang"). Language releases a world in which nothing is given, no pattern is anticipated, no conventions are acceded to, and in which the poet must find his place, as autocratic creator *and* overwhelmed observer.

It might seem risky to make some of the textual observations that I have made, particularly about punctuation, given that so few of Rimbaud's texts (aside from *Une saison en enfer* and one or two early poems) were printed with any authorial oversight. Many of the manuscripts are careful fair copies, it is true, but problems of uncertain legibility and intention remain. But two things should be said about this textual "instability": first, these texts are the only ones we have, and they are properly hedged about by scholarly caveats; second, it seems fitting to postulate that what might be regarded as inconsistencies, or doubtful or loose usage, are an integral part of that necessary linguistic flexibility by which one element might morph into another and by which perceptual states might be altered. We must not forget that Rimbaud is someone without a language ("même, quelle langue parlais-je?" (even, what language did I speak?) ["Mauvais sang"]) in search of a language ("to find a language" [letter to Demeny]), someone for whom the "*disordering* of *all the senses*" applies as much to language as to mind, for whom the vehicle of "l'hallucination simple" (the simple hallucination) is "l'hallucination des mots" (the hallucination of words) ("Délires II: Alchimie du verbe"). We must learn to read *away* from the known and the stable; we must be bold enough to inhabit linguistic delirium.

Of course, it is profitable to assess the affinities of these three poets with the literary movements that were, with the exception of Verlaine, to succeed the period of their poetic output (impressionism, symbolism, decadence, modernism), and to measure their innovations in aesthetics and verse-art/prose-art. But there is a danger that such an approach will unbalance our reading, and that our satisfactions will lie in identifying or confirming what the preoccupations of literary history dictate. The encounter with a poet is primarily a textual one, a palpation of configurations of expression and of a linguistic metabolism, an adventure in perceptual adjustment, transformation, gamble, risk. And this is the more so here, since these three poets are part of that broad modernist change of focus from subject (content) to perceiving consciousness, from unified consciousness to dispersed or multiplied consciousness, from stable moral position to temperamental variability.

NOTES

1. Baudelaire's most direct account of "spleen" is found in a letter to his mother of December 30, 1857: "Is it the ailing body that undermines the spirit and the will, or is it spiritual cowardice that exhausts the body, I have no idea. But what I do feel is an immense discouragement, an intolerable sense of isolation, a perpetual fear of some vague misfortune, a complete lack of trust in my own powers, a total absence of desire, the impossibility of finding any amusement whatsoever. . . . That is the true spirit of spleen."

2. This is not "the supernatural" in the standard sense, as Baudelaire's own definition makes clear: "The *surnaturel* includes general color and accent, that is, intensity, sonority, clarity, vibrativity, depth and reverberation in space and time. There are moments in life when time and space are deeper, and the feeling of existence hugely increased" (*Fusées* [*Rockets*]).

3. Note: The notation "//" denotes the caesura, or prosodic juncture, which occurs in the middle of the regular twelve-syllable alexandrine; the numerals denote the number of syllables in each rhythmic measure

4. Note: Once again, the notation "//" indicates the caesura, a feature of all

lines longer than the octosyllable. The tabulated numerals are the numbers of syllables in each rhythmic measure. In the third line, the impair does indeed demonstrate its capacity to "dissolve" the line's structure, erasing the caesura.

Works Cited and Recommended Further Reading

Note: All translations of passages quoted in this chapter are my own. The standard editions of Baudelaire's works and correspondence are the two-volume *Œuvres complètes*, ed. Claude Pichois, 2 vols. (Paris: Gallimard, 1975–76); and *Correspondance*, ed. Claude Pichois with Jean Ziegler, 2 vols. (Paris: Gallimard, 1973). There are many available translations of *Les fleurs du mal*, and to get some idea of the historical range, one can consult *Baudelaire in English*, ed. Carol Clark and Robert Sykes (London: Penguin, 1997); but among current translations, distinguished versions are provided by James McGowan (Oxford: Oxford University Press, 1993) and Walter Martin (Manchester: Carcanet, 1997). Baudelaire's critical writing on art and literature is well served by P. E. Charvet, trans., *Charles Baudelaire: Selected Writings on Art and Literature* (London: Penguin, 1992). For consideration of theoretical and contextual issues relating to the translation of Baudelaire, see Clive Scott, *Translating Baudelaire* (Exeter: University of Exeter Press, 2000); and Rosemary Lloyd, *Baudelaire's World* (Ithaca, NY: Cornell University Press, 2002). Lloyd is also the author of a concise and suggestive biography, *Baudelaire* (London: Reaktion Books, 2008), which can be usefully paired with Pichois and Ziegler's more detailed and larger-scale *Baudelaire*, trans. Graham Robb (London: Hamish Hamilton, 1989). Richard Burton, *Baudelaire and the Second Republic: Writing and Revolution* (Oxford: Clarendon Press, 1991) examines links between the poems and the sociopolitical context of 1848–51. A recent investigation into the architecture of both *Les fleurs du mal* and the prose poems is provided by Randolph Paul Runyon, *Intratextual Baudelaire: The Sequential Fabric of the "Fleurs du mal" and "Spleen de Paris"* (Columbus: Ohio State University Press, 2010). *Le spleen de Paris*, available in translations by Louise Varèse (New York: New Directions, 1970) and Lloyd (Oxford: Oxford University Press, 1991), has attracted searching studies by, among others, Sonya Stephens, *Baudelaire's Prose Poems: The Practice and Poli-*

tics of Irony (Oxford: Oxford University Press, 1999); and Maria C. Scott, *Baudelaire's "Le spleen de Paris": Shifting Perspectives* (Farnham: Ashgate, 2005). For discussion of Baudelaire's art criticism, see J. A. Hiddleston, *Baudelaire and the Art of Memory* (Oxford: Clarendon Press, 1999). Larger literary and artistic contextualizations of Baudelaire's work are explored in Patricia A. Ward, ed., *Baudelaire and the Poetics of Modernity* (Nashville, TN: Vanderbilt University Press, 2001); and Robert Calasso, *La folie Baudelaire*, trans. Alastair McEwen (London: Allen Lane, 2012).

Jacques Borel is the editor of the standard editions of Verlaine's poetry and prose work: *Verlaine: Œuvres poétiques complètes* (Paris: Gallimard, 1962), with Yves-Gérard Le Dantec; and *Œuvres en prose complètes* (Paris: Gallimard, 1972). Less well-served than Baudelaire, Verlaine's poetry has, nonetheless, attracted a fine body of translators, among whom one might mention Norman Shapiro (Chicago: University of Chicago Press, 1998), Martin Sorrell (Oxford: Oxford University Press, 1999), and Donald Revell (Oakland, CA: Omnidawn, 2013). Verlaine's life is explored by A. E. Carter, *Verlaine: A Study in Parallels* (Toronto: University of Toronto Press, 1969); and his place in the decadent context is assessed by Philip Stephan, *Paul Verlaine and the Decadence 1882–90* (Manchester: Manchester University Press, 1974). As a study of Verlaine's creative sensibility, Jean-Pierre Richard's essay "Fadeur de Verlaine," in *Poésie et profondeur* (Paris: Seuil, 1955) remains indispensable. The poet's relationship with Rimbaud is the subject of Christopher Hampton's play *Total Eclipse* (London: Faber, 1969, 1981), which became a film directed by Agnieszka Holland in 1995.

André Guyaux is the editor of the most recent edition of Rimbaud's work, *Rimbaud: Œuvres complètes*, with Aurélia Cervoni (Paris: Gallimard, 2009), which includes Rimbaud's correspondence, but given the importance of manuscript versions, it is a good idea to consult Steve Murphy, ed., *Arthur Rimbaud: Œuvres complètes IV: Fac-similés* (Paris: Champion, 2002). Among translators of the complete Rimbaud, one might make particular mention of Sorrell (Oxford: Oxford University Press, 2001), the unusually comprehensive Wyatt Mason (New York: Scribner, 2003), and Oliver Bernard (London: Anvil, 2012). On the problems and opportunities of translating Rimbaud's prose poetry, see Clive Scott, *Translating Rimbaud's "Illuminations"* (Exeter: University of Exeter Press, 2006). To be recommended among biographies of Rimbaud are Robb, *Rimbaud* (London: Picador, 2000); and Jean-Luc

Steinmetz, *Arthur Rimbaud: Presence of an Enigma*, trans. Jon Graham (New York: Welcome Rain, 2001); and, among general literary-critical studies, Yves Bonnefoy, *Rimbaud*, trans. Paul Schmidt (New York: Harper and Row, 1973); Edward J. Ahearn, *Rimbaud: Visions and Habitations* (Berkeley: University of California Press, 1983); and James Lawler, *Rimbaud's Theatre of the Self* (Cambridge, MA: Harvard University Press, 1992).

Mallarmé and Poetry

Stitching the Random

ROGER PEARSON

> Really, universally, relations stop nowhere, and the exquisite problem
> of the artist is eternally but to draw, by a geometry of his own, the
> circle within which they shall *happily* appear to do so.
>
> —HENRY JAMES, PREFACE TO *Roderick Hudson* (1875–76)

Stéphane Mallarmé's *A Throw of the Dice Never Shall Abolish Chance*
(1897) is arguably the most radically innovative poem in the history
of French literature. At first glance it looks like a haphazard jumble
of words flung higgledy-piggledy—and unversified—across a white
and empty space. And yet the fact that it is indeed a poem is proclaimed loudly on its title page, where "POÈME" is accorded the
largest font size and stands in bold roman type, as though indisput-
able, above the remaining information: "*Un coup de Dés jamais n'abolira
le Hasard* par STÉPHANE MALLARMÉ." In 1887, Mallarmé had
chosen the simple title of *Poésies* for his first published collection of
verse, and he planned to retain it for the revised and expanded collection he was preparing shortly before his untimely death in September 1898 (at the age of fifty-six). Characteristically mindful of ety-
mology, he was presenting his poems as simple "fashionings" or
"fabrications" (from the Greek *poieein*, "to make"), figments of language, like pieces of embroidery in which seemingly random threads
spun from sound and sense are sewn into suggestive patterns.
"POÈME," on the other hand, suggested something grander, more
ambitious. And how! For this poem numbering 664 words was intended to be published as a book.

The 1897 version of *Un coup de dés* appeared on May 4 in the Paris edition of the short-lived international review *Cosmopolis* (1896–98), alongside a poem by Rudyard Kipling and some previously unpublished letters by Turgenev and Nietzsche. This version was to be no more than a foretaste—a "progress report" Mallarmé called it in his short preface. He had already received an advance for a fine art edition of the poem with a print run of two hundred copies at 50 francs per copy (today maybe $200), and his artist friend Odilon Redon (1840–1916) had been commissioned to provide four illustrations. In the event, Mallarmé died before seeing his poem published as a book, and the contract was not fulfilled. And so, by the chance of death, we are left with a tantalizingly incomplete work. Nevertheless we can know from the extant final proofs almost—but not quite—how Mallarmé envisaged his POÈME.

As befits a poem about throwing dice, the text was designed as a cube. It was to consist of six sheets of paper, folded, presenting twelve separate "pages," each with its own recto and verso, or twenty-four sides (pages in our normal view of the matter). Pages 2, 4, and 24 were to be blank, and might have accommodated the three illustrations that Redon actually produced for the work. After the title page, the title phrase itself is dispersed in large bold capitals over pages 3 ("UN COUP DE DÉS"), 5 ("JAMAIS"), 11 ("N'ABOLIRA") and 19 ("LE HASARD") and is then followed on pages 20–23 by another statement in smaller capitals: "RIEN N'AURA EU LIEU QUE LE LIEU EXCEPTÉ PEUT-ÊTRE UNE CONSTELLATION" (nothing will have taken place but the place except perhaps a constellation). The remainder of the verbal text is "thrown," also unpunctuated, across the intervening pages: phrases, clauses, sentences, all grammatically correct but distributed seemingly at random on the page and displayed in differing cases (upper and lower), styles (roman and italic), and font sizes—like black constellations in a white sky.

As the pages are turned, the reader's eye is led by the text from top left to bottom right and must decide—if it can or ever quite does— whether to read across or down the single page, across or down the double-page, pausing to take in clusters of smaller print here and there that have the look of a qualification or an afterthought. From time to time pictorial shapes beckon from the paginal disposition of the words, not quite precise calligrams but suggestive nevertheless of the story of shipwreck that the poem begins verbally to sketch on page 5: a ship listing to starboard, righting itself, keeling over; the sails on either side of a central mast dipping now to the right, now to the left; a ship's elderly master, fist clenched above his head, gradually disappearing beneath the waves; a whirlpool or whirlwind; the solitary feather of a bird floating down toward the sea; rocks amid the foam; wreckage; and lastly a double glimpse of the Big Dipper, or of Ursa Major and Ursa Minor—"avant de s'arrêter / à quelque dernier point qui le sacre / Toute Pensée émet un Coup de Dés" (before stopping / at some last point that consecrates it / Every Thought emits a Throw of the Dice).

"Toute Pensée émet un Coup de Dés": these are the last words of the poem, taking us back to its beginning—on the title page, and on page 3 ("UN COUP DE DÉS"). For indeed, as we have just witnessed, every big thought—such as "A throw of the dice never shall abolish chance"—has need of language for its expression, and yet in that linguistic act the "masterly" intentions of the speaker may be shipwrecked by all the other random things that the words are saying. From the moment we speak (or write a poem), the die is cast: it seems that we can but watch and hear the words tumble across space in patterns of their own making. Take the word *dé*, for instance, which in French means both a single die and the thimble used in sewing. From the Latin *datum*, *dés* is the equivalent of "data," what is given—as it might be, the givens of language as well as the given numbers on some dice. But from the Latin *digitus*, *dé* also suggests a finger on the hand with which we write, and specifically denotes a cylindrical means of protection for that finger when it seeks to sew, to produce "text" or a linguistic "fabric." So from one tiny word springs the whole "memorable crisis," as the poem calls itself. "Crisis," from the Greek verb for "to decide," is here that critical, life-or-death moment in which the language-user, the poet, tries to stitch the random, to bring seemingly endless proliferations of meaning under some sort of control, into some sort of pattern—or constellation. If the poet succeeds, the poem will be the memory of a crisis.

Not only is *Un coup de dés* a cube, then, but also a cylinder: a scroll as well as a book, a long roll as well as a codex, a combination of two of the principal physical forms in which language—and particularly sacred language—has been preserved or "remembered" throughout the ages. In this way *Un coup de dés* seeks to be a Book of Books: the cube of the Holy Bible is combined with the scrolls of the Torah that are to be found in every synagogue. This scrolling nature of the text is evoked explicitly on the centerfold (pages 12–13), which is framed—top left, bottom right—by the words "COMME SI," meaning "as if." Within this frame, and spread across the double-page we read, as though of the text itself: "Une insinuation simple / au silence enroulée avec ironie" (A simple insinuation / in[to] the silence rolled up with irony). The sinuous, twisting lines of print have wormed their way into the silence and into the blank space of the page, rolled up with "irony" (etymologically deriving from the Greek word for "igno-rance," and particularly for "simulated ignorance") in the apparently contingent and meaningless muddle of this text. And the poem now describes itself also as a mystery (etymologically, that about which lips must remain closed and silent) that has been cast into "quelque proche tourbillon d'hilarité et d'horreur" (some nearby whirlpool / whirlwind of hilarity and horror) where it "voltige autour du gouffre" (flutters around the gulf). Each of these last two phrases crosses over the chasm or "gulf" that divides the double-page so that we are led to envisage the pages themselves as the concentric rings of a whirlpool and as storm-stirred waves. And the pages are also lips, simultane-ously pressed together at the center as though joined in silence and yet opening up wide to either side of the impenetrable "gulf" in gap-ing expression of both laughter and terror.

Here we are at the "dead" center of the text, the eye of the textual storm, the hollow center of a scroll, and so we are invited by implica-tion to envisage the surrounding pages of the text as concentric cir-cles—as in a rolled-up magazine, say. The inner circle of the repeated "as if" mirrors the outer circle of the repeated "A Throw of the Dice" on pages 3 and 23, as we realize when we have read the whole poem, and then we may retrospectively note that each intervening roll of text presents similarly circular and reflexive patterns. When we see, for example, that the double-page 14–15 broadly reproduces the lay-out of 10–11 upside down and back to front, we are led to consider also the reflexivity of the verbal texts: how pages 14–15 evoke the descent of a solitary feather onto a "toque," a cylindrical hat resembling a dice-box or a thimble, and how this recalls the scenario described on pages 10–11, in which the old man who is the ship's master hesitates *not* to throw the dice just before he sinks beneath the waves, "having been induced toward this supreme conjunction with probability." As it might be, the poet-master dies and becomes a quill pen, descending toward the black liquid of an inkwell.

In this way, by attending to the visual and verbal information set before us, we may come to read this multilayered text as a performance in which chaos and order compete for the upper hand. At one level, the poem depicts the experience of an old man who is "ancestrally" obliged to throw the dice; who, in doing so, loses control of the situation and becomes "heir" to the consequences unleashed by his throw—that is, to the number, already present within his fist, that the dice will eventually total: "l'unique Nombre qui ne peut pas être un autre" (the unique Number that cannot be another). When the dice finally cease to roll (and as the tumbling italics give way once more to the steady, upright roman script with which the poem began), the old man is reborn as a prince—as the heir to a new authority. In his encounter with chance he has submitted to the laws of probability, which have been confirmed rather than abolished by the throw. Nothing fundamental has changed: "nothing will have taken place but the place except perhaps a constellation." But constellations guide the mariner. Thus at another level, the throw of the dice is like a shipwreck, in that the thrower loses his mastery and flounders in the tumbling arithmetical possibilities of two dice before recovering his bearings when once the result is known.

If all this appears itself chaotic, things may become clearer if we read these various scenarios as descriptions of the poetic process itself. And this is the hallmark of Mallarmé's work: all his poems, in verse and prose, may be approached as performances of their own linguistic and textual nature—each, as he put it, an "allegory of itself." Thus the feather hovering over a toque may indeed suggest a white quill about to plunge into the blackness of an inkwell: the act of writing, of using language, is itself a throw of the dice—metaphorically, but in the case of this poem, also in the more precise sense that a throw of the word *dé* has produced the poem. "The pure work," writes

Mallarmé in *Crise de vers* (*Verse Crisis*), "implies the elocutionary disappearance of the poet, who cedes the initiative to words." The im-
pure work, by contrast, is one in which a poet sets out to impose his
own agenda on language, forcing it to behave as a medium for self-
expression, say, or for philosophical reflection. In "pure" poetry, the
poet lets the words demonstrate for themselves what they can do,
while still, though "ceding the initiative," retaining an important role
in orchestrating the demonstration. He is, as Mallarmé terms it in
some important notes that were brought to light after his death, the
"operator" who masterminds the opus.

And already in one of his earlier poems, the "Sonnet in -yx," Mallarmé had shown very cleverly how this might work. Beginning with
the apparently arbitrary decision to employ some rhymes ending in
"-yx" (sounding in French like the English "eeks!")—but perhaps to
suggest the mystery, or the "x," at the heart of all linguistic expression—he finds only three words in French to answer his purpose:
onyx, *Phoenix*, and *Styx*. Seemingly allowing these words to carry him
along, he evokes an empty room at midnight, a nowhere time, neither
yesterday nor today—and for empty room at midnight, read the as
yet unfilled sonnet form that awaits its fourteen lines of twelve syllables each (so-called alexandrines). And we learn that from this room—
or stanza!—"The Master," is absent and that the only object present
is a gilded mirror reflecting a constellation of seven stars in the onyx-
black sky: a double seven, like the repeated 4 + 3 stanzaic structure of
this Petrarchan sonnet, and itself "framed" by a rhyme-scheme that
combines "-yx" with "-or" (meaning "gold"). From the emptiness and
absence created by his initial surrender to language, the poet thus
sees a pattern come into being ("nothing will have taken place but the
place except perhaps a constellation")—like a Phoenix being born
again from the ashes, like the poet *Or*pheus first crossing and then
returning over the river Styx (the river of death surrounding the un-
derworld), like Christ rising from the dead, like the sun rising once
again at dawn. Indeed the poem presents itself as a secular Eucharist:
taking the humble wafer of a word and rendering it sacred by the
ceremony that is the poem itself.

Mallarmé adopts this strategy in many of his verse poems, the great
majority of which are in sonnet form. The dice-words differ, of

course. In one poem a swan tries in vain to take flight from a frozen lake in which it has become trapped before stoically accepting its "useless exile" from the sky. But the French for "swan"—*cygne* (denoting also the constellation Cygnus)—sounds like *signe*, meaning "sign": and we are invited to think of the linguistic sign as attempting to take poetic flight, to reach out to the ideal, the absolute, the sublime—as it may once have done in Romantic poetry—before now accepting the reality of its random nature and settling for its new poetic status as a purely earth-bound "constellation" of richly suggestive but inconclusive meanings.

In *Crise de vers*, Mallarmé describes this radically new approach to the poetic act in these terms: "I say: a flower! and, out of the oblivion to which my voice relegates any contour, as something other than the calyxes on it, musically there arises, as very idea and suave, the flower that is absent from all bouquets." When a poet—or any of us—says a word, this is first and foremost a linguistic event, an utterance with its own special reality: not a daffodil in sight! Indeed, the very act of speaking is so far removed from the physical reality named that we might just as well have forgotten this reality. But out of this oblivion, out of this simple refusal to accept the everyday referential function of language as self-evident, there arises a different phenomenon: the "poetic" flower, an "idea" or complex set of alternative relationships of sound and sense. But for Mallarmé this "idea" is not the same as the big "Thought" that "emits a Throw of the Dice." "Idea" derives from the Greek verb meaning "to see," and an idea is first and foremost a perceived shape, a form. It is the poet's duty to see, to perceive pattern, to discover new constellations. In English, for example, we might hear the word "eye" in "iris" and make a connection with the iris of the eye . . . with which we see and perceive an "eye-dea" (idea).

This is the kind of pattern making that Mallarmé regarded as "musical." In 1893, in a letter to the English poet and critic Edmund Gosse (1849–1928), he defined "music" as "basically meaning Idea or rhythm between relationships." As he concedes to Gosse, poetry is musical in the obvious sense that the poet tries to achieve harmonious sound patterns and other euphonious effects. But for him there is a much more fundamental sense: poetry creates "ideas," that is, "rhythms between relationships"—and thus relationships between relationships, a network of lace or embroidered pattern having an air of "musical" necessity. Constellations, after all, are just stars randomly distributed in space (even if that apparent randomness may one day be accounted for by astrophysicists), but to our human eye some groupings look like swans or plows or dippers. So, too, for Mallarmé, the sounds and multiple meanings of words.

As an atheist, Mallarmé acknowledged no higher authority or other source of truth than our own human thought processes. And since for him one cannot think except in language, these thought processes are highly hazardous undertakings. Take indeed the very sentence: "Un coup de Dés jamais n'abolira le Hasard." Because *hasard* derives from the Arabic word for dice (*al zahr* = the die), this simply means that a throw of the dice never shall abolish the dice. How could it? A throw of the dice implies the existence of the dice! But if one listens to (rather than seeing/reading) the French "Un coup de dés," one might just as easily hear: "un coud deux dés," meaning "one sews two dice," where "one" is the number 1 or simply the indefinite article "a." And maybe that is indeed what the poet has done in *Un coup de dés*: he has put one and one together. He has stitched the random. Quite a coup.

So is this all just a game, mere wordplay? In one of his poems ("Une dentelle s'abolit . . ." ["A piece of lace abolishes itself . . ."]) Mallarmé calls poetry "le Jeu suprême" (the supreme Game), doubtless because the use of language is a rule-bound activity (syntax, he noted, is "the sole guarantee of intelligibility") but also because it is through language that the human species undertakes the supreme endeavor of making sense of itself and its surroundings. And poetry is the language-game played for the highest stakes, a source of both laughter and terror. In *Un coup de dés*, as we have seen, the poem calls attention to itself as an "insinuation." This word signifies not only an oblique comment, a curve-ball insertion of language into silence: it is also the technical term, in English as in French, for the official registration of a document. So this poem—any poem—represents the official record, as much birth certificate as last will and testament, of a "memorable crisis" in language.

On leaving school, and before training to be an English teacher (which he remained until taking early retirement on health grounds in 1894), Mallarmé had worked briefly in the department of the Ministry of Finance that had been responsible since the 1789 Revolution for the registration and taxation of property and commercial transactions. In a famous letter to Paul Verlaine (1844–96) on November 16, 1885, Mallarmé emphasized the fact that all his ancestors since the Revolution had, both on his father's side of the family and on his mother's, worked for this department; and he noted with pride that he had managed to dodge a career "that people had meant for me since I was in diapers." With equal pride he mentions three earlier family members "who used a pen for something other than registering acts" and to whom he implies his preferred affiliation: an official overseeing the book trade under Louis XVI, a very minor poet, and the author of a "full-blooded Romantic volume entitled *Angel or Demon*." Pen-pushers come in different forms, and it is testimony to Mallarmé's characteristically keen sense of irony—and politically subversive wit—that he should present such an extraordinarily unconventional poem as *Un coup de dés* as the parody of a bureaucratic act. In his preface he compares it to a musical score, but he could just as easily have suggested that it was a balance sheet. In fact, on the very last page of the poem, the tumbling dice are said to represent "un compte total en formation" (a total account in the making), as the words, like numbers, add themselves up before our eyes.

But what indeed does all this amount to? At issue here is the question of authority, and it is in this respect that *Un coup de dés* in particular and Mallarmé's work in general constitute such an important watershed in the history of French poetry. For something quite new is being said about the status of poetry and the role of the poet. When Alphonse de Lamartine (1790–1869) published his *Méditations poétiques* in 1820, he had himself ushered in a new era in this history. Seven years earlier, Napoleonic Paris had witnessed the lavish state funeral accorded to the man then regarded as the greatest poet of the age, Jacques Delille (1738–1813), whom almost no one now reads or remembers. After an early poem about recent advances in the manufacture of prosthetic limbs, Delille had come to prominence for his verse translation of Virgil's *Georgics* in 1769 and had at once been proposed by Voltaire (1694–1778) for election to the Académie française. He then went on to publish his own long verse poem *Les jardins, ou l'art d'embellir les paysages* (*Gardens, or The Art of Embellishing the*

Landscape, 1782). Here, in imitation of Virgil and drawing on the finest examples of European horticulture, he provides useful advice on garden design and techniques, for example, on the best use of streams and cascades as water features and on the charm conferred on an artificial lake by the careful positioning of a decorative boat. The state funeral was due in large part to the helpful orthodoxy of Delille's political and religious views, while in his poetry he was simply doing—only better—what many educated people in the eighteenth century could do: write verse. Versifying was a universal practice in polite society, an accomplishment to set beside horsemanship and needlework. For everyone, the point of poetry was to express thought in as clear, elegant, and memorable a manner as possible.

But in the last decades of the century it was becoming the commonly held view that verse itself was something of an irrelevance, an artificial exercise in which true "poetry"—defined as that which stimulates the imagination and appeals to our sensibility—was lost. In 1801, the dramatist and inveterate controversialist Louis-Sébastien Mercier (1740–1814) stated unequivocally in his *Néologie* (*Neology*) that "the prose-writers are our real poets," and his evidence was *Atala*, published in the same year by François-René de Chateaubriand (1768–1848). In this prose tale recounting the tragic story of two native American Indians "poetry" was everywhere—in the descriptions of nature and personal feeling and in the brilliantly controlled power of the language that earned its creator the nickname of "enchanter"—and all without meter or rhyme.

Lamartine's *Méditations poétiques* thus constituted a literary counterrevolution. Just as Lamartine, a minor Burgundian aristocrat, and then his young rival, Victor Hugo (1802–85), the upper-class scion of a general, both supported the royalist cause when the Bourbon dynasty was restored to the throne of France in 1815, so they both arrested the decline of verse and, together with the putatively aristocratic Alfred de Vigny (1797–1863), initiated a spectacular revival in its fortunes. Marceline Desbordes-Valmore (1786–1859) was doing so also, in verse of a more intimate, lyrical, and indeed experimental kind (Charles Baudelaire [1821–67] and Verlaine were subsequently among her greatest fans), but it was the men who strutted the stage. In the wake of the 1789 Revolution, and more especially the Reign of

Terror (1793–94), reason was suspect: for this "reason" that had been championed by Voltaire and the Enlightenment had now fueled the fanaticism of Maximilien de Robespierre (1758–94) in his murderous pursuit of "pure" republican virtue. Better perhaps to trust to feeling, as Jean-Jacques Rousseau (1712–78) had argued, and how better to appeal to people's feelings than through poetry and the music of words? Lamartine's gift for writing verse that is clear, elegant, and memorable, that flows effortlessly and gives the impression that the strict and complex rules of French versification are actually helping rather than hindering this flow, proved a godsend to those who favored a Restoration, whether political or aesthetic. The nation that had spent the entire previous century seeking successors to Corneille and Racine could now look proudly on its three young poet-musketeers: Lamartine, Hugo, Vigny.

They in turn had big ideas. Both before and after the Revolution, writers and critics had been looking increasingly to the example of ancient Greece for evidence of the political power of poets. In the works of Jean-Jacques Rousseau, Étienne de Condillac (1715–80), Denis Diderot (1713–84), Jean-François Marmontel (1723–99), Mercier, and others—men who themselves had big ideas about the capacity of the writer to change society—it became almost commonplace to cite the examples of Solon and Lycurgus, the former being the politician and poet who introduced democracy to Athens, and the latter being the legal reformer who enlisted the aid of the poet Thales of Crete to persuade the inhabitants of Sparta to accept his reforms. Add in Orpheus, who could tame even wild animals with his songs, and Amphion, who could build cities by moving stone through the power of music, and here was a model for poets to follow. In the aftermath of the Revolution, for which many held writers particularly responsible, it was natural—especially for writers!—to think that the poet (in the broad sense of a creative writer, whether in verse or prose) might lead the nation forward as once Moses had led the Israelites toward the Promised Land.

And poets wrote and behaved accordingly. As events unfolded, Lamartine and Hugo moved gradually but decisively toward republicanism, and both became major public figures. For a very brief moment during the 1848 Revolution, Lamartine, as minister of foreign affairs, became the de facto head of the government—only to be side-lined by the rise of Louis-Napoleon, the future emperor. Hugo, disillusioned and (as he saw it) betrayed by this same Louis-Napoleon, went into exile, first on the island of Jersey, then Guernsey, where he became the thundering prophet of the republic, inveighing against the new emperor and proclaiming his vision of progress, of the moral restoration of humanity across the world through a gospel of love and social reform. Here was the poet-prophet writ large, the poet who listened to God and ended up more or less equating himself with God. Here was the poet who, like the shamans and soothsayers of old, had privileged, visionary access to divine truth and used the lyric, the sacred song of poetry, to convey it to the people.

Vigny, on the other hand, held a more jaundiced view. Where Lamartine and Hugo were deists of a sort, he took God's silence badly. In the face of human suffering we have to rely on ourselves, he thought, and he called his poems "pearls of thought," sedimented human knowledge handed down from generation to generation—like a message in a bottle (as one of his poems has it), a navigational chart drawn up by a doomed explorer who nevertheless can thereby consign his discoveries to the sea in the hope that they may one day be known to others—something salvaged from a shipwreck. For Vigny, poetry was wisdom: human rather than divine wisdom, but wisdom nevertheless, hard-won and independently achieved. For this reason, the poet was condemned to remain in eternal and inevitable conflict with those who held political power and for whom any "alternative" wisdom represented a threat to their authority. This is the lesson of *Stello* (1832), a prose work comprising three short historical narratives about real poets and unified by an overarching debate between feeling and reason, between a young, idealistic poet (Stello, the star) and a cynic called Doctor Black. It is also the lesson of Vigny's prose drama *Chatterton* (1835) about the English poet of that name, whose tragic fate he had already recounted in *Stello*. From Vigny the message is clear: the poet must remain aloof from society the better to guide it with his truth.

This idea of separation, stripped of the aspiration to wisdom, struck a chord with the younger generation. Théophile Gautier (1811–72) pointedly published his first book of *Poésies* at the very height of the July Revolution in 1830. Later, in his most celebrated collection, *Émaux et camées* (*Enamels and Cameos* , 1852), he included a prefatory poem explaining how he had needed to shut his window, literally and metaphorically, on the 1848 Revolution in order to write. In *Poésies*, Gautier revels in the delight of composing verse for its own sake (hence, in his case, the title *Poésies*: they have no moral, political, or philosophical messages to impart), and when critics taxed him with producing "art for art's sake," he proudly wore the insult as a badge of pride. The poet was not a prophet but an artist. Thus in *Émaux et camées*, Gautier seeks to imitate the other arts in a series of verse "transpositions." Sculpture, painting, music, dance, jewelry—all have their say. And each poem shares the same meter, stanzaic form, and rhyme scheme, as though the poet were having to hew each one from the same piece of white marble. Thus "Art," the final poem, begins: "Oui, l'œuvre sort plus belle / D'une forme au travail / Rebelle / Vers, marbre, onyx, émail" (Yes, the work emerges more beautiful / from a form that resists / being worked, / verse, marble, onyx, enamel). This approach in turn inspired a group of poets—among them Leconte de Lisle (1818–94), Théodore de Banville (1823–91), and Sully Prud-homme (1839–1907)—to publish selections of verse (their own and other people's) under the title of *Le Parnasse contemporain* (*The Contemporary Parnassus*, 1866, 1869 [1871], 1876). United in the belief that poetry should seek to reacquire the impassivity and sacred character of ancient Greek art, they were the creators of a new mountain of the Muses, a forum for contemporary verse that rejected the subjective outpourings and politico-philosophizing of the Romantic generation.

The verse poetry of Baudelaire might be said to marry the formalist aesthetic of the Parnassians and Gautier—to whom *Les fleurs du mal* (*The Flowers of Evil*, 1857) is warmly dedicated—with a subversion of Romantic poetic theory. Where Lamartine and Hugo looked to the examples of Solon and Lycurgus in seeking a role as political leaders and to Orpheus and Moses as representatives of a poetic task that consisted essentially in the exploration and communication of the mysteries of God's creation, Baudelaire adopts a less exalted and more provocative stance. For him, beauty is not intrinsic in the world but rather an effect. Thanks to poetry, the tedious becomes once again interesting. The poet's role is no longer to reveal symbolic correspondences between the terrestrial and the divine, but to produce "conjecture" in his reader. Where the symbol (etymologically, from the Greek, something "thrown together") places two things in knowing juxtaposition, Baudelaire presents comparisons, in the form of similes and metaphors, that provoke "conjecture" (etymologically, from the Latin, also something "thrown together"). And the more disparate or surprising the comparison, the greater the shock and the more resonant the reader's own conjecture: "Je suis comme le roi d'un pays pluvieux" (I am like the king of a rainy country) ("Spleen [III]"); "Quand le ciel bas et lourd pèse comme un couvercle" (When the low, heavy sky weighs down like a lid) ("Spleen [IV]"). In this way, the everyday becomes invested with novelty, the boring becomes fascinating, and we are led to view the world as through the eyes of a wide-eyed child: "Genius," Baudelaire comments in *Le peintre de la vie moderne* (*The Painter of Modern Life*), "is childhood recovered at will."

In *Les fleurs du mal*, some of the surprise comes from finding all sorts of "unpoetic" things evoked in the most accomplished of verse. In his prose poems (published posthumously as *Le spleen de Paris* [*The Spleen of Paris*] in 1869), Baudelaire reverses the trick: the banality of prose is the default, and the "poetic" is achieved through a variety of means. Urban experience itself constitutes a rich source of "conjectures," of random juxtapositions, as the poet-stroller ("flâneur") observes the incongruous and the decrepit, the dirty and the nondescript. A walk is a throw of the dice. Here poetry is born of chance encounters and the arresting incongruities of both human behavior and of a literary style that refuses to settle at any fixed point on a spectrum of linguistic register stretching from the high-flown to the colloquial and even the obscene. And in this refusal lies its enduring strength.

As a self-conscious heir to Baudelaire, Arthur Rimbaud (1854–91) also sought the "new"—bringing new words, new procedures, new images within the ambit of the poetic. By administering shock treatment to his own perceptual system—for example, by means of intoxicants and sleep deprivation—he sought out new "visions," attempting "by a long, immense and carefully thought-out disruption of the senses" to turn himself into a "seer"—not the seer who is privy to some divine reality beyond the grasp of ordinary human beings but the observer of an as yet uncharted realm of the self. "I is another," he famously wrote. In the celebrated verse poem, "Le bateau ivre" ("The Drunken Boat"), as also in his prose poems, we find a foretaste of the surrealists' later conception of poetry as an expression of the Freudian unconscious. For Rimbaud, as for the surrealists, the image is all-important: and poetry comes to consist in fabulous, extraordinary, often violently incongruous or unexpected pictures that have the strange logic and coherence of a dream. The more contingent and arbitrary the association, the more authentic the poetic experience. "La terre est bleue comme une orange" (The earth is blue like an orange), Paul Éluard would write in *L'amour la poésie* (*Love, Poetry*) in 1929: "Jamais une erreur" (Never an error), he continues; "les mots ne mentent pas" (words do not lie).

And so with the surrealists we have now begun to follow the new poetic rivers that flowed from the watershed that was Mallarmé. Previously, the poets of the nineteenth century had wanted to express what they had already thought, felt, or intuited. Even the radical and incomparable Rimbaud, having tapped into his "other" self, worried about his capacity to describe these vistas and visions—"I was noting the inexpressible" (*Une saison en enfer* [*A Season in Hell*])—and wondered if he had failed. But Mallarmé started at the other end, with language, and saw what visions—no, what *ideas*, what shapes or patterns—might spring from words. And this is the example followed by Mallarmé's young protégé and literary executor Paul Valéry (1871–1945). For him, the poem must be "just so," a unique and necessary combination of words that could not be other. A poem, he argued, is that which cannot be paraphrased. It may start out as a contingent flash of insight, but that insight has to be consciously worked on and developed through language. Take, for example, his poem "Les pas" ("The Steps") in *Charmes* (*Charms*, 1922), where the word *pas*—meaning "pace" or "step," but also "not" (as in "je n'aime pas")—is employed in the evocation of desire as the experience of an exquisite suspense between the prospect of satisfaction and the deliciousness of deferral. From the simple word *pas* emerges a delicate, carefully versified poem about tremulous approach: of a lover toward a bed, of an idea toward consciousness, of a poem toward the page.

In the work of Guillaume Apollinaire (1880–1918), however, chance is allowed to play a more central role, and the poem in unpunctuated free verse titled "Zone" with which he opens *Alcools* (*Alcohols*, 1913) contains many startling comparisons and allusions in its depiction of modern Paris. "A la fin tu es las de ce monde ancien" (In the end you are tired of this ancient world), it begins, "Bergère ô tour Eiffel le troupeau des ponts bêle ce matin" (Shepherdess O Eiffel Tower the herd of bridges is bleating this morning). As the title of the collection suggests, Apollinaire presents himself as heir to the Baudelaire and Rimbaud who saw poetry as a form of intoxication, and he employs proto-surrealist imagery to conjure strangeness and newness out of the old and familiar. Indeed, he is credited with coining the term "surrealism" (in 1917), and for many he heralds the new age of modernism in French literature. In *Calligrammes*, published posthumously in 1918 and subtitled *Poems of War and Peace 1913–1916*, the influence of *Un coup de Dés* may clearly be seen in Apollinaire's wholehearted embrace of so-called visual or concrete poetry.

And thus he in turn anticipates the coining of the latter term by the Noigrandres group of Brazilian poets for an exhibition in São Paulo in 1956. In "La cravate et la montre" ("The Tie and the Watch"), for example, the bourgeois regalia of the eponymous tie and pocket watch are depicted visually by word-pictures whose verbal constituents explicitly celebrate freedom and nonconformity and implicitly mock bourgeois philistinism. A literal-minded reader may see only a tie and a watch and remain baffled by such a highly unconventional poem. A more receptive reader, however, may note that the hands on the watch stand at five to midnight, suggesting perhaps that art alone can stay the hand of time as war and the human capacity for destruction threaten to engulf us all. In the words that visually depict "The Tie" we read: "that painful tie you're wearing and that decorates you, o civilized man, remove it if you want to breathe," while each hour on the watch-face contains a coded verbal reference in place of a number: two eyes, the child as the third member of a family, the hand with five fingers, the week with seven days, the nine muses and the nine portals of the body, the eleven-syllable line of Dante's *Divine Comedy*. The poem now resembles a puzzle, a display of ingenuity and sheer fun snatched from the jaws of global annihilation, a celebration of imagination and of the playful logic of eight o'clock: "the infinite [∞] stood on end by a crazy philosopher."

But in *Calligrammes* a certain logic thus remains. By contrast, in the first surrealist manifesto (1924), André Breton advocates for poetry and for all art the desirability of going beyond logic. For Breton, as for Mallarmé, "every thought is a throw of the dice"; but whereas Mallarmé, having thrown his dice, was minded to rearrange the numbers and create conscious patterns of his own, Breton reveled in the contingency and pursued his poetic journey guided not by the stars but by a compass that was subject to the magnetic attraction of some mysterious internal force. Chance contains its own objective truth, and the weirder the truer. Hence Breton's definition of surrealism: "Pure psychic automatism by which it is proposed to express, whether orally, or in writing, or in any other manner, the actual functioning of thought. Dictation by thought, in the absence of any control by reason, independent of all aesthetic or moral considerations."

And so for Breton anything can be a poem: "Everything is grist to the mill when it comes to deriving the desirable suddenness from certain associations. The *papiers collés* of Picasso and Braque have the same value as the insertion of a cliché into the most polished piece of literary writing. It is even permissible to give the title of POÈME to what one may obtain from the most gratuitous assembly possible (you can observe the rules of syntax if you wish) of headlines or parts of headlines cut out of newspapers." Though Mallarmé had himself been inspired by newspaper layouts and even poster art, he had never gone this far. Some thirty years after *Un coup de dés*, Breton wanted to leave poetry to its own, automatic devices. Let the random stitch itself together. But not for Mallarmé. No chance. Not if he could help it.

Works Cited and Recommended Further Reading

Note: All translations of passages quoted in this chapter are my own.

Apollinaire, Guillaume. *Alcools* and *Calligrammes*. In *Œuvres poétiques*. Edited by Marcel Adéma and Michel Décaudin. Paris: Gallimard, 1965.

Breton, André, *Manifeste du surréalisme*. In *Œuvres complètes I*. Edited by Marguerite Bonnet. Paris: Gallimard, 1988.

Éluard, Paul, *L'amour la poésie*. In *Œuvres complètes I*. Edited by Marcelle Dumas and Lucien Scheler. Paris: Gallimard, 1968.

Gautier, Théophile, *Emaux et camées*. In *Œuvres poétiques complètes*. Edited by Michel Brix. Paris: Bartillat, 2004.

Mallarmé, Stéphane, *Un coup de dés jamais n'abolira le hasard*. In *Œuvres complètes I*. Edited by Bertrand Marchal. Paris: Gallimard, 1998.

Mallarmé, Stéphane, *Crise de vers*. In *Œuvres poétiques complètes II*. Edited by Bertrand Marchal. Paris: Gallimard, 2003.

Mercier, Louis-Sébastien, *Néologie, ou Vocabulaire des mots nouveaux, à renouveler, ou pris dans des acceptions nouvelles*. Paris: Moussard and Maradan, 1801.

Rimbaud, Arthur, *Œuvres complètes*. Edited by André Guyaux. Paris: Gallimard, 2009.

Valéry, Paul, *Charmes*. In *Œuvres I*. Edited by Jean Hytier. Paris: Gallimard, 1957.

The manuscript, final proofs, and *Cosmopolis* version of *Un coup de dés* may be viewed in Stéphane Mallarmé, *Un coup de dés jamais n'abolira le hasard*, ed. Françoise Morel (Paris: La Table Ronde, 2007). For a comprehensive English translation of Mallarmé's verse and prose poems, see *Collected Poems*, trans. Henry Weinfield (Berkeley: University of California Press, 1994). Also (but without *Un coup de dés*) *Collected Poems and Other Verse*, trans. E. H. and A. M. Blakemore, Oxford World's Classics (Oxford: Oxford University Press, 2006). Both volumes include the French originals. For *Divagations*, which was first published in 1897 under Mallarmé's careful supervision and constitutes a collected edition of all his works in prose to date, including prose poems, revised newspaper articles (which he calls "critical poems"), and other writings, see *Divagations*, trans. Barbara Johnson (Cambridge, MA: Belknap Press, 2007). For a useful sample, see *Selected Poetry and Prose*, ed. Mary Ann Caws (New York: New Directions Books, 1982).

For Mallarmé's correspondence, particularly the important letters of the late 1860s and also the 1885 letter to Verlaine, see *Selected Correspondence*, trans. Rosemary Lloyd (Chicago: University of Chicago Press, 1988). For a short biography and critical introduction, see Roger Pearson, *Stéphane Mallarmé*, Critical Lives (London: Reaktion Books, 2010); and for an account of the writers and artists he knew, see Rosemary Lloyd, *Mallarmé: The Poet and His Circle* (Ithaca, NY: Cornell University Press, 1999). For critical discussion in English see Malcolm Bowie, *Mallarmé and the Art of Being Difficult* (Cambridge: Cambridge University Press, 1978); Mary Lewis Shaw, *Performance in the Texts of Mallarmé: The Passage from Art to Ritual* (State College: Pennsylvania State University Press, 1993); Graham Robb, *Unlocking Mallarmé* (New Haven, CT: Yale University Press, 1996); Roger Pearson, *Unfolding Mallarmé: The Development of a Poetic Art* (Oxford: Clarendon Press, 1996); and Pearson, *Mallarmé and Circumstance: The Translation of Silence* (Oxford: Oxford University Press, 2004). For discussion of Mallarmé's legacy, see Michael Temple, ed., *Meetings with Mallarmé in Contemporary French Culture* (Exeter: Exeter University Press, 1998).

Becoming Proust in Time

MICHAEL LUCEY

More than a few of the very first readers of Marcel Proust's *A la recherche du temps perdu* (*In Search of Lost Time*) found the novel difficult to appreciate. First readers often being the ones deciding if something will be accepted for publication, their opinions may well carry more weight than they deserve. Proust's status as a major writer appears secure these days. The jacket blurbs of recent editions of his seven-volume novel tell us that it is "indispensable," an "inexhaustible artwork," "crucial." Online and in-person Proust reading groups are not hard to find. Various published guides can be found to help readers on their journey through the more than three thousand pages that make up the novel. There is an abundant scholarly literature about Proust and his writings, and there is an immense amount of lore that circulates about the man, his life, and his novel. Among that lore is the intriguing tale of the difficulties he had finding a publisher for the novel's first volume.

It was in 1912, at the age of forty-one, that Proust started looking in earnest for a publisher for what then seemed likely to be a two-volume novel. He contacted two different publishing houses, Charpentier and the *Nouvelle Revue Française*. (The *NRF* is the publisher known today as Gallimard.) To Eugène Fasquelle at Charpentier he wrote with a caveat: "I should like to warn you very frankly in advance that the work in question is what used to be called an *indecent* one, indeed much more *indecent* than what is usually published." The reader whom Fasquelle asked to provide an expert opinion on the manuscript did not react strongly to anything in the pages he read that might qualify as indecent. He began his report in this way: "At the end of the seven hundred and twelve pages of this manuscript (seven hundred and twelve at least, because lots of pages have numbers graced with a, b, c, d)—after the utter depression of seeming to drown in fathomless complications and after irritating feelings of impatience at never being able to surface—the reader has simply no idea of what it's all about. What is all this for? What does all this mean? Where is it leading to?—It's impossible to make head or tail of it! It's impossible to comment on it!" Toward the end of the report, he sums up as best he can: "It's the study of a sickly, abnormally nervous little boy whose sensitivity, impressionable nature and reflective subtlety are in a state of irritation." As for its indecency, the reader notes, "It's hardly worth taking into account the very brief and misleading appearance of the future 'homosexual,' Baron de Fleurus. . . . If the little boy does not become a homosexual what is the point of the whole book?" (We see that in 1912 Proust had not yet fixed the name of all of his characters. Fleurus would become Charlus in the published novel.) Obviously, this reader did not recommend publication, but he did add, "In the work as a whole, indeed, and even in each unit taken on its own it is impossible not to see here an extraordinary intellectual phenomenon."

The *Nouvelle Revue Française* also turned down the manuscript. One of the moving forces at the *NRF* was André Gide. He would write remorsefully to Proust in January 1914, while reading the published volume: "For several days, I have not put down your book; I am supersaturating myself in it, rapturously, wallowing in it. Alas! why must it be so painful for me to like it so much? . . . The rejection of the book will remain the gravest mistake ever made by the *NRF*—and (for I bear the shame of being largely responsible for it) one of the most bitterly remorseful regrets of my life." Gide claimed that he barely looked at Proust's manuscript, stumbling by chance across a number of sentences he found unappealing before unthinkingly rejecting it. Contributing to his decision, he admits, was the image he had of Proust as a fellow lacking in seriousness, a socialite and a snob, an image based on a number of chance encounters between the two many years earlier. A person like the one he imagined Proust to be could have no place at the *NRF*, he wrote, since the *NRF* meant to publish only the most significant and consequential kinds of literature by serious authors. (Proust certainly had been a socialite, and indeed he authored a number of society columns for a newspaper, *Le Figaro*, in the early years of the century, which he published under a number of pseudonyms. Perhaps atypically for society columns, a couple of them made extensive reference to the novels of Balzac and Stendhal.)

Proust tried a third publisher for his novel, Ollendorff, this time offering to pay the expenses of publication himself. Ollendorff refused, on the advice of another expert reader, who complained that there was no justification for spending the thirty opening pages of the manuscript describing someone's difficulties in falling asleep. Only on his fourth attempt, would Proust find someone willing to publish him. The first volume of his novel, *Du côté de chez Swann* (*Swann's Way* or, in some recent editions, *The Way by Swann's*), would finally appear in November 1913, published by Grasset, and at the author's expense.

In the second volume of Proust's novel, *A l'ombre des jeunes filles en fleur* (*In the Shadow of Young Girls in Flower*), which would not appear until 1919, after the end of World War I (but which would, along with the rest of the volumes, be published by the *NRF*), the narrator pauses to reflect on how long it can take for a difficult new musical work to find a public that appreciates or understands those parts of it that are "newest" or most "novel": "it is always the least precious parts that one notices first. . . . The beauties one discovers soonest are also those which pall soonest, a double effect with a single cause: they are the parts that most resemble other works, with which one is already familiar. But when those parts have receded, we can still be captivated by another phrase, which, because its shape was too novel to let our mind see anything there but confusion, had been made undetectable and kept intact." Difficult works, Proust's narrator notes, have to give birth to their own publics, a process that can take years, decades, or even centuries. "The work has to create its own posterity." The reception of a work of art or of literature, its circulation, and the accumulation of value to it, the set of meanings associated with it, all happen over time and through a complicated set of processes that can be understood not only aesthetically, but also historically and sociologically. How—through what processes—does a public end up noticing, and then appreciating—giving value to—something *new*? Proust's novel represents this set of processes unfolding in the way it talks about artists, composers, actors and actresses, and writers (both real

and fictional) struggling to achieve recognition, but the novel was itself also caught up in the very processes it represents.

One of the qualities of Proust's novel that people did notice immediately was that its writing is expansive; its sentences are complex;
its thoughts and images are rich and detailed; its pace is leisurely; its
structural features emerge only slowly. ("Proust tries our patience so
long as we expect his story to move forward," Clive Bell would write
in 1928, "that not being the direction in which it is intended to
move.") The readers at Ollendorff and Charpentier obviously found
the novel's pace and density to be an overwhelming obstacle to comprehension. Gide points to a similar experience when, having finally
sat down to read the book attentively, he finds himself "supersaturating [him]self in it, rapturously, wallowing in it." With Proust, a little
goes a long way, it seems, and opening the novel with the expectation
of making quick progress turns out to be an unwise idea.

As early readers of Proust began to assimilate the novel's opening
volumes (the first volume appeared in 1913, the second in 1919, the
final one in 1927, five years after Proust's death in 1922), they quickly
found ways to relate Proust's project to other familiar reference
points. Some immediately linked it to other contemporary modernist
literary projects. J. Middleton Murry, writing in 1922, would note
"three significant books, calling themselves novels" that appeared in
1913–14, Proust's *Du côté de chez Swann*, Joyce's *A Portrait of the Artist
as a Young Man*, and Dorothy Richardson's *Pointed Roofs*. They were all
"attempts to record immediately the growth of a consciousness . . .
without any effort at mediation by means of an interposed plot or
story." What was different about Proust, for Murry, was that "he established as the starting point of his book the level of consciousness
from which the exploration actually began." That is, Proust's narrative method involved "perpetual reference to the present adult consciousness of the author." What Murry calls the author here, others
will call Proust's narrator, but the feature Murry identifies has become one that people take to be a hallmark of Proust's writing: the
subtle play of perspectives that can be found within the bounds of any
one sentence from Proust's novel, where the consciousness that seems
to be responsible for the sentence in question shifts rapidly through

time, locating itself temporarily at any one of many different points on the time line making up the narrator's life.

When Murry reaches for a figure to whom Proust could be compared or contrasted, he chooses the Rousseau of the *Confessions*. Others in the early years of Proust's reception would choose Montaigne or Saint-Simon. If Montaigne and Rousseau came to mind as part of an effort to understand the focus in Proust's novel on the workings of consciousness and memory in the elaboration of a self, Saint-Simon (whose celebrated *Memoires* chronicle the court of Louis XIV and the subsequent period of the Regency) came to mind not only because he is mentioned several dozen times throughout the novel, but because the novel also involves a great deal of sociologically acute observations of high-society people interacting within complex and carefully delineated social environments. Writing in 1923, in a special issue of the *Nouvelle Revue Française* honoring Proust after his death, the French critic Albert Thibaudet wrote: "In Saint-Simon we have a tide of history on the move, people in the mass, the whole of France and the living vehement soul of Saint-Simon ever-present and manifest everywhere. In Proust we have a psychological tide, as vast as the former but, so as to yield its full power and make headway, in need only of a soul, either the author's or the soul of a character whom it has failed to exhaust, inexhaustible as all creatures are." Thibaudet moves Proust away from the sociological to the psychological impulse in novel writing. Proust's sociological ambitions for his novel (honed through his reading of other novelists he deeply admired, such as Balzac, Flaubert, and George Eliot) were perhaps not so easily appreciated in the early years of his reception.

"The beauties one discovers soonest are also those which pall soonest," Proust's narrator had observed. In the case of *A la recherche du temps perdu*, for certain novelists of the next generation it would be Proust's intense focus on the interior life of his characters that had palled. Jean-Paul Sartre and Simone de Beauvoir would turn to American novelists of the 1930s (people like John Dos Passos) in an attempt to craft a different narrative style, a different way of representing human beings acting in the world. Instead of focusing on interior life, their intent, Sartre would write in 1939, was to arrive at an understanding of the world in which "finally, everything is outside, everything, even ourselves: outside, in the world, among all the others." Sartre would even go so far as to say in that same essay (written while he was planning his novel *L'âge de raison* [*The Age of Reason*] and Beauvoir was working on *L'invitée* [*She Came to Stay*]) that "we have put Proust behind us."

The project of writing novels with no interest in interior life would be taken a step further by someone like Alain Robbe-Grillet, a standard-bearer for the New Novel, exemplified by works such as his 1957 *La jalousie* (*Jealousy*). In an essay from 1961, Robbe-Grillet would state that the New Novelists were interested in pursuing the evolution of the form of the novel that could be traced through a line of precursors including "Flaubert, Dostoevsky, Proust, Kafka, Joyce, Faulkner, Beckett." In the course of its evolution, Robbe-Grillet affirmed, the novel was gradually shedding a concern with worn-out notions such as "character, chronology, sociological study, and so on." It now seems clear that the extent of Proust's impact on literature (both in France and around the world), and the nature of what Proust had achieved, was only starting to be felt and understood as Sartre or Robbe-Grillet wrote; it might also be noted that the clear forward-moving path of the novel's formal evolution that Robbe-Grillet thought he could point to looks decidedly less convincing from today's point of view. Proust was not part of an evolution in which the novel was *shedding* such categories as character, chronology, or sociological study. He was reinventing those categories; he was turning them to new ends.

It was around 1908, when Proust was in his mid- to late thirties, that plans for his novel began to solidify in his mind. As a younger man, Proust had published various literary essays and one collection, *Les plaisirs et les jours* (*Pleasures and Days*, 1896), which comprised a miscellany of short stories, essays, a pastiche of Flaubert, poetic portraits of painters and musicians, and poems in verse and prose. Around this time he also became fascinated with the writings of the English art critic John Ruskin, who had died in 1900. The English poet Richard Aldington wrote that the source of Proust's fascination with Ruskin lay in "Ruskin's essential appreciativeness, his capacity for the assimilation and understanding of beauty, his reverence for the arts as symbols and expressions of civilization." With the help of his mother, whose English was better than his, and a friend, Marie Nordlinger, Proust translated Ruskin's *The Bible of Amiens* (the translation was published in 1904) and also *Sesame and Lilies* (1906).

It is often in the lengthy preface that Proust wrote for *Sesame and Lilies*, called "Sur la lecture" ("On Reading"), that critics find the first premonitions of the major work that was to come. Proust's preface seems to be pursuing multiple agendas simultaneously, and it is perhaps in this multitasking quality it evinces that it most looks forward to his great novel. On the one hand, Proust offers a lusciously detailed description of what it feels like to read (or what it felt like for him to read as a child on a summer's day in his grandparent's home); how the feeling of the experience of reading was woven into the experience of interruptions to eat lunch or to go for a walk; and how the experience of reading evolved across the day, taking place in a chair near the fire in the morning, and later in bed just before falling asleep. He addresses the difference between productive and unproductive kinds of reading experiences; he discusses what it means for a mind reading to be encountering the traces of the mind that wrote the words on the page; he develops his ideas regarding what it means to think of reading as an encounter with the past. The experience of Racine's syntax, for instance, is compared to the experience of ancient architectural structures—to the walls of old cities or the baptisteries of old churches.

Roughly two years after the publication of his translation of *Sesame and Lilies*, in May 1908, Proust wrote a letter to his friend Louis d'Albufera that has become famous because of the list of projects he tells Albufera he had under way:

> I have in hand
> > a study on the nobility
> > a Parisian novel
> > an essay on Sainte-Beuve and Flaubert
> > an essay on women
> > an essay on pederasty (not easy to publish)
> > a study on stained-glass windows
> > a study on tombstones
> > a study on the novel.

The novel is, of course, a capacious genre, capable of incorporating many other kinds of discourse—poetry, essays, theoretical discourses of various kinds. Could a single novel be capacious enough to contain all the items on Proust's list? During 1908 and 1909, it seems Proust decided that yes, in fact, what he was working on was a single novel. By August 1909, Proust wrote to Alfred Vallette, husband of the novelist Rachilde and editor of the *Mercure de France* (a major publishing house that had, for example, published works by both Gide and Colette): "I am finishing a book which in spite of its provisional title: *Contre Sainte-Beuve, souvenir d'une matinée*, is a genuine novel, and an extremely indecent one in places. One of the principal characters is a homosexual.... I fancy it contains some new things.... The book does indeed end with a long conversation about Sainte-Beuve and about aesthetics . . . and once people have finished the book they will see (I hope) that the whole novel is simply an implementation of the artistic principles expressed in this final part, a sort of preface if you like placed at the end."

Charles-Augustin Sainte-Beuve was an imposing nineteenth-century literary critic, and Proust decided that it was against Sainte-Beuve's approach to authors and their works that he would build his own aesthetic position. The novel Proust was envisioning would thus contain a metafictional aspect—it would be a novel about writing novels and about reading them, a novel calling attention to its own aesthetic beliefs and its own formal procedures through a discussion of what the right method for studying literature should be. (Gide's 1925 *Les faux-monnayeurs* [*The Counterfeiters*] is another classic example of metafictional writing from these same years, containing a character who is a novelist, and including pages from that fictional novelist's journal in which he writes about his attempts to write a novel called *Les faux-monnayeurs*. Gide would then publish his own *Journal des Faux-monnayeurs* in 1926.)

Would it be fair in 1909 to call the novel Proust was writing "extremely indecent" because of the homosexual characters and behaviors it described? Perhaps for some readers, but not for others. Rachilde, to whose husband Proust was writing, had published her scandalous *Monsieur Vénus* in 1884 (a novel about a cross-dressing female aristocrat and the tortuous relationship she constructs with an effete working-class man), and other authors who dealt with nonnormative forms of sexuality were not hard to find at the time Proust was writing. Gide, for instance, had published *L'immoraliste* (*The Immoralist*) in 1902. In his *Journal*, Gide recounts a conversation from 1915 with an older novelist, Paul Bourget, in which Bourget makes a point of inquiring as to whether the protagonist of *L'immoraliste* was a "practicing pederast." People in these years were becoming familiar with the idea that literature was a place in which non-mainstream forms of sexuality could be represented, discussed, and analyzed. Between 1914 and 1922, Gide and Proust would exchange letters and have several late-night conversations regarding the representation of male homosexuality in the books they were working on (including Gide's *Les caves du Vatican, Corydon, Les faux-monnayeurs*, and *Si le grain ne meurt . . .*). Clearly for them (and for numerous other authors around them, including, of course, Colette) this topic and the kind of literary treatment it would be given could serve as key elements for cutting-edge literary writing.

The drafts Proust was working on around this time would be published after his death under the title *Contre Sainte-Beuve*. While one can recognize in them the lineaments of the novel to come, Proust's project had a good deal of evolving left to do. Not much of the writing dealing with his specific disagreements with Sainte-Beuve (regarding how to understand the relations between the works an author writes and the social life an author leads) makes its way into the published novel. But one key element of his 1909 letter to Vallette—the architectural idea of a preface that comes at the end to lay out the principle on which the whole work has been constructed—is worthy of notice. At about the same time that *Du côté de chez Swann* was published, in November 1913, Proust penned some observations about his novel that were published in the newspaper *Le Temps*. In his remarks, he insists that although only one volume of the novel was appearing at that time, it constitutes a whole—one whose effects will only be apparent at the end. "I hope that at the end of my book, some minor social event of no importance, some marriage between two persons who in the first volume belong to very different worlds, will indicate that time has passed and will take on the beauty of certain patinaed leadwork at Versailles, which time has encased in an emerald sheath." Perhaps there is a clue here to something that interests Proust that he does not fully articulate: will that minor marriage do no more than merely give us the sense that time has passed? It seems rather that Proust is gesturing at a relationship between the passage of time and certain kinds of social processes for which he has something like an aesthetic appreciation, ongoing processes that can be perceived only in the effects they produce over time, visible only in the effects they produce on the persons and the object they shape or sculpt. Different processes, Proust's novel will show us, become perceptible over different spans of time. Time holds certain things and also sculpts certain things, Proust seems to be suggesting, and part of his novelistic vision involved finding ways to show us time in its passage in order to make it possible for us to see what time holds and what it sculpts.

Along with insisting that his novelistic vision was meant, in a certain way, to make the passage of time visible, Proust emphasizes in his remarks for *Le Temps* the importance of a particular scene that occurs about fifty pages into the novel, the famous scene of the madeleine: "Already, in this first volume, you will find the character who tells the story and who says 'I' (who is not me) suddenly recovering years, gardens, people he has forgotten, in the taste of a mouthful of tea in which he has soaked a bit of madeleine." This is the scene in which Proust (or his narrator) draws a distinction between voluntary and involuntary memory. In the article in *Le Temps*, Proust writes: "For me, voluntary memory, which is above all a memory of the intellect and of the eyes, gives us only facets of the past that have no truth; but should a smell or a taste, met with again in quite different circumstances, reawaken the past in us, in spite of ourselves, we sense how different that past was from what we thought we had remembered, our voluntary memory having painted it, like a bad painter, in false colors. . . . I believe that it is really only to involuntary memories that the artist should go for the raw material of his work."

Now it turns out that the scene of the madeleine early in the novel, and the experience of involuntary memory provided in that moment, is only the first in a series of such scenes that occur periodically over the course of the novel. About halfway through the novel's final volume, a flurry of such moments occurs, provoked successively by the narrator's experience of stumbling over a paving stone, of hearing the sound of a spoon tapped against the side of a plate, of the feel of a starched napkin brushing across his face, and then, in a more complicated fashion, of the discovery on a bookshelf of a book (George Sand's novel *François le champi*) that had played a key role in an important childhood moment. The first three instances provoke a profound sense of happiness and a renewed sense of commitment to a writerly vocation. In these moments, "the past was made to encroach upon the present and make me uncertain about which of the two I was in; the truth was that the being within me who was enjoying this impression was enjoying it because of something shared between a day in the past and the present moment, something extra-temporal, and this being appeared only when, through one of these moments of identity between the present and the past, it was able to find itself in the only milieu in which it could live and enjoy the essence of things, that is to say outside of time." The long passage in which the narrator thinks over the nature of this experience of involuntary memory seems to be the kind of moment Proust described to Vallette in his 1909 letter, a preface that comes at the end, describing how intellectual apprehension (voluntary memory) will always provide an inadequate account of our passage through the world. "For the truths that the intellect grasps directly as giving access to the world of full enlightenment have something less profound, less necessary about them than those that life has, despite ourselves, communicated in an impression, a material impression because it enters us through our senses, but one from which it is also possible to extract something spiritual."

One of the most compelling and influential accounts of the importance of Proust's distinction between voluntary and involuntary memory comes from a 1939 essay by Walter Benjamin called "On Some Motifs in Baudelaire." Among the overarching themes of Benjamin's essay is the idea that the modern world (the world of standardization, of mass culture, of information) has become increasingly inhospitable to a richly reflective kind of experience capable of tying a given individual to a given place and time, to a given culture and community. Many different thinkers and artists have dealt with this problem in a variety of ways, Benjamin tells us, discussing Proust alongside the poets Charles Baudelaire and Paul Valéry, alongside

Sigmund Freud and the French philosopher Henri Bergson. In modernity, our senses are continually being shocked by stimuli from the world around us, keeping our sense of ourselves and our world in a fragmentary and unintegrated state. For Benjamin, Proust's interest in moments of involuntary memory is an interest in moments when the "atrophy of experience" so typical of modernity can, almost accidentally, be overcome, when individuals can hold meaningful images of their lives in their minds for a moment. In another essay, "The Image of Proust," Benjamin writes, "*A la Recherche du temps perdu* is the constant attempt to charge an entire lifetime with the utmost awareness."

If Benjamin's comments help us focus on that aspect of the novel that relates to coherence and an overarching unifying formal structure (sometimes difficult to perceive because of the work's enormous length), there is also the open form aspect of the book to consider, the sense that even after Proust had fixed in his mind how it was to begin and end, even after he had written the beginning and the end, the novel kept growing in the middle. Time kept passing around Proust as well. Notably, World War I intervened between the 1913 publication of *Du côté de chez Swann* and the 1919 publication of *A l'ombre des jeunes filles en fleur*. The later parts of the novel were reimagined to include the occurrence of the war and its effect on the characters. Moreover, at some point during the war, something crucial shifted in Proust's sense of the novel. A new character emerged, Albertine, whose role seemed then only to grow and grow. She became the narrator's major love interest, his obsession, his project, his prisoner. Her presence in the novel energized its treatment of certain topics, including obsessive jealousy and "indecent" forms of sexuality. She also introduced a different social class into the work (the narrator calls it "une petite bourgeoisie fort riche, du monde de l'industrie et des affaires" (a quite wealthy part of the middle class whose money came from the worlds of industry or commerce), altering its sociological ambitions as well.

Albertine first appears in the novel as one of a small group of girls whose social provenance mystifies the narrator. As he learns more about her, he finds himself falling in love not with some well-placed aristocrat (a possibility he has often dreamed of) or with someone from a cultivated and wealthy family of long-standing reputation (as was the case with Gilberte Swann, his first crush), but with a bicycle-riding, golf-playing girl whose sociological profile seems utterly alien to him: she comes from new money, she is culturally right-wing (Catholic and opposed to the secular tendencies of the Third French Republic), and, when it comes to literary, musical, or artistic taste, decidedly middle-brow. The result is that he does not, he says, even know how to talk to her: "While talking to her, I had been as unaware of my words and where they went as though I had been throwing pebbles into a bottomless well. That in general the people to whom we speak draw from within themselves the meaning they give to our words, and that this meaning is very different from the one we put into them, is a truth constantly revealed to us by everyday life. But if in addition the person to whom we are speaking is, as Albertine was for me, someone whose upbringing is inconceivable, whose inclinations and principles, even the books she reads, are a mystery to us, then we cannot tell whether our words have any more semblance of meaning for her than they would if we tried to explain ourselves to an animal. Trying to strike up a relationship with Albertine felt like relating to the unknown, or even the impossible, an exercise as difficult as training a horse, as restful as keeping bees or growing roses." We could notice any number of things about this passage: that it shows what an unpleasant fellow the narrator often reveals himself to be; that it illustrates the novel's ongoing preoccupation with mishaps in attempts at verbal communication (and with discrepancies between different varieties of French); that it indicates that the narrator's own psychosocial makeup, the structure of his own forms of taste and his own kinds of ambition, are part of the puzzle the novel presents us with.

The Albertine story, a central part of all the volumes of the *Recherche* except the first and the last, allows the novel to expand on its fascination with language as the main medium in which social identities are produced and experienced. It allows the novel more space to consider a wide range of sexualities outside the mainstream. (If the indecency Proust spoke of when referring to his novel before the war had for the most part to do with the sexual inclinations of men like Charlus, with the introduction of Albertine into the novel, someone whose sexuality will apparently remain as mysterious to the narrator as her upbringing was inconceivable, suddenly a whole range of non-mainstream sexualities between women, as well as between men who are attracted to men and women who are attracted to women, enters into the novel's purview.) It provides a new slant on the large socio-logical movements the novel traces (the seemingly endless process through which the aristocracy goes on renewing its prestige even as it heads toward inevitable obsolescence; the ascending sociocultural prominence of new segments of the middle classes). The introduction of Albertine into the novel shifts its balance, we might say, gives it freedom to pursue in new ways certain topics it already had on its agenda, to take them in new directions.

A la recherche du temps perdu is never about one thing at a time. It has an amazing ability always to be about a number of things simul-taneously. Everyone will have his or her own list of what seem to be its central topics (and of course, our collective sense of what the novel is about will change as we and it continue to move through time), but here are six promising candidates: (1) The novel is interested in what aesthetic experience is, how it works, and what it is used for; it is in-terested in how the human sensory apparatus can be captivated by beautiful things in nature or by beautiful works of art; but then it is interested in how this aesthetic capacity is used or managed by people as they move through the world and time, how people's taste evolves and why, how it might be possible (or impossible) to predict or ma-nipulate one's own taste, or the taste of others. (2) The novel is inter-ested in the faculty (or faculties) of memory, how it or they work, how they enable us to be and to become who we are, to function as the kind of people we imagine ourselves to be—or how sometimes differ-ent kinds of memory come into conflict at key moments of our lives, and leave us in a state of disorientated non-identity. (3) The novel is interested in how the social world is organized into groups (families, classes, nations, clans, religions, sexualities, professions, age cohorts), how those groups determine who we are, how they compete, repli-cate themselves through us, or are transformed, perhaps even disap-pear; the novel is persistently asking what the relationship is between the groups we belong to and the identities we imagine to be ours. (4) The novel is interested in sexuality, love, and jealousy as elements in the construction of both individual identity and social identity, as forms of energy that propel us through life, and as features of human existence that link human beings to other forms of life (animal and vegetal) and to the ecosystem around them. (5) The novel is interested in the large-scale transformations that characterize its own historic moment, in, for instance, how momentous historico-political crises (World War I being the main example) affect both the large sociopolitical institutions that organize our lives and the small structures of daily life through which we all move. Finally, (6) the novel is interested in novels, how they work, and what we use them for.

The passage of time and the instability of the experience of human subjectivity are a shared feature of all of these topics. Take just one example of this, related to the matter of how novels work—the interesting question of the way the novel deals with the narrator's name. Often critics refer to the narrator as Marcel. The narrator is given this name nowhere in the first four volumes of the novel. Other characters apparently speak his name from time to time, but the novel makes a point of never recording it. One ostentatious example (among many others) is the scene in which the narrator is announced by the doorman upon his arrival at a party thrown by the Princesse de Guermantes: "The doorman asked my name, and I gave it to him as mechanically as a condemned man allowing himself to be attached to the block. He at once raised his head majestically and, before I had been able to beg him to keep his voice down . . . he shouted out the disquieting syllables with a force capable of causing the roof of the house to vibrate." As for what those disquieting syllables were, we are given no clue.

There are only two places in the whole novel, both found in the fifth volume, *La prisonnière* (*The Captive* or *The Prisoner*), in which it could be argued that the narrator is named Marcel. The second of the two is a letter from Albertine to the narrator that begins "Dear darling Marcel," and ends "Oh Marcel, Marcel! Your very own Albertine." That might seem to be good evidence that, despite having avoided mentioning the fact for several thousand pages, the narrator is indeed named Marcel. However, earlier in the same volume the reader will have encountered a startling sentence that might make anyone wary of the truth-value of any attempt to specify the narrator's name. At the moment in question, the narrator is admiring a sleeping Albertine and watching her slowly wake up. (Note again that the confused state between sleeping and waking with which the novel began remains at the heart of its preoccupations.) "Now she began to speak; her first words were 'darling' or 'my darling,' followed by my Christian name, which, if we give the narrator the same name as the author of this book, would produce 'darling Marcel' or 'my darling Marcel.'" What is disconcerting about this sentence is the difficulty in imagining who is speaking it, who is responsible for the words that make up its second half. Can a narrator mention the existence of his author? Is the author somehow intervening here, breaking the novel's frame? Are we suddenly encountering words proffered by someone who is neither the author or the narrator, and if so—who could that be? The sentence seems intended to cause us to lose our bearings, almost as if we ourselves were being woken up, shaken out of a dream state by an occurrence that seems situated neither fully within the dream nor fully outside it.

Stop for a moment to consider this: When, in 1928, Colette's novel *La naissance du jour* [*Break of Day*] was published in *La Revue de Paris*, it had an epigraph she claimed was from Proust, but which appears to be her modification of something Proust had said in his 1913 article for *Le Temps* about his relation to his narrator. Colette's epigraph, ascribed to Proust, read "this 'I' which is me and which is perhaps not me." Colette changed the epigraph when the novel appeared in book form, replacing the passage she claimed was from Proust with one cribbed from later in her own novel: "Is anyone imagining in reading me that I am portraying myself? Have patience: This is merely my model." In reviewing *La naissance du jour*, the critic André Billy would write that this novel "offers something extremely new and daring, without precedent, I think, in literature . . . it's that the heroine of the novel is none other than the author." Billy was, of course, exaggerating: Colette always played with the discrepancy between novelistic representations of self and public ones. Yet we could certainly say that Proust's and Colette's way of creating disturbances between real and fictional persons or personas, and disturbances in our everyday understanding of the patterns of coherence that usually govern the use of the first-person pronoun proved extremely influential within French literature of the twentieth century. One might, for instance, think of Marguerite Duras in this light.

The *Recherche* performs a similar disruptive gesture in a remarkable passage from the final volume that deals with the selfless behavior of certain people during the hardest days of World War I. The narrator (or is that really who is speaking?) suddenly informs us that "in this book, in which there is not one fact that is not fictitious, not one real character concealed under a false name, in which everything has been made up by me in accordance with the needs of my exposition, I have to say, to the honour of my country, that Françoise's millionaire relatives alone, who came out of retirement to help their niece when she was left without support, that they and they alone are real, living people." How is it that the narrator, himself supposedly a fiction, suddenly knows who is "real" and who isn't?

It is as if for the novel certain questions—what is the difference between being asleep and being awake? what is the difference between the narrator and the author? what is the difference between being real and being fictitious?—are all in some way versions of the same question. It is as if in all of the different topics it treats, the novel in fact encourages us to wonder if we are awake, if we are fictions. When we are caught up in aesthetic experience, who are we? When we decide we like something, what has been decided and by whom? Who do we become thanks to the aesthetic choices we imagine ourselves to make freely? When we are lost in memory, who, where, when, and what are we? When we pursue sex or love, do we know why we do what we do? Do we know the meaning of what we do? Are our actions automatic or conscious? Do we know who or what we are as we perform them? When we use language, are we in full control of what we say and do? Are we aware of, awake to, the full significance of the way group identities transmit themselves through us? Is it possible to know the full extent of what and who we have been, what we are, what we will become, to cite the novel's closing words, "in Time"? Somehow the *Recherche* not only studies, it also offers us and is itself subject to, this complex experience of becoming. Even Proust, we could say, is still in the process of becoming who he is, as his novel goes on moving forward through time.

Works Cited and Recommended Further Reading

Benjamin, Walter. "The Image of Proust" and "On Some Motifs in Baudelaire." In *Illuminations: Essays and Reflections*, edited by Hannah Arendt, translated by Harry Zohn. New York: Schocken, 1969.

Colette. *Break of Day*. Translated by Enid McLeod. New York: Farrar, Straus and Giroux, 1961.

———. *Oeuvres, tome III*. Edited by Claude Pichois et al. Paris: Gallimard-Pléiade, 1991.

Gide, André. *The Journals of André Gide, volume 2: 1914–1927*. Translated by Justin O'Brien. New York: Knopf, 1948.

Hodson, Leighton, ed. *Marcel Proust: The Critical Heritage*. London: Routledge, 1989. (The observations by Richard Aldington, Clive Bell, J. Middleton Murry, Albert Thibaudet, and the reader's report for Fasquelle can all be found in this volume.)

Proust, Marcel. *Finding Time Again*. Translated by Ian Patterson. London: Penguin, 2003.

———. *In the Shadow of Young Girls in Flower*. Translated by James Grieve. New York: Penguin, 2005.

———. *Lettres à André Gide*. Neuchâtel: Ides et Calendes, 1949.

———. *The Prisoner* and *The Fugitive*. Translated by Carol Clark and Peter Collier. London: Penguin, 2003.

———. *Selected Letters, 1904–1909*, vol. 2. Edited by Philip Kolb. Translated by Terence Kilmartin. London: Collins, 1989.

———. *Selected Letters, 1910–1917*, vol. 3. Edited by Philip Kolb. Translated by Terence Kilmartin. New York: HarperCollins, 1992.

———. *Sodom and Gomorrah*. Translated by John Sturrock. New York: Penguin, 2005.

———. "*Swann* Explained by Proust" (from *Le Temps* in November 1913). In *Against Sainte-Beuve and Other Essays*, translated by John Sturrock. London: Penguin Books, 1988.

Robbe-Grillet, Alain. *For a New Novel: Essays on Fiction*. Translated by Richard Howard. Evanston, IL: Northwestern University Press, 1992.

Sartre, Jean-Paul. "Une idée fondamentale de la phénoménologie de Husserl: L'intentionnalité." In *Critiques littéraires (Situations, I)*. Paris: Gallimard-Folio, 2005.

The first English language translator of Proust's *A la recherche du temps perdu* was Charles Kenneth Scott Moncrieff. His translation of the first volume of Proust's novel, as *Swann's Way*, was published in 1922; Scott Moncrieff also translated the five following volumes but died in 1930 before translating the end of the novel. A translation of the final volume, *Time Regained*, was completed by Stephen Hudson, a pseudonym of Sydney Schiff. The translation of this volume was updated by Andreas Mayor in 1970. Scott Moncrieff gave the entire novel the title *Remembrance of Things Past* (a phrase he borrowed from Shakespeare's Sonnet 30), while also taking liberties with the titles of a number of the individual volumes. *A l'ombre des jeunes filles en fleur* was called *Within a Budding Grove*. *Sodome et Gomorrhe* was called *Cities of the Plain*. The sixth volume, which has been published in French both as *Albertine disparue* and as *La fugitive*, was called *The Sweet Cheat Gone*.

The Scott Moncrieff and Mayor translations were updated by Terence Kilmartin in 1981. Kilmartin abandoned the title *The Sweet Cheat Gone*, replacing it with *The Fugitive*. The same translations were further revised by D. J. Enright in 1992 after the publication of a new scholarly edition of the novel in France between 1987 and 1989. Here the English title of the whole novel became *In Search of Lost Time*, and *Cities of the Plain* became *Sodom and Gomorrah*. Yale University Press is currently in the process of publishing yet a further revision of this translation by William C. Carter.

In 2002, Penguin Books published an entirely new translation of the novel, each of the seven volumes by a different translator, and the whole edited by Christopher Prendergast. That is the version quoted from here. (*The Prisoner* and *The Fugitive* were printed together as volume 5.) The title for the second volume became *In the Shadow of Young Girls in Flower*. The final volume is called *Finding Time Again*.

There are hefty standard biographies of Proust by Jean-Yves Tadié and William C. Carter, and a useful, slimmer, recent one by Adam Watt, *Marcel Proust* (London: Reaktion Books, 2013). See also William C. Carter, *Proust in Love* (New Haven, CT: Yale University Press, 2006). Watt's *The Cambridge Introduction to Marcel Proust* (Cambridge: Cambridge University Press, 2011) is an excellent guide for further investigations. An eloquent overall assessment of Proust's achievement can be found in Malcolm Bowie, *Proust among the Stars* (New York: Columbia University Press, 1998). John Sturrock translated a handy volume containing many of Proust's other significant writings,

Against Sainte-Beuve and Other Essays (London: Penguin, 1988). Those interested in the formally innovative features of Proust's novel could profitably consult Gérard Genette, *Narrative Discourse: An Essay in Method* (Ithaca, NY: Cornell University Press, 1980). For a recent study of Proust's social and historical context, see Edward J. Hughes, *Proust, Class, and Nation* (Oxford: Oxford University Press, 2011). On the importance of the character of Albertine, see Jacques Dubois, *Pour Albertine: Proust et le sens du social* (Paris: Seuil, 1997). For a feel of the literary and artistic culture out of which Proust's novel emerged, there is Roger Shattuck, *The Banquet Years: The Origins of the Avant-Garde in France 1885 to World War I* (New York: Vintage, 1968); or Jean-Michel Rabaté, *1913: The Cradle of Modernism* (Oxford: Blackwell, 2007). Thinking about Proust and sexuality was energized by several landmark chapters in Eve Kosofsky Sedgwick, *Epistemology of the Closet* (Berkeley: University of California Press, 1990). This same aspect of Proust was studied in relation to a range of his contemporaries in Michael Lucey, *Never Say I: The First Person and Sexuality in Colette, Gide, and Proust* (Durham, NC: Duke University Press, 2006). See also Elisabeth Ladenson, *Proust's Lesbianism* (Ithaca, NY: Cornell University Press, 1999).

✳ ✳

Céline/Malraux

Politics and the Novel in the 1930s

STEVEN UNGAR

Revolutions do not make themselves, but neither do novels. So quipped André Malraux in a 1931 reply to the Marxist revolutionary and theorist Leon Trotsky, who had faulted Malraux's 1928 novel, *Les conquérants*, for lacking a natural affinity between the author—"in spite of all he knows and understands"—and his heroine, the Revolution. To which Malraux retorted that his novel was above all an accusation of the human condition. The exchange discloses assumptions concerning what novels are and what they can—or even what they should—do. Trotsky criticized Malraux's failure to recognize that the presence of Russian Bolsheviks stifled the "lava of revolution" among the Chinese masses. (Indeed, he titled his review "The Strangled Revolution.") To which Malraux replied that by making the characters of *Les conquérants* into symbols, Trotsky had removed them from time and history. Novels are products of the historical moment in which they are written, but they neither express nor reflect that moment directly. The Trotsky-Malraux exchange surrounding *Les conquérants* points to the ideological scrutiny to which novels in France were subjected during the 1930s. One way of illuminating that relation between text and context, of exerting the pressures of the one on the other is to examine two works, Malraux's *La condition humaine* and Louis-Ferdinand Céline's *Voyage au bout de la nuit*; together they constitute a window onto the social situation of the French novel between October 1932 and December 1933.

The 1930s in France have been described as a series of crises resulting from economic depression, unstable domestic rule, and autocratic regimes in Russia and in Germany that threatened the values of republican democracy. The historian Eugen Weber characterized the decade as hollow years, increasingly preoccupied, starting in 1933, by the inevitability of war with Nazi Germany. Media coverage of the period was still in large part a print enterprise. Even so, illustrated dailies and weeklies vied with newsreels screened for millions of viewers at movie theaters. Broadcast radio as a source of news and entertainment became a household staple only toward the end of the decade. Television was not yet a consumer product. Commercial programming of domestic and foreign "talkies" made cinema the primary form of mass entertainment.

In February 1934, antigovernment demonstrations near the Place de la Concorde in Paris polarized ideological differences into opposing camps. Those on the left recast themselves as antifascists; those on the right called themselves anticommunists. The conflict extended to what Herman Lebovics described as wars over cultural identity waged in the name of the true France. Two years earlier, left-leaning writers, including André Breton, André Gide, and André Malraux, had joined the Association des écrivains et artistes révolutionnaires (AEAR), whose mission to defend culture aligned with efforts among French Communist Party members and fellow travelers to promote communism outside Soviet Russia. When French authorities allowed Trotsky to enter France at the Mediterranean fishing village of Cassis in July 1933, his presence was seen by conservatives as a prelude to revolutionary overthrow. Six months earlier, Hitler's appointment as the German chancellor had heightened urgency among members of the AEAR and related leftist groups such as the Comité de vigilance des intellectuels antifascistes (CVIA). On the literary right, onetime supporters of the neoroyalist Action Française movement Robert Brasillach and Lucien Rebatet adopted a more strident tone in their articles for the anti-Semitic weekly *Je suis partout*.

In 1930, prose fiction in France was under the sway of a novel and a patriarch. The former was Marcel Proust's multivolume *A la recherche du temps perdu*; the latter was André Gide—and this despite the fact that Proust had died in 1922 before completing the *Recherche* and Gide had stopped writing fiction after *Les faux-monnayeurs* (1925). Novels by Sidonie-Gabrielle Colette, Romain Rolland, and Martin du Gard were read on both sides of the Atlantic. Prose narratives by surrealists André Breton, Louis Aragon, and Robert Desnos mixed fiction, autobiography, poetry, and essay. A year later, the Belgian-born Georges Simenon's *Pietr le Letton* appeared as the first of more than one hundred crime novels featuring Inspector Jules Maigret. The same year, the twenty-six-year-old *lycée* instructor Jean-Paul Sartre began a "factum on contingency" that would be published in 1938 as a novel, *La nausée*, after his publisher, Gaston Gallimard, rejected the original title, *Melancolia*, that Sartre had proposed as a reference to a 1514 engraving by Albrecht Dürer. Nineteen-year-old Albert Camus was studying philosophy at the University of Algiers and about to join the Algerian Communist Party.

Claims for Proust as a retrograde figure draw on literary debts ranging back in time from Gustave Flaubert's 1869 *L'éducation sentimentale* and Charles Baudelaire's 1857 *Les fleurs du mal* to the eighteenth-century memoirs of the Duc de Saint-Simon and seventeenth-century tragedies of Racine. These claims break down for Gide's portraits of star-crossed couples in *L'immoraliste* (1901), *La porte étroite* (1909), and *La symphonie pastorale* (1919), all of which challenged social and moral conventions of the period. They also weaken in light of formal experiments and social critiques in *Les caves du Vatican* (1914) and *Les faux-monnayeurs*. Each in his own way, Proust and Gide had renewed the novel. Yet by 1930, their fiction no longer spoke to the politicized culture of the new decade. Neither fulfilled the mission of Sartre's *littérature engagée* to write for one's time. Where, then, might the novel go and what might it do?

The Académie française was created in 1635 to compile a dictionary of grammar, rhetoric, and poetics intended to ensure the flourishing of the arts and sciences as expressions of a *patrimoine* (national heritage). By the mid-nineteenth century, an added measure of literary culture took the form of annual prizes such as the Prix Goncourt, awarded since 1903 by the Académie Goncourt for the best and most imaginative prose work of the year. Proust won the Prix Goncourt in 1919 for *A l'ombre des jeunes filles en fleurs*. Gide never did, but the statement accompanying the Nobel Prize in Literature awarded to him in 1947 referred to his "comprehensive and artistically significant writings, in which human problems and conditions have been presented with a fearless love of truth and keen psychological insight." In 1932, Céline's *Voyage au bout de la nuit*, an early favorite, failed to win the Goncourt. A year later, André Malraux won it for *La condition humaine*, with unanimous support on a first ballot. Cultural wars indeed!

The Prix Goncourt opens onto commercial-industrial dimensions of literary culture subject to vertical integration, ranging from the lofty status enjoyed by award-winning authors downward to the mundane practices of marketing and reception. Nowhere were these dimensions more visible in interwar France than in the Gallimard publishing house, whose assets in 1930 included the prestigious Collection Blanche of fiction and nonfiction titles as well as ZED Publications, an umbrella corporation created in 1928 to manage the illustrated weeklies *Marianne*, *Détective*, and *Voilà*. Where the latter two adopted tabloid strategies by spicing up reportage with features on sex, crime, and politics, the former billed itself as (France's? Paris's?) *grand hebdomadaire littéraire illustré*. The Editions de la Nouvelle Revue Française was created in 1911 to oversee production of *La Nouvelle Revue Française* (hereafter *NRF*), a literary monthly Gide had helped to found three years earlier. Within a decade, the Editions de la NRF became the Librairie Gallimard, under the management of publisher Gaston Gallimard. Thirty-six Goncourt and thirty-five Nobel laureates have established Gallimard's reputation as France's premier publisher.

One author and one work in particular would prove to be problematical candidates for entry into the Gallimard pantheon. Published in October 1932, *Voyage au bout de la nuit* (hereafter *Voyage*) was a first novel by the medical doctor Louis Ferdinand Auguste Destouches (1894–1961). (The pen name "Céline" adopted by Destouches had been that of his maternal grandmother.) The fact that its author seemed to appear from nowhere heightened the shock waves that the *Voyage*'s publication produced in the Parisian literary establishment. Céline began as a literary *marginal* (outsider), but he was far from an unknown quantity. When Gallimard editors asked him to summarize the manuscript he submitted in April 1932, Céline described it almost apologetically, as less of a true novel than a kind of literary symphony in which he had tried to use words to obtain emotional effects more often associated with music. As for the plot, he added, it was simultaneously complex and simpleminded, somewhat derivative from opera as a grand fresco of lyrical populism: communism with a soul, mischievous and therefore alive.

Gallimard editors already knew Céline on the basis of the manuscript of a play, *L'église*, they had rejected five years earlier after agreeing that its satirical vigor failed to compensate for a lack of continuity. Two years later, they cited the same defect when they turned down Céline's biography of Dr. Philippe Ignaz Semmelweis (1818–65), a pioneer advocate of obstetric antisepsis on whom he had based the dissertation he had written in conjunction with his medical studies. While the Gallimard staff, including Malraux, debated the strengths and weaknesses of the *Voyage*, the upstart publisher Robert Denoël moved quickly after receiving a nine hundred–page manuscript with neither signature nor return address. Rumor had it that Denoël read the manuscript straight through over a single night before setting out to identify its reclusive author. Gallimard eventually agreed to take the novel on condition that Céline cut some passages and rework others. Denoël and his partner, Bernard Steele, resolved the matter in their favor by committing to a contract without changes.

When Céline appeared in Denoël's office, he explained that when Gallimard delayed its decision, he sent the manuscript to Denoël because he had been impressed by his handling of another first novel. Winner of the first Prix du Roman Populiste, Eugène Dabit's *L'Hôtel du Nord* (1929) recounted day-to-day comings and goings among boarders at a residential hotel in a working-class neighborhood alongside the Canal Saint-Martin in Paris. Marcel Carné's 1938 film adaptation, *Hôtel du Nord*, drew in part on Dabit's novel. But it was mainly a box-office vehicle for movie stars Annabella and Jean-Pierre Aumont. Even the tart dialogues Henri Jeanson and Jean Aurenche wrote for newly added characters played by Louis Jouvet and Arletty failed to match Dabit's portraits of poverty and abjection that Céline sought to emulate. Unlike Céline, Dabit was no literary outsider. Gallimard elders Gide and Roger Martin du Gard had encouraged him to pursue literary writing in the wake of art school and failed business ventures. In the *NRF*'s December 1932 issue, Dabit hailed the *Voyage* as a tragic work in which revolt stemmed from neither aesthetic discussions nor symbols, but instead as "un cri de protestation contre la condition humaine" (a cry of rage against the human condition). Whether intended or not, Dabit's reference to the title of the novel whose "pre-original" version Malraux would serialize in the *NRF* between January and June 1933 was nothing less than prescient.

Denoël sent proofs of the *Voyage* to literary journals in order to position it favorably for the Goncourt. Initial reviews in the daily and weekly press were mostly positive. Concerns over Céline's use of nontraditional ("raw") language confirmed that his novel left few readers indifferent. Ten days before the luncheon at which the Prix Goncourt was to be announced, academy members Jean Ajalbert and Lucien Descaves offered their congratulations to Céline. Despite these signs of early support, the Goncourt went instead to Gallimard author Guy Mazeline for his novel of more than five hundred pages, *Les loups* (*The Wolves*). The final tally was six votes for *Les loups* and four votes for the *Voyage*. Céline settled for the lesser Prix Renaudot as sales of his novel soared. The *Voyage* was clearly the novel of the year, and Céline's literary career was launched. Yet what some took to calling the Goncourt affair was formative in light of subsequent rejections that hardened Céline against those he perceived as having rebuffed him. As in the photos of Goncourt candidates published in the December 9, 1932, issue of Gallimard's *Marianne* with a blank space above Céline's name, absence could serve as a determining presence (fig. 1).

The distinctive tone of the *Voyage* resulted from Céline's decision to cast the first-person account of narrator, Ferdinand Bardamu, in a mode of spoken French—Céline called it his *petite musique*—whose affective punch bordered on the visceral. For Raymond Queneau, the *Voyage*'s simulation of modern spoken French—"such as it is, such as it exists"—drew as much on syntax as on vocabulary. Céline's achievement was the skill with which he passed from written French in classical and modern forms to a *third* French (Queneau's emphasis) as it was actually spoken, although Zola was something of a predecessor in his use of working-class speech in the dialogues of *L'assommoir* and *Germinal*, as well as his matching of popular idioms and free indirect discourse. Celine's move into demotic, however, was altogether more radical and systematic. A year later, Céline corrobo-

Figure 1. Front page of *Marianne*, December 9, 1932, with Céline's photo notably missing among the candidates for the Prix Goncourt.

rated Queneau's assessment when he wrote that nothing was more difficult than transposing the spoken language of everyday emotions into writing.

The skillful yoking of vision and living language appears in the very first sentence of the *Voyage*: "Ça a débuté comme ça," to which Ralph Manheim's translation as "Here's how it started" does only partial justice. Of immediate interest is Céline's colloquial take on the standard opening, *il était une fois* (once upon a time), associated with the fairy tale and crime fiction. The verb *débuter* (to start out) conveys a conversational usage less often associated with the standard infinitive *commencer* (start). In terms of sound, the infinitive *buter* (to bump, or, in gangster slang, to bump off) is audible in the second and third syllables. The framing of the sentence by the impersonal pronoun *ça* reinforces the primacy of speech over writing. The second sentence—"Moi, j'avais jamais rien dit" (I'd never said a word)—extends the oral effect by eliding the negative particle *n'* paired with the double negative *jamais* (never) and *rien* (nothing). Céline's Bardamu initially presents himself as a *type ordinaire* (regular guy) who takes things (*ça*) as they come. The silence at its start elevates the *Voyage* into an explosive diatribe for which street French is a forceful means of expression. The novel's final words—*qu'on n'en parle plus*, translatable as "let no more be said about it," "that's enough of that," or "that'll do"—make silence integral to an ending that falls short of narrative closure. Readers attentive to Céline's skillful simulation of spoken ("street") French may also have been taken (taken aback?) by the novel's nihilist vision, whose ideological valence was hard to assess.

The *Voyage* recounts Bardamu's departures from and returns to Paris and its outskirts over a period of some fifteen years. His initial encounters with death as a soldier in battle are formative and traumatic: "You can be a virgin in horror the same as in sex." Some thirty years before US Air Force Captain John Yossarian in Joseph Heller's *Catch-22* (1963), Bardamu realized that because the war into which he walked makes no sense, efforts to understand it should not deter the primal imperative to save one's skin. The instinct to flee (*foutre le camp*) kicks in after Bardamu witnesses death at close range when a shell decapitates a cavalryman in his unit, leaving an opening at the top of his head, "with blood in it bubbling and glugging [*qui mijotait en glouglous*] like jam in a kettle." Graphic descriptions of oozing blood and mangled flesh are essential to a strain of black humor that Céline directs toward proper and place names. The commander of Bardamu's unit was a general whose name, des Entrayes, which is a homonym of *entrailles* (entrails, guts—or even embodied as Old Blood and Guts), expressed a base materialism concerned with bodily functions.

It is while wandering in the night outside the village of Noirceur-sur-Lys (literally "blackness on the river Lily") that Bardamu encounters another lost French soldier, Léon Robinson, who plans to surrender to the enemy rather than die in battle. The encounter is significant because, while Robinson and Bardamu survive the war, Robinson precedes Bardamu throughout the novel across France, Africa, the United States, and back to France into the figurative night of degradation and evil that ends with his sordid murder. The opening section of the *Voyage* also introduces the honorably discharged Bardamu to a Paris where the rich live together in adjoining neighborhoods that he likens to a wedge-shaped slice of urban cake with its tip at the Louvre and its outer edges between the Pont d'Auteuil and the Porte des Ternes. This, he concludes, is the good part of the city; "all the rest is shit." It is to the latter that Bardamu is drawn in the second half of the *Voyage*. Wartime Paris is also where Bardamu meets Lola, a young American whose job as a volunteer is to provide local hospitals with apple fritters. Bardamu states that what first had attracted him to Lola was her American body, the sight of which inspired him on the spot to make a pilgrimage to the country of its origin. Believing more in her body than in her soul, he confesses shamelessly that it was in the immediate vicinity of Lola's rear end that he received the message of a new world. Bardamu's wish comes true, but the anonymity and poverty he witnesses in New York City and Detroit quickly disabuse him of his erotic-romantic assumptions.

The long second half of the *Voyage* centers on the medical practice Bardamu sets up just outside the city limits of Paris. As in Detroit, the sky in Rancy (the place name contains the sound of the adjective *rance*, for "rancid)" is "a smoky soup that bathes the plain all the way to Levallois. Cast-off buildings bogged down in black muck. From a distance, the chimneys, big ones and little ones, look like the fat stakes that rise out of the muck by the seaside. And inside it's us." Episodes of day-to-day cruelty, greed, and pettiness harden the satirical tone of the first section toward the flat affect of resignation.

As in postwar films noirs on both sides of the Atlantic, shady ventures and dubious decisions fashion a figurative night of moral decadence whose inevitable outcome in death is punctuated by rare moments of kindness and ephemeral community. One such moment occurs when Bardamu walks back to Rancy after seeking advice from a former teacher. Crossing to the Right Bank, he notices people on the rue Lepic in Montmartre lined up outside a butcher shop in front of which an enormous pig had been tied up with a rope. People twist the pig's ears and poke it to make it squeal. The owner of the shop, who has planned the stunt to attract business brandishes a big knife and jokes around: "He couldn't have had a better time at his daughter's wedding." The passage stages an urban moment in which onlookers and passersby revert to the kind of shared experience that they, their parents, or their grandparents might have experienced in a provincial past. It reinforces Céline's treatment of working-class neighborhoods that retain occasional traces of rural (provincial) traditions. Urban landscapes are mainly oppressive spaces within which Céline depicts the daily lives of those for whom such episodes are brief respites from a daily grind whose causes they seldom have either the energy or the awareness to question.

The *Voyage* ends with Robinson's death by gunshot at the hands of his on-again off-again consort. The murder culminates a trajectory conveyed by the keywords *voyage*, *bout*, and *nuit* that the novel's second half recounts as a catalog of misery that leaves survivors exhausted and indifferent. The final paragraph of the *Voyage* conveys this indifference through the verbal equivalent of an extreme long shot of a tugboat whose sounded whistle carries across river locks, bridges, other barges, the sky, and the countryside. Two years later, Jean Vigo would likewise end his fourth and final film, *L'Atalante*, with an overhead shot of a barge. By contrast, André Malraux begins *La condition humaine* with two questions—"Should he try to raise the mosquito-netting? Or should he strike it through?"—that, as in a cinematic close-up, convey the immediacy of an act for which his reader has no context whatsoever. The questions belong to a character named Tch'en Ta Erh. They introduce a seven-page passage describing his thoughts and sensations while carrying out an assassination. The sense of immediacy throughout the passage builds on the use of free indirect speech in sentences that seem to express Tch'en's thoughts, so to speak, from within: "Oh, what a relief to fight, to fight enemies who defend themselves, enemies who are awake!"

Tch'en is part of a cell involved in an ill-fated 1927 insurrection by dissident Chinese Communists intent on preventing Chiang Kai-shek from appropriating a revolutionary movement in the name of the Kuomintang (People's Nationalist Party). Members of the cell see Chiang's goals at odds with those of the Communist International (Comintern) dedicated to establishing Soviet republics around the world. Tch'en's short-term mission is to obtain documents allowing the cell to intercept a shipment of three hundred rifles with which it would disarm the local police and arm their comrades opposed to Chiang. The questions at the start of the passage convey the complexity of motivations that drive Tch'en to kill. They show that the act he is about to commit is not only an order from his comrades, but a means of absolute self-possession. Unable to gauge the resistance of the flesh he is about to stab through a mosquito net, Tch'en presses the point of his dagger into his left arm. Despite the pain he feels, he is unsure that the arm he has stabbed is his own. When Tch'en kills his victim "with a blow that would have split a plank," he is so immersed in the moment that he initially forgets to take the document he has been sent to obtain.

Tch'en is often described as a terrorist, but it is more accurate to see him among a cell of intellectuals for whom the idea of violence in the cause of revolutionary activity is a basis of commonality. If his drive toward spectacular violence suggests a personal pathology leading to isolation and self-destruction, other members of the cell are isolated each in his or her own way. And as much as *La condition humaine* occurs mainly in the clearly defined setting of Shanghai in the early spring of 1927, the novel is often understood in abstract terms as a series of limit cases depicting the values in the cause for which an individual is willing to die. A decade before Sartre's fictional *Les chemins de la liberté* (*The Roads to Freedom*) tetralogy, *La condition humaine* illustrates an existential literature of extreme situations in which the consequences of decisions and actions are immediate and often fatal.

The isolation from the sensory world surrounding Tch'en illustrates a primary trait of what the narrator calls his humanity ("sa condition d'homme"). Yet this isolation also points to a condition of mortality to which all men and women are subject. This broader sense of the term *condition* echoes a passage from Blaise Pascal's *Pensées* (1670): "Imagine a number of men in chains and all condemned to death: some of them each day are slaughtered in full view of the others; those who remain recognize their own condition in that of their fellow men, and, looking at each other with grief and without hope, wait for their turn. This is the image of the human condition." If Pascal's *Pensées* can be read as a defense of Christian faith, assertions for Malraux's novel as an equivalent defense of revolutionary action founder on the basis of an alienation Malraux first illustrates when the cell's leader, Kyo Gisors, fails to recognize his recorded voice the first time he hears it. Kyo is arguably Malraux's most complex embodiment of the human condition understood as isolation. And this not only in terms of sensory alienation noted above, but even more in a commitment to revolutionary action that sets him apart from the Comintern leaders, whose orders to abstain from interfering with Chiang he disobeys, and from his wife, May, whose admission of a passing infidelity arouses jealousy in him that he had not foreseen.

Much as Camus wrote *La peste* (1947) as a reply to visions of absurdity he had set forth in *L'étranger* and *Le mythe de Sisyphe* (1942 for both), *La condition humaine* depicts various ways that individuals contend with isolation in the face of death. Tch'en dies by throwing himself under a car he believes is carrying Chiang Kai-Shek. Setting off a bomb he is carrying, he dies without learning that Chiang was not in the car. After Kyo is arrested and detained along with Katov to await execution, he commits suicide by taking a cyanide pellet he has been carrying. He and Tch'en die alone. Their deaths in physical isolation are tempered by a commitment to collective action that overrides the circumstances and obstacles they face on an individual basis. Katov gives his cyanide pellet away in order to ease the suffering of two comrades, knowing full well that he is about to be burned alive in the boiler of a locomotive. Hemmelrich, May, and Kyo's father survive the insurrection as witnesses to the long revolution that has cost them a wife and child, a husband, and a son, respectively.

In order to determine Malraux's distinctive accomplishment in *La condition humaine*, it is helpful to specify what his novel is not. Although it evokes a recent historical moment, the novel is neither a fictionalized account of the 1927 Shanghai insurrection, a political fable, nor a novel of ideas. It is, to a limited degree, all of these. But first and foremost, *La condition humaine* is a novel that raises fundamental questions of identity and value in conjunction with a series of events in China whose outcome at least some readers of the novel could be expected to know. Where commentators have pondered the tragic perspective on life that these questions set forth, it is at least as important to account for their presentation in a narrative mode based in cinematic montage. Claude-Edmonde Magny argues convincingly that Malraux replaces classic continuity of plot by juxtaposing "scenes" that pass without transition from one to the other in a series of flashes comparable to the projection of slides. The effect transforms verbal passages into shots and sequences whose traces the eye follows more readily and more quickly than the mind.

Much as juxtaposition-based montage inscribes individual shots and sequences within the dynamic force of a larger continuity, Malraux's verbal montage juxtaposes passages of isolation and solidarity among characters swept up in the force of circumstance. The model of cinematic montage has direct bearing on Malraux's efforts to challenge traditional treatments of fictional protagonists. Lucien Goldmann situates *La condition humaine* near the midpoint of a transition from *Les conquérants* and *La voie royale* (1930) to *L'espoir* (1938)—that is, between novels with a problematic hero and the novel more or less without individual characters. The proximity of this verbal juxtaposition to filmmaker Sergei Eisenstein's model of oppositional montage is supported by the fact that Eisenstein and Malraux collaborated on a rough screenplay of *La condition humaine* in response to a commission from a state agency. The project was abandoned in 1934 after Soviet officials withdrew support from a film whose Trotskyist vision of permanent revolution they likely saw at odds with government policies under Josef Stalin.

In line with Malraux's efforts to approximate techniques of oppositional montage in his fictional prose, *La condition humaine* can be understood as a series of verbal close-ups, extreme close-ups, and reverse tracking shots leading to action sequences of various lengths and intensities. Magny notes that the point of narrating from multiple points of view is less to tell the story of the failed Communist insurrection in Shanghai than to confront the reader with a certain total vision of the human condition through shots and sequences disclosing conditions that threaten the ability of collective action to end shared suffering: "The book's scenes are always described from the point of view of one or another of the characters: the author does not appear; the camera is always in the consciousness of a particular person, and the transitions from close-up to long shot are regulated by the oscillations of that person's attention."

Among the insurrectionist cell's protagonists Tch'en, Kyo, and Katov, none fulfills the requirements to be what critics later call an antihero. The fact that Malraux depicts all three in the mode of the problematic hero depends less on their character traits as individuals than on their shared efforts to overcome a human condition of isolation in the face of mortality. Kyo dies not simply because the self-centered "Baron" Clappique fails to warn him of his imminent arrest or because he is despondent over his wife's infidelity. Instead, he fashions his fate by disobeying orders from Comintern representatives whom he believes compromise the revolutionary activity to which he and his comrades are committed. Kyo's refusal of Comintern discipline and Tch'en's fanaticism qualify as tragic on the basis of the limited choices available to them. A full decade before Sartre's novels and essays engage a literature of extreme situations, Malraux tempers his critique of capitalism with portraits of individuals forced by circumstance to make life-and-death decisions affecting others as well as themselves.

Malraux's treatment of these decisions is inseparable from a cinematic mode of presentation that seemingly locates the reader within an action as it occurs. As an experiment in novelistic technique, *La condition humaine* explores the verbal equivalent of cinematic cross-cuts expressing an *existential* aesthetic in a narrative that is always told from *someone's* point of view (Magny's emphasis). Starting with the novel's first passage, the turn to cinematic montage approximates the direct apprehension of experience for which moving pictures provide a viable alternative to prose fiction. Over a longer duration, this turn extends to literary experimentation in modernist modes, such as Guillaume Apollinaire's efforts to evoke a series of simultaneous conversations overhead at a Left Bank café in his 1913 poem "Lundi rue Christine." But whereas Apollinaire's transcriptions approximate a sense of presence and immediacy, they have none of the urgency inherent in Tch'en's mission.

Pondering an equivalent cinematic turn in Céline's efforts to mobilize the living language of spoken French yields results that are more anecdotal than aesthetic. In 1934, Céline traveled to Los Angeles to speak with Hollywood producers about a film adaptation of the *Voyage*. Nothing came of his efforts. In 1981, film director Bertrand Tavernier combined Jim Thompson's 1964 crime novel, *Pop. 1280*, with elements of Céline's account of Bardamu in Africa. The result was *Coup de torchon* (*A Clean Slate*), which Tavernier relocated to French West Africa during a period more or less coincidental with the September 1938 Munich agreements by which Hitler annexed portions of Czechoslovakia known as Sudetenland and the outbreak of World War II. Beyond details of plot and geographic setting, the *Voyage's* dark worldview was a good match for the hard-boiled American crime fiction by Dashiell Hammett and Raymond Chandler on which Thompson drew.

The assimilation of cinematic technique in *La condition humaine* is Malraux's prelude to *Espoir: Sierra de Teruel*, the film he shot in Spain between August 1938 and January 1939 as a supplement to his 1937 novel, *L'espoir*. The progression aligned with an affinity for film that Malraux characterized in a 1936 speech as encompassing the totality of a civilization: comic with Charlie Chaplin in capitalist countries, tragic with Eisenstein in communist countries, and potentially warriorlike in fascist countries. Visual parallels for Céline's *Voyage* point instead to late medieval and early Renaissance paintings by Hieronymus Bosch and Pieter Brueghel the Elder. Where the former's *Garden of Earthly Delights* (1490–1510?) traces a trajectory from earthly paradise to damnation and exile, the latter's depiction of a peasant festival in *The Fight between Carnaval and Lent* (1559) recalls the *Voyage*'s rue Lepic episode. Both paintings fill their respective formats of landscape and street scene with multiple actions, which Bosch compresses from the panels of Brueghel's triptych to a single wide-angle take. Both contain details of grotesque physicality for which numerous passages in Céline's novel provide verbal expression.

Do all novels turn out to be political novels? Even though they do not, the question underlies the 1931 Trotsky-Malraux exchange surrounding *Les conquérants* as well as leftist critiques prompted by the *Voyage* and *La condition humaine*. Bardamu's description of the geographic slice of "good Paris" surrounded by the rest of the city discloses class differences without mentioning them explicitly. But it fails to accommodate revolutionary missions for culture in general, and the novel in particular. Trotsky wrote that the *Voyage*'s dissidence needed to be resolved in a second book in which the artist would either make peace with the darkness or perceive the dawn. Writing in the French Communist Party daily, *L'Humanité*, Paul Nizan praised the novel's sinister tableau of despair for which death was the only possible outcome. But because it lacked the revolution that explained the misery it merely described, the *Voyage* could lead anywhere: "among us, against us, or nowhere." Céline, Nizan concluded, was not "one of us." Georges Bataille resumed the *Voyage* as an account of a man's relations with his own death before noting that Céline's pitiless vision of moral decline marked a preliminary phase leading to a new fraternal consciousness among urban and exurban masses. His remarks on *La condition humaine* focused on its depiction of revolutionary activity as a state of excitation among intellectuals removed from the working class, which was destined to vegetate and die without understanding the causes of its misery. In sum, neither novel included the progression from thought to action among workers for which heightened consciousness of class was a necessary prerequisite.

In 1934, Walter Benjamin assessed what he termed the present social situation of the French writer in conjunction with fiction, essays, and journalism by turn-of-the-century figures Maurice Barrès and Charles Maurras, both of whom were associated with the neoroyalist Action Française movement. Where Benjamin's usage of the term "present" targeted the contemporary historical moment, its pairing with the adjective "social" referred to the kind of real-world engagement with the historical present that German sociologist Jürgen Habermas has referred to in conjunction with the public sphere. Much like Bataille, Trotsky, and Nizan before him, Benjamin took Céline's failure to explain the causes of suffering among the *Lumpenproletariat* as a missed opportunity. Qualifying as "treacherous" Eugène Dabit's characterization of the *Voyage* as a cry of rage, Benjamin noted, "So far so good. Were it not for the fact that the essence of revolutionary training and experience is to recognize the class structure of the masses and to exploit it." In sum, what many considered the success of the *Voyage* as a *roman populiste* represented less of an advance for the proletarian novel than a retreat on the part of bourgeois aesthetics.

Along similar lines, Benjamin saw *La condition humaine* as symptomatic of the political education and social situation of left-leaning European literary intellectuals. After noting that the failed insurrection in Shanghai was the backdrop for a depiction of individual efforts at revolutionary activity, he took Malraux to task for not having cell members realize that making cause with the workers was not the same as acting as proletarians. The lesson of Malraux's novel, he concluded, was that the insurrection failed because Kyo and Tch'en acted less from class consciousness than from a sense of tragic isolation that Benjamin attributed to the social situation of the intellectual.

Bataille and Benjamin's critiques of the *Voyage* and *La condition humaine* restate the high expectations imposed by the militant left on prose fiction. The treatment of politics in both novels is inseparable from formal innovations such as Céline's "street" French and Malraux's experimentation with cinematic techniques. In the *Voyage*, this treatment includes not only depictions of war, colonialism, capitalism, and the grinding misery of urban and ex-urban populations, but also Céline's use of vernacular French, whose revolutionary potential Trotsky immediately acknowledged. The tragic vision that Malraux situates among members of the revolutionary cell betrayed from above by the Comintern is likewise inseparable from the multiple points of view approximating cinematic or oppositional montage.

Malraux's embrace of montage aligns with Eisenstein's sense of montage in two distinct ways: first, as a powerful technique that arouse the senses and emotions of the viewer; and second, as a basic principle of making something greater than the sum of individual frames projected on screen. Eisenstein's evolving views on montage as technique and principle are driven by the prescriptive concerns of agitprop filmmaking to impel viewers to entertain doctrines related to social change. Moreover, his casting of montage in terms of dialectic extends toward the dynamic of social change his filmmaking was meant to advance. Similar claims can be made for Malraux's efforts to approximate techniques of cinematic montage in the form of fictional narration. Céline's innovative use of spoken French in the *Voyage* reverts to the long history of oral traditions at a remove from the image-based nature of cinema as an advanced mass medium of the historical and ideological present. The techniques of montage throughout *La condition humaine* posit parallels between the transformative nature of Eisenstein's oppositional montage noted above and—even more—processes of social change for which the failed Shanghai insurrection of 1927 was an object lesson. Finally, Malraux's efforts at novelistic montage marked a key phase in his intellectual trajectory toward visual cultures of cinema and the world history of graphic and plastic arts that would increasingly preoccupy him by the end of the same decade. Montage thus serves as a measure of Malraux's deviation from literary modernism that, as in Apollinaire's "Lundi rue Christine," sought to approximate unmediated experience and the speed of emergent audio-visual technologies, to committed practices that directed these technologies toward activism and social change.

In 1938, Céline wrote the first of his notorious anti-Semitic pamphlets, *Bagatelles pour un massacre*, which resolved Trotsky's question concerning dissonance in the *Voyage* in a way Trotsky would have been unlikely to endorse. Malraux was in Spain completing *Sierra de Teruel* in support of Republicans. The 1932–33 moment in France when the potential for direct denunciation and critique toward revolutionary change served as a prime measure of novels such as the *Voyage* and *La condition humaine* yielded to works of lesser scope. Winner of the 1938 Prix Goncourt, Henri Troyat's *L'araigne* reverted to psychological drama in a family setting at a remove from novelistic visions of social struggle and revolutionary change. As a symptom or document of its historical moment, *L'araigne* relocated prose fiction within the fatalism following the March 1938 demise of the leftist coalition Popular Front government and the Munich agreements six months later, the 1939–40 *drôle de guerre* (phony war), and the 1940–44 Vichy regime under German military control that followed all too quickly. The moment when Trotsky, Nizan, Bataille, and Benjamin had placed the promise and the burden of revolutionary change on the *Voyage* and *La condition humaine* had passed, resulting in the figurative equivalent of a military retreat.

Works Cited and Recommended Further Reading

For French editions of the two works discussed in this chapter, see Louis-Ferdinand Céline, *Voyage au bout de la nuit* (1932) (Paris: Gallimard "Folio," 1972); and André Malraux, *La condition humaine* (1933) (Paris: Gallimard "Folio," 1972). Cited passages from the *Voyage* and *La condition humaine* are from Ralph Manheim, trans., *Journey to the End of Night* (New York: New Directions, 1983); and Haakon M. Chevalier, trans., *Man's Fate* (New York: Vintage, 1990).

Helpful overviews of France during the 1930s include Eugen Weber, *The Hollow Years: France in the 1930s* (New York: Norton, 1994), Herman Lebovics, *True France: The Wars over Cultural Identity, 1900–1945* (Ithaca, NY: Cornell University Press, 1992), and Dudley Andrew and Steven Ungar, *Popular Front Paris and the Poetics of Culture* (Cambridge, MA: Harvard University Press, 2005). Julia Kristeva's entry on Céline in Lawrence D. Kritzman, ed., *The Columbia History of Twentieth-Century French Thought* (New York: Columbia University Press, 2006) updates the analyses in her *The Powers of Horror: An Essay on Abjection* (New York: Columbia University Press, 1982). See also Raymond Queneau, "Written in 1937," in *Letters, Numbers, Forms* (Urbana: University of Illinois Press, 2007). Claude-Edmonde Magny, "Malraux the Fascinator," in *Malraux: A Collection of Critical Essays*, ed. R.W.B. Lewis (Englewood Cliffs, NJ: Prentice-Hall, 1964) engages the major theses of Magny's *The Age of the American Novel: The Film Aesthetic of Fiction between the Wars* (New York: Ungar, 1972). On *La condition humaine*, see also W. M.

Frohock, "The Power and the Glory," in *André Malraux and the Tragic Imagination* (Palo Alto, CA: Stanford University Press, 1952); Lucien Goldmann, *Toward a Sociology of the Novel* (London: Routledge, Chapman, and Hall, 1975); and Douglas Collins, "Terrorists Ask No Questions," in *A New History of French Literature*, ed. Denis Hollier et al. (Cambridge, MA: Harvard University Press, 1987). Trotsky's "Céline and Poincaré: Novelist and Politician" and "The Strangled Revolution: André Malraux's *Les conquérants*" are reprinted in *Leon Trotsky on Literature and Art*, ed. Paul N. Siegel, ed. (New York: Pathfinder, 1970). Malraux's "Reply to Trotsky" appears in Lewis, *André Malraux*, and Walter Benjamin's "The Present Social Situation of the French Writer" is in his *Selected Writings, vol. 2 (1927–1934)* (Cambridge, MA: Harvard University Press, 1999). Georges Bataille's texts on the novels by Céline and Malraux, first published in *La Critique sociale*, are reprinted in volume one of his *Oeuvres complètes* (Paris: Gallimard, 1970). Paul Nizan's review of the *Voyage* appeared in the December 9, 1932, issue of *L'Humanité*. See also David Bordwell, *The Cinema of Eisenstein* (Cambridge, MA: Harvard University Press, 1993).

* *

Breton, Char, and Modern French Poetry

MARY ANN CAWS

André Breton and René Char are key figures in the history of twentieth-century French poetry, above all in relation to the movement—surrealism—that was to issue from predecessors such as Pierre Reverdy, Alfred Jarry, the group around Dada, and crucially Guillaume Apollinaire (who first coined the term "surrealist"). Further back in time, but no less powerfully formative, stand Lautréamont ("rediscovered" by Breton) and Rimbaud (a foundational inspiration for Char). Breton was the (often dictatorial) leader of the movement. His habit of excommunicating dissidents earned him the title "Pope of Surrealism," but he was nevertheless the leading light in the sense of being at the forefront, in both polemic and literary practice, of the surrealist project to change radically the ways in which the mind frees itself from rational baggage and correspondingly to alter the very grounds of vision. Char's relation to surrealism, on the other hand, was a more temporary and contingent affair, that of the disciple deeply—and abidingly—invested in disrupting poetic convention and renewing vision. But he was also the disciple who eventually rebels and strikes out on his own. This was partly a matter of historical location: Breton (1896–1966) belongs essentially to the period of the 1920s and the 1930s; Char (1907–88) to the time of the Second World War and the French Resistance. But there were also differences of temperament and outlook. Char had a much stronger commitment to returning poetry, via its renewed forms, to the sights and rhythms of the natural world; geographical location also mattered here (Breton was based in Paris, Char for the most part in his native Provence).

Breton's best-known work in the English-speaking world is probably *Nadja*, first published in 1928. The history of this quite extraordinary encounter, told in a quite extraordinary way, is the only work of Breton's that he rewrote: the revised *Nadja* was published in 1962, a mark of its importance for him and for the reader of surrealist writing. "Who am I," it begins, and continues with a meditation on that and related topics, for the discovery of Nadja at the beginning and the turn away from her to X at the end compose an all-engaging tale of an impossible relationship, of unreason and reason, of a couple wandering through Paris, and finally, of a narrator then moving on to someone else less mysterious. The person of Nadja is haunting ("tell me whom I haunt") to the point that many subsequent would-be Nadjas have existed. In itself, the tale gives the lie, in a sense, to the original goal of surrealism, which, in Breton's formulation, wanted to celebrate "the art of the crazed" as well as the art of the child. That it should then have, in a practical sense, come to grief when its leader and its very incarnation found, by some operation of the marvelous, a genuine madwoman in the street, whom he considered first mesmerizing and then boring, has a tragic irony to it. Nadja, who ended in an asylum in the Vaucluse (providing a case for Breton's attack on such institutions, which actually create the crazies, he said), initiates a discovery of self-knowledge in all its terribleness.

The real Nadja not only existed, as Léona-Camille-Ghislaine Delcourt (usually abbreviated to "D"), born in 1902, but her many letters to Breton indeed exist also, with their drawings, some of which are displayed in the novel. Between October 22, 1926, and February 1927, she wrote Breton twenty-seven letters and *pneumatiques*, those little blue missives that used to be sent across Paris. (One of the peculiarities of the Breton/Char confrontation that is examined in this chapter is the singular fact that in the copy of *Nadja* that Breton had given to René Char were two of Nadja's drawings and a letter. That is one of those totally unexpected objective chances. *Nadja*'s reception was prepared by the prepublication in the avant-garde journal *transition*, of the final letter to Breton's daughter, Aube, and here called "Ecusette de Noireuil," to whom he writes: "I hope you will be *MADLY* loved," the French translated by *transition*'s editor, Eugène Jolas. Breton was initially attracted by Nadja's fragility and her strangeness—her makeup was not quite completely put on, and she was accustomed to inhabiting several hotels, living partly on her earnings as a prostitute. They spent a night together, in a hotel of Saint-Germain-en-Laye, but Breton was already becoming bored. The reader may find herself on the side of Nadja, when the foreseen breakup takes place. Nadja always knew the encounter was marked by "the impossible" and always claimed that Breton—whom she had indeed madly loved—had something gigantic to accomplish, as she points out in her letter of November 30, 1926: "You will use me and I will do my best to help you to do something great." He did, and she did, giving him the basis for this all-powerful book. She took me for a god, said Breton, and for the sun.

The importance of the experience for Breton is that the *saccade* (shock) that served to jumpstart his theory of "convulsive beauty" not only ends the book *Nadja*, but transfigures itself into the first chapter of *L'amour fou* (*Mad Love*). *Mad Love*, says Marguerite Bonnet, is above all the presence of a voice, the frequent lyric repetitions serving as a "signal of intensity" in his writing-speaking here. The excitement of the madness of passion permeates the entire enterprise of surrealism, despite the irony of the real case. To impassion the dailiness of life by the expectation of the unexpected: that goal remains, from the initial dynamism of the young movement, displayed in the 1924 *Pas perdus* (*Lost Steps*) (named after a train station waiting room and the walking up and down of the one waiting), through the later lyric expanse of Breton's writing and thinking. Surrealism concerns, above all, the power of the imagination. "The imaginary is what tends to become real" ("Il y aura une fois . . ." [Once upon a time there will be . . .], in *Le revolver aux cheveux blancs* [*The White-Haired Revolver*, 1932] but published for the first time in 1930, in the first number of *Surréalisme au service de la révolution* [*Surrealism in the Service of the Revolution*]). This places surrealism in the realm of the magical and of the dream as well as the everyday, in those merging perceptions, and so it was to remain as a hinge between them, a "swinging door."

Now the integration of the disparate objects and incidents around the poet—the one who is at the center of the dream vision—comes with the attention paid to the unexpected and, precisely, the expectation that it will occur. In surrealism, as Breton conceived of it, the state of expectation, the "état d'attente" is of prime importance. It is here that the linguistic takes over, and those "lever words"—the *mots-leviers*—can guide the imaginer or dreamer straight to the facts that slide us into the marvelous, while those *faits-glissades* or "slippery facts" or, at the most surprising best, can plunge us into it: those *faits-précipices* or "cliff-facts." And exactly here is where the imaginary becomes the real, and we perceive that heart of things that holds out the thread to the one who might know how to grasp it.

The crucial conclusion of the poem "Vigilance"—that poem of keeping watch that begins with the appearance of the Tour Saint-Jacques swaying—reads in gloriously optimistic fashion:

Je ne touche plus que le coeur des choses je tiens le fil.
(I touch only the heart of things I hold the thread.)

This is a vision, leading to the work of art, that is based on an interior and not an exterior model: "man the dreamer at the heart of things." To take up that thread at the center of things is to find it more than what threads things and experiences together: it is a "fil conducteur," a conducting wire that fuses the object with the eye, placing the seer at the center of it all. Perceiver and perceived are joined.

And yet the exterior world mattered intensely, with its objects and persons you might—and certainly would—come across. Thus the importance of experiences such as those of the sculptor Alberto Giacometti and Breton in their wandering together in the Marché aux Puces, the flea market. Two objects they encountered that day inspired their interpretations: the metal mask found by Giacometti, and then a wooden spoon found by Breton, whose handle rests on a little shoe. The former they imagined to relate to a mask protecting the eyes from shrapnel during the war, and the latter served as a response (illustrating the notion of the "marvelous") to Breton's former idea of an ashtray in gray glass in the form of Cinderella's slipper, thus answering a hidden desire. So in these interpretations, death and desire, Thanatos and Eros, meet in the flea market.

Surrealism, as Breton theorizes it—and who else ever did it with such assurance?—is above all a matter of merging such opposites, having them flow one into the other as in the scientific experiment of communicating vessels. Whence the importance of the volume so titled: *Les vases communicants* (*The Communicating Vessels*, 1932), is not only influenced by the writings of Freud—a letter from whom is included therein—but is full of dream recounting and interpretation. Alas, Freud himself was more than skeptical about the surrealists' appropriation of his theory of dreams. The all-important centralizing, and for a while, crucial, matter of automatic writing, meant to show how writing could be released from conscious thought, revealing the hidden and therefore more valuable unconscious musings, was at the center of surrealist theory, even in the first Surrealist Manifesto. Take, for example, the text scribbled down by Philippe Soupault and Breton called *Le poisson soluble* (*The Soluble Fish*), in which you can actually see the speed at which the two writers penned their words. But later, it was found to be a catastrophe, quite like the meetings and correspondence of Freud and Breton.

Already in the Dada movement, binaries were conjoined, so, according to Tristan Tzara, the yes and the no would meet on the street corner. In surrealism, and in its writings and actions, night and day would be merged like swinging doors, "les portes battantes," and the irrational would be as fully privileged as the rational. This was initially the inspiration for that hyped-up presentation of automatic writing, which was to release our tightly strapped-in reasoning minds into a fully free world of imagining. A catastrophe, Breton was to say of it at one point later, but it served its purpose early on, and in its extreme popularization later, when latter-day *surrealisants* would meet in cafés here and there and try to channel the marvelous.

But in the heyday of surrealism, Robert Desnos would undertake his dream trances, and—until they were found to be menacing, and indeed, they led to fistfights, it seems—they were something to be transcribed (like the erotic fantasies of the same period) and welcomed as manifestations of the marvelous. For a while, there seemed to be a working correlation between poetry, as we think of it and read it, and the idea of spontaneous or automatic transcription. Just to take a few examples of the kind of instantaneous "discovery" yielded by that concept, we might consider these passages, in which the repetition and the wanderings of the imagination are recognizable.

Char (from *Le marteau sans maître* [*The Hammer with No Master*]):

Artine gardait en dépit des animaux et des cyclones une intarissable fraîcheur. A la promenade, c'était la transparence absolue.

(In spite of animals and cyclones, Artine retained an inexhaustible freshness. On outings, this was the most absolute transparency.)

Paul Eluard ("La terre est bleue" ["The Earth Is Blue"]):

La terre est bleue comme une orange
Jamais une erreur les mots ne mentent pas

(The earth is blue like an orange
Never an error words do not lie)

Breton ("Toujours pour la première fois" ["Always for the First Time"]):

Il y a
Qu'à me pencher sur le précipice
De la fusion sans espoir de ta présence et de ton absence
J'ai trouvé le secret
De t'aimer
Toujours pour la première fois

(There is
That leaning over the precipice
Of the hopeless fusion of your presence and absence
I have found the secret
Of loving you
Always for the first time)

Philippe Soupault ("Georgia"):

Le feu est comme la neige Georgia
La nuit est ma voisine Georgia

J'écoute les bruits tous sans exception Georgia
Je vois la fumée qui monte et qui fuit Georgia

(The fire is like the snow Georgia
The night is my neighbor Georgia
I'm listening to every single sound Georgia
I see the smoke rising and flying off Georgia)

Was Desnos making up his "dreams" in his "trances," as some have alleged? It little matters. The point is that joining of the perhaps seen to the "actually perceived," of the interior to the exterior, was the case of all the surrealist endeavors under the aegis of Breton, the "Pope" as the denigrators would call him. In any case, no Breton, no surrealism, and that is a cliff-fact, despite another fact, which is that Salvador Dalí said of himself, "Surrealism is me." He was not lacking in a sense of entitlement.

To such extent was Breton a controlling force that, when he came with his wife, Jacqueline, and daughter, Aube, to the United States in 1941, earning his living by broadcasting for the Voice of America in French, he refused to learn any English, fearing that it might damage his native language. When, in 1944, he returned to France, the atmosphere had gravely changed, and during an encounter at the Sorbonne, the former Dada leader, Tristan Tzara, accused Breton of still believing in an outdated movement: blows were exchanged, in a famous episode about what was now relevant and what was not. Surrealism had wanted, still wanted, to change the world, but that world had indeed changed on its own. The initial hope in political involvement—surrealism in the service of the revolution—was allied with the female spirit of the mermaid Melusina, demonstrating the shapeshifting freedom of the un-rational. Here, contraries were free to merge and communicate, while the belligerent male force was to be softened by the pacifying and liberating mermaid. But the metaphor seemed too optimistic for the times.

Breton's relation to the exterior world always had something in it of the aesthetic. Longing for the marvelous, the observer was able to perceive not just the mysterious meaning of an object, but its material magic: we have only to contemplate his extensive collection of objects from near and far, now making up an entire wall in the Musée National d'Art Moderne, Centre Georges-Pompidou. His daughter, Aube, in her own generous reach, not only endowed the museum bountifully, but made a voyage to Vancouver in order to return to a tribe of the First Nation what Breton had collected from that region and tribe: so she is called "The One Who Gave Back."

Breton knew how to see not just created objects, but those about him, as he always had been able to do. The excitement over the finding of an object that held in itself, by "objective chance," the answer to a question you did not know you had—as Breton put it—was a magnificent one. The many wanderings about of the group or individual participants, looking for the unlooked-for and the unexpected, continued apace, from antique stores in Paris to pebbles in the river Lot, near Breton's discovered summer place in Saint-Cirq-la-Popie. Besides these discoveries, only the proclamations and person of Breton's lifelong hero, Marcel Duchamp, could awaken in Breton that sense of excitement. What you might come across, and had not dreamed of, was what mattered, and in this the exterior and interior worlds were joined. Creation and encounter were both essential.

All description was to be eliminated, as it was shown in *Le manifeste surréaliste* (*The Manifesto of Surrealism*) to be idiotic. Nevertheless, Breton's apperception of the world about him could be—as it was in the world of art—sharp and steeped in emotion. A somewhat surprising witness to this is found in his epic *Fata Morgana* (1940): "For me, no work of art is worth this little square made of dappled grass of the vision of life." We think, as Breton surely did, of the Proust passage in which the artist Elstir fixes his last gaze on the patch of yellow roof in Vermeer's *View of Delft*.

The place names counted: as for René Char, the places would be those familiar ones in the Provençal Vaucluse, so for Breton, they would name Paris: cafés, the Hotel des Grands Hommes, the Conservatoire Renée Maubel, the Tour Saint-Jacques, and Nadja's parallel in the advertisements for the lamp Mazda. The place of their encounter was the Café à la Nouvelle France, at the angle of rue Lafayette, 92, and 91 rue du Faubourg-Poissonnière. The situation matters: its placement and its moment.

Take 1930, the year in which Breton, Eluard, and Char met in Avignon and wrote together *Ralentir travaux* (*Slow Down Men Working*) in the Rich Tavern on the Place de la République, near the Hotel Regina. In Char's recounting of it, Breton was the only one of the three who would have liked his texts to be signed, ironically. In a car, they went all around the Vaucluse, visiting Char's family home, Les Nevons, and familiar places in L'Isle-sur-la-Sorgue, in Gordes, in Chateauneuf du Pape. The title "Ralentir travaux" came from a road signal, on the way to Caumont-sur-Durance. So all experiences were to be used, like each encounter.

The relations between Breton and Char were of a complicated sort: Char felt closer to the poet Paul Eluard, who left surrealism for the Communist Party, but Breton's wife who had occasioned *Mad Love*, Jacqueline Lamba, found Char to be the "eternal poet," and took her paintings down to L'Isle-sur-la-Sorgue to visit him. That she forgot them there showed her, as she said, how important he had been and was to her.

Char and Breton both had a feeling of a message to be carried on and shared with others, albeit the difference in the message that each man felt crucial to his beliefs. For Breton, literature or writing was living; for Char, living was what led to the writing itself. For both, the feeling of the message they had to bear provided the one essential task, whether it was to be an open and political message, like that of Char's involvement in the Resistance, or a statement whose at least partial obscurity was willed, as in Breton's conclusion to the bitter and aggressive second manifesto of 1930, in a time marked by his demoralization and lack of self-assurance: "Public approbation is the first thing to flee. . . . I DEMAND THE DEEP, TRUE OCCULTATION OF SURREALISM."

But his heroic voice comes back. The end of *Le surréalisme et la peinture* (*Surrealism and Painting*) has a joyous feel to it, and one of comradeship: this is Breton's voice at its most optimistic: "Surreality is contained in reality itself, is not superior or exterior to it. . . . We are very far along, whatever anyone says, very high, up, and not at all ready to return or descend."

Born in 1907 in L'Isle-sur-la-Sorgue, where he lived most of his life, as well as in an apartment on the rue Chenaleilles, which had earlier been occupied by the writer Alexis de Tocqueville, René Char incorporated both the Mediterranean Provençal and the sophisticated and literary Parisian. He had different accents in both his living and his writing, adapted to the situation and the place. Best known for his activities as the Capitaine Alexandre in the Resistance, part of the Armée Secrete and head of the section Durance-Sud in the Basses-Alpes de Provence, he oversaw parachute landings in that region and, in 1944, served as liaison in Algeria with De Gaulle and the Allied forces. His wartime journal, *Feuillets d'Hypnos* [*Hypnos Waking*], published in 1948, tells, in aphoristic style, of his daily meditations and actions: this includes the terrible story of the time Char had to permit the shooting of his young friend Roger Bernard, in the village of Céreste, in the Basses-Alpes, by the Nazis, because otherwise the location of the *maquisards* (Resistance fighters) would have been betrayed, and the villagers massacred. Understandably, he refused ever to return to that town, and the action haunted him for the rest of his life.

His poetic works, numerous and influential on other poets, not only in France but in the United States and elsewhere, include, among other volumes, his surrealist writing: *Le marteau sans maître* (*The Hammer with No Master*, 1934), famously set to music by Pierre Boulez (as was his later poem "Le visage nuptial" ["The Nuptial Countenance," 1938]); the all-encompassing *Fureur et mystère* (*Furor and Mystery*, 1948), which includes the *Feuillets d'Hypnos* (*Leaves of Hypnos*, 1946); *Les matinaux* (*The Transparents*, 1950); *La parole en archipel* (*The Word as Archipelago*, 1962); *Le nu perdu* (*Nakedness Lost*, 1970); *La nuit talismanique* (*The Talismanic Night*, 1972); and the late poems infused with the scent of herbs: *Aromates chasseurs* (*Hunter's Aromatic Herbs*, 1975). Each title exudes a particular flavor, from that hammer, so forcible and so unmastered, to the poetic landscape in the separate islands of the archipelago, those fragmented parts of writing and living—continuous and yet distinct, exactly parallel to the style of Char's aphorisms, condensing much into a small space. One of René Char's most meaningful references is to the poetry of Hölderlin, and especially his poems to the mountaintops that correspond to each other, like so many aphoristic peaks.

Char's writing is intensely regional: we think not just of those daunting bare heights of the Mont Ventoux or the "windy mountain" in the Vaucluse (that "closed-in valley" honored by Petrarch because of his young muse Laura and the fountain where he saw her, thus the Fontaine de Vaucluse), near which Char grew up, on which he welcomed the parachutes of the partisans during the Resistance, and up which Petrarch climbed, clutching his volume of Aristotle, and which was climbed later by Thomas Jefferson, in honor of Petrarch, reminding us of another poet, Pablo Neruda, and his epic poem, *Les hauteurs de Macchu Picchu* (*Heights of Macchu Picchu*). The classical past of the Vauclusian region remains to inspire its present poetics. And indeed, in Char's country, "mon pays," the customs are foundational as well as metaphoric: the poem "Qu'il vive!" ("Long Live") refers to this land, even as it is "only a wish of the spirit, a counter-sepulcre." It summarizes, in its brief aphoristic space, the moral basis of this poet and, moreover, those who have chosen to live near him and his spirit, whose *pays* it becomes in turn:

> Dans mon pays, les tendres preuves du printemps et les oiseaux
>   mal habillés sont préferés aux buts lointains. . . .
> Dans mon pays, on ne questionne pas un homme ému.
> . . .
> Bonjour à peine est inconnu, dans mon pays.
> On n'emprunte que ce qui peut se rendre augmenté.
> Il y a des feuilles, beaucoup de feuilles sur les arbres de mon
>   pays. Les branches sont libres de ne pas avoir de fruits.
> . . .
> Dans mon pays, on remercie.
>
> (In my country, tender proofs of spring and badly-dressed birds
>   are preferred to far-off goals. . . .
> In my country, we don't question a person deeply moved.
> . . .
> A cool greeting is unknown in my country.
> We borrow only what can be returned increased.
> There are leaves, many leaves, on the trees of my country. The
>   branches are free to bear no fruit.
> . . .
> In my country, we say thank you.)

The region is rife with folklore: take the early morning risers of *Les matinaux*—the impoverished inhabitants of the Vaucluse to whom, when they called at your door, you would give bread and salt and water, and who would exchange their clothes for those on the scarecrows—such are the inherited tales of the region, passed on from family to family. Another of them is told in this way: in order to give one of the mentally less well-endowed something to do, to keep up his dignity, the town would appoint him to make a clacking noise by the water, to frighten away the frogs. The central core of much of Char's poetry is the assurance of dignity, explicit or not.

So wonderfully and terribly immersed in the daily, in wartime and peacetime, René Char somehow seems heroic in every sense of the word. Immensely tall and prepossessing, with a voice as mountainous as his person and his vision, he was the creator of a poetry, both in prose and in verse, close to the natural: the trees, the mountains, the wheat fields with their poppies, the lavender, the winding roads so particular to Provence. And yet his poetry has the tensile strength suited to its moral stance, always underlying its simplest appearance. As he wrote about we might think of as his calling, in the preface to his best-known collection, *Fureur et mystère* of 1948, "The poet, we know, mingles lack and excess, the goal and the past. From this, the insolubility of his poem." What above all he would always refuse was "the profit of being a poet." For that label would undercut his constant rebellion against any calculation, and his moral position kept him from accepting any position of ease—never becoming part of those whom his predecessor, Arthur Rimbaud, called "les assis" (the comfortably situated). Thus the "insolubility" or, indeed, the unsolvable nature of his poetry. When we contrast this with the discovery in the early days of surrealism by Breton of the "man soluble in his thought," we do not only meditate on the complexity of all poetry, but on the dissolving of all that does not matter in the universe of such men. And this is—despite what might seem to be the opposition of the terms "unsoluble" (or "unsolvable") and "soluble"—one of the strange links of the vocabulary as indicative of this kind of confrontation with the world of the conformist.

We can certainly say about both these poets that they were, in every possible sense of the word, nonconformists. In their chosen differences, both writers were deeply involved in a *world* beyond the bounds of the ordinary, in a revolt against the very notion of conformity. Their selection of images and metaphors already betokens this: Char's stated affection for "the cloud and the bird" or "fate and the primrose" is precisely a refusal of the expected: say, a cloud and a sun, a refusal that parallels Breton's insistence on imagining he might not find a pear alongside an apple in a fruit dish, but rather, say, a horse galloping on a tomato. The inventive mind is necessarily in revolt against the expected, like the surrealist denial of what has been already seen, thought, digested.

But of course, from this stems a certain pessimism, piercing through the writings and the lives. Char's poem "Wrestlers" shows both the comradeship and the burden of the metaphoric heroic deed he takes upon himself:

> Dans le ciel des hommes, le pain des étoiles me sembla
> ténébreux et durci, mais dans leurs mains étroites je lus la joute
> de ces étoiles en invitant d'autres: émigrantes du pont encore
> rêveuses, j'en recueillis la sueur dorée, et par moi la terre cessa
> de mourir.

> (In the sky of men, the bread of the stars seemed to me
> shadowy and hardened, but in their narrow hands I read the
> joust of these stars calling others: emigrants from below deck
> still dreaming; I gathered their golden sweat, and through me
> the earth ceased to die.)

Living in both places, Provence and Paris, René Char had in his makeup, then, both the sophisticated and the rural, and even had accents in his life as in his poems, of both—this bears repeating, since his poems are marked by place names, even though he wished and believed them to be as wide-ranging as the constellation of Orion, with which he so closely identified himself. That L'Isle-sur-la-Sorgue should be so close to Mont Ventoux, the windy mountain that so frequently appears in his writing, feels like no happenstance, but some sort of appropriate territory. His writing, both in wartime and in calmer times, has a feeling of rise about it. Like something overcome, surmounted, and ongoing, like a vanquishing of the heights of the Ventoux.

His moral insistence, which I am insisting on, was itself ongoing. The aphoristic mode that is recognizable in everything he ever wrote and said—that mode of tension and condensation—is responsible for what many have found "hermetic" in his poems, a term he rejected. It was instead exactly what was deliberately and yet naturally insoluble—so very much the opposite of Breton's "man soluble in his thoughts"—unsolvable, mysterious but the very opposite of mystical, which would be rather Breton's side of things. The images Char selected were themselves often difficult to put together: the cloud and the bird, rebellion and the primrose. Yet once they were there, a certain kind of sense was there also. If I dwell on the moral side of his writing, it has to do also with the part of reading, not just with the creating of it. From this point of view, his poetic theory, if you like, is similar to that of the surrealists: the double creation of the text by writer and reader. And, equally, from this point of view, both writers, Char and Breton, provide sustenance for the contemporary gaze as it has been determined by Roland Barthes and other theoreticians of literature and philosophy.

The prose texts that Char felt most strongly about, and that were the nearest to what he wanted his friends, critics, and translators to communicate, were the *Billets à Francis Curel* (*Letters to Francis Curel*), dated from 1941 to 1948. They were addressed to the son of that worker in the fields whom Char called "Louis Curel de la Sorgue," a noble title the family had inherited far back in time and that Char restored to this upright man, whom he pictures always standing in the distance, that working laborer: "Il y a un homme à présent debout, un homme dans un champ de seigle, un champ pareil à un choeur mitraillé, un champ sauvé" (There is a man now standing, a man in a field of rye, a field like a machine-gunned chorus, a field redeemed). It is perhaps worth noting that when the poet was carried out of his house, Les Busclats, in his last sickness, he was carried standing upright, as befitted his moral stance.

> Greetings to the one who walks in certainty by my side,
> to the end of the poem.
> Who will tomorrow pass STANDING under the wind.

These letters, about which he used to often speak, convey his attitude "after the disaster": not to tell on the others (let the pigs communicate with the pigs—we shall keep silent), not to betray anyone,
but to remain as far from the monstrous as possible, so as not to become a monster oneself. That he had been forced to lose the partisan
Roger Bertrand was its own excruciating punishment: there was, and
remained, no point in bringing up further punishment for the others.
To besmirch the enemy, Char thought, is to besmirch oneself, to bend
low. To remain standing in that field meant, precisely, to be true to
one's own dignity. That was the part of refusal, as he wrote in 1948, in
the last note to Francis Curel:

> Refus de siéger à la cour de justice, refus d'accabler autrui dans
> le dialogue quotidien retrouvé, decision tenue enfin d'opposer
> la lucidité au bien-être, l'état naturel aux honneurs, ces mauvais
> champignons qui prolifèrent dans les crevasses de la sécheresses
> et dans les lieux avariés, après le premier grain de pluie.

> (Refusal to sit in the court of justice, refusal to crush anyone in
> the daily dialogue taken up again, a decision finally maintained
> to oppose lucidity to well-being, the natural state of things to
> the honors, those poisonous mushrooms proliferating in the
> "cracks of aridity" and in the deteriorating places, after the first
> drop of rain.)

". . . [J]e redevenais journalier" (. . . [A]nd so I became daily again), he
concludes.

In that same year, Char wrote his "Prière rogue," his pagan prayer,
if you like, which resounds in its courageous clarity as an "Unbending
Prayer," this pagan beseeching providing a perfect description of his
position in the world of necessary decisions:

> Gardez-nous la révolte, l'éclair, l'accord illlusoire, un rire pour
> le trophée glissé des mains, même l'entier et long fardeau qui
> succède, dont la difficulté nous mène à une révolte nouvelle.
> Gardez-nous la primevère et le destin.

(Preserve for us rebellion, lightning, the illusory agreement, a laugh for the trophy slipped from our hands, even the whole lengthy burden that follows, whose difficulty leads us to a new rebellion. Preserve for us fate and the primrose.)

This is rebellion itself, and indeed, written by hand on one copy of the "Pulverized Poem" of 1947, we find these unforgettable lines:

Mon poème est mon voeu en révolte. Mon poème a la fermeté
  du désastre: mon poème est mon soufflé futur.

(My poem is my oath of rebellion. My poem has the firmness
of disaster; my poem is my future breathing.)

Something about breath and breathing, the *anima* of being, had a crucial importance for this poet. He was eager for a book being written on him to include the notion of breathing in its title, and that indeed was the inspiration—in the strong etymological sense of the word—for whatever energy it was to find.

The poem is always married to someone, says the poet. So the literal ties of the texts to the life matter, but they do not necessarily have to be spelled out in order for the text itself to resound. Think of the poem "to A***"—like Breton's "X" at the end of *Nadja*. We do not have to know specifics; we have only to believe that none of these loving texts are floating aimlessly about, as "just" literature. The fact that Breton's celebrated poem "L'union libre" ("Free Union") was used as a valentine to one woman and as a love letter to another in no way divests it of its literal weight; it remains poetry.

This consideration brings up, urgently, another issue for the translator. Take Breton's "Free Union," in which the first line begins, memorably, "Ma femme," and continues in like manner, with the anaphoric style, every line beginning the same way. So, clearly, the phrase has major importance. In my view, it cannot be translated "My woman," nor, for biographical as well as poetic reasons, can it be rendered as "My wife," because she certainly was not his spouse, each time he used it. I believe one has to say something like "My beloved" or then "My love," the gender distinction being less crucial by far than the ghastliness of the first two options.[1] Now the difference between this poem and the idea of "Mad Love" is immense. The mad love described in the volume of that name, that overcoming and deeply personalized passion for Jacqueline Lamba (who had entered the café where she knew she would find the poet, who instantly conflated his earlier poem "Tournesol" ["Sunflower"] with this experience, as a poetic premonition) is indeed attached, and permanently, to her memory. It could not be otherwise, as it recounts their voyage to Tenerife and concludes with Breton's letter to their daughter, Aube, headed "Ecureuil de noisette." The beginning explains that he has always loved the same person, in other guises ("in her red dress") and so on, but the rest leads to the unique love. What he is faithful to is the very idea of love, in every guise it might take.

On the other hand, when the specific biographical details are not urgently included in the text, the options are more numerous. In the case of the general statement, such as the concluding line of Char's memorial prose poem "Fastes" ("Annals"): "Je t'aimais, changeant en tout, fidèle à toi" (I loved you, changing in every way, faithful to you) there is no issue. Even in the magnificently difficult epic "Le visage nuptial," the end, with its religious echo of salvation and presentation: "voici, voici"—which, alas, feels very male-oriented to me, and here the hero is standing once more—poses no problem to the translator for that reason:

> Voici le sable mort, voici le corps sauvé:
> La Femme respire, L'Homme se tient debout.

> (This is the sand dead, this the body saved:
> Woman breathes, Man stands upright.)

So for this poem, this rightness. But in the super-erotic center of the poem lies a specific detail:

> Prends, ma Pensée, la fleur de ma main pénétrable,
> Sens s'éveiller l'obscure plantation.

(Take, oh my Thought, the flower of my penetrable hand,
Feel the dark planting waken.)

The poet asked if the translator knew for whom this was written (for
the then wife of Tristan Tzara, Greta Knudsen, who was a Scandina-
vian blonde) and then smiled his explanation: poetic license.

Furthermore, both poets had a firm belief in a kind of mystery.
Breton would insist on not sharing the most profound of surrealist
beliefs with just anyone, not scattering them at random: "Ne dis-
tribuez point le pain maudit aux oiseaux" (Don't distribute the *pain
maudit* to the birds)—in which case, of course, the *maudit* or "damned"
is the equivalent of "blessed." Yes, the manifestos—the first one, certainly—advocated the glories of automatic writing, which would un-
leash the too-rational of what has been already thought (the dreaded
déja pensé) because it is expected and is not the glorious unexpected
for which the surrealist was always, is always, waiting: the not-yet-
thought. But the second manifesto is already speaking to the initiated,
from whose circle those found wanting are banished, by the word of
the leader, always Breton. Along the same lines, it is crucial not to
"unfold the heart of the rose," Char would say, and, moreover: "We
wish to remain unknown to the curiosity of those who love us. We
love them." Or then, "Free birds do not let anyone look at them. Let's
remain obscure, let's renounce ourselves, near them."

One of the heights of surrealist writing and thought is surely André
Breton's *Le surréalisme et la peinture*, with its variegated essays on the
widely differing artists he contemplates. Char's writings on art and on
other writers demonstrate his closeness to certain creators, from the
classics to the contemporary, each meaningful to him for particular
reasons: Heraclitus among philosophers for his aphoristic style; Rimbaud among poets for his youthful energy and impassioned illuminations, in all the sense of the word; Van Gogh among painters for his
love of Char's own region in Provence (*Les voisinages de Van Gogh* [*The
Neighborhoods of Van Gogh*], 1985); and Georges de La Tour for his
Prisoner, a reproduction of which he kept by him throughout the Resistance, and for his Magdalen, whom the poet celebrates repeatedly,
in prose and in poetry. Her vigil-lamp lights much of his writing, and

the impossibility of any solution speaks, like any great poetry, more than it spells out. Char, a pagan, calls her Madeleine, he insists, for she is a young girl and not a statue, not a religious icon like the Magdalen, and his "Madeleine with the Vigil-Lamp, *by Georges de La Tour*" moves toward her, the girl with her hand on the skull, whom he addresses directly:

> Je voudrais aujourd'hui que l'herbe fût blanche pour fouler l'évidence de vous voir souffrir: je ne regarderais pas sous votre main si jeune la forme dure, sans crépi de la mort. Un jour discrétionnaire, d'autres pourtant moins avides que moi, retireront votre chemise de toile, occuperont votre alcôve. Mais ils oublieront en partant de noyer la veilleuse et un peu d'huile se répandra par le poignard de la flamme sur l'impossible solution.

> (I would wish today that the grass were white to trample the visible signs of your suffering: I'd not look under your hand, so young, at death's hard form without rough-cast. One discretionary day, others, though less avid than I, will remove your rough linen blouse, will occupy your alcove. But they will forget to extinguish the lamp in their departing and a little oil will spill out by the dagger of the flame onto the impossible solution.)

Now the painters he celebrates: Braque, Vieira da Silva, and Nicolas de Stael were all close to him, and he worked with each of them in close collaboration. Composed during his sleepless nights of 1972, *La nuit talismanique* reminds us of the hours in which he painted small and larger pebbles, some of which he gave as talismans—and many of which indicate the kind of flame or vigil light just seen—to celebrate the moment when a family becomes *pays*, that is, part of the countryside. The whole idea of gift is crucial to the sense of the poetic. As for the nakedness of "Le nu perdu," it reminds us of the bare heights of the windy Mont Ventoux and how everything is lost there except, perhaps, the essential that matters, even in its nudity. *Recherche de la base et du sommet* (*Search for the Base and the Summit*, 1955) expresses in its title the importance of the dynamic climb of Char's poetry at its foundation and height, in its own region, its lofty vision destined to spread outward.

These two poets, each of whom has had an immense influence on contemporary thinking and writing, take us, in a monumental climb, to the summit of which Char's title speaks. We are there with them, a stance they would permit.

NOTE

1. It was for this reason that the translation of this essential poem was removed from the *Norton Anthology of Poetry*, since it could not be changed without making a whole new edition. Too bad, but "my woman" is worse by far than the omission.

WORKS CITED AND RECOMMENDED FURTHER READING

The major work to be consulted for André Breton is *Oeuvres complètes*, ed. Marguerite Bonnet, Philippe Bernier, Etienne-Alain Hubert, José Pierre, and Marie-Claire Dumas, 4 vols., Collection Pléiade (Paris: Gallimard, 1988–2088). For a good biography, see Mark Polizzotti, *Revolution of the Mind: André Breton* (Boston: Black Widow Books, 2009). The English translations of the principal works discussed here are *Nadja*, trans. Richard Howard (New York: Grove/Atlantic, 1994); *Mad Love*, trans. Mary Ann Caws (Lincoln: University of Nebraska Press, 1988); *Communicating Vessels*, trans. Mary Ann Caws and Geoffrey T. Harris (Lincoln: University of Nebraska Press, 1997); and *Surrealism and Painting*, ed. Mark Polizzotti (Boston: Museum of Fine Arts, 2002). For the translations of poems, there are many; those used here are very often from the *Poems of André Breton*, trans. and ed. Jean-Pierre Cauvin and Mary Ann Caws (Boston: Black Widow Books, 2006).

For information on René Char and his texts, see *René Char: Oeuvres complètes*, introd. Jean Roudaut, Collection Pléiade (Paris: Gallimard, 1983; new ed., 2013). For biographies in French, see Jean-Claude Mathieu, *La poésie de René Char, ou, Le sel de la splendeur* [The salt of splendor], vol. 1: *Traversée du surréalisme* [Crossing of surrealism]; vol. 2: *Poésie et résistance* [Poetry and resistance] (Paris: José Corti, 1984); and Laurent Greilshamer, *L'éclair au front: La vie de René Char* [Lightning on his forehead] (Paris: Fayard, 2004). For critical works in English, see Nancy Piore, *Lightning: The Poetry of René Char* (Evanston, IL: Northeastern University Press, 1981); and Mary Ann Caws, *The Presence of René Char* (Princeton, NJ: Princeton University Press, 1976.) For translations, see *Selected Poems of René Char*, ed. Mary Ann Caws and Tina Jolas (New York: New Directions, 1992); *The Brittle Age and Returning Upland*, trans. Gustav Sobin (Denver: Counterpath Press, 2009); *Furor and Mystery and Other Writings by René Char*, ed. and trans. Mary Ann Caws and Nancy Kline, with an essay by Marie-Claude Char and an introduction by Sandra Bermann (Boston: Black Widow Books, 2010).

** **

Césaire

Poetry and Politics

MARY GALLAGHER

Aimé Césaire, a writer and statesman, was born in Martinique in June 1913 and died there in April 2008. He is best known as the author of the epic poem *Cahier d'un retour au pays natal* (*Notebook of a Return to the Native Land*) and as the creator—or at least co-creator—of the influential anticolonialist concept of *négritude*, to which Césaire gave a more political inflection than the cultural one perhaps more associated with the thinking of the Senegalese poet Léopold Sédar Senghor. Certainly, the value of this revolutionary slogan was subsequently decried. The Nigerian novelist Wole Soyinka, for example, dismissed it as a pious abstraction, declaring that a "tiger does not declare its tigritude," but rather springs and pounces. In the French Caribbean islands (Martinique and Guadeloupe), the battle cry of negritude was gradually replaced by less universal slogans, more culturally than racially tinged: *antillanité* (Caribbeanness) or *créolité* (Creoleness), for example.

Yet, whether it was crafted in the fiery vividness of his poetry or in the ice-clear trenchancy of his dramatic prose, Césaire's literary exposure of colonialism and of the racism on which imperial expansion and plunder were founded counter any simplistic dismissal of negritude. In his "Discours sur la négritude" ("Discourse on Negritude") delivered at a conference in Miami in 1987, Césaire admitted to not being enamored of his brainchild mantra every day of his life. More than fifty years after its launch, however, he still regarded it as necessary and valid, as addressing an undeniably real problematic.

Césaire's entire oeuvre could be read as a defense and illustration of negritude, not as a biological or metaphysical postulation, but rather as a historical reality. His writing only makes sense as an impassioned engagement with, as he puts it in the "Discours sur la négritude," "one historical shape taken by the human condition."[1] It never deviates from the fundamentally political articulation, reendorsed five decades following its first affirmation, of negritude as the voicing of "community based on a common experience of oppression." In other words, Césaire was concerned to skewer from the start the intertwined power of racism and colonialism, which diminished, violated, and even obliterated the humanity of all those whom they contaminated. The *Cahier* in particular set off an anticolonialist charge that anticipated the general global detonation of decolonization in the 1950s and 1960s, and the rest of Césaire's work charted the enduring colonialist fallout (that is, postcolonialism), as witnessed by the endless challenge of real decolonization.

The importance of Aimé Césaire's work goes far beyond the two achievements for which he is best known: the resonance of the landmark epic and the reach of a rallying cry that aimed to mobilize the oppressed of Africa and especially of its involuntary diaspora. For Césaire's literary oeuvre steadily blossomed through the *trente glorieuses*, as the three postwar decades are termed in France, before coming to a near standstill in the early 1970s (with the exceptional flashes of two poetry collections published in 1976 and 1982). As a result of those three highly productive decades, his literary legacy includes not just six major poetry collections, but also four plays and several prose essays and discourses. Césaire's poetry has often been linked to the surrealist revolution; in a much more general sense, however, all of his writing must be seen as fundamentally disjunctive, both politically and in its literary and cultural positioning. His work is part of a movement of decolonization that is at once political, cultural, and literary.

In addition to writing poetry, drama, and essays, Césaire also involved himself in three major collaborative literary ventures. In Paris in 1934, he set up the journal *L'Etudiant Noir* (The Black Student) along with his near compatriot and fellow-poet, Léon-Gontran Damas from Guyana, and another expatriate student, the future Senegalese statesman-poet, Senghor. It was in this short-lived student review that Césaire used the term *négritude* for the first time. His input into collaborative critique continued in 1939, upon his return to Martinique from Vichy France. Back in "the native land," he co-founded in 1941, along with several compatriot authors, the highly influential critical journal *Tropiques*, which was published right through the war years when Martinique was effectively blockaded under the collaborationist rule of Admiral Robert. The journal ceased publication, however, in 1945, the year when Césaire's destiny definitively changed direction. Two years later in Paris, he would once again be involved, with Alioune Diop, Paul Niger, and others, in the founding of another publication, *Présence Africaine*. This review is still flourishing, as is the prolific publishing house into which it blossomed as a space of nurture for African and African-related expression in French, based in the Latin Quarter of Paris, but with African outreach. As this cultural leadership shows, Césaire from the outset played the role of public intellectual in collaborative literary and critical activism as well as through his own poetics. Writing and publication were not destined, however, to be his sole contribution to public life.

❋ ❋ ❋ ❋

Some five years after his return to Martinique at the start of the war, Césaire became actively involved in Martinican politics and public affairs. From that point on, his political career closely shadowed, yet never completely overshadowed, his work as one of the Caribbean's foremost authors and intellectuals (in any language), work for which his formal education might be thought to have prepared him rather more fully than for a career as a statesman. The son of a tax inspector father and a dressmaker mother, Césaire had followed a prestigious academic trajectory in his studies. He attended the Lycée Schoelcher in Fort-de-France (the capital of Martinique) alongside Léon-Gontran Damas from French Guyana, who would later become a renowned poet also. Césaire subsequently studied at the famous Lycée Louis-le-Grand in Paris and thereafter at the even more renowned Ecole Normale Supérieure, where he crowned his literary studies with a thesis on the theme of the South in the "littérature négro-africaine" of the United States (the writings of Richard Wright, Claude MacKay, et al.). On his return to Martinique in 1939, he taught in the Lycée Schoelcher. It is often alleged that Frantz Fanon and Edouard Glissant, two of the most influential Caribbean writers and thinkers of their generation, were his pupils. This claim has been contested, but there seems little doubt that Césaire's work influenced both authors.

Césaire's public career as an administrator and politician quickly superseded his teaching vocation. In 1945, he was elected—on the Communist ticket—as mayor of Fort-de-France. He continued in this role for nearly sixty years, until 2001. The same year saw him take a seat in the French parliament, where he represented Martinique for more than forty-eight years, until 1993. In this latter role, Césaire was, if not instrumental, then at the very least fully cooperative, in negotiating in 1946 France's official recognition of Martinique, Guadeloupe, and French Guyana as "overseas *départements*," or direct administrative units of France rather than as less fully integrated entities.

Césaire's politics were leftist; he was, after all, for some considerable time a member of the French Communist Party. However, in the wake of the invasion of Hungary and in the face of that party's refusal clearly to denounce Stalinism—but also, and more critically, given the contradictions between the universalist class-based agenda of French communism and Césaire's more specific antiracist and anticolonialist agenda—he made a vocal exit in 1956, explaining his resignation in a published open letter to the then Party Secretary, Maurice Thorez. In the same year, disillusioned with the (neocolonial) realities of *départementalisation* as opposed to its political promises (of equality), Césaire founded the Parti Progressiste Martiniquais, which advocated increased autonomy—not outright independence—for France's former Caribbean colonies. Césaire's fraught relations with communism and their complete fracture eventually, were not, then, the only noteworthy aspects of his political profile. What was controversial both at the time and thereafter was rather the aforementioned fact that, despite being an anticolonialist intellectual of immense conviction and energy, he nonetheless supported the 1946 Act of Union. And he did so at a time when European colonies worldwide were either edging forward toward, or already involved in, movements—if not outright wars—of independence. (In 1945 there had already been rumblings of anticolonial riots and risings in Indochina and Algeria.)

Subsequent generations of Caribbean intellectuals criticized the writer's apparent support for anachronistic neocolonial tutelage. However, as Césaire's wife, Suzanne Césaire, née Roussy, a Martinican whom Césaire had married in 1937, herself also a writer and cofounder of *Tropiques*, would later argue in an article published in the wartime journal, the Caribbean islanders had themselves opted for parity (with the citizens of metropolitan France) in preference to independence, autonomy, or sovereignty. In his published conversations with Françoise Vergès, Césaire himself explains this choice in the same terms and without any notable defensiveness. While asserting the right to independence of former colonies, he also defends their right to claim what he himself clearly regards as higher imperatives, namely, equality and fraternity.

Difficult to digest as Césaire's apparently paradoxical political moderation was for some, at least one of his natural literary heirs rejected even more strongly his adoption of a particularly rarefied register of the French language as his poetic idiom. Even a cursory glance at the *Notebook* and at the subsequent poetry confirms that Césaire's poetic diction is often erudite, at times hyperbolically classical or latinate, and even abstrusely recondite. The Martinican novelist and cofounder of the Creoleness movement, Raphaël Confiant, in his diatribe *Aimé Césaire: Une traversée paradoxale du siècle* (A paradoxical journey through the century) argues that Césaire's poetic style betrays the bad faith of the anticolonialist who has in reality become so assimilated as to need to show his "more French than French" mastery of the national idiom. Confiant alleges, moreover, Césaire's rejection and/or suppression of his Creole identity, the identity championed by Confiant and his fellow-Creolists in their 1989 manifesto, *In Praise of Creoleness*. Confiant accuses Césaire's poetics of reflecting at best the political naïveté, at worst the political treachery of the thoroughly assimilated neocolonial subject. Many Caribbean writers distanced themselves, of course, from this reductive reading of Césaire's work, discredited as it was by its dogmatic policing of literary, cultural, and political authenticity and by its partial approach to Césaire's actual writing. Confiant's analysis overlooks in particular the unusual diversity of registers and idioms of Césaire's protean poetics.

A far more plausible case could be made for reading the stylistic eclecticism of Césaire's writing as evidence of a schizoid division between the uncompromising richness and resonance of the poetic language and the pragmatics of historical analysis and political activism. Certainly, toward the end of his life, Césaire himself downplayed the significance of his political contribution to his "native land." Indeed, in the interviews with Françoise Vergès, he confided not only that his real achievement was in the literary field, but that he was only able to be completely true to himself in his poetry. Moreover, forty years prior to that admission, and some time before his political career had even begun, the poet had explicitly stated the need to protect the inner life of selfhood from the pressures of political engagement. He thus refers (in "Maintenir la poésie," published in the review *Tropiques*) to the obligation to "protect oneself from the social by the creation of an incandescent aura beyond or within which the unheard-of flower of the 'I' can blossom in fierce safety." However, what is absolutely clear from the relative power of the various strata of the literary oeuvre is that the most unique, the most unforgettable, and the fiercest flower of Césaire's "I" blooms upon the axis of articulation of the poetic and the political, of the "I" and the "we."

∴ ∴ ∴ ∴

Césaire's poetics is underwritten by a profound anticolonial animus, devoid of first-degree *ressentiment*. Two principal sets of issues register in all his work: first, the need to reconstruct—in the wake of the destructive losses of colonialism—a sense of collective value and voice, community and continuity, memory and belonging; and second, the risks and challenges that ensue following decolonization, as newly independent states strive to recover from the injustices and inequalities spawned by the displacements and tyrannies of colonialism and attempt to institute just democracies. The first imperative permeates all of Césaire's writings; the second registers almost exclusively in the dramas.

The most incisive critical or theoretical analyses published by Césaire are the two that he devotes to these questions: the 1955 *Discours sur le colonialisme* (*Discourse on Colonialism*) and the 1960 study on Toussaint Louverture. In the *Discourse*, the indictment of colonialism is based on the opposition established between civilization and colonization. Blistering rhetoric links colonialism and Nazism, both underpinned by the barbaric racism through which the oppressors reify, instrumentalize, and ultimately dehumanize human beings, and in so doing decivilize and dehumanize themselves. In his analysis of the figure of Toussaint Louverture, Césaire compares the political dynamics of the French and the Haitian revolutions. Yet, however powerful these two "theoretical" texts might be, Césaire's critique of colonialism is at its most effective in his literary writing, rather than in his essays. So, unlike the two Martinican writers Edouard Glissant and Frantz Fanon (author of a definitive analysis of Caribbean racism, *Peau noire, masques blancs* [*Black Skin, White Masks*] and of the anticolonial charter *Les damnés de la terre* [*The Wretched of the Earth*]), and also unlike Albert Memmi, the Tunisian author of *Portrait du colonisé, précédé par Portrait du colonisateur* (*The Colonizer and the Colonized*), Césaire must be regarded as a poet and dramatist first and foremost and only in a secondary way as a critical analyst, theoretician, or polemicist. Although, unlike Fanon, Glissant was a poet and novelist, and while Memmi is also known as a novelist, the literary work of all three arguably serves mainly to illustrate their theories. In no way could this be said of Césaire's writing.

∗ ∗ ∗ ∗

Césaire's *Cahier* is an epic poem, a text of great stamina therefore, written both in prose and in verse. It appears to have been composed during an almost reclusive, introspective period of the poet's life in Paris and is perhaps related to a trip to Yugoslavia and to a return visit to Martinique (in 1936). Certainly, it traces a return journey, apparently from Europe to the native Caribbean—from personal, voluntary exile back to a homeland that is, itself, originally, a place both of collective exile and of mass historical transportation, enslavement, and alienation. The poem moves from the betrayal, shame, and rage aroused by the abjection of the "old negritude" (*vieille négritude*) to a rousing call for self-affirmation of "the risen black" (*le nègre debout*). Sixty years after the publication in 1939 of this searing poem in the review *Volontés*, Césaire still boiled when recalling the worst curse of colonialism: namely, the racist underpinnings of the hollowing, expropriating agenda of European imperialism. The poem is also, however, about an imaginary return to Africa, to the homeland, and this Babylonian theme lends the text considerable added depth and imaginative resonance.

Subsequently published by Présence Africaine in 1956, and never again out of print, the *Cahier d'un retour au pays natal* remains Césaire's most celebrated work. Three related features of the text make it stand out: first, its imaginative scope, which gives a richly ambitious, dense, and vigorous sense of location in space and time; second, the dramatic shift that takes place from a first movement, all prone subjection and abjection in the paradoxical image of the exhausted, butt-end of a watery dawn ("au bout du petit matin") to a second movement of revolt and upright self-affirmation; third, the power of its eruptive language: both the energetic—now sinuous, now jagged—syntax and a vocabulary that is extremely wide-ranging and various in modulation and color.

On that latter account alone, it is tempting to compare the tenor of Césaire's language with the work, written during the same period, of Saint-John Perse, the 1960 Nobel laureate also born and raised in the French Caribbean. Whereas this poet/diplomat of white Creole origin consistently wrote in the unmistakably major key of victorious conquest and colonization, Césaire's equally encyclopedic lexical reach and daring, and the equal breath and breadth of his epic poetics, are sounded in the minor key, from the perspective of the dispossessed, the disempowered. Not only does the speaker promise to be the mouthpiece of the voiceless, but he hails those who had no part in their silencing: "Eia pour ceux qui n'ont jamais rien inventé / Pour ceux qui n'ont jamais rien exploré / Pour ceux qui n'ont jamais rien dompté." (Eia for those who've never invented anything / For those who have never explored anything / For those who have never tamed anything.) Recalling the invisible "vie prostrée" (prostrate lives) of the subordinated, not just of blacks but also of "l'homme-juif / l'homme cafre" (the Jew-Man, the Kaffir Man), Césaire's representation of the biting humiliations of domination are extraordinarily vivid, as when he envisions the abjection of the plantation island as a "bedsore on the wounded waters" ("eschare sur la blessure des eaux"). Moreover, when the *Cahier* narrates the speaker's betrayal of one of his own, it underlines the fractures undermining the strength and unity of this misbegotten, aborted community: "Cette foule qui ne sait pas faire foule" (This crowd that can't be a proper crowd).

Certainly, the nostalgic poetics of a colonial childhood of the Guadeloupean-born-and-raised poet, Saint-John Perse, had—as early as 1910—put Caribbean plantation culture on the French literary map in a register that was surrealist *avant la lettre* and that broke both with amnesiac Parnassian alienation and with cloying tropical self-exoticism. The (at least) equal pungency and potency of Césaire's poetic imagination provoked, however, an incomparable poetic explosion given the radically disjunctive charge of its political engagement. Césaire gives voice to the silent servants of Saint-John Perse's *Eloges* (*Praises*). Perse's mute domestic attendants with their "faces insonores, couleur de papaya et d'ennui" (silent faces, the color of papaya and boredom) impose through Césaire their fragmented story of resurgent memories and what the poet terms, in his "Discourse on Negritude," the "debris of murdered cultures." Moreover, their projective, future-orientated timbre is radically disjunctive: from the "Antilles grélées de petite vérole" (West Indies scarred by smallpox), fried "nuit et jour d'un sacré soleil vénérien" (night and day by a fierce venereal sun), putrescent and starved, to the "éclaboussement d'or des instants favorisés" (gold splash of favored moments), to "la négraille assise / inattendûment debout" (the squatting nigger-nation / unexpectedly upright), "debout / et / libre," (upright / and / free) and to "la danse brise-carcan, / la danse saute-prison" (the dungeon-busting dance, the prison-exploding dance), and "ma noire vibration au nombril même du monde" (my black vibration in the world's very navel). What is perhaps most significant about the speaker's sense of complete centrality and self-coincidence ("Je force la membrane vitelline qui me sépare de moi-même" [I break through the egg-yolk membrane separating me from myself]) is that it has happened through his identification with the broken of all times and places. While this contributes to a sense of universal humanism, it does not cancel the sense of place marking Césaire's poetics.

Certainly, Césaire's literary language is no more stamped by the Creole language than is that of Saint-John Perse. And yet, while Africa is a presence in his writing, it is the Caribbean landscape and

Antillean history that saturate his literary imagination as a whole. From the *Cahier* onward, the omnipresence of marine imagery in the poetry foregrounds the ocean that was the theater of the traumatic Middle Passage and the amniotic source—"grand'lèche hystérique" (great hysterical lick)—both of all terrestrial life and specifically of the black Caribbean population. Thus, Césaire's ocean is at once historically resonant and also an ahistorical, universal principal of unity, a culturally undifferentiated matrix. The volcano, just as powerful and omnipresent as the sea in Césaire's poetics (as in Caribbean space) simmers, shudders, and can unpredictably explode into a roaring magma that is an objective correlative of the rage of colonial injustice so unforgettably parsed in the *Cahier*: "Et ce pays cria pendant des siècles . . . que nous sommes un fumier ambulant hideusement prometteur de cannes" (And down through the centuries this land screamed . . . that we are walking manure, so wretchedly good for the sugarcane harvest).

❖ ❖ ❖ ❖

During the war years, Césaire published poetry in *Tropiques*, and it was collected in *Les armes miraculeuses* (*Miraculous Weapons*) in 1946. Significantly, this volume also included the text of Césaire's first play, *Et les chiens se taisaient* (*And the Dogs Were Silent*). As the volume's title indicates, this poetry is surrealist and more inward and fragmented, less epic and less political than the *Cahier*. It does, however, include the highly lyrical oratorio of the collective drama, centered on the figure of a "Rebel" who relives his dreams and mistakes, defeats and triumphs as he faces up to the solitude of heroism and to the ultimate self-confrontation that is the final stand-off with death. The Rebel's interlocutors include two Madwomen, a Choir, a Mother, Bishops, Horsemen and a Narrator. However, despite the literary abstraction of the cast, there are references to the rape of Africa, and the play is clearly set against the historical backdrop of a generic colonial debacle: "les Blancs débarquent" (the white man is landing). In 1956, the text of the tragedy was published by Présence Africaine in a form "arranged for the theater."

This volume sets the tone for the fundamental post-*Cahier* bifurcation in Césaire's writing. There would be, on the one hand, several further volumes of poetry published in postwar Paris: *Soleil cou coupé* (*Solar Throat Slashed*, Editions K, 1947) and *Corps perdu* (*Lost Body*, Editions Fragrance, 1950), the latter illustrated with engravings by Picasso. Both collections were completely rearranged and abridged in a volume titled *Cadastre* (Seuil, 1961). This substantive rewriting, revision, or reedition of previously published poetry is a recurrent feature of Césaire's practice and especially remarkable in the case of the dramas, the several published versions of which were in most cases significantly different both among themselves and from the initial stage versions. As the poetry became in many ways more hermetic and inward after the *Cahier*, Césaire's more overtly politically engaged writing was for the theater. Following almost two decades of mainly theatrical writing, there were very long gaps between the publication of the final three poetry collections: *Ferrements* (Irons in ferment, or *Ferraments* as the published translation has it, Seuil, 1960); *Noria* (*Raid*, Désormeaux, 1976); and finally *Moi, laminaire . . .* (*Me, Laminary . . .* , Seuil, 1982), after which Césaire's literary voice fell silent.

In 1944, Césaire made an extended and significant visit to Haiti. It would take almost twenty years, however, for the fruits of his reflection on Haitian history to bear literary fruit, yielding his essay and his play on the respective tragedies of the captured revolutionary, Toussaint Louverture, and the postrevolutionary monarch, King Henry Christophe. It is hardly surprising that Césaire's imagination was engaged by the world's first black republic and by the Haitian revolution in particular. How could any anticolonial thinker from one of the—still—French Caribbean islands not need to understand Haiti's descent after 1792 into a hellish postindependence cycle of recidivist dictatorship (monarchic, imperial, or pseudodemocratic), of sectarianism, and eventually of economic and social stagnation and chronic debt? Césaire's historical essay (1960) on the Haitian revolutionary general who perished as an exiled captive in the Fort de Joux of the Jura Mountains is titled *Toussaint Louverture: La révolution française et le problème colonial* (*The French Revolution and the Colonial Problem*). This is the "homme seul emprisonné de blanc" (solitary man imprisoned in white) named in the *Cahier*. The other figure of fascination is Henri Christophe, the erstwhile revolutionary who had fought under

Toussaint. Upon the death of the dictator Dessalines, who was the first leader of independent Haiti, this former slave and cook turned military leader had himself crowned King Henry Christophe of the newly liberated first black republic. This figure also inspired a play by Derek Walcott.

Incisive as Césaire's historical essay is, the capacity of propositional, monological writing to explore the complexity and density of the (post)revolutionary problematic cannot be compared with that of a fully dialogical poetics. *La tragédie du roi Christophe* was first staged in 1964 in Austria and subsequently and more controversially in Paris in 1965, and it is still part of the repertoire of the French national theater, the Comédie-Française. Although this polyphonic treatment of postrevolutionary dynamics is a tragedy, there are overtones of Molièresque comedy as the king ennobles his supporters, giving them ridiculous titles, such as the Duc de Marmelade or the Duc de Limonade (Dukes of Marmalade or Lemonade), titles that reference real Haitian place-names. However, the atmosphere of farce is most uneasy, holding up, as it does, a mirror to colonialist posturing; it is, moreover, entirely absent from the second half of the play, as the king fails to coerce his subjects into the realization of his vision of a flourishing, self-confident state, and especially as he begins to execute those who have become encumbrances. He is eventually betrayed by his less loyal followers, loses his reason to disillusionment and despair, and ultimately kills himself. The play focuses therefore not on the struggle for power but rather on the struggle to govern, vividly problematizing the exercise of power and authority, charting the temptations of absolutism and self-delusion, the risks of betrayal and corruption, the fragility of genuine democracy. It also, of course, exposes the nefarious after-effects of the recklessly divisive racial engineering of colonialism.

In the anglicization of the king's name (from Henri to Henry), we can register the Shakespearean rather than the Corneillean or Racinian timbre that Césaire espoused in all of his plays apart from the T. S. Eliot–flavored oratorio style of the first. The anticlassicist stylistic capaciousness, the swings from earthiness and ribaldry to extremes of pathos and drama, all speak to a very different imaginative and literary register than the one characterizing French theatrical heroics. Césaire's next play also explores the political mines lying in wait for republican values and democratic ideals on the still-smoking battleground of decolonized states. In *Une saison au Congo* (*A Season in the Congo*), a play translated into English by the venerated postcolonial critic Gayatri Chakravorty Spivak, the action is situated in central Africa a full century and a half following Haitian emancipation. The play exposes the depth of the internecine divisions bequeathed by the impervious arrogance of the colonial plunder machine. But, unlike the Haitian *Tragédie*, which deals with a period prior to the accumulation of Haiti's astronomic national debt, the *Saison* explicitly indicts the absolute cynicism of the forces of capitalism that, far from having been swept away by independence, are represented by rapacious (world-) bankers. Of course, it also charts the other reversals and betrayals of postindependence politics, the rising power of the military, the betrayal of Dag Hammarskjöld, and the biting reality of political corruption with, at the center of the action, an antiheroic, flawed, but well-intentioned Patrice Lumumba. The language ranges from that of the ponderous, pompous statesman to the realpolitik of the military man to the weasel words of the so-called neutral men (*hommes neutres*)—and from the scatological release of unsustainable tension to lyrical outpourings, as Césaire has the idealistic secretary general of the United Nations quote to an uninspired Patrice Lumumba an unattributed string of grandiose versets from Saint-John Perse's epic poetry.

∴ ∴ ∴ ∴

It is perhaps easiest to identify Césaire's work as "postcolonial" in relation to the well-worn trope of the Empire writing back to the Imperial Power, subverting the language and the forms of empire in order to critique the latter, turning its very own (cultural) firepower against it. Césaire's most obviously postcolonial rewriting is *Une tempête* (1969), the last of his plays, first staged in Tunisia and in Paris in 1969 and two years later in Martinique. In this version of *The Tempest*, written from a point of view sympathetic above all to Caliban, the shift from the definite to the indefinite article registers the postcolonial tenor of the play, as Césaire writes back to empire, certainly, but from an oblique angle. This play is, in the author's words, adapted "pour un théâtre nègre," but what Césaire is really doing is underlining the emancipation or decolonization of his writing, set free from all "French" resonance and explicitly identifying as his model the much wilder, untamed English model of Shakespearian verve. Power, loyalty and betrayal, governance and corruption are, once more, the dominant themes, Again, the role of Caliban has little or no purchase on the central plot lines, and at the end, while the ever-opportunistic Europeans are able to forget past perfidy, cut their losses, and move on to the next promising deal, the marginalized colonial master/slave duo, Prospero and Caliban, both turn out to be utterly enslaved to their dynamic and to their domain, quite unable to let go or leave it behind them, with Caliban determined to destroy both himself and Prospero along with the whole island.

Literature and theory involve very different positionings in relation to thought. The former is far more dialogical, leaving more room not just for the imagination but also for the input of the reader. Since its meaning is not clearly stated, but remains open, plural, even contradictory, its relation to knowledge and (or as) power is entirely different from that of propositional discourse: the writer of a literary text eschews a position of dominance in relation to meaning. As the foregoing anemic abstracts of Césaire's works demonstrate, the meaning of a literary text is in radical excess of any "message" that can be abstracted from its verbal texture.

Césaire's openness to multiple voices, languages, registers, contexts, or cultures can be seen not just in his choice of three different writing genres (essay, poetry, and theater) but also in the choice of the theatrical genre itself: more specifically, in the range of dramatic situations embraced by the four different plays as well as in the range of voices and idioms within each play. The poetic oeuvre is also distinguished by its variety. First of all, each of the collections has a distinctive timbre and poetics; and second, many poems written and published by Césaire are either not included in any of the various collections, or they have been excluded from subsequent editions of collections in which they were previously included. Crucially, this lack of a unifying perspective in Césaire's oeuvre as a whole means that the meaning of each individual work is particularly open to interpretation.

Clearly Césaire felt no need to supply his work with the underpinning of a program or a manifesto. As already noted, he is far more inclined to question the slogan of negritude than to defend it—much less than to impose it either on himself or on others as a cultural or aesthetic orthodoxy. Instead he was often at pains to open it out as a pragmatic, historically situated response to oppression of any kind, rather than narrowing or limiting it as a specification. In other words, in Césaire's writing there is none of the dogmatism, none of the programmatic assertiveness or restrictiveness of the literary label, none of the imprisoning sectarianism, fundamentalism, or authoritarianism of identitarianism or essentialism. In contrast to the stamp of Creoleness, for example, which rarely surprises in terms of either form or content, Césaire's writing is stylistically multifarious.

As a corollary of this eclecticism, however, it must be recognized that some of his critical essays possess no particular poetic pitch, a fact that distinguishes them from the essays of Edouard Glissant, the sustained poetic tenor of which never drops. Césaire's choices of genres and styles is highly significant. For many politically engaged Caribbean writers, the novel is the chosen genre. Theater, being such a preeminently dialogical form, permits, *pace* Bakhtin, a very different engagement with politics than does narrative. It (re)presents thought and meaning as being entirely subject to the pragmatic, communicational constraints of relational dynamics and role playing. Furthermore, the author's text leaves space for the actors to interpret the various characters in different ways, just as it also makes room for directors and actors to stage the play according to their reading and values. Césaire's ability to cede control over the interpretation of his words in this way, his willingness to collaborate with other writers, thinkers, and artists (such as actors and stage directors), is reinforced and emphasized by his (aforementioned) predilection for (self-)revision.

Césaire's choice of poetry and drama underlines his commitment above all to direct address and to the spoken word. Perhaps the most constant feature of his writing, more fundamental even than his extraordinary linguistic and stylistic range, is his fidelity to the verbal act per se, to the quintessentially human act of speech, the proffered word. His avoidance of narrative orchestration and of theoretical pronouncements in favor of the vulnerability and openness of the I/ you relation of direct speech, can be seen both in imagined and in real discourse: in the drama and in poetry, in the voice of an imagined other, whether a "real" historical character such as Lumumba or a (re) imagined one like Caliban, or in his own voice as in the poems of *Moi, laminaire . . .* , in the *Discourse on Colonialism*, or in the valedictory conversations with Françoise Vergès. He thus eschews the monological writing style of manifestoes, which seem to stand and speak for the many but that, essentially, make proclamations in one voice, a voice represented as resounding beyond the constraints and rebounds of the relation between one person and another and as vibrating in denial of the provisional, dependent, dialogical, and only incompletely controllable reverberation of all verbal engagement.

One of the most striking aspects of Césaire's work, compared with that of almost all his fellow-Caribbean authors in French, is the diversity of language (vocabulary, register, idiom, and tone) of his writings. This reflects his ability to imagine such a variety of distinct worlds and worldviews, from the vast inwardness of the poet to the focus of the campaign-hardened military general; from the unlikely scatological remarks of the monarch, to the Ghanaian foot soldier who speaks a French/English translanguage, to the parody of rarefied courtliness in the French "maître des cérémonies" sent to refine Henry's court. This eclecticism reflects not just the flexibility of Césaire's writing across the boundaries separating different genres but is also reflected in the range of styles characterizing the different poetry collections—from the epic élan and breadth of the *Cahier* to the surrealist shards and flashes of *Les armes miraculeuses*; from the theatrical oratorio of *Et les chiens se taisaient* to the controlled fury of *Soleil cou coupé*; from the distilled distress of *Ferrements* to the more resolved introspection of *Moi, laminaire . . . .* Even though the speaker of that latter collection also has a big lump in his throat, the lump formed by "ce passé en boule non mâché" (the unchewed ball of the past), the speech act is sovereign and a statement in itself. Its constancy confirms Césaire's hallmark perspective on humans as essentially verbal beings, preeminently discursive, living within language, not as a metaphysics, but rather as the sole medium of a necessarily nontranscendent relation and engagement with the world, with history, with each other, and with themselves: as the speaker of the *Cahier* puts it: "Et si je ne sais que parler, c'est pour vous que je parlerai" (And if all I can do is speak, it is for you that I will speak). Indeed, Césaire would never, in the rest of his work, cease to speak for others, both collective and individual others, and this act of speaking for others involves both speaking to them and on their behalf, giving voice to them either directly or indirectly.

Césaire's writing occupies a central, seminal, and pioneering position in the history of literature in French. In fact, his was one of the most significant bodies of writing that eventually pried open the notion of French literature, making it impossible to confine it to a hexagonal shape, including only the work of writers from metropolitan France. He was, indeed, one of the very first authors of literature from France's overseas colonies—francophone literature as it came to be labeled for better or (mostly) for worse—to be assigned a place of honor at the high table of literature in French. In the *mère patrie*, the newness and the sharpness of his work was recognized as early as 1941 by André Breton and thereby by the surrealists in general. Breton's imprimatur, but also that of Jean-Paul Sartre, were of significant value in this respect. Important as it may have been locally, therefore, his role in representational politics pales into near insignificance in relation to his position as a writer and author, a role that propelled him onto the national, international, and even the global stage. More than any other author writing in French either before and possibly after him, Césaire put the French-speaking Caribbean or Americas on the cultural map of the world. Furthermore, he was, along with (though with greater credibility than) the Senegalese poet and statesman Léopold Sédar Senghor and prior to Frantz Fanon, one of the very first black authors to express an absolutely anticolonialist consciousness in French and to point to a radical reevaluation of the effects of racism and colonialism on the understanding of African or African-originating culture.

Beyond the field of French or francophone literary criticism, the work of Césaire has, of course, traveled widely. Thus, for example, when James Clifford was conceptualizing what he calls the "predicament of culture" in the closing decades of the twentieth century, it was to the Caribbean, and more specifically to the work of Césaire, that he looked for inspiration. It is surely significant that it was not to the novels, poetry, or essays of V. S. Naipaul or of Derek Walcott, Caribbean writers in English (both of them subsequently Nobel laureates), but rather to the effervescent poetics of a poet/dramatist working in French that Clifford turned to find a benchmark for the dying millennium's cultural ferment, which was to a very large extent the result of the crossings and interpenetration of European imperialism. Clifford's choice is perhaps not unrelated to the fact that, within the Caribbean crucible, it was in the French-speaking Caribbean specifically that the cultural magic of creolization produced not only a self-conceptualizing, exponentially impacted cultural mix, but also a viable new language, Creole. Paradoxically, however, some of the champions of Creole culture in Martinique have, as already noted, lambasted the absence of the Creole language and of Creole oral culture in Césaire's writing. And there is indeed, in that respect at least, something quixotic or even wrongheaded in the attempt by Clifford and many others to recuperate Césaire's poetics for either Caribbean or Creole cultural specificity, that is, for a culturalism that the author of the *Cahier* at no time and in none of his works sought either to defend or to represent.

In reality, Césaire's creative verve has nothing to do with the so-called politics (all too often an anti-politics) of culturalism (or cultural identitarianism). This is not to say that Césaire is not interested in culture. On the contrary, he is devoted to it, and to its even more problematic near-synonym, civilization, but as a unifying, humanizing imperative, however historically situated it might be, rather than as a separatist force of hierarchical distraction and division.

Finally, Césaire's enduringly bifocal defense both of human inwardness and of human community is particularly pertinent for an age grappling not just with the drowning of interiority in the wash of mediatization, but also with an unprecedented global attack on democracy and on the political realm per se. For our apparently postpolitical, posthistorical age, Césaire's refusal to prioritize programs of cultural or political identity over the ceaseless verbal (re)articulation of self and other(s), of introspection and extraversion, and of lived and imagined realities, is of the utmost importance, as is his mobilization of literature to galvanize and reinforce that refusal.

Note

1. This phrase is taken from the "Discours sur la négritude" first published in 2004 in Paris by Présence Africaine as a coda to the reissue of the 1955 *Discours sur le colonialisme*.

Works Cited and Recommended Further Reading

Note: All translations of passages quoted in this chapter are my own.

Bernabé, Jean, Patrick Chamoiseau, and Raphaël Confiant. *Eloge de la créolité*. Paris: Gallimard, 1989.

Clifford, James. *The Predicament of Culture: Twentieth-Century Ethnography, Literature, and Art* Cambridge, MA: Harvard University Press, 1988.

Confiant, Raphaël. *Aimé Césaire: Une traversée paradoxale du siècle*. Paris: Stock, 1993.

Fanon, Frantz. *Les damnés de la terre*. Paris: Seuil, 1961.

———. *Peau noire, masques blancs*. Paris: Seuil, 1952.

Memmi, Albert. *Portrait du colonisé (suivi de Portrait du colonisateur)*. Paris: Gallimard, 1957.

Perse, Saint-John. *Eloges*. In *Œuvres complètes*. Paris: Gallimard (Pléiade), 1975.

All of Césaire's plays and poetry collections are readily available in paperback editions, published either by Présence Africaine or Editions du Seuil. His "complete works" were somewhat prematurely collected by the Caribbean publisher Desormeaux in 1976. The still-definitive English translation of the poetry is Clayton Eshleman and Annette J. Smith, eds. and trans., *Aimé Césaire: The Collected Poetry* (Berkeley: University of California Press, 1983). A French publisher brought out a fine edition of the collected volumes of the cultural review *Tropiques* (1941–45), for which Césaire himself wrote on occasion (*Tropiques* [Paris: Jean-Michel Place, 1978]). His two most important essays in this collection are (with René Ménil), "Introduction au folklore martiniquais" (in *Tropiques* 4 [1942]) and "Poésie et connaissance" (in *Tropiques* 12 [1945]). The English translation of his play *Une saison au Congo*, mentioned in the text, is *A Season in the Congo*, trans. Gayatri Chakravorty Spivak (City: Seagull Press, 2005). The complete poetry has been collected in *La poésie*, ed. Daniel Maximin and Ernstpeter Ruhe (Paris: Seuil, 1994).

Among the many excellent studies of Césaire's work (apart from studies of individual works, such as Dominique Combe, *Aimé Césaire: Cahier d'un retour au pays natal* [Paris: Presses Universitaires de France, 1993]) are A. James Arnold, *Modernism and Négritude: The Poetry and Poetics of Aimé Césaire* (Cambridge, MA: Harvard University Press, 1981); Bernadette Cailler, *Proposition poétique: Une lecture de l'œuvre d'Aimé Césaire* (Sherbrooke: Naaman, 1976; Paris: Nouvelles du Sud, 2000); Lilyan Kesteloot, *Aimé Césaire* (Paris: Seghers, 1979); Annie Lebrun, *Pour Aimé Césaire* (Paris: Jean-Michel Place, 1994); Jacqueline Leiner, *Aimé Césaire: Le terreau primordial* (Tübingen: G. Narr, 1993); Clément Mbom, *Le théâtre d'Aimé Césaire ou La primauté de l'univesalité humaine* (Paris: Nathan, 1979); and Ronnie Scharfman, *Engagement and the Language of the Subject in the Poetry of Aimé Césaire* (Gainesville: University Press of Florida, 1987). Although some of these studies might appear dated, they provide essential insight into how Césaire's literary work was received and into its wide impact.

Other very important approaches include a chapter in Edouard Glissant, *L'intention poétique* (Paris: Seuil, 1969); Raphaël Confiant's book (listed above); Françoise Vergès's "postcolonial reading of Aimé Césaire," which follows the transcript of her conversations with Césaire in Aimé Césaire, *Nègre je suis, nègre je resterai: Entretiens avec Françoise Vergès* (Paris: Albin Michel, 2005); and Romuald Fonkoua, *Aimé Césaire 1913–2008* (Paris: Editions Perrin, 2010), a critical biography. There have also been several collective volumes, including Roger Toumson and J. Leiner, *Aimé Césaire: Du singulier à l'universel (Œuvres et Critiques* 19, no. 2 [1994]). Perhaps one of the most telling accounts of Césaire's influence is *Césaire et nous: Une rencontre entre l'Afrique et les Amériques au XXIe siècle* (Abidjan: Cauris, 2004) in which a most cosmopolitan constellation of writers, critics, and artists describe what Césaire's writing has meant to them. It is based on a gathering held in Bamako to mark the writer's ninetieth birthday. The centenary of Césaire's birth will no doubt result in a number of remarkable reassessments of the importance and impact of his work.

** **

Sartre's *La nausée* and the Modern Novel

CHRISTOPHER PRENDERGAST

"Shrove Tuesday" (*Mardi gras*) is the heading of one of the entries in the diary of the fictional character, Antoine Roquentin, who is also the first-person narrator of Jean-Paul Sartre's novel, *La nausée*, first published in 1938.[1] However, to call it a "novel," as did Sartre himself, is to beg a question or two, or at the very least to open questions of some import for the history of the modern French novel. First-person fiction in French has of course a long pedigree, directly connected to the invention of modern "interiority." Although the relevant history runs back at least to the later seventeenth century, the principal literary context that matters here is that of the Romantic period and the nineteenth-century subgenre known as the *roman personnel*, whose main practitioners were Sénancour, Chateaubriand, Constant, Musset, Sainte-Beuve, Nerval, and Fromentin. This narrative type displayed an introspective structure of varying complexity. Some of them are "frame" narratives (drawing on the earlier eighteenth-century "memoir" novel, the most famous example being Prévost's *Manon Lescaut*), with the first-person story embedded in a surrounding third-person framework that serves—not always so convincingly—as a skeptical corrective to the excesses of pure inwardness. One thing that these fictions have in common, however, is that they are all securely located in the perspective traditionally available to narrative: the retrospective view, looking back on a past completed (and generally withered); retrospection and introspection come together as if they were natural twins in the staging of the Romantic self's surveys of its own interior landscape.

In the early twentieth century, both André Gide (in *L'immoraliste*) and, above all, Marcel Proust (in *A la recherche du temps perdu*) take first-person narrative and the exploration of subjectivity into new places but without abandoning the position of retrospect. Gide would use the diary—the "journal d'Edouard"—*in* his novel *Les faux-monnayeurs* as a component of it, but that too has many precedents and is not the same as casting a novel entirely *as* a journal. Like Sartre's novel, *Les faux-monnayeurs* ends with a diary note that opens to an indeterminate future ("Je suis bien curieux de connaître Caloub" [I'm very curious to know Caloub] is its final sentence), but for the most part the experimental work of the novel remains subject to the laws of retrospect. In adopting the diary form, Sartre abandons—or at least *appears* to abandon (everything is in that "appears")—the luxury of hindsight knowledge. The entry headed "Shrove Tuesday" installs hero, narrator, and reader in an irreducible "now," blind to an unknown future and severed from the past (in his essay on John Dos Passos, Sartre claimed that the novel, even when written in the past tense, inhabits a permanent present), a work open to the sheer contingency of existence. A few years later, Albert Camus would reach for a similar effect of blank detachment from the imposing authority of narrative in the famous (and, for the translator, challenging) first sentences of *L'étranger*: "Aujourd'hui, maman est morte. Ou peut-être hier, je ne sais pas" (Today, maman died. Or perhaps yesterday, I don't know).[2] In his review of *L'étranger*, Sartre expressed his admiration of this effect, singling out for special praise Camus's use of the *passé composé* (Camus had already bestowed a large and genuine compliment on *La nausée* in his own review of the novel for *Alger Républicain*).

The diary form of writing would be used by others, including Simone de Beauvoir in her three-part tale, *La femme rompue*, in a manner designed to expose a rawness of experience that is the exact opposite of emotion recollected in tranquillity. But there is something special to the affinity of Sartre and Camus here. It marks a historical conjuncture, the one routinely expressed by the conjunction in the formula Sartre *and* Camus. That relation was to give way eventually to Sartre *versus* Camus, the moment of one of the most spectacular ruptures in postwar intellectual history. The interpretation and evaluation of that quarrel—centered on the general question of political violence, and more particularly, Soviet communism and later the Algerian War of Independence—have shifted over time and continue to this day (if, alas, with a tendency to sacrifice serious analysis to journalistic flourish). But, certainly from the point of view of twentieth-century literary history, the conjunction "and" is by far the more important term. The pairing is exemplary and involves a whole journey in the search for various answers, both theoretical and practical, to the question that was to furnish the title of a collection of essays by Sartre, *What Is Literature?* The most interesting (if not always successful) answers were not the essayistic ones, but the various attempts, in the genres of drama and narrative, to mold literary practice to the pressures of the historical moment. The plays of Sartre and Camus explored the problem of "action" as the relation of conventions of dramatic action to the urgencies of political, especially revolutionary, action (*Les mains sales* and *Les justes*). The latter also belongs with Camus's attempts to imagine a "future" for tragedy (as outlined in his Athens lecture "The Future of Tragedy"), as did Sartre's adaptation of Greek tragedy in his wartime play, *Les mouches* and later in the play *Le diable et le bon Dieu*. Politics was also at the heart of much of the narrative fiction, for example, Sartre's trilogy, *Les chemins de la liberté* and Camus's allegory of the Nazi occupation, *La peste*. But what above all remains for us of the umbilical phenomenon Sartre *and* Camus is the moment of *La nausée* and *L'étranger*, the former the big brother of the two, if only by virtue of precedence (Camus's novel was published four years after the publication of *La nausée*).

Seminal works, each raises questions about "literature" and "life," and their often contradictory and paradoxical relationship. In these terms, Sartre's novel is the more important, not only by virtue of chronological precedence, but also because its address of this paradoxical relationship and its implications is the more focused and sustained of the two (this does not mean it is the "better" novel, a pointless ranking game). One way into this unsettling space is to return to the "Shrove Tuesday" entry in *La nausée*, with reference to a particular literary detail (the devil is in the detail, as they say, and he certainly is here). The entry begins with a nightmare in which Roquentin and two friends do something decidedly vulgar with a bunch of violets to the ultra-right-wing French writer, Maurice Barres. From this flamboyant beginning the episode shifts to more mundane matters: the receipt of a letter from his former mistress Anny, lunch at the restaurant in the rue des Horloges, leaving the restaurant to walk the streets of Bouville.

The entry closes with the following passage. I shall quote it first of all from the English translation, and then from the French, since the connotations of the key term of the original are not adequately caught by the translation.

> The rain has stopped, the air is mild, the sky is slowly rolling along beautiful black pictures: this is more than enough to make a frame for the perfect moment; to reflect these pictures, Anny would cause dark little tides to be born in our hearts. But I don't know how to take advantage of this opportunity: I wander along at random, calm and empty, under this wasted sky.

> (La pluie a cessé, l'air est doux, le ciel roula lentement de belles images noires: c'est plus qu'il n'en faut pour faire le cadre d'un moment parfait; pour refléter ces images, Anny ferait naître dans nos coeurs de sombres petites marées. Moi, je ne sais pas profiter de l'occasion: je vais au hasard, vide et calme, sous ce ciel inutilisé.)

The passage contrasts two attitudes to the sky, Anny's and Roquentin's. Anny's gesture, as imagined by Roquentin, would be of an appropriating sort, domesticating the natural world in the attempt to make it conform to a literary model—the model of the "moment parfait," which is taken over more or less wholesale from the "privileged moments" in Proust's *A la recherche du temps perdu*. Anny's transformed sky is a literary sky; it is infested with metaphor, the verbal equivalents of an attempted pictorial framing, not unlike the Proustian sky filtered through the pictures of Proust's fictional painter, Elstir, for which in turn—in a closed circular movement—his narrator seeks to provide a literary version (in Proust's novel Elstir's paintings are explicitly described as "metaphorical").

Roquentin's sky is utterly different: it is merely vacant, it does not lend itself to metaphorical appropriations; it remains—this is the key term that the English "wasted" does not adequately render—it remains "inutilisé." There is however a difficulty here. The phrase "ciel inutilisé" is itself metaphorical. The negative prefix is, of course, designed to refuse the consoling, emotionally utilitarian orderings of the natural world made available by metaphor. There is nevertheless a paradox: the paradox whereby Roquentin deploys metaphor to reject metaphor. I shall return at a later point, and in greater detail, to the particular question of metaphor in *La nausée* (it was to be the main theme of Robbe-Grillet's criticism of Sartre's novel). For the moment, I simply want to use the example as an illustration of a more general paradox, for it is around this paradox that most of the interesting questions of the novel revolve. *La nausée* is a book that affirms the valuelessness of books, on the grounds that they furnish the stereotyped formulas of inauthentic living; they give the forms and alibis of ways of living that, in the terms of Sartre's existentialist morality, are manifestations of "bad faith." "It seems to me as if everything I know about life I have learnt from books," remarks Roquentin early in the novel, with the implication that the "knowledge" in question is entirely specious and that we would do better to dispense with it altogether. Yet we, as readers, know about this claim only because Roquentin has noted it in his diary, or, more pertinently, because it appears in a book by Jean-Paul Sartre. Moreover, it is perhaps one of the nicer ironies of the subsequent destiny of *La nausée* that this book, which loudly proclaims that we should not live our lives through books, was to become both myth and model for a whole postwar generation; the frequency with which intellectuals, and not only on the boulevards and in the cafés of Paris, were seized with bouts of contingency-sickness must certainly be ascribed in part to their having read *La nausée*. (This aspect of the matter is parodied in Boris Vian's very funny novel, *L'écume des jours*, where one of the characters displays a morbid enthusiasm for the writer Jean-Sol Partre, author of the influential novel *Le vomi*, and the philosophical essay "Paradoxe sur le dégeulis.")

The paradoxes thus proliferate in a variety of directions, and I shall come back at a later juncture to a few more. Their general form should, however, be clear, and indeed already familiar as one of the signposts in the landscape of the modern novel as a whole: they point to that paradoxical disposition of modern narrative to query or repudiate the genre of which it is itself a member. In this respect, it is worth recalling the date of *La nausée*'s publication: 1938. The significance of that date can be construed in a number of different ways.

Perhaps the most familiar—although in many respects unsatisfactory—is the line of inquiry that seeks to relate the novel to the philosophical themes (largely of the phenomenological and existentialist sort) engaging Sartre's attention at the time, and that would issue in what for many is Sartre's magnum opus, *L'être et le néant*. This approach does, in fact, yield a set of potentially interesting questions. They have to do with whether or not the central emphases of the philosophical endeavor are of a kind that actively command—or, conversely, militate against—a literary mode of expression: for example, the drive toward "narrative" in *L'être et le néant* arising from the detailed phenomenological descriptions of behavior that Sartre explicitly posits as methodologically crucial to the enterprise of philosophy as such. Conversely, an argument can be made that there is a fundamental tension between the claims of existentialist doctrine and the basic generic requirements of narrative: broadly, the incompatibility of, on the one hand, the existentialist proposition that the world is wholly contingent and the individual wholly free, and, on the other, the anticipatory and foreclosing operations vital to anything we might plausibly recognize as a narrative structure. These again are matters for later. The point to make here is a far more limited one: that it does not seem a particularly profitable exercise to discuss *La nausée*, as it is so often discussed, as a fictionalized version of a series of philosophical ideas. The terms of such discussion effectively reduce the text of the novel to purely illustrative status—to being, as it were, the handmaiden of another order of discourse—and hence give no framework for addressing the far more interesting question: its status as a work of fiction.

From this latter point of view, the date 1938 is a significant one in terms of twentieth-century literary history. *La nausée* stands roughly halfway between those forms of narrative experiment that, in France, we associate largely with the names of Proust and Gide, and those that later emerged under the collective, if essentially polemical, heading of the *nouveau roman*. The date marks the place of *La nausée* as a point of transition in the developing entry of the novel into what Nathalie Sarraute called its "era of suspicion," the moment of a loss of faith in the paradigms of knowledge and understanding that the novel allegedly has reflected and sustained. As an object of "suspicion," the novel can no longer be taken for granted as an instrument of discovery in the way it was for Balzac when he said of his own project, the *Comédie humaine*, that it gave supreme access to the *sens caché* (hidden meaning) of reality. In brief, the novel is no longer a reliable guide to anything, except perhaps—another paradox of course—to the absolute unreliability of everything. Sartre's novel is centrally situated within this general problematic. Part of its specific interest, however, is that its precise location in these terms is somewhat uncertain. Its position with regard to the skeptical paradigm, and the multiple paradoxes the paradigm generates, is ambiguous.

In this connection, let us consider another Sartrian metaphor, or more accurately, an analogy. Sartre once remarked that a great novel would be, inter alia, like a stone. That might not sound like a terribly promising basis on which to found a new narrative program; indeed, it might not seem to be anything we can make sense of at all. We might, however, recall that stones (and their variants, pebbles, rocks, boulders) have enjoyed a rather vigorous symbolic life in a great deal of modern French thinking. It is central to *La nausée* itself, in that Roquentin's first experience of existential nausea comes when he picks up a pebble on the beach ("that pebble," he later reminisces, "the origin of this whole wretched business"). More emphatically, he comes to see his own existence as a stone or at least as stonelike ("I existed like a stone"). Stone also provides the decisive element in Camus's allegory of the absurd, his adaptation of the story of Sisyphus, whose perpetually defeated attempt to roll the boulder up to the top of the mountain illustrates the permanent contradiction between the human desire for meaning and the world's resistance to that desire.

In the context of specifically literary theory and practice, this stone or pebble turns up in at least two other important contexts. First, in the brilliant, though nowadays little read, imaginary Socratic dialogue by Valéry, *Eupalinos*. Valéry's Socrates picks up a pebble while walking along the seashore. Washed for centuries by the sea, the pebble, in terms of smoothness and roundness, is perfect. The question it prompts is whether a perfection produced by the random forces of nature can properly be compared to the perfection of a work of art. Socrates's answer is an unequivocal no, on the grounds that its perfection is merely accidental, a result of the play of contingent forces, whereas a condition of the aesthetic artifact is the conscious, ordering activity of the human mind and the human hand. The other example is Francis Ponge's short, and deceptively simple, prose poem "Le galet" ("Beach Pebble"). Ponge's pebble is also perfect, but its status is ambiguous. It is not clear whether the real object of Ponge's attention is the thing itself or the word *galet* which denotes it; his poem oscillates ambiguously and ironically between the referential and self-reflexive functions of language, apparently miming the material properties of the thing when in fact exploring, and playing with, the material properties of the word—not so much a naming of objects as an objectifying of names. It is a deliberately cultivated, and in its implications wide-ranging, ambiguity, raising in its own low-key way the characteristic "modernist" queries about the possibilities and constraints of the relation between language and reality.

Stones thus appear to get around quite a lot in the modern French literary consciousness. But Sartre's novelistic stone or stonelike novel is quite different from either Valéry's or Ponge's respective pebbles. What Sartre has in mind is neither Ponge's ambiguous interlacing of the referential and self-reflexive, nor Valéry's rigorously classical insistence on the ordering power of imagination and convention. What Sartre envisages is a novel that would resemble the stone in its pure contingency, a novel so unself-conscious, so freed from artifice and convention, as to give us an unmediated image of the raw chaos of things, the world in its pure, meaningless "being-there." It is, of course, fantasy. What such a novel might conceivably look like and, more pertinently, to what extent *La nausée* can be intelligibly analyzed in terms of this program, are very open questions indeed.

It is nevertheless around a fantasy of this sort—a modernist reinvention of the ancient idea of *mimesis*—that a good deal of *La nausée* is organized. In the first place, what underlies it is precisely what in principle is entailed by Roquentin's experience of nausea. The emotional symptoms and consequences of Roquentin's moments of nausea—with the beach pebble, the beer glass, the tree root, and so forth—have been much discussed, generally in a philosophical context, and occasionally as representing less a philosophical outlook than a psychiatric condition. The implication of the latter view is that all Roquentin's troubles could be adequately dealt with were he to see a good doctor—the riposte to which is given by *La nausée* itself, in the figure of Dr. Rogé, voice of experience and wisdom, whose wisdom consists in "always explaining the new by the old." In the most general terms, Roquentin's nausea is the symptomatic expression of the falling away of all familiar frames of reference. It entails the abolition of difference, the breakdown of classification, the erasure of distinctions, in a process whereby identities fuse and merge to form a soft, gelatinous mess within which no structure of differentiation and intelligibility can any longer hold. In Roquentin's words, nausea spells the disappearance of "the world of human measures," the rubbing-out of the "feeble landmarks which men have traced on the surface [of things]." Nausea is akin to an experience of "melting": "The veneer had melted, leaving soft, monstrous masses, in disorder—naked, with a frightening, obscene nakedness." Or, in Roquentin's aural metaphor, the world is not so much a storehouse of information, a source of messages we can confidently decode, as the place of an "inconsequential buzzing."

Within this generalized dissolution of all human systems of ordering and representation, there is, however, one that comes in for particularly intensive treatment: the system of narrative. "Stories" (*histoires*) are at once a prop and a mask; they support us, make our world habitable, by blinding us to the pure superfluity of existence, the unmotivated or (in Sartre's slightly more moralistic way) "unjustifiable" nature of our being-in-the-world. From this point of view, the key passage in *La nausée* is the following—long, but worth quoting at length:

> This is what I have been thinking: for the most commonplace event to become an adventure, you must—and this is all that is necessary—start *recounting* it. This is what fools people: a man is always a teller of tales, he lives surrounded by his stories and the stories of others, he sees everything that happens to him through them; and he tries to live his life as if he were recounting it. But you have to choose: to live or to recount. For example, when I was in Hamburg, with that Erna girl whom I didn't trust and who was afraid of me, I led a peculiar sort of life. But I was inside it, I didn't think about it. And then one evening, in a little

café at St Pauli, she left me to go to the lavatory. I was left on my own, there was a gramophone playing *Blue Skies*. I started telling myself what had happened since I had landed. I said to myself: "On the third evening, as I was coming into a dance-hall called the Blue Grotto, I noticed a tall woman who was half-seas-over. And that woman is the one I am waiting for at this moment, listening to *Blue Skies*, and who is going to come back and sit down on my right and put her arms around my neck." Then I had a violent feeling that I was having an adventure. But Erna came back, she sat down beside me, she put her arms around my neck, and I hated her without knowing why. I understand now: it was because I had to begin living again that the impression of having an adventure had just vanished. When you are living, nothing happens. The settings change, people come in and go out, that's all. There are never any beginnings. Days are tacked on to days without rhyme or reason, it is an endless monotonous addition. . . . There isn't any end either: you never leave a woman, a friend, a town in one go. . . . That's living. But when you tell about life, everything changes; only it's a change nobody notices: the proof of that is that people talk about true stories; events take place one way and we recount them the opposite way. . . . I wanted the moments of my life to follow one another in orderly fashion, like those of a life remembered. You might as well try to catch time by the tail.

The central emphasis of this way of looking at narrative lies in the opposition of two terms: "event" (*événement*) and "adventure" (*aventure*). Much has been made of this distinction, partly because of its relation to Sartre's philosophical writings, partly because of its bearing on recurring problems of twentieth-century narrative theory. In fact, the point at issue is, on the surface at least, a relatively simple one. "Events" are what occur in real life; "adventures" are what occur in books (although they can also occur in real life to the extent that we model our lives on books). Events constitute free-floating, undetermined, discontinuous series of "happenings." Adventures, on the other hand, are happenings converted into significant order, causal sequence, meaningful pattern; in brief, adventure equals event plus intelligibility. The intelligibility in question is basically of a temporal sort. Time, in the aspect of event, is time in its "everyday slackness," where "days are tacked on to days without rhyme or reason," as "an endless monotonous addition." The time of adventure, on the other hand, is time "caught by the tail." It not only, according to the classic Aristotelian formula, has a beginning, a middle, and an end, portents and resolutions, anticipations and closures. Above all, it is time organized in function of a significant end, time organized teleologically. Narrative versions of experience occupy a structure wherein what comes before is determined by what comes after—in the world of story "the end is always there, transforming everything." In story, everything is, so to speak, back to front: life as narrative is one that "unrolls backwards: the minutes don't pile up haphazardly one after another any more, they're snapped by the story's end which draws them toward it and makes each of them draw to it in its turn the moment that precedes it."

In this conflation of remarks we can read the terms of Roquentin's (and Sartre's) critique of the presuppositions and procedures of narrative (this is also what principally caught Camus's eye when he reviewed the novel for *Alger Républicain*, an attitude to storytelling that he would carry over into the writing of *L'étranger*, if in a less explicitly advertised fashion). Narrative (or adventure) imposes factitious order on the contingent disorder of experience; it makes artificial sense of what is inherently without sense; it attributes design and purpose to what is formless and superfluous. Stories, in brief, are an epistemological confidence trick. In itself, this set of propositions is hardly news—we can find a virtually identical set of ideas in, say, Gide's notion of narrative as "forgery" or "counterfeiting," not to mention a whole number of other sources (moreover, by no means confined to what is often assigned to the preserve of "modernism"). What gives Sartre's version of this particular theme its particular edge, or sense of urgency, is that it is not limited to querying a purely epistemological order. Or rather, the epistemological doubts over the credentials of narrative are closely linked to considerations of a social and ideological character. Stories, as narrative orderings, are not just sources of error, they are also sources of dishonesty (or what Sartre calls "bad faith"). The fictions consecrated by fiction itself serve discredited utilitarian ends. For we do not simply recount or listen to "stories"; we perceive ourselves and others, we arrange our lives, construct our worlds according to their comfortable and comforting dispositions: "a man is always a teller of tales, he lives surrounded by his stories and the stories of others, he sees everything that happens to him through them; and he tries to live his life as if he were recounting it."

The life of Roquentin represents a concerted and anguished attempt to cast off the blandishments of story in order to face reality in its non-narrative "nakedness," the "obscene nakedness" that appears before one's eyes when the "veneer" of all human fictions has "melted." The difficulty with this otherwise courageous project (if we accept the assumptions that lie behind it) is that Roquentin's "life" is for us precisely a life *recounted*, directly in the form of the diary he keeps, indirectly as a "novel" written by Sartre. And the question, of course, is: How do we situate *this* story in relation to the devaluation of story proposed by Roquentin himself? What exactly is the status of this devaluation? Does the charge of bad faith refer only to a certain *class* of narratives (from which Sartre's narrative is exempt on the grounds that it gives us something radically different from the traditional fare); or does it refer to all forms of storytelling, as a disposition inherent in narrative as such, or indeed, more broadly, to any kind of articulated account of the world? Is *La nausée* a book that remains faithful to the implications of "nausea"? Or are the terms of the argument such as to make that sort of claim a contradiction in terms? And, if the latter, to what extent does *La nausée* show an awareness of this paradox? One way of putting all these questions in a kind of shorthand would be to ask: Is *La nausée* "stone" or "story"? More precisely, does this set of alternative scenarios represent a set of realistic choices?

If we follow the implication of the stone metaphor (the idea of a novel free of bad faith, which surrenders itself to the world's contingency), we will of course come up with something. We might point to the device of the story-that-crumbles: for instance, in the passage cited earlier, the story of the woman in Hamburg, Erna, reconstructed as "adventure" and then deconstructed back into "event," the latter version cancelling out the presuppositions of the former. Also, there are the ways of handling time made possible by manipulating the conventions of the diary form: first, the sense of narrative indeterminacy in the undated "first" entry and, as already noted, the wonderfully suspended yet dismal future tense on which Roquentin's manuscript closes ("Tomorrow it will rain over Bouville"); second, the frequent movements between tenses, in a manner that suggests a certain merging of narrated and narrating time, as in the Paris restaurant episode: "When I felt tired I came into this café and fell asleep. The waiter has just woken me up, and I am writing this while I am half-asleep. Tomorrow I shall go back to Bouville." This strategy of shifting temporal perspective is evidently designed to evoke a life as it is being lived. Instead of that commanding narrative preterite of classic fiction whereby, in Roland Barthes's phrase, life is converted into "destiny" (a cognate of Sartre's *aventure*), here we see an attempt to match the rhythms of writing to the texture of existential reality itself—in which past, present, and future, along with memory, experience, and project are not allowed to settle down into some prearranged design.

Finally, we could cite certain critical experiences with and in language: the famous incident connected with the tree root in the public garden, where that primary instrument of differentiation and classification, the principle of *naming*, breaks down; in Roquentin's words, "things have broken away from their names . . . I am in the midst of Things that cannot be given names" (a foretaste of the crazed, endlessly defeated attempt to name in Beckett's *L'innommable*). The implication is that, stripped of the human and humanizing labels that language confers, things appear before Roquentin in their original ontological condition of pure contingency. A similar implication could be drawn from the various hallucinated sequences of *La nausée* (for example, the episode where Roquentin roams the streets in a semi-demented state after having read the newspaper item about the raped and strangled girl); in the interpenetration of fact and fantasy, what comes under pressure is syntax itself: the sentences both proliferate and disintegrate at the same time, in a wild interchange of subjects and predicates, no longer capable of holding together that system of identity and difference from which alone the consolations of intelligible reality can be had.

These, then, would be so many marks of a narrative trying to escape from the bad faith of traditional story, in search of a new kind of narrative authenticity. But it is precisely here that we encounter all the critical paradoxes of which I have already spoken. The features I have listed may be deemed "figures" in the effort to dramatize the senselessness of existence, but they are not themselves senseless. They make sense, if only of that senselessness, in the same way that to talk of the unnameability of objects is still to name them (if only as the "unnameable"—the paradox around which Beckett's *L'innommable* endlessly circulates). That is, the linguistic and literary apparatus of *La nausée* is not like the pebble on the beach picked up by Roquentin or by Valéry's Socrates; its elements are not random and contingent, but the product of human choices made within a uniquely human medium. They are "devices" (in the strong sense given to the term by the Russian Formalists) designed to create certain impressions and effects, not the random outcomes of natural forces. One intended impression is of course what it is like to experience the world as pure contingency, but they are not themselves contingent. On the contrary, they are items in a rhetorical and narrative repertoire, as indeed is everything else in *La nausée*. Perhaps one could make the nature of the paradox a little clearer by returning to that aspect of the text with which I began: the use of metaphor.

For a text whose presuppositions would seem to demand the systematic elimination of metaphor, it is perhaps surprising that *La nausée* is absolutely saturated in it. What, for example, are we to make of bits of newspaper described as "sedate as swans," or Adolphe's braces possessing a "sheep-like stubbornness"? Is this simply Sartre, as Robbe-Grillet would have it, being unreflectingly guilty of the very anthropomorphism that his own argument would require him to refuse? One rather sophisticated account of Sartre's metaphors (Fredric Jameson's) advances the view that Sartrian metaphor is really "false metaphor." By this is meant a process of exaggeration whereby the traditional claims and implications of metaphorical representation are undermined; through the use of hyperbole, willfully exaggerated or excessive metaphorical development, Sartre decomposes metaphor; through its very excess, metaphor announces itself *as* metaphor, a literary construct whose very literariness is the mark of its distance from reality. The classic example is the elaborate figurative structure built around the episode of the tree root: ". . . that long dead snake at my feet, that wooden snake. Snake, claw or root, it doesn't matter . . . that big rugged paw . . . that hard, compact sea-lion skin . . . a small black pool at my feet . . . a greedy claw, tearing the earth, snatching its food from it."

Metaphor, in this context, is "false" in so far as our expectations of its expressive power are constantly defeated; the figures are dramatic yet impotent, a series of figures in which one displaces the others, yet where all, individually or collectively, circle around what they can never express. It is the dance of figurative language around an absence—the existential reality of the root (its "superfluity") on which metaphorical discourse (or indeed any linguistic form at all) can never gain purchase. This is an interesting argument, and it does help to make sense of some of Sartre's more baroque inventions. It does, however, have an unwarranted implication. In this view, metaphorical excess in *La nausée* not only leads us to posit a reality "beyond" metaphor (beyond the humanizing appropriations of language), it also creates the possibility of passing through that excess into direct contact with reality itself; metaphor, undone, gives the occasion for transforming absence into presence. Thus, in the example of the root, "beyond" its diverse figurative representations, so baroque as to blow up in our faces, we "somehow" (Jameson's word) sense the reality of the root as a pure physical substance. This, however, will not do (as the implied unease of the impressionistic "somehow" itself indicates). Neither in Sartrian metaphor, nor in any other, is there a "beyond" to which the text gives us access. The metaphor is the space and ground of our activity as readers; we are held within the metaphorical play of the text because there is nowhere else for us to go, except perhaps toward silence. To take the central, most extended example of the text, as readers we can know what is entailed by the experience of "nausea" only by being told what it is *like*—that is, through a set of metaphorical representations of which the key term is, precisely, "nausea" itself. *La nausée* doesn't give us nausea (unless we happen very violently to take against it); it gives us "Nausea," an abstraction as metaphor and hence as the representation of an experience rather than the experience itself.

"Nausea," in short, is a literary term, in a text for which something called "literature" is the problem. *La nausée* is one of Sartre's (several) answers to the question "What is literature?"—an answer in the mode of radical skepticism vis-à-vis the function and value of literature. "I must beware of literature," remarks Roquentin. The remark is programmatic, defining an entire stance toward the literary enterprise. But a paragraph later we find him musing, "the next day I felt as disgusted as if I had awoken in a bed full of vomit." "Vomit" is another word for "nausea." "I have no need to speak in flowery language," notes Roquentin as he defines literature as an object of wariness ("I must beware") or object of "suspicion." "Vomit" is manifestly a case in point, the antithesis of the florid. But it is certainly literary, as is the whole of the texture of *La nausée*. For the reality of *La nausée* is that of literature and not of "existence." Individual stories may crumble, but a general story is told (the life of Roquentin) in ways that do not massively offend our standard expectations of intelligibility. Time, in our ordinary experience of it, is certainly questioned, but equally certainly does not disappear. Metaphor may be made to behave in peculiar, self-deconstructing ways, but it still behaves as metaphor. Syntax, in both the strict grammatical sense and the looser sense of the syntax of narrative, may at certain junctures be threatened, but it never completely falls apart.

The main point in stating all this, however, is not to say that *La nausée* is a safe, traditional novel after all (an uninteresting, even foolish claim), but that, given the rigidities often found in the twentieth-century forms of the quarrel of the ancients and the moderns, the general categories in question, though they may be equivocated, strained, and stretched in a variety of ways, cannot simply collapse. Without those properties, narrative would be what Roquentin describes the world as being: an "inconsequential buzzing." That might be good existentialist ontology, but it is doubtful whether writing based on such a formula would retain our attention for very long. A text that was an "inconsequential buzzing" might be many things (it might, for instance, be in some way like a stone, a brute fact of nature), but it would not be a *text*. It should, of course, be clear where all this is leading us. If novels are written in bad faith, then, to some degree, they are necessarily so. As Frank Kermode argued in *The Sense of an Ending*, the truth of the world may be contingency, but it is not the truth or reality of narrative; for narrative to exist, it must possess, as constitutive conditions of its existence, properties that a contingency theory denies to the world.

One answer to such a dilemma would be to abolish narrative, or, more radically—since the extreme point of the argument touches language itself—to command silence. This is one of the alternatives of the choice starkly presented by Roquentin: "il faut vivre ou raconter" (you have to choose: to live or to recount). The choice is stark, and it confronts an entire strain of modern literature. But we have to be clear about which way Sartre here goes. He has chosen to recount, and so too will Roquentin, his exit from the novel being an entry into the literary vocation. Quite what we are to make of Roquentin's decision to write is highly uncertain. There could be an intended irony here, an ironic back-reference to the figure for whom "literature" is the royal road to salvation, and whose own novel ends with its hero embarking on the writing of a novel that is (probably) the novel we have just read: Proust. Sartre's irony would thus be anti-Proustian, and Roquentin's turning to literature as a means of personal redemption would then be understood as the adoption of a regressive escape route, modeled on the apotheosis of the Proustian narrator, just as Anny's (derided) philosophy is modeled on the Proustian epiphany of the "moment parfait."

It could, on the other hand, be taken straight, implying Sartre's belief in a form of literary consciousness and a literary practice situated beyond the infested realm of "bad faith." One suspects that the latter implication is certainly the case; Sartre seems as committed to his hero's vocabulary of "salvation" as Roquentin himself. This was one of Camus's reservations in his review of the novel, seeing in it a new version of the "salvational" conception of literature, as that which might "justify" an existence (in a mocking echo of Descartes, he summarized it in the formula "I write, therefore I exist"). The difficulty lies in squaring the decision to write with the logic that informs Roquentin's insistence that we must choose between the irreconcilables of "living" and "telling." Indeed, the exact terms in which Roquentin evokes his literary project chime oddly with what he has earlier been at pains to stress: "Another kind of book. . . . The sort of story, for example, that could never happen, an adventure. . . . A book. A novel. . . ." "Story"? "Adventure"? "Novel"?—these, of course, are the very terms, reserved in the earlier assault on human fable-making for his utmost contempt, now reappearing as the main emphases of an affirmed and affirmative literary program, one that will "make people ashamed of their existence."

But in what ways will this be "another kind of book," different from the books he has previously denounced? A further difficulty here is that we are given very little detail as to what this program will in practice involve. The chief clue is through the analogy with the haunting jazz song "Some of These Days." Yet, despite some metaphysical mutterings about transforming "existence" into "being," the analogy is not particularly informative. What, then, makes it so special? In particular, why is the jazz melody attributed "redeeming" and "cleansing" powers, whereas the "consolation" Roquentin's aunt derived from Chopin's *Preludes* after her husband's death merely fills him with disgust? What makes jazz authentic and Chopin fraudulent? There is also a further Proustian context here. Proust, a great admirer of Chopin, is also the creator of the fictional composer, Vinteuil, whose sonata and septet would prove so decisive in the aesthetic education of his narrator. "Some of These Days" looks like another ironic rejoinder to Proustian doctrine (and the drawing room world to which it belongs): cool, hip, demotic versus sophisticated, rarefied, elite.

In fact, the celebration of the jazz melody simply displaces, rather than resolves, the problem that confronts both Roquentin and the reader of *La nausée*: What does it mean to *write*? Does Roquentin's project represent a way of overcoming the problematical disjunction between "recounting" and "living" without being caught in the morass of *mauvaise foi*? If so, what grounds does *La nausée* itself offer for us to be able to believe in this as a convincing possibility? On the other hand, if Roquentin's projected book is the object of Sartre's irony, what then are the implications of the ironic stance for the fact that Sartre himself has written a book? The problem, it will be seen, is entirely circular, its logical structure akin to the conundrum of the Cretan Liar paradox (a Cretan says all Cretans are liars; if true, then false). It is not, however, a question of shredding *La nausée* in the logic-chopping machine or of turning the circle into a noose with which to hang Sartre; that is ultimately a sterile game to play, and moreover, it can be played with very many modern writers indeed. The question bears less on the fact that *La nausée* is inescapably inscribed within paradox than on how much *awareness* it shows of its own paradoxical nature. Does it generate a level of self-reflexive monitoring large enough to make the critique of fictions it contains a full-fledged auto-critique? Is it a fiction that, in questioning the value of fictions, remains alert to its own fictive character? Or does it tacitly seek to proclaim itself as "another kind of book," one that closes the gap between fiction and existence, language and thing, "story" and "stone"?

The latter, we have seen, is an impossible dream (it is also a very ancient one). It would be bizarre if Sartre, while seduced by the dream, were not also aware of its impossibility; indeed, the first section of *La nausée* itself virtually permits of no other conclusion. Yet it is not certain. *La nausée* hesitates over its relation to the paradoxes it inhabits. It is a novel that cannot quite make up its mind as to what it is, what it would like to be, what it could be. It is emphatic (even moralistically so) in its rejections (seeking to sweep away a whole tradition of narrative as the debris of a bankrupt bourgeois culture). But it is unclear in its prescriptions, explicit or tacit. For many, the hesitation is fatally disabling, the sign of a fundamental incoherence. It is, however, equally arguable that its confusions are in some ways an exemplary illustration of the dilemmas of the modern novel; that, through those very confusions, it meets head-on, if somewhat awkwardly, the difficulties that the more sophisticated ironical cleverness of other novelists tends to elide (the self-conscious shading into the self-regarding). Sartre's novel is anything but self-regarding, and it is historically decisive in taking us to where we still are—in the "era of suspicion."

Notes

1. The following is an adapted and expanded version of an essay that first appeared in *Teaching the Text*, ed. Susanne Kappeler and Norman Bryson (London: Routledge, 1983).

2. "Mother died today" is the usual translation, but there is a compelling argument for retaining the French "maman" as well the original word order: "Today, maman died." This still leaves the yawning, and perhaps unbridgeable, gap between the grammar of "est morte" and "died."

Works Cited and Recommended Further Reading

Barthes, Roland. *Le degré zéro de l'écriture*. Paris: Gonthier, 1968.

Beauvoir, Simone de. *La femme rompue*. Paris: Gallimard, 1968.

Camus, Albert. *L'étranger*. In *Théâtre, Récits, Nouvelles*. Paris: Gallimard, 1962.

———. *The Outsider*. Translated by Joseph Laredo. London: Penguin, 1982.

———. "*La nausée* de Jean-Paul Sartre." In *Essais*. Paris: Gallimard, 1965.

Field, Trevor. *Form and Function in the Diary Novel*. Basingstoke: Macmillan, 1989.

Jameson, Fredric. *Sartre: The Origins of a Style*. New Haven, CT: Yale University Press, 1961.

Kermode, Frank. *The Sense of an Ending*. Oxford: Oxford University Press, 1966.

Ponge, Francis. *Le parti pris des choses*. Paris: Gallimard, 1979.

Robbe-Grillet, Alain. *Pour un nouveau roman*. Paris: Editions de Minuit, 1963.

Sarraute, Nathalie. *L'ère du soupçon: Essais sur le roman*. Paris: Gallimard, 1956.

Sartre, Jean-Paul. "Explication de *L'étranger*" and "A propos de John Dos Passos." In *Situations 1*. Paris: Gallimard, 1947.

———. *La Nausée*. In *Oeuvres romanesques*. Paris: Gallimard, 1981.

———. *Nausea*. Translated by Robert Baldick. London: Penguin, 1965.

———. *Qu'est-ce que la littérature?* Paris: Gallimard, 1964.

Valéry, Paul. *Eupalinos, ou l'architecte*. Paris: Gallimard, 1924.

Vian, Boris. *L'écume des jours*. Paris: Union Générale d'Editions, 1965.

Beckett's French Contexts

JEAN-MICHEL RABATÉ

Usually, the question of deciding whether Samuel Beckett can be considered a "French writer" is solved by biographical explanations: The younger Beckett had absorbed too much English literature, and his first essays, stories and poems were too allusive, loaded with puns and arcane references, too self-consciously literary. In awe of his literary mentor James Joyce, to whom he owed the decision to become a creative writer instead of an academic, he upstaged the older Irish writer, who had started writing in a variety of idioms. French allowed Beckett to outgrow Joyce and forget his enormous influence. Writing in another language offered an exit, a path leading to a recognizable minimalism because French afforded the possibility of writing "without style." The story has been told often. There is now a subsidiary industry within Beckett scholarship that is devoted to analyses of Beckett's bilingualism, providing comparisons between French and English versions of the main works. While this is encouraging for the promotion of translation studies, the previous narrative can be questioned or complicated. Beckett's decision to write in French cannot be divorced from two other questions: the broader question of modernism defined as an international category, which entails the absence of a clear parallelism between high modernism in the Anglo-Saxon domain, the marginal status of "modernism" in France, and the no less different status of modernism in Ireland. Then, there is the difficult problem of understanding "style" as a term that migrates between different languages and cultures but that is inevitably referred back to specific literary traditions. Beyond the generic pigeonholing, I will argue that the idea of "writing without style" was a very "French" preoccupation at the time when Beckett became a French writer.

Beckett is often considered a modernist, albeit with qualifications: a "late" modernist, according to Tyrus Miller, or the "last" modernist, according to Anthony Cronin. If we look at one of the best collections of essays dealing with the topic—Astradur Eysteinsson and Vivian Liska's *Modernism*—we can see that Beckett occupies a special position. Anders Olsson's chapter, "Exile and Literary Modernism," gives pride of place to Beckett. Beckett is described as a "voluntary exile," like Joyce, who moreover developed a "uniquely bilingual career as a writer entirely in exile." Olsson analyzes Beckett's constant effort to "disassociate himself from the land of his birth" intent upon using the French language "as a means to conquer a plain idiom in line with his reductive vision." This entails a familiar story about losing in idiomatic freshness to gain something at another level: "Beckett's new French narration is more purified, less connotative and witty than the earlier prose, a fact that makes it possible to claim that he loses something in order to gain something else." I will return to this analysis to nuance it. What is more relevant is the fact that, within this same book, Beckett is not mentioned once in the chapter titled "French Literary Modernism," by Kimberley Healey. In it, Healey is right to start by asserting that French modernism did not exist, and she presents a competent analysis of "modernity" as a specific French tradition that takes Baudelaire, Mallarmé, and Lautréamont as its beacons. However, since Healey discusses the *nouveau roman* in terms of Alain Robbe-Grillet, Nathalie Sarraute, Michel Butor, and Marguerite Duras, one would expect at least a passing reference to Beckett, who shared with them a publisher and important ideas. This omission testifies to a difficulty facing Beckett: he is not to be situated in Irish modernism, he is not a high modernist, and his bilingual status prevents him from being claimed as a French modernist.

Can Beckett escape completely from the confines of Irish modernism? Before arguing that Beckett can and should be considered a "French author," one needs to see what his link with the Irish situation might be, even though this is a site that he is supposed to have abandoned. Here, one cannot avoid paying attention to the nagging problem of languages; Gaelic was not only a language to speak in, as for those who were advocating its return, but one to think and write in. This was a recurrent problem for the Irish "moderns." When Irish authors like Yeats and Synge began "modernizing" themselves, they faced the issue of the lost native tongue, the idiom that many of them considered a backward "dialect," especially when compared with the rest of European culture. The Irish predicament emerges clearly in an ironic account of early Irish modernism provided by George Moore, one of its main participants.

Moore had lived in Paris and knew the French scene intimately. In his autobiography, *Hail and Farewell*, Moore explains that Yeats happened to be stymied by writer's block as he planned to revise stories published in magazines for his collection *The Secret Rose*, and was then hoping to transform one into a play. Moore, always obliging, worked on one story and found a solution. Yeats was not satisfied. Moore thought that Yeats was searching for the *mot juste* but then realized that Yeats was not looking for the right word but for the right language. Moore asked whether Yeats planned to write his stories in Irish. No, Yeats did not know any Irish. He was looking for a different language and a new style as well. Yeats explained that he wanted his stories to be understood by Sligo peasants. Moore suggested writing in brogue, the comical sort of Anglo-Irish, which was rejected by Yeats. They compared the merits of dialects and major languages like Latin, English, and French, until their discussion led to an apparently absurd proposition: they would use three languages, English, French, and Gaelic, to attain what they wanted, after Moore had exclaimed: "I'd sooner write the play in French." Yeats jumped on the idea and insisted that a detour through French would provide the solution to their linguistic dilemma. First, Moore would translate Yeats's work into French. Moore continued, "Lady Gregory will translate your text into English. Taidgh O'Donoghue will translate the English text into Irish, and Lady Gregory will translate the Irish text back into English." Moore went to France and sent Yeats a French version. His memoir quotes a few pages in French, which include dialogue like this:

> GRANIA. Je ne peux te suivre. Je pense à toi, Diarmuid, nuit et jour, et mon désir me laisse sans force; je t'aime, Diarmuid, et les pommes que tu as trouvées dans cette vallée désolée ne sont-elles pas un signe que ma bouche est pour ta bouche?
>
> DIARMUID. Je ne puis t'écouter . . . nous trouverons un asile quelque part. Viens au jour. La caverne te fait peur et elle me fait peur aussi. Il y a du sang ici et une odeur de sang.

(GRANIA. I cannot follow you. I think about you, Diarmuid, night
and day, and desire leaves me exhausted; I love you, Diarmuid,
and are not the apples that you found in this desolate valley a
sign that my mouth is for your mouth?
DIARMUID. I cannot listen to you. We will find an asylum somewhere. Come into the daylight. The cave frightens you, it
frightens me too. There is blood here and a smell of blood.)

Of course, Moore pokes fun at Yeats's linguistic queasiness and literary pretention so as to parody the divided self of Irish writers.
However, this detour via a different language shows Yeats's wish to
bend and shape an idiom that does not sound universal enough. Already, then, French was a medium that allowed one to write "without
style," even though one recognizes here all the mannerisms of late
symbolist plays. If the Irish Grania and Diarmuid sound like Maurice
Maeterlinck's *Pelléas and Mélisande*, this stylistic parallel aims at heal-
ing the inner division of Irish modernists: they would blend Gaelic
legends and European modernism while creating an idiom that could
be understood by local peasants. This conflation explains the lasting
success of plays like Synge's *Playboy of the Western World*, with its synthetic and artificial brogue. The idea of Yeats, Lady Gregory, and
George Moore's translating from the French in order to launch a
Celtic Revival was fanciful but not as absurd as it seems. What this
linguistic nexus reserved for Yeats is another story, but it became a
source of worry for the young Beckett.

Beckett's decision to write in French in order to write without style
is not just the consequence of his voluntary exile to Paris in the late
thirties; neither was it caused by the accident of war, and his forced
stay in Roussillon in the forties. Beckett has followed a consistent
literary program, a program anticipated by the Irish modernists. True,
he deployed it more consistently, more rigorously, and over a longer
period of time. It was formulated early, just after a stay of some two
years in Paris, in Beckett's aborted novel, *Dream of Fair to Middling
Women*. Quoting a startling phrase ("Black diamond of pessimism")
coined by his friend Lucien (who was based on Jean Beaufret, a philosopher at the Ecole Normale Supérieure), Beckett's alter-ego Be-
lacqua finds in the expression a family resemblance with the gems of

Racine and Malherbe before generalizing about the French language: "But the writing of, say, Racine or Malherbe, perpendicular, diamanté, is pitted, is it not, and sprigged with sparkles; the flints and pebbles are there, no end of humble tags and commonplaces. They have no style, they write without style, do they not, they give you the phrase, the sparkle, the precious margaret. Perhaps only the French can do it. Perhaps only the French language can give you the thing you want." This fragment from *Dream of Fair to Middling Women* was excerpted in *Disjecta* in 1983, which testifies to its importance. What remains to be explained is the link between those verbal "diamonds"—in another context, one might be tempted to describe them as baroque metaphors—and the alleged absence of a style. It would take Beckett twenty more years to iron out the tensions or contradictions that this single passage contains.

Beckett had the advantage of having learned French very young, and of having been thoroughly immersed in the Parisian milieu of the experimental avant-garde that had gathered around Joyce and Jolas's *Transition* group as early as 1928. He witnessed the impact of Joyce's creation of a synthetic and syncretic language into which more than seventy separate idioms would be fused. However, he could also perceive that the curious idiolect of the *Wake* remained fundamentally English, at least in its grammar; it could turn into a universal language capable of absorbing all other idioms only if you knew some English. Samuel Beckett appeared then as a belated Synge who did not have to go the Aran Islands, following Yeats's suggestion, in order to forge a new Anglo-Irish idiom. Beckett found it in the street dialogues of French blue-collar workers drinking calvados in Parisian cafés, and then among the resilient French peasants of the Lubéron hills, when he and Suzanne were hiding from the Gestapo in Roussillon.

These encounters with demotic and patois turned Beckett away from the classical models that he knew so well when he taught French literature at Trinity in 1930–31. At the time, his survey of French literature gave pride of place to Racine and also to the "modern classicism" presented by André Gide and the *Nouvelle Revue Française* as a response to the avant-garde. The classical models exerted their influence for a limited duration, until surrealism and the spirit of *Transi-*

tion proved stronger. A new awareness of the potentialities of the French language as a language to think and write in was provided by poetry, especially the poets Beckett translated into English: Eluard, Rimbaud, and Apollinaire. Beckett remained a poet even when writing prose or theatrical plays, and it was poetry that he first began writing directly in French when he settled for good in Paris after 1938. One observes a new spontaneity and fluency. Feeling finally at home in Paris, Beckett wrote several poems in French. If the themes are not new (Beckett is obsessed with a dead fiancée, the sadness of physical love, and a gnawing awareness of mortality), the style is less allusive, the language less "Joycean" than the earlier poems in English. Puns are rare, litanies more insistent.

Beckett discovers a French lyrical voice that sings of loss, absence, and mourning. In "Ascension," he hears the loud radio of neighbors commenting on a football match before remembering the blood gushing from the mouth of the loved one. "The Fly" meditates on windowpanes separating the poet from the outside world, generating a vertiginous Rimbaldian invocation of the sky and the sea tumbling together. In "Prayer," silence provides a welcome shelter against fits of anxiety. Anxiety is never far off—it accompanies sexuality—but philosophy still offers some consolations. An untitled poem evokes the nominalist Roscelin, the master of Abélard, in the context of prostitution:

> être là sans mâchoires sans dents
> où s'en va le plaisir de perdre
> avec celui à peine inférieur
> de gagner
> et Roscelin et on attend
> adverbe oh petit cadeau

> (To be there without jaws without teeth / there goes the
> pleasure of losing / with the pleasure barely less / of winning /
> and Roscelin and we are waiting / adverb oh little gift)

"Waiting," is *attendant*, a participle or a gerund. With "on attend" echoing "en attendant," the verb takes on an adverbial function; such an "adverb" will be used to modify all verbs, according to an ontology of time as perpetual deferral later elaborated in *En attendant Godot*. Here, we already guess that the subject's condition is to wait, quite simply.

This new idiom, colloquial French heard with a bilingual ear, will be the stuff of the postwar plays and fiction. When Beckett wrote *Waiting for Godot* as a diversion from the relentless probing of meta-textual paradoxes in *Molloy* and *Malone Dies*, he created an instant French classic. This play is still today one of the most popular items of the French repertoire. Many details are recognizably local, in spite of the allegorical landscape. The very name "Godot," that sounds so French and so funny, and that may or may not refer to God, can be spelled "Godo" (almost "Gogo"), which evokes the simple enjoyment of the *commedia dell' arte*, praised by Beckett in his 1929 essay on Joyce, in which he mentions the Teatro dei Piccoli that brought to London and New York the traditions of that genre.

To make sense of "Godot" as a French name, we must see the layers of allusions it conceals. A notebook containing the first draft of *En attendant Godot*, kept since 2006 at the Bibliothèque Nationale de France, presents in the first draft from October 9, 1948, two old men, Lévy and Vladimir. When drafting the second act, Beckett changed Lévy to "Estragon," or "Gogo." "Didi" comes from Vladimir, a Russian name that evokes Lenin. We are told early that without Vladimir, Gogo-Lévy would be only a "little heap of bones." Beckett evokes the death camps and their freeing by Russian troops, and pays homage to his friend Alfred Péron, a Jew in the Resistance. It was Péron who brought Beckett to the partisans' Gloria network. Péron died in Mauthausen in 1945; he had survived longer than most because he had been protected by a pimp named Polo, and Polo considered Péron a poet. Estragon presents himself as a "poet" first:

> VLADIMIR. You should have been a poet.
> ESTRAGON. I was. (*Gesture towards his rags.*) Isn't that obvious?

Angela Moorjani has argued that the yellow color of tarragon is an allusion to the yellow stars worn by Jews in Nazi-occupied countries. Through these two emblematic characters, Beckett presents a recent history marked by the Shoah and the emergence of Soviet communism. In such a context, waiting, this adverb accompanying all actions, may be tedious but not unbearable. It is the simple fact of survival in a context dominated by sporadic outbursts of blind and absurd violence:

> VLADIMIR. And they didn't beat you?
> ESTRAGON. Beat me? Certainly they beat me.
> VLADIMIR. The same lot as usual?
> ESTRAGON. The same? I don't know.

Felicia McCarren has shown that one of the sources of the dialogues between Didi and Gogo, combining brotherly solicitude and bitter antagonism is the last sequence of Jean Renoir's *La grande illusion*. In the 1937 film, two French prisoners manage to escape from a German jail during World War I, Maréchal (Jean Gabin) and Rosenthal (Marcel Dallo). One is tough guy from the suburbs while the second, from a rich Jewish family, cannot stand the strain of walking day and night. Maréchal and Rosenthal bicker, try to part ways, and then are reconciled; their solidarity allows them to survive in the end. Beckett could not have missed the resemblance between Rosenthal's name and the name of an old friend from Dublin, Con Leventhal.

Waiting for Godot breaks the tedium created by repetitive exchanges between Didi and Gogo when it introduces the second couple, Pozzo and Lucky. Pozzo orders Lucky to perform "thinking" for Vladimir and Estragon. Lucky's speech is a hilarious rant that describes concentric circles, moving from considerations of God's creation to an epileptic stutter verging on aphasia ("the skull alas the stones Cunard tennis . . . the stones . . . so calm . . . Cunard . . . unfinished . . .") Thus *Godot* remains primarily a French text; the difference between "Cunard" in the English and *Conard* (*connard*) in the French is revealing: one can understand "Cunard" biographically (Nancy Cunard was a personal friend) whereas *Conard* is clearly an insult. The French text is more direct, bawdy, colloquial than its English equivalent. This divergence would tend to mark all the other texts subsequently written in the two languages.

Curiously, it is in poetry that the balance of tones and voices works perfectly in both languages, even when the lyricism of the voice branches off in different directions. In an untitled French poem from the 1940s, the musical mode of expression recalls Verlaine or Eluard:

> je suis ce cours de sable qui glisse
> entre le galet et la dune
> la pluie d'été pleut sur ma vie
> sur moi ma vie qui me fuit me poursuit
> et finira le jour de son commencement

The evocation of Ireland's rainy summers shows the speaker doggedly walking along the beach in a soft fog. Beckett translates himself without any loss, even if it seemed impossible to keep the double meaning of *je suis* ("I am" and "I am following") in English. His solution is elegant, testifying to an equal command of poetry in both languages:

> my way is in the sand flowing
> between the shingle and the dune
> the summer rain rains on my life
> on me my life harrying fleeting
> to its beginning to its end

The poet leaves behind the divided subject of the first poems to turn into a Rilkean trace, a path one follows as the flow of time is sand dripping from the hourglass. Soon, however, the two versions diverge; here is the second stanza in French:

> cher instant je te vois
> dans ce rideau de brume qui recule
> où je n'aurai plus à fouler ces longs seuils mouvants
> et vivrai le temps d'une porte
> qui s'ouvre et se referme

A literal translation would be: "dear instant I see you / through a curtain of receding mist / where I won't have to tread those long quicksand thresholds . . ." Beckett's version is different—and much better:

my peace is there in the receding mist
when I may cease from treading these long shifting thresholds
and live the space of a door
that opens and shuts.

We are now treading the treacherous quicksand of comparative translation studies. The file is immense, and most bafflingly, yields no consistent rule. At times Beckett translates himself faithfully; at times he takes huge liberties—the most obvious case being *Mercier and Camier* from 1974, not at all identical with the French *Mercier et Camier* novel from 1946. In 1974, producing more a reduction than a translation, Beckett skips entire pages, condenses dialogue, renders the quest of the two old men less delirious, more subdued, more metaphysical. The first version abounded in grotesque details that have been erased. The scenes of love-making have been expunged; tantalizing hints about a homosexual relationship between the two old men have vanished. In many instances, Beckett does not bother to translate the profanities regularly uttered by Mercier; for instance we see: "Mercier used a nasty expression," then: "He used another nasty expression."

Paradoxically, it is the English version that achieves what Beckett claims the French language can do: writing without style, erasing stylistic markers of physicality, incongruity, and intertextuality. We still have funny and bawdy exchanges between the characters, but the verbal glitter has come off. Steven Connor has analyzed the differences in great detail—what stands out is the enormity of the loss in the English version, which as a result appears weaker and more banal. The same is true of many titles: *How It Is* does not even attempt to render the obvious pun on *commencer/comment c'est* of *Comment c'est*, while *The Lost Ones* renounces the poetic echoes of Lamartine's famous line condensed by *Le dépeupleur*.

Often, it is a blank that marks a difficult spot, as we see in "Le calmant," an early short story written directly in French, containing this startling sentence: "A moi maintenant le départ, la lutte et le retour peut-être, à ce viellard qui est moi ce soir, plus vieux que je ne le serai jamais. Me voici acculé à des futurs." The English version skips the last sentence and has only: "For me now the setting forth, the struggle and perhaps the return, for the old man I am this evening, older than my father was, older than I shall ever be." Could Beckett find no equivalent for what may be glossed as "I am forced to face futures" or "I have my back against my futures"? The density of the French, with the poetic echolalia of the three /u/ sounds, was deemed impossible to render—and thus skipped.

One could multiply examples. Countless scholars of the growing field of translation studies have taken Beckett as a rare example of a bilingual author whose practice as a self-translator varies enormously from text to text, period to period, language to language. Indeed, Beckett came into his own as a French writer, and deployed all his talent there until he met a limit with "Worstward Ho." If we take the masterpiece of the first French period, *L'innommable* (*The Unnamable*), it is easy to decide that the novel is stronger and more subtle in the French original. Here is a passage from the famous lyrical ending, culminating with the famous "I can't go on, I'll go on." It comes in a long sentence of about three pages beginning with the image of a huge prison, ending with the theme of an endless flow of words that belong to no one in particular. Close to the beginning we find this:

> . . . quel halètement, c'est ça, des exclamations, ça fait continuer, ça retarde l'échéance, non, c'est le contraire, je ne sais pas, repartir, dans cette immensité, dans cette obscurité, faire les movements de repartir, alors qu'on ne peut pas bouger, alors qu'on n'est jamais parti, on le con, faire les mouvements, quels mouvements, on ne peut pas bouger, on lance la voix, elle se perd dans les voûtes, elle appelle ça les voûtes, c'est peut-être le firmament, c'est peut-être l'abîme, ce sont des mots, elle parle d'une prison . . .

Here is Beckett's English version:

> . . . what breathlessness, that's right, ejaculations, that helps you on, that puts off the fatal hour, no, the reverse, I don't know, start again, in this immensity, this obscurity, go through the motions of starting again, you who can't stir, you who never started, you the who, go through the motions, what motions, you can't

stir, you launch your voice, it dies away in the vault, perhaps it's the abyss, those are words of a prison . . .

Even if this satisfactory translation manages to add a sly joke on "ejaculations," Beckett has to battle against the drift of French grammar, which makes an explicit feminine of the "voice"; hence the last segment is clearer in French ("elle parle" refers to the voice), whereas the English has to use a deictic ("those are words"). Meanwhile the unusual or punning "on le con" is rendered weakly by "you the who." Beckett puns on "Oh le con!" a usual French insult. The bottomless stupidity ascribed to this neutral and anonymous subject pervades all language. Beckett chose to translate "on" by "you" instead of "one," which creates an interesting inner dialogism, but misses the irony of the poetic echo between "on" and "con" (a more direct translation, and one that would have to wait until *How It Is*, would be "the cunt that one is.") I highlight this tiny segment because it calls up an intractable problem of self-translation brought to Beckett by the later "Worstward Ho," from the second trilogy, a dense text beginning like this: "On. Say on. Be said on. Somehow on. Till nohow on. Said nohow on." Beckett tried hard to translate this text into French but failed, and concluded that the task was impossible: he could not find a French equivalent for the poetic and philosophical reversal of "On" into "No." He had forgotten that his previous "on le con" provided a solution, at least if one modifies "on" into "non," and admits that "cunt" (in a Joycean manner) turns into the semantic equivalent of "yes."

Thus, beyond the struggle with resistant or slippery idioms in French and English, when Beckett tried to push one language as far as he could, his work on the semantic and poetic resources of both languages was mediated by literary models. They were mostly four: Joyce, Proust, Leopardi, and Céline. From Joyce, Beckett learned that the temptation to work with several languages at once had to be resisted—he himself had indulged this game in his early work in English, and was painfully aware that *Dream of Fair to Middling Women* looked like a pastiche of *Finnegans Wake*. From Céline, whose *Journey to the End of the Night* was a major discovery for him, as it was for all the generation of writers and thinkers active in the thirties, including Leon Trotsky, Beckett learned that French could exploit its spoken, idiomatic, and demotic roots. From Proust and Leopardi, he learned that the philosophy of pessimism that he had embraced early on would not survive without adhering to a principle of formal brilliance and strict rhetorical organization. Thus when Beckett became a French writer during World War II, his solution was the paradoxical conflation of Proust and Céline, and from this pure oxymoron—the alliance of the vulgar speech emerging from the depths of the French *Lumpenproletariat* attracted by anti-Semitism and fascist values, and the entangled self-reflexive metaphors deploying social snobbism in its star-struck tropism for the higher classes—resulted a combination of opposites as workable to create a new poetic idiom as the tensions generated from similar ideological and stylistic contrasts by the mature W. B. Yeats.

One has to be cautious when rehearsing the story of Beckett's descent into minimalism thanks to a rigorous slimming cure brought about by the French language. If Beckett's desire to write without style is attested, it has to be inscribed in a broader tradition; this is not so much that of the "theater of the absurd" (a term that characterizes better Ionesco, another bilingual author) but the new modernity ushered in by contemporary writers with whom Beckett is not so often associated, like Jean Genet, Jean Cayrol, Louis-René des Forêts, and Albert Camus. There was one exception, a French author whom Beckett recognized as an equal, an alter-ego, and also a close friend: Robert Pinget.

We still have a lot to learn about the friendship between Beckett and Pinget. If we look at the opening paragraph of *Mahu, or the Material*, written before Pinget had met Beckett, the parallels with the *Trilogy* are striking, especially with its unreliable narrators like Molloy and the Unnamable: "This is the story I can't make head or tail of it, somebody said: 'You ought to write it down,' I can't remember who, perhaps it was me, I get everything mixed up, it's true sometimes when I'm being introduced to someone I concentrate so much that I take on the same face as the person and the friend who is introducing us doesn't know if it's me or the other one, he just leaves me to sort it out for myself." This novel was published in 1952 by Editions de Minuit, indeed one year after *Molloy* and *Malone Dies*, but also one year before *The Unnamable*.

Other important French predecessors were Maurice Blanchot, Louis-René des Forêts, and Albert Camus. In the 1950s, Beckett read Blanchot avidly but considered him more as a gifted literary critic than as a novelist. We do not know much about his reading of des Forêts, whose experimental novel *Le bavard* had been published in 1946 to great acclaim. Like the narrator of *The Unnamable*, in this long novella, a voice is speaking and contradicting itself. It invents stories and denies them while flaunting their lack of style: "One will remember that with an ostentation that might pass for excessive modesty, I did not avoid underlining the deliberate sparseness of my form, and I was the first to present hypocritical regrets that a certain monotony was the inevitable price to pay for its honesty." Bold metatextual games play with a fictional listener and sketch in advance the program of Beckett's trilogy: "Do you imagine me endowed with any other organ than my tongue? Can I be identified with the owner of the right hand that is now writing these letters? How can one know this? Don't wait until he denounces himself. Who wouldn't, being in his place, prefer to remain anonymous?" Here, truly, the author vanishes in a flow of words. He survives thanks to the condition of language, no matter how desperate or absurd its statements may be.

In order to avoid multiplying examples taken from the French writers of the times, I will argue that all these efforts correspond to a shift analyzed by Roland Barthes. Barthes's *Writing Degree Zero* (1953) offers a good gloss on Beckett's attempt to write in French without a style. Barthes's point of departure was a revolution in literary language brought about by the French Revolution. By highlighting the profanities that marked the style of a revolutionary like Hébert, who never began a number of *Le Père Duchêne* without introducing the exclamations "fuck!" and "bugger!," Barthes explains that such profanities do not mean anything in themselves but just signal a revolutionary situation. By dramatizing "beginnings," the stylistic markers of popular anger flaunted by Hébert, and the revolutionary regicides, Barthes splices history and text under the banner of the absence of style. Writing, according to Barthes, cannot be reduced to style, since it allows any writer a freedom of expression even when confronted with dramatic historical situations. He distinguishes Literature, the field of the literary forms; Language, a social medium granted to all speakers; and Style, the writer's singularity, a "fate" handed down by one's body. Writing deploys itself against style and language by gaining freedom from biographical determinations and social negotiations. "Placed at the center of the problematics of literature, which cannot exist prior to it, writing is thus essentially the morality of form, the choice of that social area within which the writer elects to situate the Nature of his language."

Barthes began a critical dialogue with Jean-Paul Sartre's dialectics of "engagement," which echoes with Beckett's personal tussle with Sartre and Beauvoir in *Les temps modernes*. *Writing Degree Zero* was published in 1947, just months after the publication of Sartre's *What Is Literature?*. "What Is Writing?" asks Sartre's first chapter, but it inverts its terms. Sartre defined writing as a collective response to historical situations; Barthes wrenches the term from humanistic existentialism and neo-Marxist dialectics to endow it with a new dynamism. Sartre had only two terms and relayed on the old form and content division: language communicates ideas, style gives ideas a means of expression. With three terms, Barthes escaped from this conceptual deadlock. Writing would be emancipated from a dilemma in which one had to choose between a private discourse and commitment. Defining writing as the "morality of form," Barthes lends a moral and political weight to formal invention by highlighting the work of writers like Camus, Blanchot, Cayrol, or Queneau, all of whom are called "writers without Literature."

Thus Barthes's point of departure was identical with that of Beckett, above all because of the latter's friendship with Georges Duthuit. Duthuit was a close friend of the painter André Masson and of the writer Georges Bataille. Beckett, who became a friend of Bataille after the war, had belonged earlier to the same neo-surrealist avant-garde. The friendship with those artists and intellectuals forced Beckett to reengage with a surrealism that had changed during the war (if Beckett's prewar position can be called "surrealist," as Daniel Albright argues). After 1945, this changed. Beckett then evinced a dislike of André Breton, whose smugness during the war irked him, but he refused to join the ranks of Sartre's friends, then all fellow-travelers in the French Communist Party. Beckett remained in a second avant-garde close to Duthuit, whose new journal, *Transition*, looked back to the previous avant-garde launched by Eugène Jolas after it had folded in 1938.

Beckett reminisced over his avant-gardist past in June 1949: "Here in the loft I find an old copy of *transition* (1938), with a poem of mine, the wild youthful kind, which I had quite forgotten, and an article (also by me) on a young Irish poet (young then) who had just published a volume of poems in the same series as *Echo's Bones*" (the title of his first collection of poems). Beyond nostalgia, there is a fear of repetition: could there be a new Revolution of the Word in the context of a divided Europe marked by the cold war? Duthuit did not believe in the utopia of a universal language modeled on Joyce's and Stein's experiments. The names that appear in the first issues of the new *Transition* are those of Jean-Paul Sartre, Georges Bataille, René Char, Jean Wahl, Antonin Artaud, André Malraux, Maurice Nadeau, and Jean Genet. *Transition* discusses existentialism, Marxism, the return of a left-wing and humanist Catholicism, and the emergence of René Char and André du Bouchet.

The first issue translates a passage from Sartre's 1947 *What Is Literature?*, Sartre's highly critical analysis of surrealism. However, it is introduced by a no less scathing essay by Duthuit, "Sartre's Last Class." Duthuit takes stock of the clash between Sartre and Breton and imagines an exchange of letters between Nietzsche and Louis-Ferdinand Céline; he then praises Jean Genet at the time of the scandal created by *The Maids*. Céline and Genet were read closely by Beckett at the time. Even if Beckett had expressed his admiration of the earlier writings by Sartre, such as *Nausea*, fundamentally, he followed Duthuit in his rejection of the concept of "committed" literature.

In 1953, Barthes's "degree zero of *écriture*" sketched a history of modernity moving from the Revolution to the *nouveau roman* via Flaubert and Mallarmé. Back then, modernity was equated with the *nouveau roman*: the degree zero was exemplified by its catalogs, its descriptive vertigo, its games with pseudo-objectivity that debunked a previous generation's grandiloquence. Writers like Alain Robbe-Grillet, Albert Camus, or Maurice Blanchot embodied in their "neutral" styles a resistance to political rectitude or proletarian heroism. It was crucial to bypass the idea of a plurality of "styles"; what was lost for stylistics was gained at the level of an ethics of writing, which was how Barthes and Beckett fought their way out of Sartre's neo-Hegelian dialectics.

Earlier, Barthes had found in Camus's famous present perfects in *The Stranger* a perfect "style-less style" announcing a new "writing degree zero." With *The Stranger*, according to Barthes, Camus had launched a style of "indifference," and this was to be the style of a new "absurd" because it was "flat and deep like a mirror." Barthes's review of *The Stranger* dates from 1944, and it explains why Beckett's tramps have so much in common with Meursault. With *The Stranger*, Barthes argues, "we see the beginning of a new style, style of silence and silence of style, in which the voice of the artist—equally removed from sighs, blasphemy and gospels—is a white voice, the only voice that can fit our unredeemable distress." Moreover, Barthes praised Camus's ethical stance not because of his alleged moralism or antimoralism, but because this new way of writing alone could rise to the challenge of historical catastrophes. This style-less writing finds its resources in spoken French vernacular, and its predecessor was Céline. We find it in the famous opening of *Voyage au bout de la nuit*: "Ça a débuté comme ça. Moi, j'avais jamais rien dit. Rien." This is not so far different from the first sentence of Camus's *Stranger*: "Aujourd'hui, maman est morte. Ou peut-être hier, je ne sais pas." Writing in this style-less style provided the only ethical position capable of responding to the dramas of World War II, of the Shoah, of serial betrayals among Resistance members, of the spreading use of torture in the Algerian war, of the grim face of Soviet communism, or of the dead-end of French colonialism.

Here was the site that Samuel Beckett chose to inhabit, not as a militant or a war veteran with his medal but as a French writer—a new threshold; it was a door that opened rather than shut, leading to a literary space from which he could go on as an always de-doubled and indefatigable *ego scriptor*: ". . . devant la porte qui s'ouvre sur mon histoire, ça m'étonnerait, ça va être moi, ça va être le silence, là où je suis, je ne sais pas, je ne le saurai jamais, dans le silence on ne sait pas, il faut continuer, je ne peux pas continuer, je vais continuer." Or: ". . . before the door that opens on my story, that would surprise me, it will be I, it will be the silence, where I am, I don't know, I'll never

know, in the silence you don't know, you must go on, I can't go on,
I'll go on."

Works Cited and Recommended Further Reading

Albright, Daniel. *Beckett and Aesthetics*. Cambridge: Cambridge University
Press, 2003.

Barthes, Roland. *Oeuvres complètes*. Vol. 1, *1942–1965*. Edited by Eric Marty.
Paris: Seuil, 1993.

———. *Writing Degree Zero* (1953). Translated Annette Lavers and Colin
Smith. New York: Noonday Press, 1968.

Beckett, Samuel. *Collected Poems*. Edited by Sean Lawlor and John Pilling.
London: Faber, 2012.

———. *Comment c'est*. Paris: Minuit, 1961.

———. *How It Is*. New York: Grove Press, 1964.

———. *The Complete Short Prose, 1929–1989*. Edited by S. E. Gontarski.
New York: Grove Press, 1995.

———. *Disjecta*. London: Calder, 1983.

———. *Dream of Fair to Middling Women*. Dublin: Black Cat Press, 1992.

———. *En attendant Godot / Waiting for Godot*. New York: Grove Press, 1982.

———. *Letters*. Vol. 1, *1929–1940*. Edited by Martha Fehsenfeld, Lois Over-
beck, George Craig, and Daniel Gunn. Cambridge: Cambridge University Press, 2009.

———. *Mercier and Camier*. New York: Grove Press, 1975.

———. *Nohow On: Company, Ill Seen Ill Said, Worstward Ho*. London: Calder,
1989.

———. *Three Novels*. New York: Grove Press, 1991.

Bolin, John. *Beckett and the Modern Novel*. Cambridge: Cambridge University
Press, 2013.

Camus, Albert. *L'étranger*. Paris: Gallimard, Folio, 2012.

Casanova, Pascale. *Samuel Beckett: Anatomy of a Literary Revolution*. London:
Verso, 2007.

Céline, Louis-Ferdinand. *Voyage au bout de la nuit*. Paris: Gallimard, Folio,
1972.

Connor, Steven. "'Traduttore, traditore': Samuel Beckett's Translation of

Mercier et Camier." *Journal of Beckett Studies* 11–12 (December 1989): 27–46.

Cronin, Anthony. *Samuel Beckett: The Last Modernist.* New York: Da Capo Press, 1999.

Des Forêts, Louis-René. *Le bavard.* Paris: Gallimard, 1973.

Duerfahrd, Lance. *The Work of Poverty: Samuel Beckett's Vagabonds and the Theater of Crisis.* Columbus: Ohio State University Press, 2013.

Duthuit, Georges, ed. *Transition: Forty-eight.* (Paris) 1 (January 1948).

Eysteinsson, Astradur, and Vivian Liska, eds. *Modernism,* vol. 2. Amsterdam: John Benjamins, 2007.

Fifield, Peter. *Late Modernist Style in Samuel Beckett and Emmanuel Levinas.* London: Palgrave Macmillan, 2013.

Gessner, Nikolaus. *Die Unzulänglichkeit der Sprache: Eine Untersuchung über Formzerfall und Beziehungslosigkeit bei Samuel Beckett.* Zurich: Juris, 1957.

Gontarski, Stan E., ed. *The Edinburgh Companion to Samuel Beckett and the Arts.* Edinburgh: Edinburgh University Press, 2014.

Knowlson, James. *Damned to Fame: The Life of Samuel Beckett.* New York: Simon and Schuster, 1996.

Mégevand, Martin. "Pinget Seen by Beckett, Beckett according to Pinget: The Unpublishable." *Journal of Beckett Studies* 19, no. 1 (2010): 3–14.

Miller, Tyrus. *Late Modernism.* Berkeley: University of California Press, 1999.

Moore, George. *Hail and Farewell.* Edited by Richard Allen Cave. Gerrards Cross, UK: Colyn Smythe, 2003.

Moorjani, Angela. "Whence Estragon?" *Beckett Circle* 32, no. 2 (Fall 2009): 7–8.

Pilling, John. *A Companion to "Dream of Fair to Middling Women."* Tallahassee, FL: Journal of Beckett Studies Books, 2004.

Pinget, Robert. *Mahu, or the Material.* Translated by Alan Sheridan-Smith. London: Dalkey Archive, 2005.

Djebar and the Birth of "Francophone" Literature

NICHOLAS HARRISON

In 2006, Assia Djebar was made a member of the Académie française, an institution founded in 1635 to promote and protect the French language. Its rules stipulate that there should be no more than forty Académiciens at a time, and it is an honor to join the ranks of "the immortals," as members are known, and to become associated with some great writers, thinkers, and other distinguished figures, living and dead. But by its nature it is a conservative body, and it is not difficult to treat with irony. The list of writers *not* elected is impressive. Descartes, Molière, Diderot, Balzac, Flaubert, Proust, and Sartre all remained on the outside, even though they did not face certain disadvantages of birth that Djebar overcame in being chosen: since 1635 there have been more than seven hundred Académiciens, but she was only the fifth woman to gain entry, and she was the first member from France's former North African colonies.

In the Académie's inauguration ceremony it is customary for the new member to make a speech, which is followed by a speech of welcome from another Académicien. In this instance, Pierre-Jean Rémy began by referring back to the inauguration of François Cheng, an essayist, poet, and novelist born in China in 1929, who moved to France as a young man and who, after writing initially in Chinese, began publishing in French in the late 1970s. Rémy said:

> When I pronounced my speech three years ago welcoming our fellow-member François Cheng, I remarked—and it was a euphemism—that he had arrived here from far away. You arrive here from at least as far, and perhaps further, although you have only crossed the Mediterranean. As an Algerian and a Muslim,

and what is more a Muslim woman who was born at a time when women's voices were usually silenced in your country, you started life—as a little girl born in Cherchell, about 100 miles from Algiers, between hills covered in vines and the sea—light-years away from the Académie, or so it may have seemed.

Rémy went on to say that when Djebar was elected, it was "a triumph for you and for the francophone world; and also a great moment in the life of the Académie, even if it raised a few eyebrows."

This chapter will explore how Djebar reached this point of ambiguous triumph and how her story, and her writing, may cast light on the wider story of "francophone literature." In her inaugural address, Djebar too invoked the idea of *francophonie*, recalling that when she first heard she had been elected, she was "contente pour la francophonie du Maghreb"—happy, that is to say, for French speakers in the Maghreb and for a wider culture in and around the French language in the Maghreb. The term "francophone" sometimes means simply what it appears to mean, "French-speaking": and if Djebar's election was a triumph for the francophone world, perhaps it was a triumph for all French speakers—including the French, and including members of the Parisian literary scene, which Rémy mocked for its tendency to be inward-looking and self-regarding. But the word frequently has a more coded meaning, also present in Rémy's speech, and signaled throughout this chapter by quotation marks: "francophone literature" most often designates—albeit tendentiously, as this chapter will suggest—literature in French that is not French, or not "fully" French, by an author understood to have arrived on the literary scene from a cultural distance. Such writers seem to be given a special responsibility to speak for others: for Algerian women, say, or for non-French francophones everywhere.

Djebar, who was born in 1936 and died in 2015, began writing very young, and she had published three novels before the end of the Algerian war of independence in 1962. It was beginning in 1980, with the publication of the prose collection *Femmes d'Alger dans leur appartement* (*Women of Algiers in Their Apartment*), that she really started to establish her high reputation. Her best-known work is probably *L'amour, la fantasia*, first published in 1985 and translated into English by Dorothy Blair as *Fantasia, an Algerian Cavalcade* in 1993. That book, which is central to this chapter, opens with a striking image: "A little Arab girl going to school for the first time, one autumn morning, walking hand in hand with her father. A tall erect figure in a fez and a European suit, carrying a bag of school books. He is a teacher at the French primary school. A little Arab girl in a village in the Algerian Sahel." From there it develops across a complicated structure of movements, chapters, interludes, and other subdivisions, through which different characters and different historical moments are juxtaposed, and sometimes blended together. One of its principal strands revisits episodes from the early decades of the French conquest of Algeria; another strand involves women's experiences of the Algerian war of independence; another again concerns Djebar's own life. It can be hard to tell whether the author is speaking about herself or someone else. Although there are apparently good reasons to treat some episodes as autobiographical and others as carefully historiographical, the book is positioned explicitly and implicitly as a novel, through the label on its cover and through its uses of language. All in all, the looping movement between Djebar's own story and wider histories is something that the writing itself repeatedly invites then deflects. And in doing so, as we shall see, it raises questions about the very category of "francophone literature" and its role in a "history of modern French literature."

Initially, then, there seem to be three ways in which Djebar's work, and "francophone literature" more generally, may be situated historically, and this chapter proceeds along these lines. The first approach concerns French colonial history, the second the biography of the individual writer, and the third, literary history.

This is not the place to offer an account of the French colonization of Algeria, let alone the general history of French colonialism over a long period and across the globe. All the same, it must be said that French colonialism is the unavoidable foundation of any history of "francophone literature," or at least the unavoidable foundation of any historical grasp of how "francophone literature" works as a category. As already noted, "francophone" often appears to mean "not fully French." But there is more to it than that. Plenty of eminent "French" writers were not born in France; and while some were born in French colonies—for example, Camus in Algeria or Duras in French Indochina—others were born elsewhere: the playwright and Académicien Eugène Ionesco in Romania, for example, or the non-Académicien Rousseau in Geneva. Some, including Rousseau, never had French nationality. These figures are usually treated as French authors in the sense that they form part of French literature courses, are incorporated into histories of French literature, and are shelved alongside Diderot, Sartre, and so on even in bookshops that separate "French" from "francophone" literature. (No bookshop, incidentally, separates French from "francophone" philosophy, or historiography, as far as I know—which suggests something about the peculiar burden of identity, or of cultural "representativeness," placed on literature.) None of the non-French writers just listed, nor even a figure such as Samuel Beckett, is usually referred to as a "francophone" writer.

By contrast, the "francophone" label tends to get attached, despite her objections, to a French writer such as Marie NDiaye, who was raised by her mother in France and has a surname that points to her father's Senegalese background. It is also used for writers from the French "overseas departments" such as Martinique and Guadeloupe. A Québécois author of any skin color gets to be "francophone" (if writing in French). Clearly, some sort of ethnic or pseudoethnic dimension is in play here, but that is not the whole story either. When Rémy gave his Académie française speech about François Cheng—who, as noted earlier, was born and grew up in China—the word "francophone" was never used; and there was no question of his election being a proud moment for the francophone world or, for that matter, for China. At least as strong as any tacit racial factor, then, is a tacit linking of the author figure to the French empire.

In the case of *L'amour, la fantasia*, the connection of "francophone" writing with empire is confronted head-on. The conquest of Algeria by France, which began in 1830 with battles described vividly by Djebar, is usually considered to mark the start of the second major wave of French colonialism. An earlier wave had retreated, and had left France with territories and spheres of influence that remain an important part of today's francophone world, notably Quebec, several islands in the Caribbean (among them Haiti as well as the "overseas departments"), and a scattering of other colonies, including Mauritius. In the second wave, France established and extended colonial relationships with other parts of the world, including sub-Saharan Africa, Indochina, and Madagascar, as well as Tunisia and Morocco, Algeria's neighbors in the Maghreb.

Francophone literature has emerged from all these places, and each has its own history in terms of the legacy or afterlife of French colonialism, as well as in many other ways. In the case of Algeria, the bloody war of independence that lasted from 1954 to 1962 left particularly deep scars, in both French and Algerian culture. A sense of lingering disquiet or even trauma in the relationship between the two countries is an unavoidable backdrop to Djebar's *L'amour, la fantasia* and to much Algerian francophone literature, and this helps to explain why Rémy emphasized the distance Djebar had needed to travel to the Académie, and why he saw particular significance in her election. Debates over the impact of colonialism, especially on Algeria, remain vehement in France, and a matter for formal political debate. Only in 1999 was the war of Algerian independence recognized officially in France as a war (euphemisms had always been used formerly in official documents and speeches); and a law passed by the conservative UMP (Union for a Popular Movement) government in February 2005—that is, just a few months before Djebar was elected to the Académie—stipulated that the history syllabus in schools had to "recognize the positive role of the French presence overseas, especially in North Africa." (The law was repealed, in the face of fierce opposition in France and around the francophone world, early in 2006, the year of Djebar's inauguration into the Académie.)

L'amour, la fantasia, published twenty years earlier, emphasized the appalling violence of the whole colonial period in Algeria and showed that all phases of the conquest and its aftermath, right up to the present, involved wars of opinion. The importance of the battle over representations is well known in the case of the Algerian war of independence: the French military's use of torture became a focus of international opposition to French Algeria, and a sticking point for French people troubled ethically, or in their self-perception, when they heard about the brutal work done in their name. Several chapters of Djebar's book, titled simply "Voice" or "Voices," which relate women's memories of the war, include experiences of torture; and when Djebar tells the story of two Algerian combatants who were tortured until they revealed a weapons cache, then shot, she mentions that a French soldier was "keen to show that he knew his job as a torturer"—a reminder that the use of torture was systematic and perhaps even a source of pride, rather than an aberration attributable to what today might be known as "rogue elements."

Djebar reminds us too that at the very start of the conquest, the French were already concerned with how their military actions would be depicted and remembered. She describes how the French fleet brought with it a contingent of painters, draftsmen, and engravers, and notes that numerous eyewitnesses published accounts of the first battles. Among the accounts available to Djebar, only three out of thirty-seven looked at events from the perspective of the besieged. In numerous other cases, the archives hold no written record at all from the perspective of the colonized. One moving chapter describes how 1,500 members of the Ouled Riah tribe were slaughtered in 1845: the French army lit fires in the mouth of the caves where the families had taken refuge, and they died there, crushed by their panicking animals, or burned and asphyxiated as heat and smoke billowed in on them. One of Djebar's sources, the report by the commanding officer, Lieutenant-Colonel Aimable Pélissier, sparked controversy in Paris, but his actions earned him a promotion. As Djebar notes, other officers learned from his example: thereafter, the reporting of any similar slaughters was much more discreet.

In dwelling on such episodes *L'amour, la fantasia* resembles other "francophone" novels dealing with the French empire and its legacy. It challenges Eurocentric understandings of European colonialism that were once greatly predominant and in some quarters still hold sway. (The short-lived law of 2005 reflects this.) It also enters into details and textures of the experience of conquest and colonization that may escape conventional works of history. At such moments any work of literature involves imagination, and some invention; and Djebar, while drawing on interviews and archival research, melds fiction with fact. This approach colors the stories she tells about the colonizer as well as the colonized, and complicates that opposition when, for example, she evokes currents of attraction across the two poles. But she pays particular attention to stories from the side of the colonized that might otherwise never have been heard, or captured, or imagined, especially those of illiterate women who contributed to anticolonial resistance.

Something else that *L'amour, la fantasia* shares with other "francophone" literature is the basic fact that the language in which it is written came to the author as a bequest, or imposition, of French colonialism. Indeed, as was suggested earlier in this chapter, this is fundamental to the very notion of "francophone literature." Typically, then, the so-called francophone author will have a self-conscious, perhaps uneasy relationship to French, which will remain "foreign" in some important sense, even when it is the language the author knows best, or is the author's only language.

Behind this generalization, one can glimpse further problems with the notional boundaries of "francophone literature." Literary authors who were born in France may also have a "self-conscious" relationship with language, and this may have ideological aspects, not least because the long history of regional and migrant languages unsettles any simple association of France with French. In an evocative essay titled "My Mother Tongue, My Paternal Languages," Michel Serres, another Académicien, claims that at the time of World War II, no more than half of the population of France were native French speakers. He was born in 1930, and for him too, in the mid-twentieth century, French was a "foreign" language; as a native speaker of Gascon, he encountered prejudices—and elementary problems of comprehension—when he traveled elsewhere in France as a young man. The promotion of French over other languages within France was and is a political matter, linked with the history of European nationalism; and French colonialism spread the idea of a "national language" at the same time that it spread French. If people continue to create a distinction between "French" and "francophone" literature, it is partly because of this troubled nationalist inheritance.

In other "francophone countries" too, of course, the francophone cultural and linguistic element is in truth just one among many, and those countries and cultures are diverse in many other ways. Consequently, the French linguistic legacy itself feels very different to different writers. The French speakers of Quebec are in a minority in

Canada and in North America and have reasons to consider themselves threatened by the dominance of English-language culture (which helps explain the appeal there of a linguistically based nationalism), as well as condescended to by the French, who can have trouble understanding Québécois. But within their province, French speakers are in a majority over English speakers, and over speakers of Canada's aboriginal languages, themselves decimated by European colonialism. Another part of the colonial legacy, in Quebec as in many other former French colonies, has left the French language strongly associated with the Catholic Church—which is not the case in France. The same association plays differently in Martinique, which politically remains part of France, and where Creole is the other language commonly spoken, and sometimes written; and it plays another way again in Algeria. There, Arabic, which like French is transnational and arrived in the country as the language of a colonizer, has been given privileged status as the sacred language of Islam, and it has been promoted as the official national language—partly, ironically enough, on the French model.

Not surprisingly, Djebar was not always comfortable with the rivalry between Arabic and French as national languages, or the linguistic purism associated with Arabic's status as a religious language. She was also suspicious of the politicization of religion, and as a part-Berber writer of French, she had personal as well as political reasons to object to any idea that in modern Algeria, Arabic should always trump Algeria's other languages, even if she was always drawn to Arabic literary tradition. She broached these topics in texts including *Le blanc de l'Algérie* (*Algerian White*) and *La disparition de la langue française* (The disappearance of the French language, not yet translated), both of which deal with the conflicts (or "civil war") of the 1990s that ranged Islamists against government forces and left tens of thousands of people dead. Among them were writers who were Djebar's friends, targeted for liberal views and for writing in French.

Djebar's dismay at some of the political investments in Arabic did not mean, however, that she felt wholly at home in French or could ignore the language's historical connection with the violence of colonialism, which preceded the violence of the Islamic Salvation Front. She once described *L'amour, la fantasia* as "a double autobiography where the French language becomes the main character"; the book's examination of Algerian history becomes an explanation of how history brought the French language into her hands, and how it became possible for someone like her to become a French writer, or a writer of French. If, as has already been suggested, all "francophone" literature shares something of this colonial history, *L'amour, la fantasia* could even be read as an autobiography of "francophone" literature. (Again, this is a matter of the category's connotations, rather than anything so coherent as a definition; after all, "French" literature more generally may be marked by this same history; but it is not automatically associated with it.)

In the case of Algeria, as we have already seen, the language's associations are bloody indeed, so the sense of guilt in using French can be acute. Late in the novel, Djebar writes: "I am forced to acknowledge a curious fact: I was born in *eighteen forty-two*, the year when General Saint-Arnaud arrived to burn down the zaouia of the Beni Menacer, the tribe from which I am descended." (The zaouia was a religious building at the center of the community.) The chapter in which this remark appears is named "The Tunic of Nessus," after the mythological robe, blood-stained and poisonous, that was given as a gift and then killed its recipient. The chapter ends: "The language of the Others, in which I was enveloped from childhood, the gift my father lovingly bestowed on me, that language has adhered to me [in French, the verb *coaguler* is used] ever since, like the tunic of Nessus: that gift from my father who, every morning, took me by the hand to accompany me to school. A little Arab girl, in a village of the Algerian Sahel."

Those last words echo the opening sentences of *L'amour, la fantasia*, which were quoted earlier: "A little Arab girl going to school for the first time, one autumn morning, walking hand in hand with her father. A tall erect figure in a fez and a European suit, carrying a bag of school books. He is a teacher at the French primary school. A little Arab girl in a village in the Algerian Sahel." In this "double autobiography where the French language becomes the main character," the first story is Djebar's own. In conventional biographical terms, her life started in 1936, a century after her imagined "birth" in the French conquest of Algeria and more specifically in the attack of 1842. That was why her primary school was French, as were the other schools she attended in Algeria—a middle school, then the Lycée Bugeaud. (The latter was named after the governor-general who ordered Lieutenant-Colonel Pélissier's massacre of the Ouled Riah, who told Pélissier to "smoke them out like foxes," and who later promoted him.)

Djebar shared this sort of educational experience with a high proportion of "francophone" writers, yet these individuals were in a tiny minority among the colonized in the Maghreb or other parts of Africa, where basic levels of literacy remained low right up to the end of the colonial period. Of the few "native" children who went into and beyond secondary education, a small proportion came from poor backgrounds: among eminent "francophone" writers, this was true of Albert Memmi, a Tunisian Jew whose own brilliant fictionalized autobiography, *La statue de sel* (*The Pillar of Salt*), explores how his education alienated him from his parents—a matter of class, and a particular cultural environment, as well as ethnicity—or Ousmane Sembene, who began writing only after working as a laborer in his native Senegal and then in France, where he became an active trade unionist. Djebar's case is more typical, in that her family was relatively privileged. By the same token, the readership for all these works within the authors' "native" cultures has always been limited, and for the most part elite. It was for such reasons that Sembene turned to filmmaking (as did Djebar in the 1970s), which allowed him to work in the Wolof language and to be understood by audiences who could not read French, or could not read at all.

Two different ways of placing "francophone" literature in historical context have been sketched out so far, the historical and the biographical, and, as we have seen, they are closely linked. French colonialism introduced French schooling and the French language into its colonies—albeit to a lesser extent than the rhetoric of the "civilizing mission" might have suggested. Some of the colonized became French speakers, and some became adept at writing French. In certain cases this happened at the expense of other written languages, such as Arabic, in which they might otherwise have expressed themselves. Some people, especially at the height of the anticolonial struggles, found this intolerably compromising. Many "francophone" writers, though not all, became opponents or critics of colonialism, turning their French intellectual and linguistic tools back on their colonial masters, or former masters. Against this historical backdrop, it is easy to see why many of them grew up with a difficult, often uncomfortable relationship to French culture in the broad sense. And the discomfort was not just about the contamination of French with the violent associations of colonialism. Writers who came from the "colonized" population may have identified with it and indeed remained ineluctably associated with it, but they also tended, through their unusually prolonged experiences of French education, to become distanced from their peers and their home cultures.

Consequently, the point at which historical narratives and biographical narratives converge in producing "francophone literature" is also the point at which they start to interfere, and to perturb from within the category of "francophone literature." In biographical terms, most of the writers are or were highly unrepresentative of the cultures or countries they are usually taken to represent (in Djebar's case, in the Académie française, "Algeria," "the Maghreb," and "the francophone world"); and in their works representing a "foreign" culture, they knowingly reveal themselves as products and producers of a mixed, transnational culture, albeit one with a strong French imprint.

This leads toward the third way of situating "francophone" literature historically: literary history. For other "sorts" of literature, that rubric might have provided the obvious place to start, before working out toward History in wider or grander senses. In the case of "francophone" literature, however, as we have seen, the term itself already implies, however hazily, that the literary works carry with them a nonliterary historical context. It implies that the works have something to do with French colonial expansion and discrimination, and that they should be understood in relation to a biographical "author figure" who—at least from certain viewpoints—appears marginal, and tied historically and geographically to a foreign culture. Some of the works themselves, many of which are published in Paris, may invite this approach, accepting or emphasizing the "foreignness" to their primary or imagined readership, of the culture on which they center—for instance, by explaining terms borrowed from Arabic,

Creole, or other languages. Other works, however, thwart such expectations and conventions, or imagine their first readers differently, or more openly, and leave non-French linguistic and cultural material untranslated and unexplained. Either way, the sense of "foreignness" always seems to be there for the reader who has the "francophone" category in mind; and it is hard to dispel, however far an author may have traveled, physically or intellectually, from any foreign origins, and however much a certain "Frenchness" may have become part of his or her identity. In one sense Rémy, when he welcomed Djebar to the Académie française, was correct to say that Djebar had arrived from far away, across the Mediterranean, but this was several decades after she had moved into her first flat in Paris, and a good ten years after she had taken up her first academic post across the Atlantic, in the United States.

There is more to be said about the drawbacks of a conventional literary-historical narrative about the emergence of "francophone literature." Certainly, it is possible to tell a story along those lines, starting with the first "francophone" works. One might recall that the first francophone African literary work is often reckoned to be *Les trois volontés de Malic* (Malic's three wishes), a tale written by a Senegalese schoolteacher named Ahmadou Mapaté Diagne and published in Paris in 1920. Some readers have considered it a rather crude piece of propaganda for France's "civilizing mission," though one of the ways it may qualify as "literary" is in allowing readers to interpret things differently. When the colonizers open a school in Malic's village, and an official tells the villagers they will be able to trust the teacher because he too has black skin, some readers will be less struck by the explicit message of reassurance than by the implicit recognition that the villagers may have reasons not to trust the white-skinned colonizers.

When the story was published, however, not many readers would have thought of it as "literature," and almost none would have thought of it as "francophone literature." This matters, because it seems that a fundamental part of the history of "francophone literature" is a history of reading practices. The term "francophone" was first used in print as early as 1880 by one Onésime Reclus, in a book called *France, Algérie et colonies*, but it became widely used only much later, after the main era of French colonialism was over. Accordingly, the word "francophone" was not in the title of one of the major works that, from today's perspective, would be considered influential in establishing "francophone literature" as a phenomenon, the *Anthologie de la nouvelle poésie nègre et malgache de langue française* (Anthology of new Negro and Malagasy poetry in French, 1948). Nor did it appear in the book's preface, written by Jean-Paul Sartre, "Orphée noir" ("Black Orpheus"), which hailed this poetry as "the only great revolutionary poetry" of the age, and courted controversy through its aggressive address to an imagined white reader. Sartre began: "When you removed the gag that was keeping these black mouths shut, what were you hoping for? That they would sing your praises? Did you think that when they raised themselves up again, you would read adoration in the eyes of these heads that our fathers had forced to bend down to the very ground?" The split enforced here between "us" and "them" was a matter of deliberate provocation and needs to be understood in the historical context of anticolonialism, but it also foreshadowed, in radical form, the "othering" built into "francophone literature" as a category.

The collection's editor, Léopold Sédar Senghor, would become the first president of newly independent Senegal in 1960, and he also became, in 1984, the first African and first "francophone writer" to be elected to the Académie française. There he was welcomed not only as a distinguished poet but also as an international figure who, in the immediate wake of decolonization in the 1960s, was one of the great proponents of "francophone" groupings and institutions. His achievements on all these fronts were considerable; nonetheless, it is understandable that critics of Senghor and of the wider promotion of *francophonie* (that is, the promotion of worldwide use of French, and of links between French-speaking countries) have seen it as neocolonial; and some former colonies, most notably Algeria, have kept their distance from it. Another of the difficulties of telling the story of "francophone literature," then, is that the term's connotations, and the approach to reading it implies, may be tainted by association with neocolonialism.

To express skepticism about the idea of a transhistorical, global francophone community or tradition is not to deny that there have long been fertile contacts and conversations internationally among francophone writers and their books. A salient example is the relationship between Senghor and Aimé Césaire, the Martinican poet whose long poem, *Cahier d'un retour au pays natal* (*Notebook of a Return to My Native Land*, 1939), is usually considered one of the major works of francophone literature. Most often, though, "francophone" authors have, like Djebar, dwelled on the particularities of a specific culture or history outside France—Algerian, in her case—rather than a generalized "francophone world" or a transcultural phenomenon such as *négritude* (an idea and a movement, with Césaire and Senghor as its most eminent spokespeople, that aimed to revalorize African and Caribbean cultures and the whole notion of "blackness"). As has been emphasized already, these non-French francophone cultures are scattered across the globe; involve many other languages and are internally variegated in many other ways besides; and remain disparate not least in their relations to colonialism, to French culture, and to French. For such reasons, then, questions arise not only about the relationship of francophone writers, and works, to the writer's putative "home" or original culture, but also about how much francophone works have in common besides, and by virtue of, being written in French. The skewed generality of "francophone literature"—a category encompassing very diverse literary authors who work in French, but not all literary authors who work in French—glosses over all these complexities.

Djebar is among the "francophone" writers to have recognized that to be categorized in that way is to encounter certain forms of condescension and constraint, linked to the historical domination of the francophone world by France. Some writers have responded not only by calling attention to the ethnic and colonial attitudes that have circulated around the term, but by positioning their literary works in a web of references and imagined interlocutors extending far beyond both their home culture and the "francophone" sphere. Djebar herself certainly drew on and cited other francophone writers from the Maghreb, such as Kateb Yacine, author of the experimental novel *Nedjma* (1956). She also used the term "francophone" occasionally, however alert she may have been to its ethnic and colonial associations; and she embraced Camus as a fellow Algerian and brother in writing, although he is not classified as "francophone" in the ethni-cized sense. She appeared happy to accept, then, as must any history of French literature, that to have French in common is already to have something significant in common; and for anyone who went through French schools, the common ground includes, of course, the experience of a literary education that prioritized books written in French.

Yet, breaking out of this circle, Djebar also looked elsewhere for inspiration and placed herself in other contexts. Her writing invokes Algerian writers who used other languages in the distant past, notably Augustine, who wrote in Latin, and Ibn Khaldun, who wrote in Ara-bic. The fact that these two figures wrote autobiographical works was especially important to her, as it helped her counter the idea that au-tobiography is an alien form in the Maghreb; and this became part of her wider critique of militant monoculturalism or monolingualism. In this spirit she also drew on writers with no particular link to French culture, or to Algeria, or indeed to her. Like everyone else, she also read translations; in *L'amour, la fantasia*, Agatha Christie is mentioned as an early influence. In such respects too, she and all "francophone" writers are like other French writers, who also belong to a mixed, transnational culture. Moreover, Djebar suggested that her writing had been shaped by other art forms, ranging from Algerian women's traditions of oral storytelling; to Beethoven, in whom she found in-spiration for the symphonic structure of movements in the novel; to Delacroix, whose sensual painting of women in a harem, *Femmes d'Alger dans leur appartement* of 1834, had already provided the title and cover image, and some subject matter, for the book that re-launched her writing career in 1980.

Some readers have found it disconcerting and provocative that Djebar's writing draws on such a wide range of material, especially work such as Delacroix's, given that the timing of his visit to Algeria and the nature of his imagery associate it strongly with the French conquest and even with Orientalist stereotype. Among the things she saw in the painting, however, was evidence of a fascination with oth-erness mixed with the urge to tame otherness. This too is part of the history of francophone literature. What is more, she saw the painting as transcending, at least in significant respects, its origins, which is to say the historical circumstances of its production or the intentions of the painter. However reactionary Delacroix's personal opinions on Algerian women and Algerian culture, Djebar could see in the painting, or imagine through it, something of the lost presence and even the subjectivity of the women it depicts; and she could see how it entered a tradition of representations that, rather than fixing identities definitively, always allows reinterpretation. Djebar drew as well on a series of paintings by Picasso that reworked Delacroix's images and themes, and her own literary work extends this tradition—if a singular "tradition" is still what we are talking about.

All of this casts light on the uses made by Djebar of all her sources—literary or nonliterary, from France, Algeria, or anywhere else—and on ways in which we may understand the "literature" part of "francophone" literature, or French literature. When Pélissier wrote his report on the slaughter of the Ouled Riah, he did not intend to create a scandal. According to another officer, as quoted by Djebar, "Pélissier made only one mistake: as he had a talent for writing, and was aware of this, he gave in his report an eloquent and realistic—much too realistic—description of the Arabs' suffering." From Djebar's perspective, however, both the simple fact that he committed the events to writing and his talent as a writer give reason to feel "incongruous gratitude" toward him. Pélissier, in writing well, created "terrible poetry" from his terrible material, and so brought it home and brought it to life for people in Paris who may have felt no prior sympathy for the victims of colonialism. Pélissier's writing can be and has been separated from Pélissier, Djebar is saying, just as Delacroix's paintings can be separated from Delacroix; in its emotiveness and its openness to interpretation, his report turned out to do some of the work of literature, and did so irrespective of his background and intentions.

The final problem with the category of "francophone literature," then, is that it may disguise the fact that for "francophone" writers too, or at least for some "francophone" writers, it may become important at a certain point for writing to shear away from history and biography. We may say that biographically Djebar was born in 1936, and that "historically" she was born in 1842 (this, remember, is what she herself says, late in *L'amour, la fantasia*). But we may also say, with Rémy, that "Assia Djebar was born in January 1957," the year in which she published her first novel and coined her pen name. (Her real name was Fatima Zohra Imalayène.) Djebar spoke in 1999 of the risk that the notion of "women's writing" would enclose women writers in a "pseudo-literary harem" where their work would be read always and only biographically and sociohistorically. For "francophone" women writers, the risk is doubled. Novels get treated as if they were historical documents, or as if they wished to be; fiction is treated as autobiography.

Djebar resisted this, even as she drew deeply on history and on events from her own life. Her francophone literature is a space—an exotic one, for many of her readers—in which she represents the history and culture of Algeria and evokes the perspectives of particular women whose thoughts and memories may otherwise go unrecorded. But it is also a space in which the writer can play imaginatively with any and all traditions of representation that come to hand, and gesture toward that which may not be representable in French, or in any language. It is a space in which Djebar did not have to be herself. At a certain point, for Djebar and other writers, issues of historical and biographical origin may fade into the background and other ways of reading come to the fore, as individual literary works take on an aesthetic life of their own, at a distance from their authors' lives, their "own" traditions, and even, if they are translated, from the language in which they were first written. To a significant extent, literary tradition in French, as in other languages, is defined crucially by works that succeed in such ways; and "French" or francophone literary history, drawing on and merging with other histories, is a history of exceptions.

Works Cited and Recommended Further Reading

Césaire, Aimé. *Notebook of a Return to My Native Land / Cahier d'un retour au pays natal*. Translated by Mireille Rosello and Annie Pritchard. Bilingual ed. Hexham, UK: Bloodaxe, 1995.

Diagne, Ahmadou Mapaté. *Les trois volontés de Malic*. Paris: Larousse, 1920.

Djebar, Assia. *L'amour, la fantasia*. Paris: Lattès, 1985.

———. *Fantasia, an Algerian Cavalcade*. Translated by Dorothy Blair. London: Quartet, 1989.

———. *Le Blanc de l'Algérie*. Paris: Albin Michel, 1995.

———. *Algerian White*. Translated by David Kelley and Marjolijn de Jager. New York: Seven Stories Press, 2003.

———. *Ces voix qui m'assiègent . . . en marge de ma francophonie*. Paris: Albin Michel, 1999.

———. "Discours de réception." Académie française, 2006. http://www .academie-francaise.fr/actualites/reception-de-mme-assia-djebar-f5.

———. *La disparition de la langue française*. Paris: Albin Michel, 2003.

———. *Femmes d'Alger dans leur appartement*. Paris: Editions des femmes, 1980. Expanded ed., Paris: Livre de Poche, 2004.

———. *Women of Algiers in Their Apartment*. Translated by Marjolijn de Jager and Clarisse Zimra. Charlottesville: University of Virginia Press, 1999.

Memmi, Albert. *La statue de sel*. Paris: Corréa, 1953.

———. *The Pillar of Salt*. Translated by Edouard Roditi. London: Elek Books, 1956.

Reclus, Onésime. *France, Algérie et colonies* (1880). 2 vols. with additional illustrations. Paris: Hachette, 1887.

Rémy, Pierre-Jean. "Réponse au discours de Mme Assia Djebar." Académie française, 2006. http://www.academie-francaise.fr/actualites/reception -de-mme-assia-djebar-f5.

Sartre, Jean-Paul. "Orphée noir." Preface to Senghor, *Anthologie de la nouvelle poésie nègre et malgache de langue française*. Paris: Presses Universitaires de France, 1948.

———. "Black Orpheus." Translated by John MacCombie. *Massachusetts Review* 6, no. 1 (Autumn 1964–Winter 1965): 13–52.

Senghor, Léopold Sédar, ed. *Anthologie de la nouvelle poésie nègre et malgache de langue française*. Paris: Presses Universitaires de France, 1948.

Serres, Michel. "My Mother Tongue, My Paternal Languages." Translated by Haun Saussy. In *Empire Lost: France and Its Other Worlds*. Edited by Elisabeth Mudimbe-Boyi. Lanham, MD: Lexington Books, 2009.

Yacine, Kateb. *Nedjma*. Paris: Seuil, 1956.

The texts by Djebar cited above are some of her most compelling works. Among these, *La disparition de la langue française* may be the most accessible stylistically. It is not yet translated; the same goes for her last novel, *Nulle part dans la maison de mon père* [Nowhere in my father's house] (Paris: Fayard, 2007), which is strongly autobiographical.

If drawn toward Algerian history, readers can find out more from John Ruedy, *Modern Algeria: The Origins and Development of a Nation*, 2nd ed. (Bloomington: Indiana University Press, 2005). For those wanting critical commentary on Djebar, a good place to start is Jane Hiddleston, *Assia Djebar: Out of Algeria* (Liverpool: Liverpool University Press, 2006).

The novel by Memmi and the long poem by Césaire are also classic entry points into the world of "francophone literature," and good ones, but that world, as this chapter has tried to suggest, is diverse as well as rich, and there are many other ways in. Readers interested in a particular national culture or geographical area can find pointers, and a wide-ranging overview of francophone literature, in Patrick Corcoran, *The Cambridge Introduction to Francophone Literature* (Cambridge: Cambridge University Press, 2007). Finally, it is worth remembering that the politics of *francophonie* have always been a matter for metropolitan France too; on this issue, Michel Serres's autobiographical essay "My Mother Tongue, My Paternal Languages," listed above, is moving and informative.

ACKNOWLEDGMENTS

There are many people I would like to thank for various forms of assistance in the arduous task of putting this volume together. First, of course, the contributors, without whose cooperative spirit the book would not exist. Second, the team at Princeton University Press for all the support and encouragement given. Special thanks go to Kathleen Cioffi for having steered the unwieldy vessel safely through production, Beth Gianfagna for a class act of a copyediting operation, and Jenny Lillich for her endeavors in compiling the index.

Finally, my very special thanks to Bridget Strevens Marzo, a lover of French literature, for chat, advice, game-changing input to the cover design, and above all for just being there.

INDEX

Abregé de l'art poëtique françois (Breviary of French poetic art) (Ronsard), 116, 127

absolutism: and monarchical order, 419; and opposition to monarchy, 263; and political theory, 36, 43; and rule of Louis XIV, 180, 203, 263; and *La tragédie du roi Christophe* (Césaire), 586; and Western history, 43, 85, 448

Académie française: creation of, 7–8, 536, 634; and Jacques Delille, 503; and Assia Djebar, 14, 634, 635, 638, 644, 645; Fénelon's letter to, 271; and French language, 634; and inauguration of François Cheng, 634, 637; and Eugène Ionesco, 637; La Fontaine's election to, 230–31; and *Lettres provinciales* (Pascal), 242; and poem "Le siècle de Louis Le Grand," 270; and the quarrel of the ancients and the moderns, 8; and Pierre-Jean Rémy, 634–35, 637, 638, 645; and Leopold Senghor, 646; and Michel Serres, 640; and 1782 Prix Montoyon, 337; women members of, 634

actors: and art of acting, 173–74; immorality of, 176; and improvisational style of *commedia dell'arte*, 174; and interpretation of characters, 589; as subject to excommunication, 176. *See also* Molière; theater

Africa: and Algeria, 563, 578, 636, 637, 641, 642, 646–49, 650; and anticolonial movements, 578; in Césaire's writing, 582, 583, 584; and diaspora, 576; and effects of racism and colonialism, 591, 645; and Egypt, 306; and former North African colonies, 634, 638; and literacy levels, 643; and Maghreb region, 643, 647, 648; oppressed people of, 576, 643; and *Ourika* (Duras), 347; and *Présence Africaine*, 577; and *Une saison au Congo* (*A Season in the Congo*) (Césaire), 587; and Senegal, 643, 646; and the Seven Years' War, 299; and sub-Saharan Africa, 638; and *Les trois volontés de Malic* (Malic's three wishes) (Diagne), 645; and *Voyage au bout de la nuit* (Céline), 542; and West Africa, 299, 548. *See also* Algerian war of independence

A la recherche du temps perdu (*In Search of Lost Time*) (Proust): and aesthetics, 527, 530; and artist's homeland, 13; and awareness, 525; and becoming, 530; and character Albertine, 525–27; and character of Charlus, 515, 526–27; and class, 518, 525, 527; difficulties finding publisher for, 514–16; and *Du côté de chez Swann* (*Swann's Way*), 522, 525; and first-person narrative, 595; and focus on interior life, 518–19, 595; and history of the novel, 7, 518, 595; and importance of in 1930, 535; and indecency, 514, 515, 525, 526; length of, 514, 525; and love, 525–28, 530; and madeleine scene, 523; as a multivolume novel, 514, 516, 517, 528, 535; and narrator, 517–18, 526–27, 530; and narrator's name, 528–529; and *A l'ombre des jeunes filles en fleur* (*In the Shadow of Young Girls in*

A la recherche du temps perdu (*In Search of Lost Time*) (Proust) (*cont.*)
Flower), 516, 525; and passage of time, 528; and *La prisonnière* (*The Prisoner*), 528–29; and privileged moments, 598; readership of, 514, 517; and religion, 526, 527; and sexuality, 526–28, 530; and social identities, 526, 527–28, 530; style of, 517; themes of, 527–28, 530; and World War I, 530

Algerian war of independence: as background for *L'amour, la fantasia* (Djebar), 638; end of, 635; and political violence, 596, 638–39; and torture, 631, 638–39; and view of in France, 638; women's experiences of, 636, 638–39

amour, la fantasia, L' (*Fantasia, an Algerian Cavalcade*) (Djebar): and autobiography, 641–42; and birth year of Djebar, 649; and conquest and colonization, 638–39; and French language, 642; as a novel, 636, 648; publishing of, 635–36, 638; style of, 636; themes of, 636, 637, 638; and violence in Algeria, 638–39; and women's stories, 640

amour fou, L' (*Mad Love*) (Breton), 556, 562, 570

Amours (Ronsard), 121, 124, 126, 131

Aneau, Barthelemy: as a critic of the *Deffence* (du Bellay), 140–41, 147; and French poetry, 144; and the *Quintil horatien* (Horatian Quintilius), 140

anthropology, 395–96

antiquitez de Rome, Les (*Antiquities of Rome, The*) (du Bellay): and grand monuments of ancient Rome, 149–50; and sonnets, 151

Apollinaire, Guillaume: and *Alcools* (*Alcohols*), 510; and *Calligrammes*, 510;

and concrete poetry, 510; and poetry, 4, 510; and role of chance, 510; series of conversations in poem of, 548; and surrealism, 510, 554; and translation of by Beckett, 620

Aristotle: and anagnorisis, 224; and catharsis, 207; and *diegesis*, 171; and imitation, 144–45, 443; as an inspiration, 234; and literary criticism, 39, 145, 174, 192; logic of, 47, 49; and love, 132; and a melancholy disposition, 125; and Montaigne, 158; and "pity and fear," 280; and *Poetics*, 442–43; and poetic unity, 282; and recognition plots, 198; and three unities, 171; and tragedy, 195, 198–99, 207. See also *Poetics* (Aristotle)

Arnauld, Antoine, 241, 242, 244, 245

art: and aesthetics, 277, 278, 352; and ancient Greek art, 507; and "art for art's sake," 352; and artistic progress, 287; Baudelaire on, 474; and Breton's collection of objects, 560–61; and classical verse tragedy, 270–71; and corruption of literature, science, and the arts, 395; and Diderot as critic, 383–84; and engravings by Picasso, 585; and figure of the *philosophe*, 375; and French opera, 270, 280; and going beyond logic, 511; and Constantin Guys, 475; and illustrations of Odilon Redon for Mallarmé, 496; and Italian paintings, 423; and literature, 276, 277, 286; and music, 279, 280, 362, 379, 384, 385, 516, 612; as opposed to world of finance and commerce, 441; and painting, 7, 166, 255, 277, 278, 330, 331–32, 341, 439, 441, 445, 466; and painting of Réne Char, 572; and pastel of Elisabeth Ferrand, 345; and Picasso and Braque, 511; and poet's role, 507–8; and posterity, 516; and

Quarrel of the Ancients and the Moderns, 287, 288; and sculptor Giacometti, 557; and *Le surréalisme et la peinture* (Breton), 562, 571; and Verlaine's articles in *L'Art*, 478; and visual arts, 7, 166, 255, 274–275, 277, 278. *See also* cinema; French literature; French poetry

Art poëtique françois (The French Art of Poetry) (Sébillet), 139, 140

Auerbach, Erich, 455, 466

Augustine, Saint, 241, 393

Aulnoy, Marie-Catherine d', 224, 225

autobiography, 31–32, 44, 157, 206; and *L'amour, la fantasia* (Djbar), 641–42; and diaries and journals, 339–41; and fiction, 643, 650; and *Hail and Farewell* (Moore), 617; and reading of *Le neveu de Rameau (Rameau's Nephew)* (Diderot), 384, 389; and "Manon" Roland's *Mémoires particuliers*, 340–41;and Staal-Delaunay's *Mémoires*, 340; and surrealists, 536; and work of Augustine and Ibn Khaldun, 648; and works of Jean-Jacques Rousseau, 339–40, 393–411; and writing in prison, 340

Balzac, Honoré de: and Académie française, 634; and authorial intervention, 452; and the boudoir or bedroom, 326; and *Colonel Chabert*, 441; and *La comédie humaine*, 415, 426, 601; and commodification of all aspects of life, 418; death of, 433; and *La fille aux yeux d'or*, 312; and financial speculation, 418; and French society, 415, 418, 419, 426–30, 432, 433; and *Illusions perdues (Lost Illusions)*, 9, 415, 417, 423, 429, 431, 433; and importance of Paris, 415; and marriage to noble heiresses for characters, 417; other novels of, 417,

418; and *Le père Goriot*, 414–15, 417; and poetry, 125, 477; Proust's admiration for, 518; in Proust's society columns, 516; and realism, 451, 466; and rise of self-made men, 418, 429, 431; and salons, 418, 429, 430; and self-invention, 431–32; and *Splendeurs et misères des courtisanes (A Harlot High and Low)*, 415, 417, 423, 427, 429, 430, 431, 433; and upward social mobility, 427, 431, 432

Barber of Seville, The (Beaumarchais), 361–62

Barthes, Roland: and critique of Racine, 205–6; and dialogue with Sartre's dialectics of engagement, 629, 631; and literature, 45, 567, 607, 628–29; and Literature, Language, and Style, 628–29; and *On Racine*, 195; and review of *The Stranger*, 631; and Voltaire, 302; and *Writing Degree Zero*, 628, 629, 630; and zero degree style, 13, 631

Bastille, 361, 363, 364, 365, 372, 442

Bataille, Georges, 549, 550, 552, 629, 630

Battle of the Books, The (Swift), 271–72

Baudelaire, Charles: and admiration for Marceline Desbordes-Valmore, 504; and apostrophe, 473; and beauty, 507; and the boudoir or bedroom, 326; and capital letters for allegories, 474; and correspondences in language, 471, 508; and the crowd, 472, 475, 477; and dandyism, 470–71, 472, 477, 478; and enumeration, 473, 474–76; and the *flâneur*, 508; and *Les fleurs du mal* trial, 10, 37–38; and Constantin Guys, 475, 477; hair of, 439; and imagination, 475–76; and impressionism, 477; and journal *Mon cœur mis a nu (My Heart Laid Bare)*, 472; and memory,

Baudelaire, Charles (*cont.*)
475–76, 477, 478; as a modernist,
470–71, 478; and modern urban history, 7, 470; poems of, 472–76, 479,
508; and poetry, 4, 10, 441, 470–78,
507–8, 510; and prose poem, 476–
77, 490; and relationship with
reader, 471; and self-consciousness,
471, 486; and spleen, 474, 491n1;
and *Le spleen de Paris*, 476–77, 508;
and *surnaturalisme* (supernaturalism),
471, 474, 491n2; and symbolism,
477; and synesthesia, 471, 477; temperament of, 473–74, 476; and use
of the exclamation mark, 473–74;
and vagabond consciousness, 10,
476, 508; and *vers impair*, 479; and
women, 471, 472
Beaumarchais, Pierre-Augustin Caron
de: and character of Figaro, 10, 361,
362, 368; and dramatic action, 361;
and the eighteenth century, 442; and
invention of mechanism for watches,
361; and *The Marriage of Figaro*,
362–65, 366, 368–69; plots of, 352,
362; and relationship between servants and masters, 352, 353, 368; as
a revolutionary, 361; and success of
The Barber of Seville, 361–62; and
time in Saint-Lazare prison, 365;
and traditions of Molière and the
commedia dell'arte, 352
Beauvoir, Simone de, 31, 518, 519, 596
Beckett, Samuel: as an author in exile,
616, 618; and author Robert Pinget,
627; bilingualism of, 615, 616, 621,
625; and *Dream of Fair to Middling
Women*, 618–19, 626; and *En attendant Godot* (*Waiting for Godot*), 183,
621–22; and *Ends and Odds*, 2; and
English literature, 615; and forms of
drama, 14; and friendship with
Georges Duthuit, 629; and

L'innommable (The Unnamable),
607, 608, 625–26, 627, 628; and Jolas's *Transition* group, 619–20, 630;
and learning French, 619; literary
models of, 626–27; and mentor
James Joyce, 615; and *Mercier and
Camier*, 624; as a modernist, 615–16,
631–32; as a non-French writer, 637;
and novel's form, 14, 519; as part of
avant-garde, 619, 629–30; as a poet,
620–24, 630; and rejection of Sartre's committed literature, 630; and
Sartre's dialectics, 631; and second
avant-garde group, 629–30; and self-
translation, 624–26; and spoken
French, 626–27; and stay in Roussillon, 618, 619; and surrealism, 619;
and translation of poetry, 620; and
writing in French, 615, 616, 618,
620; and writing without style, 615,
618, 619, 624, 627, 628
Béda, Noël: and attacks on Marguerite
de Navarre, 59; and correspondence
with Erasmus, 50–51; as a defender
of religious orthodoxy, 50, 51, 67;
exile of, 51; and human institutions
of the Church, 51; and persecution
of Erasmus's translator and others,
54, 66
Benjamin, Walter: and "On Some Motifs in Baudelaire," 524–25; and social situation of the French writer,
549–50, 552
Bible: and Book of Job, 296; and Book
of Revelations, 151; and flood scene
in *Heptameron* (Navarre), 94; and
garden references in *Candide* (Voltaire), 307; and Geneva Bible, 67;
and the Greek New Testament, 36,
48, 50; interpretations of, 241; and
Latin, 73; and Marie Leprince de
Beaumont as educator, 336–37;
meaning of, 54; and Montaigne,

158; and the New Testament, 73, 307, 423; and the Old Testament, 49, 73, 307; original languages of, 56, 74; and personal Christian devotion, 54; and philology, 63, 65; and *Les Prisons* (Marguerite de Navarre), 64; of Protestants, 127; reading of, 55, 56, 57, 63, 64; and relationship with Christ, 60–61, 63; stories of, 171, 172; and text of the Gospel, 57–58; and translation, 50, 63, 65–66, 67, 73–74, 91; unique authority of, 52; and Vulgate version, 73–74; and wife-husband relationship, 60–61; as work of human authors, 173; and works of Marguerite de Navarre, 65

bildungsroman: and *Candide* (Voltaire), 303; description of, 433n1; European examples of, 433–34n1; and French political and social history, 420; and *Illusions perdues* (*Lost Illusions*) (Balzac), 415, 429; and importance of appearances, 429; and *Le père Goriot* (Balzac), 415; and *Le rouge et le noir* (*The Red and the Black*) (Stendhal), 415; and social change, 432; and *Splendeurs et misères des courtisanes* (*A Harlot High and Low*), 415; and success and social prestige, 418; and youth, 417–18, 432

Blanchot, Maurice, 628, 629, 630

Boccaccio, Giovanni: and *Decameron*, 93, 94, 95; and Marguerite de Navarre, 11; and Tuscan dialect, 148

Boileau, Nicolas: and alexandrine verse form, 126; as an Ancient, 9, 270, 272, 274, 276, 281–85, 287; *Art poétique* of, 274, 282, 284, 285; and classicism, 26, 281–282; and concern for poetic creativity, 276; and Descartes, 276; and *Discours sur l'ode*, 284; and dislike for Augustan culture, 274; and dislike for Ronsard, 122; and

French language, 24, 284; and intuition, 284; and linguistic rules, 23; and literary criticism, 41, 274; and Louis XIV, 276; and Clement Marot, 65; and modernity, 275, 276; and modern philosophy, 276; and moral autonomy for literature, 285; and neoclassicism, 281, 282; and poetry, 125, 274, 276, 282; and Quarrel of the Ancients and the Moderns, 270–71, 274, 283; as a Romantic, 284; and the sublime, 283, 284–85; and support for values of clarity, reason, and moral propriety, 282; and taste for Greek art, 274–75; and tragic pathos, 285; and translation, 284

Bonaparte, Napoleon, 332, 417; and Battle of Eylau, 441; and *Bulletins of the Grande Armée*, 441; Corsican origins of, 420–21, 429; and creation of nobility, 419, 420, 428; death of, 440; education of, 421, 422; exile of, 421, 425, 440; French interest in, 420, 440; and hereditary dynasty, 419; military career of, 422, 423, 424, 425, 427, 441; and Napoleonic pose, 441; nephew of, 433; and painting of Eugène Delacroix, 439; and *Le rouge et le noir* (Stendhal), 421–25, 426, 440; and upsetting established order, 425; and upward social mobility, 422, 427

Brazil: encounters between French settlers and cultures of, 158; and *History of a Voyage to the Land of Brazil* (Léry), 158, 164, 256; and Tupi customs, 164

Breton, André: and *L'amour fou* (*Mad Love*), 556, 562, 570; as based in Paris, 554, 561; and clash with Sartre, 630; and encounters, 554–55,

Breton, André (*cont.*)
556, 560, 561; and found objects,
557, 560–61; and "Free Union"
poem, 569–70; and French poetry, 5,
554, 559, 561, 569–70, 571, 573; and
hero Marcel Duchamp, 561; as
leader of Surrealist movement, 554,
560, 571; and madness, 555, 556; as
mystical, 567; and *Nadja*, 554–56,
569; and objective chance, 561; and
Pas perdus (*Lost Steps*), 556; politics
of, 535; and recognition of Césaire's
work, 591; and relationship with
Nadja, 555–56; and role of chance,
511; and strangeness, 13; and surrealism, 511, 554–62, 565, 571, 629;
and *Le surréalisme et la peinture*, 562,
571; and truth, 511; and voyage to
United States, 560; and writing as
living, 562
Briçonnet, Guillaume, 54, 61, 91
Britannicus (Racine), 201–2
Budé, Guillaume, 49–50, 53
Buffon, Georges Louis Leclerc de,
395, 402, 426

Cahier d'un retour au pays natal (*Notebook of a Return to the Native Land*)
(Césaire), 575; and anticolonialism,
576, 581–82, 584; and Césaire, 575,
581, 590, 591, 592; as epic and political, 584; and perspective of disempowered, 582, 584; in prose and
verse, 581; as work of francophone
literature, 647
Calligrammes (Apollinaire), 510, 511
Calvin, Jean, 59, 67
Campanella, Tommaso, 253, 261
Camus, Albert: and absurdity, 545, 601;
as an Algerian, 637, 647–48; and
L'étranger, 13–14, 545, 596, 597, 605,
631; and foreignness, 13–14; and
"The Future of Tragedy," 597; and

modernity, 627, 628, 630; and neutral style, 630; as opposed to Sartre,
596; and *La Peste* (*The Plague*), 545,
597; and philosophy at the University of Algiers, 536; plays of, 597;
and review of *La nausée*, 611; and the
story of Sisyphus, 601; and writing,
629; and zero degree style, 631
Candide (Voltaire): and Leonard Bernstein's musical *Candide*, 291; and
Candide, 294, 295, 297, 299–300,
303–9; and censorship, 292; characters of, 294–95, 298–308; comic
world of, 302; and cover of book,
309, 310 fig. 2; and Cunégonde,
294, 302, 307, 308; and Eldorado,
301–2, 307; and embrace of the
concrete, 298; and English culture,
291, 300; and evil, 291, 296–98,
299, 305–6; and existence of God,
308; Aldous Huxley's opinion of,
294–95, 302; and intelligent design
of God, 304–5; and irony, 305; and
learning from experience, 295, 296,
303; and Lisbon earthquake, 297;
and Locke's tabula rasa, 303; and
metaphor of the garden, 305, 306–
7; and Muslims, 302, 305; and optimism, 292, 293 fig. 1, 297–98, 301,
304, 305, 309; and order found in
fiction, 309; and Pangloss, 291, 297,
301, 303–5, 306; and philosophy of
Leibniz, 297–98, 304, 305, 308,
309; political context of, 300–301,
306; printings of, 291, 292; and
problem of luxury, 301–2; and
Providence, 298, 306; and Mark
Ravenhill's *Candide*, 291; readership
of, 292, 297, 302, 303, 307, 308; and
references to contemporary novels
and the Bible, 307–8; and search for
truth, 296; and the Seven Years'
War, 299–300; and similarity to

Johnson's *Rasselas*, 298; and slavery, 300–301, 302; translations of, 291, 292; and travel writing, 7, 295; and treatment of Jews, 302, 305; and treatment of women, 302–3; Turkish philosopher in, 305–6; versions of, 291, 292, 309; and Voltaire, 294, 300, 303, 305, 308–9; and war with England in North America, 300; and world's randomness, 308

cannibalism: Bellay's metaphor using, 143–44, 147; and Diderot's *Encyclopédie*, 374; and essay "Of Cannibals" (Montaigne), 158, 164, 257; and giant Loup Garou (Werewolf), 56; and Tupi customs, 164; and work of Cyrano de Bergerac, 263

Caractères (La Bruyere), 230, 248

Caribbean writers: and Suzanne Césaire, 579; and Raphael Confiant, 579; in English, 592; and Frantz Fanon, 577, 581, 591; and Edouard Glissant, 578, 581, 589; and language, 590; and novel as chosen genre, 589; and Saint-John Perse, 582, 587; and Derek Walcott, 586, 592. *See also* Césaire, Aimé

Catholicism: and Antoine de Bourbon, 121; and Catholic Church, 74, 421, 423; and Catholic missionaries, 257; and *La Colombiade ou la foi portée au Nouveau Monde* (Du Bocage), 341; and Counter-Reformation, 230; and dispute between Calvinists and Catholics, 51; and the French psyche, 22; and Jesuits' attacks on Diderot, 374; and Latin, 73; left-wing and humanist type of, 630; and Marie Leprince de Beaumont as educator, 336–37; and monarchical order, 419; and Montaigne, 165; and pious culture, 225; and support of Spain, 157; and tension between

Protestants and Catholics, 160–61; and values, 379; Verlaine's conversion to, 484, 485; and wars between Protestants and Catholics, 156–57, 215. *See also* Church

Céline, Louis-Ferdinand: and absence of photo from Gallimard's *Marianne*, 539, 540 fig.1; anti-Semitism of, 551; and assault on literary writing, 13; and beginnings as an outsider, 537; black humor of, 542; and Duthuit's journal *Transition*, 630; and emotions, 541; and failure of book to win Prix Goncourt, 537; as model for Beckett, 626–27; and the 1930s, 7, 534; pen name of, 537; rejected manuscripts of, 538; and spoken French vernacular, 631; and use of spoken French in novel, 539, 541, 548, 550, 551

censorship: by the Church, 351; and the Comédie Française, 443–44; and the comte d'Argenson, 372–73; and condemnation of comedies, authors, and actors, 372–73; and Denis Diderot, 372–73; and *Index librorum prohibitorum*, 78; and Louis XVI, 363; *The Marriage of Figaro*'s attack on, 363; and Paris Parlement, 372; and problems with Diderot's *Encyclopédie*, 374; by the *Revue de Paris*, 464; and royal permission, 373, 443–44; by the state, 26, 36–38, 351, 363, 372, 374; of theater, 351, 363, 364

century: and the counterfactual, 12, 17, 18, 19; division by, 15, 42, 43

Cervantes, Miguel de: and *Don Quixote*, 86–87, 167; as a transitional figure, 157

Césaire, Aimé: absence of Creole culture in work of, 592; and anticolonialist concept of *négritude*, 575–76, 581, 583, 589; and Caribbean island-

Césaire, Aimé (*cont.*)
ers' choice regarding government, 579; and Caribbean landscape and Antillean history, 583–84; and Suzanne Césaire, 579; and charges of bad faith, 579; and collection *Les armes miraculeuses* (*Miraculous Weapons*), 584, 590; and colonialism and native land, 14, 575–76, 580–81; Confiant's critique of, 579; death of, 575; and decolonization, 576; and different genres, 588–89, 592; and direct speech, 589–90; and "Discours sur la négritude"("Discourse on Negritude"), 575–76, 583; and *Discours sur le colonialisme* (*Discourse on Colonialism*), 580–81, 590; and diversity of language, 590–91; and dramatic prose, 575; education of, 577; and effects of racism and colonialism, 591; and *Et les chiens se taisent* (*And the Dogs Were Silent*), 584, 590; and humanism, 583; and inner life protected by poetry, 580; interpretation of writings of, 588; and journal *Tropiques*, 577, 579, 580, 584; and marine imagery, 584; Martinique as birthplace of, 575; as mayor of Fort-de-France, Martinique, 578; and memory and belonging, 580, 583; parents of, 577; and perspective of disempowered, 582, 583; and pioneering nature of writings, 591–92; plays of, 576, 584, 585, 586–87, 589–90; poetry of, 575, 576, 579–80, 581, 582–84, 585, 589–90; politics of, 578–80, 583, 591; and postcolonial writing, 587–88; and *Présence Africaine*, 577, 584; as a public intellectual, 577, 591; and racism, 575–76, 581–82; and reconstruction of value and voice for community, 580; and return to Martinique, 576–77, 581; and *Une saison au Congo* (*A Season in the Congo*), 587; and seat in French parliament, 578; and situation after decolonization, 580; and *Une tempête*, 587–88; and *Toussaint Louverture: La révolution française et le problème colonial*, 585–86; and writing on Toussaint Louverture, 580, 581, 585–86. See also *Cahier d'un retour au pays natal* (*Notebook of a Return to the Native Land*)

Chansons spirituelles (Marguerite de Navarre), 61, 66

Char, René: and beloved painters, 572; and *Billets à Francis Curel* (*Letters to Francis Curel*), 567–68; and Duthuit's journal *Transition*, 630; family home of, 562; and "Fastes" ("Annals"), 570; and French poetry, 5, 122, 554, 559, 561, 562, 563–73; and French Resistance, 554, 562, 563, 564, 571; and *Fureur et mystère*, 565; and importance of place names, 561, 566; moral stance of, 565, 566, 567, 568; and *Nadja* (Breton), 555; and native Provence, 554, 561, 563, 565, 566, 571, 572; and natural world, 554, 564, 566; and notion of breathing, 569; and other writings, 571–72; and Paris, 563, 566; "Prière rogue" ("Unbending Prayer") of, 568–69; and rebellion in poetry, 569; and style of aphorisms, 563, 567; and surrealism, 571; and Vauclusian region, 563–65, 566; wartime journal of, 563

Charrière, Isabelle de, 327, 331, 338, 342–45, 347

Chateaubriand, Francois René de: and *Atala*, 504; and First Romanticism, 440; and *roman personnel*, 595; and Romantic moment, 446–47 children: and abandonment of by Rousseau, 398, 400–402; and Emma Bovary's child with Charles, 464; and education, 336–38, 399, 400, 401–2, 643; and *Emile*, 399, 400, 401; and foundling hospitals, 398, 402; Genlis as governess to, 338; and infant mortality, 402; and Rousseau's childhood, 399–400; theater for, 337–38

China: and François Cheng, 634, 637; and Chiang Kaishek versus Comintern, 544; and Chinese Communists, 544; and *La condition humaine* (Malraux), 544, 546; and failed Communist Shanghai insurrection, 546, 547, 551; and masses during revolution, 534

Christianity: and abusive priests, 93; and apologies for belief, 183–84, 244; and body of Christ, 166; and the cabal of the devout (Company of the Holy Sacrament), 181, 183; and Charles IX, 132; and Christian humanists, 49, 54, 65, 68; Christocentric vision of, 52; and Christ's new law of love, 57, 62; and Erasmus, 48–49, 67; and existence of God, 296; and faith, 57; foundational texts and principles of, 80; and grace of God, 60, 62, 66; and human institutions of the Church, 51, 80; and humanism, 79–80; and ideal Christian prince, 56; and Judeo-Christian antiquity, 50; and Marie Leprince de Beaumont's "Magasins," 335–37; and liberty, 57; and love, 66–67; and monarchy, 288; and monastic life, 83; and Pascal's defense of Christian faith, 545; and personal Christian devotion, 54, 60–61; and the *philosophia Christi* (philosophy of Christ), 48–49; and philosophy, 168;

and poems of Marguerite de Navarre, 60–61; and problem of evil, 296; and Protestantism, 156–57; and reconciliation of Epicurean naturalism with Christian principles, 230; and savage indignation, 241; and Tertullian, 176; and theater's immorality, 175–76; and translation into vernacular languages, 74; virtues of, 126; and war, 57; and way of life, 100; and writings of Pascal, 243. *See also* Bible; Church; religion

Church, 66, 68, 74, 93, 114, 156, 421, 423, 641; and the "Affair of the Placards" by Swiss radicals, 100; and canon of Le Mans cathedral, 119; and cardinal-bishop Louis de Bourbon, 119; and cardinal Jacques-Davy du Perron, 119; and Catholic missionaries, 257; and censorship, 351; and Church Fathers, 158, 241, 243; and condemnation of comedies, authors, and actors, 355; as a conservative, French power, 21–22; criticism of, 291; and the divine right of kings, 21–22; and *Don Juan* (Molière), 182; in *Don Quixote* (Cervantes), 86; of the first four centuries, 49; foundational texts and principles of, 59; and freedom of speech, 37; human institutions of, 50–51, 57, 80; and *Index librorum prohibitorum* (Index of Prohibited Books), 36, 78, 160; and intolerance of humanism, 156; and introduction of printing, 45; and Latin, 73; and medieval doctrine, 47, 49; Montaigne as faithful to, 165; and paleo-Christian church, 66; and patronage of writers, 25; and Jacques Peletier du Mans, 120; and the *philosophia Christi* (philosophy of Christ), 49; power of, 8, 38, 42, 55, 74; and Protestant Reformation, 21;

Church (*cont.*)
and relationship with state, 91; rituals of, 463; and Ronsard's poetry, 133; and scholastic, medieval fusion of Aristotelian logic and Church doctrine, 49; in the seventeenth century, 36; and social order, 28; and spread of Luther's ideas, 36; and teachings, 109; and theology, 49, 51, 57; of the twelfth through the fifteenth centuries, 49; and writings of Erasmus, 48; and written culture in the Middle Ages, 20, 25

Cid, Le (Corneille), 172, 174–75, 287

cinema: and *L'Atlante* (Vigo), 543; and "Beauty and the Beast" in Beaumont's "Magasins," 336; as a career, 28–29; and Marcel Carne's *Les enfants du paradis* (*The Children of Paradise*), 442; and Chaplin's films, 43, 548; and Cocteau's film, 336; and Assia Djebar, 643; and Sergei Eisenstein, 546, 548, 551; and film *Espoir: Sierra de Teruel*, 548, 551; and French literature, 45, 296, 546–48, 550–51; and hierarchy of genres, 44; and *Hôtel du Nord*, 538; as a male domain, 31; and moving pictures, 46; in the 1930s, 535; and postwar film noirs, 543; and Jean Renoir's *La grande illusion*, 622; and Ousmane Semene, 643; and social change, 551; and use of Céline's Bardamu in *Coup de torchon* (*A Clean Slate*), 548

class: and aristocracy, 156, 157, 191, 203, 214–15, 221, 222, 231, 312, 320, 327, 344, 417, 419, 420, 527; and aristocracy in *Le rouge et le noir* (Stendhal), 417, 421–22; and aristocratic blood, 363; and aristocratic spaces, 312–13, 316, 317, 322, 381, 414, 428; and aristocratic values, 418, 432; and aristocratic writers, 504; and artisanal class, 361; and Bonaparte's creation of nobility, 419, 420, 427–28; and bourgeoisie, 178, 180, 184, 191, 222, 255, 315, 438, 439, 441, 525–26; and bourgeois values, 206; and *Burial at Ornans* (Courbet), 466; and class consciousness, 549, 550; and class identity, 359, 420; and commoners in Switzerland, 246; and Communist Party agenda, 578; and Corsican nobility, 421; and different sectors of society, 180; and early modern caste system, 102, 363; and *L'école des filles*, 222; and European aristocracy, 374; and false noble identity, 424; and family relationships, 367; and feudal system, 121, 420; and Franks, 363; and *The Game of Love and Chance*, 358–59; and Gauls, 363; and high society, 177, 185, 377, 379, 381, 415, 416, 428, 429, 430, 518; and hoods of Limousin women, 255; and Julien in *Le rouge et le noir* (Stendhal), 425; and La Fontaine, 231, 255; and *Lettres trouvés dans les portefeuilles d'émigrés* (Charrière), 344; and lower classes, 353, 358, 359, 366, 367, 368, 442; and *The Marriage of Figaro* (Beaumarchais), 365, 366, 368–69; and middle class, 341, 368, 429, 442, 527; and *Le noble* (Charrière), 344; and noble ancestry required for army career, 364; and nobles, 98, 159, 203, 230, 246, 263, 340, 344, 346, 347, 356, 359, 363, 366, 419, 420; and noble titles, 418, 419, 424, 428, 567, 586; and Parisian upper class, 542, 549; and *Le paysan parvenu* (Marivaux), 314, 315; and

Peers, 441; and poverty, 425; and proletariat, 550, 627; and protection of the court and aristocracy for *philosophes*, 376–79; and the Restoration, 420, 427–28; and royal patent, 418, 428; and Lucien de Rubempré in *Illusions perdues* (*Lost Illusions*), 427; and self-invention, 428, 429; and servants and masters in theater, 352–60; and seventeeth-century theater, 199; and sixteenth-century aristocratic society, 94; and *Slave Island* (Marivaux), 359–60; and social status in *Candide* (Voltaire), 303; and Staal-Delaunay's *Mémoires*, 340; and *La statue de sel* (*The Pillar of Salt*) (Memmi), 643; and theater, 178, 199, 354, 358; in theater presentations, 442; and upper classes, 187, 191, 199, 335, 354, 358; and working class, 34, 539, 543, 549. *See also* monarchy; salons

classicism: Nicolas Boileau as voice of, 26, 281–82; and the century, 42; and Cicero's ideal of *homo humanus*, 78–79; and class, 191; consolidation of, 29; French, 190–99, 209; and Gide's modern classicism, 619; and moralists, 231; and national classics, 9; and neoclassicists, 40, 190, 275, 281, 284, 437, 439, 444, 445; and the Restoration, 40; and return to ancient sources, 79; and Romanticism, 438, 448; and Ronsard's imitation of the Ancients, 116; and standards of appropriateness for genres, 78; and theorists' authority, 40; universal rules of, 22; and values of the seventeenth century, 9, 12, 29, 39; and Vauclusian region, 564. *See also* Greek culture; *Phèdre* (Racine); Roman culture

Clélie (Scudéry), 215–216, 221

Colette, Sidonie-Gabrielle, 7, 30, 521, 522, 529, 535

Collectanea (Erasmus), 47–48

Colloquia (*Conversations*) (Erasmus), 48, 54–55, 67

colonialism: and Algeria, 637–39, 642–43; and anticolonial writers, 643–44; and Britain and France in Quebec and India, 299; and Caribbean injustice, 583–84; and Caribbean islands, 637; and Aimé Césaire, 14, 575–76, 578, 580–81, 583–84, 591; and colonial North Africa in *L'étranger*, 14; and colonial wars, 299–300, 578; and colonies' choice regarding government, 578–79; and conquest of Algeria, 637, 638–39; and dehumanization, 581; effects of, 591; and *Et les chiens se taisent* (*And the Dogs Were Silent*) (Césaire), 584; and European imperialism, 582, 592; and former French colonies, 641; and France's colonies, 302, 575, 578–79, 591, 637–38; and French colonialism, 631, 636–40; and French language, 640–42; and Haiti, 585–86, 587, 637; and illiterate women's stories, 640; and Maghreb region, 643; and master/slave duo in *Une tempête* (Césaire), 588; and "overseas departments," 578, 637–38; and Saint-John Perse, 583; and situation after decolonization, 580, 587; and sub-Saharan Africa, 638; sympathy for victims of, 649; and *Toussaint Louverture: La révolution française et le problème colonial* (Césaire), 585–86; and violence, 641, 644; and *Voyage au bout de la nuit* (Céline), 550. *See also* racism

Comédie de Mont-de-Marsan (Marguerite de Navarre): and evangelism, 61; and humanism, 63; and shepherdess as ravished by God's love, 64, 65

comedy: and Aristophanes's *Clouds*, 81; Athenian comedy, 80; and autonomy, 356, 357; and *The Barber of Seville* (Beaumarchais), 361–62; and class and gender cross-dressing, 365; and *The Colony* (Marivaux), 359; and comedy of character, 184–85, 188–89; and *commedia dell'arte*, 352, 356; and *divisio*, 80, 81; and Erasmianism, 68; and family relationships, 355, 361, 366–67; and farce, 191, 351, 353; and fear of being cuckolded, 76; and *The Game of Love and Chance*, 357–59; and happiness, 361, 362, 365, 366, 367; and heroine's sexual bliss, 175; and identification, 204; and immorality, 352; and *L'impromptu de Versailles* (*The Versailles Impromptu*), 173–74; and improving society, 352; and jokes, 81, 383, 387; and love, 354–61, 362, 365; and Marivaux, 352–61, 365; and marriage, 357–61, 365–68; and *The Marriage of Figaro* (Beaumarchais), 362–69; and modern situation comedy, 188; and Molière's comedies, 8, 76, 173–74, 202, 222, 352–53, 586; and openly comic theater, 44; and physical comedy, 351, 353, 365; and *Poetics* (Aristotle), 442–43; popularity of, 353; and power, 361, 389; as a public mirror, 175, 352; and Rabelais's comic epics, 52, 80; and relationship between servants and masters, 352–61, 368; and relaxation of standards of decorum, 80–81; and Pierre de Ronsard, 123; royal permission for, 362; and Scarron's *Roman comique*, 33; and sentiment,

360–61; seriousness of, 81–82; and the seventeenth century, 8, 174; and Shakespeare, 305; and the sixteenth century, 80; and *Slave Island* (Marivaux), 359–60; themes of, 353; theory of, 174–75; vs. tragedy, 175; and utopian comedies, 359

Condillac, Etienne Bonnot de: and desperate Rousseau, 407; and *Traité des sensations*, 345; and writers' role in society, 505

condition humaine, La (Malraux): and assassination, 544; and character Tch'en Ta Erh, 543–45, 547, 550; and cinematic montage, 546–48, 551; and context's relationship with text, 534; and existential literature, 544–45, 547–48; and failed Communist Shanghai insurrection, 546, 547, 551; and free indirect speech, 544; and isolation, 544–45, 547, 550; and Kyo Gisors, 545, 547, 550; leftist critiques of, 549–50, 552; and mortality, 545, 547; and the Prix Goncourt, 537; and problematic heros, 547; and questions raised in relation to China, 546; and revolutionary action, 544, 545, 547, 550; and revolutionary vision, 546; and suicide, 545; and tragedy, 546, 547; and violence, 544

confession d'un enfant du siècle, La (*Confession of a Child of the Century*) (Musset), 16–17, 441, 448

Confesssions (Rousseau): and attack on in d'Epinay's memoirs, 402–3; and author before God with his book, 403; and autobiography, 398–405; and failed first-person justification, 405; and figure of the outsider, 377; and goodness of author, 403–4; and human nature, 393, 403; and morality, 402, 404–5; posthumous publishing of, 402; public reading motif in,

403–4, 407; and readings of in Paris, 403, 404; and self-knowledge, 408–9, 518

consciousness: different states of, 485, 488; and drugs, 471; and modernism, 491, 517; and poetic language, 472–73, 485; and revolution, 470; and the self, 518; and self-consciousness, 471; and shift from content to perceiving consciousness, 491; and *surnaturalisme* (supernaturalism), 471, 477; and vagabond consciousness, 10; in Verlaine's poetry, 483–84

Contes (*Tales*) (Perrault), 281, 224

Continuation des amours (Ronsard), 126

Corinne, ou l'Italie (Staël), 330–31

Corneille, Pierre: and alexandrine verse form, 126; career of, 25; characters of, 198, 233, 285; and *Le Cid*, 172, 174–75, 287; cultural role of, 505; and emotional speech, 200; heroism in plays of, 203, 204; and "male" passions of ambition and revenge, 204; and Rabouillet salon, 221; and tragedy, 202, 204; tragicomedy of, 443

coup de Dés jamais n'abolira le Hasard, Un (*A Throw of the Dice Never Shall Abolish Chance*) (Mallarmé), 496; and book form, 495; and calligrams, 497; and competition between chaos and order, 499; and cube design, 496, 497–98; and illustrations, 496; and influence on Apollinaire, 510; and music, 503; and poetry, 511; random layout of, 496–97; and shipwreck story, 497, 499; and thought's need for language, 497

Crébillon, Claude-Prosper Joylot de, 314, 315–16

Crise de vers (*Verse Crisis*) (Mallarmé), 13, 127, 128, 499–501

Critique de L'école des femmes (*The Critique of the School for Wives*) (Molière), 175, 177, 178

Cyrano de Bergerac, Savinien de: Tommaso Campanella as guide in novel of, 253; and career as dramatist and novelist, 230, 250, 261; daimon of Socrates in novel of, 252, 253, 260, 261; and Descartes in travel novel, 253, 261; as a detractor of Descartes, 251; and "esprits animaux," 237, 238; and *Les Etats et Empires de la Lune* (*The States and Empires of the Moon*), 252, 256, 259, 260, 261, 262–63, 264; and *Les Etats et Empires du Soleil* (*The States and Empires of the Sun*), 252–53, 256, 258, 259, 260, 264; and explorer narratives, 256, 258, 259; and freethinking, 230, 231; and hero on the moon, 231, 252, 253, 261, 264; and Hobbes's body politic, 238; and imagination, 237, 238, 252, 253, 260, 265; and inversion, 257, 263; as a libertine, 251; literary references of, 261; and love of all creatures, 265; and Lucian's *True Story*, 261; and mythology, 253, 264–65; and narration, 239, 252, 253, 259, 260–61; and narrator as stateless and foreign, 262–63, 265; and philosophy, 253, 260, 263, 264–65; and principle of reversal, 253; questions raised in fiction of, 253, 264–66; and Rostand's play *Cyrano de Bergerac*, 252; and satire and critique, 256, 260, 263; and science fiction, 237; and shifting states of matter, 265; and the Thirty Years War, 230; and travel writing, 254, 259, 260–61, 265–66; and violence, 263; and world on the sun, 253, 261, 263, 264

Decameron (Boccaccio), 93, 94, 95

Deffence et illustration de la langue francoyse, La (*The Defense and Illustration of the French Language*) (du Bellay): and borrowing from other languages and literatures, 152; criticism of, 140–41, 147; and dreams for France, 121, 143; and French language, 137–40; and French language as vehicle for poetry, 23; and French poetry as a hybrid, 144; and French state, 139, 140, 143; and heroic verse, 127; and idea of imitation, 149–50; and imitation of other languages, 140; and imitation of the poets of Greco-Roman antiquity, 138–39, 140; as a manifesto of the Pléiade poets, 147; and the Merchant Taylors' School, 152; and military might and expansion, 138, 140; poetic language of, 147; and revitalization of French poetry, 137; and Pierre de Ronsard, 122; rules of, 139; and second Renaissance, 68; and series of rivalries, 139–41; and translation, 139, 145–47; and use of Roman works, 146

Delille, Jacques, 503–4

Descartes, René: and Académie française, 634; and authority of methods of knowledge, 75; and Cartesian mechanism, 173; and Cartesian method, 155–56, 163, 250–51, 279; as contrary to pantagruelism, 86; and "esprits animaux," 237–38; and love for "jardins de Touraine," 118; and modern philosophy, 155–56, 272, 276, 611; in novel of Cyrano de Bergerac, 253, 261; Pascal's feelings on, 241; and Charles Perrault, 279; and rational thought, 168, 224–25, 269; and relationship with Montaigne, 168; and self-knowledge, 235; and separation of reflection

from bodily experience, 166; and thinking as defining humans, 43, 250–51; travels of, 251

Desnos, Robert, 536, 558

Dialogo delle lengue (Dialogue on languages) (Speroni), 147, 148

Dialogue en forme de vision nocturne (Marguerite de Navarre), 59, 61

Diderot, Denis: and Académie française, 634; and artisanal class, 361; and attack on Rousseau's *Confessions*, 402–3; and *Les bijoux indescrets* (*The Indiscreet Jewels*), 372; death of, 382; and "De la poésie dramatique," 286; as an editor, 371, 372, 373; and the eighteenth century, 442; as a French author, 637; incarceration of, 26, 372, 373; and Malesherbes, 374; and materialist determinism, 410; as a Modern, 286; and *Le neveu de Rameau*, 373; and patronage of Catherine the Great, 382; readership of, 381–82; and *Le rêve de D'Alembert* (*D'Alembert's Dream*), 339, 371, 383; and role in the Enlightenment, 371, 389; and Romanticism, 438; and royal council's problems with *Encyclopédie*, 374; and social codes of men of letters, 384; and the sublime, 286; and *Supplément au voyage de Bougainville*, 3, 295; as target in play *Les philosophes* (Palissot), 380; thought of, 272, 286; unpublished works of, 371, 373, 381, 383; and vagabond-beggar, 10; work of, 294, 337, 371–72, 380, 381–83; and writers' role in society, 505

Discord estant en l'homme par contrarieté de l'espérit et de la chair (*Discord between the Spirit and the Flesh*) (Marguerite de Navarre), 60

Discours de la méthode (*Discourse on Method*) (Descartes), 279

Discours des misères de ce temps (Ronsard): and alexandrine line, 132; and defense of Catholic France, 132, 134; and defense of monarchy, 132, 134; and *Institution* for Charles IX, 133

Discours sur le colonialisme (*Discourse on Colonialism*) (Césaire), 580–81, 590

Discours sur les sciences et les arts (*First Discourse*) (Rousseau), 286–87, 395

Discours sur l'origine et les fondements de l'inégalité parmi les hommes (Rousseau), 393, 395, 397–98

Djebar, Assia: and Algeria, 634–35, 641, 647–48; as an Algerian, 634–35, 647; and Algerian women's stories, 648; birth year of, 635, 642, 649–50; and *Le blanc de l'Algérie* (*Algerian White*), 641; death of, 635; and descriptions of battles, 637; and *La disparition de la langue française* (*The disappearance of the French language*), 641; education of, 642–43; and *Femmes d'Alger dans leur appartement* (*Women of Algiers in Their Apartment*), 635; and French language, 641–42; and life in Paris and the United States, 645; and Maghrebian writers, 647; as member of Académie française, 634, 638, 645; as a Muslim, 634–35; novels of, 635, 639–40, 642; and postcolonial writing, 14; real name of, 650

Don Juan (Molière): and cabal of the devout (Company of the Holy Sacrament), 181, 183; dramatic conflict of, 182, 187; and human nature, 182, 184; and hypocrisy, 180–81; and immorality of Don Juan, 181–82, 184; and link with *Tartuffe*, 181; and Molière's vision, 189; and religious themes, 180–84; and servant characters, 353; and *vraisemblance* (verisimilitude), 183–84; and world of Molière's time, 188

Don Quixote (Cervantes): and *Candide* (Voltaire), 308; and conformity to status quo, 86; and human will, 86–87; and undermining heroic ideals, 157

drama: and absence of narration, 171; and action, 184, 207; and Aristotelian tradition, 207, 442–43; and Beaumarchais's plays, 361, 442; and Samuel Beckett, 14, 183; bourgeois, 205, 206, 442, 443; and catharsis, 207; and Aimé Césaire, 576, 580; and comedy, 8, 20, 44; and dramatic action, 597; and *Et les chiens se taisent* (*And the Dogs Were Silent*) (Césaire), 584; and five-act structure of plays, 36; and French classical drama, 197; and French opera, 280; as a genre, 256; and Hugo's Romantic dramas, 437–38; and melodrama, 442; and national literary culture, 274; and poetic practice, 199–200; Romantic, 443; and *Ruy Blas* (Hugo), 443; theory of, 207; and tragedy, 8, 20, 39, 44, 171, 192, 207; and unities, 39, 171; and *vraisemblance* (verisimilitude), 39, 171. *See also* Beckett, Samuel; theater; tragedy

du Bellay, Joachim: and *Les antiquitez de Rome* (*The Antiquities of Rome*), 149–50, 151; and borrowings from Speroni, 147, 148; and cannibalism metaphor for literature, 143–44, 147; and creation and destruction in Petrarch's work, 151; and criticism, 39, 140–41, 147; and cyclical notion of history, 147, 151; death of, 139; and *La deffence et illustration de la langue francoyse*, 68, 121, 122, 127, 137, 138–48, 149, 152; education

du Bellay, Joachim (*cont.*)
of, 159; and *The Faerie Queene*
(Spenser), 152; and French language, 7, 8, 23, 24, 137–41; and
Greek and Roman antiquity, 137–47,
148, 151; and idea of imitation, 144–
46, 147, 148, 151; and imitation of
the ancients, 138, 139, 143, 144, 148;
and importance of language, 142–43,
145; and international and multilingual literature, 151–52; and literary
nationalism, 11, 137–38; and metaphor for literature, 146–47; and
Olive, 117, 121, 131, 148–49; as a
Pléiade poet, 4, 137–38, 139; poetic
language of, 138, 147, 149–50; poetry of, 113, 158; and polyglotism,
144; and the Quarrel, 8; and *Les regrets*, 130, 149; and rivalry with
Marot, 138, 139; and role of translation, 145–46, 151; and Romans' cultivation of Latin, 141–42; and series
of rivalries, 151–52; and sonnet sequence *Songe* (*Dream*), 149, 150–51;
Edmund Spenser's translation of,
152; and texts in foreign languages
as sources, 146, 148, 150–51; and
translation and poetry in Latin, 139;
and the word "Gaul," 153n2
Duras, Marguerite, 530, 637
Duthuit, Georges, 629–30

école des femmes, L' (*The School for Wives*)
(Molière): action of, 185; and Agnes,
176, 185; and fear of being cuckolded, 176–77; and love's lessons,
177; and morality, 177; public controversy over, 175, 176, 181, 287;
and sex, 177
education: and Aristophanes's *Clouds*,
81; and authors as members of society, 25; and censure of Erasmus by
Faculty of Theology, 50; and
Charles IX's religious education,
133; of children, 336, 337–38, 399,
401–2; and the Collège de France,
50; and *Conversations d'Emilie*
(d'Epinay), 337; and creationism in
American schools, 297; and *L'école
des femmes* (*The School for Wives*)
(Moliere), 176; and Erasmus's works
on pedagogy, 56; and Francois I's
plan for institution of higher learning, 50; and francophone writers,
643; and the French Church, 21;
and French colonialism, 642–44;
and French language, 648; and
French university syllabus, 44; and
Greek ideals, 79, 158; and humanism, 50, 58, 63, 64–65, 158–59; and
Jansenist school at Port-Royal, 203;
and Julien in *Le rouge et le noir* (Stendhal), 424; and liberal studies, 64–65;
under Louis XIV, 273; and Marie
Leprince de Beaumont's "Magasins,"
335–37; and Marie Leprince de
Beaumont's novels, 342; and medieval practices, 83; of Michel de
Montaigne, 158–59, 166; and *Pantagruel* (Rabelais), 71, 159; and Richard Mulcaster of the Merchant Taylors' School, 152; and *La philosophie
dans le boudoir* (*Philosophy in the Bedroom*) (Sade), 325; and *Les Prisons*
(Marguerite de Navarre), 64–65;
Rousseau's programs for, 398; Rousseau's view of, 402; and *La statue de
sel* (*The Pillar of Salt*) (Memmi), 643;
and spread of French, 23, 34; and
universal primary education, 23, 24,
31, 34; and the University of Paris,
36, 49, 50, 51; and upper-middle
class, 341; and women, 327, 335–37,
338, 341; and writings of Erasmus,
48, 50–51, 56. *See also* Rousseau,
Jean-Jacques; Sorbonne

égalité des deux sexes, L' (*The Equality of Both Sexes*) (La Barre), 348

égarements du coeur et de l'esprit, Les (*The Wayward Head and Heart*) (Crébillon): and the boudoir or bedroom, 316–17; and interiorization, 316; and libertine novel, 315; and private spaces, 315–16; and social settings, 315, 316

Eliot, T. S., 2, 451, 470, 586

Eluard, Paul, 559, 562, 620, 623

En attendant Godot (*Waiting for Godot*) (Beckett), 621–22

Encyclopédie, ou Dictionnaire raisonné des arts, des sciences et des métiers (Diderot): and accusations of plagiarism, 374; Jean le Rond d'Alembert as an editor of, 371, 377; and arts, sciences, and technology, 373; and censorship, 374, 375; composition of, 371; contributors to, 371; and definition of the *philosophe*, 376, 378; and Diderot as author, 371, 380, 382; Diderot as editor of, 371, 372, 373; and figure of the *philosophe*, 376, 377; and freethinking, 373; and Malesherbes, 375; and rational thought, 373–74; and Voltaire's entry "Men of Letters," 377

England: and Anne Boleyn, 101, 223; and George Canning, 292; and decision on banning books, 36; and the Declaration of Vienna, 425; as a dominant colonial power, 299, 300, 333; and Anne-Marie Du Bocage, 341; and *L'école des filles*, 222; and the eighteenth century, 22, 299–300; and English philosophy and literature, 300; and French obsession with the English, 12; and Henri II's peace with England, 123; Henry VII of, 97; and influence of Petrarch, 117, 152; and international trade, 299,

301; and *Lettres philosophiques* (Voltaire), 295; and *Lettres sur les Anglais* (Voltaire), 12; and Marie Leprince de Beaumont as educator to upper classes, 335; and Mary Queen of Scots, 119, 121; and Richard Mulcaster of the Merchant Taylors' School, 152; and publishing of *Candide* (Voltaire), 291, 292, 309; and Quarrel of the Ancients and the Moderns, 271–72; and readers of *Candide* (Voltaire), 292; and Marie-Jeanne Riccoboni's novels, 342; Rousseau's time in, 399; and Scotland's James V, 119; and the Seven Years' War, 299–300; and Shakespeare as master of theater, 12; and Edmund Spenser, 152; and support of French Protestant movement, 157; and translation of *Le miroir de l'âme pécheresse* by Princess Elizabeth, 101, 109; Voltaire's travels in, 292, 294. *See also* Shakespeare, William

Enlightenment: and aesthetic experience, 288; and artistic genius, 288; and *Candide* (Voltaire), 292; and censorship, 37; and the century, 42; comedy in, 351–69; and conjectural histories, 394, 397, 411; and consciousness in Europe, 6; and critique by Adorno and Horkheimer, 405; and empiricism, 295, 395; and encyclopedists, 395; and the European Enlightenment, 371; French, 371, 389; and French obsession with the English, 12; and French thought, 22, 241, 333, 389; and happiness, 351; and knowledge, 378, 395; and the "noble savage," 275; and novel writing, 295; and origins, 393; and pedagogy, 335–38; and *philosophes*, 29, 271, 336, 339, 375–89;

Enlightenment (*cont.*)
and primitivism, 288, 397; and problem of evil, 309; and Quarrel of the
Ancients and the Moderns, 286; and
reason, 43, 336, 341, 505; and religion, 337; and the republic of letters, 332, 333, 377; and science of
man, 393, 395; and the social self,
43, 394–96; and state of nature as
goal, 411; and the sublime, 288; and
travel writing, 12; and universalism,
394; women's contributions to, 30;
and writers' roles, 28, 241. *See also*
Candide (Voltaire); Diderot, Denis;
Rousseau, Jean-Jacques; salons;
Voltaire

epic narratives: and the *Aeneid* (Virgil),
73, 204–5; and Aristotle, 443; and
heroic values, 20, 204–5; and heroism's resistance to erotic temptation,
204–5; and hierarchy of genres, 39,
44; and "high" subject matter, 80;
and the *Iliad* (Homer), 271, 308; and
Jerusalem Delivered (Tasso), 204–5;
medieval chivalric epics, 308; and
the *Odyssey* (Homer), 204–5; orality
of, 286; and passions, 204–5; scene
of war in, 162; and storytellers, 21;
and Swift's satire *The Battle of the
Books*, 271–72; and tragedy, 171;
warrior epics, 21. *See also* Rabelais,
François

epic poems: and alexandrine verse
form, 126, 127, 130, 132; and
Agrippa d'Aubigne, 132; and *Cahier
d'un retour au pays natal* (*Notebook of
a Return to the Native Land*), 575,
576, 581–84; and René Char, 570–
71; and Christian verse epic, 280–81;
and *La Colombiade ou la foi portée au
Nouveau Monde* (Du Bocage), 341;
and decasyllabic line, 127; and "De
la poésie dramatique" (Diderot),

286; and Guillaume du Bartas, 132;
and *The Faerie Queene* (Spenser),
152; and 1550 odes of Ronsard,
123–24; and *La Franciade* (Ronsard),
121, 123, 129; and Greco-Latin epic
hexameter, 127; and *Les hauteurs de
Macchu Picchu* (*Heights of Macchu
Picchu*), 564; and Homer, 125, 128;
and Saint-John Perse, 587; and *La
Pucelle* (Chapelain), 280, 281; *Les regrets* as a counter to, 130; and Pierre
de Ronsard, 127–28, 129, 132; and
the sixteenth century, 132; and Virgil, 128; and Voltaire, 294

Erasmus: and *Adagia*, 48, 68; as an Augustinian monk, 47; as an author, 35,
52, 54–55, 68; and brotherly love,
48, 55; and censure of work by Faculty of Theology, 50; and classical
literature, 47–49; and *Colloquia* (*Conversations*), 48, 54–55, 67; correspondence of, 49–51, 53–54, 59, 65, 99,
161; death of, 51, 68; and dialogue
form, 54, 68; enemies of, 59, 67; and
experience in Paris, 47, 49, 50; and
the Faculty of Theology, 47, 50;
faith of, 47; as a famous Christian
humanist, 49, 53; and French translator Louis de Berquin, 53–54; and
fusion of classical learning with
Christian texts, 48, 49, 68; and the
Greek New Testament, 48, 50, 67;
and history of French literature, 11;
and human institutions of the
Church, 50–51, 57; and humanism,
59, 63, 64–65, 68, 78, 156, 166; influence of, 51, 54, 56–57, 58; and
irony, 54, 55; and Latin, 47, 52, 54,
84; literary devices and modes of,
54; and Lucianic style, 54; and *Moriae encomium* (*Praise of Folly*), 48, 55;
and the *philosophia Christi* (philosophy of Christ), 48–49, 55, 63; and

praise of folly, 189; and publishing of *Collectanea*, 47–48; and return to ancient sources, 49; and satire, 48, 54, 66; and shaping of the Renaissance, 49; and study of ancient Greek, 48; and toleration of ambiguity, 85; and use of Latin, Greek, and Hebrew, 52; women and marriage in works of, 67; and works of Marguerite de Navarre, 65; and works on pedagogy, 56; writings of, 47–48, 52, 54–55, 56, 68

Essay Concerning Human Understanding (Locke), 295

Essays (Montaigne): and body linked to text, 163, 166; and customs and cultures, 155, 157–58, 164, 257; different editions of, 160, 162; on education, 166; and Erasmus, 68; and essay "Apology for Raymond Sebond," 165; and essay "Of a Monstrous Child," 164–65; and essay "Of Books," 166; and essay "Of Cannibals," 158, 164, 257; and essay "Of Cripples," 164; and essay "Of Cruelty," 164; and essay "Of Experience," 167; and essay "Of Friendship," 160; and essay "Of Idleness," 162, 163; and essay "Of Moderation," 158; and essay "Of Physiognomy," 166; and essay "Of Practice," 163; and essay "Of Presumption," 165; and essay "Of the Useful and the Honorable," 165; and ethics, 155, 164, 165; and form of the essay, 161; and humanism, 156, 165; and knowledge, 155, 164–65; and moral themes, 158, 164–65; and nature, 164–65; as personal and public, 161; and philosophy, 155, 158, 159, 161–68; and process of self-revision, 165; and Renaissance, 156; and the self, 155, 393

étranger, L' (*The Stranger*) (Camus): and absurdity, 545, 631; and colonial North Africa, 14; and Meursault, 631; and narrative, 596, 597; and outsider figure, 13

Euripides, 193, 197

existentialism: and Duthuit's journal *Transition*, 630; and engagement, 41; and *L'étranger* (Camus), 13; and existential literature, 544–45, 547–48, 600; and French thought, 22, 629; and *La nausée* (Sartre), 13, 600, 610

fables: adaptation of, 229; and authority of scholars, 234; and fable "The Power of Fables" (La Fontaine), 240; and fictional fabliaux, 102; and the *Heptameron* (Marguerite de Navarre), 102, 104; and La Fontaine, 230–32, 236, 238–39, 240, 250, 264; moral lessons from, 20, 236, 239; and origin of politics, 247

fairy tales: adaptation of, 229, 336; and authority of scholars, 234; and "Beauty and the Beast" in Beaumont's "Magasins," 336; and *Contes de ma mere l'oye* (*Mother Goose's Tales*) (Perrault), 336; and Marie-Jeanne L'Heritier de Villandon, 225; and love and happiness, 336; and oral traditions, 224, 336; and Perrault's *contes des fées*, 281; printed editions of, 224; and telling of at court and salons, 224, 225; and women's conversation, 223–24; and women's role as mothers, 225; and women writers, 224, 336. *See also* Aulnoy, Marie-Catherine d'; Perrault, Charles

fausse suivante, La (Marivaux): and absence of family, 357; and gender and cross-dressing, 357, 358; and names of servants, 353–54; and Trivelin's identity, 354

faux-monnayeurs, Les (*The Counterfeiters*) (Gide), 521, 522, 535, 536, 596
feminism, 31, 103, 223, 295, 367, 468.
    See also women's writing
Fénelon, François, 271, 285–86
Flaubert, Gustave: and Académie française, 634; and ancient Carthage in *Salammbo*, 466; and autonomy of literature, 10; and the bildungsroman, 433n1; and *Bouvard and Pecuchet*, 460, 467; and clichés of language, 459–62, 467; and *Un coeur simple* (*A Simple Heart*), 462; devotion to writing of, 460; and free indirect discourse, 452; and history of modernity, 630; and impersonality of narration, 451–52, 466–67; and importance of language, 466–67; and *Madame Bovary* trial, 10, 37–38, 462, 463, 464–66, 468; and Montaigne as a prose writer, 168; and morality, 452, 464–66; and novel's form, 519; philosophy of creation of, 452; and problematic nature of realism, 465–66; and Proust, 518, 519; and religious themes, 466; and *Sentimental Education*, 466, 536; style of, 452, 461, 466–67; and use of pronoun *on* (one), 466–67. See also *Madame Bovary*
fleurs du mal, Les (Baudelaire): architecture of, 472; and dedication to Gautier, 507; and the *flâneur*, 508; and literary debates, 536
Foucault, Michel: and *Le neveu de Rameau* (*Rameau's Nephew*) (Diderot), 389; and sex as part of identity, 201; work of, 156, 168
Fouquet, Nicolas, 254, 262, 263
France: and abstraction and reason, 25, 40; and abuses of Church and Parliament, 66; and the "Affair of the Placards" by Swiss radicals, 100; as

an agrarian society, 353; and authorization of public speaking, 243; and Anne Boleyn, 101, 223; and capitalism, 550; and Caribbean islands Martinique and Guadeloupe, 575, 637; and Catholicism, 22, 66, 67, 132, 223; and the centralizing principle, 22, 23, 25, 36; and Christianity, 132; and civil war, 4, 113, 114, 123, 128, 263, 264; and the Collège de France, 50; and colonialism, 299, 300, 550, 636–44, 647; and colonization, 256–57; and the Comédie Française, 436, 441–42; and conquest of Algeria, 636, 637, 642, 648; and conquest of Occitania, 16; and crises of the 1930s, 534–35; as cultural center of Europe, 11; and cultural identity, 535; and cultures of Brazil, 158; and the Declaration of the Rights of Man and of the Citizen, 419; and the Declaration of Vienna, 425; and dispute between Erasmus and Béda, 51; and divine reason, 126–27; and the Dreyfus affair, 12; and early capitalism, 418; as egalitarian, 419; and the eighteenth century, 234, 257, 286, 295, 299–302, 330, 335, 338–39, 345; and Empire, 143, 299, 419, 433, 438, 444, 466, 637; and expansion of reading public, 33–35; and former North African colonies, 634; and French Indochina, 637, 638; and French literacy, 23–24, 32, 33, 34, 339; and Frenchness, 21, 22; and French Resistance, 554; and Fronde era, 178, 203, 263, 264; and Henri II's peace with England, 123; and Huguenots, 121; and humanism, 49, 50, 143, 156, 157; and imperial expansion, 140, 146, 575; and importance of sentiment, 40; in the "Indies," 124;

and infant mortality, 402; and influence of Petrarch, 117; and international trade, 299, 300, 301; and Italian wars, 118; and Jesuit accounts of Americas and Near East, 257; and John Locke, 295; languages spoken in, 23, 24; and leftist coalition Popular Front, 552; and liberty, 334–35; and literary history, 6–12; and Lyons, 3, 36, 71, 140; and Madagascar, 638; and the Maghreb, 638; and Marie Antoinette, 333–34; and media in the 1930s, 535; and meritocracy, 419; and military might and expansion, 138, 140, 143; and modern language, 24; and monarchies, 419, 436–37; and Montaigne's politics, 165–66; and Napoleon Bonaparte, 332, 417, 420; and national-cultural institutions, 11, 21–22; national identity of, 21, 379; and national literary culture, 7, 20, 536; and native French speakers, 640; and Newtonian ideas, 338; and the nineteenth century, 330, 333, 433; and noble ancestry required for army career, 364; and "overseas *departements*," 578, 637, 638; and poetry in Provençal, 149; and politics of novels in 1930s, 534–36; and post-Napoleonic society, 432; and power of self-interest, 234–35; and prepublication censorship, 36–37; and President Sarkozy, 213; and the public figure of the intellectual, 244, 375–76; and the *querelle des bouffons*, 379; and Racine as foremost tragedian, 191; and the Reign of Terror, 504–5; and religious zealots' cruelty, 164; and Renaissance, 147, 150; and Republics, 419, 433; and respect for literary heritage, 44; and the Restoration, 420, 423, 426, 432–33, 438, 441,

444; and Ronsard's poetry, 132–33; and second wave of colonization, 637–38; and "seigneurial rights," 366; and the seventeenth century, 168, 203, 220, 224, 225, 233, 234, 257, 269; and the Seven Years' War, 299–300, 374; sexual mores of, 295, 327; and shaping of French culture, 21–22, 140, 375; and the sixteenth century, 20, 21, 32, 73, 94, 137, 141, 144, 151, 156–57, 160, 199, 233, 234; and social conduct of politeness, 234; as source for Djebar, 649; and status as a world power, 302; and theater, 199–200, 351–69; and the Thirty Years War, 230; and travel writing, 256; and treaty with Spain, 91; and the twentieth century, 257; and Vichy regime, 552; and *Voyage au bout de la nuit* (Céline), 541, 542; and Wars of Religion, 7, 51, 85, 156–57, 160, 215; and war with England, 299–300, 302; and widows, 356–57; and women's conversation, 220–23; and women's rights, 334–35; and the word "Gaul," 152–53n2. *See also* colonialism; French Revolution; Lyons, France; Paris, France

Franciade, La (Ronsard): and alexandrine line, 128–29, 134; and decasyllabic line, 123, 127, 132; as epic, 121, 129; and poetry, 125, 126; royal orders for composition of, 127

François I: and Cartier's expeditions to North America, 256; and centralized state formation, 8; and Claude de Bretagne, 67; death of, 120; and dispute between Erasmus and Béda, 51; and letter to Erasmus, 50; and Marguerite de Navarre, 25, 51, 91; and Clement Marot, 123; and marriage of Marguerite de Navarre's daughter, 99; and printing, 36 francophone literature: and Algerian francophone literature, 638; and the *Anthologie de la nouvelle poésie nègre et malgache de langue française*, 646; and *Cahier d'un retour au pays natal* (*Notebook of a Return to the Native Land*), 647; and Aimé Césaire, 14, 591, 647; and decolonization, 646; and Assia Djebar, 14, 635–50; and fiction, 44; and foreignness, 644–45; and France's colonies, 591, 638, 639; and francophone culture, 14, 644, 646, 647; and francophone writers' homelands and culture, 647; and French colonialism, 636–44, 646; and French language, 640–44, 646, 647; and Frenchness of authors, 645; and history, 643–44, 648, 649; and history of modern French literature, 636; and Marie NDiaye, 637; readership of, 45, 643, 644; and Leopold Senghor, 646–47; and term "francophone," 645–46; and true lives, 44; and women writers, 650; and writer's biography, 636, 643, 644, 649. *See also* Césaire, Aimé; *amour, la fantasia, L'* (Djebar)

French literature: and aesthetics, 521, 530, 538, 548, 550; and ancient literature as battleground, 447; and antiquity, 151, 330, 447; and authors not born in France, 636–37; and Samuel Beckett, 14, 615–32; Beckett as teacher of, 619; and beginnings of in sixteenth century, 16, 18; and *bienséance*, 39; and bourgeois values, 205, 206; and Emma Bovary's readings, 455; and Caribbean plantation culture, 583; and censorship, 36–38, 288, 291, 443–44; and centralizing tendency, 42; and Césaire's poetry, 575, 580–84; and characters in theater and novels, 202–3; and Cioran,

166; and clarity and reason, 13, 22, 28, 40; and classicism, 22, 26, 29, 40, 42; and colonialism and native land, 14, 575–76, 580–81; and commercialization, 44–45; and *Correspondance littéraire* (Grimm as editor), 374, 382; and *Un coup de Dés jamais n'abolira le Hasard* (Mallarmé), 495–99; and courtly writing, 21, 166; and *créolité* (Creoleness), 575, 589; and criticism, 39–42; and culturalism, 592; and deaths of writers, printers, and translators, 100; and *De la littérature* (*On Literature*) (Staël), 332; and Joachim du Bellay, 68; and eavesdropping, 222–23; and the eighteenth-century novel, 312–28; and Enlightenment, 22, 28, 29, 42, 43, 241, 298, 333; and existentialism, 22, 41, 544–45; and first-person fiction, 595–96; and Flaubert's devotion to writing, 460; and Flaubert's realism, 451–68; and foreignness, 13–14; and francophone culture, 14, 635, 640; and francophone literature, 44, 45, 591, 635–50; and free indirect discourse, 206, 452; and French language, 648; and fusion of classical and biblical antiquity, 48, 49, 68; and André Gide, 155, 521, 522; and "good taste," 39; and Greek and Roman antiquity, 137; and Horace's idea of usefulness, 40; and humanism, 151; identity of, 14, 21; and immigration, 45; and immorality, 352, 464; and importance of moralists, 238; and importance of sentiment, 40; and improving society, 352, 398, 465; and influences of other countries and ideas, 22–23; and internationalism, 11–12; and introduction of printing, 21; and journalism, 27–28, 33, 39; La Fontaine as emblematic figure of, 252; and *Landmarks of French Literature* (Strachey), 2; and La Rochefoucauld, 166; and *Lettres provinciales* (Pascal), 241–42; and literacy, 229; and literary nationalism, 11; and literary trials, 10, 37–38, 452, 462–68; and literature in European languages, 137; and *littérature engagée*, 110; and medieval literary forms, 52, 59, 61, 62, 102; and membership in canon, 5, 9, 332; and metafiction, 521; and metaphor, 17, 393, 508; and modern literature, 157, 451, 470, 510; and modern novel, 595–613; and modern subject, 266; and the modern writer, 615–16; and modes of philosophical narrative, 96; and *mondain* writers, 225; and moral and religious beliefs as relative, 257; and moral indignation, 241, 470; and moralist writers, 248; and morality, 280, 464, 471, 477; and movements after 1820, 41; and music, 537–38, 612; and Napoleon Bonaparte, 419–23; and national classics, 9; and national identity, 11; and national literary culture, 12–13, 14, 270; as a national literature in competition with others, 144; and new careers with the rise of the middle class, 26; and *Le neveu de Rameau* (*Rameau's Nephew*) (Diderot), 384; and New Criticism, 22, 29, 38; and new forms of writing, 45–46; and opposition to power, 28, 33; and oral traditions, 224, 227; and Paris Parlement, 372; and Pascal as an engaged intellectual, 243–44; and philosophy, 286–87; and Pipelet's public reading at the Lycée des Arts, 335; and poem *Chatelaine de Vergy*, 105–6; and poem "Le siècle de Louis Le Grand" (Perrault), 270; and poetry, 3–5, 27, 28, 59–61, 64–65, 91–92, 97, 101, 113–35; and polyphony, 342, 586; and postcolonial writing, 14, 576, 587–88; and postmodernism, 42; and prepublication censorship, 36–37, 38; and principle of immanence, 171; and printing revolution of 1830s, 35; prizes for, 536–37, 539; and progressive ideas, 28, 38–39; and prose, 13, 39, 127, 128, 130, 147, 152, 168, 242; and prosecution for obscenity, 38; and public figure of the intellectual, 332, 376; and Quarrels, 8–9, 39–40, 172, 213, 270–86, 375, 379; and race problems, 45; and Racine, 619; and readership, 1–3, 26–28, 31–35, 38–39, 212–13, 229; and realism, 102, 415, 416–18, 420, 426, 429, 451–68; and relation with nation, 14, 38; and the Renaissance, 42, 43, 68–69, 137–38, 151; and the republic of letters, 332; and the Restoration, 439; and revolutionary change, 551–52; and rise of the Internet, 45; role and power of, 113, 139; and *Roman de la Rose* (*Romance of the Rose*), 138; and Romanticism, 42, 394, 436–48; and Ronsard's prosody, 4; and Jean-Jacques Rousseau, 393–94; and Rousseau's modern, divided self, 394–95, 411; and scholar-printer-publishers, 36; and the seventeenth century, 212–27, 229, 245, 253; and shaping of French culture, 143–44; and shaping of individual and collective life stories, 241; and the sixteenth century, 71, 72, 73, 85, 92, 139; and social lives of authors, 522; and social situation of the French writer, 549–50; and stream-of-consciousness, 206; and structuralism and deconstruction, 42; and

French literature (*cont.*)
theological tradition, 61; and travel
narratives, 250–66; and Troyat's
L'araigne, 551–52; and the true, the
good, and the beautiful, 40, 465; and
use of *je* (I), 529–30; and values of
honnêteté, 33; and vanity of existence,
264; and vernacular literature, 52,
54; and *vraisemblance* (verisimilitude), 39; and vulgar style, 52; and
widows, 356–57; and women, 45,
330–48, 356–57; and women in pedagogy, 335–38; and women's conversation, 220–23; and work of Pierre
Boiastuau, 92; and world literature
in French, 11; and writing without
style, 615. *See also* classicism; drama;
French poetry; genre; New Criticism; printing; theater; women's
writing

Frenchness: and centralizing principle,
22; and clarity and reason of art and
thought, 22; and diversity, 45; of
France, 21; and French formalism,
22; and importance of Catholicism,
22; and Mallarmé, 13; and national
literary culture, 7, 11, 13, 14; and
Occitan troubadour poetry, 16; and
readership, 31

French poetry: and alexandrine verse
form, 4, 116, 119, 122, 123, 126–34,
151, 479, 491n3; and amity/love,
132, 134, 569–70; and *Les antiquitez
de Rome* (*The Antiquities of Rome*) (du
Bellay), 150; and Guillaume Apollinaire, 4, 510; and Apollinaire's
"Lundi rue Christine," 548, 551; and
the apostrophe, 473, 489; and "art
for art's sake," 507; and *Art poétique
françois* (The French Art of Poetry)
(Sébillet), 139; and Charles Baudelaire, 4, 470–78, 507–8; and Samuel
Beckett, 620–21, 623; and André

Breton, 5, 554–62, 569–70; and caesura, 491–92n4, 491n3; and Aimé
Césaire, 575, 576; and civil war polemics, 128; and René Char, 5, 122,
554, 559, 562, 563–73; and classical
poetry, 68, 113–17, 122, 123; and
Vittoria Colonna, 91; and concrete
poetry, 510; and *Un coup de Dés jamais n'abolira le Hasard* (Mallarmé),
503; and courtly poet Théophile de
Viau, 230; and decadence, 491; and
decasyllabic line, 4, 115–16, 118,
126, 127, 128, 129, 132, 134, 151,
479; and decolonization, 576; and *La
deffence et illustration de la langue
francoyse* (du Bellay) as Pléiade manifesto, 137, 147; and Jacques Delille,
503–4; and *Discours sur l'ode* (Boileau), 284; and Joachim du Bellay,
113, 117, 130, 137–52, 158, 159; in
the eighteenth century, 504; and
Emaux et camées (*Enamels and Cameos*) (Gautier), 507; and *L'enfer*
(Marot), 66; and feminine and masculine rhymes, 116, 127, 133, 480;
and 1550 odes of Ronsard, 121–24;
and *Les fleurs du mal* (Baudelaire),
472; and foreignness, 13, 133; and
free verse, 4, 484, 510; French language as vehicle for, 23, 68, 140; and
Fureur et mystère (Char), 565; and
genres, 116, 122–23; and geometric
principles of the Moderns, 279–80;
and Guillaume de Lorris, 138; and
heroic register, 123; and heroic
verse, 4, 126, 127, 134; and Homeric
and Virgilian epic, 123; and imitation of the poets of Greco-Roman
antiquity, 138, 140; and imperial expansion, 140, 146; and impressionism, 491; and *Institution* for Charles
IX, 133; and *Jadis et naguère* (*Long
Ago and Not So Long Ago*) (Verlaine),

478–79; and *Les jardins, ou l'art d'embellir les paysages* (*Gardens, or the Art of Embellishing the Landscape*), 503–4; and Jean de Meun, 138; and Louise Labé, 3, 29, 117; and Etienne de La Boétie, 160; and La Fontaine, 252; and love poetry, 124, 126, 128, 559, 569–70; and lyric poetry, 113, 116, 125; and Malherbe, 122, 125; and Stephane Mallarmé, 4, 13, 122, 128, 495–503; and Marguerite de Navarre, 59–61, 91–92; and Clement Marot, 4, 65–67, 113–14, 117, 150–51; and *Méditations poétiques* (Lamartine), 503, 504; and metaphor, 508; and military might and expansion, 140, 143; modern developments in, 5, 471; and modernism, 491, 554–73; and morality, 472, 477; and music, 127, 128, 479, 505; and national cadence, 127; and the nineteenth century, 27; and notion of breathing, 569; and Occitan troubadour poetry, 16; and odes, 113–17, 121, 123, 124–25, 126; and "On Some Motifs in Baudelaire" (Benjamin), 524–25; and Parnassians, 507, 583; and pastoral poems, 118–19; and Peletier's *Oeuvres poétiques*, 120; and Petrarch, 4, 69, 117, 122, 123, 148–49; and Petrarchan sonnet, 148–49, 500; and Constance Pipelet's poems on men and marriage, 335; and Pléiade poets, 4, 29, 43, 68, 69, 137–38, 139; and "Poème sur le désastre de Lisbonne" ("Poem on the Lisbon Disaster") (Voltaire), 297; and poem "Le siècle de Louis Le Grand" (Perrault), 270; and poems of Marguerite de Navarre, 59–61, 64–65, 92, 97, 101; and poem "The Man of the World" (Voltaire), 301; and poetic forms, 68–69, 116, 123, 139, 149; and poetic meters, 36, 116, 126, 127, 128, 129, 130, 131, 134, 151; and poetics as cultivation, 142–43; and poetic sense, 44, 121; and poetry of praise, 138; and poet's role, 28, 29, 113–14, 116–17, 264, 506–8; political, 132; and prose poem, 4, 10, 13, 476–77, 489, 490, 508, 509, 570; and prose writers, 504; prosodic forms of, 3, 4, 5, 116, 123; in Provençal, 149; and Quarrel of the Ancients and the Moderns, 277; and *rejets*, 481–82; and the Renaissance, 151, 152; rhythmic forms of, 3, 121, 130, 554; and Arthur Rimbaud, 4, 155, 485–92; and rising status of France, 138; and role of the poet, 503; and Pierre de Ronsard, 113, 114, 115–35, 137, 138; and Ronsard's golden-age renewal, 113, 117, 121, 129; and Ronsard's poetry, 158, 159; and Maurice Scève, 3; and series of rivalries, 139–44; and the sixteenth century, 138; and sonnets, 4, 68–69, 121–24, 126, 127, 128, 130, 131, 132, 134, 139, 148–51, 206; and *Le spleen de Paris* (Baudelaire), 441, 476–77; and the sublime, 283–86, 501; and surrealism, 509, 554–62; and symbolism, 491; and syntax, typography, and page layout, 5; and *Le temple de Cupido* (Marot), 66–67; and translation, 127, 133; and troubadour poetry, 16, 117; and truth, 511; and the unconscious, 13; and the vagabond consciousness, 10; and Paul Valery, 2, 3, 18–19, 123, 509; and Vauclusian region, 564–65; and Paul Verlaine, 4, 123, 478–84; and vernacular, 113–14, 141; and versification, 5, 116, 122, 123, 126, 127, 133–34; and *vers impair*, 478–80, 492n4; and voice, 482–83; and

French poetry (*cont.*)
women writers, 29, 91. *See also* epic poems; La Fontaine, Jean de; Marguerite de Navarre; national literature; Quarrel of the Ancients and the Moderns; Ronsard, Pierre de; Valéry, Paul

French Revolution (1789), 22, 402, 419, 503, 504–5; and authors' rights, 27; and the citizen, 312, 334, 419; and *Considerations sur les principaux événements de la Révolution française* (Staël), 333; and the Declaration of Vienna, 425; and democratic participation, 42–43; and female education, 338; and figure of the *philosophe*, 375, 377; and freedom of speech, 37; and French people, 23, 34, 156; and the guillotine, 444; and historical consciousness, 394; and literary history, 43; and literary language, 628; and meritocracy, 364; and natural laws, 43; and *Nouvelle Clarice* (Leprince de Beaumont), 342; and religion, 43; and Republican calendar, 18; and rights of blacks or slaves, 334; and the Terror, 344; and theatrical and media monopolies, 335; and violence, 419; and women's rights, 30, 334–35

Freud, Sigmund, 41, 525, 558

Fronde, the, 178, 203, 263, 264

Gallimard, 514, 536, 537–38, 539

Game of Love and Chance, The (Marivaux): and autonomy, 357; and class, 358–59; and love, 357–59; and marriage, 357–59; and masters and slaves, 360; popularity of, 357; and Silvia's exchange of roles with maid, 358–59; and social hierarchy, 359

Gargantua (Rabelais): and anti-monastic community, 83; and anti-monk Frère Jean, 62; and education, 79, 159; and Erasmus, 52, 58; and fabulous events, 84; and human institutions of the Church, 59; and interpretation, 81–82; and language of colors, 75; and *Pantagruel*, 71; and religion, 58, 59, 83; style of, 53, 58–59; and theology, 59; in vernacular language, 53; and violence, 59

Gassendi, Pierre: as a libertine, 182; and maxim *ambulo ergo sum*, 250–51; and modern philosophy, 276; and opposition to Descartes, 250–51; and reconciliation of Epicurean naturalism with Christian principles, 230; and role of sensory experience, 251; travels of, 251

Gautier, Théophile: and *Emaux et camées* (*Enamels and Cameos*), 507; and first book of *Poesies*, 506–7; and Hugo's *Hernani*, 436, 438; and Romantic legend, 442

Genius of Architecture; or the Analogy of That Art with Our Sensations (Le Camus de Mezieres), 313

Genlis, Félicité de, 337–38, 341

genre: and ancient genres, 122–23; and aphorism, 229, 245; and autobiography, 31–32, 44; and the bildungsroman, 433n1; and Césaire's different genres, 588–89; and characters, 229, 238; and cinema, 44; and comedy, 44, 80, 123, 174, 184–85; and comedy of character, 184–85; and context, 18; and dialogue form, 229, 261, 271, 287; and *divisio*, 80, 81; and drama, 81, 256, 442, 597; and epic, 39, 44, 56, 80, 204–205; and epic poetry, 294, 341; epistemic novels, 253; essays, 161–62, 536; and *Les Etats et Empires de la Lune* (*The States and Empires of the Moon*), 254; and *Les Etats et Empires du Soleil* (*The States and Empires of the Sun*), 254; explorer narratives, 256–60; and fables, 229, 230, 234, 238, 239, 240, 247, 250; and fairy tales, 223–25, 229, 234, 270, 281, 336; and fiction, 44, 168, 213, 215, 216, 223, 227, 229, 259, 260, 280, 294, 308, 309, 312, 314, 342, 347, 535–36; and the fifteenth century, 21; and form of the essay, 161–62, 165, 234; and freedom of speech, 37; and French opera, 191–92; and hierarchy of genres, 39, 44; and historical novel, 214; historical prose, 443; and horror genre, 208; and investigative journalism, 242; and the letter, 161, 229, 234, 241–42, 243, 254–56, 312; love sonnet sequences as, 132; and lyric poetry, 39, 113, 116; and Marguerite de Navarre, 59; and maxims, 229, 234, 238; and melodrama, 442; and the memoir-novel, 314–17; and modern fiction, 308; and Montaigne's essays, 68, 161–62; and narrative fiction, 597; newspapers, 213; and *nouvelle historique* (historical short stories), 216–17; novel, 44, 212–17, 224, 254, 309, 312–28, 442, 521, 589; and one genre in French sequences, 131; opera, 270; and *Pantagruel* (Rabelais), 71; and poetic genres, 116, 122, 123, 256, 442; and political satire, 123; and popular fiction, 29; and pornography, 208; and portrait, 229, 234, 238; and proimetrum, 254; and prose, 147, 152, 168, 215, 216, 220, 223, 227, 242, 254, 287, 308, 535–36; and romance, 21, 29–31, 202, 215, 216, 219–20, 223; and Pierre de Ronsard, 125; and satire, 241, 261, 298; and science fiction, 254; and short stories, 216–17, 229, 230, 337; standards of appropriateness for, 78;

and term *nouvelles*, 30, 104; and tragedy, 39, 44, 80, 123, 171, 193–94, 204, 294, 341; and travel writing, 3, 12, 229, 250–62, 264; and utopias, 229, 253, 254, 261, 264; and verse, 254; and *vraisemblance* (verisimilitude), 216; and work of Cyrano de Bergerac, 261, 265. *See also* novel

Germany: autocratic regime in, 534–35; and control of Vichy regime, 552; and *De l'Allemagne* (*On Germany*), 332; and Hitler's annexation of Czechoslovakian Sudetenland, 548; and Hitler's appointment as chancellor, 535; and influence on France, 22; and Nazis in World War II, 563; and occupation of France, 38; and the Seven Years' War, 299; Voltaire's travels in, 294

Gide, Andre, 7, 155, 515, 517, 521; and diary form, 596; and *Les faux-monnayeurs*, 535, 536, 596; and *L'immoraliste* (*The Immoralist*), 522, 536, 595; and importance of in 1930, 535; and male homosexuality, 522; as a member of the Gallimard staff, 538; and modern classicism, 619; and narrative as forgery, 605; and narrative experiments, 600; and Nobel Prize in Literature, 536–37; and *La Nouvelle Revue Française* (*NRF*), 537; politics of, 535

Godwin, Francis, 261, 262

Gouges, Olympe de, 334–35

Graffigny, Françoise de, 327–28, 346–47

Greek culture: and the *Aeneid* (Virgil), 66, 73, 163; and ancient Greece, 466, 505, 507; and antiquity, 50, 68, 137, 195, 270, 272–73, 274, 388; and Aristotle, 39, 132, 158, 171, 192, 195, 224, 280, 282, 442–43; and *Art poétique* (Horace), 120, 140; and

Greek culture (*cont.*)

Athenian comedy, 80; and Athenian democracy, 505; and Athenian polis, 240, 270, 272; and beauty, 20; and Cicero, 78–79, 132, 158, 161; and comedy, 20; and depictions of emotion, 206; and Diogenes, 378, 381, 388, 409; and Euripides's plot in *Phèdre* (Racine), 193, 195, 197; and Galen, 53; and gods, 80, 81, 87, 124, 129, 167, 341, 396; and gods in Racine's plays, 192–95, 196, 197; and Greco-Latin epic hexameter, 127; and Greek language, 23, 71, 73, 74, 140, 141–42, 253; and Greek sources of Erasmus, 49; and group of Alexandrian poets, 138; and Hellenist Anne Dacier, 30, 271, 285; and Hippocrates, 53; and *Hippolytus* (Euripides), 195; and Homer, 82, 113, 117, 122, 123, 124, 125, 126, 128, 138, 144, 261, 271, 273, 280; and Homeric world, 272, 273, 274, 275, 285–86; and Homer's *Iliad*, 271, 285; and Homer's Odysseus, 261, 308; and Horace, 113, 120, 122, 124, 140, 144, 158, 162, 167, 192, 282; and humanism, 151; and idea of imitation, 144–45; and legal reforms, 505; and literature, 143, 144, 271, 282–83; and Longinus's *On the Sublime*, 282–83; and Lucian of Samosata, 48, 54; and Lucretius, 124; and lyric poetry, 113; and military leaders, 138; and moderation, 78–79; Montaigne's love of, 158; and Muses, 124, 507; and mythology, 253, 264–65, 281; and the *Odyssey* (Homer), 204–5; and Ovid, 124, 138, 158, 261, 262; and paganism in poetry and the arts, 286–87; and Perrault view of ancient poetry as flawed, 280; and Pindar, 78, 80, 113, 115, 116, 117, 122, 123, 124, 125, 144; and Plato, 81, 82, 158, 171, 277, 396; poets of, 68, 78, 81, 113, 123, 124, 125, 138–39, 144; and Rabelais, 78; and seeking of wisdom, 65, 78–79, 167, 396; and Socrates, 81, 82, 158–59, 166, 167, 252, 260, 261, 396, 456, 601–2, 608; and title of Marguerite de Navarre's *Heptameron*, 92; and tragedy, 20, 80, 81, 194–95, 282, 597; and translation of poems, 145; and truth, 20; and usefulness, 20; and Venus, 313; and Virgil, 66, 73, 113, 123, 124, 125, 128, 138, 144, 158, 273, 285, 503. *See also* Aristotle; language; Petrarch; Seneca

Grimm, Friedrich Melchior, 374, 382, 402

Hegel, Georg Wilhelm F., 193, 208, 383, 389
Henri IV, 8, 21, 161
Heptameron (Marguerite de Navarre): and author's life, 99, 103, 108; and Boccaccio's *Decameron*, 59, 93, 94, 96; as a collection of stories, 92, 93, 94, 101, 102, 103; and dialogue form, 93, 105; and discussions between storytellers, 93, 94, 95, 96, 102, 103, 104, 105, 107–8; and early modern caste, 102; and education of author, 97; and equality, 105; and exemplarity of tales, 104; and faith, 94; and flood scene, 94; and group of travelers, 93, 94, 95, 104–5; and Pierre Gruget's *Heptameron*, 93, 104; and human nature, 94, 110; interpretations of, 104; and irony, 107; Italian sources of, 93, 94, 95, 96, 105; and *litterature engagée*, 110; and love, 93, 106, 107; and love and friendship, 93; and Luther's sermons, 107; and marital fidelity, 93, 94; and mar-

riage, 93, 98–99, 103; and meaning of title, 92; and monastic life, 100; and monks listening to stories, 108–9; narrative contract in, 105–6; and narrator Hircan, 107, 108–9; and Oisille as leader, 95, 106, 107; and Parlamente's identification with Marguerite, 96; and *La passion secrète d'une reine* (Chardak), 109; and *La Princesse de Clèves* (Lafayette), 101; and poem *Châtelaine de Vergy*, 105–6; publication of, 100–101; and realist French narrative, 102; and reception history, 103, 104; reception of, 101–2, 106; and religious themes, 93–94, 102, 108, 109, 110; and satire, 109; and sexuality, 93, 94, 95–6, 102, 103, 106–7; and sixteenth-century aristocratic society, 94; and stories of *Histoires des amans fortunez* (Boiastuau), 92–93; structure of, 102, 103, 104; and theology, 110; and transition from oral to written narrative, 106; and truth of accounts, 96, 102–4, 105, 106, 107, 108; and women as advocates of parental control, 98; and world-historical change, 97

Hernani (Hugo): battle of, 436–38, 440, 443–44; and censorship, 443–44; as a love story, 444; and play's first night, 8; shock of, 446

Histoire d'un voyage fait en terre de Bresil (*History of a Voyage to the Land of Brazil*) (Léry), 158, 256

Histoire naturelle (*Natural History*) (Buffon), 395, 402

Histoires des amans fortunez (Boiastuau), 92–93

history: and addition of Navarre to France, 21; and the "Affair of the Placards" by Swiss radicals, 100; and Africa, India, and South America, 257; and Algerian history, 641, 642, 650; and Algerian War, 38, 596, 631, 635, 636, 638; and ancient history, 161, 446, 447; and anticolonial movements, 578; and Antillean history, 584; and Battle of Eylau disaster, 441; and breakup of Roman Empire, 20; and *Bulletins of the Grande Armée*, 441; and capitalism, 85, 587; and Cartier's expeditions to North America, 256; and censorship during a national crisis, 38; as a chain of causes and effects, 43; and civil war, 113, 114, 123, 128; classical history, 158; and the cold war, 630; and colonization, 256–57, 578; and Communist Party, 578; and consciousness in Europe, 6, 272; and Cortez's violence against Aztec Empire, 87; and the Council of Trent, 156; and coverage, 2, 3; and the Crusades, 257; cyclical notion of, 147, 151; and Cyrano de Bergerac, 265; and deaths of writers, printers, and translators, 100; and the Declaration of the Rights of Man and of the Citizen, 419; and the Declaration of Vienna, 425; and decolonization in the 1950s and 60s, 576; and Diet at Haguenau, 120; and different governmental systems, 433; and English-language histories, 1; and *Essays* (Montaigne), 158; and European histories, 158; and Europe's civil and religious wars, 233; and failed Communist Shanghai insurrection, 546, 547, 551; of France in Middle Ages, 21; and France's Italian wars, 118; and French army's murders, 639, 643; and French colonialism, 636–44; and French crises of the 1930s, 534–35; of French literature, 11, 17, 42–43, 45, 155, 238, 242; and French history (*cont.*)

poetry, 3–5, 554; and French Resistance, 621; and French Revolution, 630; and the Fronde era, 178, 203, 263, 264; and Girondin government, 340; of Haiti, 585–86, 587; and Haussmann's changes to Paris, 470; and Henri II's peace with England, 123; and historiography, 172, 191; and Hitler's appointment as German chancellor, 535; and humanism, 156; and introduction of printing, 21; and July Monarchy, 436–37; and the July Revolution in 1830, 507; and leftist coalition Popular Front, 552; and Lisbon earthquake, 297; of literature, 2–7, 11, 238; and membership in canon of French literature, 5; and modern history, 7, 161; and modernity, 15–16, 84–85; and Montaigne's *Essays*, 155, 168; and Munich agreements, 548, 552; and Napoleon Bonaparte, 419–23, 425, 427; and Napoleon III's Second Empire, 466, 470; and natural history, 239; and the New World, 97, 256–57; and perspective of colonized Algerians, 639; and power of the Terror of 1974, 38; and presentism, 2, 446; and readership, 1–3, 45; and realist bildungsroman, 420; and the Reign of Terror, 504–5; relation of literature with, 272; and repressive Second Empire, 37–38; and the Restoration, 420, 423, 426, 427, 432–33, 441, 444, 505; and revolution of 1848, 466, 470, 505–6, 507; and royal historiographers, 26, 191; and Saint-Simon, 518; and the Seven Years' War, 299–300, 374; and the sixteenth century, 119, 132, 156–57, 233, 256; and St. Bartholomew's Day massacre, 132, 157; and territo-rial expansion, 256, 257; and treatment of women, 85; and War of Austrian Succession, 372; and wars of King Francois I, 91; and Wars of Religion, 7, 51, 85, 156–57; and women writers, 30–31; and World War I, 516, 525, 528, 530, 622; and World War II, 548, 554, 563, 621, 627, 631, 640. *See also* colonialism; French Revolution; literary history

Hobbes, Thomas, 173, 182, 187, 238, 245, 396

Holland: and Isabelle de Charrière, 343–44; and Anne-Marie Du Bocage, 341; and Erasmus of Rotterdam, 47; and publishing, 37

honnêteté, 187–88, 189, 376, 377

Horace: *Art poétique* of, 120, 140; cultural role of, 144; and literary criticism, 192; and moderation, 78; and Montaigne, 158, 162, 167; odes of, 114–15; and poetry, 282; and Pierre de Ronsard, 113, 114–15, 122, 124

Hugo, Victor: and censor Briffaut, 443–44; and *Les contemplations*, 442; and *Cromwell*, 443; cultural role of, 123, 436, 505, 507; death of, 128; and dictionary, 24; exile of, 506; and first night of *Hernani*, 8; and God's creation, 507; and love and social reform, 506; and philosophy, 130; as a poet, 3, 28; and protests at the Comédie Française, 436, 437–38; public funeral of, 10; and republicanism, 505, 506; and rise of Louis-Napoleon, 506; and Romanticism, 436, 437, 438, 440, 441; Romantic dramas of, 437–38; and *Ruy Blas*, 443; and support for royalist cause, 504; and truth, 506. See also *Hernani* (Hugo)

humanism: and Christian humanists, 49, 54, 63, 64–65, 68; and classical

antiquity, 156; and disapproval of the Gothic, 79; and *divisio*, 80, 81; and Dutch humanist Justus Lipsius, 165; and education, 58, 63, 64–65, 79, 97, 158, 159; and Erasmus, 35, 51, 52, 53, 58, 59, 63–65, 156; and free will, 83; and French humanists, 48, 51, 53, 147; and the Gothic world, 83; and Greek and Roman literature, 143; and human relations, 59; and ideals of heroism, 156, 157, 159; and Italian humanists, 48, 49, 183; Italian roots of, 156; and Etienne de La Boétie, 159–60; and Latin, Greek, and Hebrew, 52, 56; and legacy of Greece and Rome, 151; and mastering many fields of knowledge, 157; and military virtue, 159; and Montaigne, 157, 162, 166, 167–68; and northern Europe, 156; and *Oration on the Dignity of Man* (Pico della Mirandola), 183; and Paris, 49, 50; and philology, 58; and political crisis, 157; and political rhetoric, 159; and Rabelais, 78, 156; and Renaissance humanism, 78–80, 275; and return to ancient sources, 49, 156, 272; and scholasticism, 83; and the sixteenth century, 156; and tension with Christianity, 79–80; and the twentieth century, 84; and use of vernacular language, 35; and virtue, 156. *See also* Erasmus; Renaissance
Hume, David, 272, 399

Illiad (Homer), 271, 285
Illusions perdues (Balzac): and characters' lack of principles, 423, 430; and chronicles of the nineteenth century, 9; and crime, 417, 430; and financial speculation, 417; and high society, 428, 429, 430, 431; and marriage to aristocratic heiress, 430–31; and Na-

poleon Bonaparte, 418, 427, 428, 430; and Paris, 415, 420, 428, 429–30, 437; and Parisian theater, 437; and the Restoration, 427, 428; and Lucien de Rubempré, 416, 417, 420, 427–33, 437; and self-made noblemen, 429, 430; and sexual exploits, 417, 430; and social capital of noble name, 428; and Julien Sorel, 427, 431
immanence, principle of, 171, 172–73
impromtu de Versailles, L' (*The Versailles Impromptu*) (Moliere), 173–74, 177–78
Index librorum prohibitorum (Index of Prohibited Books) (Vatican), 36, 78, 81, 160
Italy: and Giorgio Agamben, 446; and ancient Rome, 149–50, 151; and beginnings of the Renaissance, 20; and Boccaccio's *Decameron*, 93, 94, 95; and *commedia dell'arte*, 174, 352, 356; and Tommaso Campanella, 253; and competition with France, 132, 144; and *Histoire de la peinture en Italie* (*The History of Painting in Italy*), 445; history of, 158; and humanism, 156; and influence of Petrarch, 117, 144, 151; and Italian humanists, 48, 49; and Italian Renaissance, 152; literature and civilization in, 151, 160; medieval culture of, 445; monasteries in, 423; and Montaigne's travels to Rome, 160; and Pico della Mirandola, 183; poetry of, 140, 144, 150, 151, 152; and the *querelle des bouffons*, 379; and Ronsard's ode, 124; and the seventeenth century, 269; and the sixteenth century, 22, 149, 152; and sociability of Italian courts, 269; and Stendhal's appointment as consul, 433; and wars with France, 118. *See also* Petrarch; Roman culture; Speroni, Sperone

Jacques le fataliste (*Jacques the Fatalist*)
(Diderot): and figure of the *philosophe*, 375, 376; posthumous publishing of, 371
Joyce, James: as an author in exile, 616;
Beckett's essay on, 621; as Beckett's
mentor, 615; bilingualism of, 616;
and creation of a synthetic language,
619; and Joycean language, 620, 630;
as model for Beckett, 626
Julie ou la nouvelle Héloïse (*Julie, or the
New Heloise*) (Rousseau): and architecture of bourgeois house, 322–23;
copies of, 32; and the epistolary
novel, 320–24, 327; and intimacy of
the salon of Apollo, 322–23; and
marriage and family, 320, 321–22,
324; and nature, 322, 323–24; and
La philosophie dans le boudoir (*Philosophy in the Bedroom*) (Sade), 326; and
private spaces, 320–22; and Saint-
Preux in Julie's dressing room, 320–
22, 323; and Saint-Preux in the Elysée garden, 323–24; and sentiment,
40, 320; and transparency, 320, 322

Labé, Louise, 3, 29, 117, 149
La Boétie, Etienne de, 159–60
La Bruyère, Jean de: as an Ancient, 271;
Caractères of, 230, 235–36; as a moralist, 230, 235–36; professions of, 230
Laclos, Pierre: and academic competition, 338; and the eighteenth-
century novel, 314; and *Les liaisons
dangereuses* (*Dangerous Liaisons*), 32–
33, 317, 337, 343; and women's freedom, 30
Lafayette, Madame de: and anonymous publishing of novel, 217–18;
and characters' passions, 202, 203,
206, 212, 213–14, 216, 217, 220; and
eavesdropping culture, 222–23; and
the *nouvelle historique*, *Princesse de
Montpensier*, 216; and psychological
novel *La Princesse de Clèves*, 202, 203,
212, 213, 215–20, 223; and Rabouillet salon's conversation, 221; and
Versailles, 218–19; and women's
conversation, 212, 220, 222–23; and
Zayde, 202
La Fontaine, Jean de: and the Académie française, 230–31, 252; as an
Ancient, 271; and animal nature of
humans, 235; and description of
Richelieu's chateau, 255, 258, 264; as
a detractor of Descartes, 251; and
ethics of writing, 238; and explorer
narratives, 256, 258–60; and fable
"An Animal in the Moon," 231–32;
and fables, 230, 231–32, 236, 238–
39, 250, 252; and *Fables*, 252, 264;
and fable "The Power of Fables,"
240; and imagination, 240, 260; and
Lettres à sa femme (*Letters to Madame
de La Fontaine*), 254–56, 259–60,
262; as a libertine, 230; as a moralist,
230; on politics and war, 263–64;
and power of language, 238–39; as
protégé of Nicolas Fouquet, 254;
questions raised in fiction of, 265–
66; and satire and critique, 256,
260, 263; and sense perception with
reason, 231–32; and seventeenth-
century poetry, 252; and short stories, 230; and travel writing, 261–62,
265–66; and *Voyage d'Encausse* (Chapelle and Bachaumont), 262; and
wife Marie Hericart, 254
Lamartine, Alphonse de, 503, 504; and
God's creation, 507; as minister of
foreign affairs, 505–6; and poet's
role, 507; religion of, 506; and republicanism, 505–506
language: and aboriginal languages in
Canada, 641; and ancient Greek,
282; of antiquity, 122, 140, 141, 148,

161; and Arabic, 641, 643, 644, 648; and Aramaic, 56; and authors as members of society, 25, 643; and authors' choices, 24–25, 146, 616–17; and Beckett's self-translation, 624–25, 626; and borrowing from other languages and literatures, 152; and Breton, 23; and the century, 15; and classical languages, 156; and clichés in Flaubert, 459, 460, 461, 462, 467; and communication between francophone nations, 24, 646; and correspondences, 471; and *Un coup de Dés jamais n'abolira le Hasard* (Mallarmé), 497; and Creole, 583, 592, 641, 645; and *La deffence et illustration de la langue francoyse* (du Bellay), 137–43, 145–47; and dialects, 72, 73, 617; and dictionaries, 23, 24; and direct speech, 589–90; and Dutch, 52, 72, 336; and English, 336, 641; and "Essai sur l'origine des langues" ("Essay on the Origin of Languages") (Rousseau), 286; and francophone culture, 24, 635, 640; and French as a national language, 7, 11, 23; and French as suitable for poetry, 140; and French in the Maghreb region, 635; and French language, 3, 7, 11, 13, 22–24, 35, 56, 68, 71, 72, 113, 114, 128, 137–38, 140–41, 145, 158, 221, 287, 526, 640, 641, 647; and French literacy, 23–24, 33, 34, 339; and Gaelic, 616–17; and Gascon, 640; and German, 71, 336; and God, 403; and the Gothic world, 79, 84; and Greek, 23, 35, 48, 50, 52, 53, 56, 71, 74, 78, 138, 140, 142, 143, 148, 336, 501; and Hebrew, 50, 52, 56, 97; and imitation of other languages, 140, 146; and interpretation, 73, 74; and issues of translation and interpretation, 73–75,

145–46, 151; and Italian, 11, 71, 73, 97, 148, 149, 151, 158, 347; and Joyce's creation of a synthetic language, 619; and Latin, 23, 35, 47–48, 50, 52, 54, 56, 71, 72, 73, 79, 83–84, 97, 138, 139, 140, 143, 148, 158, 648; and Latin in *Le rouge et le noir* (Stendhal), 421, 423; and limits of for expression, 459–60; and Limousin, 71, 72; and literary language, 628; and literature in European languages, 45, 71, 72, 148, 149; in *Madame Bovary* (Flaubert), 456–61; and making sense of self and surroundings, 502; as medium of relation and engagement, 590–91; and modern francophones, 71; and modern French argot, 24; and modern Italy, 23; and modern languages, 148; and moving pictures, 46; and "My Mother Tongue, My Paternal Languages" (Serres), 640; and naming of things, 607, 608; and national heritage, 536, 640; and nationalism, 640–41; and national language, 132, 640, 641; and national literary culture, 7, 11, 23, 536, 640; and native French speakers, 640; nature of, 134; and Occitan, 23; and *Pantagruel* (Rabelais), 71–73, 87; and poetic language, 472, 483, 486, 490, 502; and polyglossia, 11, 84; and polyphony, 266; and process of cultivation, 141–43; and Proust's writing, 526, 530; and reality, 602; and relationship with author, 628; and *Remarques sur la langue française* (Vaugelas), 221; and rhythm and meter, 128, 134; and Romans' cultivation of Latin, 141–42; and Ronsard's odes, 115, 134; as a rule-bound activity, 502; and sacred language, 498; of seduction, 461; and sonnets, 131; and

language (*cont.*)
  Spanish, 72, 97, 336; and spoken
    French vernacular, 631; standardiza-
    tion of, 35–36, 72; and the sublime,
    283; and translation, 72, 73–74, 145,
    279, 282, 284, 287, 291, 294, 343,
    347; and translations of Marie Le-
    prince de Beaumont's "Magasins,"
    336; and Tuscan dialect of Italian,
    148; and universal language, 630;
    and use of pronoun *on* (one), 460–
    61, 466–67, 626; and use of spoken
    French in novel, 539, 541, 550; and
    use of vernacular language, 24, 35,
    51, 52, 54, 73–74, 550; and women's
    conversation, 221; and writing, 619,
    629; and writing without style, 615.
    See also *deffence et illustration de la
    langue francoyse, La* (du Bellay);
    French poetry
La Rochefoucauld, Francois de: apho-
    risms of, 8; as a celebrated moralist,
    230; *Maximes* of, 235, 248; and self-
    interest, 234; and self-love, 232, 235;
    on virtue and vice, 233
Leibniz, Gottfried: and divine order,
    308; and Leibnizian optimism, 296,
    297, 298, 304, 305, 309; and philoso-
    phy, 306; and problem of evil, 298
Lettres à sa femme (*Letters to Madame de
    la Fontaine*) (La Fontaine): as an
    epistolary narrative, 254, 256; and
    imprisonment of Fouquet, 254, 262;
    and narrator as an exile, 262; and
    places visited, 255–56; and religious
    subjects, 255; and travel writing,
    259–60; and *Voyage de Paris en Li-
    mousin*, 254, 256, 262
Lettres d'une peruvienne (*Letters from a
    Peruvian Woman*) (Graffigny), 295,
    327–28, 346–47
Lettres persanes (Montesquieu), 295,
    345

Lettres provinciales (Pascal), 241–43
Lettre sur les aveugles (*Letter to the
    Blind*) (Diderot), 372
Leviathan, The (Hobbes), 182, 238
liaisons dangereuses, Les (*Dangerous Liai-
    sons*) (Laclos): and the boudoir or
    bedroom, 317–18, 319, 320, 324,
    copies of, 32–33; and the epistolary
    novel, 317, 318–20; and immorality
    of Marquise de Merteuil, 343; and
    libertines' use of space, 317–20; and
    observation of Mme de Tourvel,
    318–19; publishing of, 337; and ren-
    dezvous between Mme de Merteuil
    and Prévan, 319; and smallpox, 326;
    and Valmont's seduction of Mme de
    Tourvel, 318–19
libertines: and adventures of the self,
    232; and belief in God, 244–45; and
    cultural authority, 234; and Cyrano
    de Bergerac, 251–52; and freethink-
    ing, 182, 229, 230, 231; and Gas-
    sendi, 182; and human excesses, 231;
    and illusions about oneself, 235; and
    La Fontaine, 230–31; and liberti-
    nage, 229, 230; and libertine writers,
    230–32, 235, 238; and libertine writ-
    ing, 229, 230, 313, 315–20, 324–27;
    and matter, 238; Pascal's feelings on,
    241; and people's motivations, 232;
    and politics, 247; and power of
    imagination, 235, 238; and search
    for secrets, 327; and self-love, 231;
    and site of the bed, 324, 326; and
    spatial strategies in novels, 317–19;
    and violence, 326
literary career: and alienation, 10; and
    authors as members of society, 25,
    28, 29; and authors' copyrights, 28;
    and authors' wages, 25, 26, 27–28;
    and dictionary, 26; and encyclope-
    dists, 26; and journalists, 26, 27–28;
    and literary self-consciousness, 9;

and patronage of court and Church, 25–27; and personas or pseudonyms, 25, 37; and professional writers, 27–31, 42; and rise of the middle class, 26, 30; and royalty payments, 27; and value of independence, 25; and writer as intellectual, 28, 29; and writer as rebel and outsider, 9, 28
literary history: and aesthetics, 234, 288; and attack on Rousseau's *Confessions*, 402–3; and Charles Baudelaire, 470; and beginnings of modernization, 8; and Benedictines of Saint Maur, 6; and border-crossing, 12–13; and censor Briffaut, 443–44; and the century, 15, 42, 43; and context, 6, 7, 18, 92; and cosmopolitanism, 12; and criticism, 39–42, 213; and dating of chronology, 18; and discussion about *La Princesse de Clèves* (Lafayette), 213; and dominant, emergent, and residual stages, 16–17; and the eighteenth century, 6, 9; and the fifteenth century, 21; and First and Second Romanticism, 440; and the "first Renaissance," 51, 54; and Francois I's plan for institution of higher learning, 50; and francophone literature, 591, 636, 644, 645, 650; and French arts, 287–88; and French literary prose, 241–42; and French literature, 45, 242, 287–88; and French poetry, 3–5; and French world, 7; and the *Heptameron* (Marguerite de Navarre), 92; as a history of readings, 18–19; and influence of a work, 19; and Jean-Jacques Rousseau, 394–95; and *Lettres provinciales* (Pascal), 241–42; and literary criticism, 39–42, 591; and the literary marketplace, 9–10, 11; and literary movements, 491; and literary self-consciousness, 9;

10–11; and literary trials, 10, 37–38, 452, 462, 463, 464–66, 468; and *The Marriage of Figaro* (Beaumarchais), 362; and *Méditations poétiques* (Lamartine), 503; and membership in canon, 6, 9; and modern Western literary history, 206; and Montaigne's *Essays*, 155, 168; and Montesquieu, 43, 288; and national literary culture, 12–13, 14, 20; and new forms of writing, 45–46; and the nineteenth century, 3, 4, 6, 7, 9, 10, 12–13, 16; as opposed to history of literature, 5–7; and patronage of writers, 25–27; and pioneering nature of Césaire's writings, 591–92; and political change, 43; and prepublication censorship, 36–37; and presenting interiority, 206–7; and Quarrel of the Ancients and the Moderns, 272, 275, 277, 287–88, 440; and the Renaissance, 15–16, 43, 269, 438; and revolution of printing, 35; and rise of books on moral doctrine, 234; and the seventeenth century, 7–9, 11–12, 13, 16, 17, 43, 234, 266; and the sixteenth century, 3, 4, 11, 16, 51; and story's reproduction, 19; and term Renaissance, 137; and travel writing, 266; and the twentieth century, 3, 11, 13, 22, 43, 596–97, 600; and the twenty-first century, 11, 44, 46; and vocation of literature, 21; writer or work's place in, 18, 19. *See also* classicism; history; Quarrels
literary trials: and Baudelaire's *Les fleurs du mal*, 10; and Flaubert's *Madame Bovary*, 10, 452, 462–66, 468; and trial of Théophile de Viau, 230
Locke, John: and empiricism, 295; and *Essay concerning Human Understanding*, 295; and human mind as a blank tablet, 295, 303; and natural laws, 396

Louis XIV: absolute rule of, 180, 203, 263, 269; and Anne of Austria, 180, 203; and centralized state formation, 8; and Jean Chapelain, 122; and classical culture, 273, 275, 276; court of, 81, 178, 214, 222, 225, 263, 518; and fashion, 444–45; and imprisonment of Fouquet, 254; and incorporation in *Tartuffe* (Molière), 178–80; and marquise de Montespan, 225; and patronage of writers, 26, 174; and Charles Perrault, 15, 275; and poem "Le siècle de Louis Le Grand" (Perrault), 270; Racine as historiographer for, 191; and Versailles, 22, 214, 225, 270; and wife Mme de Maintenon, 225

Louverture, Toussaint, 580, 581, 585–86

Lucian of Samosata, 48, 54, 55, 58, 261

Luther, Martin, 36, 60, 61, 91; sermons of, 107; and treatise on monastic vows of celibacy, 100. *See also* religion

Lyons, France, 3, 36, 71, 117, 140, 330

Madame Bovary (Flaubert): and Emma Bovary, 452–59, 461–65, 467, 468; and censorship by editors, 464; and clichés of language, 459–62; and detail of description, 451, 452–55, 460, 463; and Emma's child with Charles, 464; and Emma's debt, 462–63; and Emma's lovers, 454, 458–64; and Flaubert's impersonality of narration, 451–52; and influence of romance novels, 456; and language, 456–61, 467; as modern, 455, 467–68; and realism, 7, 451–56, 465–68; and reality of marriage, 462, 465, 467; and scandal, 452, 464–66; serial publishing of, 464; and suicide, 463; and sympathy for main character,

456–57, 468; themes of, 451, 456–57, 464–66, 467, 468; and trial concerning public and religious morality, 10, 452, 462, 463, 464–66, 468; and use of pronoun *on* (one), 460–61. *See also* language

Mallarmé, Stephane: and alexandrine verse form, 4; as an atheist, 502; and authority, 503; careers of, 502–3; and *Crise de vers* (*Verse Crisis*), 13, 127, 128, 499–501; death of, 495, 496; and difficult modes of expression, 28; family of, 503; and history of modernity, 630; and language, 509; and music, 128, 501–2, 503; and *Poésies*, 495; and poet as seer, 501; and poetic meters, 134; and poetry, 4, 122, 128, 495–503, 511; and prosody, 126; and sonnets, 500–501; and versification, 122

Malraux, André: and challenge to traditional treatment of protagonists, 546; cinematic montage in novel of, 546–48, 550–51; and *Les conquerants*, 534, 549; and Duthuit's journal *Transition*, 630; and film *Espoir: Sierra de Teruel*, 548; and literature of extreme situations, 547; as a member of the Gallimard staff, 538; and the 1930s, 7, 534, 535; politics of, 535, 551; and Prix Goncourt for *La condition humaine*, 537; and "the human condition," 539; tragic vision of, 550

manifestos: and conflict with the state, 10; and *La deffence et illustration de la langue francoyse* as Pléiade manifesto, 137, 147; and French authors, 25, 190, 466, 590; and Goethe's *Weltliteratur* and globalization, 11; and modernizing impulse, 8; and Perrault's modern-party manifesto, 271, 273; and *In Praise of Creoleness*, 579;

for realism, 466; and Romantic manifesto *Racine and Shakespeare* (Stendhal), 190, 444, 445; and surrealist manifestos, 511, 558, 561, 562, 571

Marguerite de Navarre: as Marguerite d'Angoulême, 52, 59, 96; as anti-Erasmian, 52, 62–65, 99; attacks by Béda on, 59, 67; and belief in Bible, 52, 63, 97, 109–10; and Guillaume Briçonnet, 54, 61, 91; and Jean Calvin, 59, 67; and correspondence with social network, 54, 61, 91; and court in Nérac, 100; courtly and medieval works of, 59, 94; and daughter Jeanne, 121; death of, 68, 92; diplomatic skill of, 91; and education, 63, 97; and Erasmus's letters, 53–54, 59, 65; as evangelical, 61, 62, 63, 110; farces and songs of, 52, 61–64, 66; and Henri d'Albret, king of Navarre, 107; and the *Heptameron*, 92, 93, 100–101, 103, 110; husbands of, 97–98, 107; and imitation in English, 102–3; influence of, 101–2, 109; and innovations to narrative traditions, 104–6; and interaction with Boccaccio, 11; and marriage, 98–99, 103; and Clément Marot, 66, 123; and mother Louise de Savoie, 97; and mystico-Lutheran ideology, 61, 62; and *La passion secrète d'une reine* (Chardak), 109; and patronage of writers, 91–92, 99, 100; piety and faith of, 52, 60–62, 97, 99; plays of, 92; poetry of, 59–61, 64–65, 92, 97, 101; and political change, 91, 97; as queen of Navarre, 53, 96–97; readership of, 59; and relationship with brother, 108; and relationship with Rabelais, 100, 109; and religious themes, 60–65, 108, 109; and Mellin de Saint-Gelais, 123; and salvation,

62, 64; as sister of François I, 25, 51, 52, 59, 91, 97, 99; and translations of seditious writings, 100; writing style of, 59, 60, 61, 62

Marivaux, Pierre Carlet de: and absence of gender hierarchy, 357; and authority, 352; and autonomy, 352, 357, 361; and characters' names, 353–54, 356; and cross-dressing, 357, 358; and discovery of the self, 361; and family, 352, 356–57; and *La fausse suivante* (*The False Lady's Maid*), 353–54, 357, 358; and *The Game of Love and Chance*, 357–59; and gender equality, 359; and happiness, 361; and love, 352, 354–61; and marriage, 352, 355, 356–57, 360–61; and novel *Le paysan parvenu* (*Up from the Country*), 314–15; and relationship between servants and masters, 352–60, 365; and second *Surprise of Love*, 354, 356–57; and self-determining female characters, 356–57; and sentiment, 360–61; and servants as twins of upper-class characters, 354–55; and social hierarchy, 359, 360, 368; social views of, 357; and *Surprise of Love* (1722), 354–57; and traditions of Molière and the *commedia dell'arte*, 352, 356; and widows, 356–57; and women's marital status, 356, 357. *See also* class

Marot, Clément: allegories of, 52, 66; death of, 67, 68; enemies of, 67; and *L'enfer*, 66; as Erasmian, 66, 67; and evangelism, 66, 67; and human institutions of the Church, 66; and lyric stanzas, 66; and patronage of Marguerite de Navarre, 99, 123; as a poet, 4, 52, 65–67, 113–14, 117, 138, 139; and poetic forms, 68–69; and refuge at Marguerite's court, 100; and sonnets, 139, 151; and *Le temple*

Marot, Clément (*cont.*)
de Cupido, 66–67; and translation of Petrarch, 139, 150–51; and translations of biblical psalms into French, 65–66, 67; as a vernacular poet, 113–14

Marriage of Figaro, The (Beaumarchais): and attack on censorship, 363; and attack on judicial system, 364; and character of Count Almaviva, 362, 363, 365–68; and character of Fanchette, 367; and character of Figaro, 363, 364, 365–68; and class and gender cross-dressing, 365; as a critique of the ancien régime's values, 363, 365; and family, 366–67; and happiness, 365, 366, 367; and lack of economic opportunity for women, 364; and love, 368–69; and marriage, 365–68; and meritocracy, 364; popularity of, 364; and public opinion, 364–65, 368; and relationship between Figaro and Suzanne, 366, 367, 368; and relationship between servants and masters, 365, 368; and "seigneurial rights," 366; and struggle to stage, 362–64

Martinique: and *antillanité* (Caribbeanness), 575; and Aimé Cesairé, 575, 576–77, 578, 581, 647; and Raphael Confiant, 579; and Creole language, 641; and *créolité* (Creoleness), 575, 579, 592; and French "overseas *departements*," 578, 637, 641; and *négritude*, 575; politics in, 577, 578; and rule of Admiral Robert, 577; and works of Glissant and Fanon, 581

Marx, Karl, 32, 41, 383, 389

Maximes (La Rochefoucauld), 203, 230, 233

Méditations poétiques (Lamartine), 503, 504

Mercier, Louis-Sebastian, 504, 505

Mericourt, Theroigne de, 334–35

Middle Ages: and authority of the Ile de France, 21; authorship in, 25, 29; and courtly love, 29; and Italian republics, 445; and medieval history, 440, 445, 447; and medieval romance, 8, 29; and monastic life, 83; and Occitan troubadour poetry, 16; or "dark ages," 56; poetry of, 137; and *querelles des femmes*, 29; as a regression to moderns and ancients, 272; and the *Roman de la Rose*, 8, 29, 32; and Romanticism, 439–40; and *Tristan et Iseut*, 440; and François Villon, 25; and written culture in the Church, 20, 25

Miroir de l'âme pécheresse, Le (*The Mirror of the Sinful Soul*) (Marguerite de Navarre): and Bale's version *The Glasse of the Synnefull Soule*, 101; and feminine first-person speaker, 60; and love of Christ, 61; and Marot's psalm translation, 66; and path to salvation, 60; publishing of, 60, 101; and relationship with Christ, 60–61; and translation of by Princess Elizabeth of England, 109

misanthrope, Le (Molière): action of, 188; and Alceste, 185–86, 188, 189; and Alceste's friend Philinte, 185–87, 188; and Célimène, 185, 186, 188; and comedy of character, 184–85, 188–89; and Hobbes's idea of man as a wolf to others, 187; and *honnêteté*, 187–88; and human nature, 186–87, 188; and hypocrisy, 186, 187; and public controversy, 175

modernism: and *A la recherche du temps perdu* (*In Search of Lost Time*) (Proust), 517; and Guillaume Apollinaire's importance, 510; and Apollinaire's series of conversations, 548, 551; and Charles Baudelaire, 470,

471, 478, 491; and *Candide* (Voltaire), 294–95, 308; and comedy of character, 188; and cosmopolitanism, 12; and dilemma of the human condition, 208; and *Du côté de chez Swann* (*Swann's Way*) (Proust), 517; and early modern period, 201, 250, 361; as emerging, 470; in England, 615; and Europe, 272; and existentialism, 13–14, 41; and Eysteinsson and Liska's *Modernism*, 616; and fiction, 361; and foreignness, 13–14; French modernism, 615, 616; and French poetry, 5, 13, 270, 491; and imitation in English, 102–3; and impersonality of narration, 451; as international, 615; Irish modernism, 615, 616–18; and levels of historicity, 446–47; and *Madame Bovary* (Flaubert), 455; and *mimesis*, 602; and the modern as the new, 8; and modern novel, 595–613; and modern period, 5, 7; and modern public, 39; and modern situation comedy, 188; and modern stage, 171, 194, 443; and the modern writer, 302; and narrative, 605; and national literary culture, 7; and Perrault's modern "method," 279; and *Phèdre*, 208; and *Pointed Roofs* (Richardson), 517; and *A Portrait of the Artist as a Young Man* (Joyce), 517; and Quarrel of the Ancients and the Moderns, 16, 272; and Arthur Rimbaud, 491; and the self, 201; and the seventeenth century, 269–70; and shift from content to perceiving consciousness, 491; and surrealism, 13; and theater, 361; and Paul Verlaine, 491. *See also* modernity; surrealism

modernity: and acceptance of uncertainty, 88; and ancients versus moderns, 16, 209n2; and Baudelaire, 478, 616; and beginnings of in 1960s, 85; and Maurice Blanchot, 630; and Albert Camus, 627, 628, 630; and challenge to theology, 16; and civilization, 20–21, 42, 84–85, 273; and comparison between Rome and Greece, 273; and the degree zero of writing, 630; and *divisio*, 88; and *Don Quixote* (Cervantes), 87; and ethics of writing, 630; of European humanist learning, 143; and French classical tragedy, 173; and French Revolution, 630; and Jean Genet, 627, 630; and importance of the future, 447; and information, 524; and introduction of printing, 21; and Lautréamont, 616; and Mallarmé, 616; and Marivaux's plays, 361; and mass culture, 524; and modern subject, 266; and Molière's comedies, 174, 179–80; and northern melancholy, 332; and the *nouveau roman*, 630; and the Ossianic model, 332; and pantagruelism, 88; and the "progress" story, 16; and Quarrel of the Ancients and the Moderns, 273, 275; and question of starting point, 84–85, 273; and Racine, 209n2; and the Renaissance, 15–16, 84; and secularism, 16, 173; and shocks to the senses, 525; and social sciences, 411; and style of writing, 630; and theater, 172–73; and theory of human progress, 273; and Virgil as modern before his time, 273; and work of Molière, 173; and work of Rabelais and contemporaries of, 19, 85; and work of Racine, 206; and work of Rousseau, 411. *See also* modernism

Molière (Jean-Baptiste Poquelin): and Académie française, 634; as actor, 173, 174, 180–81, 188, 189; and actors of troupe, 173–74; and *Amphi-*

Molière (Jean-Baptiste Poquelin) (*cont.*)
tryon, 184; and Armand de Bourbon,
prince of Conti, 181; and *Le bourgeois
gentilhomme* (*The Would-be Gentleman*), 188–89; burial of, 176; career
of, 25, 173; characters of, 202, 352–
53; and comedy of character, 184–85,
188–89; and *Critique de l'école des
femmes* (*The Critique of the School for
Wives*), 175, 177; as director, 173,
174, 189; and *Don Juan*, 175, 180–84,
189, 353; and dramatic action, 361;
and *L'école des femmes* (*The School for
Wives*), 175, 176–77, 181; enemies of,
184; and family relationships, 355;
and farce, 184, 353; and *George Dandin*, 184; and *honnêteté*, 189; and
L'impromptu de Versailles (*The Versailles Impromptu*), 173–74, 177–78;
and improvisational style of *commedia
dell'arte*, 174; and justice, 182, 184;
and Louis XIV, 174, 178, 179–80;
and *Le malade imaginaire* (*The Imaginary Invalid*), 188–89; as a materialist,
182, 184; and *Le misanthrope*, 175,
184, 202; and modernity, 173, 174,
179–80; and morality, 182–83, 184;
and obsession with medicine, 175;
plays of, 40, 43, 76, 173–74, 179–80,
184–85, 353, 379; as playwright, 173,
174, 189, 351; and *Les précieuses ridicules* (*The Pretentious Young Ladies*),
222; and religious themes, 182–84;
and rival theater company, 178; royal
patronage of, 176, 180; sex in plays
of, 177, 185; and *Tartuffe*, 175, 178,
180, 189, 353, 380, 423; and theatrical professionalism, 173–74; tradition of, 352; and *vraisemblance* (verisimilitude), 173, 174–75
monarchy: between 1790 and 1870,
419; and annexation of Occitania,
16; and anti-royalist Fronde era,
178, 203, 263, 264; and Armand de
Bourbon, prince of Conti, 181; and
Bourbon dynasty, 181, 419, 437, 504;
and caste system, 363; and Catherine de Médicis, 121, 123, 132, 133,
134; and Catholicism, 157; and censorship, 351, 363; and Charles IX,
132, 133, 134; and Charles X, 432,
436; and coalition of European
monarchies, 425; and concentration
of power with king, 263, 269; and
the court, 8, 113, 121, 123, 214–15,
218–19, 224, 353, 361, 363, 428; and
death of François I, 120; and death
of Louis XII, 99; and death of Mazarin, 203; and defense of by Ronsard,
132; devotion to, 126, 165; and the
divine right of kings, 21–22, 45, 121;
and duties to king and feudal hierarchy, 21, 120; and essay "Of the Useful and the Honorable" (Montaigne), 165; and feudal system, 21,
45, 121, 269; and François I, 118,
123, 138, 256; and François II, 114;
and François's death, 119; and
French royal dynasty, 124; and Haitian government, 585; and Henri II,
113, 114, 121, 123, 126, 129, 214,
223; and Henri IV, 121, 161; and
Hobbes's body politic, 238; imperial
ambitions of, 159; and July Monarchy, 436–37, 441; and justification
for regicide, 160; and king in Diderot's novel, 388, 389; and liberal
monarchies, 432, 433; and Louis XI,
418; and Louis XII, 118; and Louis
XIV, 174, 178, 203, 214, 254, 255,
263, 269, 444–45, 518; and Louis
XV, 361, 374; and Louis XVI, 362,
363, 364, 365, 503; and Louis
Philippe, 432–33, 436–37; and Marguerite de Navarre's mother Louise
de Savoie, 97; and Marie Antoinette

as Queen, 333–34, 343, 363; and marriage of Marguerite de Navarre, 99; and monarch's administration, 8; and Napoleon Bonaparte, 419; and Orleans branch of royal family, 436; and painting of Eugène Delacroix, 439; and patronage of writers, 25–26, 91–92, 99, 121, 123, 176, 377; and Philippe d'Orleans, 340; power of, 203; and problems with issues raised by ancient works, 288; and proposals for Reform, 100; and protection of the court and aristocracy for *philosophes*, 376–77; and the Restoration, 428, 432; and royal council's problems with Diderot's *Encyclopédie*, 374; and royal permission for theater, 362, 364; and the seventeenth century, 11–12, 178–80, 203; and the sixteenth century, 119, 120–21, 132; and social order, 4, 28, 100, 179–80; and *Tartuffe* (Molière), 178–80; and theater, 178–180; and Turkish royal court, 338; and *Of Voluntary Servitude* (La Boétie), 160. *See also* absolutism; class; England; François I; Louis XIV

Montaigne, Michel de: as adviser to Henri of Navarre, 161; ancestral home of, 160; and anthropology, 164, 168; and the body, 166, 167; career of, 9, 25, 159, 160; and classical culture, 156, 158–59, 161, 162–67; and criticism, 39; and customs and cultures, 155, 157–58, 164, 257; death of, 162; and death of friend Etienne de La Boétie, 159–160, 161; education of, 158–59, 166; ego of, 230; and Epicureanism, 230; and essay "Apology for Raymond Sebond," 165; and essay "Des Cannibales," 3, 96, 257; and essay "Of Books," 166; and essay "Of Friendship," 160; and essay "Of Physiognomy," 166; *Essays* of, 68, 155–62, 408; and essay "The Apology for Raymond Sebondus," 159; and ethics, 155, 164, 165–66; and the everyday world, 167–68; and the familiar letter, 161; father of, 158, 159; and form of the essay, 161–62, 165; and French language, 23, 158; and humanism, 157, 158–59, 162, 166, 167–68; and importance of conversation, 166, 167; and inversion, 257; and judgment, 162, 164, 165, 165–66, 167; and knowledge of Latin, 158, 161; and limits of knowledge, 164–65; literary personality of, 155, 157, 158, 159, 165; as mayor, 160, 166; as a modern, 157, 164; and moral philosophy, 158, 164–65; and myth of "noble savage," 257; and philosophy, 130, 155–58, 159, 161–68, 257; as a political mediator, 160–61, 166; and prose style, 102, 152, 161–63, 168; and Pyrrhonism of Sextus Empiricus, 159; religion of, 165; and role of the face (countenance), 166, 167; and the self, 161, 165, 167–68, 241, 518; and skepticism, 157, 159, 168, 230; and sung poetry, 125; and toleration of ambiguity, 85, 164, 168; as a transitional figure, 157; and *Travel Journal* from Roman trip, 160; and Wars of Religion, 7, 156–57, 160–61; writers influenced by, 168

Moore, George, 617–18

moralists: and adventures of the self, 232; and brevity of writing forms, 238; and *Caractères* (La Bruyère), 248; and cultural authority, 234; and the eighteenth century, 229–30; and human excesses, 231; and illusions about oneself, 235; and La Fontaine,

moralists (*cont.*)
   230, 231–32; and life after death,
   248; and moralist writers, 230, 232,
   236, 248; and moralist writing, 229,
   230, 248; and people's motivations,
   232, 236; and power of imagination,
   235, 237, 239; and Saint-Evremond,
   233; and self in society, 236; and
   self-love, 231, 236; and truths of living, 234
More, Thomas, 54, 84, 85
Moriae encomium (*Praise of Folly*) (Erasmus), 48, 55
Musset, Alfred de, 16, 17, 28; and *La
   confession d'un enfant du siècle* (*Confessions of a Child of the Century*), 441,
   448; and play *Lorenzaccio*, 440; and
   roman personnel, 595; and Romantic
   movement, 448

Nadja (Breton), 554–56
Napoleon: and censorship, 37, 38; and
   court patronage, 27; and women's
   rights, 30
nation: and canon of the national classics, 9; and censorship during a national crisis, 38; and centralized state
   formation, 22; and communication
   between francophone nations, 24,
   646; and conservative nationalism,
   12; cultural life of, 29, 36; and
   French nationality, 637; and imperial competition, 147; and leaders,
   156; literary excellence as related to
   power of, 274; moral norms of, 284;
   and national identity, 21; and national language, 640, 641; and national literary culture, 7, 9, 11, 12–
   13, 14, 274; and national literature,
   46, 147; and national security, 100;
   and nation-state, 11, 113; and patronage of writers, 25–27; and Pléiade poets, 68; power of, 270; and

Proust's writing, 527; and relation
   with literature, 14, 26, 38, 270; and
   Ronsard's defense of religion and
   nation, 134; and Ronsard's golden-
   age renewal, 113, 117, 121; and Jean
   Vilar's *Théâtre national populaire*, 34;
   and Voltaire's funeral, 9–10
national literature: and alexandrine
   verse form, 127; and antiquity, 141;
   and competition between traditions,
   140, 141, 143, 144; and cyclical process of competition, 143, 147; and
   French poetry, 137, 140, 144; and
   French Renaissance, 141; as a hybrid
   of forerunners, 144; international
   nature of, 144; and national language, 23, 132
naturalism: and Gassendi, 230; and illusion of reality, 171–72, 174–75;
   and literary criticism, 41; and
   Molière, 173–74, 182; and natural
   limits, 171; and period of "nature"
   for theater, 172; and Racine, 191,
   198–99, 205–6, 208; and reconciliation of Epicurean naturalism with
   Christian principles, 230
nature: and *Atala* (Chateaubriand),
   504; and botany, 409–10; and *Les
   jardins, ou l'art d'embellir les paysages*
   (*Gardens, or the Art of Embellishing
   the Landscape*), 503–4; and metaphor
   of self-portraiture, 393; in relation
   to man, 395, 397; Rousseau's descriptions of, 394, 410; Rousseau's
   philosophy of, 405; and state of nature, 393–98; and *surnaturalisme* (supernaturalism), 471. *See also* Char,
   René
nausée, La (*Nausea*) (Sartre): and adventures, 604–5, 606, 612; and author
   Sartre, 630; and bad faith, 608, 612;
   and contrasting attitudes to the sky,
   598; and Cretan Liar paradox, 612;

and diary form, 595, 596, 597, 599, 606–7; and existential reality, 607, 609; and feeling of nausea, 601, 602–3, 609–10; and first-person narrator, 595, 596; hero of, 13, 595, 596, 602–8, 610, 611–12; and importance of stories, 603–6; and language, 607, 608, 609, 610; and metaphor, 598–99, 601, 608–9; and music, 612; and narrative as part of bourgeois culture, 613; original title of, 536; publication year of, 595, 599, 600; readership of, 599; and Russian Formalists, 608; and tension between living and telling, 611; and time, 605, 607, 610

negritude: and *Cahier d'un retour au pays natal* (*Notebook of a Return to the Native Land*), 581; and Aimé Césaire, 647; Césaire's questioning of, 575, 589; and "Discours sur la négritude"("Discourse on Negritude") (Césaire), 575–76, 583; and journal *L'Etudiant Noir* (The Black Student), 576; and Leopold Senghor, 647

neveu de Rameau, Le (*Rameau's Nephew*) (Diderot): and anti-*philosophes*, 387–88; and dialogue form, 383; and eighteenth-century Parisian culture, 389; and figure of the *philosophe*, 381, 384–89; framing narrative of, 384–86; and Goethe's *Rameaus Neffe*, 382, 383, 389; and jokes, 383, 387; and label of *philosophe*, 385–89; and mimes, 383–84, 388; narrator of, 384–86, 388–89; and the *pauvre diable* (poor devil), 389; and posterity, 381, 383; posthumous publishing of, 371, 383; and revenge on Palissot, 384; and satire, 383, 384, 389; secret existence of, 382; and social codes, 385, 389; and space of the cafe, 386,

387; and title *Satire seconde* (Second satire), 383; translations of, 382–83, 389

New Criticism, 22, 29, 38

newspapers: and absence of photo from Gallimard's *Marianne*, 540 fig. 1; and elections of 1824, 445–46; and fiction, 27, 213, 226, 464; *Le Figaro*, 515–16; *L'Humanité*, 549; and media in the 1930s, 535; *Mercure Galant*, 213, 226; and sensational serials, 27, 464; and social realities, 45; *Le Temps*, 522, 523, 529

Nietzsche, Friedrich: and Duthuit's journal *Transition*, 630; and language, 460; and moralists, 231; and *Will to Power*, 229; work of, 168, 496

novel: and adultery, 462, 464–65, 467; and American novelists, 518; and anglophone reader, 102; and architecture, 313, 317–19, 322–23; and aristocratic spaces, 316, 322; and bad faith, 610–11; and Balzac's *La comédie humaine*, 415; and Samuel Beckett, 14; and the bildungsroman, 303, 415, 417, 418, 420, 429, 432, 433n1; and the boudoir or bedroom, 312–21, 324–27; and *Candide* (Voltaire), 303, 309; comic novels, 254, 295, 296, 302, 383; and conversations, 213, 226–27; and *Corinne, ou l'Italie* (Staël), 330; and crime novels, 548; and *Delphine* (Staël), 342; and Assia Djebar, 14; and *L'écume des jours* (Vian), 599; and the eighteenth century, 312–28, 342, 353, 385; and emotions, 313, 315, 320–21, 342, 343; and enigma of love, 326–27; and enigma of the woman, 326–27; epistemic novels, 253; epistolary novel, 206, 312, 317, 318–24, 327, 342–43; and era of suspicion, 600–601; and experiments of Maurice novel (*cont.*)

Blanchot, 14; as favored by Caribbean writers, 589; and first-person
narrator, 239, 312, 314; Flaubert's
elevation of, 451–52; and Flaubert's
style, 10–11, 451–52, 461; and Félicité de Genlis, 337; and hierarchy of
genres, 44; and historical subject
matter, 214–17; and identification,
204; inclusiveness of, 521; and indecency, 77–78, 464, 514, 515; and interiority, 327; and interiorization,
312–13, 315, 316; and James Joyce,
517, 519; and Madame de Lafayette,
206, 212–13, 216–18; and Marie Leprince de Beaumont, 342; and libertine novel, 313, 315–20, 324–27; and
marriage, 212, 217, 320, 321–22,
324, 462, 467; and *Mémoire de Madame de Valmont* (Gouges), 334; and
memoir forms, 314–17, 342, 595;
and metafiction, 521; and metaphor
of stone, 601, 602, 613; and modern
novel, 595–613; and narration from
many points of view, 547; and narrative theory, 604–5; and narrator as
an exile, 262; and *Nedjma* (Yacine),
647; and *Le neveu de Rameau* (*Rameau's Nephew*) (Diderot), 373, 381–89;
and New Novel, 519; and the nineteenth century, 7, 217, 312, 326,
432–33, 455, 464; and the 1930s,
534, 535–36, 546–52; and the *nouveau roman*, 13, 600, 616; and novels
of Sade, 313, 314, 324–27; picaresque, 7, 312, 314, 315, 324; plots
of, 308–9, 312–13, 317–18, 343, 344;
and *La Princesse de Clèves* (Lafayette),
101–2, 212–17, 225; and printing industry, 27, 36; and private lives of
individuals, 30, 213, 315, 317–18,
321–24, 345; and private spaces, 312,
314, 315–22, 324–25; and problematic heros, 547; and Proust's writing,
519, 528; and psychological drama,
551–52; and the psychological impulse, 518; and psychology of character in fiction, 30, 317; and public
consumption of private conversation, 212, 213, 218; and Richardson's
Clarissa, 342; and Robbe-Grillet, 14,
519; and romances, 202, 215, 216,
219–20, 221, 342, 456; and *roman
feuilleton*, 27, 34; and Rousseauist
novel, 313, 320–24; and salon conversations, 215, 221; sentimental
novel, 320, 327; and Madeleine de
Scudéry, 202, 215; and the seventeenth century, 8, 202, 212–17; and
Simenon's crime novels, 536; and
Tencin's *Mémoires du comte de Comminge*, 342; and use of *je* (I), 529–30;
and *vraisemblance* (verisimilitude),
225, 343; women as readers of, 30;
and women's bodies, 313, 314–15;
and women's writing, 347. *See also*
Balzac, Honoré de; Flaubert, Gustave; *Princesse de Clèves, La* (Lafayette); women's writing

On the Sublime (Longinus), 282–83
Oraison à nostre seigneur Jesus Christ
(Prayer to Our Lord Jesus Christ)
(Marguerite de Navarre), 60

painting: and aesthetics, 278–79; and
Leon Bonnat, 441; and Bosch and
Brueghel paintings, 548–49; and
Boucher, 321; and *Burial at Ornans*
(Courbet), 466, 467 fig. 1; and cele-
brated painting *Le verrou* (Frago-
nard), 319; and *Corinne au Cap
Misène* (*Corinne at Cape Misenum*) by
Gérard, 330, 331–32; and Gustave
Courbet's realism, 466; and Jacques-
Louis David, 331; of Eugène Dela-

croix, 439, 471, 477, 648–49; and English painting, 255; and *Histoire de la peinture en Italie* (*The History of Painting in Italy*), 445; and liberty, 439; and the nineteenth century, 7; and *La peinture* (Perrault), 277; by Picasso, 649; and portrait by La Tour, 374; and portraits in *Le noble* (Charrière), 344; and portraits of great men, 166; and "Manon" Roland, 341; and Van Gogh, 571

Palissot, Charles: and accusations of plagiarism by Diderot, 374; and patrons of *philosophes*, 378–79; and play *Les philosophes*, 380, 387; and revenge on by Diderot, 384; work of, 381, 397

Pantagruel (Rabelais): and abolishing of human institutions of the Church, 57; and the Bible, 56, 57–58; characters of, 56, 71, 72, 75–77, 83, 86–87; and education, 159; and Erasmus, 52, 56, 57, 58; and fabulous events, 84; and faith, 57; and fear of being cuckolded, 76–77; genre of, 56; and humanistic education, 56, 79; and ideal Christian prince, 56; and language, 71, 72, 73, 87; and marriage advice for Panurge, 75–77; as medieval and popular, 56; and mockery, 82; and the moral life, 56, 58; and Pantagruel, 71, 72, 76, 83, 84; and pantagruelism, 85–86; prequel and sequels to, 58, 71; and the *Quart Livre Pantagruel*, 67–68, 71, 86; and silent debate, 75; themes of, 56, 71, 83; and the *Tiers livre*, 75–77, 83, 85; and toleration of ambiguity, 87–88; and Utopia, 56, 57, 58, 83; in vernacular language, 53, 56; and vulgar style, 53; and war, 56–57, 67, 71

Paris, France: academies in, 22, 117, 120, 577; in *Alcools* (*Alcohols*) (Apollinaire), 510; and Apollinaire's series of conversations in poem, 548; archdiocese of, 176; and author Césaire, 577, 581; and Balzac's hero Rastignac, 414–17; and Beaumarchais, 361; and Samuel Beckett, 14, 618, 619, 620; and the bildungsroman, 416–17, 420, 421; Emma Bovary's interest in, 458; and André Breton, 554–56, 561; and Canal Saint-Martin, 538; as center of French culture, 22, 25, 42, 270; and centralizing tendency, 45; and the Collège de France, 50; and court in Sceaux, 340; and Cyrano de Bergerac, 230; and Delille's funeral, 503; and the eighteenth century, 301–2, 353, 389; and Erasmus, 47, 55; and fashion, 266n2, 439–40; and figure of the *philosophe*, 375, 389; and francophone literature, 644, 645; and French language, 23; and Gassendi, 251; and Françoise de Graffigny, 346; Haussmann's changes to, 470, 476; high society of, 185, 414–15, 431; and Hugo's *Hernani*, 437; and humanism, 49, 50; and *Illusions perdues* (*Lost Illusions*) (Balzac), 428; and introduction of printing, 45; and Jolas's *Transition* group, 619; and journal *L'Etudiant Noir* (The Black Student), 576; and jurisdiction over Marguerite's court, 100; and La Bruyère, 230; and La Fontaine, 231, 254–55; and life of Mme de Staël, 332; major theaters of, 351, 441–42; and Marche aux Puces (flea market), 557; and Napoleon Bonaparte, 425; and nation's affairs, 22; and *Le neveu de Rameau* (*Rameau's Nephew*) (Diderot), 373, 382–83, 389; and opening of *Phèdre*, 191; and *Pantagruel* (Rabelais), 56, 72; and Paris Parlement,

Paris, France (*cont.*)
372, 374; and *Le paysan parvenu*
(Marivaux), 314; and *philosophes*, 339;
power transfer from Versailles to,
33; and printing, 36; and public
opinion, 288, 335; and public transportation system, 230; and publishing of *Candide* (Voltaire), 291; and
publishing of *Le neveu de Rameau*
(Diderot), 382; and realism, 416,
417; and review *Cosmopolis*, 496; and
Marie-Jeanne Riccoboni, 343; and
Romanticism, 437, 441–42, 446; and
Rousseau's books, 399, 403; and the
sixteenth century, 3; size of cultured
public of, 32; social scene of, 415–
16, 420; and spleen, 470; and St.
Bartholomew's Day massacre, 157;
and subscription libraries, 34; and
tale in newspaper *Mercure Galant*,
226; and theater, 351, 380; and *La
tragédie du roi Christophe* (Césaire),
586; and *Le spleen de Paris* (Baudelaire), 476; unrest in, 372; and Voltaire, 292; and *Voyage au bout de la
nuit* (Céline), 541, 542–43. *See also*
Bastille; Sorbonne
Parnasse contemporain, Le (*The Contemporary Parnassus*), 507
Pascal, Blaise: and death, 236; death of,
245, 246; and defense of Antoine Arnauld, 241, 242–43, 245; and *De
l'ésprit géometrique*, 232; and divine
grace, 245, 247, 248; and efforts to
convert libertines and skeptics, 244–
45; as an engaged intellectual, 243–
44; and fate of humanity, 247; and
God, 239–40, 241, 244–45, 247; and
humans' desires, 244, 247; and illusions about oneself, 235; as inventor
and designer, 230; and *Lettres provinciales*, 241–43; as a lone voice, 243–
44; as a moralist, 230, 233; and ori-

gin of politics, 246–47, 248; *Pensées*
of, 184, 244–47, 248; and power of
imagination, 237, 246, 247; readership of, 243; and the seventeenth
century, 168, 243; and theological
and political issues, 243, 247–48; and
writings on math and physics, 245.
See also *Pensées* (Pascal)
paysan parvenu, Le (Marivaux): and encounter between Jacob and Mme de
Ferval, 314–15; and interiority, 315;
and married life, 315; and the
memoir-novel, 314; and the picaresque novel, 314, 315; and private
spaces, 314–15, 317; and the psychological novel, 314
peintre de la vie moderne, Le (*The Painter
of Modern Life*) (Baudelaire), 474–75,
508
Pensées (Pascal), 184; and apologies for
Christian religion, 244; as a collection of reflections, 244, 245; as a defense of Christian faith, 545; fragmentary nature of, 245–46, 247, 248;
and headings of reflections, 245,
247; and the human condition, 545;
and imagination, 246, 247; and origin of politics, 246, 247; two copies
of, 246, 247
Pensées philosophiques (Diderot), 337,
372
Pensées sur l'interpretation de la nature
(*Thoughts on the Interpretation of Nature*) (Diderot), 373
père Goriot, le (Balzac): and hero Rastignac's social ascent, 414–17, 429,
431; and Paris, 415–16, 420
periodization, 15, 18
Perrault, Charles: and aesthetics, 277,
278, 280, 281, 283; and the century,
15; and *Contes de ma mere l'oye*
(*Mother Goose's Tales*), 336; fairy tales
of, 224, 225, 270, 281, 336; and geo-

metric principles, 279; and immorality of classical tragedy, 287; and importance of intellectual design, 278–79; and literary and artistic criticism, 277; and literary criticism, 277, 278; and Louis XIV, 275; as a Modern, 8, 271, 272, 273, 274, 277–81, 283–84; and modern "method," 279; and moral point of literature, 280, 281; and music, 279; and neoclassicism, 281; and *Parallèle des anciens et des modernes* (Parallel of the ancients and the moderns), 271, 273, 277, 278, 280; and poem "Le siècle de Louis Le Grand," 270; and reason on top, 277, 278; religious epic of, 280–81; and *Le siècle de Louis le Grand*, 8; and theory of human progress, 273; and translation, 284

Petrarch: and *Canzone delle visioni* (*Song of Visions*), 150–51; creation and destruction in work of, 151; cultural role of, 144; diversity of, 131; and Joachim du Bellay, 121–22, 148, 149, 150; and emptiness of earthly beauty, 150; imitations of, 69, 117, 121, 148, 149; and love poetry, 117, 123, 149; as a modern European poet, 4, 11; and Montaigne, 158; and Petrarchan sonnet, 4, 121, 123, 139, 148–49, 152, 500; and Pierre de Ronsard, 113, 117, 121, 122; and Tuscan dialect, 148; and Vauclusian region, 564; and versification, 150

Phèdre (Racine): and Barthes's critique, 205–6; and characters' uncertainty, 200; and destiny, 193–94, 202; and divine agency, 192, 194–95; and early modern period, 7, 194; and Euripides's plot, 192–93, 195, 197; and fate of Hippolytus, 194–95, 207; and French classicism, 190–91, 197; and heroine's desire, 190, 192–96,

207, 208; and heroine's tragedy, 195, 207, 208; and *Hippolyte* (Gilbert), 197; and identification, 207; and myth of Phaedra, 194–95, 202; and name of play, 208; and opening of in Paris, 191; and pagan gods, 192–93, 194, 196, 197–98; and passions, 194–98, 207; and Phèdre's suicide attempt, 196; popularity of, 191; and speaking, 195–99; as a tragedy, 190–98, 205

philosophe: and d'Alembert on relationship with patron, 377–78; and anti-*philosophes*, 387–88, 389; and atheism, 379; and autonomy as not important, 377; and eighteenth century Parisian culture, 375; and figure of in *Le neveu de Rameau* (Diderot), 385–89; and Lespinasse's letters, 339; and *Nouveaux mémoires pour servir a l'histoire des Cacouacs* (Moureau), 379; and the *pauvre diable* (poor devil), 384; and play *Le café ou l'Ecossaise* (Voltaire), 380–81; and play *Les philosophes* (Palissot), 380, 387; and poverty, 378, 381; and protection of the court and aristocracy, 376–79, 381; and rise of the anti-*philosophes*, 380–81; and salons, 381; and satire, 375, 381; as a sociable figure, 376, 377–78; as speaking truth to power, 375–76

philosophy: and abstraction, 166, 167; aesthetic philosophy, 208; age of, 269; and Jean le Rond d'Alembert, 371, 377–78; and antiquity, 269–70; and Aristotle, 125, 207, 224, 234; and Henri Bergson, 525; and the body, 166; and Tommaso Campanella, 253; and Cartesian method, 155–56, 163, 168, 232; and Catholic faith, 337; and Christianity, 168, 233; and classical ideals, 167, 168, philosophy (*cont.*)

729, and condemnation of torture, 164; and *Contes philosophiques* (Voltaire), 40; and corporeal existence, 251; and Descartes, 250–51, 276, 279; and *Discours sur l'origine et les fondements de l'inégalité parmi les hommes* (Rousseau), 393; and *divisio*, 77, 80, 81, 82; and empiricism, 22, 39, 269, 295, 395, 409; and English philosophy and literature, 300; and Enlightenment, 405; and Epicureanism, 230, 261; and *Essays* (Montaigne), 155, 158, 159, 161–68, 393; and ethics, 155, 165–66; and European literature, 155; and existentialism, 41, 600; and fairy tales, 224; and free will, 183; and French thought, 22, 39, 49, 96, 460; and Gassendi, 250–51, 276; and Hegel, 208; and Hobbes, 86, 182, 247, 396; and human experience, 232; and humanism, 49, 64, 183; and human nature, 29, 43, 94, 110, 186–187, 188, 229, 230, 393, 395–96, 398, 407, 411; and human rationality, 224–25; and ideal of poet as seer and intellectual, 116–17; and illusions about oneself, 235; and immanence, 171, 172–73, 247; and Italian Giorgio Agamben, 446; and Kant, 208, 378; and knowledge, 75, 155, 251, 378; and Etienne de La Boétie, 160; and learning from experience, 304; and Leibniz's divine order, 308; and *Lettres philosophiques* (Voltaire), 294; and libertines, 182, 229–32, 234; and Lisbon earthquake, 297; and literature, 286–87; and John Locke, 295, 396; and love and friendship, 265; and Marguerite de Navarre, 97; and materialism, 182, 184, 261, 325, 409–10; and maxim *ambulo ergo sum*, 250–51,

261, 266; and metaphysics, 171, 234, 266, 373; and modern philosophy, 155–56; and modern science, 251; and modes of philosophical narrative, 93, 96; and Montaigne, 130, 155–58, 159, 161–68, 257, 393; and Montesquieu, 294, 295; and moral and religious beliefs as relative, 257; and moralists, 229–34; moral, 49, 158, 168, 229; and natural laws, 43, 327, 348, 396; and natural man, 393–94, 396, 398, 405–6; and *Le neveu de Rameau* (*Rameau's Nephew*) (Diderot), 383; and novel *Le triomphe de la verité ou histoire de M. de La Villete* (Leprince de Beaumont), 337; and optimism, 292, 296, 297, 298, 301; and *Pantagruel* (Rabelais), 71; and Pascal, 168; and pessimism, 627; and philosopher Raymond Sebondus, 159; and *philosophes*, 294, 375–76; and the *philosophia Christi* (philosophy of Christ), 48–49; and *La philosophie dans le boudoir* (*Philosophy in the Bedroom*) (Sade), 324–26; and philosophical poetry, 113, 130; and poetry, 125, 277–78; and positivism, 6, 22, 40; and postmodernism, 156; and power, 168; and power of imagination, 235, 237; and problem of evil, 296, 297; and the "Province of the Philosophers," 253; and Pyrrhonism of Sextus Empiricus, 157; and Quarrel of the Ancients and the Moderns, 270, 272–73; and rational thought, 43, 168, 269, 273, 277, 373–74; and reason, 232, 237, 244, 269, 270, 273, 277, 376, 505; and revolutionary disenchantment, 172; and the sciences, 278, 396; and the seventeenth century, 8, 33, 43, 229, 234, 266; and shaping of French culture, 375; and skepticism,

157, 159, 168, 230, 304; and social and political order, 236, 351, 398; and social engagement, 167–68; and state of nature, 393, 394–98, 406, 411; and Stoics, 165; and thought of Montesquieu, Vico, and Hume, 272; and *Traité des sensations* (Condillac), 345; and trust in human will, 83; and truth claims, 155, 251; and truths of living, 234, 408–9; and Turkish philosopher in *Candide* (Voltaire), 305–6; and virtue, 159, 165, 167; and work of Cyrano de Bergerac, 260; and the world of the everyday, 167–68, 234; and writing in the Enlightenment, 351. *See also* Aristotle; Diderot, Denis; existentialism; Foucault, Michel; humanism; Montaigne, Michel de; nature; Rousseau, Jean-Jacques

philosophy dans le boudoir, La (*Philosophy in the Bedroom*) (Sade), 324–26, 327

Pindar: cultural role of, 144; and lyric poetry, 125; and Ronsard's odes, 124

Pizan, Christine de: and defense of women's rights, 29; and representation of women, 8

Plato: and denunciation of Homer, 277; ideas of, 171; and *The Republic*, 277, 280, 287, 396

Pléiade poets: *La deffence et illustration de la langue francoyse* as manifesto for, 147; and Joachim du Bellay, 4, 137–52, 138; and imitation of the poets of Greco-Roman antiquity, 138; and king and nation, 68; and the Merchant Taylors' School, 152; and mission to establish sonnet, 139; and Petrarchan sonnet, 149; poets of, 137; and the Renaissance, 68, 69, 137; and the Romantics, 43; and Pierre de Ronsard, 4, 125, 137, 138; and women writers, 29

Poe, Edgar Allen, 470, 471, 477

Poetics (Aristotle): and *anagnorisis*, 224; and classical rules for theater, 442–43; and comedy, 442; and compassion and horror, 195; and imitation, 144–45, 443; and three unities, 171; and tragedy, 224, 442

poetry: and the *Aeneid* (Virgil), 66, 73; and aesthetics, 279–80; and Alexandrian poets, 138; and ancient poetry as flawed to Perrault, 280; and *Les antiquitez de Rome* (*The Antiquities of Rome*), 149–50, 151; and Aristotle, 125, 282; and *Canzone delle visioni* (*Song of Visions*), 150–51; and Christian verse epic, 280; and classical poetry, 68, 78, 114–17, 162; and collage and paste-up poetics, 162; and collection *Les armes miraculeuses* (*Miraculous Weapons*) (Césaire), 584; and Vittoria Colonna, 91; and Gontran Damas, 577; and decasyllabic line, 115–16, 118, 126, 128, 151; versus dialectical logic, 49; and *Discours sur l'ode* (Boileau), 284; and Etienne Dolet, 100; and English blank verse, 119; and free verse, 4, 484; French language as vehicle for, 23, 68; and geometric principles of the Moderns, 279–80; and Edmund Gosse, 501; and Greco-Latin epic hexameter, 127; and Homeric and Virgilian epic, 123; and Homeric world, 275, 276; and ideal of poet as seer and intellectual, 116–17; and imagination, 504; and imitation, 144–46, 285; and impressionism, 483; and indecency, 77–78; and influence of Petrarch, 4, 117; and influence of Poe on Baudelaire, 470; and intuition, 284, 288; and Italian poetry, 140, 152; and Gustave Kahn, 484; and Etienne de La Boétie, 160; and La Fontaine, poetry (*cont.*)

252; and Latin poets, 274; and
Lettres à sa femme (*Letters to Madame
de La Fontaine*) , 260; and love and
peace, 124–25; love, 117, 121, 123,
124, 126; lyric, 21, 39, 113, 117,
125, 506; as a male domain, 31; of
Marguerite de Navarre, 59–61, 64–
65, 92, 97, 101; of Clement Marot,
65–67, 117; and meter, 21, 126, 128,
151, 477; Montaigne's love of, 158;
and morals of the ancients, 285–
286; and music, 113, 116, 121, 122,
124, 125–28, 270, 501–2; and national literary culture, 274; and
Noigrandres group of Brazilian
poets, 510–11; and odes, 113, 114,
115–16, 117, 121, 123, 125, 126,
284; and odes of Horace, 78, 114–
15; and order, clarity and correctness, 278; and origins of poetic language, 472; and pastoral poems,
118–19; and Jacques Peletier du
Mans, 120; and Petrarchan poems,
121, 158, 500; and philosophical
poetry, 113, 116–17, 123, 125, 297;
and Pléiade poets' promotion of the
sonnet, 139; and poetic theory, 567;
and poet's role, 503, 506–8; and political poetry, 113, 132, 139; popularity of, 27; and prosodic and
rhythmic forms, 116, 476–77; and
"pure" poetry, 499–500; and Quarrel of the Ancients and the Moderns, 277; and relation with political
good, 270; and Renaissance poets, 3,
21; as revolutionary, 470; and rhythmic forms, 3, 127, 501–2; and Romanticism, 438, 441, 470, 507; and
Leopold Senghor, 575; and shape of
alexandrine, 475; and sonnet form,
148–151, 152, 206, 500–501; and
Sonnets (Shakespeare), 152; and

Spanish poetry, 140, 152; and the
sublime, 283–86; and *surnaturalisme*
(supernaturalism), 471, 474; and
surrealists, 536; on tombstones, 107;
and translation from Latin, 139; of
the twentieth century, 162; and vanity, 264; and *vers impair*, 478–80;
and Western tradition, 122. *See also*
Boileau, Nicolas; Césaire, Aimé;
epic poems; French poetry; Marguerite de Navarre; Petrarch

politics: and absolutism, 36, 43, 263;
and Action Française movement,
535, 549; and Algerian Communist
Party, 536; and Algerian conflicts
with Islamists, 641; and anticolonialist concept of *négritude*, 575–76;
and Aristotle, 125; and attack on
democracy, 592; and authors as
members of society, 25, 28, 113,
165–66, 376; and battle of *Hernani*
(Hugo), 440; and Caribbean islanders' choice regarding government,
579; and Catholic Church, 156; and
censorship, 36–38; and Aimé Césaire, 577–80; and Chiang Kai-shek
versus Comintern, 544; and chief
minister Richelieu, 221; and Chinese Communists, 544; and coalition of European monarchies, 425;
and communism in *Voyage au bout
de la nuit* (Céline), 538; and *La condition humaine* (Malraux), 546–47;
and conquest via expeditions, 256–
57; and *Considérations sur les principaux événements de la Révolution
française* (Staël), 333; and crises of
the 1930s, 534–35; and Cyrano de
Bergerac, 263; and *Déclaration des
droits de la femme et de la citoyenne*
(Gouges), 334; and democratic participation, 43; and different governmental systems, 419; and "Discours

sur la négritude" ("Discourse on Negritude") (Césaire), 575–76; and elections of 1824, 445–46; and Eluard in Communist Party, 562; and epic poetry, 132; and *Essays* (Montaigne), 158; and European nationalism, 640; and failed Communist Shanghai insurrection, 546, 547, 550, 551; and fascist values, 627; and French and Haitian revolutions compared, 581; and French Communist Party, 535, 549, 578, 629; and French Resistance, 562, 564, 631; and the Fronde, 178, 203, 263; and *Gargantua* (Rabelais), 58; and Girondin government, 340; and Hobbes's version of man as a wolf to other men, 247; and importance of salons, 221; and issues of translation and interpretation, 74; and La Fontaine, 263–64; and Lamartine as minister of foreign affairs, 505–6; and leftist coalition Popular Front, 552; and leftist critiques of novels, 549; and *The Leviathan* (Hobbes), 182; and literature, 151–52, 534–35, 549–50; and Machiavelli's thought, 158, 173; and Marie Antoinette as Queen, 333–34; and Marguerite de Navarre, 91, 96, 97; and marriage, 99; and *The Marriage of Figaro* (Beaumarchais), 368; and Marxism, 630; and modern conception of self, 29; and Montaigne, 165–66; and moral doctrine, 233; and Napoleon Bonaparte, 419–23; and the 1960s, 85; and novels, 549; and Pascal's *Pensées*, 246–48; and persecution, 306; and pessimism of the aristocracy, 203; and *philosophes*, 381; and poet's role, 28, 505, 506; and political change, 43; and political engagement, 155,

376; and political legitimacy, 419, 420; and political passions, 204; and political poetry, 113, 132, 139; and political rhetoric, 159; and political satire, 123, 586; and power, 33, 38, 423, 436, 587, 588; and Quarrel of the Ancients and the Moderns, 270, 285; and rebirth in Renaissance, 137; and republicanism, 288, 470; and the Restoration, 426, 432–33; and revolutionary action, 597; and revolutionary disenchantment, 172; and Revolution as heroine of novel, 534; and revolution of 1848, 466, 470; and rise of Louis-Napoleon, 506; and "Manon" Roland's *Mémoires particuliers*, 341; and Roman culture, 275; Rousseau's programs for, 398; and salons as havens for men of letters, 377; and the Seven Years' War, 299–300, 374; and sexual politics, 102; and social contract, 247; and socialist principles, 28; and Soviet communism, 596, 621–22, 631; and stable state, 122, 178; and surrealism, 560; and *Tartuffe* (Moliere), 178, 179; and territorial expansion, 256; and the *Theologico-Political Treatise* (Spinoza), 182; and theory of human progress, 272; and *La tragédie du roi Christophe* (Césaire), 586; and training for public service, 156; and uncertainty, 427; and universally valid laws, 351; and violence, 596; and Wars of Religion, 156–57, 166; and works of Sartre and Camus, 597; and writings of Erasmus, 48. *See also* Césaire, Aimé; monarchy; nation; state

Pope, Alexander, 271, 296
Port-Royal group, 8, 245
Portugal, 256–57

Princesse de Clèves, La (Lafayette): anonymous publishing of, 217–18; aristocratic conversation in, 222; aristocratic families in, 214–15; and attack by critic Valincour, 213; and central character's interiority, 217, 220; central scene of, 212, 213, 214; and characters' emotions, 212, 216, 217, 220; and court culture, 214–15, 220, 223, 226; and drawing on romance tradition, 219–20; and eavesdropping culture, 212, 220, 222–23; fame of, 202, 212–13; form of, 215, 216–17; impersonal narrative of, 217; and newspaper *Mercure Galant*, 213, 226; and pessimism, 203; plot of, 213–14, 216–17, 218, 220, 223; and public consumption of private conversation, 212, 213, 218; readership of, 212–15, 216, 218; and role of gossip, 214, 218, 220; and surveillance scenes, 218–19, 220; and *vraisemblance* (verisimilitude), 225; and women's conversation, 223; and women's writing, 109, 217

printing: and authors' wages, 25; and censorship, 26, 36–37; and chapbooks, 33–34; and clandestine printing of *Candide* (Voltaire), 292; and the Declaration of the Rights of Man, 37; and Estienne dynasty, 36; and Gutenberg, 35; introduction of, 21, 31, 35, 45; invention of, 9; and licenses required to print, 26; and poetic meters, plays, and novels, 36; and printing press, 59; and printing revolution of 1830s, 35; and Renaissance scholars, 35; and rise of books on moral doctrine, 234; and runs for novels, 27; in the sixteenth century, 32; and spread of Luther's ideas, 36; and

standardization of language, 35–36; state control of, 26; and technologies, 27, 35

Prisons, Les (Marguerite de Navarre), 59, 61, 64–65

Prix Goncourt, 536–37, 539–40, 551–52

prosody: details of, 5; forms of, 3, 20, 123, 126; and Pierre de Ronsard, 4, 113, 122, 123; rules of, 122. *See also* genre

Protestantism: and Lyons, 36; and Protestant orthodoxy, 67; and Protestant Reformation, 257; and support of England, 157; and tension between Protestants and Catholics, 160–61; and wars between Protestants and Catholics, 156–57, 215

Proust, Marcel: and Académie française, 634; and comparisons with Rousseau, Montaigne, and Saint-Simon, 518; and *Contre Sainte-Beuve*, 522; death of, 517, 518, 535; and distinction between voluntary and involuntary memory, 523–24; essays and collection of, 519; and exploration of consciousness, 517–18; and fictional painter Elstir, 598; and French prose, 13, 536; and historical time, 18; and indecency, 521; and *A la recherche du temps perdu* (*In Search of Lost Time*), 13, 514–18, 520–30; and *A l'ombre des jeunes filles en fleur* (*In the Shadow of Young Girls in Flower*), 536; and main character's homosexuality, 521; and male homosexuality, 522; and metafiction, 521; as model for Beckett, 626–27; and music, 612; and narrative experiments, 600, 611; and novel's form, 519; and "On Some Motifs in Baudelaire" (Benjamin), 524–25; and passage of time, 522–23; and pessimism, 627; and preface "Sur la lecture" ("On Reading"), 520; and the Prix Goncourt, 536; and social realities, 45; society columns of, 515–16; and translation of Ruskin's works, 519–20

publishing industry: and advent of Internet, 38; and alliance with writers, 35; and authors' copyrights, 25, 27; and book trade supervised by royal officials, 36; and censorship, 26; and centralizing tendency, 36; and Césaire's *Présence Africaine* , 577; and clandestine printing of *Candide* (Voltaire), 292; and the comte d'Argenson, 372–73; and different genres, 44; and e-forms of books, 46; and eighteenth-century book market, 292; and eighteenth-century publishers, 9; and Estienne dynasty, 36; and expansion of reading public, 9, 27, 31–35; and Pierre Gruget's *Heptameron*, 93; and indecency, 514–15; Jesuits in, 373; and *A la recherche du temps perdu* (*In Search of Lost Time*), 514–16, 518; and the *libraires'* offer of editorship to Diderot, 372; and licenses to print, 26; and literary market, 44; and new careers with the rise of the middle class, 26; and *Nouvelle Revue Française* (*NRF*), 514, 515, 516, 518, 537, 538–39, 619; and obscenity, 222; and printing, 9, 21, 25, 26, 35; and the Prix Goncourt, 537; as a production line, 29; and readership, 31, 43, 44, 46; and rise of the Internet, 45; and scholar-printer-publishers, 36; and technologies, 9, 35; and Voltaire's *Candide*, 291, 292; and women's writing, 345–47; and work of Pierre Boiastuau, 92. *See also* Gallimard; printing

Quarrel of the Ancients and the Moderns: and the ancien regime, 440; and ancient literature as battleground, 286, 288, 447; and the Ancient party, 275, 282, 283, 287; and ancient values, 273, 280; and arguments of Diderot and Rousseau, 286–87; and artistic progress, 287; Nicolas Boileau as central figure of, 270–71, 272, 274–76, 281–85; and classical verse tragedy, 270–71; and didacticism, 284–85; and the eighteenth century, 272, 288; and emergence of aesthetics, 277, 288; and English debate, 271–72; and French opera, 270; and geometric principles of the Moderns, 279–80; and Greco-Roman divide, 275; and Homeric Greece as apex for Ancients, 273, 274, 275; and literary history, 275, 288; and modernity, 275; and Modern party, 273, 275, 283, 284–85, 287, 288; and *Parallèle des anciens et des modernes* (Perrault), 271; and Charles Perrault, 271, 272, 274, 277–81, 283, 284, 285; and poem "Le siècle de Louis le Grand," 270; and public opinion, 288; and reading public, 287–88; and relation of literature with history, 272; and relation of literature with the philosophical good, 270; and role of literature and the arts, 277, 288; and split between humanities and sciences, 276–77; and the sublime, 283, 285, 286; and support for values of clarity, reason and moral propriety, 281, 282; and Swift's satire *The Battle of the Books*, 271–72; and theory of human progress, 272–73; and the twentieth century, 610

quarrels: of the Ancients and the Moderns, 8–9, 16, 30, 40, 270–88, 440, quarrels (*cont.*)

445; and *Le Cid* (Corneille), 172,
287; and *De l'Allemagne* (*On Germany*) (Mme de Staël), 12; and
Diderot at center of culture war,
375; and discussion about *La Princesse de Clèves* (Lafayette), 213; and
hierarchy of genres, 39; and literary
self-consciousness, 9; and Molière's
L'école des femmes, 287; and morality
of theater, 175–76, 178; and pastoral
and satirical as losers, 39; and poem
"Le siècle de Louis le Grand" (Perrault), 270; and the quarrel du
Roman de la Rose, 8, 29; and the *querelle des amyes*, 29; and the *querelle des
bouffons*, 379; and Rousseau's problem with Hume, 399; and spread of
from Paris, 22; and superiority of
noble and heroic, 39; and *Tartuffe*
(Molière), 287; and verse over prose,
39

Quatre premiers livres des odes (Ronsard): of 1550, 121, 122; *First Book*
of, 116, 123, 126; and France's
wealth and power, 121; and lyric poetry, 113; and odes of Horace, 114–
15; success of, 114; third book of,
126

Quebec, Canada: and authors, 637;
Britain and France in, 299; and language choice, 24; as part of francophone world, 637, 640–41

Rabelais, François, 56; and (anti)mo-
nastic community in *Gargantua*, 83,
95; and the body, 166; and character
of Panurge, 77, 86–87; and Christianity, 80, 83; as a comic author, 51–
52, 71, 76, 80, 86; death of, 68, 71,
78; and *divisio*, 82; as a doctor, 25,
71; and education in *Pantagruel* and
Gargantua , 159; education of, 53,

78; enemies of, 67, 100; and Erasmus's influence, 52, 59, 62, 63, 68,
78; as evangelical, 62, 63; and the
Gothic world, 83, 84; as a Hellenist,
53, 78; and the *Heptameron* (Marguerite de Navarre), 102; and
human institutions of the Church,
66, 80; and humanism, 62, 63, 83,
156; and human will, 83, 86–87; and
irony, 58; and issues of translation
and interpretation, 75; and language,
83–84; and letter to Erasmus, 53;
misogynist elements of, 85; and
modern elements, 85, 88; and pantagruelism, 85–88; and polyglossia,
11, 84; and popular culture, 62–63;
and prose style, 102, 152; and the
Quart Livre Pantagruel, 58, 67–68,
71; and relationship with Marguerite de Navarre, 100; and Renaissance evangelism, 63; and ribald
epics, 52; and road to modernity, 18,
19; and satire, 66; scholarly works
of, 53; and seriousness of works, 81–
82; and Sorbonne's banning of
books, 78; and toleration of ambiguity, 85, 87–88; and translations of
works, 72, 74; and Wars of Religion,
7; writing style of, 62–63, 71–72. See
also *Gargantua* (Rabelais); *Pantagruel*
(Rabelais)

race: and anticolonialist concept of
négritude, 575–76, 647; and Caribbean blacks, 584, 647; and journal
L'Etudiant Noir (The Black Student),
576; and problems, 45; varieties of,
395. *See also* negritude; racism;
slavery

Racine, Jean: and alexandrine verse
form, 126, 205–6; as an Ancient, 9,
205, 209n2, 271; and aposiopesis,
200; and Aristotelian tradition, 207;
and Barthes's critique, 195, 205–6;

and *Britannicus*, 201–2; and characters' motivations, 205; and characters' naturalness, 198–99, 205, 206, 208, 233; cultural role of, 505; and destiny, 205; and divine agency, 192, 194; and emotional speech, 200, 201, 202; as ennobled, 26; as France's foremost tragedian, 191; and French classicism, 209; and French language, 619; and guilt, 196, 205; heroes of, 203, 207; and human will, 193–94; and identification, 202, 204, 207, 208; and Jansenism, 193, 203; and job of royal historiographer, 191; and mindset of his time, 191; as modern in his day, 191, 205; and myth as source, 192, 194–95, 202; and pagan gods in plays, 192–95, 205; and *Phèdre*, 9, 190–95, 197, 199–202, 205, 207–9; plots of, 206; and preface "Sur la lecture" ("On Reading") (Proust), 520; and representations of passions, 191, 194, 195–96, 201–5, 206, 207–9; and Romantic manifesto *Racine and Shakespeare* (Stendhal), 190; and seventeenth-century Christian theatergoers, 192; and tragedy, 204, 204–9, 536; verse of, 206

Racine et Shakespeare (Stendhal), 190, 191, 444, 445

racism: and analysis of Caribbean racism, 581; and colonialism, 581–82; and dehumanization, 576, 581; effects of, 591; and imperial expansion, 575

reading public: and anglophone reader, 190; and chapbooks, 33–34; and the common reader, 1–2; composition of, 33, 34, 35, 43; and demand for emotion, 40; and demand for fiction, 229, 240; and divisions of readers, 31; expansion of, 9, 27, 34, 35, 229,

240; industrial working class as market for, 34; liberal views of, 38–39; and literacy rates, 32, 33, 34; and literary and theatrical quarrels, 271, 287; and Pascal's letters, 243; and posterity, 516–17; and *La Princesse de Clèves* (Lafayette), 212–15; and readers of *Candide* (Voltaire), 291, 292; and reception theorists, 32; and salon speech, 222; in the seventeenth century, 33, 203–5, 229, 240, 282; in the sixteenth century, 32; and values of *honnêteté*, 33; and Voltaire's *Candide*, 291–92, 294; and writing on practical ways of life, 229, 240

realism: and Balzac, 451, 466; and bildungsroman, 420, 429; in *Don Quixote* (Cervantes), 86; and expansion of reading public, 34; and French literature, 415–418; and French narrative, 102, 466; and importance of language, 466–67; and *Madame Bovary* (Flaubert), 451–68; and the nineteenth-century novel, 7, 465–68; and painter Courbet's realism, 466; as a radical concept, 465–66; and Reformist theology, 110; and role of literature, 41, 465; and Scarron's *Roman comique*, 33; and sensual uses of the body parts, 463; and Stendhal's aesthetics, 426; and the Universal Exposition of 1855, 466; and women writers, 31; and work of Flaubert, 451–68; and Zola, 451

religion: and actors as subject to excommunication, 176; and the "Affair of the Placards" by Swiss radicals, 100; and Algerian conflicts with Islamists, 641; and Arabic as sacred language, 641; and atheism, 230, 241, 373; and authority of Church teaching, 182; and authors as mem-

religion (*cont.*)
bers of society, 25, 80, 94, 230, 239–
40, 373; and Marie de Beaumont as
educator, 336–37; and belief in God,
44, 57, 60, 63, 64, 94, 240, 244–45;
and belief in pagan gods, 194–95;
and the Bible, 50, 52, 53, 55, 73–74,
498; and Emma Bovary's readings,
455; and the cabal of the devout
(Company of the Holy Sacrament),
181; and Catholic Church, 74, 114;
and Catholicism, 22, 66, 67–68, 73,
230, 484; and Catholic missionaries,
257; and censorship, 36–37, 372,
373; and Christian environment in
France, 229; and Christianity, 52, 54,
79–80, 233, 244, 296; and Christian
sects and heresies, 466; and Christian verse epic, 280–81; and chronology in the Christian era, 18; and
clash between moral philosophy and
scholastic theology, 49; and *Colloquia*
(*Conversations*) (Erasmus), 54–55;
and *Comédie de Mont-de-Marsan*, 64;
conflicts in, 21, 67–68, 74, 91, 93,
156, 160–61, 215; and convents, 361,
368, 373; and the Council of Trent,
156; and Counter-Reformation, 86,
230; and creationism in the U.S.,
297; and creatures of God, 254; and
criminal character of Vautrin, 430;
and cruelty of zealots, 164; and the
Crusades, 257; and debate over quietism, 30; and destiny, 193–94; and
Diderot's *Encyclopédie*, 374; and dispute between Calvinists and Catholics, 51; and divine Creator, 171,
297; and divine Providence, 296–97;
and *Don Juan*, 180–84; and du Bellay's metaphor for literature, 146–
47; and Enlightenment, 337, 351;
and *Les Etats et Empires de la Lune*
(*The States and Empires of the Moon*),

260, 262; and *Les Etats et Empires du
Soleil* (*The States and Empires of the
Sun*), 253, 260; and evangelism, 57,
61, 62–63, 66, 67, 110; and execution of Lutherans, 66; and exiled papacy in Avignon, 149; and existence
of God, 296, 297, 304–5, 308; and
faith, 94, 108, 184, 230, 337, 341,
374, 423, 545; and the Fall, 478; and
female mysticism, 61; and the
French Church, 21–22; and French
Renaissance, 49; and French Revolution, 43; and *Gargantua* (Rabelais),
58, 59, 62; and God as no longer
center of universe, 231; and God in
Don Juan (Molière), 182; and God in
his place, 297; and God/Jupiter, 129;
and the gods, 20, 129, 192–94; and
grace of God, 60, 62, 63, 66, 109,
193, 241, 245, 247; and the *Heptameron* (Marguerite de Navarre), 95,
102, 108–9; and Victor Hugo, 506;
and human institutions of the
Church, 50–51, 57, 59; and human
will, 193–94; and humor, 68; and
ideal of poet as seer and intellectual,
116; and identification of Nature
with God, 118; and immortality,
260; and inquisitions, 68; and Islam,
634–35, 641; and issues of translation and interpretation, 73–75; and
Jansenism, 193, 203; and Jesuit missionaries, 257; and Jesuit priests,
241, 243; and Jesuits' attacks on
Diderot, 374; and Judaism, 51; and
Judeo-Christian antiquity, 50; and
Judgment Day for Rousseau, 403;
and Julien in *Le rouge et le noir*
(Stendhal), 421, 422, 423, 429; as
king as God's surrogate in defense
of secular society, 179–80; and Leibniz's divine order, 308; and *Lettres à
sa femme* (*Letters to Madame de La*

Fontaine) (La Fontaine), 255; and libertines, 229, 230; and Lisbon earthquake, 297; and literary history, 43, 266; and love, 57, 62, 66–67, 236; and Lutheranism, 50, 61, 62, 66, 68; and monastic life, 83; and Montaigne, 165–66; and Moses, 505, 507; and original sin, 231, 236, 340; and paganism in poetry and the arts, 288; and *Pantagruel* (Rabelais), 56, 67–68; and *philosophes*, 375, 381; and the *philosophia Christi* (philosophy of Christ), 48–49; and poems of Marguerite de Navarre, 60–61; and poetry, 60–61, 506, 508; and Port-Royal group, 8; and power, 94; and printing of works, 32, 35, 35–36; and *Les Prisons* (Marguerite de Navarre), 65; and problem of evil, 296, 297; and proposals for Reform, 100; and prosecution for possession of condemned works, 100; and Protestantism, 156–157; and Protestant orthodoxy, 67; and Protestant Reformation, 21, 32, 35, 36, 74, 97, 100, 257; and Providence, 297, 298; and Quarrel of the Ancients and the Moderns, 285–86, 287; and the *Quart Livre Pantagruel* (Rabelais), 67–68; and reason, 245; and reformers, 191; and the representation of the "Other," 257; and Ronsard's poetry, 132–34; and rule of St. Benedict, 83; and salvation, 51, 64, 193, 241; and scholastic theology, 47, 49; and secularism, 173; and seventeenth-century Christian theatergoers, 192; and Spinoza's critique of holy writ, 173; and spread of Luther's ideas, 36; and tension between Protestants and Catholics, 160–61; and territorial expansion, 257; and theological disagreement, 157; and theological

power, 233; and the *Theologico-Political Treatise* (Spinoza), 182; and theology, 16, 35, 39, 47, 48–52, 56, 59, 61, 64, 97, 110, 230, 234, 241, 242, 297; and the Torah, 498; and translation into vernacular languages, 73–74; and translation of *Le miroir de l'âme pécheresse*, 101; and violence, 74, 79; and Voltaire's skepticism about religious belief, 294; and war, 57; and writings of Erasmus, 48–49. *See also* Augustine, Saint; Bible; Church; Erasmus; *Pensées* (Pascal); Sorbonne; Wars of Religion

Renaissance: and antiquity as writers' model, 151–52, 195, 269, 272; and beginnings of in Italy, 20, 93; and Boccaccio's *Decameron*, 93; and the century, 42; and clash between moral philosophy and scholastic theology, 49; and classical antiquity, 20, 49, 56, 68, 78–79, 138–39, 157; and classical ideals, 167; and conquest, 250; and criticism, 39; and cultural encounter, 250; and deference to divine creator, 43; and depictions of emotion, 206; and Joachim du Bellay, 7, 137–52; and duties to God and king, 21; and English Renaissance, 152, 167; and Erasmus, 49, 51, 53, 54, 59, 66, 67, 68, 78; and *Essays* (Montaigne), 156; and evangelism, 54, 61–63, 66, 67, 110; and the "first Renaissance," 51, 54; and French Renaissance, 49, 51, 91, 141, 148, 149, 151, 152; and fusion of classical learning with Christian texts, 49; and the *Heptameron* (Marguerite de Navarre), 97; and history of French literature, 11, 14, 18, 62; and humanism, 78–80, 158, 159, 167, 282; and ideals of courtly

Renaissance (*cont.*)
love and honor, 21; and imitations of Petrarch, 148–49; Italian foundation of, 148–49; and Italian Renaissance, 152, 199; and languages of Greek, Latin, and Hebrew, 56; and Marguerite de Navarre, 101, 110; and modernity, 15–16, 56; and Montaigne, 102, 156, 160; and morality, 233; poets of, 3, 68–69, 101; and prose writers, 102; and Rabelais, 84, 102; and religious and philosophical oppositions, 49; and the Renaissance man, 116; and role of the face, 166, 167; and Romanticism, 438; and scientific exploration, 250; and second Renaissance, 68–69; and separation of Christian and secular influences, 68; and sixteenth century France, 11, 49; and "the age of discovery," 250; and *Theatre for Worldlings* (van der Noot), 152; and travel writing, 3, 250; in the twelfth century, 21; and unfinished narratives, 102; and usage of term by Jules Michelet, 137; and the word "Gaul," 153n2

Republic, The (Plato), 277, 280, 287, 396

republic of letters: epistolary circuits of, 12; and freedom of speech, 37; and replacement of kings' empire, 35; and salons, 377; and Mme de Staël, 332, 333

rêve de D'Alembert, Le (*D'Alembert's Dream*) (Diderot), 371, 383

Riccoboni, Marie-Jeanne, 342–43

Richelieu, Armand-Jean du Plessis, Cardinal: and the Académie française, 7–8; chateau of, 255, 258, 264; and concentration of power with king, 263; and royal edict of 1643 about theater, 176

Rimbaud, Arthur: and the apostrophe, 489; on the bourgeoisie, 441, 565; and consciousness, 488; and difficult modes of expression, 28; and disordering of all the senses, 486, 490, 508–9; and exclamation marks, 489; and "I is an other," 485, 509; *Illuminations* of, 487, 488, 489; and motivation for writing, 32; and poet as seer, 508–9; and poetic language, 490, 509; and poetry, 4, 10, 470, 485–91, 508–10; and prose poem, 489, 490, 509; and recklessness, 486–89; and self-consciousness, 485–86; and surrealism, 554; and symbolism, 486; and translation of by Beckett, 620; and use of the dash, 488–89; and the vagabond consciousness, 10; and youthful energy, 571. See also *saison en enfer, Une* (*A Season in Hell*) (Rimbaud)

Robbe-Grillet, Alain, 14, 519, 599, 608, 616, 630

Roland, "Manon," 338, 340–41

Roman culture: and ancient Rome, 142, 149, 151, 164, 270, 273; and antiquity, 50, 68, 137, 149–50, 158, 270, 272–73; and cycles of civilizations, 151; and depictions of emotion, 206; and gods, 341; and Greco-Latin epic hexameter, 127; and Holy Roman Emperor Charles V, 68; and Horace, 140; and humanism, 151; and imitation of Greek writers, 143; and Latin poets, 274; and law, 49; and literature, 56, 78, 143, 144; and Lucian of Samosata, 261; and lyric poetry, 113; and military leaders, 138; and numismatics, 49; and paganism in poetry and the arts, 286–87; poets of, 68, 113, 138–39, 144; and Romanticism, 439; and Seneca, 158, 160, 161, 194, 195; and translation of poems, 145, 147; and Virgil, 117

Roman de la Rose (*Romance of the Rose*), 8, 29, 32, 138, 141

Romanticism: and adversaries the neo-classics, 444, 445; and aesthetic experience, 288, 440, 444; and *Angel or Demon*, 503; and artistic freedom, 442; and artistic genius, 288; and authors' use of Bonaparte as a model, 440–41; and battle of *Hernani* (Hugo), 440, 443–44, 446; and the century, 42; and challenge to conservative nationalism, 12; and the color red, 438–39; and consciousness in Europe, 6, 40, 446; and cosmopolitanism, 12; and *De l'Allemagne* (*On Germany*), 332; and democratic forces, 22; and dominant, emergent, and residual stages, 16–17; and First and Second Romanticism, 440; and the fragment in literature, 246; and the great quarrels, 16, 440, 445; and Hugo's *Hernani*, 436–38, 440, 443–44, 446; and Hugo's Romantic dramas, 437–38; and imagination and feeling, 40, 444–45; and importance of the future, 447; and influence of romance novels, 456; and Italian Giorgio Agamben, 446; and Julien in *Le rouge et le noir* (Stendhal), 426; and levels of historicity, 446, 447–48; and medieval culture, 439–40, 445; and middle or low social classes in plays, 442; and moral and religious beliefs as relative, 257; and Alfred de Musset, 28, 440, 441; and the past, 445–46, 470; and Pléiade poets, 43; and poetry, 43, 501, 507; and primitivism, 288; and promotion of the present, 446–47; and protests at the Comédie Française, 436, 441; and Quarrel of the Ancients and the Moderns, 275; and return to Renaissance and antiquity, 438; and *roman personnel*, 595; and Romantic manifesto *Racine and Shakespeare* (Stendhal), 190, 444, 445; and Rousseau as pre-Romantic, 394; and Shakespeare as Master of theater, 12; and subjectivity, 507; and the sublime, 288, 443, 501; and taste for *Memorial de Sainte-Hélène*, 440; and youth, 436, 439, 444, 448. See also *Racine et Shakespeare* (Stendhal)

Ronsard, Pierre de: and alexandrine line, 4, 116, 119, 122, 123, 126, 127, 128–34; and attack by Mellin de Saint-Gelais, 123; and beloved home as theme, 115, 116, 117–18; and Catholic Church, 114, 132; Christian sources of, 126; and decasyllabic line, 4, 115–16, 118, 123, 126, 127, 128, 129, 131, 132; and defense of monarchy, 132–34; and *discours*, 128, 131, 132, 134; education of, 117, 119, 120, 159; elegies of, 128, 131, 132, 134; family of, 117, 118, 119, 120; father of, 118, 119, 120; and feminine and masculine rhymes, 116, 133; and French language, 113, 115, 134; and golden age of France, 123–24, 129; and golden era of French poetry, 113, 117; and Greek and Roman lyricists, 113, 115–16, 117; and heroic verse, 126, 127, 134; and Homeric and Virgilian epic, 123, 125, 128; hymns of, 121, 129–32, 134; and ideal of poet as seer and intellectual, 116–17; and identification of Nature with God, 118, 121; and imitation of the Ancients, 114, 116, 117, 122, 126; and *Institution for Charles IX*, 133; as the king's poet, 114, 121, 124; as leader of Pléiade poets, 4; and love for "jardins de Touraine," 118–19; and love poetry, 121, 123, 124–25, 128, 130–31;

Ronsard, Pierre de (*cont.*)
and lyric poetry, 113; and Montaigne, 158; and music, 113, 116, 121, 122, 125, 128; odes of, 113–16, 117, 120–26, 131, 134; and ode to Michel de l'Hôpital, 123, 124–25; on order of kinship, 4; as page to dauphin François and Charles, 119; and pastoral poems, 118–19; patrons of, 121, 123–24, 134; Jacques Peletier du Mans as tutor to, 120; and philosophical poetry, 113, 121, 123, 130; poetic themes of, 116, 117, 121, 123, 124–27, 132–34; and poetry of praise, 115–116, 117, 121, 123–24; and political poetry, 113, 132; prosody of, 4, 113, 122, 123; as a public intellectual, 4, 113, 114, 123, 135; and *Quatre premiers livres des odes*, 113, 114, 117, 118, 121, 126; and relationship with Joachim du Bellay, 120, 125; as royal counselor, 113, 114; in service to dauphin Henri, 120; and sung poetry, 124, 125–26; and teacher Jean Dorat, 120, 125; and versification, 123, 126, 129–30, 131, 133–34

rouge et le noir, Le (*The Red and the Black*) (Stendhal): and character Julien's infatuation with Napoleonic example, 421–26, 440; and the color red, 439; and false noble identity, 424; and hypocrisy, 423, 424–25; and Napoleon Bonaparte, 417, 421, 422, 423, 424, 426; and Paris, 421; and realism, 426; and Mme de Rênal, 421, 424–25, 426, 432, 440; and Romanticism, 426, 439; and Julien Sorel, 416, 417, 420, 421–25, 426, 429, 432–33, 440; and upward social mobility, 417, 426

Rousseau, Jean-Jacques: abandonment of children of, 398, 400–401, 402;

and architecture of bourgeois house, 322–23; and artisanal class, 361; and authorship, 406–7, 408; bed in novel of, 326; bohemian status of, 377, 378, 381; and botany, 409; celebrity of, 371, 395; childhood and parents of, 399–400; *Confessions* of, 377, 393, 398–405, 409; and conjectural history, 397; and *Contrat social* (*The Social Contract*), 398, 399; and corruption of literature, science, and the arts, 395; and corruption of literature from social state, 395, 398, 411; death of, 402; and denunciation of women writers, 335; and desire to revert to state of nature, 397–98; and development of autobiography, 44, 339–40, 393, 394, 407; and devotion to truth, 408–9; and dialogues *Rousseau juge de Jean-Jacques* (*Rousseau Judge of Jean-Jacques*), 394, 404–8; and *Discours sur l'origine et les fondements de l'inégalité parmi les hommes*, 393, 395, 397–98; and education, 337, 398, 399, 401–2; and education of children, 399–402; and the eighteenth-century novel, 314, 320–24; and *Emile*, 398–99, 401, 402; and encyclopedists, 395, 399, 402; and end of friendship with Diderot, 380, 410; and the epistolary novel, 320–24, 327; and "Essai sur l'origine des langues" ("Essay on the Origin of Languages"), 286; and essays on by Mme de Staël, 332; as an exile, 26, 399, 403; and fatherhood, 401, 402; and fictionality, 396, 411; and the first person, 10, 393, 394, 405; and First Romanticism, 440; and Geneva, 401, 637; and Homer, 286; and human nature, 396, 398, 407, 411; and immorality of classical tragedy, 287; and importance of sentiment, 40, 320, 505; and interiority, self, and society, 10, 43, 394–98; and making drafts of work public, 245; and man's natural goodness, 394, 399, 400, 405–6, 409; and metaphor of self-portraiture, 393, 394, 398; and Montaigne, 168, 393, 408; and moral and political function of literature, 286–87, 397–98; and natural man, 393–94, 396, 398, 405–6; and nature, 322, 323–24, 380, 393, 394, 397, 405, 410–11; and orality of epics, 286; and origins, 393, 395, 396, 397; and philosophy, 130, 272, 276, 393–411; and political programs, 398; and postscript to *Rousseau juge de Jean-Jacques*, 408; and primitivism, 397, 398; and "public" virtues, 320; and Quarrel of the Ancients and the Moderns, 286; and the *querelle des bouffons*, 379; and rationalism, 322; and refusal of patronage, 377; and reverie, 398, 399, 409, 410–11; and *Rêveries du promeneur solitaire* (*Reveries of the Solitary Walker*), 402, 403, 406, 408–11; and Rousseauist novel, 313, 320–24; and self-knowledge, 395, 408–9, 518; and social codes of men of letters, 384, 388; solitude of, 394, 398, 405, 408, 410; and state of nature, 393–98, 406, 411; as target in play *Les philosophes* (Palissot), 380; work of, 294, 381, 393, 394, 408. See also *Julie ou la nouvelle Héloïse*

Rousseau juge de Jean-Jacques (Rousseau), 394, 404–8, 409

Ruskin, John, 519–20

Russia: autocratic regime in, 534–35; and Bolsheviks, 534; and communism, 535, 544, 596, 621–22; and Stalin's policies, 546

Sade, Marquis de: and the eighteenth-century novel, 313, 314, 324–27; incarceration of, 10; and motivation for writing, 32; and philosophical experience, 313, 324–26; and private space for sex, 324; and prosecution of publisher for obscenity, 38; and violence, 326. See also *philosophie dans le boudoir, La*

Sainte-Beuve, Charles-Augustin: and beginnings of French literature, 16; and critical journalism, 6, 40; and national literary culture, 13; opposition from Proust to approach of, 521, 522; and prose as medium of French literature, 242, 339; and Riccoboni's novels, 343; and *roman personnel*, 595; and seventeenth-century classicism, 12

Saint-Simon, Duc de, 518, 536

saison en enfer, Une (*A Season in Hell*) (Rimbaud), 486, 487–88, 490, 509

salons: and aristocratic salons, 428; and authors as celebrities, 26; and Balzac's Rastignac, 415, 417; and Catherine the Great, 382; and Célimène in *Le misanthrope* (Molière), 185; codes and manners of, 8, 39, 414, 429; and conversations as a novel's beginning, 215; and *divisio*, 81; and Enlightenment, 29, 377, 382; and fairy tales, 224; games of, 227; hostesses of, 29, 30, 221, 224, 330, 332, 339; and intimacy of the salon of Apollo, 322–23, 324; in the novel, 316, 322, 323, 324; and *philosophes*, 381; and play *Les philosophes* (Palissot), 380; political significance of, 221; and Rabouillet salon, 221; salon hostess Marie du Deffand, 339; satires of conversations of, 222; and success and social prestige, 418; and women's conversation, 221

Sand, George, 440, 462

Sarraute, Nathalie, 600, 616

Sartre, Jean-Paul: and Académie française, 634; and "adventure," 606, 607; and *L'âge de raison* (*The Age of Reason*), 519; and American novelists, 518; and bad faith, 599, 605–6, 611; and *Les chemins de la libérté* (*The Roads to Freedom*), 544, 597; and committed literature, 630; cultural role of, 123; and definition of writing, 629; and dialectics of engagement, 629; and diary form, 595, 596; and Duthuit's journal *Transition*, 630; and *L'être et le néant*, 600; as a French author, 637; and literature of extreme situations, 544–45, 547; and *litterature engagée* (engaged literature), 536; and metaphor of stone for novel, 601; and *Les mouches*, 597; and *La nausée*, 536, 595–613, 630; as opposed to Camus, 596; and "Orphée noir" ("Black Orpheus"), 646; philosophical writings of, 604, 646; plays of, 597; and recognition of Aimé Césaire's work, 591; and use of metaphor, 608–9; and *What Is Literature?*, 597, 629, 630

Scève, Maurice, 3, 117, 131

science: and Jean le Rond d'Alembert, 371; and atheism, 373; and authors' aims, 28; and Beaumarchais's invention, 361; and botany, 410; and comparative science of man, 393, 395–96; and concern for creativity, 276; and corruption of literature, science, and the arts, 395; and Emilie du Châtelet, 338; and experimental and human sciences, 29; and Bernard Le Bovier de Fontenelle, 271; and Galileo, 269; and happiness, 351; and imagination of fiction, 260; and Linnaeus's system of classification, 410;

and modern science, 276; and natural history, 395; and natural science, 172, 269, 351; and Newtonian ideas, 338, 351; as part of philosophy, 278; and political science, 173, 182, 187; and the scientific method, 295; and scientific revolution, 277; and the seventeenth century, 8, 251, 269; and social sciences, 411; and split between humanities and sciences, 276–77; and theory of human progress, 272; and the universe, 253, 260; and work of Cyrano de Bergerac, 260; and zoology, 426. *See also* anthropology

Scudéry, Madeleine de: as a celebrated novelist, 202; and heroic romances, 202, 215; and *Lettres provinciales* (Pascal), 243; and map of tenderness, 215–16, 226; and Rabouillet salon, 221

Sébillet, Thomas, 139, 140, 144

self: autonomy of, 232; awareness of, 43, 201, 220; and Emma Bovary, 455; centralization of, 472, 486; and community, 43, 235, 239; and dandyism, 470–71, 486; and discovery of in Marivaux's plays, 361; and divided self of Irish writers, 618; and expression, 161, 235; and "I is an other," 485, 509; and inner life protected by poetry, 580; and language, 239; and memory, 518; and metaphor of self-portraiture, 393, 398; and modern period, 29, 201, 231, 239, 394; and Montaigne's self-exploration, 159, 165, 167; multiplication of, 471–72; and nature, 395, 410–11; nature of, 155, 235, 393–95; and others, 238, 394; and personal identity, 44, 220, 233; and public life, 220, 233; and race, 201; and reading, 31; and reputation, 236, 238; and Romantic self,

595; and Rousseau, 43, 44, 394–95, 409–11; and self-interest, 236; and self-knowledge, 395, 408–9; and self-love, 231, 232, 235, 236, 248n1; and the seventeenth century, 231, 233–34; solitude of, 410; study of, 168, 395–96; and virtue and vice, 233; and writing about public service, 44; and written confession of sins, 44, 393. *See also* Rousseau, Jean-Jacques

Seneca, 158, 160, 161, 194, 195
Senghor, Leopold, 575, 576, 591, 646
Sévigné, Mme de, 224, 338
sexuality: and adultery, 197, 462, 464–65, 467; and ancient works, 288; and anxiety, 620; and *Les bijoux indiscrets* (*The Indiscreet Jewels*), 372; and Anne Boleyn, 223; and the boudoir or bedroom, 313–21, 324–27; and Breton's relationship with Nadja, 555–56; and Isabelle de Charrière's Caliste, 331; and celebrated painting *Le verrou* (Fragonard), 319; and Célimène in *Le misanthrope* (Molière), 185; and character Albertine, 525; and character of Fanchette, 367; covering up of, 327; and criminals in Saint-Lazare prison, 365; and culture of *galanterie*, 226; and *L'école des femmes* (*The School for Wives*) (Molière), 176–77; and *L'école des filles*, 222; and erotic passions, 205, 253, 320–21, 323–24, 326–27; and femininity, 315, 320–21; and feminism, 31, 103; and the *Heptameron* (Marguerite de Navarre), 93, 94, 95–96, 98, 102, 103; and heroine's sexual bliss, 175; and homosexual character in *Candide* (Voltaire), 302–3; and homosexuality, 515, 521, 522; and *L'immoraliste* (*The Immoralist*), 522; and incest, 93, 103, 106–7, 108, 197;

and indecency, 525, 526; and Louise Labé's poem in Italian, 149; and Lucien's exploits in Balzac novels, 417, 430; in *Madame Bovary* (Flaubert), 454, 461, 462; and male sexual hypocrisy, 364; and marital fidelity, 93, 98; and *The Marriage of Figaro* (Beaumarchais), 367; and masculinity, 94; and *Mercier and Camier*, 624; and Montaigne's *Essays*, 166; and novels of Sade, 324–27; and passions, 459, 461, 462; and *Phèdre* (Racine), 194; and power, 94; and prostitution, 620; in Proust's writing, 527–28; and public and private contrast, 327; and rape, 93, 103; and *Le rêve de D'Alembert* (*D'Alembert's Dream*), 383; and "Manon" Roland's *Mémoires particuliers*, 341; and "seigneurial rights," 366; and sex as part of identity, 201; and sexual humiliation, 399; and sexual love as subject of theater, 176; and sexual mores, 295, 327; and tale in newspaper *Mercure Galant*, 226; and *Tartuffe* (Moliere), 178; and treatment of women, 302–3; and trial of poet Théophile de Viau for atheism and homosexuality, 230; and Valmont's seduction of Mme de Tourvel, 318–19; and vows of celibacy, 100; and women's bodies, 314–15. See also *Phèdre* (Racine)

Shakespeare, William: and the body, 166; and the century, 15; and character of Edmund in *King Lear*, 201; and character of Hamlet, 157; comedy of, 305; and discovery of in the eighteenth century, 12; and the French seventeenth century, 17; lovers in work of, 308; and Montaigne, 102, 152, 168; plays of, 152; and Romantic manifesto *Racine and*

Shakespeare, William (*cont.*)
　　Shakespeare (Stendhal), 191; and
　　Sonnets, 152; and *Une tempête* (Cé-
　　saire), 588; as a transitional figure,
　　157; and work of Pierre Boiastuau,
　　92
Slave Island (Marivaux), 359–60
slavery, 300–301, 334, 347, 581, 584;
　　and Haiti, 586; and master/slave
　　duo, 588. *See also* class; racism; *Slave
　　Island* (Marivaux)
Socrates, 166, 167, 252, 260, 261, 396
Songe (*Dream*) (du Bellay), 149, 150,
　　151
Sorbonne: and banning of books, 78;
　　and encounter between Breton and
　　Tzara, 560; and *Index librorum pro-
　　hibitorum*, 78; persecutions of, 50,
　　91–92; and theology, 36, 47, 49, 50,
　　51, 241, 242; traditionalism of, 51,
　　91–92, 276
Spain: and Africa, India, and South
　　America, 257; and colonization,
　　256–57; comic novels from, 261; and
　　the Declaration of Vienna, 425; and
　　film *Espoir: Sierra de Teruel*, 548, 551;
　　and French princes as hostages, 118;
　　and influence of Petrarch, 117; and
　　philosopher Raymond Sebondus,
　　159; poetry of, 140, 144, 152; and
　　Ronsard's poetry, 121, 124; and the
　　seventeenth century, 22; and support
　　of Catholics in France, 157; and
　　treaty with France, 91
Speroni, Sperone, 147, 148
Spinoza, Baruch, 173, 182, 187
spleen de Paris, Le (Baudelaire), 476–77,
　　508
Staël, Mme Germaine de: and
　　Bonaparte's creation of nobility, 420;
　　and *Considerations sur les principaux
　　événements de la Révolution française*,
　　333; and the Coppet group, 332–33;

as a cosmopolitan, 343; and *De la lit-
　　térature* (*On Literature*) , 332; and *De
　　l'Allemagne* (*On Germany*), 12, 332;
　　and *De l'influence des passions sur le
　　bonheur de l'individu et des nations*,
　　333; and *Delphine*, 342; and early life
　　in Paris, 332; and economic and so-
　　cial prejudice, exploitation, and in-
　　equalities, 347; emotions in work of,
　　333–34; as an exile from France,
　　332–33; and First Romanticism,
　　440; and husband's diplomatic sta-
　　tion, 334; and influence of political
　　writings, 333–34; and letter writing,
　　338; and novel *Corinne, ou l'Italie*,
　　330, 333; and painting *Corinne au
　　Cap Misène* (*Corinne at Cape Mise-
　　num*) by Gérard, 330, 331–32; par-
　　ents of, 332; and portrayal of as
　　Corinne, 331–32; and *Réflexions sur
　　le procès de la reine* (*Thoughts on the
　　Queen's Trial*), 333–34
state: and authors' copyrights, 28; and
　　black republic of Haiti, 585–86; and
　　Caribbean islanders' choice regard-
　　ing government, 579; and censor-
　　ship, 26, 36, 37–38, 351; and central-
　　ized state formation, 8, 22; and Aimé
　　Césaire representing Martinique,
　　578; and the comte d'Argenson,
　　372–73; and condemnation of com-
　　edies, authors, and actors, 355, 372–
　　73; and cultural power, 11, 21–22;
　　and dangers of royal patronage, 26;
　　and different governmental systems,
　　419, 433, 548, 585; and the divine
　　right of kings, 21–22; and essay "Of
　　the Useful and the Honorable"
　　(Montaigne), 165; expansion of, 138;
　　as following empire, 166; and free-
　　dom of speech, 37–38; French as of-
　　ficial language of, 138; and French
　　Revolution, 419; and Haitian revo-

lution, 585; and Italian republics,
445; and Lamartine as minister of
foreign affairs, 505–6; and laws covering sedition, obscenity, or slander,
38; and liberties, 178; and literary
trials, 10, 37–38, 462, 463, 464–66,
468; and Napoleon III's Second Empire, 466; and national literary culture, 12–13, 25–26; and nation-state,
11, 113; and new democracies, 580,
586; and newly independent Senegal, 646; and political interests of in
poetry, 139; and printing, 26; and
rebirth of culture of antiquity, 137,
138; and the Reign of Terror, 505;
and relationship with church, 91;
and relationship with literature, 42,
122, 134, 138, 139, 470; and republican democracy, 535; and republicanism, 505–6, 551; and revolution of
1848, 470; and revolution replacing
the Bourbons, 432–33; and rise of
Napoleon, 419, 420–21; and Ronsard's poetry, 134; and secular pleasures, 178; and situation after decolonization, 580, 587; in the sixteenth
century, 138, 139; and spread of Luther's ideas, 36; and Stalin's policies,
546; and support of writers, 28; and
La tragédie du roi Christophe (Césaire), 585–86; and well-ordered society, 132. *See also* monarchy
Steiner, George, 191, 192
Stendhal, Frédéric de, 9; and attachment to Italian medieval culture,
445; and biography of Napoleon,
421, 422; and character Julien's infatuation with Napoleonic example,
421–26; and classical imitation contrasted with imagination, 444–45;
and French society, 419, 431, 433,
444; and importance of appearances,
429; and importance of Paris, 415;

and marriage to noble heiresses for
characters, 417; and the past, 445–
46; and promotion of the present,
446; in Proust's society columns,
516; and Racine, 205; and realism,
426; and rise of self-made men, 418;
and Romantic manifesto *Racine and
Shakespeare* , 190, 191, 444, 445; and
Le rouge et le noir (*The Red and the
Black*), 415; and the social world, 10,
424
Strachey, Lytton, 2, 6
Supplément au voyage de Bougainville
(Diderot), 3, 295
surrealism: and Guillaume Apollinaire,
510, 554; and automatic writing,
558, 571; and Samuel Beckett, 629;
and André Breton, 5, 13, 511, 536,
554–62, 565, 566, 571; and Caribbean plantation culture, 583; and
Césaire's poetry, 576, 584; and
René Char, 5, 554, 561, 563; and
Dada, 554, 558, 560; and Salvador
Dalí, 560; and Desnos's dream
trances, 558, 560; and dreams, 41,
556–57, 558, 560; and first Surrealist Manifesto, 558, 561; and Freudian unconsciousness, 509; and
imagination, 556–57, 558, 566; and
importance of encounter and creation, 561–62; and importance of
place names, 561; and the irrational,
558, 560; and Lautreamont, 554;
and madness, 555, 556; and the
marvelous, 557, 558; and merging of
binaries, 557–58; and painting, 562;
and passion, 556, 557; and poetic
theory, 567; and poetry, 4, 509, 554,
557, 558, 560; project of, 554, 562;
and Rimbaud, 554; and Sartre's
analysis, 630; second manifesto of,
562, 571; and struggles of the avant-
garde, 440

symbolism: aspects of, 484; and
  Charles Baudelaire, 477, 491; and
  literary criticism, 41; and Arthur
  Rimbaud, 486, 491; and Paul Ver-
  laine, 484, 491
Synge, John Millington, 616, 618, 619

Tartuffe (Molière): banning of, 180;
  and deus ex machina device, 180; and
  Dorine, 353; and hypocrisy, 178,
  179, 181, 423; and king as God's surrogate, 179–80; and Louis XIV, 178–
  80; and Molière's vision, 175, 189;
  plot of, 178–79; political stake of,
  178, 179; public controversy over,
  287; and religion, 178; and vraisemblance (verisimilitude), 180; and
  world of Molière's time, 188
theater: and actors, 173–74, 355, 362,
  437, 589; and alexandrine verse
  form, 190, 205–6; and Les amazones
  (Du Bocage), 341; and Amphitryon,
  184; and Aristophanes's Clouds, 81;
  and Aristotelian theory of mimesis
  (imitation), 171; audience of, 442,
  443; and The Barber of Seville (Beaumarchais), 361–62; and Samuel
  Beckett, 183; and bienséance (seemliness), 172; and Leonard Bernstein's
  musical Candide, 291; and Le bourgeois gentilhomme (The Would-be Gentleman), 188–89; and bourgeoisie,
  178, 180; and Cartesian mechanism,
  173; and censorship, 351–52, 443–
  44; and Césaire's politically engaged
  plays, 584, 585, 586–87, 588; and
  Isabelle de Charrière's plays, 344; and
  Chatterton (Vigny), 506; for children,
  337–38; and Le Cid (Corneille), 172,
  174–75; and claques, 437; and class,
  351, 356, 442, 443; and classical
  rules, 442–43; and classical theater,
  43, 80–81, 171–72, 173, 190–94,

199; and the Comédie Française,
  334, 362, 365, 380, 383, 436, 441–42,
  586; and comedy, 44, 80–81, 173–74,
  184–85, 191–92, 202, 204, 351–69;
  and comedy of character, 184–85;
  and commedia dell'arte, 174, 352, 621;
  and Critique de l'école des femmes
  (The Critique of the School for Wives)
  (Moliere), 175, 177; and Cyrano de
  Bergerac (Rostand), 27; and destiny,
  193–94, 205; and deus ex machina device, 172, 180; and divine agency,
  192, 194; and divisio, 81; and Don
  Juan (Molière), 175, 187, 188; and
  dramatic action, 184–85, 188, 361,
  597; and L'école des femmes (The
  School for Wives) (Molière), 175–77,
  185; and emotions, 198, 200–2, 207–
  9, 360–61; and enjambment, 442;
  and French opera, 191–92; and Félicité de Genlis, 337–38; and George
  Dandin, 184; and guilt, 205; and heroic characters, 200–2; and Hippolyte
  (Gilbert), 197; and Hippolytus
  (Euripides), 195; and Victor Hugo,
  3, 10; and Hugo's Hernani, 8, 436–
  38, 446; and Hugo's Romantic dramas, 437–38; and human nature, 21,
  181; and human will, 193–94; and
  hypocrisy, 178, 179, 180–81; and
  identification, 202, 204, 206; and
  immorality, 352; and L'impromptu de
  Versailles (The Versailles Impromptu),
  177–78; and indecency, 77–78; and
  Italian and Spanish influence, 12;
  and Le malade imaginaire (The Imaginary Invalid), 188–89; as a male domain, 31; and The Marriage of Figaro
  (Beaumarchais), 362–69; and melodrama, 442; morality of, 175–76; and
  Le misanthrope (Molière), 175, 184–
  88; and obscenity, 177; and passions,
  176, 190, 191, 192–97, 201, 202,

203–7; and play *Les philosophes* (Palissot), 380; and play *Lorenzaccio* (Musset), 440; and plays of Marguerite de Navarre, 92; and plays' scripts, 174; and playwrights, 21, 25, 26, 171, 172, 173, 191, 193, 198, 352, 437; and poetic practice, 199–200; popularity of, 27, 353; and principle of immanence, 172–73; and professionalism, 173–74; and the professional stage, 199–200; and psychological dimension, 205; and Mark Ravenhill's *Candide*, 291; and realism, 191; and recognition plots, 198; and religion, 175–176, 182–84, 192–95, 196; and role playing, 589; and royal edit of 1643, 176; and Royal Shakespeare Company, 291; and *Ruy Blas* (Hugo), 443; and *Une saison au Congo* (*A Season in the Congo*) (Césaire), 587; and secularism, 173, 178, 179–80, 182; and sense of nature, 171–72; and seventeenth-century Christian theatergoers, 192; seventeenth-century theory of, 199, 207; and sex, 175, 176, 177, 185, 201; and Shakespeare's plays, 152; and speaking in *Phèdre* (Racine), 195–98; and symbolist plays, 618; and *Tartuffe* (Molière), 175, 178, 188, 380; and theory of comedy, 174–75, 188; and tragedy, 44, 80–81, 132, 171–75, 191–92, 199–200, 206–9, 282, 597; and tragicomedy, 443; and transfer of emotion, 207, 282; and twentieth-century productions, 205; and unities, 39, 171, 172, 199; and Jean Vilar's *Théâtre nationale populaire*, 34; and violence, 199, 207; and virtue, 177, 179; and *vraisemblance* (verisimilitude), 39, 171, 172, 173, 174–75, 180; and widows, 356–57; and work of Aristotle and Horace, 192; and *Zamore et Mirza* (Gouges), 334. *See also* classicism; drama; Hugo, Victor; Shakespeare, William

Tom Jones (Fielding), 307–8

tragedy: and alexandrine verse form, 205–6; and ancient tragic sense of life, 191; and Aristotle, 224, 442–43; and catharsis, 207; and *Le Cid* (Corneille) as problematic, 172; and classical French theater, 43, 171, 190–201, 202; classical tragedy, 270–71, 294; vs. comedy, 175; and Pierre Corneille's Medea, 285; "death of," 192; and "De la poésie dramatique" (Diderot), 286; and destiny, 193–94, 205; and *divisio*, 80, 81; and Anne-Marie Du Bocage, 341; and early modern period, 7, 194; and emotions, 198, 200–201, 202, 207, 208; and *Et les chiens se taisent* (*And the Dogs Were Silent*) (Césaire), 584; and Euripides's plot, 192–93; and "The Future of Tragedy" (Camus), 597; and Greek mythology, 192–95, 205; and Greek tragedies, 80, 81, 194–99, 205; and guilt, 205; and heroic characters, 174–75, 193, 194–95, 198, 204–5, 207; and hierarchy of genres, 39; and *Hippolyte* (Gilbert), 197; and *Hippolytus* (Euripides), 195; and historical subject matter, 192, 586; and Hugo's *Hernani*, 436; and identification, 202, 204, 207, 208; and immorality of classical tragedy, 287; and the individual, 207; and modern literature, 207; and modern rules, 190–91; and modern stage, 171, 173; and Moliere's comedies, 191; morality of, 176; and naturalism, 173, 191; and neoclassicists, 437; and the nineteenth century, 44, 436, 437; passions of, 282; and performance, tragedy (*cont.*)

127; and *Phèdre* (Racine), 7, 191–98; and *Poetics* (Aristotle), 442–43; politics of, 132; and Racine, 204–9, 536; and Pierre de Ronsard, 123; royal permission for, 362; and Sartre's *Les mouches*, 597; and secularism, 192; and the seventeenth century, 8, 171, 172, 190, 191–92; and sexuality, 201; theory of, 174–75; and tragic action, 207; and *La tragédie du roi Christophe* (Césaire), 586; and tragic monologue, 206; and twentieth-century productions, 205; and *vraisemblance* (verisimilitude), 171, 172, 225; and Western tradition, 207

travel writing: and antiquity, 250; and "Des Cannibales" (Montaigne), 3, 257; and conquest, 257; and cultural encounters, 251, 257, 266; and Cyrano de Bergerac, 250–54, 256, 258, 259, 260–61, 265–66; and drive of curiosity and "fantasy," 255; and early science fiction, 260–61; in the eighteenth century, 295; and *Les Etats et Empires de la Lune* (*The States and Empires of the Moon*), 252–54; and *Les Etats et Empires du Soleil* (*The States and Empires of the Sun*), 252–54; and explorer narratives, 256–59; and "galant" travel writing, 261–62; and generic hybridity, 266; as a genre, 253–54, 256, 259, 260; and *History of a Voyage to the Land of Brazil* (Léry), 158, 256; and Homer's Odysseus, 261; and La Fontaine, 250, 251, 252, 254–56, 258–266; and maxim *ambulo ergo sum*, 250, 254, 261, 266; and *Nouveaux mémoires pour servir à l'histoire des Cacouacs* (Moureau), 379; and the "Other," 12, 253, 257, 263, 266;

philosophical questions of, 251, 253, 261–66; political, religious, and scholarly functions of, 256–57, 260, 266; and political power, 265–66; and polyphony, 266; and prejudices, 3; and "primitive" peoples, 395; and problems of explorer narratives, 258–59; and relativity of customs and beliefs, 257, 265, 295; and the seventeenth century, 229, 250–66; and *Supplément au voyage de Bougainville* (Diderot), 3, 295; and transmission of knowledge, 259, 260; and travel as metaphor, 295; and *Travel Journal* (Montaigne), 160; and travelogues of expeditions, 256–57, 266; and Voltaire's *Candide*, 7; and *Voyage d'Encausse* (Chapelle and Bachaumont), 261–62

Trotsky, Leon: and criticism of *Les conquérants* (Malraux), 534, 549; and political novels, 549, 550, 551; and presence in France, 535; and revolutionary vision, 546, 552; and *Voyage au bout de la nuit* (Céline), 626

Tzara, Tristan, 558, 560, 571

United States: and bestsellers, 31–32; René Char's influence in, 563; and Assia Djebar, 645; and "littérature négro-africaine," 577; and novelists of the 1930s, 518; and the twentieth century, 22; and *Voyage au bout de la nuit* (Céline), 542

Valery, Paul: cultural role of, 123; and *Eupalinos*, 601, 602; and "On Some Motifs in Baudelaire" (Benjamin), 524–525; and poem "Les pas," 509; and reading, 2, 18–19; and the twentieth century, 3

Vergne, Marie-Madeleine Pioche de La. *See* Lafayette, Madame de

Verlaine, Paul: and admiration for Marceline Desbordes-Valmore, 504; and articles in *L'Art*, 478; and consciousness, 483, 484, 485; and cultivation of *vers impair*, 478–80; and dreams, synesthesia, and silence, 484; and enumeration, 484; and feminine and masculine rhymes, 480; as an impressionist, 483; and *Jadis et naguère* (*Long Ago and Not So Long Ago*), 478–79, 484; and letter from Mallarmé, 503; and literary movements, 491; and musical mode of expression, 623; and poetry, 4, 10, 123, 470, 478–85; and *rejets*, 481–82; religion of, 484, 485; and Rimbaud, 484; and self-pity, 478, 484; and vagabond consciousness, 10; and voice, 482–83

Vigny, Alfred de, 504, 505, 506

Virgil, 66, 73, 163, 503, 504

Voltaire: and birthplace in Paris, 292; and *Candide*, 292, 294, 297–300, 308–9; career of, 26, 272, 294; and Catherine the Great, 382; celebrity of, 292, 294, 371; and *Contes philosophiques*, 40; and criticism of Rousseau, 397, 398, 400–401; cultural role of, 123, 244; death of, 292, 294, 402; and Jacques Delille, 503; and different genres, 294; and divine designer or creator, 297; and *Encyclopédie* entry "Men of Letters," 377; and the ethics of luxury, 301–2; as an exile, 9, 26; and female correspondents, 339; and freethinking, 304; and intelligent design, 304–5; and Leibnizian optimism, 309; and *Lettres philosophiques*, 294, 295; and *Lettres sur les Anglais*, 12; and Mme du Châtelet, 30; narration of, 308; and national classics, 9; in *Le neveu de Rameau* (Diderot), 387; original

name of, 294; and picaresque narrative, 7; and play *Le café ou l'Ecossaise*, 380–81; and play *Les philosophes* (Palissot), 380; and "Poème sur le désastre de Lisbonne" ("Poem on the Lisbon Disaster"), 297; and poem "The Man of the World," 301; and problem of evil, 297–98, 309; and Providence, 297, 298, 306; public funeral of, 9–10; and reason, 505; and residence at the Château de Ferney, 294; and Romanticism, 438; secular worldview of, 298; and size of cultured public of Paris, 32; and skepticism, 294, 309; and social codes of men of letters, 384; and travels in Germany, 294; and travel writing, 7; writings of, 294, 381

Voyage au bout de la nuit (Céline): and American Lola, 542; and capitalism, 550; and class, 543, 549, 550; and colonialism, 550; and context's relationship with text, 534; and death, 549; and emotions, 537, 541; and failure to win Prix Goncourt, 537; and French soldier Leon Robinson, 542, 543; leftist critiques of, 549–550, 552; as model for Beckett, 626; and narrator Ferdinand Bardamu, 539, 541–43, 549; nihilist vision of, 541; and parallel with Bosch and Brueghel paintings, 548–49; and poverty, 542; publishing of, 537–39; suffering described in, 549, 550; as a tragic work, 538–39; and use of spoken French in novel, 539, 541, 551, 631; and war, 541–42, 550

Voyage d'Encausse (Chapelle and Bachaumont), 261–62

voyages de la Nouvelle France occidentale, dicte Canada, Les (*Voyages to New France*) (Champlain), 256 *vraisemblance* (verisimilitude), 39, 171, 172, 173; and *Don Juan* (Moliere), 183–84; and *Les liaisons dangereuses* (Laclos), 343; and naturalism, 174–75; and the *nouvelle historique*, 216; and novels, 225; and *Tartuffe* (Molière), 180; and tragedy, 225

Wars of Religion: and France, 51, 156–57; and Montaigne, 7, 160, 161, 166; and *nouvelle historique*, 216; and Rabelais, 7; and Ronsard's poetry, 132–33; and St. Bartholomew's Day massacre, 132, 157; and wars between Protestants and Catholics, 156–57, 215; and Western history, 85

Williams, Raymond, 16–17, 207

women's writing: and anonymous publishing of works, 217–18, 333, 345, 347; and antiquity, 330; anxiety about propriety of, 217–18; and Marquerite Audoux, 31; and autonomy, 327–28; and black women, 347; and the boudoir or bedroom, 327; and the *Caquets de l'accouchée*, 221; and Isabelle de Charrière, 327, 331, 338, 342, 343–45; and Christine de Pizan's defense of women, 29; and Colette, 7, 30, 535; and *La Colombiade ou la foi portée au Nouveau Monde* (Du Bocage), 341; and concerns of Djebar, 650; and customs and cultures, 346; and *Déclaration des droits de la femme et de la citoyenne* (Gouges), 334; and denunciation of women writers, 335; and Marceline Desbordes-Valmore, 504; and Catherine Des Roches, 68; and Anne-Marie Du Bocage, 341; and *L'école des filles*, 222; and economic and social prejudice, exploitation, and inequalities, 347; and *écriture feminine*, 31; and George Eliot, 518; and En-lightenment women, 330–48; and Louise d'Epinay, 337; and the epistolary novel, 327–328, 342–343, 346–347; and *Epître aux femmes* (Epistle to women) (Pipelet), 335; and essays on Rousseau by Mme de Staël, 332; and female authors' pay, 346; and female mysticism, 61; and the female voice, 330; and feminism, 31, 68, 109; and Elisabeth Ferrand, 345; and Félicité de Genlis, 337–38; and Olympe de Gouges, 334–35; and Françoise de Graffigny, 327–28, 346, 347; and Graffigny's novel about Peruvian princess Zilia, 346–47; and Hellenist Anne Dacier, 30; and the *Heptameron* (Marguerite de Navarre), 101, 102, 109; and hostile public opinion, 30–31, 345; and Mme de Lafayette, 30, 101; and Louise Labé, 149; and Marie Leprince de Beaumont's "Magasins," 335–37; and Julie de Lespinasse, 339; and letter writing, 29, 338–39, 341; and *Lettres neuchâteloises* (*Letters from Neuchatel*) (Charrière), 345; and *Lettres trouvées dans les portefeuilles d'emigrés* (Charrière), 344; and love letters of Mme de Villedieu, 218; and Marguerite de Navarre, 60–61, 101–2, 109; and *Mémoire de Madame de Valmont* (Gouges), 334; and men developing women's ideas, 345; and Lady Mary Montagu's Turkish letters, 338; and mythology, 330, 336; and *La naissance du jour* (*Break of Day*) (Colette), 529; and *Le noble* (Charrière), 344; and novel "*Le triomphe de la verité ou histoire de M. de La Villete* (Leprince de Beaumont), 337; and *Ourika* (Duras), 347; and poet Constance Pipelet, 335; and *Pointed Roofs* (Richardson), 517; and political and societal questions, 344–45; and post-1945 intellectual writers, 31; and *La Princesse de Clevès* (Lafayette), 101–2, 109; and the public sphere, 348; and publishing, 44, 101, 345–47; and *querelles des femmes*, 29; readership of, 347; and realistic, naturalistic tradition, 31; and Marie-Jeanne Riccoboni, 342–44; salon hostess Marie du Deffand, 339; and George Sand's *Une conspiration en 1537*, 440; and Mlle de Scudéry's sentimental romance, 29–31; and sentimental novel, 327; and the short *nouvelle*, 30; and social prejudice, 345; and Théroigne de Méricourt, 334–35; and translation, 336, 338; and translator Steck-Guichelin, 345; and women as foreigners, 347; and women in pedagogy, 335–37, 338; and women's condition in society, 344–45; and women's conversation, 220–23; and *The Women's Decameron* (Voznesenskaya), 109; and women's fiction, 45, 327–28; and women's rights, 30, 334–35; and women writers of the *nouvelle historique*, 216; and work of Assia Djebar, 634–50; and work of Mme de Staël, 330–34; and *Zamore et Mirza* (Gouges), 334

Woolf, Virginia, 1–2, 84

Yeats, William Butler: French as language for play of, 617–18; and modernism, 616, 619, 627

Zola, Emile: and the boudoir or bedroom, 326; cultural role of, 244; and free indirect discourse, 539; and journalism, 28; and realism, 451; and working-class speech, 539